THROUGH A GLASS DARKLY

Through a Glass Darkly

REFLECTIONS ON PERSONAL

IDENTITY IN EARLY AMERICA

EDITED BY RONALD HOFFMAN,

MECHAL SOBEL, & FREDRIKA J. TEUTE

Published for the Omohundro Institute of Early American

History & Culture, Williamsburg, Virginia, by the University

of North Carolina Press, Chapel Hill & London

The Omohundro

Institute of Early

American History and

Culture is sponsored

jointly by the College

of William and Mary

and the Colonial

Williamsburg

Foundation. On

November 15, 1996,

the Institute adopted

the present name in

honor of a bequest

from Malvern H.

Omohundro, Jr.

Library of Congress Cataloging-in-Publication Data
Through a glass darkly : reflections on personal
identity in early America / edited by Ronald
Hoffman, Mechal Sobel, and Fredrika J. Teute.
p.   cm.
Includes index.
ISBN 0-8078-2336-8 (cloth : alk. paper). —
ISBN 0-8078-4644-9 (pbk.: alk. paper)
1. United States—History—Colonial period, ca. 1600–
1775—Congresses.   2. United States—History—
Colonial period, ca. 1600–1775—Biography—
Congresses.   3. United States—Social conditions—To
1865—Congresses.   4. United States—Social life and
customs—To 1775—Congresses.   5. Identity
(Psychology)—United States—History—17th
century—Congresses.   6. Identity (Psychology)—
United States—History—18th century—Congresses.
7. Group identity—United States—History—17th
century—Congresses.   8. Group identity—United
States—History—18th century—Congresses.
I. Hoffman, Ronald, 1941–   .   II. Sobel, Mechal.
III. Teute, Fredrika J.   IV. Omohundro Institute of
Early American History and Culture.
E189.T43   1997
973—dc21   96-52036
                CIP

This volume received indirect support from an
unrestricted book publication grant awarded to the
Institute by the L. J. Skaggs and Mary C. Skaggs
Foundation of Oakland, California.

01   00   99   98   97   5   4   3   2   1

For continuing the

traditions of the Institute

this book is dedicated to

TIMOTHY J. SULLIVAN

President, College of William and Mary

and

ROBERT C. WILBURN

President, Colonial Williamsburg Foundation

PREFACE

This volume's genesis was a conference held in Williamsburg, Virginia, on November 2–4, 1993, to mark the fiftieth anniversary of the Institute of Early American History and Culture. The idea of an institution supporting a broad program of research and publication in colonial history arose out of proposals for closer collaboration between the College of William and Mary and the Colonial Williamsburg Foundation during the late 1930s and early 1940s. In 1943, a group of distinguished historians who were then serving the Foundation in an advisory capacity—Charles M. Andrews, Virginius Dabney, Samuel Eliot Morison, Richard L. Morton, Arthur M. Schlesinger, Earl Gregg Swem, and Thomas J. Wertenbaker—endorsed the idea of a cosponsored organization put forward by the College and Foundation presidents, John E. Pomfret and Kenneth Chorley.

Under their auspices, the Institute emerged as an autonomous center for promoting the study of all phases of American life, thought, and institutions from contact to 1815. As one of its vehicles for disseminating historical knowledge, the Institute assumed responsibility for publishing the *William and Mary Quarterly,* reformulated in a third series as *A Magazine of Early American History, Institutions, and Culture,* under the editorship first of Richard L. Morton and then of Douglass Adair. Lester J. Cappon as editor of publications presided over a book program whose monographs were published through the University of North Carolina Press. Concerned that the field of early American history had been languishing, Carl Bridenbaugh as first director made the Institute's objective to reinvigorate interest in the early period of American history and to stimulate and support scholarship of the highest standards in the field.

Consistent with the intentions of the Institute's founders that it encourage important lines of innovative research, the fiftieth-anniversary conference focused on scholars' growing interest in the ways people defined themselves in early America, the meanings of those measures of self-definition, and what the process of self-definition and the categories it employs reveal about the character of that society and how it changed over time. Beginning in the 1970s, the field of early American scholarship has witnessed spectacular advances in understanding because of the new social history. What impressed me as the decade of the 1990s began, however, was a perceptible turning from that emphasis to a concentration on individual life experiences and how they could be probed for deeper meaning. During the preceding decade, a number of historians had begun to approach these questions from a biographical perspective informed by anthropology, psychology, literary analysis, and material culture. A common purpose seemed to mark their investigations—an endeavor to discern through the lives of individuals or families the broader contours of the social and cultural landscape. Such work as that of John Demos on Eunice Williams, Rhys Isaac on Landon Carter, Kenneth Lockridge on William Byrd II, and Laurel Thatcher Ulrich on Martha Ballard pointed to an effort by scholars, some of whom had begun their careers with town studies and other new social history forms, to reach a different level of apprehension. As scholars turned away from aggregate studies based in institutions and demography, they seemed to seek meanings for colonial experiences from patterns embedded in individuals' lives. My sense of a scholarly movement into historical explorations of personal existence convinced me that the time had come to convene a forum focused on this work.

My own work on the Carroll family of Maryland also served as a catalyst in shaping the ideas that became this program. As part of my sabbatical in 1991, I spent several months in Israel, with the result that my first thoughts about the topic that has culminated in this volume came to me during a bus ride from Tel Aviv to the University of Haifa, where Mechal Sobel had invited me to speak to her graduate students. Mechal had asked me to address the most terrifying question a historian can be asked—namely, What is the significance of your scholarship? Wrestling with this proposition as the bus sped along the coastal highway, I mused that my current project on the Carrolls had not turned out as originally intended. Initially, I had planned to do a brief documentary edition, but that idea had expanded until it encompassed forty reels of microfilm, three heavily annotated volumes of correspondence, and a separate monograph on the family in Ireland and Maryland, 1500–1782. Here my mind started to wander, as it often does when I look at the landscape of the Galilee, to the continuity of the contemporary Arab-Israeli conflict with the bloody record of warfare that characterized ancient Israel.

My reflections brought me quite suddenly and unexpectedly to a new understanding about the Carrolls. I had long appreciated their outsider status—Maryland's Catholic community constituted less than 10 percent of the population, and its members lived under the threat that, at any time, the Elizabethan penal statutes could be invoked, a process that in England and Ireland had led to the confiscation of virtually all Catholic-held lands. What I had not previously grasped was that the Maryland Carrolls' conscious memory of their family's long, bitter, and ultimately futile struggle against conquest and dispossession in their native Ireland also signified something profoundly important about the way they thought about themselves, how they structured themselves internally, how they developed a sense of self, and how memory and powerful social forces working in tandem over considerable expanses of time established behavioral patterns and character traits that surfaced over and over again in response to similar dangers. Threatened perennially between 1500 and 1782, first by the territorial ambitions of rival clans, then because of their stubborn attachment to their Gaelic Irish heritage, and finally for their defiant adherence to Catholicism, the Carrolls consistently developed comparable strategies, confronting each particular peril with a mixture of compromise, implacable will, cunning, and a tenacious determination to devise some mode of survival. Memory explained part of the family's parallel reactions over centuries of time, but the deeper level of continuity in their behavior stretched well beyond that. As if in response to an inexorable nudge, each generation seemed to be living out the unfinished lives and carrying on the unfinished business of its predecessor.

Discussing these insights with Mechal Sobel during the next several days proved to be an extraordinarily fruitful experience. Mechal pointed out Carl Jung's relevance for my work, especially his writings that focus on how strong family figures, predominantly but not exclusively male, establish behavioral characteristics that carry over multiple generations. This observation led us into a series of conversations about the methods through which human beings structure their identities and the important implications such behaviors hold for the study of history. Mechal shared with me her insights regarding the changing patterns of self-definition that she had extracted from her close reading of more than two hundred autobiographies ranging from the seventeenth through the early nineteenth century. She spoke with particular conviction about how the stories and dreams of people recorded in their autobiographies revealed the deep societal transformations in the conception of self that had occurred over the course of three centuries. As we grew increasingly excited about the potential of this approach and began to talk about the work of other scholars in this area, we decided to lay the groundwork for a conference that would extend these areas of mutual interest. It is this idea that I, with Mechal's enthusiastic support and advice, appropriated for the Institute's fiftieth-anniversary conference.

In developing the possibilities inherent in historicizing self-identity, Sally Mason, the associate editor of the Carroll Papers, was an indispensable colleague. She imaginatively grasped and extended the topic's potential. As the plans for the conference progressed, I also discussed its structure and implications with the Institute's editor of publications, Fredrika J. Teute. Her counsel proved invaluable, and the meeting's final format was hers. The same can be said of the book. Both Mechal and I recognized that Fredrika's exacting standards and analytical grace were essential for giving the volume the shape and coherence we had originally envisioned.

All three editors believe that *Through a Glass Darkly: Reflections on Personal Identity in Early America* attests to the creativity and imagination that presently characterize the scholarship in the field of American studies. We are confident that this gratifies the Institute's sponsors—the College of William and Mary and the Colonial Williamsburg Foundation—and that it honors the faith they have sustained in the Institute for more than half a century. Without their support, neither the conference, this volume, nor the continuing work of the Institute would be possible. For their short-term investment in the fiftieth-anniversary conference and their long-term investment in early American history and culture, we thank them.

The editors also wish to acknowledge the important contributions made by other participants at the Institute's fiftieth-anniversary conference: Joyce O. Appleby, James L. Axtell, Cary Carson, David Brion Davis, John Demos, Robert A. Gross, Barbara E. Lacey, Laura Rigal, Robert St. George, Julius S. Scott, Thad W. Tate, Gordon S. Wood, and Alfred F. Young. Finally, no acknowledgments for an Institute book can be complete without recognizing the scholarly care and expertise brought to bear in copyediting and preparing the manuscript for publication. Editing fourteen different authors' prose and subjects into a collected volume of essays is a challenging task, and Virginia Montijo Chew has executed it with style and skill.

Ronald Hoffman

CONTENTS

THROUGH A GLASS DARKLY

INTRODUCTION:

IN SEARCH OF A METAPHOR

Greg Dening

"Early America" is a notion in search of a metaphor. True, there are metaphors enough inscribed on the American landscape: names that celebrate something "new" with a memory of something old, names that proclaim some ideal of classical republicanism. Names that make narrative out of some sacred text or catch the pain and triumph of encounters with an alien land and peoples. There is a procession of saints, heroes, dreams, and sorrows across the land, from east to west, from west to east.

Time and space need not preoccupy us in that search for a metaphor, although they raise a puzzle or two relevant to any question of identity. How early is "early"? Back to the origins of human settlements, twenty thousand years ago? How far does "America" reach? To the West Coast and its Spanish experiences? To the Arctic and Aleut experiences? To Yucatán and Mayan? Historical periodization, however, is never just a matter of time and space. It is more a matter of dynamic and synthetic understanding. A metaphor makes sense of the whole.

"Marchlands," Bernard Bailyn has suggested in *The Peopling of British North America*, might be that metaphor that makes sense of the whole.[1] "Marchlands" replaces "frontier." "Frontier" has accrued too many connotations of progress, anticipation, and liberation, too many unresolved historical questions to be thought to catch the actual experience of strangers' making a place familiar. "Marchlands," on the other hand, is a name for regressive, bizarre, and wild places dominated by violence. They were boundary places where being "civilized" was always compromised by the realpolitik of the harsh environment, where everybody went a little savage to survive. "Early America" found its identity in a fierce mélange of order and disorder, of idealistic and yet bloodied reality, of novel and yet accustomed experience, of regressive and yet progressive ambitions. The metaphor that makes sense of the whole of early America will need to include irreconcilable polarities.

1. Bernard Bailyn, *The Peopling of British North America: An Introduction* (New York, 1986), 112–113.

1

In the essays that follow, the authors are in search of qualities that gave identity in early America. The self they are looking for is primarily in the individual, but it is extended too to the group. They do not align themselves behind any one metaphor to describe the processes of making that individual, be it marchlands, frontier, or anything else. They do, however, discover a common characteristic or state in early America. None of them, I think, give that feature a name. I, by privilege of introducing them, will give it one. I will call that characteristic or state in which early America found reflection of its identity "limen," or liminality. Early America was a place of thresholds, margins, boundaries. It was a place of ambivalence and unset definition. The search for identity in that place was multivalent and unending. Such a space is like a hall of mirrors. It is made for reflection. But when reflections are made off so many surfaces and from so many angles—from sailor towns and trapper tracks, from settlements and camps, from parlors and courtrooms—which is the reflection of self?

Perhaps the very mention of words like limen or liminality will put many historians on edge. That is partly because the words have the feel of the Latinized mystifications of the social sciences. Partly it is because thresholds, margins, boundaries, beaches are edgy places. Edginess is what one feels in limen. Edginess is what one feels about limen. That's all right. Edginess is the quintessential feel of early America.

The notion of limen comes to us out of the writing of Arnold van Gennep and Victor Turner, but some structuralists like Edmund Leach will use it too.[2] Biological living, they tell us, is a continuous flow, but social living is a series of discontinuous jumps. It is a sequence of definitions and redefinitions. The discontinuities are constant. In becoming adult, or married, or healthy, or educated, or criminal, and in all the specifying of roles, gender, age, status, and kin, the normal times of living are interrupted by times of definition, moments of marking, occasions of abnormality. We sometimes call these marking and abnormal times ritual. Sometimes we refer to them as theater. They are moments in between. They are points of defining rather than of definition, when, for example, one's identity is neither that of being single nor married but in between for a time, bride and groom. They are threshold moments, limen. The quintessential feel of early America was that. It was in between, always in defining rather than definition mode, always on the edge of being something different.

2. Arnold van Gennep, *The Rites of Passage* (1909; reprint, London, 1960); Victor Turner, *From Ritual to Theatre: The Human Seriousness of Play* (New York, 1982); Edmund Leach, *Culture and Communication: The Logic by Which Symbols Are Connected* . . . (Cambridge, 1976).

Edginess is certainly the paramount concern of that scriptural metaphor that is used to entitle this collection of essays—*Through a Glass Darkly*. It comes from what is known as *Paul the Apostle's First* (but probably his second) *Epistle to the Corinthians,* written in A.D. 57. The Corinthian Christians were marginalized in their own Hellenistic society by what they had come to believe. They were poor, too, amid considerable wealth, and they had become strangers to their fellow citizens. So they had questions to put to Paul about marriages that crossed social and religious boundaries, about whether virginity was an ordinary or extraordinary state of virtue, about where authority lay when the spirit whirled through them in tongues. Should they share food that had been sacrificed to idols? Should they submit to civic power? Paul told them that it was the human condition to be uncertain but that they were on the edge of something better. They should live by that hope and find their identity in what was to come. "For we know in part, and we prophesy in part. But when that which is perfect is come, then that which is in part shall be done away. When I was a child, I spake as a child, I understood as a child, I thought as a child; but when I became a man, I put away childish things. For now we see through a glass darkly; but then face to face; now I know in part; but then shall I know even as I am known" (1 Cor. 13:9–13).

Maybe edginess is the paramount feeling of the human condition itself. Perhaps it is not necessarily specific to such situations as early America and early Christianity. Ever since George Mead drove a distinction between "I" and "Me"—"I," the impulsive tendency of the individual, "Me," the incorporated other within the individual—self and society have been understood in a symbiotic relationship. The definitiveness of the "Me," reflecting the organized sets of attitudes, understandings, and expectations common to the group, is in harness with the spontaneous, undirected tendencies of the individual.[3] The resulting interplay is not so much a closure of identity as a process of identifying. The self is always on edge, always contingent, dependent on all the exchanges with otherness around. Identity is an appreciation that "I" am not now what "I" was then. Anyone pondering bons mots and faux pas in the early hours of the morning knows that. "That was not me at the dinner party, or at the seminar, last evening. I spake like a child; now (at 3.00 A.M.) I am a man."

Perhaps we should think of identity as being those snapshots of self, inevitably different by the time and the occasion they are taken. Living is the moving film made out of a series of stills. Each still is defined by a boundary. That boundary, like every boundary, has no space of its own, just a separating function. It is untenable by any other quality than that of defining. There is no

---

3. George Herbert Mead, *Mind, Self, and Society: From the Standpoint of a Social Behaviorist* (Chicago, 1934).

definition in it. Definition belongs to what is on either side of it. In social and cultural life, we invent such a defining space in ritual and theater. That space with no space we call limen. Our authors, looking through a glass darkly, will find reflections of identity in early America in limen of different sorts. But the abiding sense is that there is nothing indigenous to this environment, not even those indigenes who had been there since the time-before of early America. The mutual otherness of all the groups made a space without a space, a time without time, a limen, a place of much inventiveness.

The uneasy relationship between contingency and universality in self has long been an understanding of American social philosophers—George Mead, William James, John Dewey among them. William James once wrote of a "certain blindness in human beings." On a trip through the Appalachian Mountains, he had come across a clearing in the forest where the trees had been replaced with a muddy garden, a log cabin, and some pigpens.

> Because to me the clearings spoke of naught but denudation, I thought that to those whose sturdy arms and obedient axes had made them they could tell no other story. But when *they* looked on the hideous stumps, what they thought of was personal victory. . . . In short, the clearing which to me was a mere ugly picture on the retina, was to them a symbol redolent with moral memories and sang a very paean of duty, struggle, and success. I had been as blind to the peculiar ideality of their conditions as they certainly would also have been to the ideality of mine, had they had a peep at my strange indoor academic ways of life at Cambridge.[4]

We have to think that at this moment William James was experiencing liminality. He discovers himself in the otherness of what this forest clearing meant for those Appalachian farmers. He has to change himself, to enlarge himself with an understanding of a contradiction he cannot resolve. That landscape is neither one thing nor the other. Its contradictions prompt reflection. James will know himself differently in that reflection. Maybe the farmers did too. James has to resolve it by dramatizing it in some way—lecturing about it, using its story as parable for something else he has to say. How the farmers resolved their contradictions we cannot say. We do know that, the more the contradictions became conflictual, the more likely they were to create social drama in a court, on a hustings, in a riot, in the memory in a ballad. We do know that the farmers would come to redefine their identities in some social drama.

4. William James, "On a Certain Blindness in Human Beings," in Frederick Burkhardt and Fredson Bowers, eds., *Talks to Teachers on Psychology and to Students on Some of Life's Ideals* (Cambridge, Mass., 1983), 134, quoted in Richard Rorty, "The Contingency of Selfhood," in Rorty, *Contingency, Irony, and Solidarity* (Cambridge, 1989), 38.

You will see that the places where the authors in *Through a Glass Darkly* discover liminality are greatly varied—in trials and executions, in courts, in commonplace books, in dreams, in new communities, in personal pain, in diasporic experiences, to name just a few. What is common to them all is that they turn around some experience of otherness. It is otherness that prompts self-description. That self-description is caught in the texts that the early America players made of their lived experience, their autohistories, their stories, their diaries. But self-description, even when it is caught in texts, is much more transient than that, as we are aware from our everyday cultural experience. It was Erving Goffman who developed the metaphor of theater in his *Presentation of Self in Everyday Life*. To see the role and persona in identity, we need to be, not just observers, but theater critics too.[5]

Historians have to be observers also. They cannot just be readers of texts. They have to observe the behavior in the texts. And they have to be theater critics. In *Through a Glass Darkly*, the historians move naturally to those moments of ambiguity that otherness presents. They are theatrical moments par excellence. Self-presentations are dramatized—in a courtroom, in a soothsayer's interpretation of a dream, in the carving of a piece of furniture. Thus dramatized, the events are closed around in some way. They are pulled out of the babble and noise of every moment's consciousness and are given a beginning and an end. A space is contrived for presenting that dramatization and interpreting it. That is its theater. There are audiences and performers in this act of viewing. And if there is theater, there is theatricality. There is a sense of contrivance and staging. And there is performance consciousness, a sense of personal distance in the acting and of audience. The self, whether of group or of individual, given identity is thus not merely reflected in the drama; it is reflected upon.

No historian would ever believe that there is one self reflected in one great mirror of society or that the many selves reflected are statuesque, frozen in time. So, inevitably, thirteen authors will find thirteen theaters for their descriptions of selves in early America. In order that the presentations of the selves have some theater of their own, the whole of *Through a Glass Darkly* has been divided into three acts. The first, "Histories of Self," contains narratives of the self-describing in early America. They are written with a sense of the process in and dialogic nature of culture. They make theater of the ambiguities created by otherness. The second, "Texts of Self," offers readings of the ways that selves in early America were inscribed—in writing, in stories told, in material things. The third, "Reflections on Defining Self," presents efforts to

5. Erving Goffman, *The Presentation of Self in Everyday Life* (New York, 1959).

fulfill the historian's obligation not merely to tell the story of self-defining but to explain it. Each act is preceded by a prologue, which, like all prologues, is an invitation to the audience to be a theater critic of what it sees.

Deep in the wilderness of southwest Tasmania, an island to the south of continental Australia, is a cave. Fraser Cave, it is called. On the walls of the cave are imprints of hands, traced with red ochre. They are the signatures of those who visited the cave twenty thousand years ago. These visitors had walked across the land bridge that the lowering of the sea levels in the Ice Age had left between island and continent. The visitors would have seen from the cave the icebergs that had drifted off the Antarctic ice cap. It reached far to the north of where it is today. The men and women had left a witness with their handprints of their presence in a place farther south on the globe than any other human being had gone. Their own ancestors, forty thousand years before them, had made their own way across a whole continent.

In the last moments before the SS snatched him away to strangle him, Dietrich Bonhoeffer, the Lutheran theologian who had resisted Nazism and was caught up in Hitler's last annihilating forces, scribbled his signature on the flyleaf of a Bible. "Dietrich Bonhoeffer," just that.

Human beings make great efforts to leave their signatures on life—in the children they bear, in the constitutions they write, in the things they build. I have always felt that the great privilege of a historian has been to be guardian of the signatures everyone desires to leave. I feel honored to have been invited to introduce to you the selves that the historians in these pages have saved.

PART I: HISTORIES OF SELF

"Tell me, sir," Herman Melville has his confidence man ask his mark as he sets him up with feigned innocence. "Do you really think that a white man could look the negro so?" "For one, I should call it pretty good acting." "Not much better than any other man acts," the mark replies, displaying his worldliness. "How? Does all the world act? Am I, for instance, an actor? Is my reverend friend here, too, a performer?" "Yes, don't you perform acts? To do, is to act; so all doers are actors." "The Sham is evident, then?" the confidence man asks. "To the discerning eye," the mark replies—with a horrible screw of his gimlet eye.[1]

Melville, in this the most despairing and skeptical of his novels, has us believe that there is no "discerning eye" sharp enough in the theater of self. Life, he suggests, is a trickster's stage. So it is, of course. It is "wink upon wink upon wink," as Clifford Geertz has remarked in a famous phrase.[2] Knowing the reality behind the wink is always a problem for each of us but especially for the historian. Self, as far as we can know it, is not to be seen. It has no reality other than in relationship to something else. Yet that something else, that otherness, is always changing in the time of living and in the space of sociality. That otherness can never be the Other. That self can never be the Self. The Other and the Self belong to the imagination of the theoretician, not the actualities of the historian. One needs to be blinkered in some way to see them. History, professedly the most unblinkered of sciences, will try to represent the experiencing self rather than the model. Histories of self will always discover the ambivalence in relationships, the multiple meanings in an act, the processes and fluidities in any definition. Histories of self will discover these things, then make stories of them.

Of course, the actualities of self and otherness created in these relationships past and present are not random or unique. They are cultural. Being cultural, they are public in the sense of being shared, public by being recognizable, having some system. No matter that there are errors in the recognition, no matter that there are facades and subterfuges. To those experiencing the rela-

1. Herman Melville, *The Confidence-Man: His Masquerade,* ed. Hershel Parker (1857; reprint, New York, 1971), 27.
2. Clifford Geertz, *The Interpretation of Cultures: Selected Essays* (London, 1975), 7.

9

tionship between self and otherness there are certainties that we call cultural. And if those who experience them have some certainty in their recognition, then an outsider, a historian for example, can have the same certainty, or nearly. The outsider, the observer that the historian is, is likely to see these cultural events differently from the insider. The outsider tends to see culture as a map. "[The map] is the analogy," Pierre Bourdieu writes, "which occurs to an outsider who has to find his way around a foreign landscape and who compensates for his lack of practical mastery, the prerogative of the native, by the use of a model of all possible routes."[3] The insider, the native, has a sense of practical space, of journeys actually made, of the ways systems are related to a personal body, time lived, distances seen. Histories of self will lessen the disadvantages of being an outsider by simulating the perspectives of an insider. Not just the perspectives of the rational agent, mind you. The emotions as well and the sense that the stage on which the actors perform is given to them and made by them at the same time.

There are two words that come from the same Greek word *theasthai*, meaning to "watch, contemplate, look at." They are *theater* and *theory*. That prompts Herbert Blau to write: "Theater is theory, or the shadow of it. . . . In the act of seeing, there is already theory."[4] In the dramas of living, reflections are made. Self is reflected in, self is reflected upon in the dramas of living—"through a glass darkly." Historians are attracted to dramas of living like moths to a lamp.

Theater does not need a building, but it needs a social space. It needs a space closed down by the willingness of an audience to watch and of performers to play. In the Susquehannah Valley, in James H. Merrell's history of self, an "unintelligible person," Andrew Montour, made such a space. He made a self that required "reading," in Merrell's phrase. With many a contradictory badge of identity in the color of his skin, his languages, and his names, Montour (or Sattelihu or Echnizera) crafted himself into something new, neither French, British, nor Indian, neither genteel colonist, Iroquois warrior, nor frontiersman, but all of them—and all of them merged into something new. His was a special sort of constructed otherness. Men could lose their lives, and did, not seeing it. He had a dream that was especially threatening. He dreamed that he could make a community in which this new merged self of his would not be other at all. That was his theater of self. But there were many who did not like what they saw in his otherness. They did not let him make himself old or new. They made him stay just in between.

3. Pierre Bourdieu, *Outline of a Theory of Practice*, trans. Richard Nice (Cambridge, 1977), 1–2.
4. Herbert Blau, *Take Up the Bodies: Theater at the Vanishing Point* (Urbana, Ill., 1982), 1.

Thomasine/Thomas Hall has to be reduced to a *T* to describe his/her merged self. And Mary Beth Norton, in token of the misfit of categories of sex and gender T represented, had to invent a language to tell the history of how a Virginia community invented a self for this in-between person. The General Court was the theater of this self. The General Court became the drama of living and reflected the selves of the collectivity in the otherness it made of T. When the contradictions in the communal systems of sexuality, gendered power, external symbols of status, and privacy were found to be irresolvable, the collectivity, through the Court, materialized T in a man's apparel worn with a woman's coif and apron. The Virginians, it might be noted, had had some experience that sex and gender might be otherwise related in the otherness of Algonquin gendered roles they saw around them.

How a collectivity summoned the strength to change itself through "publick opinion" is T. H. Breen's history of self. Three Massachusetts slaves—Bristol, Arthur, and Quock Walker—are the performers in this theater. The trial and execution of the first two and the successful defense of the third against the charges of a brutal master were *catharsis*—in Aristotle's word of the theater. They were an "enlightenment" in the community's reflections on the contradictions created by slavery in a free society. Arthur was the trickster in this trio, "too clever by half," says Breen. He assaulted traditional boundaries, had sexual relations with women of different races, traveled across Massachusetts and the Caribbean, exposed various masters as fools. He was a most free unfree person. The enlightenment of this theater was to make the belief that "all men are born equal and free" a matter of common sense as well as law.

There are denouements in Alan Taylor's story of "the unhappy Stephen Arnold" that need to be respected. If the history of self is discovered in the theater of life, that history itself is likely to be theatrical. The ostensible stage for Arnold's theater was upstate New York, with its volatile community of new migrants. The drama was his trial and execution for the cruel murder of his stepdaughter because she could not pronounce the word "gig." But the real stage was the volatility itself, the swirling movements of these migrant peoples in search of their identity. Arnold was a schoolteacher and by that calling held in his person the ambitions of the community to shape its future self. These ambitions were divided at the time between an older patriarchal desire to create the proper self by breaking the pride and will of the child, violently if necessary, and a newer view of nurturing the innate innocence of children with love. Then when Arnold told his own story of his victimization at the hands of his father, "a cult of sensibility" could hardly distinguish victim and criminal. But the story is more complex than that by far.

The Dutch notary who is the subject of Donna Merwick's history is, she says, like the smallest figure on the farthest edge of a Brueghel painting. Deceptively, he seems inconsequential to the central figures—West India Company men, English governors—usually given attention in New York's early history. Adriaen Janse van Ilpendam made much history by "putting reality into writing" in his notarial papers. Yet the history that is to be made of him has to be made out of the shadows in the scenes of life around him. Perhaps it is only a small man who can be destroyed so hugely by an English conquest and military occupation that reached so deeply into his Dutch soul. The story of this self-made scribe who tragically self-murdered is a story of an occupation in every sense of the word.

These histories of self break away from the impossible pursuit of an Identity, or a Self, or an Other. Otherness and self are always seen in a complex and shifting set of public and private, cultural and political, social and psychological relationships. The identities defined in these relationships are refracted as much as reflected "through a glass darkly" in the images of the self in the otherness around.

Greg Dening

~

"THE CAST OF HIS COUNTENANCE":

READING ANDREW MONTOUR

James H. Merrell

On the morning of October 25, 1755, a band of forty-nine men sat on their horses at a fork in the road along the east bank of the Susquehanna River. They were discussing how best to get downstream. The path to the right led to a ford across the river, an easy ride down the western shore, and another ford taking them back across the Susquehanna to their homes at Paxton, some fifty miles away. Straight ahead was "the old Road" down the east side, a shorter but harder ride.[1]

Ordinarily the choice would have been easy; the right-hand path was the conventional route, and the one the men had come up two days before. But this was no ordinary time. Just nine days earlier, Indian war had come to Pennsylvania, igniting a conflagration of hatred, bloodshed, and sorrow that would last for a generation. In the Susquehanna Valley, the first blows had fallen upon the Penn's Creek settlements on the west side of the river. On hearing the terrible news, these forty-nine "Paxton people," led by the fur trader and storekeeper John Harris, had come north to bury the dead, search for the missing, and scout the enemy. From Penn's Creek the burial party had forded the river and headed to Shamokin, an Indian town at the confluence of the North and West Branches of the Susquehanna. "There is a Body of Indians assembled" in that village, it was said, Indians who had sent word that they

For helpful comments on earlier versions of this paper, I am grateful to Clyde Griffen, Alison Duncan Hirsch, Michael McConnell, Alice Nash, Ann Marie Plane, and Daniel K. Richter, and to the Department of History at Princeton University and the Colonial History Workshop at the University of Minnesota.

1. The number in the party is in *Minutes of the Provincial Council of Pennsylvania, from the Organization to the Termination of the Proprietary Government*, 16 vols. (Harrisburg, 1851–1853), VI, 657 (hereafter cited as *MPCP*); *Pennsylvania Archives*, 138 vols. (Philadelphia and Harrisburg, 1852–1949), 1st Ser., II, 459 (hereafter cited as *PA*). Unless otherwise noted, the story of these events is derived from *MPCP*, VI, 645–701, and *PA*, 1st Ser., II, 443–493. For the paths, see Paul A. W. Wallace, *Indian Paths of Pennsylvania* (Harrisburg, 1965), 122–123, 158.

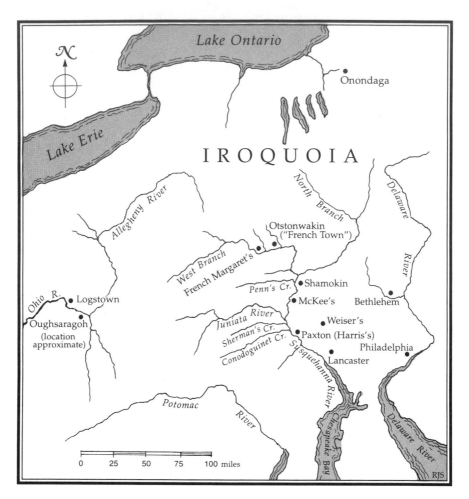

FIGURE 1. Andrew Montour's World. *Drawn by Richard Stinely.*

"want to see their [Pennsylvania] Brethren's faces" in these dark times. So the band of Pennsylvanians pushed on upstream in order "to know their [the Indians'] minds."[2] Were those natives preparing to help colonists stop the invasion, or plotting to join it?

It was hard to tell from the look of things at Shamokin, where Harris's party arrived on the evening of October 24. On the one hand, the Paxton men— some of them, like Harris and the fur trader Thomas McKee, well acquainted with the Susquehanna Valley Indian peoples—saw a number of familiar faces and were "seemingly well received." On the other hand, amid the familiar faces were many "strange Indians, . . . all painted Black" for war. Worse still, during

2. *MPCP,* VI, 648, 649, 653, 658.

the night some of Harris's men overheard Delawares plotting to call in rein-forcements against these colonial visitors, talk followed by "the War Song" and then by four Indians, "well armed," paddling off into the darkness. The next morning, Harris and his companions, no fools, "got up early in order to go back." As the party prepared to leave, another familiar face in those parts, a man named Andrew Montour, stepped forward to warn the travelers "not to go the same Road they came, but to keep this side Sasquehannah and go the old Road" in order to slip a trap. And so, at "the parting of the Roads" just outside Shamokin, the forty-nine men talked, that autumn day, about the safer course to take.[3]

The question framing the discussion was simple: Can we trust Andrew Montour? Some in the party, having known the man for more than a decade, said yes. Over the years, Montour had traveled hundreds of miles on errands for Pennsylvania and her sister colonies. His work on behalf of the English—carrying messages, delivering gifts, translating speeches—earned him the du-bious distinctions of having a French bounty on his capture (or his scalp), serving with George Washington at Great Meadows, and marching toward even worse disaster with Edward Braddock. So trusted was Montour by Penn-sylvanians that, when he had arrived at the Paxton settlements late in 1754 bearing a commission to raise a body of Indian troops for the English, so many "River Men" volunteered (including John Harris's brother, William) that Montour filled his ranks with Pennsylvania colonists instead.[4] Interpreter,

3. Ibid., 648, 657–658. Although the weight of the evidence favors Montour's giving the warning, it should be noted that another colonist in the party said simply that they "were advised" to avoid the western shore (648); Delaware Indians later said it was Scarouyady, an Ohio Oneida, who had issued the warning (James Sullivan et al., eds., *The Papers of Sir William Johnson*, 14 vols. [Albany, 1921–1965], IX, 334–335 [hereafter cited as *PWJ*]). John Harris, in his reports of the episode, said nothing about any warning, leading me to suspect that he was instrumental in disregarding this advice; *MPCP*, VI, 654–655; Harris to Isaac Norris, Oct. 27, 1755, Pierre Eugene Du Simitiere Papers, 966.F.49, 21, Library Company of Philadelphia (hereafter cited as LCP). The details of the debate about which course to take were not recorded. I have reconstructed its likely character from other information, par-ticularly from comments about Montour offered by John Harris and other Paxton folk in the days following the discussion.

4. For a summary of Montour's public career, see Howard Lewin, "A Frontier Diplomat: Andrew Montour," *Pennsylvania History*, XXXIII (1966), 153–186. For Montour's work on behalf of the English, see Lois Mulkearn, ed., *George Mercer Papers Relating to the Ohio Company of Virginia* (Pittsburgh, 1954), 16–17, 256; [Bernhard A. Grube], "A Missionary's Tour to Shamokin and the West Branch of the Susquehanna, 1753," *Pennsylvania Magazine of History and Biography*, XXXIX (1915), 443–444; *MPCP*, VI, 397–398; *PA*, 8th Ser., V, 3978, 4008. On Montour's commission to raise Indian troops, see *PA*, 1st Ser., II, 230; R. A. Brock,

adviser, soldier—Montour, some of the Paxton men argued, had proven his loyalty too many times to be doubted now. Heed his warning; stay on this side of the Susquehanna.

Others disagreed. After all, this "French Andrew," this "Monsieur Montour," was the son of a "Madame Montour," with a brother who acted like "a perfect French Man" and a cousin called "French Margaret."[5] Moreover, the man's recent behavior clearly betrayed him. "Montour knew many days of the Enemy's being on their March against us before he informed me," John Harris said. And, if such silence did not speak loudly enough, when Montour came forward at Shamokin that morning to warn the Pennsylvanians about the risks of the river's west side, he was "painted as the rest." Although admitting that "tis hard to tell," colonists urging the western route insisted that Montour could not be trusted; he was "an Enemy in his heart."[6]

And so the men argued, knowing that their lives might depend upon their reading of Montour. Ultimately, those mistrusting him won the day; the horsemen, "fearing a snare might be laid on that [east] side," forded the river—and

---

ed., *The Official Records of Robert Dinwiddie, Lieutenant-Governor of the Colony of Virginia, 1751–1758 . . .* , 2 vols. (Virginia Historical Society, *Collections*, N.S., III-IV [Richmond, Va., 1883–1884]), I, 450, II, 7; William Hand Browne, ed., *Correspondence of Governor Horatio Sharpe*, I, *1753–1757*, Archives of Maryland, VI (Baltimore, 1888), 144–145 (hereafter cited as *Corr. Sharpe*).

5. For "French Andrew," see *MPCP*, V, 660. For "Monsieur Montour," see *PA*, 1st Ser., III, 42. For reference to Montour's brother, see Richard Peters to the proprietaries, Nov. 6, 1753, Penn Manuscripts, Official Correspondence, VI, 115, Historical Society of Pennsylvania (hereafter cited as HSP). For "French Margaret," see Witham Marshe, *Lancaster in 1744: Journal of the Treaty at Lancaster in 1744, with the Six Nations*, ed. William H. Egle (Lancaster, Pa., 1884), appendix, 28; William C. Reichel, ed., *Memorials of the Moravian Church* (Philadelphia, 1870), I, 330n. Colonists variously called French Margaret Andrew's sister and his cousin. My reading of the evidence suggests that she was his cousin—the daughter of Madame Montour's sister—but the closeness of the relationship (see below) is more important than her precise status. For the varying accounts, see *Dictionary of Canadian Biography*, III (Toronto, 1974), 147, s.v. "Couc, Elizabeth?"; *MPCP*, III, 501; John W. Jordan, ed., "Spangenberg's Notes of Travel to Onondaga in 1745," *PMHB*, II (1878), 429–430; Shamokin Diary, Sept. 18, 1745, Moravian Church Archives: Records of the Moravian Mission among the Indians of North America, microfilm (1970), reel 28, box 217, folder 12B, item 1 (hereafter cited as Mor. Arch. reel/box/folder/item numbers); [Grube], "Missionary's Tour," *PMHB*, XXXIX (1915), 442–444.

6. *MPCP*, VI, 654, 658. Montour himself had spoken of meeting at Great Island on the West Branch with enemy Delaware and Shawnee warriors (*PA*, 1st Ser., II, 451–452; *MPCP*, VI, 673). On Montour as enemy, see *PA*, 1st Ser., II, 458. See also Adam Hoops to Isaac Norris, Oct. 31, 1755, Du Simitiere Papers, 966.F.49e, 27. Two years earlier, Conrad Weiser had pronounced Montour "a French man in his heart" (Peters to the proprietaries, Nov. 6, 1753, Penn Mss., Off. Corr., VI, 115).

rode straight into the ambush that Montour knew was there.[7] Four men fell to the first volley; several more drowned trying to make it back to Montour's side of the Susquehanna. The rest staggered home to Paxton to tell their story to family, to neighbors, to provincial officials, and to us.

The men who misread Andrew Montour that day were neither the first nor the last to make this mistake; they just paid a higher price than others. Richard Peters, an Anglican clergyman and provincial secretary to the Penn family who was deeply involved in the colony's Indian affairs, considered Montour "really an unintelligible person"; many others felt the same way. Conrad Weiser, Pennsylvania's Iroquois specialist who knew Montour even better than Peters did, "found him faithful, knowing, and prudent" in June 1748, but, by summer's end, was "at a lost [sic] what to say of him."[8]

Historians, like Peters, have generally thought Montour unintelligible, and, like Weiser, they are often at a loss for what to say about him. Most confine themselves to a sketch of Montour's colorful family and his checkered career: his birth to the Oneida leader Currundawanah and "the celebrated" Madame Montour, a Canadian métis who, among other adventures that brought her fame from Albany to Philadelphia to Detroit, dined with an English governor and bedded a French commandant;[9] his attachment to French Margaret, who once traveled from the Susquehanna Valley to New York accompanied by "her Mohawk husband and two grandchildren, . . . with an Irish groom and six relay and pack-horses";[10] his appearance on the Susquehanna frontier in 1742 as an interpreter and guide for Moravian missionaries; his performances over the years that followed at councils and other intercultural conversations in Pennsylvania, Iroquoia, New York, Virginia, and the Ohio country; his status

7. *MPCP,* VI, 648, 658.

8. Peters to the proprietor, Feb. 7, 1753, Penn Mss., Off. Corr., VI, 7; *MPCP,* V, 290; *PA,* 1st Ser., II, 12.

9. For Madame Montour, see *DCB,* III, 147, s.v. "Couc, Elizabeth?"; Alison Duncan Hirsch, "Métis Women and the Struggle to Survive on the Middle Ground: Madame Montour and Her Family" (paper presented to the First Annual Conference of the Institute of Early American History and Culture, Ann Arbor, Mich., June 4, 1995); I am grateful to the author for providing me with a copy of this paper. The quotation is from [Witham Marshe], "Witham Marshe's Journal of the Treaty Held with the Six Nations by the Commissioners of Maryland, and Other Provinces, at Lancaster, in Pennsylvania, June, 1744," Massachusetts Historical Society, *Collections,* 1st Ser., VII (Boston, 1801), 189 (hereafter cited as "Marshe's Journal").

10. Reichel, ed., *Memorials,* I, 331n. For his attachment to her, see [Grube], "Missionary's Tour," *PMHB,* XXXIX (1915), 443; Richard Peters, "Diary No. 15, 27 7ber [September], 1758–7th Nov. 1758," Oct. 13, 1758, Peters Papers, HSP (hereafter cited as Peters, "Diary").

as a commander of colonial or Indian troops and a member of the Iroquois council; his bitter arguments with provincial officials; his battles with the bottle; his narrow escapes from debtor's prison; and his murder by a Seneca in 1772, thirty years after he first stepped onto the public stage.[11]

That Montour has befuddled both his contemporaries and later scholars is not surprising. Because he rarely spoke for himself, because he usually translated words others uttered and marked pages others wrote, it is hard to get beneath the surface of his career—this trip, that treaty—in order to study the man, to look upon his face or see into his heart.

More than the lack of sources, Montour's anomalous life gets in the way of a clear view. His very existence goes against the habit of thought, then and since, accustomed to consider the colonial frontier a dividing line between Europeans and native Americans. Trying to locate Montour on either side of that frontier—like the related guessing game devoted to determining whether he favored France or England—preoccupied British colonists, who seemed to spend as much time trying to label Montour as they did trying to understand him. Richard Peters considered him an Indian, but others called him "white," and Conrad Weiser even referred to Montour as Indian on one page of a letter and white on another.[12]

The first encounter with Montour to find its way into the historical record reveals one important source of the confusion about him: his appearance. "Andrew's cast of countenance is decidedly European," wrote the Moravian leader Count Nikolaus Ludwig von Zinzendorf after meeting Montour in September 1742,

11. See Lewin, "Montour," *Pa. History,* XXXIII (1966), 186, on his death. Treatments of Montour can be found in Reichel, ed., *Memorials,* I, 95n; John G. Freeze, "Madame Montour," *PMHB,* III (1879), 79–87; William M. Darlington, "The Montours," *PMHB,* IV (1880), 218–224; Charles A. Hanna, *The Wilderness Trail; or, The Ventures and Adventures of the Pennsylvania Traders on the Allegheny Path . . . ,* 2 vols. (New York, 1911), esp. I, chap. 8; Paul A. W. Wallace, *Conrad Weiser, 1696–1760: Friend of Colonist and Mohawk* (Philadelphia, 1945); Nicholas B. Wainwright, *George Croghan, Wilderness Diplomat* (Chapel Hill, N.C., 1959); and Marshe, *Lancaster in 1744,* ed. Egle, appendix. The latest, and best, study of him is Nancy Hagedorn, " 'Faithful, Knowing, and Prudent': Andrew Montour as Interpreter and Cultural Broker," in Margaret Connel Szasz, ed., *Between Indian and White Worlds: The Cultural Broker* (Norman, Okla., 1994), 43–60. I saw Hagedorn's work only after coming to my own conclusions about our shared subject.

12. *MPCP,* VI, 151, 160. For Montour as Indian, see *MPCP,* VI, 588, VII, 64; *Corr. Sharpe,* I, 342. For Peters's views, see *MPCP,* V, 431, 435, 440–441; Peters, "Diary," Sept. 30, Oct. 1, 26, 1758. For Montour as white, see Reichel, ed., *Memorials,* I, 102; *PWJ,* III, 301. As if the man was sui generis, another colonist noted that a party heading out to war consisted of "Thirty five Rangers, five or Six [European colonial] inhabitants and as many Indians, accompanied by Mr. Montour" (*PWJ,* III, 316).

and had not his face been encircled with a broad band of paint, applied with bear's fat, I would certainly have taken him for one. He wore a brown broadcloth coat, a scarlet damasken lappel-waistcoat, breeches, over which his shirt hung, a black Cordovan neckerchief, decked with silver bugles, shoes and stockings, and a hat. His ears were hung with pendants of brass and other wires plaited together like the handle of a basket. He was very cordial, but on addressing him in French, he, to my surprise, replied in English.

To people like Zinzendorf, accustomed to reading European badges of identity—such as color of skin and cut of hair, language (or accent) and literacy, kin and clothes—Montour sent out mixed signals. Even his reply to Zinzendorf's greeting is hard to read: was Montour showing off his English? Trying to avoid being thought French? Relishing the visitor's surprise? No easier to decipher is the fashion statement Montour made by combining hat and waistcoat with earrings and paint. Nor does his impressive collection of names—not just Andrew Montour and French Andrew but Henry Montour, Andrew (or Andreas) Sattelihu, and Echnizera (or Oughsara)—help to fix his identity.[13]

No wonder those skeptical Paxton men, like others reading Montour in their day and our own, admitted that it is "hard to tell" about him. Hard, yes, but not impossible. By venturing into the shadowy Susquehanna world that Montour called home, by listening with care when he did speak his mind, by letting his actions speak as loudly as his words, one can attempt a reading of Andrew Montour. Those shadows, those words, those actions suggest that Montour, nurtured in a distinctive cultural milieu, fashioned himself into a new sort of person, someone who drew from several traditions in order to craft a life. More than that, he might have been groping his way toward a new sort of society, one nestled in the interstices between Indians and colonists, one inhabited by people like him. Reading Andrew Montour, then, offers a sense of

13. For Zinzendorf's description, see Reichel, ed., *Memorials*, I, 95–96. For a variant translation, see Edmund De Schweinitz, *The Life and Times of David Zeisberger: The Western Pioneer and Apostle of the Indians* (Philadelphia, 1870), 112, n. 1. In contrast to Montour, French Margaret expressed her delight at finding French-speakers during a visit to Bethlehem in 1754 (Reichel, ed., *Memorials*, I, 332n). An excellent discussion of how frontier peoples used clothing as social markers is Timothy J. Shannon, "Dressing for Success on the Mohawk Frontier: Hendrick, William Johnson, and the Indian Fashion," *William and Mary Quarterly*, 3d Ser., LIII (1996), 13–42. Echnizera is in *MPCP*, VII, 491; "The Treaty of Logg's Town, 1752: Commission, Instructions, etc., Journal of Virginia Commissioners, and Text of Treaty," *Virginia Magazine of History and Biography*, XIII (1905–1906), 165. For Oughsara, see Hanna, *Wilderness Trail*, I, 245.

the possibilities open to people in that place at that time and a sense, too, of the limits of the possible, the harsh realities on which Montour foundered.[14]

The best way to approach Montour is to visit the Susquehanna River Valley where he spent much of his life. When Montour lived there, from the 1720s to the 1760s, the Susquehanna country was a debatable land, a place marked by confusion and contention.[15] Too few "natives" remained there to serve as a charter group that could determine the character of life in the region, the Susquehannocks having been all but destroyed by their Iroquois neighbors in the late seventeenth century.[16] The Six Nations—Mohawks, Oneidas, Cayugas, Onondagas, Senecas, and (after 1722) Tuscaroras—claimed the area by virtue of that victory and, after 1700, oversaw a repeopling of the valley's lower reaches not only by Seneca, Oneida, and Cayuga emigrants but also by Indian refugees fleeing European colonial intrusions.[17] From Maryland came Conoys and Nanticokes, from Carolina Tutelos and Tuscaroras; from farther south still, and from the west, came Shawnees, and from the east came Delawares.

Out of the east, too, came colonists from various European lands. English and French, German and Scots-Irish, Swiss and Welsh moved into the valley during the first half of the eighteenth century, pursuing their own versions of happiness and drawing sustenance from faiths as various as Catholic, Quaker,

14. On the limits of possibility in another context, see John Shy, "The Spectrum of Imperial Possibilities: Henry Ellis and Thomas Pownall, 1763–1775," in Shy, *A People Numerous and Armed: Reflections on the Military Struggle for American Independence* (New York, 1976), chap. 3.

15. Montour's date of birth is unknown. I estimate that he was born about 1720, an estimate based on his appearance in the records as a young man in 1742 and the fact that, in 1754, Weiser, then 58 years old, remarked that Montour was "a Young Man and in the best of his time"; see Conrad Weiser to Richard Peters, Mar. 15, 1754, Correspondence of Conrad Weiser, I, 44, in Papers of Conrad Weiser, HSP (hereafter cited as Corr. Weiser).

16. Scholars disagree about the Susquehannocks' fate. Some argue that the Iroquois never defeated them but did absorb them; others stand by the traditional interpretation of a conquest. Whatever the course of events, the end result by 1700 was the same: the Susquehanna Valley was virtually emptied of the Indian peoples who had lived there 50 or 100 years before. See Francis Jennings, "Glory, Death, and Transfiguration: The Susquehannock Indians in the Seventeenth Century," American Philosophical Society, *Proceedings,* CXII (1968), 15–53; Elisabeth Tooker, "The Demise of the Susquehannocks: A 17th-Century Mystery," *Pennsylvania Archaeologist,* LIV, nos. 3–4 (September-December 1984), 1–10; Barry C. Kent, *Susquehanna's Indians,* Anthropological Series, no. 6 (Harrisburg, 1989), 21–58. The Susquehannocks survived, with considerable additions of Senecas, as Conestogas.

17. The histories of these groups deserve fuller treatment. But see Paul A. W. Wallace, *Indians in Pennsylvania,* ed. William A. Hunter, rev. ed. (Harrisburg, 1986); Peter C. Mancall, *Valley of Opportunity: Economic Culture along the Upper Susquehanna, 1700–1800* (Ithaca, N.Y., 1991); Kent, *Susquehanna's Indians.*

Presbyterian, and Moravian. Added to this mix were African Americans, some of them runaway slaves, others owned by colonial fur traders, still others bought or stolen by Indians. Whatever their status, like "Delaware Negroes" visiting a provincial fort on the riverbank one winter day in 1758, African Americans were an everyday feature of the Susquehanna social landscape.[18]

"Delaware Negroes"? The phrase is puzzling, accustomed as we are to painting the colonial scene in the standard primary colors of red, white, and black. Indeed, to our eye the look of the whole Susquehanna Valley in Montour's time seems strange, because the conventional mental maps for finding our way in early America are of little use there. Here was a world that found nothing remarkable in three very different Indian peoples—Siouan-speaking Tutelos, Algonquian-speaking Delawares, and Iroquoian-speaking Oneidas—living in one town; a world where a Pennsylvania trader, drinking with some Delawares, ended up "singing and dancing with the indians after their manner"; a world where another colonial fur trader, Jonas Davenport, sold his servant, Henry Hawkins, to an Indian trader named Chickoonkoniko; a world where European visitors found some Delawares at Shamokin "so buisy at Cards, that they had no Time to look at us"; a world where a Tutelo wrote a letter to a Pennsylvania colonist and received a string of wampum beads in return.[19]

The sense of the Susquehanna Valley as a decidedly unusual place grows when we tune in to the babel of voices, accents, dialects, and languages echoing

18. For runaways, see *MPCP*, III, 211–212, 215. For Africans belonging to traders, see *PA*, 1st Ser., I, 311; Correspondence of James Logan, box 2, files 18, 30, Papers of James Logan, HSP (hereafter cited as Corr. Logan); Will of John Harris, Will Book B-1-542, Lancaster County Archives, Lancaster, Pa.; Accounts, 1754, in Corr. Weiser, I, 49; John Harris, Account Book, 45, Papers of John Harris, HSP; Indian Records Collection, Papers Relating to Indian Losses, 39, HSP; Richard Peters Papers, II, 32, HSP. For Indians who captured and sold blacks, see *PA*, 1st Ser., I, 295. For "Delaware Negroes," see Journal of Captain Joseph Shippen at Fort Augusta, Shamokin, 1757–1758, Jan. 9–10, 1758, Shippen Papers, HSP. These three might have been servants or slaves of Nutimus, a Delaware leader; see Travel Journal, Mor. Arch., 30/225/2/1, Oct. 11, 1748. For other blacks living as free people among the Indians, see William M. Beauchamp, ed., *Moravian Journals Relating to Central New York, 1745–66* (Syracuse, N.Y., 1916), 163–164; Deposition of Patrick Burns, Nov. 17, 1755, Penn Mss., Indian Affairs, II, 44, HSP; *PA*, 1st Ser., III, 57; *PWJ*, XI, 165–166, 174–175.

19. *MPCP*, III, 285. This text reads "Signing," but, in an earlier edition (Harrisburg, 1840, 302), it is "Singing." That the Indians were Minisink Delawares is revealed in *MPCP*, III, 314. On the sale of Henry Hawkins, see Chester County, Court of Quarter Sessions, Indictments, May 1723–August 1729, indictments of February 1724/5, Chester County Archives, West Chester, Pa. My use of "Indian trader" here denotes Indians who traded with colonists; those colonists I call "colonial fur traders." For the Delawares' playing cards, see Shamokin Diary, Oct. 12, 1745, Mor. Arch., 28/217/12B/1. On Tutelo's letter, see *MPCP*, IV, 684 (mis-

through the valley. Newcomers trying to get their bearings amid the noise were profoundly disturbed by the clamor and clash of competing tongues. We "have hear [sic] So many Languages that we find it verry Diffical[t] to larn anything," one Moravian missionary at Shamokin observed; "its rare to hear two Indians talking in one language." Other missionaries, having made some progress in sorting things out, happily sang hymns during a service at Shamokin in "Indian" as well as German and English. Still others built bridges across the linguistic gulf; one span started with a German-speaker and made its way through Mohican and Shawnee to Oneida. Increasingly, however, such makeshift structures were unnecessary, for the mingling of groups brought in its train more people conversant with languages other than their own. Although few could match Ousewayteichks (Captain Smith), a Conoy able to speak "to perfection" Delaware, Conestoga, and Shawnee as well as Conoy, many learned enough to get by. "They mostly all Spake English," a Pennsylvania colonist said of some Delawares, and "one spake as good English as I can."[20]

Strange as the Susquehanna country may seem to us—and strange as it seemed to many in colonial America—this was the world Andrew Montour knew, the world where he began to make something of himself. To a person of his background and upbringing, the future must have looked rich in possibilities, for Montour was singularly well equipped to chart a life's course that would take him in a number of different directions.

One of those directions led, through his mother, toward European colonial society. From Madame Montour Andrew picked up more than French and English; he also learned how to behave in polite provincial circles. Despite her many years among the Indians, colonists still considered Montour's mother "a French lady[,] . . . genteel, and of polite address," who "was . . . very much

---

spelled or misprinted "Tridolow"); *PA*, 1st Ser., I, 649. This Tutelo wrote on behalf of the Oneida leader Shickellamy and the Delawares; the wampum was for a formal reply to the Delawares. For another letter from an Indian, see Shamokin Diary, Jan. 17, 1748, Mor. Arch., 6/121/4/1.

20. Shamokin Diary, Sept. 29, 1745, Jan. 7–8, 1748, Mor. Arch., 28/217/12B/1, 6/121/4/1 (quotation); John W. Jordan, ed., "Bishop J.C.F. Cammerhoff's Narrative of a Journey to Shamokin, Penna., in the Winter of 1748," *PMHB*, XXIX (1905), 174. On the Conoy, see *MPCP*, III, 93, 102. For Indians' speaking English, see *PA*, 1st Ser., II, 724, III, 107; "Marshe's Journal," 180; Beauchamp, ed., *Moravian Jnls.*, 225; *PA*, 1st Ser., III, 397 (quotation). My depiction of the Susquehanna country here is, in some ways, akin to Richard White's treatment of the Great Lakes country (*The Middle Ground: Indians, Empires, and Republics in the Great Lakes Region, 1650–1815* [New York, 1991]). As I suggest below, however, my sense is that, in the Susquehanna country, any such middle ground was less firmly planted and much shorter-lived—indeed, more illusory—than what White has found beyond the mountains.

caressed by the gentlewomen of" Philadelphia, "with whom she used to stay for some time" during treaties there. Along with the social and linguistic skills, Montour's mother would also have told him that being a Montour in Indian country was sometimes dangerous: in 1709, angry warriors had assassinated a Montour for leading Indian traders to Iroquoia and Albany instead of French Canada, and, twenty-five years later, a Seneca hinted that he hoped to do the same to Madame Montour herself.[21]

Montour would have known, too, his mother's unhappiness, in her old age, with her fate. "She was weary of Indian life," she confided to a Moravian visitor in 1742. Three years later, besieged by Indians—who, she said, "know of nothing but drinking and Dancing"—Madame Montour told another guest from Bethlehem of "a great Desire in her heart to come and die there, and she believd she sho.d than [sic] die happy." Whether her son shared that desire to spend his days in a Pennsylvania town, his own disillusionment with Indian country occasionally surfaced. "He had never lived so poorly in his Life," Montour informed visitors to his "very poor Hut" at Shamokin that same fall of 1745.[22] With his appearance and his knowledge of European ways, he could have wiped the paint off his face, pulled the spangles from his ears, and found a home in the colonial world.

Alternatively, Montour could have recast his countenance, adding more paint and turning his face away from Philadelphia or Bethlehem and toward Logstown or Onondaga, deeper into the Indian cultures and countries. After all, along with French and English he could speak Delaware, Shawnee, and one or more Iroquois languages. In addition, his mother, whatever her longings for colonial company, was to all appearances "in mode of life a complete Indian," and, in his youth, Montour was apprenticed in his father's trades of hunting and war. An added incentive to look west or north rather than east was the knowledge that colonial society, too, could be a dangerous place. Although Madame Montour might be a "lady" in the eyes of many colonists, she was also branded a "French lady," her family "the French people," her settlement "French Town," in an age when a hint of anything French automatically made

21. "Marshe's Journal," 189–190; Daniel K. Richter, *Ordeal of the Longhouse: The Peoples of the Iroquois League in the Era of European Colonization* (Chapel Hill, N.C., 1992), 224–225; Peter Wraxall, *An Abridgment of the Indian Affairs Contained in Four Folio Volumes, Transacted in the Colony of New York, from the Year 1678 to the Year 1751*, ed. Charles Howard McIlwain (Cambridge, Mass., 1915), 64–68; *MPCP*, III, 572, 578.

22. Reichel, ed., *Memorials*, I, 97; Shamokin Diary, Sept. 17, 26, Nov. 3, 1745, Mor. Arch., 28/217/12B/1. See also Beauchamp, ed., *Moravian Jnls.*, 174. For hints of Madame Montour's earlier isolation, see Conrad Weiser, "Narrative of a Journey, Made in the Year 1737 . . . from Tulpehocken to Onondago . . . ," trans. Hiester H. Muhlenberg, Historical Society of Pennsylvania, *Collections*, I (1851–1853), 8.

one suspect in Anglo-America.[23] The suspicions Andrew faced at Shamokin in October 1755 had been part of his life since the very beginning.

A third possibility was that Montour could choose neither path. Instead, he could stay in the Susquehanna Valley, where a person like him was, if not common, at least not some freak of nature and culture. As it turned out, Montour did just that. Although he never stayed in one spot for long, his life remained centered in those parts of the Susquehanna where he had grown up.[24] There, the rhythms of his existence resembled those of most other Susquehanna peoples, whether their native soil was along the Delaware or the Rhine, the Savannah or the Thames. Montour hunted and traded, grew corn and raised sheep, and went off to war against both the Susquehanna Indians' traditional enemies, like Catawbas, and England's old foes, the French.[25] And, like many Susquehanna colonists of every description, he drank a lot and piled up debts, habits that sometimes took him from tavern to jail and back again.[26]

23. Weiser, "Narrative," 8. See also "Marshe's Journal," 189–190 (where Madame Montour is called "almost an Indian"). For other references to Madame Montour as French, see MPCP, III, 271, 295; PA, 1st Ser., I, 227. For reference to her family as French, see Penn-Physick Manuscripts, IX, 12, HSP. On "French Town," see Hanna, Wilderness Trail, I, 200; George P. Donehoo, A History of the Indian Villages and Place Names in Pennsylvania . . . (Harrisburg, 1928), 139–140.

24. It is hard to pin down someone as peripatetic as Montour. However, except for a few years in the late 1740s and another span of perhaps eight years at the end of his life—times when he lived in the Ohio country—Montour's home base was on a stretch of the Susquehanna running from John Harris's through Shamokin and up the West Branch 30 miles to Otstonwakin ("French Town").

25. For Montour's hunting, see Reichel, ed., Memorials, I, 97; Jordan, ed., "Spangenberg's Notes," PMHB, II (1878), 428, 430. For his farming, see MPCP, VI, 151. That in the 1750s Montour lived on a farm rather than in a village seems clear enough; less clear is whether he adopted the colonial practice of working the fields himself. My guess is that he did not. His travels, as well as his upbringing, worked against so fundamental a change. On Montour's going to war against native enemies, see "Marshe's Journal," 191; PA, 1st Ser., I, 662; Weiser to Joseph Spangenberg, May 5, 1746, Mor. Arch., 6/121/8/1. I use the term "Susquehanna Indians" here in the fashion it was used in the 18th century: to denote the many Indian peoples living in the Susquehanna River Valley, whatever their tribal affiliation. ("Susquehannocks," used earlier in this paper, refers specifically to the tribe living along the lower Susquehanna River in the 17th century.)

26. On Montour's drinking, see PA, 2d Ser., VII, 260–261; Peters, "Diary," Oct. 7, 25, 1758; John W. Jordan, ed., "The Journal of James Kenny, 1761–1763," PMHB, XXXVII (1913), 429. On Montour's debts, see Wallace, Conrad Weiser, 339–340; Lewin, "Montour," Pa. History, XXXIII (1966), 158; Penn Mss., Accounts, II, 5, Doc. 80a, 10, Doc. 85b, HSP. For a tavern debt, see PWJ, X, 148. For colonial fur traders' debts, see Francis Jennings, "The Indian Trade of the Susquehanna Valley," APS, Procs., CX (1966), 406–424.

At the same time, however, Montour was no ordinary inhabitant of the valley. What distinguished him from his neighbors was not only his exceptional linguistic skill but also his ability to fashion himself from more than one template: genteel colonist, Iroquois warrior, frontiersman. Moreover, he drew on those resources to make connections to peoples near and far. Some of those connections he inherited and then nurtured; others, he manufactured. Montour's father linked him to the Oneidas, and to a martyr whose death in 1729 at the hands of the hated Catawbas lived on in Iroquois memory for a generation. From his mother he received with his surname a far-flung network of kin, including a brother in Canada, cousins wed to Iroquois and living at various places in the Susquehanna Valley, an uncle linked by marriage to a Delaware family at the forks of the Delaware River, and, near Lake Erie, an aunt among the Miamis. Montour's own marriages—to the granddaughter of a Delaware leader at Shamokin and, later, to the kinswoman of a Conoy headman—spun additional strands in the human web that bound him to the Indian countries. In the spring of 1746, Montour, comfortably enmeshed in that web, headed deeper into those countries, crossing the mountains with his mother and family in tow.[27]

Two years later, however, this band was back on the Susquehanna, living near John Harris, where Montour could make more of his ties to the European colonial world. Here his extended family, which gave him such an advantage among Indians, might have been a hindrance, given how English colonists felt about the French. But Montour, overcoming the handicap of hailing from French Town, developed connections with the Anglo-American world founded, not on kinship, but on patronage. Besides Count Zinzendorf, Montour cultivated Conrad Weiser, the expert on all things Iroquois who in 1748 "presented Andrew to the Board [Pennsylvania Council] as a Person who might be of Service to the Province," George Croghan, a prominent fur trader and Pennsylvania's man across the Appalachians, the Virginia land speculators

27. On Montour's father, see James H. Merrell, "'Their Very Bones Shall Fight': The Catawba-Iroquois Wars," in Daniel K. Richter and James H. Merrell, eds., *Beyond the Covenant Chain: The Iroquois and Their Neighbors in Indian North America, 1600–1800* (Syracuse, N.Y., 1987), 124, 128. On Montour's uncle, see *PA*, 2d Ser., VII, 156. On his aunt, see *MPCP*, III, 295. For his marriage to a Delaware, see *MPCP*, VII, 95–96. There is considerable uncertainty about Montour's second wife. Some have said she was an Oneida (Hagedorn, "Montour," in Szasz, ed., *Between Indian and White Worlds*, 48, drawing upon *DCB*, VI, 7, s.v. Sarah Ainse), and indeed she was clearly connected to the Oneidas (*PWJ*, IX, 661– 662, 871, X, 481). But she also knew the Conoy language (*PWJ*, IX, 633–634) and was identified by Montour himself as a kinswoman of a Conoy headman (Peters, "Diary," Oct. 25, 1758). On Montour's crossing the mountains, see Weiser to Spangenberg, May 5, 1746, Mor. Arch., 6/121/8/1; *MPCP*, V, 762.

of the Ohio Company, and, after 1755, Sir William Johnson of New York, the crown's superintendent of Indian affairs for the northern department.[28]

Montour's pursuit of all of these relationships sharpened his ability to negotiate the cultural terrain of colonial America. At home in a longhouse and at a governor's dinner table, able to perform the Iroquois condolence ceremony and explain baptism to Indians, bearing a provincial captain's commission and a wampum belt with his credentials as an Iroquois leader, wearing a hat on his head and paint on his face—Montour made a name for himself as "a very useful Person" with "a good Character, both amongst White people and Indians." "Montour would be of singular use to me here at this present, in conversing with the Indians," a worried George Washington wrote from the frontier in June 1754; "I am often at a loss how to behave and should be reliev'd from many anxious fear's of offend[in]g them if Montour was here to assist me."[29] Many people involved in similar conversations during these years sought in Montour the same assistance, the same relief from "anxious fear's."

No one serving so many masters was going to please all of the peoples all of the time, however. Amid the testimonials to Montour were tirades, sometimes by the very people praising him, about his behavior. A "dull stupid creature," raged Richard Peters, an "untractable," "extravagant," and "expensive man." "An Impudent felow" with "great pride" who was "very hard to please," agreed Conrad Weiser. "I am Sorry that ever I recomended him . . . in the least thing."[30]

28. *MPCP,* V, 290.

29. *PWJ,* VII, 173, IX, 494; *PA,* 1st Ser., III, 42, 2d Ser., VI, 491–492; Mulkearn, ed., *Mercer Papers,* 11–12; Peters to Weiser, Feb. 6, 1753, Corr. Weiser, I, 38; *Corr. Sharpe,* I, 139; William P. Palmer, ed., *Calendar of Virginia State Papers and Other Manuscripts, 1652–1781 . . . ,* I (Richmond, Va., 1875), 245 (hereafter cited as *CVSP*). For his importance to Ohio Indians, see *MPCP,* V, 455, 497, 540, 683; *CVSP,* I, 245–247; Richard Peters to the proprietor, [Sept. 1753], Penn Mss., Off. Corr., VI, 105. For his being a member of the Iroquois council, see "Treaty at Logg's Town," *VMHB,* XIII (1905–1906), 165; Peters to Weiser, Feb. 6, 1753, Corr. Weiser, I, 38; Peters to the proprietor, Feb. 7, 1753, Penn Mss., Off. Corr., VI, 7; *MPCP,* V, 540, 607, 683. Croghan wrote that Montour was "look'd on amongst all the Indians as one of their Chiefs" (*MPCP,* V, 54), although this might have been hyperbole. In 1744, Witham Marshe said that he was a war captain and councillor ("Marshe's Journal," 191). That seems unlikely, given Montour's probable age in 1744. Marshe was wrong about a number of details in his report of a conversation with Madame Montour; this, too, he might have got wrong. For Washington's letter, see W. W. Abbot et al., eds., *The Papers of George Washington,* Colonial Series, I (Charlottesville, Va., 1983), 124.

30. Peters to the proprietaries, Nov. 6, 1753, Penn Mss., Off. Corr., VI, 115; Lewin, "Montour," *Pa. History,* XXXIII (1966), 158; Letterbook of Richard Peters, 1737–1750, in

Weiser was not the only one to be sorry. "I cannot Trust . . . Montour," said one leader of the Susquehanna Delawares. Neither, it turned out, could the Iroquois, who once doubted the man enough to ask colonists, in his presence, for a second translation of a message he had brought from Virginia. In the middle of another translation, he inspired, not doubt, but scorn. When a Delaware council speaker asked colonists to continue the liquor traffic because his people "loved" rum, Montour, concluding his interpretation of the speech, added that he "loves it too," an aside that "made the Indians laugh so hearty, that some of the young men could hardly stop."[31]

When war came to the Susquehanna in the fall of 1755, the grumbling and laughter turned ugly. A month after the first strike at Penn's Creek, riding with the Oneida Scarouyady from Philadelphia to Iroquoia in order to enlist the Six Nations' help, Montour waded into an elemental sea of hatred and anger. Lining the Susquehanna road were several hundred armed colonists, "enraged against all the Indians" and eager to "kill them without Distinction." "Why must we be killed by the Indians and we not kill them!" they shouted as the two rode past under guard. "Why are our Hands so tied?"[32]

Montour and Scarouyady got through to the Susquehanna "with much adoe," but heading upriver toward Iroquoia they again heard angry words, this time from Indians launching attacks on Pennsylvania. At one council house, the envoys sat with local leaders while "the rest cried out of doors, let us kill the Rogue; we will hear of no Mediator, much less of a Master; hold your Tongue and be gone, or you shall live no longer." "Montour informs me," wrote a colonist in January 1756, after the two men had arrived in New York, "that if the Delawares had known their Business to the Five Nations, Scarrooyady and he had never come thro' their Settlements [alive]."[33]

Montour escaped the Susquehanna peoples' anger this time, but thereafter he always had to watch his back. The following spring, Ohio Delawares "particularly threatned that . . . they . . . would burn" Montour if they ever caught him. There was no telling when the blow might come. One summer night in 1764, while he accompanied British forces and native warriors on their way

---

Peters Papers, HSP, 365 (hereafter cited as Peters Letterbook); Peters, "Diary," Oct. 13, 1758; Weiser to Peters, February[?] 1753, Weiser to ——, [1753–1754?], Corr. Weiser, I, 17, II, 25; PA, 1st Ser., II, 12.

31. PWJ, III, 778; Beauchamp, ed., Moravian Jnls., 175; Kenny, "Journal," PMHB, XXXVII (1913), 429.

32. PA, 1st Ser., II, 505.

33. MPCP, VII, 13, 49, 53, 65–66.

west, some of the "Indians got drunk in their Encampment and were going to kill Montour."[34]

It is hard to tell whether this was a drunken brawl or a sober assassination attempt, but it is clear that many peoples had plenty of reasons to hate Andrew Montour. Part of the problem was that the man kept changing the cast of his countenance. With the likes of Zinzendorf he could be so civil that the haughty reichscount remarked how "at times we have observed signs of grace in Andrew"; yet, at other times, he was so "[i]ll natured" that colonists thought it "a habit he took from the Indians and Indian traders." Conrad Weiser was particularly confused. In 1753, Weiser, predicting that Montour would "put on a brazen face and go on" against Pennsylvania's Indian policies, wondered aloud whether "prehaps [sic] he wishes me death, to have the Menagment of Indian affairs all to him Self"; yet, the following spring, Weiser reported a visit from Montour, who, "free and open," acted "as if there had never been nothing amiss between him and me." Only a few months later, however, a drunken Montour again "abused me very much," a shocked Weiser wrote, even as he added that when sober the man, "with shaking hands, Called me a[t] one side, [and] Asked pardon for offence given."[35]

Montour's abrupt changes bespoke more than the rum in his belly or the interests of his audience. They were one expression of a habit he had—a nasty habit, in the view of the people he ostensibly served—of changing not only his countenance but his mind. In 1751, he said nothing when George Croghan happily announced to his Pennsylvania superiors that Indians had given the British permission to build a fort in the Ohio country to counter the French, then infuriated Croghan (and, presumably, pleased Ohio Indians) by claiming the opposite: the tribes there had expressly forbidden a fort. A year later, Montour was instrumental in getting Ohio leaders gathered at Logstown to accept Virginia's expansive interpretation of a land sale, then reversed himself again, embarrassing Weiser (and, again, pleasing Ohio nations) by insisting that "the Indians never Sold nor released it [the Ohio land.] If they did they were imposed upon by the Interpreter"—none other than Weiser himself.[36]

34. Deposition of John Craig, Mar. 30, 1756, Penn Papers, Indian Affairs, II, 78 (these Indians also targeted George Croghan and Monacatootha [Scarouyady]); "Journal 1764—To Niagara—John Montresor," in G. D. Scull, ed., The Montresor Journals (New-York Historical Society, Collections, for the Year 1881 [New York, 1882]), 263.

35. Reichel, ed., Memorials, I, 99; PA, 2d Ser., VII, 261 ("Indian traders" here means colonial fur traders); Weiser to Peters, February[?], Mar. 15, 1753, Corr. Weiser, I, 17, 44; PA, 2d Ser., VII, 261. See also below for Montour's encounter with Weiser.

36. Wainwright, George Croghan, 41–44; Peters to the proprietor, Feb. 7, 1753, Peters to the proprietaries, Nov. 6, 1753, Penn Mss., Off. Corr., VI, 7, 115; "Treaty of Logg's Town,"

Such bold assertions of Indian rights misled those who saw in Montour a consistently staunch defender of native sovereignty, however. In December 1758, when British troops had taken Fort Duquesne and were determined to remain there, Montour helped George Croghan twist Ohio Indian speeches demanding the army's withdrawal into an invitation to stay. Similarly, at Easton four years later, he helped Sir William Johnson side with the Pennsylvania proprietors against Delaware charges of land fraud by condensing a four-hour reading of the proprietary defense into a brief summary for the Delaware ambassadors.[37]

No wonder so many people despised Montour. The man was more than hard to read; he was, in some alarming way, unfathomable. His true nature, the wellsprings of his behavior, remained hidden. Indeed, what made Montour so mistrusted is also what made him so indispensable. His gift, and his curse, was that his habits of dress and address allowed many different readings of him. People saw in him what they hoped (or feared) to see: French spy or British puppet, Christian convert or Iroquois warrior, land agent or defender of Indian domain, "Dupe" of "low Company" (according to colonial authorities) or of the provincial elite (according to Indians defending their lands).[38] Montour could be all things to all peoples—he got along with governors and "Woods Men," led war parties and missionaries, negotiated Indian land sales and then renounced them—but he belonged to no one. His behavior frustrated attempts to label him, to co-opt him, to render him loyal to someone or something, to make him predictable and safe.

There were, then, as many reasons to doubt Montour as there were reasons to rely on him. But perhaps the truest source of the dislike and distrust he inspired, the real reason he rubbed so many people the wrong way, ran deeper than his drinking or his spending, his impertinence or his pride, his changes of countenance or changes of mind, his affinity for "low Company" or for provincial elites. That reason is the way Montour tried to define himself and to shape the future character of Susquehanna society. His vision, inchoate and never stated outright, can be retrieved from an unlikely place: his land dealings

VMHB, XIII (1905–1906), 171–172; Peters to Weiser, Feb. 6, 1753, Weiser to ——, [1753–1754?], Corr. Weiser, I, 38, II, 25 (quotation); Wallace, Conrad Weiser, 348.

37. Christian Frederick Post, "Two Journals of the Western Tours . . . ," in Reuben Gold Thwaites, ed., Early Western Travels, 1748–1846 . . . , I (Cleveland, Ohio, 1904), 283–285; PWJ, III, 769–772, 777–778. For the treaty, see Anthony F. C. Wallace, King of the Delawares: Teedyuscung, 1700–1763 (1949; reprint, Salem, N.H., 1984), chap. 18; Francis Jennings, Empire of Fortune: Crowns, Colonies, and Tribes in the Seven Years War in America (New York, 1988), 435–436.

38. PA, 1st Ser., II, 385; Peters Letterbook, 1737–1750, 361. See also Corr. Sharpe, I, 144–145.

at midcentury. In these negotiations, Montour's signature, his hand, can be read more clearly—and clearly puts him at odds with most native Americans and most European colonists of his day.

Montour's land speculation first surfaced in 1748, when he left the Ohio country and brought his family back to the Susquehanna—and back, he thought, to stay. "Andrew Montour has pitched upon a place in the Proprietor's mannor, at Canatqueany [Conodoguinet Creek, across the Susquehanna River from John Harris's]," reported Weiser that August. "He Expects that the Government shall build him a house there, and furnish his family with necessarys." Intentionally or not, Montour had touched a sore spot in Pennsylvania's history with its native neighbors. In 1731, the province, trying to lure disaffected Shawnees back over the mountains from the Ohio, had set aside land along the Conodoguinet in the proprietaries' name "in order to Accomodate the Shaawna Indians or such others as may think fit to Settle there."[39] The Shawnees never came back, but—apparently considering himself one of those "others"—Montour did.[40] Believing "the Land to belong Still to the Indians," he explained, "he only Soposd he Might Live there for his Life." He even hired a colonist to build him a house, promising payment from Philadelphia. From Philadelphia instead came word that Montour was in trouble. "What consummate Impudence is this?" thundered Richard Peters as he "put a stop to it directly" and made the would-be homesteader "very uneasy[,] Expecting to be putt in Jale for the money he owed" the builder.[41]

Montour managed to avoid prison, but his first attempt to live on a patch of native ground amid European colonists was a fiasco. He did not give up on the idea, however. In 1751, he had set his sights on some Indian land "over the hills"

39. *MPCP*, III, 462–463; *PA*, 1st Ser., I, 299, II, 12. See Donehoo, *Indian Villages*, 42–44; Draught of the Manor of Lowther, *PA*, 3d Ser., IV, #34; Barry C. Kent et al., "A Map of 18th Century Indian Towns in Pennsylvania," *Pa. Archaeologist*, LI, no. 4 (December 1981), 4, fig. 2.

40. In the late 1740s, however, there were rumors that Shawnees did plan to return, to the colonists' dismay (they had come to count on having the land themselves and were angry at the Shawnees for allying with the French). "Those troublesome creatures the Shawanese have the Impudence to talk of returning to the Manor," wrote Richard Peters, adding that Weiser felt that "the best way to prevent it is to begin a Town there directly"; Peters Letterbook, 1737–1750, 327.

41. Croghan to Peters, Aug. 27, 1750, Peters to Croghan, Sept. 8, 1750, Penn-Physick Mss., V, 10, XI, 15. Montour was, by colonial law, correct. See Donehoo, *Indian Villages*, 42–43. (Montour claimed that Weiser had encouraged this project.) The two-year gap between Weiser's report of the plan and Peters's sharp response is puzzling. It could be due to a misdating of Weiser's letter or to slow work building the house. Montour was in the Ohio country much of the time between August 1748 and August 1750. Several years later, the proprietor was still fuming about Montour's scheme (Thomas Penn to Peters, Feb. 21, 1755, Peters Papers, IV, 4).

north of the Conodoguinet, and this time he visited both Onondaga and Philadelphia to seek approval. The Iroquois apparently were noncommittal; Pennsylvanians, lobbied "earnestly and repeatedly" by Montour, had reasons to go along.[42] In the spring of 1752, the governor, seeing here an opportunity to keep squatters out of Indian country and the colony out of trouble, issued him a commission "to go and reside . . . over the Kittochtinny Hills . . . in order that you may by your personal Care and Vigilance preserve those Lands ['not purchased of the Indians'] from being settled as well as warn off all who have presumed to go there."[43]

Commission in hand, a delighted Montour moved to Sherman's Creek, just south of the Juniata River. Once there, however, he began to depart dramatically from his instructions, sketching on the land his vision of the region's future and his own place in that future. Instead of driving out European colonial settlers already there and warning off others on their way, Montour actually began to recruit these people, inviting them into the valley and setting them up as his tenants. "He aims of haveing a large piece of ground over the hills and a good Number of Setlers on it to pay Contribution to him," Weiser wrote to Richard Peters. "How he will bring it about is a Mistery to me."[44]

Weiser and Peters were determined to solve that mystery in order to thwart

42. It is difficult to learn much about Montour's negotiations with the Iroquois; we have only colonial suspicions and fears about those conversations; see Peters to Weiser, Sept. 19, 1751, Peters Papers, III, 47; Weiser to Peters, February[?] 1753, Peters to Weiser, Feb. 6, 1753, Corr. Weiser, I, 17, 38; Peters to the proprietor, Feb. 7, May 3, 1753, Penn Mss., Off. Corr., VI, 7, 47. Weiser wrote in 1754 that Montour had got from Ohio Indians some lands along Sherman's Creek or the Juniata River, but the nature of that grant is unclear (Wallace, *Conrad Weiser*, 355).

43. *MPCP*, V, 566–567. In the past, the province had granted licenses permitting European colonists to settle on unpurchased Indian lands, although these were for specific tracts of land and did not come with the charge of keeping other settlers out; see Donna Bingham Munger, *Pennsylvania Land Records: A History and Guide for Research* (Wilmington, Del., 1991), 68–70. Provincial efforts to oust squatters tended to backfire. In the 1740s, Indians were furious when officials sent to remove colonists from Susquehanna lands started to survey those lands instead. "They are in League with the Trespassers," said native spokesmen, who insisted that "more effectual Methods may be used, and honester persons employ'd"; see *MPCP*, IV, 570, 572 (quotation; see also V, 435–436). Whether these Indians considered Montour "more effectual" and "honester" is unclear.

44. Hanna, *Wilderness Trail*, I, 226–227; Wallace, *Indian Paths*, 49, 115; Weiser to Peters, February[?] 1753, Peters to Weiser, Feb. 6, 1753, Corr. Weiser, I, 17, 38; Peters to the proprietor, Feb. 7, May 3, 1753, Penn Mss., Off. Corr., VI, 7, 47; Wallace, *Conrad Weiser*, 355. At one point, Peters began to believe Montour's denial of these charges; see Peters to the proprietaries, Nov. 6, 1753, Penn Mss., Off. Corr., VI, 115. Weiser, however, remained convinced that Montour was up to something; see Weiser to Peters, Feb. 7, 1754, Berks and Montgomery Counties, Miscellaneous Manuscripts, 1693–1869, 55, HSP.

Montour's "Scheme." Anxious themselves to buy more territory for Pennsylvania—"The whole Province will clamour in case an Indian Purchase be not made," Peters had fretted in 1751—they had their eye on those very lands. So desperate was Weiser to expand Pennsylvania's boundaries that he advocated having Pennsylvanians move onto Indian territory in order to precipitate a crisis—and a sale. In February 1754, he urged that "our people Should be lett loose to Set[tle?] upon any part of the Indian lands upon giveing Security for their Complying with the proprietary terms after pu[rchase?]." The humble Moravians might best disguise this ploy; or perhaps colonial fur traders should go and "under Colour of Trade take Possession of the Lands and build Houses." Whoever went, Weiser saw the outcome clearly: "The Indians would Come in and demand Consideration . . . and what Can they Say, the people of pensilvania are their Brethren according to the treatys Subsisting."[45]

Montour's speculations included Pennsylvania settlers, too, but not as undercover agents of a land grab. Rather, drawing from his experiences in the Susquehanna Valley—his home village "a promiscuous Indian population," his wives Delaware and Conoy, his neighbors Shawnees, Germans, Tutelos, and Irish—he envisioned a place that brought different peoples together, a place that, to him, looked like nothing more than the next step down a path that the Susquehanna peoples already seemed to be traveling—a place, in short, where he felt at home.[46]

That Montour might become the landlord and neighbor of European colonists, that he might start a society in which Indian peoples and European peoples lived peaceably together, was Conrad Weiser's worst nightmare. It was true that an Indian war might erupt over these lands, Richard Peters had admitted in a 1749 letter to the Pennsylvania proprietors,

> but Mr. Weiser apprehends a worse Effect, that is that they [what Peters called "the Lower sort of People" in the province] will become tributary to the Indians and pay them yearly Sums for their Lycence to be there—he says positively that they are got into this way on the East side of Sasquehanna beyond the Hills [above John Harris's] and receive acknowledgments and are easy about those Lands, and that if they do the same on the West side of that River the Proprietors will not only have all the abandoned People of the Province to deal with but the Indians too and that they will mutually

45. Peters to Weiser, Sept. 19, 1751, Peters Papers, III, 47; Peters Letterbook, 1737–1750, 363; Weiser to Peters, Feb. 7, 1754, Berks and Montgomery Counties, Misc. Mss., 55; Weiser to Peters, Oct. 12, 1754, Corr. Weiser, I, 47. Although never official policy, land sales in Pennsylvania during these years routinely "came about as a direct result of settlers' encroaching on the unpurchased Indian land" (Munger, Pennsylvania Land Records, 59–61, 65, 68).

46. Reichel, ed., Memorials, I, 98 (quotation).

support each other and do a vast deal of Mischief. This consideration, [Peters concluded,] has alarm'd me more than any other.[47]

As Peters and Weiser came to see, they were in a contest with Montour not just for land but for the power to determine what sort of society was to be born on the Susquehanna—and, perhaps, beyond it. Would it resemble the Delaware Valley, now virtually empty of Indians? Or would it be something new, forged by various refugee and emigrant groups—European and Indian—from the common Susquehanna experience of the past generation and led by men like Montour?

The answer to these questions came at Albany in July 1754 when Weiser and Peters purchased from the Six Nations the land beneath Montour's feet. Pennsylvania won in part because the Iroquois were as unhappy with Montour's plan as Weiser and Peters were. In the past, Iroquois sales of land had served to affirm the Six Nations' authority over other native peoples and to keep European colonists at arm's length. No wonder Onondaga refused to go along with his scheme. Certainly Peters was convinced that giving Montour a Pennsylvania commission to occupy unsold Iroquois lands "will cut him up with the Indians." Weiser, too, hoped that Montour's "great pride," expressed in land speculation, "will soon render him odious to the onontago Counsil."[48] How odious Montour was remains unclear, but the Iroquois sale of the Juniata Valley (and more) at Albany suggests that their view of the region's future was closer to Weiser's than to Montour's; it was to be a land of lines dividing Indians from Europeans, not a place where lines blurred and peoples came together.

Just how important this speculative venture was to Montour, just how great a blow the Albany purchase was, became abundantly clear when he next crossed paths with Weiser, at John Harris's in the early fall of 1754. Weiser, headed west, persuaded Montour to go along; the Pennsylvania interpreter soon had reason to regret issuing that invitation. "When he meet me at John Harris," Weiser reported, "he called for so much punch that himself . . . and other Indians got drunk, the same at Tobias Hendricks [on the road west]. I bought 2 quarts of Rum there to use on our Journey, but he drunk most all the first day." The liquor unleashed a torrent of anger. Montour "Cursed and swore . . . , damned me more than hundred times," Weiser continued. "He is vexed at the new purchase. Told me I cheated the Indians. He says he will now

47. Peters Letterbook, 1737–1750, 363. For further discussion of this alleged tribute, see Peters to the proprietaries, Sept. 11, 1749, May 5, 1750, Penn Mss., Off. Corr., IV, 236, V, 2, 9.

48. Peters to Weiser, Apr. 17, 1753, Peters Papers, III, 67; Weiser to Peters, February[?] 1753, Corr. Weiser, I, 17.

kill any white men that will pretend to settle on his Creek, and that the Governor and Mr. peters told him so much, saying *he was a Warrior—how he could* [sic] *suffer the Irish to encroach upon him*—he would now act according to advice, and kill some of them. . . . I left him drunk," Weiser concluded; "on one legg he had a stocking and no shoe, on the other a shoe and no stocking. . . . He swore terrible when he saw me mount my horse."[49]

The image of that drunk and disheveled figure hurling abuse at Weiser's retreating back exposes how badly Montour had misread the realities of the colonial frontier. Perhaps his mistake was taking the Susquehanna country at face value; the cacophony of voices and the kaleidoscope of cultures might have blinded him to enduring differences between Europeans and Indians. He went from trader's store to missionary's hut to hunter's camp to headman's lodge without missing a step; did he notice that few could match his ability to make himself at home in so many different places? Did he wonder why one Susquehanna town had Tutelos, Delawares, and Oneidas but none had, say, Germans, Swiss, and Senecas, or Irish, Cayugas, and English? The creation of new cultural features on the Susquehanna landscape overlay a fault line between Indian and colonist that was only obscured, not erased.[50]

Others saw this fault line, even if Montour did not. Pennsylvanians expressed their belief in fundamental differences between colonists and Indians by drawing a distinction between "the woods" (Indian country) and "the Inhabited Parts" (areas dominated by European settlers), a fiction that ignored the woods a short walk from Philadelphia and the many clearings—and many inhabitants—in "the woods." This distinction was common among officials in Philadelphia—"The woods are so dark and private," shuddered more than one governor—but, as a shorthand way of ordering the world, it was also common currency among colonial fur traders, interpreters, and other frontier folk.[51]

That Anglo-American colonists had no intention of living in "the woods" or becoming one people with Indians is clear enough. Less well known is the Indians' own resistance to such an idea. Beneath the metaphors of harmony and unity that decorated the treaty minutes—the talk of becoming one people

49. *PA,* 2d Ser., VII, 261.
50. It is hard to fathom why Montour, so well versed in Susquehanna ways, apparently did not detect this fault line. Among the many possible reasons for his blindness is his experience in the Ohio country just before he embarked on his speculative voyage in the Susquehanna. Across the mountains, perhaps, he became acquainted with multi-ethnic communities and was trying to translate his impressions of the Ohio social landscape back to the Susquehanna. I am grateful to Richard White for suggesting this possibility.
51. *MPCP,* V, 149, III, 275.

with one body, one heart, and one mind—ran a chorus of dissonance and dissent. During a council at Lancaster in 1744, an Iroquois speaker informed his audience: "The World at the first was made on the other side of the Great water different from what it is on this side, as may be known from the different colour of Our Skin and of Our Flesh. . . . You have your Laws and Customs and so have we." "You know I am not as you are," an Oneida from the upper Susquehanna reminded Pennsylvania officials in 1762. "I am of a quite different Nature from you."[52]

Not only were natives different, but they wanted to stay that way. "We are Indians," one Susquehanna headman replied when a missionary broached the subject of conversion, "and don't wish to be transformed into white men. The English are our Brethren, but we never promised to become what they are. As little as we desire the preacher to become Indian, so little ought he to desire the Indians to become preachers." Another Susquehanna Indian leader lost authority once his people began to suspect that he "wants to make English Men of the Indians."[53]

Just how little native peoples relished the prospect of a European embrace came to light vividly in November 1755, when the Ohio Delaware leader Shingas, once an inhabitant of the Susquehanna Valley, paused in his return from a raid on Pennsylvania to explain to his colonial prisoners on what terms the Indians would stop fighting. Peace is possible, the warrior said, if the English colonies will send five families to live with the Indians in order to "Promote Spinning for Shirts and In Gen'l" to "Bring all Kinds of Trades among them that they [the Indians] might be Supplied with what they want near home." "They and the English shou'd Live Together in Love and Freindship and Become one people," the Delaware continued, but then he quickly backed away from this standard rhetorical device, adding that "the Indians did not Insist nor Desire that the English sho[ul]d Be obliged to Intermarry with them."[54] A mere five families, an island of alien expertise in an Indian sea—this was all the contact Shingas wanted.

It was possible, of course, that the Susquehanna Valley would go against the powerful current of opinions and events dividing Indians from Europeans; apparently Montour hoped (and Conrad Weiser feared) that it would. But any chance of that happening, already remote when Montour berated Weiser in

52. *MPCP*, IV, 720, 742.

53. Jordan, ed., "Spangenberg's Notes," *PMHB*, II (1878), 428; *MPCP*, VIII, 120. See also Gregory Evans Dowd, *A Spirited Resistance: The North American Indian Struggle for Unity, 1745–1815* (Baltimore, 1992).

54. Beverley W. Bond, Jr., ed., "The Captivity of Charles Stuart, 1755–1757," *Mississippi Valley Historical Review*, XIII (1926–1927), 65 (emphasis added).

the fall of 1754, perished with the farmers on Penn's Creek a year later. If Montour did not know that his dream had died before then, he certainly knew it when his old friend Thomas McKee, a survivor of the ambush on Harris's party, made his way back to Shamokin with the news that the Paxton men had heeded Montour's facial paint—probably applied as protective coloration amid all those "strange Indians"—rather than his past performances. The party's fatal decision to take Montour at face value was a defining moment, not just in Montour's life but in the life of the frontier, for it exposed the abiding sense of a chasm between Indian and colonist and exposed it in the heart of the Susquehanna country, where the seeds of something new had seemed most likely to take root.

In the years to come, Susquehanna peoples, native American and Euro-American alike, would scrawl in blood the epitaph for Montour's dream by using knowledge acquired during a generation of peaceful intercourse to kill each other without mercy. *"Be still we wont hurt you,"* an Indian warrior herding German children together a month after Penn's Creek said in "High Dutch"—before burying a hatchet in their mother's head, stepping on her neck to tear off her scalp, and joining his companions to cut down the fleeing boys and girls.[55]

In the Susquehanna Valley eight years later, the tables were turned when some troops from Paxton came upon three Indians. "Dont shoot brothers, dont shoot," the three cried; they proclaimed their friendship for Pennsylvania, and, personifying it, one was even "named George Allen," a Paxton man recalled, "after the George Allen that was with us." Blind to such signs of attachment, the soldiers took the Indians prisoner and, after ordering them to walk on ahead, shot them in the back. George Allen (the Indian), wounded in the arm, played dead while they scalped him; then, as the killers began to strip his leggings off, he jumped up and escaped, even though "the skin of his face, the scalp being off, came down over his eyes so that he cou'd not see." This George Allen, recovering his vision and his health, lived to talk of gaining revenge on his namesake.[56]

55. *PA,* 1st Ser., II, 512; see also III, 283.

56. Archibald Loudon, *A Selection of Some of the Most Interesting Narratives of Outrages, Committed by the Indians in Their Wars with the White People . . . ,* 2 vols. (1808–1811; reprint, New York, 1971), II, 186–188. See also *MPCP,* IX, 140; *PA,* 2d Ser., VII, 469; Edward Shippen to Gov. James Hamilton [draft], Sept. 1, 1763, Burd-Shippen Papers, APS. Indians had a custom of swapping names with colonists as "a seal of friendship" (Post, "Two Journals," in Thwaites, ed., *Early Western Travels,* I, 253 n. 96; see also *MPCP,* VII, 6). Whether that exchange happened in this case is unclear.

For the Indian George Allen trading at Fort Augusta, see Fort Augusta, Ledger A, 37, 66,

In a world where George Allen shot George Allen, where Indians spoke German while killing Germans, where was Montour to fit? He had set about defining himself as a denizen of this debatable land. Only after Montour had made it his life's ambition to become the leading citizen of the territory between the woods and the inhabited parts, only then did he discover that he had pitched his camp, had pitched his life, in a no-man's-land.

Montour was not completely alone, of course. Besides his extended family, besides those peoples on the east side of the Susquehanna living together amicably enough (or so it seemed to Weiser), a few others did articulate this search for a meeting of minds, hearts, and souls that, in Indian metaphor, bound societies one to the other. Among the Iroquois in 1750, the Moravian bishop John Christian Frederick Cammerhoff mused that he "sometimes felt like saying to myself: [']I am dwelling among my own people,['] and when I shall be able to say that in its true meaning, my heart will rejoice." But Cammerhoff never saw that happy day; indeed, virtually no one did. Although many crossed the cultural divide between Indians and Europeans, few really felt at home on the far side. Croghan, Weiser, the Oneidas Shickellamy and Scarouyady—these and the other go-betweens of the Pennsylvania theater were firmly anchored on one side of the frontier or the other. Like Thomas Gist, a frontiersman whom the Wyandots in 1758 captured, stripped, shaved, painted, and adopted, European colonists in the Indian countries were only "acting the part of an Indian." "I could do [this acting] very well," Gist boasted after he— "determined to be what I really was"—made good his escape.[57]

69, 109, Gratz Collection, case 17, box 2, HSP. The colonist named George Allen was among Pennsylvania scouts who "dressed as Indians" during the summer of 1756. Later in the war, he was "Master of the Batteaus" on the Susquehanna River (*PA*, 1st Ser., III, 432). His career can be followed in William A. Hunter, *Forts on the Pennsylvania Frontier, 1753–1758* (Harrisburg, 1960), 497, 499, 500, 511; [Charles Beatty], "Journal Kept in 1756," in William Henry Egle, *History of the Counties of Dauphin and Lebanon in the Commonwealth of Pennsylvania: Biographical and Genealogical* (Philadelphia, 1883), 54–55; *MPCP*, VII, 154; *PA*, 1st Ser., IV, 113, 2d Ser., II, 643, 646, 647, 676, 691, 695, VII, 462, 8th Ser., VI, 4867.

Whether one George Allen actually shot the other is not clear. George Allen from Paxton apparently was against shooting the Indians, arguing that they should be taken to a frontier fort instead. It is hard to tell whether, on being overruled, he was one of the six to open fire, although a soldier at Fort Augusta later spoke of the three scalps as "them Allen brought" (*PA*, 2d Ser., VII, 469), and Allen was the officer in charge of the party. Certainly, George Allen, the Indian, held Capt. Allen and one other man responsible, for these were the two men in the Paxton party he knew. The colony's attempt to placate this native by returning his gun and giving flour to his family failed to cool his resentment (Accounts, box 3, folder 19, George Croghan Section, Cadwallader Collection, HSP).

57. Beauchamp, ed., *Moravian Jnls.*, 35. Only two weeks later, Cammerhoff wrote that he

Gist, like Weiser and Croghan, like Shickellamy and Scarouyady, knew what he really was. Did Montour? Here the answer is less clear; it is as hard to read the man now as it was 250 years ago. What can be said is that Montour was never able to borrow or to fashion a vocabulary that would define him as neither Indian nor European but something new, something else altogether. Lacking that working vocabulary, Montour spent his life maintaining his credentials as both an Indian and a European. In March 1762, for example, he and his son John planned to set up a trading post near Shamokin, arguing "that being Indians, they had a Right to settle anywhere upon Indian Lands." In the years to come, Montour sought still other ways to connect to his roots in Indian country. He moved back to his original West Branch homeland and claimed tracts where Montour villages once had stood. When those lands went to creditors, Montour moved to a site on the south side of the Ohio a few miles below Pittsburgh—land that he called, not Montoursville, but Oughsaragoh (place of Oughsara).[58]

At the same time, Montour was also adopting more trappings of European colonial culture, trappings that went well beyond the "Silver Laced hatt" and other finery he continued to fancy. He wore the surname of his mother and maternal uncle, but his children bore his name rather than their mother's. Moving farther still away from matrilineal habits of thought he had known in his youth, in the mid-1750s Montour sent his children to school in Philadelphia and Williamsburg so that they were "independent of the[ir] Mother."[59] Well before then, he had abandoned the village communities he had grown up in and settled a farm instead. Finally, he stopped going off to kill Catawbas and

and his Moravian companion "spent a very happy evening, and were especially glad to be alone and not to have any Indians with us" (61). For Gist, see Howard H. Peckham, ed., "Thomas Gist's Indian Captivity," *PMHB*, LXXX (1956), 302.

58. Lt. Caleb Graydon to Col. James Burd, Apr. 10, 1762, Shippen Family Papers, V, 466, HSP; see also Graydon to Burd, Mar. 5, 1762, 463. For his West Branch home and his site below Pittsburgh, see Hanna, *Wilderness Trail*, I, 245; J. F. Meginness, *Otzinachson; or, A History of the West Branch Valley of the Susquehanna* (Philadelphia, 1857), 38, 39, 139, 157; *PWJ*, VI, 596–597, VII, 335–336, 568, 575, 690. For his farm above the Shamokin site, see *PA*, 2d Ser., VII, 472; Loudon, *Narratives of Outrages*, II, 174; Sylvester K. Stevens et al., eds., *The Papers of Col. Henry Bouquet*, series 21653 (Harrisburg, 1940), 193.

59. "Mr. Mitchell's Receipt for Capt. Montour," July 7, 1762, box 1, folder 18, Croghan Section, Cadwallader Collection (see also 1/13, 1/14); Peters to Thomas Penn, Apr. 25, 1756, Penn Mss., Off. Corr., VIII, 73; *MPCP*, VII, 95–96. Glimpses of the Montour children's lives in Philadelphia can be gained from accounts submitted to the Assembly for their lodging, food, clothing, schooling, and medicines. At least one of these children, Debby Montour, remained in Philadelphia until 1766. See *PA*, 8th Ser., V, 4093, 4183, VI, 4656–4657, 4859–4860, 5146, 5151, 5272, 5362–5363, VII, 5853, 5933, 5944, 5968, 6224–6226.

other traditional foes of Susquehanna Indians, marching to war instead with the likes of George Washington and Sir William Johnson.[60]

Trying to be both Indian and European, Montour ended up being neither. The life that he made for himself, the path he traveled, turned out to be a dead end in English America, not an avenue to some new social order. There was no place in between, there were no words to describe the sort of person he was, there was no critical mass of people like himself sufficient to weave new social patterns from the fraying edges of the old.[61] "Will not it be impossible for Indians and White people to live together?" asked Richard Peters, even as he worked with Weiser to keep those unraveling margins from being stitched into new designs. "Will not there be an eternal Intercourse of Rum and a perpetual Scene of quarreling?"[62] Two centuries after Andrew Montour and a century after Wounded Knee, the questions linger.[63]

60. Montour was also going to war in new ways. In 1764, for example, he led an expedition of Indians and colonists into the upper Susquehanna Valley that—in its scope and its wholesale destruction of Indian towns, crops, and livestock—was a precursor to the Sullivan campaigns of the Revolutionary War. His role in this campaign warrants further investigation. *PWJ*, IV, 321–322, 324, 336–337, 349–352, 361, 374, 392, 399, 403, 405–406, XI, 51–52, 74–76, 86–88, 131–132.

61. For an introduction to the successful construction of such identities elsewhere in North America, see Dennis F. K. Madill, "Riel, Red River, and Beyond: New Developments in Métis History," in Colin G. Calloway, ed., *New Directions in American Indian History* (Norman, Okla., 1988), 49–78.

62. *PA*, 1st Ser., II, 214.

63. With apologies to Edmund S. Morgan (*American Slavery, American Freedom: The Ordeal of Colonial Virginia* [New York, 1975], 387).

COMMUNAL DEFINITIONS

OF GENDERED IDENTITY IN

SEVENTEENTH-CENTURY

ENGLISH AMERICA

Mary Beth Norton

On February 12, 1628/9, three Virginia women—Alice Longe, Dorothy
Rodes, and Barbara Hall—went to the home of John Atkins, a planter who had
recently purchased a maidservant named Thomasine Hall. There they found
the servant asleep, examined her body stealthily while she slept, and pronounced her to be "a man." They quietly called to Atkins to "see the proof
thereof," but, before he could join them in looking at Thomasine's body, she
seemed "to starre as if shee had beene awake." Thus, Atkins left and "Could see
nothing."[1]

The abortive inquiry did not stop the female searchers. The following Sunday, their ranks augmented by two other women, they "againe assembled" at
Atkins's house. This time Thomasine Hall was awake, and the five women
openly examined the maid's body in Atkins's presence. Once more, they did

Portions of this essay draw on material presented in *Founding Mothers and Fathers: Gendered Power and the Forming of American Society* (New York: Alfred A. Knopf, 1996).

1. The case is printed in H. R. McIlwaine, ed., *Minutes of the Council and General Court of
Colonial Virginia, 1622–1632, 1670–1676* (Richmond, Va., 1924), 194–195 (hereafter cited as
Va. Ct. Recs.). Unless otherwise indicated, all quotations about the case in this article come
from these pages. My interpretation has benefited substantially from the advice of the Cor-
nell Sex and Gender Study Group, and I wish to acknowledge the work of Tom Foster, Cor-
nell University, 1991, whose term paper on the Hall case in 1989 first alerted me to its impor-
tance. The other extended treatments of the case are Alden T. Vaughan, "The Sad Case of
Thomas(ine) Hall," *Virginia Magazine of History and Biography*, LXXXVI (1978), 146–148;
Jonathan Ned Katz, *Gay/Lesbian Almanac: A New Documentary* (New York, 1983), 71–72;
Kathleen M. Brown, *Good Wives, Nasty Wenches, and Anxious Patriarchs: Gender, Race, and
Power in Colonial Virginia* (Chapel Hill, N.C., 1996), 75–80; and Brown, "'Changed . . . into
the Fashion of Man': The Politics of Sexual Difference in a Seventeenth-Century Anglo-
American Settlement," *Journal of the History of Sexuality*, VI (1995), 171–193. My interpreta-
tion in part coincides with Brown's article and in part differs sharply from it.

"finde him to bee a man." When Atkins asked his maid "if that were all hee had," Thomasine replied, "I have a peece of an hole." Atkins directed Hall "to lye on his backe and shew the same[.] And the said woemen searching him againe did againe finde him to bee a man." So, Atkins reported to the Virginia General Court, he "did Comaunde him to bee put into mans apparell."

A few days or weeks later, Hall, now dressed as a man and known as Thomas, encountered two men, Roger Rodes (who might have been Dorothy's husband) and Francis England. Roger said to Hall, "Thou hast beene reported to be a woman and now thou art p[ro]ved to bee a man, I will see what thou carriest." With that, Rodes and England "threw the said *Hall* on his backe, and then [England] felt the said *Hall* and pulled out his members whereby it appeared that hee was a p[er]fect man."

What had prompted three groups of male and female Virginians to scrutinize the body of a servant so carefully? Clearly, people were confused about Hall's sexual identity. At times, Hall dressed as a man; at other times, as a woman. What sex was this person? other colonists wanted to know. The vigor with which they pursued their concerns dramatically underscores the significance of gender distinctions in seventeenth-century Anglo-America. The case also provides excellent illustrations of the powerful role the community could play in individuals' lives and of the potential influence of ordinary folk, both men and women, on the official actions of colonial governments.

The Hall case offers compelling insights into the process of defining gender in early American society—a process as much communal as it was personal. Categorizing a person of indeterminate sex, like Hall, poses perplexing questions for any society. An analysis of seventeenth-century Virginians' attempts to come to grips with the problems presented to them by a sexually ambiguous person can accordingly reveal their fundamental beliefs about gender identity.[2]

After narrating the story of the person known variously as Thomas or Thomasine Hall, this account will reflect on what that tale shows about the relationship among formal governmental institutions, colonists' self-definitions, and the position of individual Anglo-Americans within communities of peers. The concern is less with Hall's personal dilemma than with other Virginians'

2. Anthropologists have been in the forefront of the investigation of the various relationships of sex and gender. A good introduction to such work is Sherry Ortner and Harriet Whitehead, eds., *Sexual Meanings: The Cultural Construction of Gender and Sexuality* (New York, 1981). The handling of cross-sexed individuals in native American societies is analyzed in Walter L. Williams, *The Spirit and the Flesh: Sexual Diversity in American Indian Culture* (Boston, 1986). For an account of how contemporary American society handles sexually ambiguous babies at birth, see Suzanne J. Kessler, "The Medical Construction of Gender: Case Management of Intersexed Infants," *Signs: Journal of Women in Culture and Society,* XVI (1990), 3–26.

reactions to this person who resisted being defined irrevocably by both sex and gender.[3]

Describing my usage of personal pronouns and names is essential to the analysis that follows. The other historians who have dealt with the case have referred to Hall as "Thomas" and "he," as do the court records (with one significant exception). Yet the details of the case, including Hall's testimony, make such usage highly problematic. Therefore, the practice here shall be the following: when Hall is acting as a female, the name "Thomasine" and the pronoun "she" will be used. Conversely, when Hall is acting as a male, "Thomas" and "he" are just as obviously called for. In moments of ambiguity or generalization (as now) "Hall" or the simple initial "T" will be employed (the latter as if it were an ungendered pronoun).

A BRIEF NARRATIVE OF THE LIFE OF THOMAS(INE) HALL IN ENGLAND, FRANCE, AND VIRGINIA

Thomasine Hall was born "at or neere" the northeastern English city of Newcastle upon Tyne. As the name suggests, Hall was christened and raised as a girl. At the age of twelve, Thomasine went to London to stay with her aunt, and she lived there for ten years. But, in 1625, her brother was pressed into the army to serve in an expedition against Cádiz. Perhaps encouraged by her brother's experience (or perhaps taking his place after his death, for that expedition incurred many casualties), Hall subsequently adopted a new gender identity. Thomas told the Virginia General Court that he "Cut of[f] his heire and Changed his apparell into the fashion of man and went over as a souldier in the *Isle of Ree* being in the habit of a man." Upon returning to Plymouth from army service in France, probably in the autumn of 1627, Hall resumed a feminine identity. Thomasine donned women's clothing and supported herself briefly by making "bone lace" and doing other needlework. That she did so suggests that Thomasine had been taught these valuable female skills by her aunt during her earlier sojourn in London.[4]

3. There are, of course, other aspects of communal definitions of gendered identity that could be discussed here, like beliefs about "ideal" men and women, their behaviors and roles, but, for the purposes of this article, I have chosen to concentrate on an incident that is especially fascinating because of its violation of so many modern sensibilities. I think of this essay rather like Robert Darnton's joke about killing cats—trying to understand its meaning opens a "strange and wonderful world." See Darnton, *The Great Cat Massacre and Other Episodes in French Cultural History* (New York, 1984), 5.

4. Clive Holmes and Nicholas Canny alerted me to the fact that "Cales Accon," in which

Plymouth was one of the major points of embarkation for the American colonies, and, "shortly after" arriving in the city, Thomasine learned that a ship was being made ready for a voyage to Virginia. Once again, Hall decided to become a man, so he put on men's clothing and sailed to the fledgling colony. Thomas was then approximately twenty-five years old, comparable in age to many of the emigrants to Virginia, and, like most of his fellows, he seems to have gone to the Chesapeake as an indentured servant.

By December, Hall was settled in Virginia, for on January 21, 1627/8, a man named Thomas Hall, living with John and Jane Tyos (T's first master and mistress), was convicted along with them for receiving stolen goods from William Mills, a servant of one of their neighbors. According to the testimony, Hall and the Tyoses had encouraged Mills in a series of thefts that began before Christmas 1627. Some of the purloined items—which included tobacco, chickens, currants, a shirt, and several pairs of shoes—were still in the possession of Hall and the Tyoses at the time their house was searched by the authorities on January 14. Although Thomas Hall is a common name (and indeed John Tyos knew another Thomas Hall, who had arrived with him on the ship *Bona Nova* in 1620), a significant piece of evidence suggests that T and the man charged with this crime were one and the same. William Mills had difficulty carrying the currants, which he piled into his cap during his initial theft. Since that was clearly an unsatisfactory conveyance, when Mills was about to make a second foray after the desirable dried fruits he asked his accomplices to supply him with a better container. Thomas Hall testified that Jane Tyos then "did bring a napkin unto him and willed him to sowe it and make a bagg of it to carry currants." It is highly unlikely that an ordinary male servant would have had better seamstressing skills than his mistress, but Thomasine was an expert at such tasks.[5]

T's brother participated, was the attack on Cádiz (anglicized at the time as "Cales") in October 1625. The expedition in which Thomas later took part was an ill-fated English attack on the Île de Ré during the summer of 1627. The troops who futilely tried to relieve the French Protestants besieged in the city of La Rochelle embarked on July 10, 1627; most of them returned to Plymouth in early November. It is possible, however, that Hall returned sooner than that.

5. *Va. Ct. Recs.*, 159, 162–163 (quotation on 163). Yet, it is possible that the Thomas Hall in this case was the other man, the one who came to Virginia in 1620. (For him, see Virginia M. Meyer and John Frederick Dorman, eds., *Adventurers of Purse and Person: Virginia, 1607–1624/5*, 3d ed. [Richmond, Va., 1987], 42, which places Thomas Hall and John Tyos as residents of George Sandys's plantation in James City on the muster of 1624/5 and identifies them as 1620 immigrants on the *Bona Nova*. Also, in March 1625/6, Tyos mentioned Thomas "Haule" in a deposition [*Va. Ct. Recs.*, 96].) In the theft prosecution, Thomas Hall

Although thus far in Hall's tale the chronology and the sequence of gender switches have been clear—for T specifically recounted the first part of the tale to the Virginia General Court, and the timing of the thefts and their prosecution is clearly described in court testimony—the next phase of the story must be pieced together from the muddled testimony of two witnesses and some logical surmises.

A key question not definitively answered in the records is: What happened to raise questions in people's minds about Hall's sex? Two possibilities suggest themselves. One is that John and Jane Tyos, who obviously recognized that Hall had "feminine" skills shortly after T came to live with them, spoke of that fact to others, or perhaps visitors to their plantation observed Hall's activities and drew their own conclusions. Another possibility is that, after traveling to Virginia as a man, Hall reverted to the female clothing and role that T appears to have found more comfortable. The court records imply that Hall did choose to dress as a woman in Virginia, for Francis England, a witness, reported overhearing a conversation in which another man asked T directly: Why do you wear women's clothing? T's reply—"I goe in weomans aparell to gett a bitt for my Catt"—is difficult to interpret and will be analyzed later. In any event, a Mr. Stacy (who cannot be further identified) seems to have first raised the issue of T's anomalous sexual character by asserting to other colonists that Hall was "as hee thought a man and woeman." Just when Stacy made this statement is not clear, but he probably voiced his opinion about a year after T arrived in the colony.[6]

In the immediate aftermath of Stacy's statement, a significant incident occurred at the home of Nicholas Eyres, perhaps a relative of Robert Eyres, who

---

is not explicitly identified as a servant, although he was living with T's eventual master and mistress. Thus, he could have been the free man who was Tyos's earlier acquaintance, perhaps a partner. Moreover, the birthplaces differ: T, as already indicated, described a birthplace "at or neere" Newcastle; this Thomas Hall identified his birthplace as a village in Cambridgeshire—not especially "neere" Newcastle, yet still in the same general area northeast of London. But the conclusion that the later T and this Thomas are the same seems justified not only by the thieving Thomas's sewing abilities but also by the difficulty of believing that, within the same year, two *different* persons both named Thomas Hall—who were approximately the same age (25 or 26) and who both knew how to sew—lived at the house of John and Jane Tyos, which would be a remarkable coincidence. Vaughan, "The Sad Case of Thomas(ine) Hall," *VMHB*, LXXXVI (1978), 146–148, and Katz, *Gay/Lesbian Almanac*, 71–72, do not link the Thomas Hall of the theft case with T. Brown, "'Changed . . . into the Fashion of Man,'" *Journal of the History of Sexuality*, VI (1995), 179 n. 18, rejects the linkage.

6. Since the conversation overheard by England took place at Atkins's Arbor, the home of T's second master, it possibly occurred *after* T had been officially ordered to don women's clothing (see below). But then the element of voluntarism in both the question and the

had recently become John Tyos's partner. "Uppon [Stacy's] Report," Alice Longe, Dorothy Rodes, and Barbara Hall examined Hall's body for the first time. Their action implied that T was at the time dressed as a woman, for women regularly searched other women's bodies (often at the direction of a court) to look for signs of illicit pregnancy or perhaps witchcraft. They never, however, performed the same function with respect to men—or anyone dressed as a man. And John Tyos both then and later told Dorothy Rodes that Hall was a woman. Even so, the female searchers, having examined Hall, declared that T was a man. As a result of the initial disagreement between Tyos and the women about T's gender, T was brought before the commander of the region, Captain Nathaniel Basse, for further examination.[7]

Questioned by Basse, T responded with a description of a unique anatomy with ambiguous physical characteristics. (The text of the testimony is mutilated, and the remaining fragments are too incomplete to provide a clear description of T's body.) Hall then refused to choose a sexual identity, instead declaring that T was "both man and woeman." Captain Basse nevertheless decided that Hall was female and ordered T "to bee put in woemans apparell"—thus implying that T was, at that moment at least, dressed as a man. The three women who had previously searched T's body were shaken by the official ruling that contradicted their own judgment; after being informed of the commander's decision, they reportedly "stood in doubte of what they had formerly affirmed."

John Tyos then sold Hall, now legally a maidservant named Thomasine, to John Atkins, who was present when Captain Basse questioned T. Atkins must have fully concurred with Basse's decision; surely he would not have purchased a female servant about whose sex he had any doubts. Yet questions were again raised about her sexual identity, for Alice Longe and her two friends subsequently went to Atkins's house to scrutinize Thomasine's body for a second time, in the first of the three incidents described at the beginning of this essay.

---

answer would seem misplaced, unless T's wearing women's apparel on that occasion was recognized as one of a number of similar episodes rather than a break with a past pattern that had occurred only because of orders from a superior.

7. Little can be discovered about the three women. At the time of the muster in 1624/5, Alice Longe was listed as living with her husband Richard on Nathaniel Basse's plantation. Roger Rodes, probably Dorothy's eventual husband, was then a servant of Thomas Allnut. The name Barbara Hall does not appear. A "boy" named Nicholas Eyres was resident on the Sandys plantation with John Tyos and the other Thomas Hall (see Meyer and Dorman, eds., *Adventurers*, 32, 41, 48). In *Va. Ct. Recs.*, the name of Tyos's partner is rendered as "Eyros," not "Eyres," but, since handwriting styles at the time make it difficult to distinguish *o* and *e*, and the presence in Virginia of men surnamed "Eyres" is well documented, I have altered that spelling.

As was already noted, they examined Thomasine twice during the ensuing week (once accompanied by two additional female helpers), unhesitatingly concluding that Hall was a man. Atkins thereupon ordered his servant to don men's clothing, which then led the curious men, Roger Rodes and Francis England, to search Thomas's body.[8]

By this time, not only Hall but also everyone else was undoubtedly confused, and a rumor that Hall "did ly with a maid of Mr Richard Bennetts called greate Besse" must have added considerably to the uncertainty. Hall accused Alice Longe of spreading the tale. She denied the charge, blaming the slander instead on an unnamed male servant of John Tyos. If the story were true, what did it imply about Hall's sexual identity? Whether Hall were male or female would obviously have a bearing on the interpretation of any relationship with Bennett's maid Bess. Virginians now had reason to seek a firm resolution of the conflict. Since Captain Basse, the local commander, had been unable to find an acceptable solution, there was just one remaining alternative—to refer the dilemma to the General Court.[9]

That court, composed of the governor and Council, was the highest judicial authority in the small colony. The judges heard from Hall and considered the sworn depositions of two male witnesses (Francis England and John Atkins), who described the events just outlined. Remarkably, the court accepted T's own self-definition and, although using the male personal pronoun, declared that Hall was

> a man and a woeman, that all the Inhabitants there may take notice thereof and that hee shall goe Clothed in mans apparell, only his head to bee attired in a Coyfe and Crosecloth wth an Apron before him.

Ordering Hall to post bond for good behavior until formally released from that obligation, the court also told Captain Basse to see that its directives were carried out. Since most court records for subsequent years have been

---

8. The two female newcomers were the wife of Allen Kinaston and the wife of Ambrose Griffen. Allen "Keniston" is listed as a single man and a resident of Pasbehays in James City on the muster of 1624/5 (Meyer and Dorman, ed., *Adventurers,* 25). There is no mention of Griffen or his wife.

9. Vaughan, "The Sad Case of Thomas(ine) Hall," *VMHB,* LXXXVI (1978), 146–148, and Brown's discussion of the case in *Good Wives, Nasty Wenches, and Anxious Patriarchs,* 75, and " 'Changed . . . into the Fashion of Man,' " *Journal of the History of Sexuality,* VI (1995), 171, argue that the fornication rumor was the key to the case; T would first have to be defined as male before a fornication charge could be filed. I disagree that the fornication rumor was central but agree that the gossip must have been part of the reason why T was brought to court.

lost (they were burned during the Civil War), it is impossible to trace Hall's story further.[10]

The Hall case raises many questions, prime among them the relationship of physical characteristics and gender identity in the minds of early Americans. All those who examined T, be they male or female, insisted that T was male. Thus T's external sex organs resembled male genitals. Roger Rodes and Francis England, for example, pronounced Thomas "a perfect man" after they had "pulled out his members." Still, T informed Captain Basse "hee had not the use of the mans parte" and told John Atkins that "I have a peece of an hole" (a vulva). Since T was identified as a girl at birth, christened Thomasine, and raised accordingly, T probably fell into that category of human beings who appear female in infancy but at puberty develop what seem to be male genitalia. Such individuals were the subjects of many stories in early modern Europe, the most famous of which involved a French peasant girl, Marie, who suddenly developed male sex organs while chasing pigs when she was fifteen, and who in adulthood became a shepherd named Germain. It is not clear whether early Virginians were aware of such tales, but if they understood contemporary explanations of sexual difference, the narrative of Marie-Germain would not have surprised them. Women were viewed as inferior types of men, and their sexual organs were regarded as internal versions of male genitalia. In the best scientific understanding of the day, there was just one sex, and, under certain circumstances, women could turn into men.[11]

10. On February 9, 1632/3, the administration of Thomas Hall's estate was awarded to a man named Francis Poythres, but there is no way of knowing which Thomas Hall had died (*Va. Ct. Recs.*, 202). A Thomas Hall also appears occasionally in the Lower Norfolk County records in the early 1640s; see Norfolk County Deeds and Orders, I, microfilm 1a, Virginia State Library, Richmond.

11. The best discussion of the one-sex model of humanity and its implications is Thomas Laqueur, *Making Sex: Body and Gender from the Greeks to Freud* (Cambridge, Mass., 1990). See 126–130 for an analysis of Marie-Germain. See also, on persons with ambiguous sexual organs, John Money and Anke A. Ehrhardt, *Man and Woman, Boy and Girl: The Differentiation and Dimorphism of Gender Identity from Conception to Maturity* (Baltimore, 1972), chaps. 6, 8; Julia Epstein, "Either/Or—Neither/Both: Sexual Ambiguity and the Ideology of Gender," *Genders,* no. 7 (Spring 1990), 99–142; and Anne Fausto-Sterling, "The Five Sexes: Why Male and Female Are Not Enough," *Sciences,* XXXIII, no. 2 (1993), 20–24. Fausto-

What, then, in the eyes of Virginia's English residents, constituted sufficient evidence of sexual identity? For the male and female searchers of T's body, genitalia that appeared to be normally masculine provided the answer. But that was not the only possible contemporary response to the question. Leaving aside for the moment the persons who saw Hall as a combination of male and female (they will be considered later), it is useful to focus on those who at different times indicated that they thought T was female. There were three such individuals, all of them men: Captain Nathaniel Basse, who ordered T to wear women's clothing after T had appeared before him; John Atkins, T's second master, who purchased Thomasine as a maidservant; and, most important of all, T's first master, John Tyos.

It is not clear from the trial record why Captain Basse directed Hall to dress as a woman, for T asserted a dual sexual identity in response to questioning and never claimed to be exclusively female. Perhaps the crucial fact was T's admission that "hee had not the use of the mans parte." Another possibility was that Basse interpreted T's anatomy as insufficiently masculine. As was already indicated, the partial physical description included in this portion of the record survives only in fragmentary form and so is impossible to interpret, especially in light of the certainty of all the searchers.

John Atkins acquired Thomasine as a servant after Captain Basse had issued his order, and he at first accepted her as a woman, referring to how "shee" seemed to awaken from sleep. Yet Atkins changed his mind about his servant after he and the five women subjected Hall's body to the most thorough examination described in the case record. It involved a physical search by the women, then questioning by Atkins, followed by an order from Atkins to Hall to "lye on his backe and shew" the "peece of an hole" that T claimed to have. When the women "did againe finde him to bee a man," Atkins issued the directive that contradicted Captain Basse's, ordering T to put on men's clothes. He furthermore now referred to his servant as "him." For Atkins, Hall's anatomy (which he saw with his own eyes) and the women's testimony were together decisive in overriding his initial belief that T was female, a belief presumably based at least in part on his presence at Basse's interrogation of T.

Unlike Atkins, John Tyos had purchased T as Thomas—a man. And for him the interpretive process was reversed. After just a brief acquaintance with Thomas, John and his wife Jane learned that he had female skills. Approximately a year later, Tyos "swore" to Dorothy Rodes that Hall "was a woman," a

<hr>

Sterling believes that T was either a true hermaphodite or what she calls a "ferm"—a female pseudohermaphrodite, or a person with XX chromosomes and female sex organs but also with masculinized genitalia (personal communication, 1993).

conclusion that contradicted the opinion of the female searchers. It also seemingly flew in the face of what must have been his own intimate knowledge of Hall's physical being. The lack of space in the small houses of the seventeenth-century Chesapeake is well known to scholars.[12] It is difficult to imagine that Tyos had never seen Hall's naked body—the same body that convinced searchers of both sexes that T was male. So why would Tyos insist that T was Thomasine, even to Dorothy Rodes, who forcefully asserted the contrary? The answer must lie, not in Hall's sexual organs, but in T's gender—that is, in the feminine skills and mannerisms that would have been exhibited by a person born, raised, and living as a female until reaching the age of twenty-two and that would have been immediately evident to anyone who, like John Tyos, lived with T for any length of time.

Here the distinction between sex and gender developed by feminist scholars proves particularly useful in explaining Tyos's reasoning. The term "gender," as currently employed by many, is not a synonym for "sex" but rather describes its cultural construction—that is, the definition of masculinity and femininity. Although every society believes that its gender definitions stem "naturally" from biological sexual identity, in practice different cultures define the sexes' modes of behavior and appropriate roles in widely varying ways. Unlike the searchers of Hall's body, then, John Tyos was judging his servant's identity by applying cultural (and therefore gendered) rather than anatomical (and therefore sexual) criteria.[13]

English migrants to North America learned that gender was culturally constructed immediately upon their arrival in their new homes, for the practices of eastern Algonquian peoples confronted them with a direct challenge to

12. See Lois Green Carr, Russell R. Menard, and Lorena S. Walsh, *Robert Cole's World: Agriculture and Society in Early Maryland* (Chapel Hill, N.C., 1991), 90–114, on "the standard of life" in the early Chesapeake.

13. For the most thorough and influential examination of the concept of gender as it applies to historical works, see Joan W. Scott, *Gender and the Politics of History* (New York, 1988). Feminist scholars have increasingly questioned the utility of a rigid distinction between "biological" sex and "cultural" gender, arguing that sex is also culturally constructed. Although agreeing with such caveats, I find the precision of the two terms too useful to discard completely. See Gisela Bock, "Women's History and Gender History: Aspects of an International Debate," *Gender and History,* 1 (1989), 7–30, esp. 10–15. Insightful works by anthropologists include Peggy Reeves Sanday, *Female Power and Male Dominance: On the Origins of Sexual Inequality* (New York, 1981); Carol MacCormack and Marilyn Strathern, eds., *Nature, Culture, and Gender* (New York, 1980); Ortner and Whitehead, eds., *Sexual Meanings;* and Stephanie Coontz and Peta Henderson, eds., *Women's Work, Men's Property: The Origins of Gender and Class* (London, 1986). Linda J. Nicholson, a philosopher, addresses some of the same issues in *Gender and History: The Limits of Social Theory in the Age of the Family* (New York, 1986).

the gender system with which they were familiar. In the English sexual division of labor, men worked in the fields, whereas women occupied themselves with household and children.[14] But, in North America, Algonquian women performed agricultural duties, and their menfolk, one colonial observer remarked, engaged in "no kind of labour but hunting, fishing and fowling." Such activities supplied protein crucial to the villagers' diet, but English people viewed them solely as elite leisure-time diversions. Thus, colonists uniformly and inaccurately interpreted the Algonquian gender system as one in which women were "in great slavery" and men "extraordinary idle." The Algonquians, in return, appear to have been just as startled by the gender system of the interlopers. Thomas Lechford, an early New Englander, reported that Algonquian men called English women "Lazie *squaes*," accusing male colonists of "spoiling good working creatures."[15]

Gender systems like those of the English and the Algonquians did more than simply assign work roles to men and women; gender terminology also described the social relationships between the sexes, thus supplying (in the words of Joan Scott) "a primary way of signifying relationships of power." A 1666 comment from the Marylander George Alsop reveals as much. He described the Algonquian gender system as one in which women were "Butchers, Cooks, and Tillers of the ground," and men thought it "below the honour of a Masculine" to do anything but hunt. He then exposed his own assumptions about the connection between gender and power by remarking, "I never observed . . . that ever the Women wore the Breeches, or dared either to look or action predominate over the Men."[16]

To Alsop's European mind, those who tilled the soil normally "wore the Breeches" and "predominate[d] over" the other sex. Therefore, he had to assure both himself and his English audience that, despite their work roles, Algonquian women were simply—in his words—"ingenious and laborious

14. For a useful summary of current scholarship on the work roles of English women, which varied somewhat by region, see Brown, *Good Wives, Nasty Wenches, and Anxious Patriarchs,* 24–27; and Brown, "Gender and the Genesis of a Race and Class System in Virginia, 1630–1750" (Ph.D. diss., University of Wisconsin, Madison, 1990), I, 20–32.

15. J. Franklin Jameson, ed., *Johnson's Wonder-Working Providence, 1628–1651* (New York, 1910), 262; Thomas Lechford, *Plain-Dealing; or, Newes from New-England* (London, 1642) (Massachusetts Historical Society, *Collections,* 3d Ser., III [1833]), 103. A book exploring such contrasts is James Axtell, ed., *The Indians of Eastern America: A Documentary History of the Sexes* (New York, 1981).

16. Scott, *Gender and Politics of History,* 42; George Alsop, *A Character of the Province of Mary-land, 1666,* in Clayton Colman Hall, ed., *Narratives of Early Maryland, 1633–1684* (New York, 1910), 370–371, 377. See also Joan Kelly, "The Social Relationship of the Sexes," in Kelly, *Women, History, and Theory* (Chicago, 1984).

Housewives" rather than competitors for the power that properly resided in male hands. By asserting that a European-style gender system prevailed in Algonquian as well as English families, Alsop rendered an alien form of social organization both more familiar and less threatening. William Wood took a similar tack later in the century when, after criticizing "lazy" Indian men, he praised Algonquian women for "not presuming to proclaim their female superiority to the usurping of the least title of their husband's charter, but rest themselves content under their helpless condition, counting it the woman's portion."[17]

Therefore, Alsop and Wood, confronted in North America with a disturbing challenge to their assumptions about gender, interpreted what they saw to avoid disrupting their notions of proper relationships. They could not deny that Algonquian women performed tasks that in the English gender system were assigned to men, but they downplayed the significance of that reversal by insisting that, even in Algonquian families, women recognized their natural inferiority and obeyed their husbands, unworthy though their menfolk were by English standards. Accordingly, the English colonists convinced themselves that the gender hierarchy they saw as appropriate was maintained even in the very different culture they had encountered in their new homeland.

For the colonists, then, two components combined to comprise one's identity as man or woman. The first was physical: the nature of one's genitalia. The other was cultural: the character of one's knowledge and one's manner of behaving. The English observers' remarks about the Algonquians demonstrate how they were able to resolve the conundrum presented to them by biological females who acted "like men" by performing masculine tasks. The Europeans accomplished that feat by referring, not to work roles, but rather to another gendered aspect of feminine identity—that is, wives' necessary and "natural" submission to their husbands—which they interpreted in such a way as to accord with their own preconceptions about properly gendered behavior.

In T's case, the female and male searchers applied the physical criterion, John Tyos the cultural. John Atkins initially adopted the second approach but later switched to the first. Nathaniel Basse might have agreed with Tyos, or he might have refused to interpret Hall's anatomy as unambiguously as did the searchers; it is not clear which. But it is certain that two distinct tests of sexual identity existed in tandem in early Virginia and elsewhere in the colonies. One relied on physical characteristics, the other on learned, gendered behavior. On most occasions, of course, results of the two tests would accord with each other. Persons raised as females would physically appear to be females; persons

17. William Wood, *New England's Prospect,* ed. Alden T. Vaughan (Amherst, Mass., 1977), 112, 115.

raised as males would look like other males. Hall acted like a woman and physically resembled a man. Thus, in T's persona, the results of the two independent criteria clashed, and that was the source of the confusion. Moreover, that confusion was less easily resolved than was the contrary example of the Algonquian women—who were physically female but behaved like men—because one aspect of the Indians' behavior (seeming submission to their husbands) could easily be interpreted as more significant than another aspect of their behavior (their agricultural duties). T's unique identity did not permit the drawing of such convenient distinctions.

In addition to clarifying the sex/gender distinction, Hall's case also points up the importance of clothing as a gendered marker in seventeenth-century society. At first glance, it seems remarkable that the official determinations of Hall's identity took the form of comments—both in and out of court—about what clothing T should wear, men's or women's. Captain Basse and John Atkins did not say to T, "You are a man," or, "You are a woman"; instead, they issued instructions about what sort of apparel T was to put on. Likewise, although the General Court declared explicitly that Hall was both male and female, its decision also described the clothing T was to wear in specific detail.

Clothing was so central because in the seventeenth century it served as a key identifier of persons. Not only did males and females wear different garb, but people also were expected to reveal their social status in their dress. Distinctions in gender and rank were of crucial importance in seventeenth-century England, where, as the historian Keith Wrightson has observed, "the most fundamental structural characteristic" of the society was "its high degree of stratification, its distinctive and all-pervasive system of social inequality." Displaying visually one's sex and rank to everyone else was even more essential in America than in the mother country, because the geographical and social mobility inherent in colonization rendered people anonymous. In the colonies, it was particularly requisite that new acquaintances know how to categorize each other even before exchanging a word of greeting. In a fundamental sense, seventeenth-century people's identity was expressed in their apparel. Therefore, the English colonists attempted to control who could wear certain garments. Virginia never went so far as Massachusetts, which passed laws regulating what clothing people of different ranks could wear, but the Virginia colonists were clearly determined to uphold the same sorts of rules.[18]

18. Keith Wrightson, *English Society, 1580–1680* (London, 1982), 17 (quotations), 21. See Nathaniel B. Shurtleff, ed., *Records of the Governor and Company of the Massachusetts Bay in New England, 1628–1674* (Boston, 1853–1854), IV, pt. 1, 60–61, IV, pt. 2, 41–42, for sumptuary laws; and George F. Dow, ed., *Records and Files of the Quarterly Courts of Essex County,*

Although no statutes anywhere in the colonies formally prohibited cross-dressing, several court cases in New England involved challenges to gendered conventions of clothing. In 1652, for example, Joseph Davis of Haverhill, Massachusetts, was convicted in the court at Strawbery Banke of "puttinge on woemans apparell and goeinge about from house to house in the nighte"; in 1677, Dorothy Hoyt of Hampton, New Hampshire, was likewise convicted of "putting on man's apparel." A prominent resident of Maine thought that such a charge, circulating in gossip about his wife, was sufficiently damaging to *his* reputation to warrant filing a defamation suit. Mr. Edward Godfrey accused Mistress Ellen Raynes of saying of his wife Anne that "twas the prid of her hart to wearre her husbands hatte about and a waskoat." He further declared that Ellen's husband Francis Raynes had then repeated the slander "att a publique meting one the Lords day." This matter "Consernd them not," Godfrey asserted.[19]

Why would Mr. Godfrey contend that such a statement had left him, rather than his wife, "damnified in his reputation"? The answer lies in the colonists' insistence on women's inferiority. A woman who wore a man's hat and waistcoat out of "pride" was questioning the familial hierarchy by asserting her equality to (if not superiority over) her husband. Since the English social system consisted of a series of interlocking hierarchies, it was essential that proper subordination be maintained in that most basic of all hierarchical relationships, marriage. A man of Godfrey's standing (he was then the governor of the province) could not permit a tale of his wife's misbehavior to be repeated without challenge, just as George Alsop and William Wood could not let stand the implication that Algonquian women might claim superiority in the household on the basis of their work roles.[20]

So clothing, which was sharply distinguished by the sex of its wearer, served as a visual trope for gender and thus for one's position in the specific status

Massachusetts (Salem, Mass., 1911–1921), I, 303–305, for a series of 1653 prosecutions under the laws (hereafter cited as *Essex Ct. Recs.*). Carolyn Merchant, *The Death of Nature: Women, Ecology, and the Scientific Revolution* (San Francisco, 1989), 174–177, points out the importance of clothing in establishing status in Francis Bacon's 1624 utopia, *The New Atlantis*.

19. Otis Hammond, ed , *New Hampshire Court Records, 1640 1692*, New Hampshire State Papers Series, XL (1943), 96 (hereafter cited as *New Hamp. Ct. Recs.*); *Essex Ct. Recs.*, VI, 341; Charles Libby and Robert Moody, eds., *Province and Court Records of Maine* (Portland, Maine, 1928–1947), I, 174.

20. Male colonists repeatedly demonstrated that they believed women inferior to men by their comments in letters and other writings. See, for example, John Underhill, *Newes from America; or, New and Experimentall Discoverie of New England* (MHS, *Colls.*, 3d Ser., VI [1837]), 5–6; Samuel Eliot Morison et al., eds., *Winthrop Papers, 1498–1649* (Boston, 1929–),

hierarchy governing men and women. Gender itself was one of the two most basic determinants of role in the early modern world (the other was rank, which was never at issue for Hall, who was always a servant). People who wore skirts nurtured children; people who wore pants did not. People who wore aprons could take no role in governing the colony, whereas other people could, if they were of appropriate status. People who wore headdresses performed certain sorts of jobs in the household; people who wore hats did other types of jobs in the fields. It is hardly surprising, therefore, that Virginians had difficulty dealing with a person who sometimes dressed as a man and other times as a woman—and who, on different occasions, did both at the direction of superiors. Nor, in light of this context, is it surprising that decisions about T's sexual identity were stated in terms of clothing.[21]

Just as the authorities' pronouncements reveal their understanding of the key role of apparel as a gender marker, so too the actions of Hall's fellow colonists disclose their understanding of what would today be termed personal privacy—or, more precisely, the lack thereof. Judging by their behavior in this case, seventeenth-century Virginians had few hesitations about examining the genitalia of another colonist, with or without official authorization from a court and regardless of whether they did so forcibly, clandestinely, or openly. The physical examinations were nominally by same-sex individuals: women when the object was Thomasine, men when the object was Thomas. There was one exception: John Atkins joined the women in scrutinizing the body of his maidservant. Clearly, a master's authority over the household extended to the bodies of his dependents. If a master like Atkins chose to search the body of a subordinate of either sex, no barrier would stand in his way.[22]

The concern over Hall's identity extended beyond the boundaries of Atkins's household. It became a topic of discussion for the community at large, particularly for individuals of the same sex. What would today be regarded as a

---

I, 222; and Glenn W. LaFantasie, ed., *The Correspondence of Roger Williams*, 2 vols. (Providence, R.I., 1988), II, 666 n. 10. As for women, even the well-educated poet Anne Bradstreet did not disagree; see verse 7 of her famous "Prologue," in Jeannine Hensley, ed., *The Works of Anne Bradstreet* (Cambridge, Mass., 1967), 16.

21. Laqueur observes, in *Making Sex*, 124–125, that "in the absence of a purportedly stable system of two sexes, strict sumptuary laws of the body attempted to stabilize gender— woman as woman and man as man—and punishments for transgression were quite severe." A relevant study is Marjorie Garber, *Vested Interests: Cross-Dressing and Cultural Anxiety* (New York, 1993).

22. For another case in which a master ordered a maidservant's body searched (it is not clear by whom), see Samuel Eliot Morison, ed., *Records of the Suffolk County Court, 1671–1680*, pt. 2 (Colonial Society of Massachusetts, *Publications, Collections*, XXX [1933]), 690 (hereafter cited as *Suffolk Ct. Recs.*).

personal question—the determination of one's sexual being—was in this case seen as properly subject to collective decision making. Hall was not an autonomous individual with the ability to make fundamental choices about selfhood independently; rather, T's identity—and, by extension, the identities of other people as well—belonged to the community as a whole, which took a key role in shaping it. Indeed, Edward Godfrey was unusual in his insistence that the clothing his wife wore should not concern his neighbors; few other colonists would have agreed with him. Even with respect to many aspects of married life that today would be thought most obviously private, the settlers concurred in a belief that the behavior of their peers was appropriately subject to collective commentary and judgment. Accordingly, the wider colonial community had a great deal to say about how people defined themselves and their personal lives.[23]

Some Anglo-Americans actually appeared to invite the community's intrusion into their affairs. From the former Rhode Island resident who complained to several people that his wife had refused to sleep with him, to the New Haven man who, describing his wife as "barren," approached two other married women to see if they could "teach him to gett a boy," colonists showed little hesitation about involving others in their most intimate problems. One particularly fascinating example of such behavior occurred in the Uffitt household in New Haven in the mid-1650s. The recently married son of the family, John, was experiencing sexual impotence, and so his parents and other household members observed a fast day "to seeke God to fitt him for his duty toward" his bride. They thus collectively attempted to solve what today would be seen as the most personal of all marital difficulties. (His unhappy wife Hannah, though, told several female friends: "I did not fast, but filled my belly as full as I could, and when they prayde one way I prayde another way.")[24] In the context of such incidents, the intrusive searches of T's body seem commonplace instead of remarkable.

One of the most significant aspects of T's story is the initiative taken throughout by Hall's fellow colonists. They not only brought their doubts about Hall's sex to the attention of the authorities; they also refused to accept Captain Basse's determination that Hall was female. Both men and women joined in the effort to convince Virginia's leaders that T was male. Nearly

23. For a contrasting, more expansive interpretation of the colonists' sense of privacy, see David H. Flaherty, *Privacy in Colonial New England* (Charlottesville, Va., 1972), pt. 1.

24. *Winthrop Papers*, IV, 259–260; Charles J. Hoadly, ed., *Records of the Colony and Plantation of New Haven, 1638–1649* (Hartford, Conn., 1857), 238; Charles J. Hoadly, ed., *Records of the Colony or Jurisdiction of New Haven, from May 1653 to the Union* (Hartford, Conn., 1858), II, 209 (hereafter cited as *New Hav. Recs.*).

uniformly rejecting T's self-characterization as "both" (the only exception outside the General Court being Stacy), Virginians insisted that Hall had to be either female or male, with most favoring the latter definition. They wanted a sexual category into which to fit T, and they did not hesitate to express their opinions about which category was the more appropriate.

Women in particular were active in this regard. Three times groups of women scrutinized T's body, whereas a group of men did so only once. After each examination, women rejected T as one of their number. Because of the vigorous and persistent efforts of female Virginians, Hall was deprived of the possibility of adopting unambiguously the role with which T seemed most comfortable, that of Thomasine. Here Hall's physical characteristics determined the outcome. Women thought T did not physically qualify as female— regardless of the gendered skills T possessed—and they repeatedly asserted that to any man who would listen. For them, T's anatomy (sex) was more important than T's feminine qualities (gender).

Seventeenth-century women were accustomed to viewing the bodies of other females. Midwives, not male physicians, supervised all births, and the other attendants of women in labor were also female. As is true in all populations that do not practice contraception, most adult, married women in the early Chesapeake would have experienced pregnancies every two to three years during their period of fertility. Even in small communities, births—and thus gatherings of women by the bedsides of parturient females—would have been commonplace occurrences, given the frequency with which each sexually active female adult became pregnant. Women as a group, and midwives especially, would accordingly have been familiar with the appearance of many other women's bodies beside their own and, because of their extensive experience tending each other in childbirth, with external female genitalia in particular.[25]

Indeed, women often searched other women's bodies at the direction of a court or a master, looking for signs of illicit pregnancy, concealed childbearing (and possible infanticide), or witchcraft. Sometimes judges formally convened women's juries; at other times, the process was more informal. But seventeenth-century court records demonstrate that the sorts of searches women conducted of Thomasine Hall's body were notable only in two respects: their precise object (determination of sex rather than potential illegal activity) and their number (most searches were performed only once, at most twice). An abundance of

25. An insightful overview is Adrian Wilson, "The Ceremony of Childbirth and Its Interpretation," in Valerie Fildes, ed., *Women as Mothers in Pre-Industrial England* (London, 1990), 68–107. I have discussed the assumed regularity of births in a later period in *Liberty's Daughters: The Revolutionary Experience of American Women, 1750–1800* (Boston, 1980), 72–84.

evidence pertaining to such incidents suggests that women felt considerable confidence in their ability to reach judgments about the usual appearance of women's external genitalia.[26]

The same was true of the female Virginians who scrutinized Thomasine, all of whom agreed that the servant was not physically a woman. Male opinion, by contrast, was divided. To be sure, the three male searchers of T's body—Roger Rodes, Francis England, and John Atkins—agreed with the women's conclusion. But other men applied other criteria. John Tyos and Nathaniel Basse thought T more appropriately classified as a woman, whereas Stacy and the members of the General Court said T displayed aspects of both sexes. It seems plausible to infer from their lack of agreement about T's sex that men as a group were not entirely certain how to create the categories "male" and "female." Some relied on physical appearance, others on behavior.

Moreover, the complacency of the male searchers can be interpreted as quite remarkable. They failed to police the boundaries of their sex with the same militance as did women. It is possible that men were not as accustomed as women to scrutinizing the bodies of other members of their own sex and that the physical standards the Virginia men employed in their examination of T were therefore somewhat less demanding than those the women used. Certainly, in sharp contrast to women, men rarely had the experience of searching another man's body at the direction of a court—at least, not a living body (coroners' juries composed of men did examine corpses of both sexes).[27] That Hall, if a man, was a very unusual sort of man indeed did not seem to bother Rodes, Atkins, and England. For them, T's physical resemblance to other men was adequate evidence of masculinity, despite their knowledge of Hall's feminine skills and occasional feminine dress. That opinion was, however, in the end overridden by the doubts of higher-ranking men on the General Court, who were not so willing to overlook T's peculiarities.

26. For examples of such searches, see William Hand Browne et al., eds., *Archives of Maryland* (Baltimore, 1883–1972), X, 457, XLIX, 233 (hereafter cited as *Md. Archs.*); New Haven Colonial Records, I-B, fols. 328–330, Connecticut State Library, Hartford; *New Hav. Recs.*, II, 81–83. I have discussed the role of female searchers of women's bodies in "Gender, Crime, and Community in Seventeenth-Century Maryland," in James Henretta et al., eds., *The Transformation of Early American History* (New York, 1991), 144–148.

27. An unusual example of a physical examination of a man by a group of men is reported in Martin Duberman, "Male Impotence in Colonial Pennsylvania," *Signs,* IV (1978), 395–401. Another is the case of Nathaniel Clarke of Plymouth, cited in Nathaniel B. Shurtleff and David Pulsifer, eds., *Records of the Colony of New Plymouth, in New England,* 12 vols. (Boston, Mass., 1855–1861), VI, 191–192. *Md. Archs.*, IV, contains many reports of coroners' juries. Such juries concerned themselves with determining cause of death, so they did not focus on the reproductive organs of the men or women they examined.

Biological sex and interpretation of gendered behavior were not the only issues raised in the prosecution of Thomas(ine) Hall. Indeed, twice, and in quite different ways, the case record addresses questions of sexuality. Both references have been alluded to briefly: the rumor of Thomas's having committed fornication with "greate Besse," and Hall's explanation for wearing women's clothing—"to gett a bitt for my Catt."

A judgment about Hall's body would imply a judgment about Hall's sexuality as well. Yet, was it possible to reach a definitive conclusion about Hall's sexuality? If T were Thomas, then he could potentially be guilty of fornicating with the maidservant Bess; if T were Thomasine, then being in the same bed with Bess might mean nothing—or it could imply "unnatural" acts, the sort of same-sex coupling universally condemned when it occurred between men and occasionally penalized when women were the delinquents. Two times colonial courts punished women for what was termed (in 1642) "unseemly and filthy practises betwixt hir and another maid, attempting To Doe that which man and woman Doe" or (in early 1649) "leude behavior each with other upon a bed." Thus, the rumor about Bess, which for an ordinary male servant might have led to a fistfight (with the supposed slanderer, Tyos's servant), a defamation suit, or a fornication presentment, raised perplexing questions because of T's ambiguous sexual identity, questions that could apparently only be resolved by a court decision.[28]

T's phrase "to gett a bitt for my Catt," as reported by Francis England, was even more troubling. What did it mean, and was that meaning evident to England and the members of the General Court? As an explanation for wearing female apparel, it could have been straightforward and innocent. One

28. For the 1642 case, see *Essex Ct. Recs.*, I, 42, and Essex Quarterly Courts, Record Books, 2d Ser., I, fol. 123, Phillips Library, Peabody Essex Museum, Salem, Mass. George F. Dow expurgated most of the details of this prosecution from his published text, and the quotation is from the manuscript. For the 1649 case, see Shurtleff and Pulsifer, eds., *Records of the Colony of New Plymouth*, II, 137. In the first case, a maidservant was fined and whipped; in the second, two free women (one of them married) were publicly admonished. An excellent article focusing primarily on the prosecutions of men for same-sex activity is Richard Godbeer, " 'The Cry of Sodom': Discourse, Intercourse, and Desire in Colonial New England," *William and Mary Quarterly*, 3d Ser., LII (1995), 259–286. A good general discussion of the colonists' attitudes toward sexuality is John D'Emilio and Estelle B. Freedman, *Intimate Matters: A History of Sexuality in America* (New York, 1988), 1–52, esp. 27–38 (on the regulation of deviance).

In " 'Changed . . . into the Fashion of Man,' " *Journal of the History of Sexuality*, VI (1995), 186, Brown has speculated that "great Besse" might have been of African origin. If Brown's speculation is correct, the racial difference would presumably have made a court decision seem even more imperative to contemporaries.

historian reads it literally, as indicating that Hall wore women's clothing to beg scraps for a pet cat. Hall might also have been saying that because T's skills were feminine, dressing as a woman was the best way for T to earn a living, "to get a bit (morsel) to eat." But some scholars have read erotic connotations into the statement. Could T, speaking as a man, have been saying that wearing women's clothing allowed T to get close to women, or, in modern slang, "to get a piece of pussy," by masquerading as a female?[29]

There is another more likely and even more intriguing erotic possibility. Since Hall had served in the English army on an expedition to France, T could well have learned a contemporary French slang phrase—"pour avoir une bite pour mon chat"—or, crudely put in English, "to get a prick for my cunt." Translating the key words literally into English equivalents (bite = bit, chat = cat) rather than into their metaphorical meanings produced an answer that was probably as opaque and confusing to seventeenth-century Virginians as it has proved to be to subsequent historians.[30] Since much of Francis England's testimony—with the exception of his report of this statement and the account of his and Roger Rodes's examination of T's anatomy—duplicated John Atkins's deposition, England could have been called as a witness primarily to repeat such a mysterious conversation to the court.

If T was indeed employing a deliberately misleading Anglicized version of contemporary French slang, as appears probable, two conclusions are warranted. First, the response confirms T's predominantly feminine gender, for it describes sexual intercourse from a woman's perspective. In light of the shortage of women in early Virginia, it moreover would have accurately represented T's experience: donning women's garb unquestionably opened sexual possibilities to Thomasine that Thomas lacked. At the same time, second, Hall was playing with T's listeners, answering the question about wearing women's apparel truthfully but in such an obscure way that it was unlikely anyone would

29. Brown accepts Hall's statement at face value in "Gender and Genesis of a Race and Class System," I, 88, and does not try to explain it in *Good Wives, Nasty Wenches, and Anxious Patriarchs,* 76. The suggestion that the phrase might have meant "earning a living" is mine, developed after consulting the *Oxford English Dictionary,* s.v. "bit." Katz speculates that T's phrase had the erotic meaning suggested here, although he recognizes that such an interpretation is problematic (*Gay/Lesbian Almanac,* 72).

30. I owe the identification of the probable French origin of this phrase to Marina Warner and, through her, to Julian Barnes, whom she consulted (personal communication, 1993). My Cornell colleague Steven Kaplan, a specialist in the history of early modern France (and scholars he consulted in Paris) confirmed that "bite" and "chat" were used thus in the late 16th century and that the interpretation appears plausible. My thanks also go to the many historians who futilely tried to assist me in interpreting the phrase when I thought it was English in origin.

comprehend T's meaning. In other words, Hall was having a private joke at the expense of other Virginians. Hall's sly reply thus discloses a mischievous aspect of T's character otherwise hidden by the flat prose of the legal record.

Finally, the most surprising aspect of the case might appear to be the General Court's acceptance of Hall's self-definition as both man and woman. By specifying that T's basic apparel should be masculine, but with feminine signs—the apron and the coif and crosscloth, a headdress commonly worn by women at the time—Virginia officials formally recognized that Hall contained elements of both sexes. The elite men who sat as judges thereby demonstrated their ability to transcend the dichotomous sexual categories that determined the thinking of ordinary Virginians. But their superficially astonishing verdict becomes explicable when the judges' options are analyzed in terms of contemporary understandings of sex and gender.

First, consider T's sexual identity. Could the court have declared Hall to be female? That alternative was effectively foreclosed. Women had repeatedly scrutinized T's anatomy and had consistently concluded that T was male. Their initial determination that Hall was a man—in the wake of Stacy's comment that Hall was both—first brought the question before Captain Basse. Subsequently, their adamant rejection of Captain Basse's contrary opinion and their ability to convince John Atkins that they were correct, coupled with the similar assessment reached by two men, was the key element forcing the General Court to consider the case. A small community could obviously not tolerate a situation in which groups of men and women alternately stripped and searched the body of one of its residents or in which the decisions of the local commander were so openly disobeyed. Declaring T to be female was impossible; ordinary Virginians of both sexes would not accept such a verdict.

Yet, at the same time, could anyone assert unconditionally that Hall was sexually a man? Francis England, Roger Rodes, John Atkins, and the five female searchers thought so, on the basis of anatomy; but John Tyos, who was probably better acquainted with T than anyone else, declared unequivocally that Hall was a woman. And T had testified about not having "the use of the mans parte." Hall, in other words, revealed that, although T had what appeared to be male genitalia, T did not function sexually as a man and presumably could not have an erection. To Captain Basse and the members of the General Court, that meant that—whatever T's physical description—Hall would not be able to father children or be a good husband to a wife.

The ability to impregnate a woman was perhaps the key indicator of manhood in seventeenth-century Anglo-America. In the eyes of contemporaries, the best evidence of a proper marriage was provided by its offspring. An appropriately consummated sexual relationship was deemed crucial to successful matrimony, and the birth of children confirmed the existence of such a relationship. That was all the more true because of the contemporary belief that women could not conceive without reaching orgasm. (The New Haven justices, for example, informed a young woman who claimed to have been impregnated while in "a fitt of swooning" that "no woman can be gotten with child without some knowledg, consent and delight in the acting thereof.")[31]

Accordingly, the absence of children called into question the character of a marriage and, in particular, the husband's ability to satisfy his wife sexually. On several occasions, childless colonial wives reported facing insults directed more at their husbands than themselves. In 1639 in the Bay Colony, for example, a man approached a woman "and offered to put his hands under her coats and sayd he came of a woman and knew what belonged to a woman and because her husband was not able to give her a great belly he would help him." In the minds of the colonists, in short, childlessness indicated a husband's failings as a man and the unsatisfactory nature of a marriage.[32]

Moreover, impotence was one of the few permissible grounds for divorce in the seventeenth-century colonies. New Haven statutes made explicit what was implicit in the jurisprudence of the other colonies. As that province's divorce law delicately put it, if a woman "needing and requiring conjugall duty, and due benevolence from her husband" found "after convenient forbearance and due tryall" that he "neither at the time of marriage, nor since, hath been, is, nor by the use of any lawfull means, is like to be able to perform or afford the same," she could sue for divorce and permission to remarry. The statute also provided that, if the man had known of his incapacity before marriage and had deceived her, she could be awarded monetary damages. Hence, women whose husbands were impotent insisted to colonial courts that their marriages were a sham, referring in their divorce petitions to a "pretended Contract of marriage" with a man "altogether deficient" in the "performance of an husband" or to a man "incapable of doing the duty and offices of a husband to a Wife." Marriages not physically consummated were only "pretended," women be-

31. *New Hav. Recs.*, II, 123. On 17th-century scientific opinion about conception, see Laqueur, *Making Sex*, esp. 99–103.

32. Edward Everett Hale et al., eds., *Note-Book Kept by Thomas Lechford, Esq., 1638 to 1641* (1884; reprint, Camden, Maine, 1988), 177. John Demos's emphasis in *Entertaining Satan: Witchcraft and the Culture of Early New England* (New York, 1982), 72–73, on the negative implications of childlessness for women is thus partially misplaced, because husbands shared the blame for that condition. See Linda Pollock, "Embarking on a Rough Passage: The Experience of Pregnancy in Early-Modern Society," in Fildes, ed., *Women as Mothers*, 40–41.

lieved, expressing their agreement with the definition contained in the New Haven statute.[33]

Accordingly, not only in New Haven did women cite their spouses' alleged impotence as grounds for divorce, and sometimes they won their cases. In March 1662/3, for example, Elias White reluctantly admitted to the Massachusetts Court of Assistants: "I find myself Infirmous not able to performe that office of marriage." His wife had previously asked him in the presence of two men "whither or no he had ever made use of hir"; he had been forced to reply, "no." Twenty-three years later, Nathaniel Clarke of Plymouth Colony proved less willing to accept his wife Dorothy's description of their marriage. After he disputed her statement that he was "misformed, and is always unable to perform the act of generation," the court ordered him examined by three physicians. Evidently the doctors concurred with him, for the court rejected her petition for a divorce. The judges did, however, acknowledge the "uncomfortable difference" between the two and so allowed them to separate if not to divorce and remarry.[34]

Gaining a reputation for "insufficiency" could be ruinous. A traveler encountered such a man in a state of "distress for want of a wife." He wrote to another that the man "Entertained me with nothing but the talk of his own Sufficiency, and is raving mad at all the world that wont be of the same mind with him in that regard." He "dos vehemently assert, and will stand by it to the last breath," the traveler commented, that he is capable of sexual intercourse, "and would have it published [publicized], that he may be under the greater Advantage, to get an Agreable companion." Perhaps in this case the gossip was so widespread that its target thought a defamation suit would achieve nothing, but other colonists did employ that mechanism to stop the telling of similar sorts of stories. Thus, a New Hampshire widow sued a man who had declared that "if she be with child it wilbe a bastard for it is not her husbands Getting for he wase not a man sufficient," and John Waltham, a Virginian, sued two women who had jeered his wife, sneering that since "he was not able to gett a child" he "hade his Mounthly Courses as Women have."[35]

33. *New Hav. Recs.*, II, 479, 586; Anna Keayne Lane, quoted in Edmund S. Morgan, "A Boston Heiress and Her Husbands: A True Story," Colonial Society of Massachusetts, *Publications, Transactions*, XXXIV (1937–1942), 503; Duberman, ed., "Male Impotence," *Signs*, IV (1978), 398. For Cotton Mather's summary of justifiable grounds for divorce in New England, see *Magnalia Christi Americana . . .* (Hartford, Conn., 1853), II, 253–254.

34. John F. Noble, ed., *Records of the Court of Assistants of the Colony of the Massachusetts Bay, 1630–1692* (Boston, 1901–1928), III, 132; Shurtleff and Pulsifer, eds., *Records of the Colony of New Plymouth in New England*, VI, 191–192.

35. N.S. to [Thomas Cotton], Feb. 28, 1710/11, Curwen Papers, box 2, folder 1, American

One woman's insistence on the importance of sexual intercourse to a marriage became evident in the Suffolk, Massachusetts, county court in the late 1670s. Mary Drury, twice presented by the grand jury for refusing to live with her husband, Hugh, as the law required, readily admitted that she would not live with "her outward husband." She informed the court that Hugh "never had a fellow ship with me, nor was abull" and that he had been "incapasitated for a mariage Estate" at the time of their wedding. Explaining that she had "loged with [him] six weekes or thear abouts" after their wedding, Mary revealed that he "[ne]ver had fellow ship with me as a husband thou[gh] he did indevor [it] the two first nites I lay with him." For the other months she resided there, "he never offered to have fellow ship with me," and so she left his house. Subsequently, she had resisted neighbors' repeated and persistent attempts to persuade her to return to Hugh, although evidently without revealing exactly why she had departed. Eventually, she petitioned the Bay Colony's Court of Assistants for divorce, supplying testimony from several witnesses who had spoken to Hugh's first wife, Lydia, "some yeares since." One woman disclosed that, when she told Lydia she looked pregnant, Lydia had responded that that was impossible, because "alas my husband hath a great weaknes upon him along time." But Hugh Drury had fathered a son during that first marriage, and so the Court of Assistants—evidently regarding the evidence as inconclusive—refused to nullify Mary Drury's marital union. She, however, adhered to her belief that she could not be said to be properly married to an impotent man, and she resolutely refused to resume living with him. Mary Drury was fifty-four years old, so procreation per se was not at issue in the case, but basic sexual functioning clearly was.[36]

Accordingly, a person who could not father a child was by that criterion alone an unsatisfactory male. T had admitted being incapable of male orgasm. Given that physical incapacity and its implications, declaring Hall to be a man was as impossible as declaring T to be a woman.[37]

Moreover, consider T's gender identity. In seventeenth-century Anglo-America, as in all other known societies, sexual characteristics carried with them gendered consequences. In Hall's life history, those consequences were especially evident, because what T did and how T did it were deeply affected by whether T chose to be Thomas or Thomasine.

Antiquarian Society, Worcester, Massachusetts; *New Hamp. Ct. Recs.*, XL, 253; Susie M. Ames, ed., *County Court Records of Accomack-Northampton, Virginia, 1632–1640* (Washington, D.C., 1954), 85.

36. *Suffolk Ct. Recs.*, II, 754–755, 837–841.

37. On the importance of marital sexuality in the colonies, see D'Emilio and Freedman, *Intimate Matters*, 16–27.

Whenever Hall traveled far from home—to France in the army or to Virginia—T became Thomas. Men had much more freedom of movement than did women. Unlike other persons raised as females, Hall's unusual anatomy gave T the opportunity to live as a male when there was an advantage to doing so. Even though T seemed more comfortable being Thomasine—to judge by frequent reversions to that role—the option of becoming Thomas must have been a welcome one. It permitted Hall to escape the normal strictures that governed early modern English women's lives and allowed T to pursue a more adventurous lifestyle.[38]

Thus, whether T chose to be male or female made a great difference in T's life. As Thomas, Hall joined the army and emigrated to the colonies; as Thomasine, Hall lived quietly in London with an aunt, did fancy needlework in Plymouth, and presumably performed tasks normally assigned to women in Virginia. T's most highly developed skills were feminine ones, so T was undoubtedly more expert at and familiar with "women's work" in general, not just seamstressing.

It was, indeed, Hall's feminine skills that convinced some men that T was female; and those qualities, coupled with Hall's physical appearance, must have led to the court's decision. T's gender was feminine but T's sex seemed to be masculine—with the crucial exception of sexual functioning. Given T's sexual incapacity, all indications pointed to a feminine identity—to Thomasine. But Virginia women's refusal to accept T as Thomasine precluded that verdict. On the other hand, the judges could not declare a person to be male who had admitted to Captain Basse an inability to consummate a marriage. Ordinary men might possibly make a decision on the basis of physical appearance alone, but the members of the General Court had a responsibility to maintain the wider social order. If they said Hall was a man, then Thomas theoretically could marry and become a household head once his term of service was complete. That alternative was simply not acceptable for a person of T's description.

So, considering sex (incompletely masculine) and gender (primarily feminine), the Virginia General Court's solution to the dilemma posed by Hall was to create a unique category that combined sex and gender for T alone. Unable to fit Hall into the standard male/female dichotomy, the judges preferred to develop a singular definition that enshrined T's dual identity by prescribing clothing that simultaneously carried conflicting messages.

The court's decision to make Hall unique in terms of clothing—and thus gender identity—did not assist the community in classifying or dealing with T.

38. See, on this point, Rudolf M. Dekker and Lotte C. van de Pol, *The Tradition of Female Transvestism in Early Modern Europe* (London, 1989).

After the verdict, Virginians were forced to cope with someone who, by official sanction, straddled the dichotomous roles of male and female. By court order, Hall was now a dual-sexed person and was prevented from assuming either a masculine or a feminine persona. T's identity had no counterpart or precedent; paradoxically, a society in which gender—the outward manifestation of sex—served as a fundamental dividing line had formally designated a person as belonging to both sexes. Yet, at the same time, it was precisely because gender was so basic a concern to seventeenth-century society that no other solution was possible.

Hall's life after the court verdict must have been lonely. Marked as T was by unique clothing, unable to adopt the gender switches that had previously given T unparalleled flexibility in choosing a way of life, Hall must have had a very difficult time. T, like other publicly marked deviants—persons branded for theft or adultery or mutilated for perjury or forgery—was perhaps the target of insults or assaults. The verdict in the case, in its insistence that Hall be constantly clothed as *both* sexes rather than alternating between them, was therefore harsh, though it nominally accorded with T's own self-definition. Hall's identity as "both" allowed movement back and forth across gender lines. The court's verdict had quite a different meaning, insisting, not on the either/or sexual ambiguity T had employed to such great advantage, but rather on a definition of "both" that required duality and allowed for little flexibility.

It is essential to reemphasize here what necessitated this unusual ending to a remarkable case: the opinions and actions of the female neighbors of John Tyos and John Atkins. Captain Nathaniel Basse, confronted with basically the same information that the General Court later considered, concluded that Hall should be dressed and treated as a woman. In a sexual belief system that hypothesized that women were inferior men, any inferior man—that is, one who could not function adequately in sexual terms—was a woman. Thus, charged the women at an Accomack cow pen in 1637, John Waltham "hade his Mounthly Courses as Women have" because his wife had not become pregnant. Undoubtedly the General Court's first impulse would have been the same as Captain Basse's: to declare that T, an inferior man, was female and should wear women's clothing. But Virginia women had already demonstrated forcefully that they would not accept such a verdict. Hall's fate, therefore, was determined as much by a decision reached by ordinary women as it was by a verdict formally rendered by the elite men who served on the General Court.

This unique case considered by the highest Virginia court in April 1629 accordingly supplies compelling evidence of the importance of examining the context in which colonial self-definitions were shaped. Thomas(ine) Hall, in a more dramatic way than most, was affected by the colonial community's determination of gendered identity. But others no less than Hall accomplished a final resolution of their gendered identity not only through individual contemplation and reflection but also as a result of the opinions and actions of their fellow colonists. Gendered selves, like other aspects of personal identity in the seventeenth century, must be studied, not in isolation from, but in conjunction with the collectivity of colonial people—elites and persons of ordinary rank. Only then can a full picture of the process of self-definition be obtained.

~

MAKING HISTORY: THE FORCE OF
PUBLIC OPINION AND THE LAST YEARS
OF SLAVERY IN REVOLUTIONARY
MASSACHUSETTS

T. H. Breen

How exactly do ordinary people make history? The question is as old as the discipline itself, and over the centuries historians have advanced responses that contemporaries found more or less persuasive. For some, of course, the problem of inclusion has never seemed particularly compelling. These writers have produced familiar narratives of the past in which ordinary men and women scarcely appear, let alone enjoy a significant role in the making of history. For those of Marxist persuasion, however, the issue has always been of paramount concern. At risk of gross oversimplification, one could assert that Marxists maintained that ordinary men and women entered history as they acquired class consciousness. A shared understanding of economic and political interest provided individuals with social meaning, situating biography within a potentially revolutionary framework. Class consciousness effectively linked the personal experience of material culture to the larger social forces—to capitalism and nationalism, for example—that inevitably shaped that experience.

In recent years, the collapse of Marxism as well as the rejection of other grand interpretive schemes has radically transformed the intellectual landscape. It is no longer quite so clear how ordinary people in early modern society—the focus of attention in this chapter—made history. Even as they proclaim the importance of human agency, insisting upon the capacity of marginal men and women to fashion their lives, many modern social histo-

An earlier version of this essay was presented as the Gilbert Osofsky Memorial Lecture, University of Illinois at Chicago, Mar. 31, 1993. Gary Nash, Linda Kerber, James Oakes, Robert Wiebe, Alfred Young, James Axtell, George Fredrickson, and Nell Painter read various drafts of the manuscript and offered helpful suggestions for revision. Also, while completing the research for this project, I received invaluable assistance from Albert Clark of Barre, Massachusetts, Robert Williams and Lise Compton of Taunton, and Daniel Mandell, Eric Slauter, Russell Maylone, and Charles S. Fineman.

rians seem ill-prepared to answer our initial question. They have separated everyday experience from political and economic structures and thereby isolated quotidian concerns from external sources of power. Such accounts teach us a lot about the construction of self, often within the context of family and community, but not much about society. No doubt, by chronicling what might be called "lifestyle" decisions, we gain a heightened appreciation of how ordinary people established cultural identities. But to what purpose? However much it might have enriched the stories we tell ourselves about the past, the interpretive move away from broad economic and social structures might have come at too great a price. It has divorced the individual from major external systems of power, leaving the impression that, for ordinary men and women, making history was simply a matter of personal choice.

This essay argues that public opinion provides an appealing as well as timely solution to the general question of how ordinary people make history. The German historian and philosopher Jürgen Habermas first drew scholarly attention to the invention of the concept of public opinion in his *Structural Transformation of the Public Sphere*.[1] Habermas's name now appears in the literature with the same enthusiasm that social historians once mustered for Clifford Geertz, the anthropologist who seemed to invite the production of ever thicker cultural description. Like Geertz, Habermas is regularly misinterpreted, and the notion of a "public sphere" has been pressed into interpretive service in ways that suggest a tenuous understanding of what he actually wrote about: radical changes in the structure of eighteenth-century intellectual life.

The public sphere was emphatically not a physical space. It was a useful abstraction, a form of Enlightenment discourse, a reification created by newspaper writers and pamphleteers who claimed to speak for the public. During this period, no one actually polled the public to discover what ordinary men and women believed. Rather, by assuming the voice of an imagined public, authors sought legitimacy as well as authority. After all, as these writers regularly explained, they did not represent the church, or the army, or the crown, all traditional European institutions identified with coercive state power and narrowly partisan interests. By contrast, public opinion was reasonable and independent, virtuous and reflective, a powerful perspective from which popular authors presumed to criticize the workings of established institutions. As the philosopher Charles Taylor has explained, "Public opinion, as originally conceived, is not just the sum of our private individual opinions, even where

1. Jürgen Habermas, *The Structural Transformation of the Public Sphere: An Inquiry into a Category of Bourgeois Society,* trans. Thomas Berger (Cambridge, Mass., 1989). Historians have applied Habermas's insights to other societies; see Craig Calhoun, ed., *Habermas and the Public Sphere* (Cambridge, Mass., 1992).

we spontaneously agree. It is something which has been elaborated in a debate and discussion, and is recognized by us all as something we hold in common. This element of common recognition is what makes it public in the strong sense."[2]

For historians of eighteenth-century America, Habermas's insights into the development of public opinion would seem to have considerably less analytic purchase than for European historians working in the same period. Neither church nor state in colonial society could pass for genuine institutions of an ancien régime; government power was generally weak and even established churches had to compete with aggressive dissenting sects. But, in point of fact, these conditions in no way reduced the force of public opinion in Britain's mainland provinces. A robust commercial press encouraged authors to adopt the innovative discourse, in other words, to presume to speak *to* a colonial public as well as *for* it. When they entered hotly contested debates, journal writers and pamphleteers swore that neither party nor faction had influenced their views. They claimed to have brought an independent perspective to the divisive issues of the day. Unlike hireling scribblers who attempted to mask private designs, those in touch with public opinion presented themselves in print as honest and virtuous, as the authentic voice of common sense. During the 1740s, religious controversies associated with the Great Awakening generated many examples of the new rhetorical strategy. The anonymous author of one embattled essay entitled *The Examiner, or Gilbert against Tennent* directed his arguments specifically to the "impartial Reader." The public could trust him, or so the writer insisted, since, "the whole essay is submitted to the Judgment of Common Sense."[3] By the time of the Revolution, the concept of public opinion had become commonplace, as familiar to the British colonists as it was to contemporary Europeans.

Presented in this manner, as essentially a rhetorical strategy or form of print discourse, public opinion seems ill-suited to help us understand better how

2. Charles Taylor, "Invoking Civil Society," *Working Papers and Proceedings of the Center for Psychosocial Studies*, no. 31 (1990), 11. In addition to Taylor, see J.A.W. Gunn, "Public Opinion," in Terence Ball, James Farr, and Russell L. Hanson, eds., *Political Innovation and Conceptual Change* (Cambridge, 1989), 247–265; and Mono Ozouf, "Public Opinion at the End of the Old Regime," *Journal of Modern History*, LX (Supplement, September 1988), S1–S21.

3. *The Examiner, or Gilbert against Tennent*, cited in T. H. Breen, "Retrieving Common Sense: Rights, Liberties, and the Religious Public Sphere in Late Eighteenth Century America," in Josephine Pacheco, ed., *To Secure the Blessings of Liberty: Rights in American History* (Fairfax, Va., 1993), 60–73. A valuable study of the "public sphere" in late colonial American culture is Michael Warner, *The Letters of the Republic: Publication and the Public Sphere in Eighteenth-Century America* (Cambridge, Mass., 1990).

ordinary people made history. What is missing—and this is the central methodological thrust of this chapter—is a persuasive link between abstract public opinion and the specific social conditions in which public opinion acquired persuasive force. What, in fact, drove public opinion? Was it merely a device allowing traditional leaders to speak in the name of the people? Did ordinary men and women have no significant role in shaping public opinion? It would appear inconsistent to insist that such obscure persons possessed meaningful agency—the ability to shape their material and moral environments—while simultaneously depicting them as largely passive figures in the formation of public consciousness. For our purposes, the concept must somehow be brought into effective contact with actual historical events.

One way of addressing the interpretive problem is to observe the obvious. Ordinary people have in fact regularly thrust themselves into the realm of public opinion. They might not always have intended to achieve that end, but by rioting, or by protesting oppression, or by demanding freedom and equality, or simply by engaging in activities that disrupted daily life they brought rhetorical strategy into critical contact with events. Perhaps the eighteenth-century writers who spoke *to* and *for* the public might have imagined themselves as insulated from such mundane influence. But intellectual dreams of pure objectivity were fantasy. Humble contemporaries always had ways of penetrating public consciousness. During the early modern period, for example, dramatic trials often shaped public opinion by exposing ideological contradictions, crystallizing political issues, and exposing widespread doubts about traditional social practice.[4] Such defining moments served to channel debate, simultaneously constraining and provoking discussion and, in a profoundly interactive conversation, drove public opinion toward conclusions that elite writers would never have championed unless pressured by ordinary people intent on making their own history. Public opinion thus broadly conceived became a point of intersection between biography and structure; it was an imagined interpretive space in which personal decisions acquired larger social and historical meaning.

The collapse of slavery in Massachusetts during the Revolutionary era provides an instructive example of the transforming force of public opinion. The process began sometime during the early 1760s. At first, free white colonists regarded racial bondage merely as an irritant or as a slightly embarrassing reminder that their own demands for political freedom and equality within the British empire smacked of hypocrisy so long as they continued to enslave black men and women. The legal and moral assumptions that had previously

4. An excellent example of this kind of analysis is Sarah Maza, *Private Lives and Public Affairs: The Causes Célèbres of Pre-Revolutionary France* (Berkeley, Calif., 1993).

sustained the institution were steadily eroded and, by the 1770s, no longer commanded popular assent. By the time the nation had won independence, state courts throughout Massachusetts had abolished slavery. As we shall discover, contemporaries insisted that public opinion made it impossible for the judges to reach any other decision. If we take a narrow or "weak" view of public opinion, we might conclude that freedom came to enslaved blacks as a gift of white leaders, thoughtful, moral, reflective members of a professional elite who expressed their growing abhorrence for slavery in print and thereby determined the course of public consciousness.

But, as I shall argue, a broader, more inclusive conception of public opinion attempts to take account of the participation in this process of black Americans. In various ways, they drove the debate forward, often simply by registering personal anger but also sometimes by petitioning for freedom using exactly the same language as white colonists employed against the British Parliament. At a critical moment in the development of Western liberal political thought, the slaves of Massachusetts brought the testimony of their own lives before a public increasingly unwilling to defend social and economic categories of unfreedom.

This essay reconstructs the story of three Massachusetts slaves. The documentary record is thin. Two of them have not even left surnames and are known to us only as Arthur and Bristol. Because Arthur prepared a short, disturbing personal statement written shortly before his execution for allegedly raping a white woman, he figures centrally in the investigation of public opinion. The object of this study is not to excuse violence—both Arthur and Bristol attacked women—or to suggest that brutality is somehow less objectionable if committed by persons who themselves have been brutalized. Rather, the narrative of their experiences dramatically recounted at the moment of death revealed widespread white defensiveness about the institution of slavery. Quite unintentionally, these black men thrust themselves into the realm of public consciousness and transformed obscure life stories into history.

CONFLICTING ACCOUNTS OF FREEDOM

Emancipation in Massachusetts has a peculiar history of its own. We do not know exactly when white citizens of the new state first perceived the elimination of slavery as a significant interpretive moment. No doubt, individual black men and women spun out highly personal stories about freedom, but, for our purposes, the conscious construction of a shared narrative of abolition dates from early 1795, when the respected Virginia jurist St. George Tucker dispatched a provocative letter to a Massachusetts scholar whom he knew only by reputation. Tucker asked the Reverend Jeremy Belknap, director of the newly founded Massachusetts Historical Society, how the northern state had managed to rid itself of the burden of slavery. If he could discover the economic and cultural details of this great achievement, Tucker concluded, he might better be prepared to assist fellow Virginians in the eradication of "the same evil from among ourselves."[5]

In his selection of a correspondent, Tucker was lucky. Belknap was not only a first-class scholar—his *History of New Hampshire* (1784–1792) later won Alexis de Tocqueville's praise—but also a child of the Enlightenment. For him, the letter from Virginia required an objective, almost scientific response, and Belknap dispatched a formal questionnaire entitled "Queries Respecting the Introduction, Progress, and Abolition of Slavery in Massachusetts" to approximately forty persons whom he knew to be especially knowledgeable on the subject. For the most part, the composition of the list was safe and predictable. It included judges, merchants, and political figures, the elders of the Revolutionary generation. But the curious Belknap also sent his questionnaire to Prince Hall, a former slave whom the clergyman described as "a very intelligent black man, aged fifty-five years." Probably born in 1735, Hall founded the nation's first lodge of black Masons, and, throughout his long life, he worked sedulously to bring freedom to "a Great Number of Blackes detained in a State of slavery in the Bowels of a free and Christian Country."[6] Hall came of age in the same social environment as did Arthur and the other obscure black men who will figure prominently in our exploration of public opinion.

Although the responses that Belknap gathered contained conflicting information—different men remembering different pasts—they suggested two general strategies for interpreting events in Massachusetts. One of these quickly became the dominant explanation, and, to this day, it remains the favored account. This story of abolition might best be termed the "heroic legal narrative." A second explanation put forward in the various answers tied the eradication of slavery to the evolution of a powerful new force in New England society that Belknap's correspondents called "publick opinion."[7]

The "heroic legal narrative" chronicles the professional activities of judges

5. Massachusetts Historical Society, *Collections*, 1st Ser., IV (1795), 191–192.

6. "Jeremy Belknap," in Clifford K. Shipton, *Sibley's Harvard Graduates: Biographical Sketches of Those Who Attended Harvard College* (Boston, 1873–), XV, 175–195; "Queries Respecting Slavery and Emancipation of Negroes in Massachusetts. . . ," MHS, *Colls.*, 1st Ser., IV, 192, 199. Prince Hall is discussed in Sidney Kaplan, *The Black Presence in the Era of the American Revolution, 1770–1800* (Washington, D.C., 1973), 181–192 (quotation on 182).

7. "Queries Respecting Slavery," MHS, *Colls.*, 1st Ser., IV, 201.

and legislators. It depicts reasonable white men in positions of authority gradually coming to an appreciation of the unconstitutionality, if not the profound immorality, of human bondage. The majority of Belknap's respondents would have found this explanation for the extinction of slavery in late-eighteenth-century Massachusetts entirely plausible. They generally agreed that a series of suits brought before the state courts between 1781 and 1783 did, in fact, deliver what Belknap termed "a mortal wound to slavery."[8] The problem with the traditional legal narrative is, not that it is somehow wrong, but, rather, that it condescends to the ordinary people of late eighteenth-century Massachusetts—to blacks as well as whites—who are either excluded from the story of liberation or who appear as hapless victims of social injustice. After all, the legal narrative portrays freedom as a gift to the long-suffering slaves from the judges, lawyers, and legislators. In this reconstruction of events, only the courts and the legislative assembly possessed effective political agency.

Belknap's correspondents advanced a second explanation for the eradication of slavery in Massachusetts, one that has not received serious attention since being put forward in the late eighteenth century. In their answers to the questionnaire, several respondents claimed that "slavery hath been abolished here by *publick opinion*." This is an arresting line of argument. The very concept of public opinion—at least as a force in New England culture—was a recent innovation. Belknap thought that public opinion had first come into play in Massachusetts during the Stamp Act Crisis. "At the beginning of our controversy with Great-Britain," he informed Tucker, "several persons, who before had entertained sentiments opposed to the slavery of blacks, did then take occasion *publickly* to remonstrate against the inconsistency of contending for our liberty, and at the same time depriving other people of theirs." In another passage of the summary report sent to Tucker, Belknap traced how "opinion" had acquired ever greater persuasive force in this society. It radiated out from Boston to the colony's smaller farming communities. It overcame opposition. It gained momentum. "During the revolutionary-war," the clergyman wrote, "the *publick opinion* was so strongly in favour of the abolition of slavery, that in some country towns, votes were passed in town-meetings, that they would have no slaves among them."[9]

What Belknap's correspondents seem to have had in mind was an evolving white consciousness, a principled discussion about the evils of slavery carried on in "pamphlets and news-paper essays." This was a limited and essentially self-serving model for the diffusion of ideas. A few good men had stepped forward in a good cause. Their efforts no doubt helped persuade men and

8. Ibid., 203.
9. Ibid., 201, 203.

women living in small villages that public opinion really did condemn slavery. Other people appearing on Belknap's list, however, remembered a different, more inclusive debate.[10] Respondents such as Prince Hall reminded Belknap that slaves had participated in shaping public opinion. Indeed, during the run-up to national independence, unfree blacks accelerated the erosion of a mental framework that had sustained slavery for as long as anyone could remember. They bore witness to personal experience; they managed to translate their aspirations and sufferings into a liberal language of natural rights shared by white judges and legislators. Some blacks were more marginal, bringing troubled and troublesome lives to public view. However criminally violent they might have been, they provoked doubt—a defensive reaction—among whites already uneasy about slavery. It is within this interpretive context that one can recount the stories of Bristol, Arthur, and Quock Walker, obscure persons who call forth a forgotten tale of historical agency and who invite us to explore the pluralistic possibilities of a history of public opinion.

IMAGINING THE MEANINGS OF VIOLENCE

An account of the end of slavery told from the perspective of an inclusive public consciousness might begin early on the morning of June 4, 1763. That was the moment when Bristol, a sixteen-year-old African then living in Taunton, turned on the family that had come to trust the boy. Without warning he brutally murdered a young woman who happened not only to have been his master's sister but also his closest companion during the eight years since being sold in the British colonies as a slave. The details of this horrific attack need not detain us. Following the bloody assault on Elizabeth McKinstry, Bristol rode off on his master's horse to a nearby town and was arrested there without offering the slightest resistance.[11]

Although Bristol readily confessed the crime, the white people of Taunton demanded to know what had motivated such a savage attack. The young African either could not or would not satisfy their curiosity. To be sure, he expressed profound regret for what he had done, but the only explanation that he ever offered was that "he was prompted to it by a Negro Boy of his Acquaintance, who threatened to kill him if he did not do it." This admission—and no

10. Ibid., 201. Surviving responses can be found in "Letters and Documents Relating to Slavery in Massachusetts," MHS, *Colls.*, 5th Ser., III (1877), 373–444.

11. The fullest account of the McKinstry murder is in Stephen T. Riley and Edward W. Hason, eds., *The Papers of Robert Treat Paine*, 2 vols. (MHS, *Colls.*, LXXXVIII [1992]), 256, 283–285.

one in Taunton seems to have believed Bristol—hardly put the matter to rest. "These Circumstances," wrote Robert Treat Paine, a local lawyer respected throughout Massachusetts, "naturally fill us with more Astonishment and Indignation, than if the same had happened after repeated Resentments, settled Malice, or sudden Provocation; for it seems difficult to conceive how one, who never shew'd ill-nature on any Occasion, and who always appeared chearful and contented, should on a sudden, without Provocation, commit the most barbarous Cruelty on one who never offended him."[12]

The phrase "never offended him" strikes an oddly discordant note. Without intending to justify Bristol's violent crime, we might ask whether Paine and other residents of Taunton considered slavery itself an offense. Did not the denial of freedom count as provocation? Might being sold out of Africa not suggest a possible motive for assault? Since we assume that reflections of this sort are by their very nature anachronistic, it comes as a surprise to discover that such questions were already beginning to destabilize traditional justifications for black enslavement—at least, in this particular Massachusetts community.

Bristol's actions exposed a shadow of doubt about race and freedom, a hint of uncertainty, a sign that white uneasiness over the enslavement of blacks was moving from private guilt into a larger, more abstract realm of public consciousness. In the long history of colonial New England, other dependent workers had killed their masters, actions that inevitably concluded with execution, but on no previous occasion had anyone described the villainy as anything other than an expression of human depravity. In 1751, for example, the Reverend Mather Byles delivered an execution sermon for a young black man convicted of poisoning an infant. Byles admonished his auditors to avoid a host of sins, but in more than a score of pages published under the title *The Prayer and Plea of David*, he never bothered to mention the race of the man about to be hanged.[13]

In Bristol's case, however, one suddenly senses a shadow of defensiveness. Minutes before Bristol was scheduled to hang, a local Congregational minister admonished the young African slave: "You are not to imagine, that you are treated with any greater Severity meerly because you are a black Boy, bro't from your native Country among us, for you are not: If any of us had done such a

12. Ibid.

13. See Lawrence W. Towner, "True Confessions and Dying Warnings in Colonial New England," in *Sibley's Heir: A Volume in Memory of Clifford Kenyon Shipton* (Colonial Society of Massachusetts, *Publications*, VIX [Boston, 1982]), 523–539; and Daniel A. Cohen, *Pillars of Salt, Monuments of Grace: New England Crime Literature and the Origins of American Popular Culture, 1674–1860* (New York, 1993). Mather Byles's sermon was published in Boston in 1751.

horrid Thing as you have, we should be treated as you are: Your being of a different Colour from us, makes no Odds in this Matter."[14] Who, the modern reader wonders, was the Reverend Sylvanus Conant trying to persuade? Had Bristol somehow introduced categories of race and slavery into the court's proceedings? Was Conant really speaking directly to a slave or was he responding to a new, fugitive discourse just then taking root within this frightened town?

Standing on the gallows, Bristol delivered a curious little speech. Although the original text has not survived, Conant noted that the slave directed his last comments "particularly to those of his own Colour." Again, we can only guess how the blacks scattered through the huge crowd interpreted Bristol's dying words. But for Conant—and, no doubt, for many anxious whites in Taunton—the lesson was clear. In *The Blood of Able, and the Blood of Jesus Considered and Improved,* the clergyman contradicted his own assurances to Bristol that race made no difference in these matters. He insisted that Africans hated their masters, and, if not closely watched, slaves would seek revenge.

> It naturally calls upon those who have the Care of Negroes to be very vigilant in removing the Prejudices of their barbarous Disposition by Instruction, and to instill into their Minds such Christian Principles as may influence their Actions when absent from the Eye of their Masters; and particularly to inspect their companying together, that grand Source of all the Evils that have arisen so frequently from this Nation, when in their Conspirings they cry out, *Let us lay wait for Blood, let us lurk privily for the Innocent without a Cause.*[15]

We should pause here to consider the complex evolution of public consciousness. The process involved different, even conflicting, concerns. Individuals of all sorts were perfectly capable of voicing contradictory opinions. And so it was in Taunton. The brutality of the assault on Elizabeth McKinstry clearly provoked anger and revulsion. Conant's racist rhetoric addressed the white community's deep fear of black assault. Like his neighbors, he railed against "this Nation's" dark conspiracies and insatiable blood lust. But although Conant condemned violence, he also raised the possibility of another, more reflective interpretation. Perhaps slavery itself was the problem. Perhaps being transported from Africa against one's will and sold into bondage drove young black men like Bristol to lash out at those who were responsible. Public opinion in eighteenth-century Massachusetts—and no doubt in our own time

14. Sylvanus Conant, *The Blood of Able, and the Blood of Jesus Considered and Improved, in a Sermon Delivered at Taunton, December the First, 1763; Upon the Day of Execution of Bristol, a Negro Boy of about Sixteen Years Old . . .* (Boston, 1763), 20–21.

15. Ibid., 34, 35.

as well—could accommodate competing views: loathing as well as guilt, self-righteousness as well as defensiveness, desire for immediate revenge as well as hope for eventual reform. Bristol did not bring down slavery, but his widely publicized story introduced uncertainty into a debate that extended far beyond the boundaries of Taunton.

THRUSTING AUTOBIOGRAPHY INTO HISTORY

Major Richard Godfrey, a Taunton gentleman, undoubtedly witnessed Bristol's execution. And in all likelihood so too did Godfrey's slave Arthur. It is around Arthur's life that I shall develop a more dialectic interpretation of public opinion. The task is not easy. About Arthur we know only what he bothered to communicate to the Reverend Thaddeus Maccarty several years later on the eve of his own execution.[16]

Poverty of sources is, of course, an annoying problem. Our central piece of evidence is a four-column broadside published in 1768 under the title *The Life, and Dying Speech of Arthur, a Negro Man*. Throughout the statement, the author employs the first person pronoun. Indeed, the opening sentence commands attention as a perfectly straightforward declaration of fact: "I was born at *Taunton*, January 15, 1747, in the House of *Richard Godfrey*, Esq.; my Mother being his Slave . . ."[17] The inclusion of the precise date is a nice touch. Specificity always enhances narrative credibility. But even as we attempt to draw meaning from this initial passage, we must maintain a skeptical distance. Are the words really Arthur's? Is the document a genuine autobiography, or has an elusive interpreter silently placed himself between us and Arthur's own interpretation of his life? This is a matter of some significance, because, insomuch as Arthur was catapulted into public consciousness, he commanded attention not as a person but as a text.

Our assessment of the autobiography depends heavily on what we make of the relation between Arthur and the Reverend Thaddeus Maccarty, the leading Congregational minister of Worcester, Massachusetts. Maccarty enjoyed a modestly successful career. Among parishioners, he seems to have inspired respect rather than affection. One account depicts him as "a man tall of stature, slender of habit, [and] with a black penetrating eye." Contemporaries also claimed that, as a preacher, Maccarty was "solemn, loud, searching, and rous-

16. *The Life, and Dying Speech of Arthur, a Negro Man Who Was Executed at Worcester, October 20th 1768, for a Rape Committed on the Body of One Deborah Metcalfe* (Boston, 1768).

17. Ibid.

ing."[18] Whatever his character might have been, he devoted long hours visiting Arthur in prison. The clergyman wanted to fashion the miscreant at the moment of death into a good Christian servant. And it was he who oversaw the final publication of a rough manuscript.

Whether Arthur interpreted his life and death through Maccarty's religious lens is less clear. At the conclusion of the autobiography, the condemned slave specifically thanked the minister for spiritual guidance. "I cannot conclude this my Narrative," the writer declared, "without gratefully acknowledging the unwearied Pains that was taken by the Rev. Mr. *Maccarty*, to awaken me to a proper Sense of my miserable and wretched Condition." Although Arthur claimed to be fully literate, we cannot be sure that he actually wrote the document. The somewhat stilted, highly moralistic vocabulary—especially in the concluding paragraph—rings false. It is hard to imagine a young man who had enjoyed no formal education and who spent so much of his life on the run crafting phrases such as "ignominious Death," "my notorious Wickedness," and "never-ending Eternity."[19]

The interpretive problem can be addressed from another perspective. Much of the autobiography (perhaps 80 percent of the published document) recounts in remarkable detail Arthur's adventures from approximately his fourteenth birthday to the moment of his final arrest. This section not only contains many specific names—a series of masters, people from whom he purloined goods, and magistrates who tried him for various petty crimes—but also an inventory of the actual items he picked up along the way. From "a Store of Mr. *Roach's* [Rotch]" on Nantucket, for example, Arthur took "a Quantity of Rum, a pair of Trowsers, a Jacket, and some Calicoe." After escaping from a Worcester jail, he and his friends "broke into a Barber's Shop, from whence we stole a Quantity of Flour, a Comb, and a Razor: We then set off for *Boston*. At *Shrewsbury*, we stole a Goose from Mr. *Samuel Jennison;* and from the Widow *Kingsley*, in the same Place, we stole a Kettle, in which we boiled the Goose."[20]

And so it went, material objects precisely described, an inventory of larceny and desire. Maccarty would have had no incentive—professional or otherwise—to alter most of the account. In fact, the execution sermons for thieves

18. Zephaniah Willis, quoted in Shipton, *Sibley's Harvard Graduates*, X, 380.

19. *Life, and Dying Speech of Arthur*. On the difficulties of interpreting such a problematic document, see James Clifford and George E. Marcus, eds., *Writing Culture: The Poetics and Politics of Ethnography* (Berkeley, Calif., 1986); Lawrence W. Levine, "The Folklore of Industrial Society: Popular Culture and Its Audiences," *American Historical Review*, XCVII (1992), 1369–1399; Stephen Greenblatt, *Marvelous Possessions: The Wonder of the New World* (Chicago, 1991); and Eric J. Sunquist, *To Wake the Nations: Race in the Making of American Literature* (Cambridge, Mass., 1993).

20. *Life, and Dying Speech of Arthur*.

published during the Revolutionary period often included this kind of detail. In his *Brief Account of the Life and Abominable Thefts* (1768), Isaac Frasier, one of Arthur's partners in crime, announced, "The articles from each store, are particularly mentioned at his [Frasier's] desire, that the owners may know the articles taken by him, in order to exculpate others."[21]

Finding the actual people whose names appeared in Arthur's autobiography proved extremely difficult. Nineteenth-century courthouse fires in Taunton and Barnstable destroyed records that might have confirmed incidents recounted in the published narrative. But whenever the eighteenth-century materials have survived—as many have in Worcester County—the slave seems to have controlled the character and flow of his own story. These passages are as close to Arthur's version of the truth as we shall ever get. The central figures in the slave's short life were real men and women, and, although Maccarty might have acted as scribe and entreated the condemned sinner to repent, he did not invent memory for another man. The proud voice that told of hair-raising escapes, bragged of sexual escapades with white and Indian women, and censured various masters for foolish trust was undoubtedly Arthur's.

African Americans who lived in colonial Taunton were part of the community but not of it. They went about their business, slaves working as domestics in the homes of the wealthier Taunton families. Their names appear as property in probate records; occasionally, a church official noted the baptism of a black child. During the 1740s, the Great Awakening swept through this region of Massachusetts, and a minor evangelical, the Reverend Josiah Crocker of Taunton, reported, "Being desired by the negroes, I preached to them." His efforts to bring the word of God to the local "negroes" pleased Crocker. "We had a crowded assembly," he observed, "and much of the gracious presence of God. The whole assembly seemed to be under the influences of the Holy Spirit. . . . They appeared not to be careless hearers, but to hunger after the Word."[22] Arthur's mother might well have attended Crocker's Negro revival. About her we know almost nothing, not even her name.

Unlike Bristol, Arthur had been born in America. In fact, the two blacks were exactly the same age, both adolescents and slaves, young men briefly thrown together in Taunton. It is hard to tell whether Arthur and Bristol were friends, but, in a town with a small black population, they probably associated on a regular basis. Perhaps it was meetings of this sort that caused a Boston

21. *A Brief Account of the Life and Abominable Thefts of the Notorious Isaac Frasier, Who Was Executed at Fairfield, Sept. 7th, 1768, Penned from His Own Mouth, and Signed by Him, a Few Days before His Execution* (New London, 1768), 15.

22. Josiah Crocker, cited in Samuel Hopkins Emery, *The Ministry of Taunton*, 2 vols. (Boston, 1853), I, 361.

newspaper to blame the McKinstry murder on "the bad Effects of Negroes too freely consorting together."[23]

The identity of Arthur's father remains a mystery. Although he seems to have maintained a close relation to his mother, he mentioned his parents only once. In *The Life*, Arthur recounted a particularly threatening series of misadventures, and, after stealing a horse in Dorchester, he paid "a Visit to my [par]ents; who suspecting my Situation, insisted [on me] returning to my Master." At the time of his own death in 1792, Richard Godfrey did not appear to have owned an adult black man who might have been Arthur's father. One other piece of evidence is tantalizing. Arthur described himself as "a Negro Man," and perhaps most of his white contemporaries accepted that classification. But when he was indicted for a capital offense in Worcester, the clerk of the superior court termed the defendant a "Malato."[24] Perhaps Godfrey, who treated the rebellious teenager with surprising patience, was Arthur's father. The connection is worth consideration if only to remind ourselves that public opinion during the 1760s might have known far more about Arthur's life than he bothered to recount in the published autobiography.

By the time of Bristol's trial, Arthur had already begun to challenge comfortable white assumptions about slavery. He was too intelligent and too independent for his own good, a teenager unwilling to defer to any adult, even to his own master. After spending his first fourteen years in the Godfrey household, where his mother also served as a slave, Arthur broke loose, not through violence, but simply by running away. He later claimed that he had been illtreated by Godfrey's wife, Theodona. Whatever the conditions in the Taunton household might have been, Arthur developed an insatiable taste for freedom and adventure. Before his departure, he had acquired sufficient literacy to make his way among strangers. Had Arthur grown up in vastly different circumstances, we might depict him as the kind of charming roustabout that frequently appeared in contemporary British fiction, in other words, a daring,

23. *Boston Evening-Post,* June 13, 1763.

24. *Life, and Dying Speech of Arthur.* Arthur mentions that he visited his "[par]ents" in Easton, a small village north of Taunton. During the late colonial period, some slaveowners of Taunton, such as Richard Godfrey, seem to have transferred their African Americans to Easton for the summer months. In his *History of the Town of Easton, Massachusetts* (Cambridge, Mass., 1886), William L. Chaffin reports that one member of the Godfrey family stated "that his grandfather use to come up with his slaves from Taunton and cultivate his lands in summer in the south part of the town near the Bay road, and then take them back with him to spend the winter" (435). For the superior court's designation of Arthur as a "Malato," see Worcester Files Collection, Supreme Judicial Court, Boston, Massachusetts, no. 152339, vol. 1073. I want to thank Elizabeth C. Bouvier, head of Archives, for helping me find records of Arthur's trial.

sometimes foolish lover and confidence man, a person forever skirting personal disaster.

By 1763, Arthur had already lived briefly among the native Americans of nearby Sandwich, experienced sex, sailed out of Nantucket on a vessel owned by Captain Nathan Coffin, and been arrested several times for minor theft. However far he wandered, of course, he remained the property of Richard Godfrey. From time to time, Arthur reappeared in Taunton—one such moment coinciding with Bristol's public execution—but no sooner had he reestablished contact with his master and his mother than Arthur took off again. He crewed on a ship bound for the West Indies, where by his own admission he drank heavily and loved indiscriminately. When he next turned up in Taunton late in 1764—brazenly flirting with a local white woman and threatening to burn the house of a man who interrupted his amorous designs—Godfrey decided to send Arthur "out of the country." This possibility must have genuinely frightened the young slave. He might have seen the hellish sugar plantations of the Caribbean. As the Reverend Jeremy Belknap observed in his report to Tucker, "A house of correction, to which disorderly persons of all colours were sent, form one object of terror to them [the slaves of pre-Revolutionary Massachusetts]; but to be sold to the West-Indies, or to Carolina, was the highest punishment that could be threatened or inflicted."[25]

Native Americans figured prominently in Arthur's life during this period. They provided "safe houses" for the slave when pursued by white authorities or angry masters. Arthur also took Indian lovers, and, although he never seems to have seriously contemplated living permanently in one of the Indian communities scattered throughout southeastern and central Massachusetts, he established close ties with Mashpees, Nipmucks, and Wampanoags among others. These were remnant groups, struggling desperately in the late eighteenth century to survive. The death of so many native American males during the Seven Years' War had profoundly disturbed sex ratios in these villages, and, by the 1760s, Indian women substantially outnumbered the men. In this demographic situation, it is not surprising that the women sometimes welcomed companions of other races, a practice that white outsiders sometimes condescendingly interpreted as promiscuity. The Reverend Gideon Hawley, for example, a long-time minister at Mashpee and a state-appointed guardian of the Indian community, claimed that the females "are loose in their morals." In fact, the clergyman reported, "many of our women have found negroe husbands, as they were strolling in the county[,] bro't them home; and too many of them have not been good in their morals." Although Arthur probably did

25. *Life, and Dying Speech of Arthur;* "Queries Respecting Slavery," MHS, *Colls.*, 1st Ser., IV, 200.

not comprehend the forces that were destroying the Indians of New England, he accepted their hospitality. And on one occasion, a native American woman saved him from certain arrest. "By Advice for my Companion (who like the rest of her Sex, was of a very fruitful Invention)," Arthur explained, "I had recourse to the following Expedient: I dressed in the Habit of a Squaw, and made my own Cloaths a Pappoose; in this manner we proceeded to H[adl]ey undiscover'd w[here] I was introduced by my Companion, to an Indian Family, where I tarried."[26]

Without recounting a series of miraculous escapes, breathless chases, and spectacular intrigues that rescued Arthur from involuntary exile, we might briefly consider the general political environment in which he came of age. Whatever Godfrey's wishes might have been, this strong-willed young African American defined himself in public exchanges as an almost-free person. Although legally a slave, he traveled widely, acquired a taste for British imported goods, and enjoyed intimate relations with whites and Indians. Although none of the people with whom he came into contact anticipated a war for national independence, they felt the tremors that were beginning to shake an empire that most white colonists had come to equate with liberty, prosperity, and security. The Stamp Act riots shocked this complacent provincial world, and, even in small country villages, ordinary people developed a heightened consciousness of freedom and equality in their lives. It was in this highly uncertain political atmosphere that Arthur learned to interpret the faces of white contemporaries for weakness, for signs of doubt, and for moral misgivings about enforcing a system of human bondage that, in Massachusetts at least, made no economic or ideological sense.

Like the late-twentieth-century blacks of South Africa who struggled against apartheid, Arthur pushed against a traditional institutional structure and felt it give just a little. One might speculate that this was the moment when he—and perhaps many other anonymous African Americans throughout New England—thrust themselves into a broader public consciousness. They were

26. Gideon Hawley to James Freeman, Nov. 2, 1802, Gideon Hawley Papers, Massachusetts Historical Society, Boston, Massachusetts. Daniel Mandell kindly brought this correspondence to my attention. Useful studies of the local native American groups living in this area include Daniel Richard Mandell, "Behind the Frontier: Indian Communities in Eighteenth-Century Massachusetts," June 1993, manuscript; Mandell, " 'To Live More Like My Christian English Neighbors': Natick Indians in the Eighteenth Century," *William and Mary Quarterly*, 3d Ser., XLVIII (1991), 552–579; Jean Maria O'Brien, "Community Dynamics in the Indian-English Town of Natick, Massachusetts, 1650–1790" (Ph.D. diss., University of Chicago, 1990); Stephen Badger, "Historical and Characteristic Traits of the American Indians in General, and Those of Natick in Particular," MHS, *Colls.*, 1st Ser., V (1798), 43; *Life, and Dying Speech of Arthur*.

no longer quite so invisible as they had been during earlier generations. Their own desire for freedom intersected with a larger political debate that energized and legitimated their own fondest hopes.

Every day, the almost theatrical elements of Arthur's life, his curiously elastic bondage in a society aggressively proclaiming liberty, helped transform the context of public opinion. He drew attention to the conditions of enslavement, and, as he did so, he was probably encouraged by the general swirl of liberal ideas transforming colonial Massachusetts. It is possible that Arthur was aware of what James Otis, Jr., a radical proponent of American rights, had recently written about slavery. By the same token, of course, Otis might have known of Arthur, or, if not Arthur himself, then of other slaves cut from the same cloth. Otis came from the same region of Massachusetts as Arthur; Otis's father had sat as a magistrate in a case involving the footloose slave. Whatever their relation might have been, the younger Otis published a highly regarded pamphlet in 1764 titled *The Rights of the British Colonies Asserted and Proved*, which insisted, "The colonists are by the law of nature freeborn, as indeed all men are, white or black." And he asked readers who would have daily encountered people such as Arthur, "Does it follow that 'tis right to enslave a man because he is black? Will short curled hair like wool instead of Christian hair, as 'tis called by those whose hearts are as hard as nether millstones, help the argument?"[27]

During the mid-1760s, Arthur was sold from master to master, an object of commerce in a yeoman society. Each new owner was apparently willing to take the risk that a talented but high-spirited slave might become more tractable. He finally came into the possession of Edward Clark, a farmer and owner of a sawmill who lived in a sparsely populated community then known as the Rutland District, some twenty miles west of Worcester. For a person described as a "gentleman" by the clerk of the superior court, Clark achieved a level of obscurity rivaling that of Arthur and Bristol. His most notable achievement might have been service as a minor provincial officer with the Anglo-American forces at Crown Point during an early campaign of the Seven Years' War. It was there that Clark seems to have befriended Major Godfrey, and this shared military experience might have influenced the sale of Arthur a decade after the two men had departed the military.

The Rutland District had not yet become an independent New England town when Arthur arrived. Curiously, when it achieved status as a legal township some years later, supporters of the royal governor named it Hutchinson.

---

27. *Life, and Dying Speech of Arthur;* James Otis, Jr., *The Rights of the British Colonies Asserted and Proved* (Boston, 1764), reprinted in Bernard Bailyn, ed., *Pamphlets of the American Revolution: 1750–1776* (Cambridge, Mass., 1965), I, 439.

But no Massachusetts community wanted to be identified with a despised loy-
alist, and, in 1774, Hutchinson was reborn Barre, in honor of Colonel Isaac
Barre, a member of Parliament who spoke in favor of colonial rights. The Rutland District must have seemed a very unpromising home for an adventurous
young slave, and Arthur soon made Clark's life as difficult as he had Godfrey's.
Fewer African Americans resided in this area of Massachusetts than in Taunton. According to a history of Worcester County—of which the Rutland District was part—"The blacks in the region were a scattered people, less than 1
percent of the population. They lived in lonely isolation in the households of
ministers and other gentry, or as servants in taverns, with clusters of fifteen to
twenty in some of the leading towns." A primitive census completed in 1754
lists only two slaves in the Rutland District. Contemporary whites believed that
blacks were treated markedly better in such communities than in major port
cities such as Boston and Salem. Belknap's correspondents claimed, for example, that "in the country, they [slaves] lived as well as their masters, and often
sat down at the same table, in the true style of *republican equality*." We should
probably not make too much of this sentimental image, for, in the same report,
Belknap also observed that no sooner were blacks freed from slavery than they
deserted the countryside, flocking to commercial centers along the coast where
they found opportunities to work for wages. "Having been educated in families," the minister wrote in 1795, "where they had not been used to provide for
themselves in youth, they know not how to do it in age. Having been accustomed to a plentiful and even luxurious mode of living in the houses of
their masters, they are uncomfortable in their present situation."[28]

The chronicle of these years of Arthur's life is the stuff of pure fiction. When
Clark decided that he too would try to sell the troublesome slave out of the
country—specifically, to a Maryland planter—Arthur bolted, seeking refuge
among black friends in the Boston area. Throughout the autobiographical
statement, he provided tantalizing glimpses into a lost world in which blacks
communicated over long distances, provided sanctuary when possible, and
relaxed in each other's company. One evening a group of them attended a local
"husking," a traditional harvest festival where strong drink flowed freely and
people frolicked in ways deemed inappropriate during most of the year. According to Arthur, "I went with some Negroes to a Husking, at Mr. *Thomas*

28. John L. Brooke, *The Heart of the Commonwealth: Society and Political Culture in
Worcester County, Massachusetts, 1713–1861* (Cambridge, 1989), 45; "Number of Negro Slaves
in the Province of the Massachusetts-Bay . . . ," MHS, *Colls.*, 2d Ser., III (1847), 95–96. For
the early 1760s, see "Misc. 1640–1775," Massachusetts Archives, Boston, Massachusetts,
LXVIII, 305. For Belknap's report, see "Queries Respecting Slavery," MHS, *Colls.*, 1st Ser.,
IV, 200.

Parkes's in *Little Cambridge,* where they on the same Night introduced me to a white Woman of that Place. And as our Behaviour was such, as we have [illegible] Reason to be ashamed of, I shall for her sake [pass] it over in Silence." It is possible that the autumn revelers were thoroughly drunk; perhaps Arthur misread the woman's participation in a village bacchanalia as an invitation to have sex. Perhaps he misinterpreted passivity for assent. We shall never know, but whatever occurred that night at Little Cambridge, a similar situation a few months later involving a white woman from the Rutland District would bring him before a Worcester court on charges of rape. When the husband heard what had allegedly happened at the husking, he vowed revenge on the slave who had slept with his wife, and, in a frenetic effort to save face, he pursued Arthur from town to town, waving an arrest warrant and demanding personal satisfaction. Although Arthur successfully eluded local authorities, he did engage the angry husband in an all-out fistfight. As the insouciant runaway later explained, "I coming off Conqueror, [I] put on for *Cambridge*[, and] the next Night I went to another Husking."[29]

News of Arthur's high jinks did not amuse his master in Barre. Clark seemed more determined than ever to sell the slave to a Maryland planter, and Arthur beat another hasty retreat, this time on a horse stolen from a Dorchester farmer. The fugitive rode as fast as he could toward Taunton, south to his mother and to the safety of a Mashpee village on Cape Cod. "When I got to *Sandwich,*" Arthur later recounted, "I went to an Indian House, where I had been formerly acquainted, and with the Squaws there, spent my Time in a manner which may be easily guessed."[30] Local whites soon became suspicious. No doubt, the sight of a young black man riding a good horse sparked curiosity, and, after Arthur had confessed to the obvious crime, Barnstable authorities locked him in the county jail.

The indomitable Arthur was not easily discouraged. He soon escaped, and, after hiding for six weeks among the Indians—a period during which he was frequently intoxicated and continued to steal small items from the local shops—Mr. Clark's slave found himself back in the Barnstable prison. Once again luck and charm carried the day. As Arthur told the story, "I was tried and sentenced to receive twenty Stripes; but being unwell, the Man from whom I stole the Horse at *Dorchester,* coming to *Barnstable,* and by paying the [Court] Cost, took me out of Goal, so that I again got off unpunished: With him I lived about three Weeks, and behaved well."[31] One can well imagine that Arthur had already entered a larger public consciousness. People throughout the colony

29. *Life, and Dying Speech of Arthur.*
30. Ibid.
31. Ibid.

must have gossiped about the recent huskings, the fight between husband and lover, the audacious theft of a horse, and, finally, the curious reconciliation between victim and criminal. From Worcester to Cambridge, from Dorchester to Taunton, an area that encompassed most of settled Massachusetts, the farce played itself out before a large audience. And, in the end, Clark transported the truant slave back to the Rutland District. For Arthur few options remained. He was like a caged bird, flapping himself to exhaustion against the legal constraints that defined him as another man's property.

The great crisis in Arthur's short life occurred one chilly night in 1767. "Another Negro of my Master's," related Arthur, delivered a message, informing him "that the young Squaw, so often mentioned, was very desirous of seeing me." As the Reverend Aaron Hutchinson, a Congregational minister from Grafton who delivered one of Arthur's execution sermons, noted, the slave's lust overcame good sense, for, instead of remaining in cozy bed, Arthur decided to ride out into the cold darkness to meet his lover. A bottle of rum pilfered from Clark's house helped keep the amorous slave warm. But the tryst did not come off as planned. The Indian woman failed to appear at the rendezvous, and, for reasons clear only to Arthur, he decided to ride several miles to a small, isolated farmhouse owned by Deborah Metcalfe (nee Adams), a widow then probably in her mid-forties. We do not know when Metcalfe's husband Joseph died. By him she seems to have had four children, the most recent a daughter born in 1752. Although town records make it hard to estimate her wealth, she does not appear to have prospered in the Rutland District. The surviving foundation stones from the Metcalfe house—found today deep in the woods near a Ware River flood-control dam—suggest a very modest structure.[32] Although in an economic sense she was probably a marginal person in this community, no one seems to have accused her of loose moral behavior.

Nor did anyone ever question whether Arthur and Deborah Metcalfe had sex that night. At issue was the charge of rape. The next morning Metcalfe told Clark her side of the story, and when he asked if she wanted to obtain a formal warrant for Arthur's arrest, she balked. The stakes were high. Arthur provided an explanation for her hesitation. Since she was unwilling to have him hanged for the offense, she "proposed making up the Matter for a proper Consideration, providing my Master would send me out of the Country."[33] Clark

32. Ibid.; *Vital Records of Barre, Massachusetts* (Worcester, 1903), 61; "Baptisms of the First Church of Holden," *New England Historical and Genealogical Register*, LVIII (1904), 372; "Births in Medway, Mass.," ibid., XLIX (1895), 446. Albert Clark of Barre has located the site of Deborah Metcalfe's house. He kindly shared his research and knowledge of local history with me throughout the project.

33. *Life, and Dying Speech of Arthur.*

quickly accepted Metcalfe's terms, no doubt pleased for reasons of his own to free himself from the burden of Arthur's slavery.

Metcalfe's reluctance to press charges in a capital case does not argue for Arthur's innocence. Rape victims often prefer silence to public interrogation, and Metcalfe might have been painfully aware of her own vulnerability in a patriarchal society. As we shall see, Arthur felt that he had been wronged. Although he never offered a full explanation for what had occurred, he drew attention to Metcalfe's demand for "a proper Consideration," as if that request should somehow have raised doubts about her credibility. Perhaps Arthur misread the situation. He might have concluded that a poor white woman— the kind of person he had encountered at several huskings where the rum flowed freely—would welcome his advances. Metcalfe's dilemma might have been that she had slept with a black man, an unacceptable act in a predominantly white farm community where secrets were hard to keep.

One cold March morning, Edward Clark and Arthur set off for Albany, the place selected for Arthur's sale. The road across western Massachusetts took the two men through territory that remained even in the late eighteenth century wild and unsettled. They had not traveled many miles, however, when they were overtaken by Nathaniel Jennison, a well-known figure in the Rutland District. He carried a warrant for Arthur's arrest. It seems unlikely that Jennison acted as Deborah Metcalfe's agent. After all, she had not wanted to have the slave hanged. But events in the small community might have spun out of her control. Jennison was a large slaveholder, an anomaly in this section of Massachusetts, and, like white southerners who would later lynch black men for allegedly defiling white women, Jennison might have taken it upon himself to enforce a rural code of masculine honor. Moreover, he might have concluded that, if Arthur escaped punishment so easily, other African Americans might follow his example.

Whatever the motive for Jennison's gratuitous intervention might have been, Arthur could not resist playing him for the fool. When Jennison stopped at a tavern in Hardwick for refreshment, he ordered his prisoner to continue walking down the road toward the Rutland District. Jennison was riding a horse, and he informed Arthur that he would soon overtake the slave. Arthur seized the opportunity. "I went out of the Door," he recounted, "and seeing his Horse stand handily, what should I do, but mount him, and rode off as fast as I could, leaving *Jennison* to pursue me on Foot. I got home before Bed-time, and took up my Lodging in my Master's Barn for the Night, where I had a Bottle of Cherry Rum (which I found in Mr. *Jennison's* Baggs) to refresh my self with." The humiliation of Jennison appears to have been an entirely spontaneous act, the kind of thing that Arthur had been doing for years. It was good fun, a splendid story to amuse his friends. But as contemporaries observed, the black trickster always returned "home." Whites apparently reasoned that Arthur could have run to New York, where he might have presented himself as a free man. The Reverend Aaron Hutchinson assumed that the devil must have corrupted Arthur's common sense. How else could one explain the fact that the fugitive "not only returned home, after his atrocious villainy, (tho' so well practised in running away) but after he was arrested by the officer and gave him the slip, with a good horse, sillily for himself, went home and so was retaken."[34] Perhaps Arthur did not comprehend the seriousness of the charges lodged against him. More likely, he chose to take his chances in the only world he had ever known.

Jennison eventually delivered Arthur to the Worcester jail. His incarceration began on March 30, 1767, and it was there that Arthur made a new friend. The slave found himself in the company of Isaac Frasier, colonial New England's most notorious burglar. Frasier had been born on February 9, 1740, the child of an impoverished family living in North Kingston, Rhode Island. At the time of Frasier's execution in Fairfield, Connecticut (September 9, 1768), the Reverend Noah Hobart observed that "from stealing Trifles, [Frasier] proceeded to steal things of Value. At length he went into the practice of breaking open and robbing Houses; and was in near thirty Instances guilty of Burglary."[35]

Arthur could not believe his good fortune. He and another adolescent fell under the spell of the "celebrated FRASIER," and the three men soon broke out of the Worcester jail. The little gang set off in the direction of Boston, taking needed food and clothing along the way. From Samuel Jennison—no doubt, Nathaniel's relative—they stole a goose. But, for Arthur at least, freedom proved elusive. He seemed incapable of imagining another life, of severing personal connections, and, once the other two men left Arthur, turning south toward Connecticut, the young slave appeared unable to devise a plan that would successfully keep him out of the Worcester jail. In his autobiography, Arthur tells of his final arrest: "I went to Mr. *Fisk's* in *Waltham*, who knew me. And having heard of my Escape from *Worcester* Goal, immediately secured me, and with the assistance of another Man, brought me back again." Like Frasier, Arthur had become a momentary celebrity; by now people had "heard" of his exploits throughout Massachusetts. As Hutchinson stated complacently, "So [Arthur] was at last infatuated, to meet his deserved end."[36]

34. Ibid.; Aaron Hutchinson, *Iniquity Purged by Mercy and Truth; A Sermon Preached . . . after the Execution of Arthur, a Negro Man . . .* (Boston, 1769), 22, 25.

35. Noah Hobart, *Excessive Wickedness, the Way to an Untimely Death . . .* (New Haven, Conn., 1768), 2.

36. *Life, and Dying Speech of Arthur*; Hutchinson, *Iniquity Purged*, 25.

This time the county jail held its prisoner. To the original charge of rape, Arthur pleaded not guilty. In court documents, the king's attorney described the accused as a "labourer and servant of Edward Clark of Rutland District," but presumably everyone knew that Arthur was in fact a slave. A parade of local witnesses journeyed to Worcester, a distance of about twenty miles, to testify against Arthur. Nathaniel Jennison came forward; so too did Jennison's neighbor, John Caldwell. Four Metcalfes were present, all of them apparently Deborah Metcalfe's children, but the trial records do not mention her participation in the proceedings against Arthur. On September 17, 1767, a jury convicted the slave of the crime, a capital offense in Massachusetts. Arthur immediately requested benefit of clergy—a motion that would have allowed him to avoid the death penalty—but after the prosecuting attorney Jonathan Sewall consulted with other crown officials in Boston, the superior court denied the slave's petition. The execution took place on October 20, 1768, more than a year after the trial, and drew a large crowd from the surrounding countryside. The Reverend Ebenezer Parkman of Westborough, a tiny community located many miles to the east of the Rutland District, noted sadly in his diary: "The Day of the Execution of Arthur, who was condemned for committing a Rape, but I could not go to *Worcester*."[37]

Although the court documents are sparse—no depositions or direct testimony survives—one senses that contemporaries were concerned about the fairness of the Worcester trial. There was, of course, the matter of Deborah Metcalfe's attempt to negotiate a private settlement. Moreover, in an unusual move, the court postponed the date of hanging for almost a year, allowing Arthur an opportunity to appeal on new evidence. "Perhaps there never was an execution like to this," Hutchinson announced, "wherein mercy and truth, or mercy and justice, were better united. A whole year passed after he was found guilty, before his sentence. This gave room for mercy, if any way could be hit upon, for mercy to rejoice against judgment. No way was found."[38]

Court officials put Arthur in an impossible situation. Twice they asked him directly whether he knew any reason why the hanging should not be carried out. It is not clear what would have constituted a persuasive response. The slave had no witnesses to bring forward; his earlier brushes with the law told against him. And so, as the chief justice noted, "the prisoner having nothing else to

37. Indictment no. 152339, vol. 1073, Supreme Judicial Court. Also, see *Massachusetts Gazette*, Oct. 15, 1767; Ebenezer Parkman Diary, Oct. 20, 1768, American Antiquarian Society, Worcester, Massachusetts. Thomas Knoles, curator of manuscripts, brought this entry to my attention.

38. Hutchinson, *Iniquity Purged*, 18–19.

offer why sentence of death should not be pronounced against him: Sentence of death is pronounced against him."[39]

Neither sermon preached at the time of Arthur's execution allays doubts about the fairness of the verdict. Thaddeus Maccarty and Aaron Hutchinson, two Worcester County ministers, excoriated Arthur for many vices, for heavy drinking, for lust, for idleness, for sexual relations with Indians, but, curiously, neither of the published accounts made much of the alleged rape of Deborah Metcalfe. It is hard to imagine that the ministers found the discussion of explicit sexual matters embarrassing. Whatever their thoughts about what happened that winter night in the Rutland District, they seemed to argue that, whether or not Arthur actually harmed the woman, he certainly deserved to die. "And thus the land is purged," Hutchinson thundered, "and we hope will still be purged, and that all our Israel will hear and fear, and do no more so wickedly." In another convoluted passage, Hutchinson assured his readers, "They that were most acquainted with his high-handed wickedness, were obliged to say, what they maliciously said of Paul, *away with such a fellow from the earth, for it is not fit that he should live.*"[40]

Comparing Arthur to a celebrated saint might have struck some contemporary New Englanders as far-fetched—as if Hutchinson had not fully worked out the logic of his biblical examples—but, surely, the minister outdid himself by transforming the condemned black man into a modern-day Lot's wife. Arthur, insisted Hutchinson, "is set up as a Lot's wife for us to remember, and be cautioned and warned." Perhaps the slave's escape in the habit of an Indian woman impressed itself on the preacher's mind. Whatever Hutchinson might have been thinking about cross-dressing, he employed the bizarre trope of Lot's wife in other passages and, ignoring Arthur's race and gender, informed a congregation of rural white farmers that Arthur "is designed by heaven for a monument to warn us, and that all the natives, negroes, and all people, *may hear and fear, and do no more so wickedly.*"[41] As in the sermon delivered at Bristol's execution, this lecture betrays white uncertainty. The story of Arthur's life somehow threatened the stability of Hutchinson's moral order. The black trickster beckoned across racial lines, inviting white colonists to consider the joys of Sodom, in a word, to incorporate a slave biography into broad public consciousness.

The Reverend Thaddeus Maccarty experienced even greater difficulty placing Arthur comfortably within a traditional interpretive framework. The problem was that the condemned slave would not cooperate; he refused to

39. Indictment no. 152339, vol. 1073, Supreme Judicial Court.
40. Hutchinson, *Iniquity Purged,* 18–19.
41. Ibid., 19, 27.

legitimate the justice of the court's decision. Maccarty spent long hours visiting Arthur in the Worcester prison, and, although he tried to reform the slave, to fashion him at the moment of death into a good Christian servant, the minister sensed that Arthur secretly mocked his efforts. Minutes before Arthur was hanged, Maccarty was still begging him to exonerate not only the "honourable Court" but also to forgive the woman who had accused him of rape. "And even supposing you think you was [sic] unfairly and injuriously treated in the matter," argued the anxious minister, "yet do you find a disposition freely and heartily to forgive her?—Such a disposition as this, however contrary to corrupt nature, the gospel of Christ makes absolutely necessary, even in cases of the greatest injuries."[42] What injustice? Had Deborah Metcalfe lied? Had Jennison manipulated events to suit his own purposes? Had the court treated the slave unfairly? Was it evidence of a corrupt nature or lack of common sense to protest "the greatest injuries"? In the published sermon, *The Power and Grace of Christ Display'd to a Dying Malefactor*, one can almost hear Arthur sparring with Maccarty, protesting his innocence, and thereby forcing the minister and a large anonymous public who read the published work to weigh the possibility of an alternative story.

As in the legal proceedings against Bristol—only this time more forcefully and more widely—we encounter the muffled language of communal uncertainty. Without elaboration a Boston newspaper reported: "We hear that a negro fellow was tried at the Assizes held lately at Worcester, for a rape, and found guilty, and received a sentence of death.—A white man was also tried and found guilty of attempting the same crime, and sentenced to sit on the gallows." Perhaps the juxtaposition of these two stories was fortuitous. Perhaps Arthur's crime was in fact far more serious than that committed by the white man. Perhaps the journal recognized that Arthur's major problem was that he had been tried as "a negro fellow." The execution sermons—it was extremely rare for a single criminal to spark two independent publications—and the newspaper coverage provide hints to a richer, highly problematic narrative that thrust itself into public consciousness. What seems clear at this distance is that, like the ancient Egyptian slave Aesop, who was murdered by the freemen of his community, Arthur might have been too clever by half.[43] He might have paid his life for assaulting traditional boundaries, for having sex with women of different races, for traveling about the Massachusetts countryside at will, for

42. Thaddeus Maccarty, *The Power and Grace of Christ Display'd to a Dying Malefactor* (Boston, 1768), 22.

43. *Boston Chronicle*, Sept. 26, 1768. A model of the kind of analysis I am attempting is Keith Hopkins, "Novel Evidence for Roman Slavery," *Past and Present*, no. 138 (Feb. 1993), 3–27.

exposing a village official as a fool, in a word, for making a mockery of his status as an unfree person.

In the unstable political environment of the late 1760s, highly publicized incidents such as Arthur's execution—not only the actual hanging but also the several published narratives—fed directly into a new political force that the Reverend Jeremy Belknap called "publick opinion." The details of the life of an obscure slave flowed into a larger debate about parliamentary oppression and the morality of slavery. Arthur compelled interpretation not simply by a few well-educated ministers but also by ordinary people throughout Massachusetts, black as well as white. Popular consciousness in colonial society consisted of many different fragments of thought. As we have seen, Arthur continually turned to "Negro" friends for counsel and support: tales of his adventures spread through a wide oral network of historically invisible men and women. And, even though he had not defined his life as a political statement, it found meaning for these people within a liberal discourse of rights and liberties. Only a few years after Arthur's execution, a group of black men living in Worcester County—men who surely had known Arthur—announced "that we abhor the enslaving of any of the human race, and particularly of the Negroes of this country, and that whenever there shall be a door opened, or opportunity present for anything to be done towards the emancipation of the Negroes, we will use our influence and endeavor that such a thing may be brought about." And, in 1767, the moment of Arthur's indictment, Worcester became one of the first communities in Massachusetts specifically to instruct its representatives in the colonial assembly to "use your Influence to obtain a law to put an End to that unchristian and Impolitick Practice of making Slaves of the Human Species in this Province." Whatever one may think of Arthur's behavior—especially of his treatment of Deborah Metcalfe—one can appreciate that he made history by intruding himself powerfully into a continuing, colony-wide debate about the meaning of freedom.

Insistent local voices had the capacity to sustain a larger critique of slavery. The driving engine of protest was autobiography, the experiences of unfree people who managed to enter the public consciousness, who insisted in print that they too could define self in terms of natural rights. During this period the rhetorical blasts against human bondage in Massachusetts became ever more strident, more uncompromising. "Blush ye pretended votaries for Freedom!" announced the Reverend John Allen in 1774. "Ye trifling patriots! who are making a vain parade of being advocates for the liberties of mankind, who are thus making a mockery of your profession by trampling on the sacred rights and privileges of *Africans.*" Allen was a recent Baptist immigrant—an artisan of sorts—from Wilkesite London, and, as such, he was an outsider to Boston who picked up on the emancipation theme and prefigures Thomas Paine's angry condemnation of slavery in the colonies. Or consider the words of "A Lover of Constitutional Liberty." The anonymous pamphleteer declared in 1773 that "many will object to the freeing the *Slaves* among us, by saying, If they are set at Liberty they will turn Vagrants, and thereby become a Pest to Society; that our Streets will be filled with Robbers, House-breakers, etc. In Answer to which I would ask this Question, What Right had we to bring those People among us, or to encourage so iniquitous a Trade?"[45]

Such statements have a familiar ring. Not surprisingly, they often find their way into modern document collections. But they should be read with care. Their inclusion inevitably creates an impression that it was a few Boston intellectuals who generated revolutionary notions of freedom and equality and, by extension, that the ideological proclamations of the metropolis filtered down eventually to smaller, less cosmopolitan communities, such as Worcester and the Rutland District. But what we have uncovered in Arthur's story are much more complicated patterns of interaction. The people of Worcester County might have self-consciously situated themselves within a general liberal discourse, but divorced from local and personal histories—abstracted from the story of Arthur, for example—external explanations carried little persuasive power. Messages of freedom flowed in all directions, from Boston to the countryside, from the Rutland District to Boston, and from black people to whites. What Belknap and others called public opinion was a shared story mediated by local experience.

The transformation of personal experience into public opinion included a third person. Quock Walker also made history. His personal experiences at the hands of a violent master entered public consciousness in Massachusetts during the final years of the American Revolution. His insistent demand for

---

45. [John Allen], *Watchman's Alarm to Lord N——h* . . . (Salem, Mass., 1774), 27. Winthrop D. Jordan presents a masterful account of the rising protest against slavery and the slave trade in *White over Black: American Attitudes toward the Negro, 1550–1812* (Chapel Hill, N.C., 1968), 269–311. Also valuable for understanding the historical context of this debate is Gary B. Nash, *Race and Revolution* (Madison, Wis., 1990), 3–24; and Peter H. Wood, " 'Liberty Is Sweet': African-American Freedom Struggles in the Years before White Independence," in Alfred F. Young, ed., *Beyond the American Revolution: Explorations in the History of American Radicalism* (Dekalb, Ill., 1993), 149–184; A Lover of Constitutional Liberty, *The Appendix; or, Some Observations of the Expediency of the Petition of the Africans, Living in Boston . . .* (Boston, 1773), 7.

freedom dramatically exposed the moral bankruptcy of the institution of slavery. It no longer enjoyed the sanction of public opinion. The defensiveness that we encountered during the early 1760s had gradually become a source of genuine embarrassment and, finally, an object of general condemnation. Unlike Bristol and Arthur, Walker was not a criminal. Since being sold into slavery in 1754 with his mother and father, Dinah and Mingo, Walker had lived quietly in the Rutland District, renamed Barre in 1774. He almost certainly knew Arthur. He might have even witnessed Arthur's execution, as Arthur had Bristol's. And, like his contemporaries, Walker undoubtedly imbibed the liberal language of rights and equality intensified by political revolution. Sometime during the War for Independence, Walker decided on his own that he was no longer a slave, indeed, that he was free to work for wages just like any other person in Massachusetts. The catalyst might have been a new state constitution that, among other things, declared, "All men are born free and equal." Whatever his reasoning, Walker left his master's house and accepted a job with James Caldwell, the brother of the man who had originally brought Walker's family to the Rutland District as slaves and who had appeared as a witness at Arthur's trial.[46]

Although the Caldwells sensed that the times were changing, Walker's master decided to dig in his heels, angrily insisting on his rights as an owner of human property and thumbing his nose at public opinion. That man was none other than Nathaniel Jennison, the neighbor who a few years earlier had taken it upon himself to bring Arthur to justice and who at the conclusion of the Revolution still listed ten slaves—including Walker's brother—as part of his taxable estate. One spring day in 1781, Jennison confronted Walker in Caldwell's field, and, when the former slave refused to return to bondage, Jennison physically attacked him, beating Walker and then holding him captive on his own farm less than a mile away. When white people in the region learned of Jennison's actions, they made it clear that they no longer tolerated such brutality. Surprised and hurt, Jennison responded to criticism with the reflexive arguments of all beleaguered slaveholders: "that the black was his slave, and that the beating, etc., was the necessary restraint and correction of the master."[47]

Jennison soon discovered that the traditional defense of human property had lost most of its persuasive force in this society. Walker's courage made a

46. Arthur Zilversmit, "Quok Walker, Mumbet, and the Abolition of Slavery in Massachusetts," WMQ, 3d Ser., XXV (1968), 614–624; D. Hamilton Hurd, comp., History of Worcester County . . . , 2 vols. (Philadelphia, 1889), II, 341–342; James Sullivan to Jeremy Belknap, Apr. 9, 1795, MHS, Colls., 5th Ser., III (1877), 403.

47. Cited in Moore, Notes, 218–219; for excellent insights into the Walker affair, see 211–217.

difference. His resistance in Caldwell's field solidified public opinion, and, instead of allowing himself to be bullied, this black engaged capable legal counsel. In a series of civil and criminal proceedings brought before the Worcester courts between 1781 and 1783, Walker's defenders shredded Jennison's various claims. Freedom, Jennison insisted, would expose his loyal slaves—"some of them young and helpless, others old and infirm"—to needless suffering. He whined that, if the white people of Massachusetts had realized that the "free and equal" clause in the state constitution would abolish slavery, they would never have ratified the document. And Jennison warned darkly that victory in the courts for Walker would offend the southern states and endanger the fragile national union.[48]

The judges of the Massachusetts Supreme Court would have none of it. Faced with humiliating defeat, Jennison seems to have transferred his remaining slaves to Connecticut, where he assumed that the law still respected his own version of the rights of property. Walker's brother deserted Jennison almost immediately, returning to Barre, where the two men—Africans who demanded freedom in America—survived into the nineteenth century. Their stories, like those of Bristol and Arthur, briefly influenced the course of public opinion, shaping it, driving it forward, exposing tensions, crystallizing doubts, so eroding the institution of slavery that, at some critical moment in the history of Massachusetts, emancipation became common sense.

48. Ibid., 218–219.

"THE UNHAPPY STEPHEN ARNOLD":
AN EPISODE OF MURDER AND PENITENCE
IN THE EARLY REPUBLIC

Alan Taylor

On the morning of June 16, 1806, in the rural village of Cooperstown in Otsego County, in upstate New York, James Cooper eagerly anticipated a total eclipse of the sun. Sixteen years old, he had yet to become the great American novelist of his generation (and had yet to add "Fenimore" as his middle name). Young Cooper wandered through the streets, keenly examining the faces and movements of the villagers, as if on this day they would reveal something new and profound as they reacted to the dimming light. An industrious, utilitarian, commonsensical people, they seemed, at first, disappointingly unaware of and unaffected by the approaching spectacle:

> Many were busy with their usual tasks, women and children were coming and going with pails of water, the broom and the needle were not yet laid aside, the blacksmith's hammer and the carpenter's plane were heard in passing their shops. Loaded teams, and travellers in waggons, were moving through the streets; the usual quiet traffic at the village counters had not yet ceased. A farm-waggon, heavily laden with hay, was just crossing the bridge, coming in from the fields, the driver looking drowsy with sleep, wholly unconscious of the movement in the heavens.

Then, at about 9:50, as the moon slowly began to slide across the sun, the villagers put down their tools and crowded into the streets, gazing upward. As Cooper recalled that moment, the eclipse revealed and reinforced the roles properly played by the villagers, according to their age, occupation, and sex:

> As the light failed more and more with every passing second, the children came flocking about their mothers in terror. The women themselves were looking about uneasily for their husbands. The American wife is more apt than any other to turn with affectionate confidence to the stronger arm for support. The men were very generally silent and grave. Many a laborer left his employment to be near his wife and children, as the dimness and darkness increased.

To Cooper's remembered relief and delight, everything seemed orderly, harmonious, and contemplative on the ground as the rupture in the heavens proceeded. In describing men and women reacting to the eclipse, Cooper celebrated his culture's prevailing contract between the sexes: husbands would govern and protect in return for love and obedience from their wives and children.[1]

However, as Cooper roamed through Cooperstown, he found one great, jarring exception to his reassuring picture of the peaceable village. Quietly but firmly saying, "Come with me!" a "man of few words" took James by the arm, leading him up the main street to the jailer's house beside the courthouse and jail. There, at a window, gazing skyward, stood the jailer and a "man with haggard face, and fettered arms, a prisoner under sentence of death." For a year he had languished in a dungeon cell without direct sunlight. Now the jailer permitted the prisoner out to see its eclipse.

> That striking figure, the very picture of utter misery, his emotion, his wretchedness, I can never forget. I can see him now, standing at the window, pallid and emaciated by a year's confinement, stricken with grief, his cheeks furrowed with constant weeping, his whole frame attesting [to] the deep and ravaging influences of conscious guilt and remorse. Here was a man drawn from the depths of human misery, to be immediately confronted with the grandest natural exhibition in which the Creator deigns to reveal his Omnipotence to our race. The wretched criminal, a murderer in fact, though not in intention, seemed to gaze upward at the awful spectacle, with an intentness and a distinctness of mental vision far beyond our own, and purchased by an agony scarcely less bitter than death. It seemed as if, for him, the curtain which veils the world beyond the grave, had been lifted. He stood immovable as a statue, with uplifted and manacled arms and clasped hands, the very image of impotent misery and wretchedness. . . . It was an incident to stamp on the memory for life.

In the prisoner's misery and awe, Cooper did find something striking and revealing within the familiar and prosaic village: a most horrific and sobering disruption in the expected patterns of family and order. Named Stephen Arnold, the wretched prisoner was a country schoolteacher who had beaten his adopted daughter to death. Not all American children and wives could be so confident in protection from "the stronger arm."[2]

During 1805–1807 in New York State, public attention and anxieties became

1. James Fenimore Cooper, "The Eclipse," *Putnam's Magazine*, 2d Ser., IV (1869), 352–356; Charles Holt, *Holt's New-York Register, for 1806* . . . (Hudson, N.Y., 1805), 3.

2. Cooper, "The Eclipse," *Putnam's Magazine*, 2d Ser., IV (1869), 355–356.

focused on Arnold's dramatic flight, sensational trial, conspicuous penitence, and suspenseful execution. Indeed, a close narration of his fate reveals the especially powerful cultural and social tensions in the many new villages of the early Republic. First, as a parent who had killed in an act of corporal punishment, Arnold evoked an emerging conflict between the traditional notions of strict patriarchy and the newer ideals of nurturing love. Second, the rituals at his execution provoked a conflict between the common spectators and the legal authorities over the proper scripting for publicly staged deaths. Third, as a trusted neighbor and teacher, who erupted in deadly rage only to cultivate exemplary penitence, Arnold epitomized prevailing confusions over the relationship of external appearances to internal character. He fed public anxieties that were especially acute at a time when, and in places where, an unprecedented and increasing migration obscured the origins and identities of so many new neighbors. Fourth, at a time of profound cultural change, he evoked conflicting narratives meant to explain the nature of murder. Whereas Arnold's enemies cast him as an unfeeling, inhuman monster, he attracted numerous supporters, who regarded him as a pitiable victim warranting compassion.

The people of upstate New York tried to decipher Stephen Arnold in order to understand themselves and their apparently uncertain and unstable social order. A disappointment as a child who succeeded in becoming a frontier householder and teacher, Arnold failed as a parent but ultimately triumphed in the role of public penitent. In a new Republic that so celebrated the self-made man, Arnold's life constitutes a peculiar success story.[3]

MURDER

In his confession published in 1805, Arnold narrated his own life as a tale of brilliant prospects frustrated by a deceitful and disorderly world. Born in 1771 as the son of a prosperous farmer (and indulgent father) in Rhode Island, Arnold enjoyed initial advantages that promised a bright future of property and influence. As a teenager, Arnold attended a nearby academy, where he won renown as "the best scholar in school." Unusually proficient in Latin and Greek, mathematics and English, Arnold joined the academy's faculty at age eighteen as an assistant preceptor. "I bid fair to be not only a comfort to my parents in their declining years, but likewise an ornament to my country." A year later, his father became ill and bedridden, obliging young Arnold to

3. For a similar capsule biography, see Paul E. Johnson, "The Modernization of Mayo Greenleaf Patch: Land, Family, and Marginality in New England, 1766–1818," *New England Quarterly*, LV (1982), 488–516.

return home to manage the family farm. Embittered by this twist of fate, Arnold denounced the farm's hired hands as "abandoned and vicious characters," who recklessly drank, gambled, and profaned the Sabbath. In response, they cursed Arnold and ignored his orders. Fortunately for all concerned, the father recovered to resume command and restore order, which freed Arnold to leave home and study medicine as an apprentice to a country doctor. After five months of intense study, he apparently suffered a nervous breakdown. Returning home, Arnold spent nearly two years "doing little or nothing."[4]

Unable to fulfill his father's high expectations, Arnold yearned for escape. He listened with keen interest to a cousin who, during a brief return visit to Rhode Island, extolled his new home on the frontier in upstate New York as "an excellent place for young men tolerably educated." In 1794, at the age of twenty-three, Arnold followed his cousin back to Burlington in Otsego County, where an uncle provided the prodigal son with a place to board. Like many a young man fleeing eastern disappointment, Arnold was delighted with Otsego as a land of frontier opportunity: "There was business in plenty for people of every description; villages and towns were in want of Physicians, School-Masters, etc., and Merchants and Land Speculators in want of Clerks." Arnold went to work clerking for a local land speculator, probably Adolphus Walbridge, from whom he bought a small farm (fifty acres) in Burlington for $250 in 1800. After two years in the speculator's employ, Arnold accepted an invitation from the Burlington school committee to become a teacher.[5]

Sober young men with a modicum of education were rare and highly prized as teachers in the Yankee settlements of upstate New York. The pious folk worried that their children would deteriorate morally unless instructed every winter by a teacher from New England. Too often, Otsego communities had to settle for ill-educated men of dubious morality and violent temper. One New Englander sojourning in upstate New York described the teachers as "worthless wretches! Drunken sots! Profane wretches!" Henry Clarke Wright bitterly recalled the abusive schoolmaster from his youth in Otsego during the first decade of the nineteenth century. Although also an evangelical preacher, "very moving in prayer, earnest in exhortation, and terrible in his rebukes to sinners," the teacher was "fiery tempered" and "a hard drinker of whiskey," who

4. Stephen Arnold, *Life and Confession of Arnold, Who Inhumanly Whipped to Death Betsey Van Amburgh, His Little Niece—Aged Six Years* . . . (Albany, [1805]), 3–8 (copy at American Antiquarian Society, Worcester, Mass.); Louis C. Jones, "The Crime and Punishment of Stephen Arnold," *New York History*, XLVII (1966), 249–250.

5. Arnold, *Life and Confession*, 9–10; Willard V. Huntington, "Old Time Notes Relating to Otsego County and the Upper Susquehanna Valley," New York State Historical Association, Cooperstown, typescript, 1069.

imbibed steadily through every school day. "He always grew savage as he grew more drunken; and the children were sure to feel his heavy rod, towards evening, without mercy. His anxiety to have us converted, was in proportion to the degree of his drunkenness." He sat in the middle of the room with a "long whip in his hand, giving the children a most tender exhortation, and telling us how he loved our souls—the tears streaming down the while." He earnestly prayed to God "to give ease and comfort to our souls, while he was inflicting pain and misery upon our bodies." Given this low standard, the Burlington school committee was delighted to hire the abstemious, well-educated, and severely self-disciplined Stephen Arnold.[6]

Over the course of seven winters conducting school, Arnold attracted growing numbers of children of diverse ages. Eager for money and paid per student, Arnold readily accepted new children. His school grew from a barely manageable 50 to an impossible 150 students. Prospering materially, he bought 50 acres of land in 1800 and another 101 acres a year later. Worth only $350 in 1800, his taxable property nearly doubled to $662 in 1803. Shortly after 1800, he married Susannah Van Amburgh, a local farmer's daughter. Apparently unable to conceive their own children, they adopted her young niece, Betsey, "a lively child, always dancing, and good natured." It seemed that Arnold would become an ornament to his country after all.[7]

But his material prosperity came at a severe and increasing emotional cost exacted by the excessive number of students attending his school. Their fees endowed Arnold's new farm and made possible his new family, but their numbers and defiance took a toll on his self-control. His unprepossessing appearance, easily agitated nerves, and obsession for detail ensured disrespect and provocations, especially from the older boys. Arnold was, the *Otsego Herald* explained, "about 34 years of age, sandy hair, a little bald, speaks through his nose, has something of a down look, shews his upper teeth when

6. Jones, "Crime and Punishment," *New York History*, XLVII (1966), 250–251; Nahum Jones, Diary, Aug. 22, 1795, American Antiquarian Society ("worthless"); "Philo Patria," *Otsego Herald*, Dec. 29, 1796; George Peck, *The Life and Times of Rev. George Peck, D. D., Written by Himself* (New York, 1874), 19–21; Henry Clarke Wright, *Human Life: Illustrated in My Individual Experience as a Child, a Youth, and a Man* (Boston, 1849), 49–50.

7. Arnold, *Life and Confession*, 10–11; Jones, "Crime and Punishment," *New York History*, XLVII (1966), 252; Otsego County Conveyances, D, 71–72, Otsego County Registry of Deeds, Otsego County Clerk's Office; Burlington Tax Assessment Lists, 1800, 1803, Series B-0950-85, boxes 37, 38, New York State Archives, Albany; Sally Adams testimony, in Elihu Phinney, ed., *The Trial of Stephen Arnold; For the Murder of Betsey Van Amburgh, a Child of Six Years of Age . . .* (Cooperstown, N.Y., 1805), 16–17. Arnold does not appear on the Federal Census of 1800 for Burlington—which suggests that he was then still an unmarried boarder in someone else's household.

speaking, [and] is very abstemious as to strong drink." When his precious self-control gave way, it was frightful to behold. A neighbor saw Arnold "beat a cow very severely for a trifling cause." Unable to maintain order in his overcrowded school, Arnold blamed "a country newly settled," where the children "did not appear to be really civilized." As with his father's rowdy farm laborers, Arnold again found enemies bent on humiliating him. But, this time, Arnold could physically chastise his tormentors. Finding "argument of little or no use," Arnold daily resorted to the rod in a futile bid to regain control. He especially recalled January 10, 1805: "The day on which I committed the dreadful act for which the sentence of death has been pronounced on me, I was provoked even to madness, through the ill-behaviour of my pupils. . . . My accursed temper got the better of my reason."[8]

Arnold returned home in a rage at his loss of control over his classroom. It was the misfortune of his six-year-old ward, Betsey Van Amburgh, that he decided to make her the critical test of his waning power to control and to instruct. Arnold meant to conquer, once and for all, her speech impediment that he found so vexing. He demanded that she read and pronounce the word "gig." When she replied, "jig," he deemed her obstinate. Arnold and his wife had whipped Betsey once or twice before with, to their minds, good effect. After collecting a bundle of eight beechwood switches, each three feet long, he hauled Betsey out into the cold, dark night. He pulled her dress up over her head and clenched it in one fist, leaving her backside naked and her hands bound as he beat her with the switches held in his other fist. After one beating, Arnold drew the crying girl inside and again demanded that she read and pronounce "gig." Again she failed and again he took her outside for a whipping. During the course of an hour and a half, she failed seven times and received seven thrashings, each more painful than the one before. Consumed with mounting fury, Arnold announced that "he had as leave whip her to death as not." For the last beating, he heated and hardened the switches in the fire before devoting a half hour to striking the girl. Neither Susannah Arnold nor their servant girl, Sally Adams, tried to halt the beatings. After the seventh thrashing, Betsey pronounced "gig" to his satisfaction.[9]

Betsey became delirious and feverish, passing in and out of consciousness.

8. [Elihu Phinney], "A Savage Ruffian!" *Otsego Herald,* Jan. 31, 1805; Hubbell testimony, in Phinney, ed., *Trial of Stephen Arnold,* 16; Arnold, *Life and Confession,* 12.

9. Arnold, *Life and Confession,* 12; [Phinney], "A Savage Ruffian!" *Otsego Herald,* Jan. 31, 1805; Sally Adams and Dr. Gaines Smith testimony, in Phinney, ed., *Trial of Stephen Arnold,* 10, 13–15; Cooper, "The Eclipse," *Putnam's Magazine,* 2d Ser., IV (1869), 355; James Kent's trial notes, June 4, 1805, in New York State, *Journal of the Assembly of the State of New-York: At Their Twenty-Ninth Session . . .* (Albany, 1806), 70–71.

For two days, Stephen and Susannah Arnold delayed calling a doctor, vainly hoping that their daughter would heal. On the third day, they consulted a doctor but restricted his examination, insisting that Betsey only suffered from worms. At last, on January 13, Stephen Arnold sought out Dr. Gaines Smith, pleading, "*I will tell you, I have whipped it to death, and if you will go and cure it and keep it a secret, I will give you half of my property, even all.*" To rescue his imperiled girl, character, and life, Arnold was willing to forsake the cherished farm purchased at the expense of his own sanity. Smith and two other doctors entered Arnold's home, examined Betsey, and found "the child was cut and mangled shockingly from the calves of her legs up to the middle of her back." They concluded "that the girl was out of her head" because she "begged of them not to whip her to death." The doctors could do nothing to save Betsey, who died the next day, January 14. "Arnold! a dreadful moment awaits you," Smith muttered.[10]

Fearing arrest, Arnold bolted into the woods and fled down the Susquehanna River, out of Otsego County and New York State into Pennsylvania. As with any other public emergency, the town fathers of Burlington reacted by calling a public meeting to elect a committee and raise funds, by voluntary subscription, to offer a two-hundred-dollar reward for Arnold's capture. Published in Elihu Phinney's Cooperstown newspaper, the *Otsego Herald,* on January 31 and then reprinted "in almost every newspaper published in the United States," the pathetic story of Betsey's death and the alluring reward for Arnold's capture generated "a fervid excitement through the length and breadth of the land." Seeking the reward, Thomas Cahoon of adjoining Chenango County set off in pursuit, tracking Arnold south and west across Pennsylvania. Finding Arnold at a tavern in Pittsburgh on March 4, Cahoon made the arrest, abetted by two local assistants. Reaching into his pocket, Arnold pulled out a pistol, which he cocked, placing the muzzle to his left ear, determined to kill himself. One of Cahoon's assistants quickly knocked Arnold's arm aside and the pistol discharged into the air. Subdued, disarmed, and conducted through an angry crowd to a justice of the peace, Arnold confessed to killing Betsey Van Amburgh.[11]

Apprised of Arnold's arrest, the Burlington committee sent two men to

10. Testimony of Dr. Gaines Smith, Dr. Ezra S. Day, Rebecca Hubbell, and Sally Adams, in Phinney, ed., *Trial of Stephen Arnold,* 9–13, 17; James Kent's trial notes, June 4, 1805, in New York State, *Journal of the Assembly . . . Twenty-Ninth Session,* 70–71; Smith, quoted in Arnold, *Life and Confession,* 13.

11. Arnold, *Life and Confession,* 13–18; [Phinney], "A Savage Ruffian!" *Otsego Herald,* Jan. 31, 1805; Nathaniel Stacy, *Memoirs of the Life of Nathaniel Stacy, Preacher of the Gospel of Universal Grace* (Columbus, Pa., 1850), 161; Thomas Cahoon to Burlington Committee, Mar. 5, 1805, in *Otsego Herald,* Mar. 28, Apr. 25, May 23, 1805; Testimony of Eliphaz Alexander, in Phinney, ed., *Trial of Stephen Arnold,* 16.

Pittsburgh to conduct him back to Otsego for trial. Returning to Cooperstown on May 17, they entrusted Arnold to the dungeon cell of the county jail. The local newspaper publisher, Elihu Phinney, served as the foreman of the grand jury that indicted Arnold for murder on June 3. The grand jurors did not indict Susannah Arnold, despite evidence that she had abetted the fatal beating and had subsequently attempted to hide Betsey's wounds. As the person who inflicted the fatal blows and as the head of household in a patriarchal society, Stephen Arnold was deemed solely responsible for his daughter's death.[12]

Chief Justice James Kent traveled west from Albany to preside when the Otsego County Court of Oyer and Terminer convened in Cooperstown on June 4, 1805, to try Stephen Arnold for murder. Otsego's three resident judges, led by Jedediah Peck, served as Kent's assistants on the bench. Because rural New Yorkers rarely killed one another, this was the first murder trial in the county's fourteen year history. Arousing keen interest throughout the county, Arnold's trial attracted an unprecedented crowd to the courthouse. Fewer than half the people could crowd into the jammed courtroom, obliging the jailer to post guards at the door to keep out the rest.[13]

That Stephen Arnold had beaten Betsey Van Amburgh to death was not at issue. Nor did the prosecution dispute Arnold's parental right corporally to punish his ward. Instead, the trial pivoted on the appropriate degree of pain that a parent could inflict to chastise a child. The prosecution argued that Arnold used grossly excessive force by employing eight long sticks "as big as ox goads" to whip Betsey seven times during an hour and a half: long enough to reconsider his passion. "Such an outrageous correction as this," the district attorney insisted, "can never be allowed by law." The defense conceded: "The sticks, it is true were too large—larger perhaps than either of the jurors would have used, in correcting a child." Nonetheless, her death was an accident provoked because "the child persisted in its perverseness, when it could and [in the past] had pronounced the word right." According to the defense, Betsey provoked her own death.[14]

The trial came during a period of cultural transition, when there was no longer a clear consensus in upstate New York on the appropriate degree of

12. Phinney, ed., *Trial of Stephen Arnold*, iii, 5–6, 16; *People* v. *Arnold*, Otsego County Court of Oyer and Terminer, Record Book I, June 4, 1805, Otsego County Clerk's Office, Cooperstown, N.Y.

13. Phinney, *Trial of Stephen Arnold*, iii, 5–6; *People* v. *Arnold*, Otsego County Court of Oyer and Terminer, Record Book I, June 4, 1805. For the rarity of murder in rural New York, see John Theodore Horton, *James Kent, a Study in Conservatism, 1763–1847* (New York, 1939), 35 n. 43.

14. Phinney, ed., *Trial of Stephen Arnold*, 17–21.

corporal punishment. Among rural Yankees, the traditional ideal was the family as a little commonwealth sternly governed by a strict patriarch. Recalling his childhood in Otsego during the first decade of the nineteenth century, Henry Clarke Wright described his father as the consummate patriarch:

> In the government of his children he allowed but little familiarity on their part towards him, never allowing us to speak to him or of him, as thou, or you, he or him; but only by the appelation of father. . . . When in his presence, a look, or a tap of his foot on the floor, was enough to guide us and keep us quiet.

Every morning before breakfast, Wright's father summoned the family together with the call, "Come to duty." After reading a chapter from the Bible, he led the family in prayer. "I regarded my father with a feeling of awe. . . . There he stood, his back towards us, his face to the wall, leaning his hands on the top of a chair, talking in a solemn, deliberate and earnest tone of voice to a Being whom I could not see." Such traditional patriarchs (and their wives) thought it their parental and religious duty to break the pride and will of their children with as much force as necessary. Loyal to that tradition, Arnold had insisted "that he wished he was like the old country people, that he could whip her to death; meaning . . . that he wished he possessed a hard heart." According to that old country standard, Betsey sowed and reaped her own death by stubbornly persisting in her willful mispronunciation. More than the word "gig" was at stake. By defying her parent, despite increasing pain, Betsey clung to the innate sinfulness that, unless broken, would culminate in an eternal fate worse than death: hell.[15]

But in the early Republic there was also a newer, more sentimental understanding of children as innately innocent and in need of nurturing rather than physical pain. Imported from the genteel circles of England, those new ideas of child-rearing found a newly receptive audience among the Yankees of New England and New York in the late eighteenth and early nineteenth centuries. Patriarchal control had begun to weaken in New England in the mid-eighteenth century, when population growth and the limited supply of arable land jointly meant dwindling resources that dutiful children could inherit from their demanding fathers. At the end of the century, after the Revolution, impatient sons had even less reason to honor their fathers, because they could

15. Arnold quoted by Sally Adams, in Phinney, ed., *Trial of Stephen Arnold*, 17; Wright, *Human Life*, 22, 81–84, 91–92; Philip Greven, *The Protestant Temperament: Patterns of Child-Rearing, Religious Experience, and the Self in Early America* (New York, 1977), 32–51; Mary P. Ryan, *Cradle of the Middle Class: The Family in Oneida County, New York, 1790–1865* (New York, 1981), 32–33.

more readily emigrate west to obtain a farm in the abundant lands newly available to settlers in upstate New York. Growing numbers of Yankee families began to favor "love" over discipline and submission to bind children to their parents. Arnold's trial commanded such intense interest in upstate New York because there was so much new uncertainty about, and dissonance over, the proper relationship of children to their parents.[16]

After one long day hearing and examining six witnesses, all called by the prosecution, both sides presented their closing arguments. In his charge to the jury, Chief Justice Kent agreed with the prosecution that the duration and severity of the beatings amounted to murder. After deliberating for two hours, the jury returned at 10:30 in the evening to announce their verdict: "*Guilty of Murder.*"[17]

The next day, June 5, Kent pronounced sentence. Oblivious to the source of Arnold's rage, Kent reasoned that, "having been a schoolmaster; and having the care of children, he ought surely to have known how to treat them." In fact, it was because Arnold had charge of too many children that he had learned to treat them so violently. Concluding "that it was necessary to make a public example of him, to deter others from the like offense," Kent sentenced Arnold "*to be hanged by the neck until you are DEAD! and* [may] *the Lord have mercy on your soul!*" Kent scheduled the execution for July 19.[18]

SENSIBILITY

Because murder was so rare and shocking in the northeastern states of the early American Republic, a killing deeply troubled the public, demanding some story that would explain the crime and reaffirm the social order. But Stephen Arnold's crime, flight, arrest, trial, conviction, and sentence occurred at a time of confusion and transition in how Americans narrated and accounted for murder. Most Otsego residents had grown up in eighteenth-century New England, in a culture that understood murder and evil in Calvinist terms. Regarding all humans as morally depraved, leading ministers demanded that the audiences at executions recognize their own kinship as sinners with the unfortunate murderer. The ministers also held out a hope that

16. Robert A. Gross, *The Minutemen and Their World* (New York, 1976), 98–102; Ryan, *Cradle of the Middle Class*, 54–59.

17. Phinney, ed., *Trial of Stephen Arnold*, 21–22; James Kent to Governor Morgan Lewis, July 8, 1805, New York State Assembly Papers, XXXIII, 743, New York State Archives.

18. Phinney, ed., *Trial of Stephen Arnold*, 22–23; *People* v. *Arnold*, Otsego County Court of Oyer and Terminer, Record Book I, June 5, 1805.

the condemned man might, at this last moment, truly repent and receive divine grace, sparing the soul, even as the body died. But, at the close of the eighteenth century, Calvinist theology became less compelling and unifying as growing numbers of people embraced the individualism and voluntarism promoted by revivalist denominations and by the American Revolution. As more people thought of themselves as free agents capable of choosing independence, morality, prosperity, and salvation, they felt ever more alienated from those who, it seemed, chose dependence, crime, poverty, and damnation. Consequently, at the turn of the century, it became more difficult for ministers to evoke a sense of community in original and enduring sin with the condemned. The execution sermon faded in popularity, giving way to secularized and sensationalized narratives and trial reports ordinarily prepared by newspaper journalists or editors. Indeed, no one published an execution sermon to explain the meaning of Arnold's crime and fate; instead, Elihu Phinney published a trial report.[19]

No longer the archetypal sinner, the criminal became a peculiar monster, inexplicably capable of malignant choices horrifying to an audience newly prepared to feel moral superiority. As the criminal became alien and inhuman, the public developed a growing empathy for, and fascination with, the pain and suffering of the victim. Indeed, they indulged in what Karen Halttunen labels "the pornography of pain": a self-indulgent voyeurism in scenes of pain and suffering. People felt better about themselves by reacting with a medley of overt horror and covert pleasure to graphic and gory depictions of torture and murder.[20]

By whipping to death a child, his own adopted daughter, Arnold touched upon the rawest nerves of a public especially repulsed and drawn to scenes involving the flagellation of the relatively weak and seemingly passive. The public empathized with the victim and constructed Arnold as an abhorrent monster. The Universalist minister Nathaniel Stacy recorded the sentiments of his fiancée, Susan Clark:

19. For the cultural transition, see, especially, Karen Halttunen, "Early American Murder Narratives: The Birth of Horror," in Richard Wightman Fox and T. J. Jackson Lears, eds., *The Power of Culture: Critical Essays in American History* (Chicago, 1993), 67–101; Halttunen, "Humanitarianism and the Pornography of Pain in Anglo-American Culture," *American Historical Review*, C (1995), 304. For the shift away from execution sermons, see also Daniel A. Cohen, *Pillars of Salt, Monuments of Grace: New England Crime Literature and the Origins of American Popular Culture, 1674–1860* (New York, 1993), 24–26; Louis P. Masur, *Rites of Execution: Capital Punishment and the Transformation of American Culture, 1776–1865* (New York, 1989), 33–35.

20. Halttunen, "Humanitarianism," *AHR*, C (1995), 303–334.

She was a great lover of children, and the least cruelty practiced upon them excited her indignation even to revenge. She had read the heart-rending story of the poor child's sufferings till her heart bled with pity, and burned with indignation against her savage and cruel murderer, and nothing could satisfy her but his protracted death, wherein he should feel as much pain, in proportion to his strength to bear it, as the poor innocent child did. Hanging was too good for him,—he ought to be whipped to death; and she could see it done—she would exult in seeing him cut into shreds.

Clark's anger reveals how an emotional identification with the suffering and passive victim could evoke a deep longing to *see* extreme pain inflicted upon the criminal, who was reimagined as an utter outcast from a community redefined by a shared sensibility to suffering.[21]

But, following his imprisonment, and especially after his sentencing, something odd and striking happened: a growing minority began to pity and sympathize with Arnold, rendering the victim a fading memory. A steady stream of the curious visited the notorious murderer, the condemned man. They were surprised and gratified to find him conspicuously wracked with remorse and contrition. The Episcopal missionary Daniel Nash observed: "When I first saw him, I could never have formed an idea of the misery of the damned to have excelled the horror and distress he endured—poor, unhappy Mortal! Altho' deserving severe punishment, yet I pitty him from my Soul." Similarly, James Fenimore Cooper recalled, "He was deeply, and beyond all doubt unfeignedly, penitent for the crime into which he had been led, more, apparently, from false ideas of duty, than from natural severity of temper. He had been entirely unaware of the great physical injury he was doing the child." By so thoroughly and convincingly displaying misery and remorse, Arnold gradually substituted himself for Betsey as the prime victim of his act. His pain and suffering became more conspicuous and compelling as her death receded in time and his own approached.[22]

Arnold's new sympathizers included Elihu Phinney who, as editor and publisher of the *Otsego Herald*, had whipped up outrage against Arnold the fugitive and who, as foreman of the grand jury, had indicted Arnold of murder. Phinney was the quintessential Yankee and village editor, a type that James Fenimore Cooper came to loathe in life and to blacken in novels. Born in Connecticut in 1755, Phinney served in the Continental army before emi-

21. Stacy, *Memoirs of the Life*, 162.
22. Daniel Nash to Bishop John H. Hobart, June 3, 1805, Hobart Papers, reel 8, Protestant Episcopal Church Archives (copy in the New-York Historical Society); Cooper, "The Eclipse," *Putnam's Magazine*, 2d Ser., IV (1869), 355.

grating in 1795 to Cooperstown, where he established, edited, and published the county's first (and, as of 1805–1806, only) newspaper and book press. Phinney aptly described himself in a letter to his hero, former president John Adams:

> My turn of mind is rather serious, occasionally facetious, fond of knowledge (where is it?) and true Wit, even in an enemy, [I] began 'the world' $20 in debt, am now worth Thousands of dollars, gained by my own industry and attention to business. You, sir, have now a sketch of my character.

Measuring his own character in dollars, Phinney confidently anticipated meeting Adams "in paradise," because "Hell was not ordained for Elihu Phinney, nor the great and good John Adams." Sharing Adams's deism, Phinney wrote and published essays that mocked evangelical religion as vulgar superstition and that denounced ministerial influence as "spiritual oppression and intolerance." In 1796, he founded, and subsequently governed, Cooperstown's Freemasonic Lodge, a haven for aspiring men skeptical of scriptural religion and convinced of their superior rationality. Shrewd, witty, entrepreneurial, eclectic, and opportunistic, Phinney was a tireless champion of Enlightenment rationality, favorite politicians, village improvements, and his own self-interest.[23]

According to Karen Halttunen, the emerging liberal order nurtured a "cult of sensibility" that "took for its hero 'the man of feeling,' whose tender-hearted susceptibility to the torments of others was the mark of his deeply virtuous nature." Determined to fulfill that ideal, Phinney seemed ever in need of some subject to bear his formidable sympathies and crusading energies. At first he invested them in the murder victim, but the imprisonment, and especially the conviction, of her killer reversed Phinney's polarity. His restless empathy and enthusiasm became attached to the convict's compelling performance as a suffering penitent: "The unhappy Stephen Arnold appears to be possessed of many amiable qualities, such as truth, sincerity, affection, honesty, sobriety, etc. etc. to which may be added a respect for the Laws, which he is sensible he has violated." By capturing Phinney's sympathy, Arnold converted the *Otsego Herald* from the engine of his disgrace and arrest into the principal vehicle for

23. Ralph Birdsall, *The Story of Cooperstown* (Cooperstown, N.Y., 1948), 147; Kathryn Klim Sturrock, "The Phinneys of Cooperstown, 1795–1850" (master's thesis, State University of New York at Oneonta, 1972), 2; Madeleine B. Stern, "Books in the Wilderness: Some Nineteenth Century Upstate Publishers," *New York History*, XXXI (1950), 262–264; Elihu Phinney to John Adams, July 21, 1809, Adams Papers, reel 407, Massachusetts Historical Society, Boston; [Elihu Phinney], "Modern Quack Preaching," *Otsego Herald*, Mar. 22, 1798, June 30, 1800.

pleading his cause. In Phinney's newspaper, the "Savage Ruffian" of the winter became "the unhappy Arnold" of spring and summer.[24]

Led by Phinney, Arnold's friends circulated petitions urging Governor Morgan Lewis to postpone, if not cancel, the execution. In late June and early July, about two thousand Otsego County inhabitants, including two hundred from Burlington, signed the petitions for clemency. According to Phinney, Arnold's sympathizers included "a great majority of the leading and most respectable characters." Many of the same people who had moved heaven and earth to capture and convict Arnold had become too taken with his new role as public penitent to curtail his performances at the Cooperstown jail.[25]

EXECUTION

The county was deeply divided over Arnold's impending fate. Whereas the county notables were more apt to visit Arnold's cell and to appreciate his performance, the county's rustic majority continued to think of Betsey as the victim and Arnold as a monster. On his execution day, it became evident that thousands wanted to see the murderer die for his crime. Coming from as far away as the Chenango and Mohawk Valleys, at least twelve thousand spectators thronged into Cooperstown. Looking down from a second-story window, James Fenimore Cooper saw the main street as "paved with human faces." Never before had so many people come into Cooperstown. Never before had the state hanged anyone in Otsego County.[26]

Multiple, and sometimes conflicting, motives drew thousands into Cooperstown for Arnold's execution. Among a rural people who ordinarily lived scattered on farms and who knew little public amusement, a hanging promised a rare and exciting spectacle, an opportunity to share in, and contribute to, the electric anticipation of a large crowd watching a ritualized death. Parents also brought their children to see the bitter wages of sin, disobedience, and crime. In 1794, a rural Yankee mother traveled to see an execution at Albany, explaining, "she had come *ten miles* to see the *show,* and brought little *Obadiah* and

24. Halttunen, "Humanitarianism," *AHR,* C (1995), 303; *Otsego Herald,* May 23, June 27, July 4, 18, 1805.

25. Elihu Phinney to Governor Morgan Lewis, July 12, 1805, and Jedediah Peck to Lewis, July 13, 1805, in New York State Assembly Papers, XXXIII, 893, 897, New York State Archives; *Otsego Herald,* May 23, June 27, July 4, 18, 1805.

26. [William Leete Stone], "Hiram Doolittle, Jun.," *Freeman's Journal* (Cooperstown, N.Y.), Sept. 21, 1829; *Otsego Herald,* July 25, Aug. 1, 1805; Cooper, "The Eclipse," *Putnam's Magazine,* 2d Ser., IV (1869), 355.

Tabitha that they might take warning." Attending Arnold's execution was a family affair, drawing men, women, and children keen to see their first legalized killing. The Middlefield blacksmith Luther Peck brought his young sons George and Luther, Jr., to Cooperstown for "the hangin.'" Ultimately, the crowd came to complete their voyeurism in Betsey's imagined pain by watching Arnold suffer public humiliation and death.[27]

In conducting Arnold's ritualized death, the Otsego authorities carefully cleaved to precedent, to the traditional conventions for the procession, religious service, last words, and fatal drop. Because new hinterland counties like Otsego bore unwanted reputations as social and cultural backwaters, the Otsego leaders were determined to prove their regularity by conducting a rigidly proper execution. At noon, Solomon Martin, the county sheriff, mounted his horse and led the formal parade that escorted the prisoner from the jail eastward along Second Street, past Otsego Hall and over the Susquehanna bridge to the gallows at the edge of town. The sheriff was followed in careful order by "the Reverend Clergy and other gentlemen," a band playing funeral dirges, a wagon bearing the prisoner seated on his coffin, and two companies of Cooperstown militia armed with muskets and bayonets. The ritualized procession symbolized the restoration of order and security after the violent rupture wrought by the murder of Betsey Van Amburgh. On execution day, the people received vivid instruction in the humiliating and fatal consequences of sin and crime. The solemn parade also affirmed that vengeance was the monopoly of the legal authorities. By surrounding and escorting the prisoner, the legal and religious leaders distinguished themselves from all others, who were rendered the audience; the audience's passive approval as witnesses was essential to the procession's success in reaffirming the legal order and in marginalizing private vengeance. But, although devoutly sought by the ministers and magistrates, this stark dichotomy between performers and audience proved elusive; the crowd insisted on their own activism in judging the proceedings.[28]

After crossing the bridge, Arnold, the sheriff, and the clergy took as their stage the wooden gallows newly built on the flat land beside the river. The militia stood guard around the raised platform. To the east, the ground ascended gradually to form "a vast natural amphitheatre filled with all gradations of citizens, from the opulent landlord to the humble laborer." Phinney marveled at the spectacle: "The display of about 600 umbrellas, of various colors; the undulating appearance of silks and muslins of different hues; the vibration of thousands of fans, in playful fancy . . . the roofs of the buildings,

27. *Albany Register,* Jan. 27, 1794; Peck, *Life and Times,* 30.
28. Jones, "Crime and Punishment," *New York History,* XLVII (1966), 264; *Otsego Herald,* July 25, 1805; Cohen, *Pillars of Salt,* 24–26; Masur, *Rites of Execution,* 26–27, 33–35.

which commanded a view, covered with spectators; the windows crowded with faces; every surrounding point of view occupied, and the gleam of swords, bayonets, etc. in the centre." On the periphery, peddlers worked the crowd, hawking gingerbread and water. At center stage, three grave clergymen solemnly conducted two prayers and delivered a brief sermon.[29]

Then it was Arnold's turn to perform. James Fenimore Cooper recalled, "I have seen other offenders expiate for their crimes with life, but never have I beheld such agony, such a clinging to life, such mental horror at the nearness of death, as was betrayed by this miserable man." Invited by the clergy to address the people, Arnold earnestly urged "them to improve by his fatal example, to place a strict guard upon their passions"—exactly what the clergy and sheriff wanted a condemned man to say in departing the planet. Projecting his own response onto the multitude, Phinney insisted that Arnold's penitent speech "drew forth the tears of sympathy from the surrounding spectators." But one of those spectators, George Peck, remembered the scene very differently: "Popular indignation was strong. A great concourse of people assembled on the hill-side east of the outlet of the lake, and, with lively satisfaction, waited to see the wretched man die."[30]

Placing the noose over Arnold's head, the sheriff drew taut "the fatal cord." The crowd grew tense and still, anticipating the sudden spring of the trap floor that would drop Arnold's body and snap his neck. At that climactic moment, Sheriff Martin pulled from his pocket and read aloud a letter from the governor postponing the execution indefinitely. Borne by a special courier, the letter had reached the sheriff in the morning, but he had decided to let the show proceed. Martin deemed it prudent to satisfy the crowd with a measure of the spectacle that they had come so far to see, from fear of a riot if he canceled the entire proceedings. To ensure convincing performances, especially by Arnold, Martin kept the letter secret until the fateful moment. As it turned out, he should have canceled the execution early in the day, before people's expectations had been aroused by the pageantry of impending death.[31]

Delighted with the reprieve (and concerned for Cooperstown's reputation), Phinney implausibly reported that the crowd "dispersed without any tumultuous conduct" and that "the village assumed its accustomed tranquility." In fact,

29. Jones, "Crime and Punishment," *New York History,* XLVII (1966), 264; [Stone], "Hiram Doolittle, Jun.," *Freeman's Journal,* Sept. 21, 1829; [Elihu Phinney], *Otsego Herald,* July 25, 1805.

30. [Phinney], *Otsego Herald,* July 25, 1805; Cooper, "The Eclipse," *Putnam's Magazine,* 2d Ser., IV (1869), 355; Peck, *Life and Times,* 31. For the formulas of criminal addresses, see Masur, *Rites of Execution,* 34–35, 41–42.

31. Peck, *Life and Times,* 30–31; [Phinney], *Otsego Herald,* July 25, 1805.

pandemonium erupted around the gallows. Arnold collapsed, and the shocked crowd clamored with angry disappointment. Indeed, Phinney contradicted himself in adding that, on his way back to prison, Arnold "requested that the Sheriff might command silence." Then Arnold "warned the multitude to govern their passions, declaring that ANGER had brought him to the shameful condition in which they saw him." Lacking Phinney's motives, George Peck recalled the scene in more vivid and telling detail:

> Wild excitement followed. Arnold fell as if he had been shot through the heart. Women shrieked; some of them wept aloud; some fainted; men raged and swore. The criminal was so detested for his cruelty that his escape from execution provoked a storm of fury. So indignant were the people that some rough fellows captured a dog, named him "Arnold," and hung him on the gallows which had failed to do justice to his namesake.

They were, after all, a thrifty, industrious people who did not like squandering a workday for no good end. "Many had come a great distance, their curiosity had been much excited, a day had been lost, besides incurring considerable expence, for which they had no corresponding return," Levi Beardsley remembered. Implicitly confirming Peck's account of the dog surrogate, Beardsley concluded that the crowd "acted and talked as if they must have a substitute." A third spectator concluded, "The multitude went grumbling homewards because of their disappointment," for "they had come to see a man hanged."[32]

Quite rightly, the people felt manipulated as well as deprived. They had played their expected role as spectators, deferring to the authority of the sheriff and clergy, only to be cheated of the dramatic death that had lured them into Cooperstown. Wrought up to an emotional crest by the procession and service, they had been denied the catharsis of completion. By cursing Arnold, heckling the sheriff, and hanging the dog, they reminded the authorities that an execution day was also the property of the common people, who brought their own expectations to the gallows. If leaders meant to retain their authority, they should not toy with audiences who had played their part so perfectly.

A public execution was supposed to restore familial order, which civil and religious leaders deemed essential to social and political stability. In 1799, the Reverend John McDonald had assured the villagers of Cooperstown that their families were "the pillars on which the edifice of government rests, and from their polish, order, and strength, the whole structure receives beauty and stability." Ministers and magistrates assumed that every criminal had fallen by

32. [Phinney], *Otsego Herald*, July 25, 1805; Peck, *Life and Times*, 31; Levi Beardsley, *Reminiscences; Personal and Other Incidents; Early Settlement of Otsego County . . .* (New York, 1852), 79; [Stone], "Hiram Doolittle, Jun.," *Freeman's Journal*, Sept. 21, 1829.

rebelling against parental instruction. It was a commonplace of printed confessions for convicts to lament their defiance of paternal authority as the root of their downfall. But, as a parent who killed in the act of disciplining a disobedient child, Arnold presented a paradox. Moreover, although his confession exhorted children to obey their parents without question, Arnold depicted his own father as unworthy and the font of his troubles. What instruction, then, did children take from Arnold's public humiliation? And what message did they receive from his sudden reprieve? What was reaffirmed: a child's right to disobey or a parent's right to punish?[33]

COMMUTATION

Because the governor had not pardoned Arnold but had merely postponed his execution, the prisoner returned to his dank, dark cell in the basement of the Otsego County jail. To discourage escape, the jailer manacled Arnold's hands and chained one leg to a heavy log. His notoriety and his conspicuous despair continued to attract the curious and continued to arouse their sympathy. In February 1806, Nathaniel Stacy took his fiancée, Susan Clark, to see the hated Arnold and to test her capacity to forgive. Stacy recalled that they found Arnold "in a state of helpless despair! and the deep dolorous groans that escaped from his dark cell, as we entered the jail, mingled with the rattling of his chains as he writhed about; were enough to appall the boldest spirit, and draw sympathy from a heart of stone! His wife was by his side; . . . a groan accompanied [his] every word, and his poor wife wept aloud!" Upon departing, Stacy asked the shaken Clark whether she still wished to see Arnold hang. " 'No' she said, bursting into tears, 'he has suffered enough; I wish they would let him go.' " The reply gratified Stacy, who had already become taken with Arnold's penitence.[34]

In late 1805 and early 1806, Arnold's sympathizers continued to write and petition the governor and state legislature seeking a pardon or, at least, the commutation of his sentence to life imprisonment. Led by the persistent Elihu Phinney, they argued that "once suffering the ignominy, the horror, and the certain anticipation of an immediate death, is sufficient to reclaim the of-

33. John McDonald, *The Duty of America Enforced: An Exhortation Delivered at Cooperstown, on the Evening of the National Fast, April 25th, 1799* (Cooperstown, N.Y., 1799), 89; "A Friend to the Rights and Duties of Men and Women," *Whitestown Gazette*, Oct. 25, 1796; Masur, *Rites of Execution*, 35–36; Arnold, *Life and Confession*, 19.

34. "Letter of E. Phinney, Esq., to the Governor" (Feb. 10, 1806), *Historical Magazine*, 2d Ser., VIII (1870), 301; Stacy, *Memoirs of the Life*, 163–164.

fender, to operate as an example, and to deter others from the commission of similar acts of barbarous cruelty."[35]

Arnold contributed a contrite petition to the state legislature and a confessional autobiography published by the obliging (and profit-seeking) Phinney. On the surface, Arnold said all the right things: he expressed profound sorrow and guilt while exhorting youths to pray, read the Bible, attend church, keep the Sabbath, obey their parents, eschew profanity and gambling, and, especially, to avoid vicious and licentious companions. More subtly, Arnold sowed mitigating and exculpating considerations through his text. He rooted his crime in a childhood ruined by indulgent parents and "the company of youths of corrupted morals"—those rowdy hired hands on the family farm. Arnold insisted, "It is to this vice that I alone attribute my own unhappy fate; it was not my choice, however, to associate with men of abandoned and profligate characters, but the situation of my father's business rendered it necessary." By failing to exercise patriarchal power to reform or exclude vicious laborers, Arnold's father was ultimately to blame for Betsey Van Amburgh's subsequent death in distant Burlington. Finally, Arnold also belied the sincerity of his contrition by smuggling into his confession a covert justification for the fatal beating:

> Little do children know the anxiety which they occasion their parents, and how afflicting to them is their misbehavior. . . . Nothing is more unbecoming in children than to exhibit a stubborn willfulness, and unwillingness to obey their parents when commanded. If indulged in this habit, they soon become of depraved dispositions, and seek means to inflict their parents rather than [to] comfort them.

Therefore, young people must strictly and promptly obey their parents' orders. Arnold championed the harsh discipline of the traditional New England patriarch.[36]

Closely examined, Arnold betrayed more determination to cheat death than sincerity to lament Betsey Van Amburgh's demise. Although his confession vociferously regrets the criminal act and his own plight, he barely mentions the victim, never describing her in life, never mentioning his own

35. [Phinney], *Otsego Herald*, Aug. 1, 1805, Feb. 20, 1806; "Letter of E. Phinney, Esq., to the Governor" (Feb. 10, 1806), *Historical Magazine*, 2d Ser., VIII (1870), 301; "To the Honorable, the Legislature of the State of New York . . . the Petition of the Subscribers, Freeholders and Inhabitants of the County of Otsego" [1806], Broadside Collections, box 1894, John Carter Brown Library, Providence, R.I.

36. [Stephen Arnold], "Petition of the Prisoner" (Feb. 1806), *Historical Magazine*, 2d Ser., VIII (1870), 301; Arnold, *Life and Confession*, 18–23.

sense of loss in her death. She is merely the unnamed object of his own rage: he refers to Betsey as "the child" or "it," never giving her a name. As Arnold tells the story, he is his own victim (or the victim of his parents and their laborers or the victim of the stubborn defiance of "the child"). Arnold implicitly portrays himself as the injured and misunderstood innocent undone by his association with more artful and more vicious men (and child)—a theme characteristic of self-presentation in the early Republic.[37]

Arnold shaped his confession and biography to manipulate his sympathizers. With more desperation than logic, Arnold sought a pardon by arguing that his painful, daily contrition was a greater and more enduring punishment than the execution he longed to avoid. Arnold also posed as an only son ruined by overly indulgent parents, even though he had a sister and two brothers back home in Rhode Island. Indeed, at his sentencing in June 1805, Arnold had sought a prolonged delay in his execution to permit his brothers to visit him. Heeding that plea, Kent allowed a six-week interim, which had proved critical to the successful petition drive that saved his life without a day to spare.[38]

Arnold's new friends were blind to the signs that he was manipulative—as well as in considerable real distress. Elihu Phinney proved especially gullible, despite, or because of, a conceited pride in his own cunning. After an interview with the convict in the jail cell, Phinney went into raptures when Arnold confided that his will would compensate the Burlington Committee for the two-hundred-dollar reward they had paid, "observing that they had done right." Paying "careful attention [to] his eyes, those faithful interpreters of the heart," Phinney concluded that Arnold was sincere. In fact, his will, written five days later, contained no such clause. Arnold's deception of Phinney confirms a point that Stephen Burroughs made so often and so cleverly in his famous and popular *Memoirs:* Yankees were peculiarly gullible because of their excessive pride in their own skepticism and because of their overreliance on reading the superficially visible. Did Phinney belatedly learn this lesson by 1810, when he published a condensed version of Burrough's popular and profitable *Memoirs?*[39]

37. Arnold, *Life and Confession,* 3, 19. For the ubiquitous theme of injured innocence, see Cohen, *Pillars of Salt,* 143–163; Robert A. Gross, "The Confidence Man and the Preacher: The Cultural Politics of Shays's Rebellion," in Gross, ed., *In Debt to Shays: The Bicentennial of an Agrarian Rebellion* (Charlottesville, Va., 1993), 313.

38. Arnold, *Life and Confession,* 3, 19; Phinney, ed., *Trial of Stephen Arnold,* 22; "Letter of E. Phinney, Esq., to the Governor" (Feb. 10, 1806), *Historical Magazine,* 2d Ser., VIII (1870), 301.

39. "Letter of E. Phinney, Esq., to the Governor" (Feb. 10, 1806), *Historical Magazine,* 2d Ser., VIII (1870), 301 (in his letter to the governor, Phinney referred to Arnold's three siblings); Stephen Arnold, last will and testament, written Feb. 15, 1806, and proved Apr. 16,

In early 1806, Governor Lewis again rallied to Arnold's cause, assuring the state legislature: "His right to correct the child cannot be contested—the instruments used were not unlawful." Arnold was guilty of manslaughter, not murder, Governor Lewis argued. Reacting cautiously, the legislature consented only to postpone Arnold's execution for another year, leaving him in the Otsego County jail—where James Fenimore Cooper found him during the eclipse of June 16, 1806. In March 1807, the legislature reviewed the case and commuted Arnold's death sentence to life imprisonment at hard labor. A month later, Arnold departed "the old dark and rotten dungeon" of the Otsego County jail, bound for "Newgate," the New York State prison located in Greenwich Village within New York City. There, at least, he could see the sun through the bars.[40]

The public remained much agitated over, and conflicted about, the commutation of Arnold's death sentence. In 1807, when Governor Lewis broke with the Republicans and ran for reelection as an independent (with Federalist support), his political foes made an issue of his prominent role in sparing Arnold's life. Posing as an offended mother, a Republican newspaper essayist argued:

> I live in a retired place in the country, and am obliged to send two of my little children to a school-house situated in a solitary place, under the care of such tutors as our neighbors are able to pick up; sometimes pretty good, and sober—sometimes vicious and passionate. Without a protector, out of the hearing of any neighbor, the only security of my dear little ones, against brutality and intemperence resides in the laws of the state and in the laws of God.

Blaming the governor, the author complained: "The murderer is yet on the land of the living. The blood of the innocent victim, whom he has tortured to death for a trifling fault, has called in vain for vengeance—*and that blood remains upon us.*" This rhetoric effectively combined a traditional biblical call for vengeance, lest God punish the entire community for the innocent blood spilled, with a newer sentimentality in which mothers could venture into the

---

1807, Otsego County Will Book, B, 114–115, Surrogate's Office, Cooperstown, N.Y.; Stephen Burroughs, *Memoirs of Stephen Burroughs* (1924; reprint, Boston, 1988); Cohen, *Pillars of Salt*, 155.

40. Governor Morgan Lewis, speech to the legislature, Jan. 28, 1806, *Otsego Herald*, Feb. 6, 1806; New York State, *Journal of the Assembly . . . Twenty-Ninth Session* (Albany, 1806), 11–13, 99, 102, 128, 130, *Thirtieth Session* (Albany, 1807), 242; New York State, *Journal of the Senate . . . Twenty-Ninth Session* (Albany, 1806), 120, *Thirtieth Session* (Albany, 1807), 109; *Otsego Herald*, Apr. 10, May 29, 1806, Mar. 19, 26, 1807; [New York State], *Laws of the State of New-York . . .* (Albany, 1809), chap. 56 (Mar. 21, 1807), 76.

public sphere to protect their innocent and fragile children. Bridging a culture in transition, this powerful appeal helped alienate the electorate from the governor. Although many Republican state legislators had supported the commutation, they successfully made Lewis the scapegoat for a public that wanted Arnold neither to live nor to die. In late April, a political neophyte, Daniel D. Tompkins, handily upset the sitting governor.[41]

MASKS

Everyone involved in the Arnold drama had reason to feel deceived. The participants took on shifting identities as they pursued and compounded their various miscalculations. Determined to win respect as an "old country" patriarch, Arnold ruled with a desperate and clumsy severity that instead rendered him a hated and hunted fugitive. The people of Burlington believed that they had secured an unusually self-disciplined and competent teacher—only to discover his homicidal rage. After tracking down the "Savage Ruffian," his Otsego neighbors learned that he was, in fact, the complete penitent. Indeed, he so convincingly vented his suffering and so thoroughly bore the sins of a deceitful world that hundreds of people, including most county leaders, longed to prolong his life. The grand jury foreman and assistant judge who helped convict Arnold thereafter became his champions for a pardon. He polarized the inhabitants into those who still saw him as a "monster in human shape" and those who reimagined him as the "unfortunate Arnold": a majority keen to see his death and an influential minority determined to spare his life. Arrested and convicted as a murderer, Arnold became, at last, a perverse "ornament of his country," the best-known and most compelling figure in his county. Twelve thousand came from far and near, crowding into Cooperstown, to hear him speak and see him die. Never before had anyone in Otsego County commanded such a large and rapt audience—no small accomplishment for an

41. "A Mother," *Albany Register*, Mar. 16, 1807; Desiah Van Amburgh Rolo, affidavit, Jan. 27, 1807, ibid., Apr. 9, 1807; *Republican Crisis* (Albany), Mar. 12, Apr. 6, 1807; "Learned Traveller," *Hudson Balance*, June 23, 1809; Beardsley, *Reminiscences,* 80; Jabez D. Hammond, *The History of Political Parties in the State of New York, from the Ratification of the Federal Constitution to December 1840,* 2 vols. (Albany, 1842), I, 231–232. For Republican support for commutation, see New York State, *Journal of the Senate . . . Thirtieth Session,* 109. During the gubernatorial election, Betsey's biological mother, Desiah Van Amburgh Rolo, made her only appearance in the historical record. She was still alive, in Burlington, and illiterate: she marked her document with an X instead of a signature. In an affidavit published in a newspaper hostile to Governor Lewis, she simply denied a rumor that she had signed the petition for Arnold's reprieve.

obscure and homely teacher. Following the standard conventions for his last speech, Arnold presented himself as a child gone astray, when in fact he was a parent who had grossly abused his patriarchal power. Relishing the first judicial killing in Otsego's history, thousands flocked to Cooperstown only to find that they were participants in an initially compelling but ultimately frustrating charade. Heeding petitions signed by hundreds and appeals from Otsego's leaders, Governor Lewis rescinded the execution, believing that he would win popular applause. Instead, he became a political pariah as disingenuous Republicans made him the scapegoat for the unpopular commutation that they helped legislate. Although Arnold had brutally beaten a helpless girl to death, he successfully posed as an injured innocent betrayed by his father, youthful companions, frontier students, and his stubborn victim. In his confession, Arnold aptly observed, "This is a deceitful world, which on first view appears to abound with sweets and flowers, but alas, too soon are they converted into thorns and thistles."[42]

Arnold's story illustrates the array of illusions and masks so characteristic of the early American Republic. In the many new towns emerging along the frontier, it was difficult to know whom to trust among the many strangers newly arrived from a diverse array of eastern towns. Stephen Arnold was one of many men who migrated to the frontier, seeking a new start far from most of those who knew his early missteps and frustrations. On the frontier, newcomers hoped to obtain more property and greater respect than they had known, or could ever obtain, in their old towns. The migrants found both opportunity and inspiration in the vast new lands newly conquered from the natives, in the proliferation of new political offices, and in the liberal rhetoric of the recent Revolution that invited common men to seek higher status, political influence, and increased prosperity. With more places and more reasons to go, Americans moved farther and more often than ever before, shifting into and out of a series of communities, where diverse strangers far outnumbered kin and old acquaintances. The rising velocity of movement and the increased competition for honors and resources meant that nothing seemed certain, stable, and predictable. In a new nation of strangers, nothing was quite what it seemed. Indeed, impostors, swindlers, con men, and counterfeiters proliferated in the many new towns of the early Republic, exploiting the pervasive uncertainty over character where there were so few old neighbors who could affix lasting reputations.[43]

42. Stacy, *Memoirs*, 163; Arnold, *Life and Confession*, 22.
43. Gordon S. Wood, "The Significance of the Early Republic," *Journal of the Early Republic*, VIII (1988), 1–20; Richard R. Beeman, *The Evolution of the Southern Backcountry:*

During the manhunt for the fugitive Arnold in the winter of 1805, two cunning farm laborers hit upon a clever scheme to obtain free food and drink from a tavern in Middlefield. One posed as a deputy sheriff and the other as his prisoner, the notorious Stephen Arnold. Eager to assist the alleged captor, who promised future compensation from the county, the tavernkeeper fed their horses, served the men two heaping meals, and poured them six drinks: two glasses each of gin, brandy, and rum. Subsequently detected and arrested, the putative Arnold landed in the Otsego County jail, occupying a cell next to the real Arnold; "a wooden partition is now all that parts them," Elihu Phinney commented. The play of false identities in the Arnold episode reached its absurd culmination in the laborer's attempt to impersonate a suspected murderer.[44]

In the end, Arnold assumed the ultimate mask: the utter anonymity of a distant penitentiary. Upon entering the state prison, never to depart, Arnold became legally dead. On April 16, 1807, the Otsego County surrogate approved Arnold's last will and testament bequeathing all his estate, real and personal, to his "beloved wife Susannah." That same day, she sold their Burlington farm for eight hundred dollars and subsequently moved to Middlefield. When the buyer defaulted, she foreclosed, and Elihu Phinney bought the property at auction for two hundred dollars. Apparently, he acted on her behalf, for she resold the same property for seven hundred dollars in March 1809. Although declared dead, Stephen Arnold was still alive in Newgate prison on December 31, 1810—when the surviving register for that prison ends and he disappears from the historical record.[45]

Paradoxically, Arnold's public performance as a suffering penitent won numerous and influential sympathizers who secured a commutation that meant

<hr />

A Case Study of Lunenburg County, Virginia, 1746–1832 (Philadelphia, 1984), 88–95; Andrew R. L. Cayton, "Land, Power, and Reputation: The Cultural Dimension of Politics in the Ohio Country," *William and Mary Quarterly*, 3d Ser., XLVII (1990), 266–286; Gross, "The Confidence Man and the Preacher," in Gross, ed., *In Debt to Shays's*, 303–309. For some disturbing consequences of the early Republic's geographic mobility and social upheaval, see also Daniel A. Cohen, "Homicidal Compulsion and the Conditions of Freedom: The Social and Psychological Origins of Familicide in America's Early Republic," *Journal of Social History*, XXVIII (1995), 725–764.

44. *People* v. *Eli Spears and Gardner Carpenter,* June 5, 1805, Otsego County Indictments, 1805 folder, Otsego County Clerk's Office, Cooperstown, N.Y.; *Otsego Herald,* July 17, 1806.

45. Stephen Arnold, last will and testament, Otsego County Will Book, B, 114–115; Otsego County Mortgages, C, 63, and Otsego County Conveyances, G, 291, K, 441, Otsego County Registry of Deeds; Newgate State Prison Ledger, 1797–1810, New York State Archives, Albany. For Arnold's final home, see W. David Lewis, "Newgate of New York: A Case History (1796–1828) of Early American Prison Reform," *New-York Historical Society Quarterly*, XLVII (1963), 137–172.

his incarceration in a distant prison, where he vanished from sight and publicity. After his removal to Newgate, Arnold's name never reappeared in the pages of the *Otsego Herald* or in any source other than the incomplete prison register. The reminiscences of four Otsego residents—Levi Beardsley, James Fenimore Cooper, George Peck, and William Leete Stone—discussed Arnold's story, but none seemed to know his ultimate fate. In the substitution of a secluded incarceration and indeterminate fate for a communal and finite ritual of public pain and death, Arnold lived out another important cultural transition of the early Republic: the invention of institutions meant to identify deviant people and isolate them. Indeed, by privatizing and prolonging punishment, the invention of the asylum helped to avoid the conflicts manifest in Otsego's divided response to Arnold; once secluded and forgotten, the prisoner could divert little empathy from memory of his victim. Hidden punishment preserved the stark dichotomy of monstrous criminal and tormented victim newly desired by the American public.[46]

EPILOGUE

There would be one last, lingering, and culminating inversion as one of the disappointed spectators later replaced Arnold as the county's first executed convict. Twenty-two years would pass after the Arnold fiasco before there was another murder trial and conviction in Otsego County. In December 1827, the state would successfully kill the convicted murderer, Levi Kelley, a cabinetmaker, who, as a resident of Cooperstown in 1805, must have attended Arnold's near-execution. Delighting in public executions, Kelley had traveled to Albany for a hanging there in August of 1827. Despite this supposedly edifying spectacle, just ten days later Kelley angrily shot through the heart a tenant who worked his farm outside Cooperstown. Kelley was the first and last person ritually hanged in Otsego County before New York State abolished public executions. Two decades after the Arnold spectacle, Kelley belatedly provided the county with the public death that he and his neighbors had felt cheated of in 1805.[47]

Kelley apparently fulfilled the fear of humanitarian reformers that scenes

46. Halttunen, "Humanitarianism," *AHR*, C (1995), 333–334; David J. Rothman, *The Discovery of the Asylum: Social Order and Disorder in the New Republic* (Boston, 1971); Michael Meranze, *Laboratories of Virtue: Punishment, Revolution, and Authority in Philadelphia, 1760–1835* (Chapel Hill, N.C., 1995).

47. Shaw T. Livermore, *A Condensed History of Cooperstown* (Albany, 1862), 140; Birdsall, *The Story of Cooperstown*, 201–210.

of public pain would brutalize spectators, compounding violence in society. Indeed, his quick resort to murder attests that public executions could no longer fulfill their traditional function of rallying a community to renew their covenant with a saving God. As humanitarian reformers saw more men and women treating public executions as a voyeuristic entertainment, they became resolved to privatize executions behind penitentiary walls far from an audience. In New York State, Kelley helped abolish the public executions that had been his fascination.[48]

Because Levi Kelley was James Fenimore Cooper's first cousin, he was buried in an unmarked grave within the Cooper family plot in the Christ Church cemetery at Cooperstown. In June 1806, Kelley probably stood beside his Cooper relatives to witness the solar eclipse, for his cabinetry shop lay on Fair Street—where that family watched the dimming sun. In December 1827, when Kelley died, James Fenimore Cooper was far away in Paris, but he certainly knew of his cousin's fate, and that knowledge probably informed his reminiscence of a previous convicted murderer and the eclipse of 1806. It is tempting to speculate that Levi Kelley was the "man of few words," who on June 16, 1806, led young James Fenimore Cooper to observe the jailed Arnold. This speculation has some plausibility because Kelley, like the mysterious guide, was taciturn, a family intimate, and especially fascinated with criminals and executions. Just as the eclipse transformed day to night, Kelley's preoccupation with public punishment eventually converted him into Arnold's substitute on the Otsego gallows.[49]

48. Halttunen, "Humanitarianism," *AHR*, C (1995), 330, 333–334; Masur, *Rites of Execution*, 88–90.

49. Wayne Wright, "The Cooper Genealogy: Compiled from Materials in the Collection of the New York State Historical Association Library," New York State Historical Association, Cooperstown, N.Y., 1983, typescript; Birdsall, *Story of Cooperstown*, 202–203.

THE SUICIDE OF A NOTARY:
LANGUAGE, PERSONAL IDENTITY,
AND CONQUEST IN COLONIAL
NEW YORK

Donna Merwick

Adriaen Janse van Ilpendam hanged himself in Albany, New York, on March 12, 1686. Dutch people called it "self-murder." It was a rare occurrence among them, both in New Netherland and the Low Countries. In Leiden, for example, the magistrates handled only thirty cases of self-murder during the whole of the seventeenth century. In the Albany area, the court recorded the case in 1677 of a woman who might have taken her own life in order to end the life of her unborn child. Otherwise, Janse was alone among the hundreds of people who had lived there since the 1630s and, as Dutch doctors of law put it, criminally robbed himself of his own life.[1]

We know nothing of the circumstances of Janse's dying. Whether he hanged himself in his house or walked outside beyond the town palisades—unseen? noticed by someone?—we do not know. No one recorded where his body was buried or by whom. Seven families paid for the Reformed church's pall that year. No one paid for him. We have to think that, following custom, no one tolled the bell, no one invited friends to the funeral. Earlier, in the summer of 1664 in New Amsterdam, one of the resident burghers hanged himself. His

I am grateful to Colleen and Rhys Isaac and to Greg Dening for reading earlier versions of this essay.

1. The date of Janse's suicide is given in Deposition of Willem Bancker, May 19, 1693, Notarial Archives 2342, Collections 51–69, Notary Jacob de Winter, Gemeentearchief Amsterdam (hereafter cited as GA). For reported suicides in Leiden, see inventory of H. M. van der Heuvel, De Criminele Vonnisboeken van Leiden, 1530–1811, Gemeentearchief Leiden (hereafter cited as GL). The Leiden data are supported by research on nearby Delft published as, Dirk Jaap Noordam, "Strafrechtspleging en criminaliteit in Delft in de vroegmoderne tijd," *Tjidschrift voor sociale geschiedenis*, XV (1989), 209–244. Extraordinary Session, Dec. 24, 1677, in A.J.F. van Laer, ed., *Minutes of the Court of Albany, Rensselaerswyck, and Schenectady, II, 1675–1680* (Albany, N.Y., 1928), 285 (hereafter cited as *CRA, 1675–1680*), presents the possible suicide of Maria Brill.

near neighbors successfully petitioned the burgomasters to give his body a decent burial. Whether anyone spoke for Janse, we do not know.[2]

Only one man that I know of has puzzled over Janse's suicide. Writing in the early twentieth century, he guessed that it was related to the English conquest of Janse's home, New Netherland, in 1664. Since Janse earned his livelihood as a notary by writing legal papers in Dutch, the increasing demand that they be written in English moved him to his tragic decision.[3]

The archivist was, I believe, correct. And perhaps he was right too in leaving the matter at that. I am still puzzled, however, at how it was that an imperial power's designs for territorial acquisition, military invasion and occupation, how these forces met with and made a casualty of so small a life as Janse's. England's grand visions did not include the obsolescence of his role as notary. They did not include his death. He was so incidental.

In a situation of colonial conquest, personal identities are redefined. The ways of natives become a scandal to the strangers. Their behaviors as workers, as wives, as worshipers are seen as contradictions. But, in the same exchange of meanings, the strangers are a contradiction to the natives. The new arrivals do not necessarily make the settled peoples feel inferior. Below the surface of acquiescence, resentment may privately persist, feeding off a more reflective sense of self-esteem and a determined identification with traditional ways. We cannot say that for Adriaen Janse the English conquest was a series of occurrences that fatally shook his self-esteem. Nothing tells us that he felt diminished as a member of the Reformed congregation. He appeared to be the same husband to his wife, the same friend to his neighbors. However, slender clues suggest that, as a man respected for his competency with language, the loss of that fluency was real. The professional edge it gave him as a legal scribe and as a counselor to townspeople about the law was gone.

I

On April 28, 1621, six men met in the rooms of the orphanmasters of Leiden to draw up a contract. Three officials appeared for the *weesvaders,* or guardians. Two friends accompanied a young hatmaker from Delft, Jan Janse van

2. For the suicide of Hendrick Janse Smitt in 1664, see Berthold Fernow, ed., *The Records of New Amsterdam from 1653 to 1674 Anno Domini,* V, *Minutes of the Court of Burgomasters and Schepens, Jan. 8, 1664, to May 1, 1666, Inclusive* (1897; reprint, New York, 1976), 93.

3. "Preface," in Arnold J. F. van Laer, ed., *Early Records of the City and County of Albany and Colony of Rensselaerswyck,* III, trans. Jonathan Pearson, New York State Library, History Bulletin 10 (Albany, N.Y., 1918), 17 (hereafter *ER3*).

Ilpendam. He was there to arrange matters on behalf of his thirty-month-old son Adriaen. The child's mother had died several months before and provided a small sum for his upbringing. The usual businesslike contract was agreed upon. The sum would be invested by the orphanmasters and kept until the boy married or was twenty-five years of age. His name was put on their books and kept there until at least 1646. Their definition of him was among the first of all the descriptions—those made of Adriaen Janse by others, those made by himself—that would give him his self-identity. He was written down as "Jan Janse's orphan."[4]

Adriaen Janse's father appears to have been something of a rolling stone. By the time the boy was eight, Jan had remarried and was soon working the small ships plying the country's rivers, canals, and inland seas. He had moved his family out along the Mare, Leiden's most distant encircling canal. Yet the course of his career would soon lead him farther and farther from Leiden. The city was responding to the allure of the Indies and untold wealth. Along with thousands of others, he too yielded to that call, casting his fortunes with the newly formed overseas trading venture, the West India Company.[5] Everyone knew that doing so was like trying your luck on the stock market. It could mean great profits. Or it could mean entering the bankruptcy chamber in the Amsterdam town hall and reflecting on its ominous reliefs: scenes of empty chests and unpaid bills strewn around a room filled with scuttling and hungry rats.

By 1635, Jan Janse was in the service of the company. He was working the Recife coast of Portuguese Brazil as a supercargo on the yacht *Pernambuco*. Yachts were armed cruisers. They menaced the coast, sometimes supporting large military operations, at other times engaging in hit-and-run attacks on forts or sugar plantations. Everyone on them was in danger. In 1636, at Porto Calvo, Jan Janse was taken prisoner. Somehow he earned his release and returned to Amsterdam. There he petitioned the company directors for back pay and was refused. Still, the company had plans for him. He would sail for New Netherland on *Rensselaerswijck*, a vessel being fitted out for almost immediate departure.[6] In September 1636, he found himself with Captain Jan Tiepkesz as

4. Penningboek van de Weeskamer, May 6, 1646, 7e PB, f. 133vo., GL. For a biographical sketch of Jan Janse van Ilpendam, see H. M. Kuypers, "Jan Joachimsz. van Ilpendam, een Leidse bezitter van de Barbara-prebende in de 16de eeuw," *Genealogische bijdragen Leiden en omgeving*, VII (1992), 476–479.

5. See Kuypers, "Jan Joachimsz," *Genealogische bijdragen Leiden en omgeving*, VII (1992), 477–478, and William J. Hoffman, "An Armory of American Families of Dutch Descent: Van Lodensteyne," *New York Genealogical and Biographical Record*, LXVI (1935), 376–382.

6. Janse's exploits in Brazil and his return to Holland are briefly mentioned in Kuypers, "Jan Joachimsz," *Genealogische bijdragen Leiden en omgeving*, VII (1992), 478, and I. N.

the commander took the ship from Amsterdam to Texel and joined it to a fleet of twenty-two vessels making their way down the channel. It was five and a half months before the ship reached what they simply called "the Manhatans."[7] There Jan Janse probably found what he expected: a fort with walls of mud as much as stone, several warehouses, a scattering of workplaces for company employees. Nothing much to be seen. Still, it was what it should have been: a fortified anchorage for oceangoing vessels and a trading station for commerce with the indigenous peoples. Eventually—if profits made remaining worthwhile—the fort's walls would be properly reinforced and expanded to enclose other spaces: houses for traders of other nations, marketplaces, a church, all the customary buildings of the workers' quarters, ship repair shops. It was all a matter of future trade. Here in New Netherland that meant furs. Everyone was into the trade in one way or another. Many traded illegally.

Jan Janse allowed himself to become one of the illegal traders. Within a year, he was caught defrauding Kiliaen van Rensselaer, a brilliant entrepreneur who had established a patroonship (or *colonie*) on the Hudson River. He was required to make repayment but seemed to be as dismissible as his misdeed. "Jan Janse van Ilpendam," van Rensselaer wrote to one of his officers: "This man is in the service of the Company. If he pays you, I have nothing to say about him."[8] Three years later, in 1641, he was appointed commissary at Fort Nassau along the Delaware River. He was in charge of the company's trading goods and furs. In its customary way, the company was advancing him up the ranks by giving him command of a fortified outpost. His commission, however, took him to a place of violence. The river and the wilderness were distant meeting places for traders, mercenaries, river Indians, Swedes, English, and Dutch. Yet it was not the violence of the place or the riverine pirates that soon undid him. It was his own dishonesty. He was found to be defrauding the company by carrying on his own trade and benefiting private traders. By 1645, he was in court on Manhattan Island defending himself. Yet he did it badly: he seemed

---

Phelps Stokes, *The Iconography of Manhattan Island, 1498–1909* . . . (New York, 1915–1928), IV, 84. A more elaborate context for his experiences is found in S. P. L'Honore Naber, ed., *Joannes de Laet: Jaerlyck Verhael van de Verrichtingen der Geoctroyeerde West-Indische Compagnie in derthien Boecken*, III ('s-Gravenhage, 1934), 84, 108, 136, 197, 204–213, and S. P. L'Honore Naber and J.C.M. Warnsinck, eds., *Joannes de Laet: Jaerlyck Verhael van de Verrichtingen der Geoctroyeerde West-Indische Compagnie in derthien Boecken*, IV (s'Gravenhage, 1937), 25–31, 152–161, 212–216. See also C. R. Boxer, *The Dutch in Brazil, 1624–1654* (Oxford, 1957), 58–70.

7. Log of the ship *Rensselaerswyck*, in A.J.F. van Laer, ed., *Van Rensselaer–Bowier Manuscripts, Being the Letters of Kiliaen van Rensselaer, 1630–1643, and Other Documents Relating to the Colony of Rensselaerswyck* (Albany, N.Y., 1909), 355–389 (hereafter cited as *VRBM*).

8. Kiliaen van Rensselaer to Jacob Albertsz Planck, May 12, 1638, *VRBM*, 417.

not to be trying very strenuously, or he was again dealing carelessly with his life. Within months, he was condemned for "grossly wronging" the company and ordered to Holland for final judgment. However, before he could face banishment, further interrogation, and punishment, some time before August of 1647 both he and his wife died on Manhattan Island.[9]

Four years later, two young Amsterdam men testified that, yes, they knew Jan Janse. When he died, he left behind "more debts than profits." And they knew his son Adriaen. He had to refuse all association with his father's estate in order to protect himself from creditors. They knew something more about him. He too was at "the Manhatans." He was a schoolmaster.[10]

Janse has left in mystery how and why he came to the New World and why he chose to be a schoolmaster, a life so different from his father's, a career that affirmed the structures that Jan Janse seemed determined to flout. An admired writer on Dutch schooling, Dirck Adriaensz Valcooch, expected such a man to be nothing less than meek.[11] Yet Janse betrays some idea of the way he meant to fashion his life in 1649. He had been in New Netherland for about two years and now had his family and business concerns in Leiden in the forefront of his mind. Leiden was something of a lodestar, and it would continue to be for the remainder of his life. Or, rather, the magnetic point was an uncle, David Janse van Ilpendam, who lived there until 1644. David's remembrance of him in his last will and testament was a reality to which the young man returned for strength again and again.

David Janse might have been the young man's "Dutch uncle" in the full meaning of that term. His two sons had died in 1635, exactly the year when Jan Janse entered the service of the West India Company and chose, or found it necessary, to leave his son Adriaen fatherless. They shared, too, a way of being bookish. In all the moments when Adriaen Janse left a trace on the pages of New Netherland history, he was teaching, looking for employment as a scribe of some kind, or getting a commercial world on paper as a notary. In this he was as much like David Janse as anyone who would come into his life.

As much as it did the cloth industry, Leiden took pride in its university. Adjuncts to the university were the nearby bookstores. The books in the great library of the university were pointed to with extraordinary pride; similarly

---

9. Entry of Feb. 8, 1646, in Kenneth Scott and Kenn Stryker-Rodda, eds., *New York Historical Manuscripts: Dutch*, IV, Arnold J. F. van Laer, trans., *Council Minutes, 1638–1649* (Baltimore, 1974), 299; see also 282, 285–286, 289, 297.

10. Deposition of Willem Thomas and Jan Hendrickss, Dec. 8, 1651, Not. Arch. 2279, III, fol. 18, Nots. Jac. de Winter, GA.

11. D. Wouters and W. J. Visser, *Geschiedenis van de opvoeding en het onderwijs vooral in Nederland* (Groningen, 1926), 90.

valued were those trafficked in nearby bookshops like "Solomon's Temple" and, also within walking distance, the shop of David Janse. His establishment was on Breestraat, one of Leiden's best streets. He was in fact also a publisher, and his widow continued the business after his death.[12]

In 1640, David Janse signed his name to the last of seven folio pages that were *not* displayed in his shop for the pleasure of bibliophiles but were his last will and testament. Among other stipulations, he bequeathed one thousand guilders to each of six young members of the family. Among them was Adriaen Janse.

Jacob Franz van Merwen notarized the document. He was one of at least thirty-one notaries practicing in a city whose commercial enterprises were generating notarized papers in which tens of thousands of guilders were being negotiated.[13] Such attestations were made for local merchants traveling or dispatching agents to cities like Bruges or Hamburg and for strangers arriving to conduct business in this and other Dutch mercantile centers. For all, the proof of good faith was the signature of the licensed notary. Although the real professionalization of the *notariaat* did not occur until the eighteenth century, notaries were already essential to the Dutch domestic economy and overseas empire. Seventeenth-century city governments were careful to restrict their ranks to trustworthy men. They regulated their fees, established rules for their protocols, and policed the requirement that they write acts only for those known to them. Apprenticeships, examinations, surveillance of notaries' private lives—all were measures adopted to ensure that burghers could proceed in their affairs confident of the notary's reputation and of what he had put in writing.[14] Kiliaen van Rensselaer would have spoken for most merchants, and

12. The establishment of David Janse is listed in J. A. Gruys and C. de Wolf, *Thesaurus, 1473–1800: Nederlandse boekdrukkers en boekverkopers, met plaatsen en jaren van werkzaamheid [Dutch Printers and Booksellers, with Places and Years of Activity]* (s'Gravenhage, 1989), 257. Kuypers offers sketchy information on David Janse taken largely from public records; see "Jan Joachimsz," *Genealogische bijdragen Leiden en omgeving*, VII, no. 4 (1992) 477. J. J. Orlers wrote a fascinating guidebook to Leiden and commented on the university library, *Beschrijvinge der Stad Leyden, inhoudende 't begin den voortgang, ende den wasdom der selver: De stichtinge van de kerken, cloosteren, gasthuysen, ende andere publycque gestichen, etc., desgelijcx de oprechtinge van de Academie, ende de Collegien Theologie . . .* (Leyden, 1641), 180–195. For Leiden's bookfairs, see B. van Selm, *Een menighte treffelijcke boeken: Nederlandse boekhandelscatalogi in het begin van de zeventiende-eeuw* (Utrecht, 1987), 31–42.

13. Van Merwen's papers from 1633 to 1644 are held in Oude Notariele Archief, Nos. 533–542, GL. See Testament de eersmen David Jansz. van Ilpendam ende de eerbare Aefjen Dammasdr. vander Horn echteluijden, 1640 juni 20 [inventory number 538, f. 29ro.], GL.

14. The work of the Dutch historian A. Pitlo provides entry into the compendious literature on the *notariaat*. Especially useful are *De zeventiende en achttiende eeuwsche*

Dutch people generally, in praising his specialist skills. "Oral promises" were either useless or the work of papists. Memory was fallible. Precisely "because words are forgotten or can be twisted," he wrote, "written instruments are made."[15]

A family notary like van Merwen often drew up such instruments knowing they were likely to be tried before the courts. Municipal courts in places like Amsterdam or Leiden were in effect courts merchant. They met with remarkable frequency and were conducted by magistrates who were ordinarily merchants and who expected litigants or their notaries to have accounts or notarized acts to present as legal evidence. They moved cases quickly, encouraging settlement by arbitration, but in all instances unashamedly serving the interests of their own and other merchant communities. There was no national sovereign law. It was local, with magistrates calling upon a limited set of commentaries on Roman law and early Dutch rulings but essentially interpreting law in order to protect all classes in their immediate community—especially merchants. English observers in the Low Countries had no difficulty understanding the purposes and widespread acceptance of such courts. But by the mid-seventeenth century, the difference between them and their own courts was becoming marked. And although not all commentators were as critical of courts merchant as Sir William Blackstone in his later *Commentaries on the Laws of England* (1765–1769), his appraisal was gaining ground: "Merchants ought to take their law from the [common law] courts, and not the courts from the merchants." They should not be allowed to suppose that "their crude and new-fangled fashions . . . become the law of the land." Sir Edward Coke had argued earlier that law merchant was merely "foreign law."[16]

---

notarisboeken; en wat zij ons omtrent ons oude notariaat leeren (Haarlem, 1948), and *Taal en stijl der notariële akten* (Wageningen, 1953). Others who detail the social history of the profession are Wim Heersink, '*Van oude tijden bij alle volkeren geacht*': *Amsterdamse notarissen van schriftafel tot schepenbank, 1600–1800,* in Sjoerd Faber, ed., *Nieuwe licht op oude justitie: misdaad en straf ten tijde van de republiek* (Muiderberg, 1989), 48–64; H. A. Warmelink, *De notarissen, de calligraphie en de drukkunst: de bibliographie van het notariaat* (Wageningen, 1952); A. Fl. Gehlen, *Het Notariaat in het tweeherig maastricht: Een rechtshistorische schets van de inrichting en practijk van het maastrichtse notariaat vanaf zijn opkomst tot ann het einde van de tweeherigheid over de stad* (Assen, 1981).

15. Kiliaen Van Rensselaer to Johannes Megapolensis, Mar. 13, 1643, *VRBM,* 648.

16. Blackstone and Coke, quoted in Daniel R. Coquillette, "Legal Ideology and Incorporation, II: Sir Thomas Ridley, Charles Molloy, and the Literary Battle for the Law Merchant, 1607–1676," *Boston University Law Review,* LXI, pt. 1 (1981), 354; and "Legal Ideology and Incorporation, III: Reason Regulated—The Post-Restoration Civilians, 1653–1735," *Boston University Law Review,* LXVII, pt. 1 (1987), 296. Coquillette and the following authorities are useful because they compare early modern England and the Low Countries on interna-

To the Dutch, of course, their operative laws of the land had nothing to do with crude and newfangled fashion. So the courts of newly established overseas cities and towns like New Amsterdam and Beverwijck in New Netherland were courts merchant as well. As they did at home, court secretaries hastened to sessions twice, sometimes three times, a week. The pages of their minutes filled up with stories of aggrieved plaintiffs and uneasy defendants often disputing the sort of matters that come before small claims tribunals today. They also told tales about the clerks themselves and the legal system they actualized, about the proprieties of keeping detailed minutes, about meeting the protocols of recordkeeping at home. And until 1669 when he became a notary and gave us pages and pages of stories about himself, court secretaries inscribed accounts of Janse, the only ones we have.

Sometime before 1647 when he first appeared in New Netherland, Janse copied the will that van Merwen had so meticulously composed. We know that Janse could read and write and was confident that he would understand the will's legal words and meanings. But there is nothing to tell us of his education. Perhaps he already aspired to be a notary. Everyone knew that for someone who had earned great honor as a doctor of law being a notary was a step down: comparatively, he was a lesser functionary. But for many it was a step up. Having some knowledge of provincial laws and perhaps a bit of Latin made a young man (as scholars would say later) a "half-intellectual."[17] The office often carried even greater respect in the overseas stations, where doctors of law and a sizable bureaucracy were often absent. At the same time, everyone knew too that being a notary was almost a family affair. A father passed on his clients to his son or nephew, and so it went, from one generation to the next. This was happening in Leiden. It would not happen to Janse.

In 1649 on Manhattan Island, Janse was putting his life in order. He arranged with a friend who was sailing to Holland to make inquiries about his inheritance. He closed off whatever chapter of his life he had shared with his father, publicly acknowledging Jan's failure to provide for him. Citing a saying filled with as much meaning about a shattered personal relationship as an encumbered estate, he declared that he had "kicked . . . [his father's estate]

---

tional law: R. C. van Caenegem, "The English Common Law: A Divergence from the European Pattern," *Tijdschrift voor rechtsgeschiedenis,* XLVII, no. 1 (1979), 1–7; Leon E. Trakman, "The Evolution of the Law Merchant: Our Commercial Heritage," *Journal of Maritime Law and Commerce,* XII (Oct. 1980), 1–24, and "The Evolution of the Law Merchant: Our Commercial Heritage—Part II," *Journal of Maritime Law and Commerce,* XII (Jan. 1981), 153–182; Jonathan Clark, "Sovereignty: The British Experience: Blackstone, Bentham, and the Origins of Parliamentary Absolutism," *Times Literary Supplement,* Nov. 29, 1991, 15–16.

17. Pitlo, *Zeventiende en achttiende eeuwsche notarisboeken,* 7.

away with his foot."[18] Instead, he was making his way as a local trader's servant—and perhaps trading a bit himself—and earning something as a schoolmaster. Yet the times were difficult, full of dissension. The previous director general had created chaos in the community, even war with the natives, and now Petrus Stuyvesant had arrived to bring some order. He was only thirty-seven and had not had much success. Disputes raged between the company and the local merchants who were growing powerful and who recognized that it was time Stuyvesant provided them with the safeguards that had always protected the affairs of entrepreneurs in Dutch port cities. They demanded to be denizens of an independent city.

Janse did not take sides. Fate, he might well have thought, had brought him to New Netherland when others *were* taking sides vengefully. They turned to writing, composing their lengthy remonstrances against Stuyvesant and sending them off to Holland. Writing had become a kind of sorcery. To see the end of a wicked man, it was only necessary to fashion a damaging representation of him, a deadly word doll, and run him through there. The company and the States-General were always in the market for observations. Written information was a commodity they could not resist. Especially letters about their officials, their good behavior or their treachery, were warmly received. They could see the future of New Netherland, and its profits, only in reports and accounts, in the empire of signs. In the early 1650s, the States-General read the merchants' complaints and shared their conviction that the hesitant probing of the wilderness was giving way to the customary structures of trade: long-term credit, joint partnerships, the appearance of some wholesale merchants, overseas investment. They determined that Stuyvesant was throttling this and overruled him by effectively redefining New Netherland. They established New Amsterdam as a city and made it the "capital" of the province.[19] At the same time, they set the stage for the everyday practices that would ensure its independence. A court of burgomasters and *schepen*, or aldermen, was allowed—and they sent the merchants their first notary.

This hopeful future was to Janse's advantage. He had begun to live as a

18. Kenneth Scott and Kenn Stryker-Rodda, eds., *New York Historical Manuscripts: Dutch*, III, Arnold J. F. van Laer, trans., *Register of the Provincial Secretary, 1648–1660* (Baltimore, 1974), 166.

19. "Additional Observations on the Preceding Petition," July 26, 1649, in E. B. O'Callaghan, ed., *Documents Relative to the Colonial History of the State of New-York* . . . (hereafter cited as *DRCH*), I (New York, 1856), 265 n. 11. Henri van der Zee and Barbara van der Zee, *A Sweet and Alien Land: The Story of Dutch New York* (New York, 1978), 109–234, offer a readable account of this period, but the documents printed in *DRCH* give the best sense of it. See also Oliver A. Rink, *Holland on the Hudson: An Economic and Social History of Dutch New York* (Ithaca, N.Y., 1986), 172–213.

schoolmaster. The company's insatiable craving to get things in writing was now clear. Merchants and many tradespeople had the same need, even farmers. There was a good market for the ABC's and legible writing and numeracy. Officials were expected to cooperate with local churchmen in establishing schools, and private schools for the younger children were available. Janse chose to conduct one of these and seems to have been a good schoolmaster. He went by the rules: he did not keep an inn, collect the excise on spirits, or write legal documents, especially in a public house. He was called "Master" and was, like the minister, expected to keep in mind that he was a public figure. We have to think that it would have been noticed if he had tarnished the schoolmaster's reputation. People would have talked, and it would have come to the court's attention. Stuyvesant's secretary, Cornelis van Tienhoven, had done that, brought disrespect upon the office of secretary. Partly it was his greed, but people also saw him running around like a native, almost naked, they said. It was lewd. Such "loose people" provoked them into thinking about the place as a "wild . . . country."[20]

If Janse was earning modest approval, he was nonetheless not earning a substantial income. There were only about 120 households on Manhattan Island, so perhaps there were no more than two hundred children and, among these, only a portion would have been of lower-school age. He had at least two competitors for pupils; there might also have been dame schools. Even in ten years' time and when the population was almost tripled, a master would think himself fortunate to have twenty-five pupils. Adriaen Janse probably had closer to fifteen. With the fee set at between 8 and 16 guilders for the year's four quarters of instruction, his income would not have exceeded 240 guilders. It would have met the cost of renting a small house—something like 52 guilders a year—and little more than the necessities of bread and beer. The earnings of a cartman in 1658 (2.10 guilders a day, when he had a day's work) were more than his.

20. "Remonstrance of New Netherland, and the Occurences There . . . ," Oct. 13, 1649, in *DRCH*, I, 309. William Heard Kilpatrick, *The Dutch Schools of New Netherland and Colonial New York* (Washington, D.C., 1912), offers the best synthesis of schooling during the period, although his work has minimal interpretive value; see 111, 118, 120–122, for Adriaen Janse. E. van Vechten's not entirely reliable study picked up Janse as well; see *Early Schools and Schoolmasters of New Amsterdam*, 2d Ser., II, Maud Wilder Goodman et al., eds., *Historic New York* (1897–1898; reprint, Port Wasington, N.Y., 1969), 328. Because of inadequate sources, much about schooling has to be inferred from prescriptive material on education in the Low Countries. Most commentators rely on Dirck Adriaensz Valcooch; see Pieter Antonie de Planque, *Valcooch's Regel der Duytsche Schoolmeesters: Bijdrage tot de kennis van het schoolwezen in de zestiende eeuw* (Groningen, 1926). I found it helpful to consider matters of education in New Amsterdam with Walter J. Ong's work on Petrus Ramus in mind; see "Ramist Method and the Commercial Mind," in *Rhetoric, Romance, and Technology: Studies in the Interaction of Expression and Culture* (Ithaca, N.Y., 1971), 171, 173.

In 1650, the colonists of van Rensselaer's patroonship—some 120 miles up-river from Manhattan Island—decided their children needed proper school-ing. For some reason, they knew of Janse. He was called, and he accepted. In the course of their discussions, the colonists had defined the schoolmaster's importance in a way that undoubtedly accorded with the thinking of the New Amsterdam parents whom he had left behind. They lived, they reminded themselves, in a "republic."[21] The presence of a schoolmaster brought order to such a way of living. They said this, but they did not elaborate further.

Janse began a life on the margins of Dutch settlement but nonetheless within the recurring cycles of living at Rensselaerswijck. He learned about the trading season and the routines of the farmers. He became part of the slowed-down activities of winter and, because it had become something in which all were caught up, the contest for control of the fur trade, carried on between the resident director of the patroonship and the company's officers at their trading station, Fort Orange. It had become a dangerous game of chess, with the direc-tor even claiming the land on which the fort was built. But the game changed early in 1652. Stuyvesant took the chess pieces into his own hands. There would be an independent fort and a town around it; beyond would be van Rensse-laer's lands. Those who wished might be burghers of the town and, subject to company regulations, free to trade. Let the new *peltrij handelaars,* the dealers in furs, make of the town what they would. He named it Beverwijck.

Stuyvesant's first act was to set up a court. Through it, the new magistrates dispensed justice. Over the years, the notion of an additional assembly or town meeting townspeople seemed never to entertain; never once did they gather together politically as a community. They sought their rights, as they did so much else, individually or as families, within the walls of the courtroom. In four months' time, Janse put his name forward as secretary of the court. He proposed that as a schoolmaster he was suitably credentialed, and he must have felt that he could follow the procedures of the court and fulfill the pro-tocols of keeping minutes. The magistrates supported him, but Stuyvesant felt the presiding officer could keep his own records.[22] Janse did not put his name forward again. Also at some point during these or earlier months, he married.

21. G. Beernink, *De Geschiedschrijver en Rechtsgeleerde Dr. Arend van Slictenhorst en zijn vader Brant van Slictenhorst, Stichter van Albany, Hoofdstad van der Staat New-York* (Arn-hem, 1916), 294; Ext. Sess., Nov. 28, 1650, in A.J.F. van Laer, ed., *Minutes of the Court of Rensselaerswyck, 1648–1652* (Albany, N.Y., 1922), 132; see also Arthur James Weise, *The History of the City of Albany, from the Discovery of the Great River in 1524, by Verrazzano, to the Present Time* (Albany, N.Y., 1884), 91.

22. Ordinary Session, Aug. 6, 1652, in A.J.F van Laer, ed., *Minutes of the Court of Fort Orange and Beverwyck, 1652–1656* (Albany, N.Y., 1920), 29 (hereafter cited as *CMFO*).

His wife, Tryntje Jans, was a widow. She was not of an important family, and that undoubtedly said that he too was socially unimportant. They were not blessed with children. Within eighteen months, however, he owned land.

Over the next eight years, Janse established himself as a trustworthy burgher of Beverwijck. By 1660, the market town probably had more than a hundred households. He was now the owner of a house lot and brickyard; he was a schoolmaster and probably a small-time trader. These were elements of a strange self-fashioning, one might think. In one way, however, they were the cards he was playing in the risky game of survival that everyone in Beverwijck had to pull up a chair to join. Others played with different cards: a yacht, a pair of partnerships, three properties. No one could know when or why a fellow player's hand would change, with a lot discarded for a cargo of merchandise or a brickyard purchased. Staying in the game meant not showing one's hand. In another way, these portfolios of investments or employments were a stimulus to the imagination.[23] They let a man or woman experience a range of skills and practical knowledge.

The community was growing. The trade in furs fluctuated but was still generating wealth. The town palisades now enclosed about twenty-four acres; the population was nearly six hundred men, women, and children. Access to New Amsterdam and destinations in Holland was easy and well organized. As the market developed, the burghers wanted the protection of business papers properly notarized. In 1660, they welcomed the arrival of the first notary, Dirck van Schelluyne. Immediately his skills were in demand. Townspeople came at all hours of the day: 8:00 in the morning, 4:00 in the afternoon, 9:00 in the evening. They found him every day of the week but mostly on Tuesdays and Saturdays. Over the next four and a half years, he drew up at least 321 docu-

---

23. For Janse's propertyownership, see, inter alia, Jonathan Pearson, ed., *Early Records of the City and County of Albany, and Colony of Rensselaerswyck (1656–1675)* (Albany, N.Y., 1869), 56–57, and see 7, 183 n. 1, 228, 229, 440, 452–453. The Huntington Library holds the original of Stuyvesant's land grant to Janse dated simply October 1653. A transcript is in the Special Collections, New York State Library, Albany. The location of his house and lot (and another he rented) can be pieced together only from scattered and inconclusive data; see A.J.F. van Laer, ed., *Early Records of the City and County of Albany and Colony of Rens-selaerswyck, IV, Mortgages 1, 1658–1660, and Wills 1–2, 1681–1765,* trans. Jonathan Pearson, New York State Library, History Bulletin 11 (Albany, N.Y., 1919), 154–157 (hereafter cited as *ER4*); Jonathan Pearson, *Diagrams of the Home Lots of the Village of Beverwyck,* in Joel Munsell, ed., *Collections on the History of Albany from Its Discovery to the Present Time, with Notices of Its Public Institutions, and Biographical Sketches of Citizens Deceased, IV* (Albany, N.Y., 1871), 203. For evidence of Janse's keeping a day and night school, see Ord. Sess., Feb. 2, 1655, *CMFO,* 200. For the relationship between by-employments and imagination, see A. Th. van Deursen, *Het kopergeld van de Gouden Eeuw III: Volk en overheid* (Assen, 1979), 28.

ments, but of these he also made an untold number of copies. In 1662 alone, he met with 196 contracting parties and 101 witnesses. A large number of his clients and witnesses were literate, 78 percent of the men and 40 percent of the women: they could sign their names.[24]

In 1669 and at the age of fifty-one, Adriaen Janse qualified as a notary. It is impossible to know how he acquired this learning, although probably he apprenticed himself to van Schelluyne, whose routine was certainly demanding enough to require a clerk. In any case, when van Schelluyne left the town in about 1668, Janse took up the role that he had played.[25] It was a role that took Janse from one day's small drama with clients to another. Small ceremonies they were. But they bound him closely to the past—to the past of the *notariaat*, to the past of the town and people's lives. They lent dignity to his relations with the townspeople. Taken together, the brief encounters comprised much of what was important in his world.

For those of us who see some connection between the construction of self and cultural performances, the words that initiated each of Janse's acts must have a ringing significance. At the top of each page, he wrote, "Appeared before me," and then named himself, sometimes the magistrates, and always those seeking his assistance and witnesses. The phrase can be regarded as simply a prefabricated word cluster that ensured the act's authentication. Nonetheless, it also described a tableau, the coming together of people in a meeting in which Janse became, not just a player, but a leading figure.

The notary assembled a clutch of men and women who had come before him, settled into known parts—as vendor, buyer, or deponent—and taken up their lines. He incited storytelling, looking for the particulars of the narratives—*verhaelstof* they called it. So in 1672, Janse elicited from two men the terms of a partnership in a brewery: exact details about purchase money and the laying in of grain, the responsibilities of one partner's young son. On another occasion, he enticed details from witnesses to an alleged act of fornication. One witness said he saw the young couple "go into the garret together." Another: the young woman said, "Well, Roelof, how shall this go? I am preg-

---

24. Van Schelluyne's papers have been edited and given revised translations by A.J.F. van Laer in *ER3*, 29–308. Like Janse's papers, they are not complete; van Laer conjectures that they were somehow given into Janse's care (15). Van Schelluyne served as notary from 1660 to 1665, after which he was for some time town secretary. Martha Dickinson Shattuck, "A Civil Society: Court and Community in Beverwijck, New Netherland, 1652–1664" (Ph.D. diss., Boston University, 1993), has tested the level of literacy in Beverwijck using a larger sample and supplies the figures of 66% for males and 49% for females (59–61).

25. Janse's papers were collected and published by van Laer in *ER3*, 308–588.

nant."[26] Either during the play or later, Janse transformed such narrative fragments into legal prose.

The papers that Janse inscribed became his notarial register. They were kept in his house and preserved in the confidentiality required by his oath as notary. In a way, they made him a town archivist. He was a custodian of the town's written past. Clients, of course, could come to him for copies of documents inscribed on their behalf. A written page cost about a guilder. For the legal protection they offered, such acts were highly prized. However, the *look* and *form* of the papers were valued as well. We know from Jan van Eyck's *Arnolfini Portrait* (1434) that the artist inscribed his name in the painting in the manner of a notary in order to enlarge its merit as a marriage *document*. And Janse's rendition of his material, always with a view to external exactness and to the documentation of (mere) everyday life, set his work alongside that of the artists at home who were then producing thousands of paintings popular because of their selection, or seeming unselection, of similar common scenes. From the point of view of consumption, such scenes, his and theirs, gave the impression that what was represented was, "not the dramatic highpoint of an exceptional event[,] but a fairly arbitrary moment taken from an incident in daily life." They represented deeply laid Dutch values, like domesticity and the pleasures taken in material things.[27]

As notary, Janse was expected to guide his clients toward recitations that were adequate for the requirements of the law. This expectation was part of Dutch society's larger requirement that he master the *ars notariatus,* the art of the notary. As a component of the medieval *ars dictaminis,* it required competence in taking notes and calligraphy as well as in drafting and formatting a range of attestations into acceptable legal form. For this schooling, *notarisboeken* were becoming increasingly available in the seventeenth century. Most were rudimentary manuals, some presenting theoretical matters, all offering simple models of acts like a will, power of attorney, or inventory. At one end of the scale was a manual like Jacob Verwey's *Ars Testandi* (1656). It was essentially a guidebook for those who would write up wills and handle inheritances.

---

26. Contract of Partnership between Goose Gerritsz van Schaick and Pieter Lassen, Feb. 28, 1672, Depositions of Jacobus Gerritsen van Vorst and Pieter Pietersen Winne, Junior, May 1, 1676, both in *ER3,* 340–342, 390–391.

27. Lyckle de Vries, "The Changing Face of Realism," in David Freedberg and Jan de Vries, eds., *Art in History, History in Art: Studies in Seventeenth-Century Dutch Culture* (Santa Monica, Calif., 1991), 225 (quotation). For Dutch picture making, see Svetlana Alpers, *The Art of Describing: Dutch Art in the Seventeenth Century* (Chicago, 1983). For the discussion of the *Arnolfini Portrait,* see Margaret D. Carroll, " 'In the Name of God and Profit': Jan van Eyck's *Arnolfini Portrait,*" *Representations,* no. 44 (Fall 1993), 99; and Alpers, *Art of Describing,* 178.

Verwey made few concessions to ordinary learning. A sample will contained no fewer than sixty-eight clauses. Jacques Thuys's *Ars Notariatus*, on the other hand, was a popular do-it-yourself kit, perhaps because it presented material in question-and-answer form and, although something of a "wonderful hotch-potch," offered simple models. Salomon Lachaire, a notary practicing in New Amsterdam in the early 1660s, cited another book of this sort, Gerard van Wassenaer's *Practyk Notariael* (Utrecht, 1660). He also referred to the commentators on civil and criminal law as well as admiralty law: Joost de Damhouder, Barent van Zutphen, Hugo Grotius, Gerard Rooseboom, Justinian, all of whose works he'd made available to himself.[28] Kiliaen van Rensselaer had sent a copy of Thuys's *Ars Notariatus* to his law enforcement officer in Rensselaerswijck in 1634 and a further copy would have seemed essential to van Schelluyne.[29] Janse gave no direct indication of owning such a text, but his papers, although not as schooled as van Schelluyne's, were letter-perfect.

In 1672, the magistrates took the unusual step of awarding Janse a special seat in the church "in consideration of his long citizenship." Townspeople would have known why he had received his honored place. It was not that he had grown rich or made himself important in church affairs.[30] His achievement had been to have served well, year after year, in all the small particulars of being something of a lesser civil servant. Still, his livelihood remained an insecure one. We cannot say that he was poor, but certainly he felt the need to

28. Pitlo, *Zeventiende en achttiende eeuwsche notarisboeken*, is an excellent introduction to the early modern manuals. See, for Verwey, 39; for Thuys, see 30. The full title of the 1590 edition of Jacques Thuys's treatise is *Ars notariatus, dat is: Conste en stijl van notarischap: begreven in theorijcke ende practijcke; allen practisienen, rentieren, cooplieden, ende andere, seer nut, oirboor een de dienstelijck* (Antwerpen, 1590). Gehlen, *Het notariaat in tweeherig maastricht*, 97, points to Thuys's plagiarism of other writers, which was common enough and indicates the number of manuals beginning to appear. For Lachaire's citations, see Kenneth Scott and Kenn Stryker-Rodda, eds., *New York Historical Manuscripts: Dutch*, E. B. O'Callaghan, trans., *The Register of Salomon Lachaire, Notary Public of New Amsterdam, 1661–1662* (Baltimore, 1978), 20, 25, 54, 80, 105, 118, 119, 148, 160, 178, 195, 200, 201. Jacob Adriaen Schiltkamp has reconstructed from incomplete evidence a list of treatises on civil and criminal law that either arrived in New Netherland for officials like Stuyvesant or were in the possession of notaries; see *De geschiedenis van het notariaat in het octrooigebied van de West-Indische Compagnie* ('s-Gravenhage, 1964), 47, 48.

29. Kiliaen van Rensselaer to Wouter van Twiller, Apr. 23, 1634, and Instructions to Jacob Albertsz Planck, Apr. 27, 1634, *VRBM*, 281, 283, 294. Paul M. Hamlin suggests that van Schelluyne had his library with him; see *Legal Education in Colonial New York* (New York, 1939), 73.

30. Ord. Sess., Apr. 18, 1672, in A.J.F. van Laer, ed., *Minutes of the Court of Albany, Rensselaerswyck, and Schenectady, I, 1668–1673* (Albany, N.Y., 1926), 298 (hereafter cited as *CRA, 1668–1673*).

retain his position as schoolmaster and seek a trifling income as clerk of the town's militia, the burgherguard. During his seventeen years as notary, he wrote at least 256 acts. His clients were the ordinary men and women of the town. Most of the wealthier traders brought their business to other notaries, one or another on Manhattan Island or perhaps to the secretary of the patroonship who had ex officio notarial privileges.

Until 1676, Adriaen Janse was, or seemed to be, very much alone in the fashioning of his life in the town. Then suddenly a letter arrived from Haarlem in Holland. His family and home country became real again. He had come into his inheritance.

The news of his good fortune was an obvious joy. David Janse's bequest—and another added in a codicil—would allow him and his wife financial security. He was, after all, now fifty-eight years of age—just two years away from the age when a man could qualify for admission to the old men's home in a place like Amsterdam. He welcomed the inheritance but also the opportunity to write the letters that would secure it. He could demonstrate his professional skills. So he was careful to show himself a man of learning as he now began a correspondence that was to last for nine years. He composed letters to his cousin Dammas Guldewagen, who was secretary of the city of Haarlem and ready to administer a yearly annuity from his inheritance, and to Jan Sijbinck, a wealthy wholesale merchant of Amsterdam. Equally gratifying, Sijbinck could now send him the best materials for his important role as notary.

First, there was the letter to Sijbinck. He arranged that the merchant would receive his yearly interest as credit on needed merchandise, and he presented an order for clothing, household goods, and the things he needed as notary, like fine sealing wax and a ream of High Dutch foolscap paper. He could not suppress how eagerly he wanted everything to go smoothly: remember to calculate the costs of customs, read the letter enclosed for Guldewagen and send it along, seal it with a wafer of wax.[31]

He wrote to Guldewagen as befitted his cousin's status as a member of Haarlem's regent class. To emphasize his own trustworthiness, he drew attention to his notarial skills. Guldewagen could have confidence in him from his "writing style and signature." Considerable paperwork would have to be undertaken on his account, he realized, and a transcription of a codicil to the will sent. A copy of the will itself was unnecessary. He had kept his copy for more than thirty years. "In my youth," he explained, "I copied the same from an authentic copy and till this date have it by me." Closing the letter, he excused Guldewagen in advance for delays that would occur in yearly accounts of

31. Adriaen Janse van Ilpendam to Sijbinck, June 19, 1676, in *ER3*, 335, 336.

interest payments: after all, he was "here 36 [Dutch] miles inland from New York, where the ships arrive."[32]

By 1678, arrangements were faltering, and he held great fears. Again he wrote the two men. The past year's consignment had been delayed, and he had convinced himself that marauding Turks had seized the ship carrying it across the seas. But, no, everything had come out all right. He placed another order for himself and his wife. He required a fine penknife with a long white handle and "a turned horn pocket inkstand to contain 3 or 4 pens." He also needed "4 fine spectacles with large lenses and silver rims." These were, he said, "for the use of people who are over 60 years old."[33]

In 1681 and 1683, his worries were more intense. His cousin had been ill, and it made him melancholy. He feared for his total dependence on him. Now he knew no one else in Holland who could collect what was due to him. Yet, he wrote, "I and my wife are both over 63 years of age and can not earn much here and have need of the [money], but I do not know where it is, nor who has possession of it, nor how I can obtain it." He constructed a simple account for Guldewagen. The annuity had never been a large one, but now it was mysteriously diminishing. At first his interest had been 204.8 guilders. Now it was 69.8. He did not complain but merely set out the disturbing figures.[34]

By 1685, Janse's inheritance had become a source of desperation. He no longer needed to worry for his wife's sake. He had rented the pall for her coffin three years earlier. In the first days of October, he wrote an agitated and worried letter to Amsterdam. Both men who were his contacts in Holland had now died. He had written desperately to Guldewagen's widow, but she had ignored his letters. Jan Sijbinck's wife had at least answered his appeal for information about his income. He pointed to his sense of helplessness. It was "with great grief and sorrow" that he had learned of his cousin's death and that she had been unable to obtain his interest. He had heard nothing from Guldewagen's widow, although, as he put it, "I do not seek another's goods, but only what is justly due to me. I am now past 67 years of age, so that I can not earn much more and said interest is my chief means of support." He did not know in what city the son-in-law who was handling his affairs was living, or even his name. He took care to place his plight within a Christian view of rewards and punishment. Whoever is at fault, he recalled, "will not easily answer for it hereafter, for the present is but a short portion of life and we ought always to think of eternity."[35]

32. Van Ilpendam to Guldewagen, June 19, 1676, in *ER3*, 334.
33. Van Ilpendam to Sijbinck, Sept. 19, 1678, in *ER3*, 337.
34. Van Ilpendam to Guldewagen, Nov. 4, 1681, in *ER3*, 494, and see 495.
35. Van Ilpendam to Madame Jan Sijbinck, Oct. 2, 1685, in *ER3*, 584.

He also looked to the future. He placed an order for foolscap paper, an ink horn, and "an almanac which will be good for the next few years." He commended Madame Sijbinck to God and looked forward to receiving the goods, with God's help, "this summer."[36] Three months before the summer came, he hanged himself.

II

The elements in Adriaen Janse's life that seem most deeply implicated in his suicide appear to have been lack of family support in a community where that counted heavily, financial insecurity, loneliness and age, perhaps an essentially passive temperament, even too great a geographical distance from sources of comfort and promise. On the edges of his career and death, however, and like a light fog that rolled in and became imperceptibly and threateningly thick, was another factor.

Janse was never licensed as a notary by a *Dutch* director general of New Netherland. Unlike van Schelluyne and Lachaire, he was commissioned for the *notariaat* by Englishmen, governors Francis Lovelace, Edmund Andros, and Thomas Dongan.[37] He served his seventeen years as notary during the earliest years of English military occupation in Albany. They were marginal years in the town's and the colony's existence. Ironically, he began to create himself as Dutch in a special way just when it was becoming irrelevant. To discover what that meant is important, although it is like trying to clutch handfuls of the surrounding fog in which he had to make his way.

An English squadron seized New Amsterdam in 1664, about thirteen years after Janse moved north to Beverwijck. In many ways, it was a marauding act more typical of the naval activities of European nations in the Caribbean than anything seen along the coast of northeastern North America. In this case, an amphibious landing and possible burning and pillaging of the fort and city were threatened but prevented by Stuyvesant's surrender. New Netherland became New York. The following twenty-five years in northern New York were not, however, marked by English colonization, the introduction of those cultural ways that would have been initiated by the arrival of families and the

36. Ibid., 583, 584.
37. Ord. Sess., June 10, 1669, in *CRA, 1668–1673*, 80; Ord. Sess., Sept. 7, 1675, in *CRA, 1675–1680*, 22. We can only surmise that Janse was recommissioned by Dongan, since he was practicing well after his arrival in New York.

establishment of peaceful settlements. Rather, people lived under military government and military occupation. In the usual way, the new authorities held local magistrates responsible for the collaboration of their communities with the new English ways. Often they intervened directly in people's lives.

In Albany, the officers and men of the garrison—usually about thirty— shared with the burghers the day-to-day experience of making the best of it. They were quartered on a people made sullen by their presence and, at times, violent in their resistance. The troopers picked fights with one another and with the men of the local burgherguard. They also earned resentment by muscling into the fur trade. Most were miserably poor. They shared the toils of a subsistence living with most of the residents while facilitating a culture of coercion as unnatural to them as to the townspeople.[38]

How Adriaen Janse would tell the story of the English conquest and the years of occupation we do not know. The English had their stories to tell: the people had settled into cooperating, but many were surly and ignorant, certainly they pleaded ignorance of English ways whenever it suited them. Still, as an early governor general commented to the local commanding officer, they could not be expected to "love us."[39]

Janse was part of daily happenings, nothing to which exception could be taken. Until 1669, his presence was unremarkable, witnessing an agreement to sell land, acting as trustee for a friend's estate. Immediately after his appointment as notary, he seemed to be coping with the presence of the English, although initially he didn't know how to seek his commission. He seemed to think that along with the governor general the local magistrates still had some authority in the matter. He also persisted in writing "Nieuw Albanij" instead of "Albanij," as though, like Amsterdam and New Amsterdam, Albany was an English city of which New Albany was a recent overseas version. By the close of the year, he had a few clients, and the magistrates were still making it clear that they wanted papers brought before them to be in proper "notarial form." He felt comfortable before the court and was chosen as one of the "good men" sought to arbitrate disputes. He might have been frightened if he had known that within six months Lovelace had forgotten that he had commissioned him

38. I have tried elsewhere to interpret the early years of English occupation in *Possessing Albany, 1630–1710: The Dutch and English Experiences* (New York, 1990), 148–219, and "Becoming English: Anglo-Dutch Conflict in the 1670s in Albany, New York," *New York History,* LXII (1981), 389–414. See also Weise, *History of the City of Albany,* 135–183.

39. Instructions for Capt. John Baker, Oct. 1672, in Peter R. Christoph, ed., *New York Historical Manuscripts: English,* XXII, *Administrative Papers of Governors Richard Nicolls and Francis Lovelace, 1664–1673* (Baltimore, 1980), 32.

as notary for Albany and approved another man. Still, his own appointment was not revoked.[40]

Yet there were other worrying misunderstandings. Everyone knew that a "poor community" existed in Albany—"poor community" were the court's own words. To avoid sliding into it, Janse needed to put his earnings as school-master alongside his small income from the *notariaat*. But in mid-1670, Love-lace surrounded that with uncertainty. Someone got to Lovelace about school-teaching in Albany. They put it in his ear that schoolmasters other than a burgher named Jan Juriaensz Becker gave instructions only when it conve-nienced them, whereas Becker made it his business year-round. Lovelace was persuaded, seemingly unaware that the townspeople counted on having many day and night schools and that these were kept by perhaps as many as six masters. He ordered that no one other than Becker might keep a school.[41]

Then, but only after two months, Lovelace came upriver to Albany and attended a court session held in the old Dutch fort. (He and the soldiers now called it Fort Albany—later he stated that the burghers should consider it "their Mother and greatest concern," which was a strange phrase that no one ever used.) Among other things, he revoked Becker's commission. He now felt that it had been solicited by someone without proper qualifications.[42]

Late in 1674, Edmund Andros became the military governor of New York. Soon he came upriver to inspect the garrison and town of Albany. He issued directives meant to make the town like other "English places" in New York.[43] He was intent on change. There were dangers from the French and hostile natives. Defenses were necessary, and taxes had to be exacted. All householders were pressed very hard. Farmers faced hardships. The Reformed congregation could no longer support the minister on weekly contributions.

The vulnerability of Janse's position increased. The townspeople's need for his services was diminishing. There were new expectations, and new uncer-tainties, about legal papers: just a change here and another there, no pattern but enough to be unsettling. One trader, confused about the security of a contract, turned for advice to the governor's English secretary in New York

40. Ord. Sess., Sept. 30, 1669, in *CRA, 1668–1673*, 106; Commission of Jan Juriaensz Becker, Nov. 1, 1669, in Peter R. Christoph and Florence A. Christoph, eds., *New York Historical Manuscripts: English, Books of General Entries of the Colony of New York, 1664–1673* . . . (Baltimore, 1982), 309, 310.

41. For "poor community," see Ord. Sess., Oct. 29, 1668, in *CRA, 1668–1673*, 31. For Lovelace's role in Becker's appointment, see Order for Jan Juriaensz Becker, May 16, 1670, in Christoph and Christoph, eds., *General Entries*, 345.

42. Lovelace, quoted in Berthold Fernow, ed., *DRCH*, XIII (New York, 1881), 464. For revoking Becker's approval, see Ext. Sess., July 20, 1670, in *CRA, 1668–1673*, 171.

43. Ord. Sess., Aug. 24, 1675, in *CRA, 1675–1680*, 16, and see 16–23.

City rather than a notary. In 1677, the governor issued new regulations on another matter. In future, no depositions might be taken except in court. Before that, one could take it for granted that statements could be made before a notary—in his house, in any number of public places. Now, for some reason, everyone had to face up to the court secretary—in this case, Robert Livingston—and watch the notary's business go to him. The status of mortgages was uncertain as well. One respected burgher had appeared before the court demanding fulfillment of a bond "written by a notary public in the form of a mortgage." He assumed the document's validity, but the magistrates denied his suit. The bond had not been executed by a secretary and in the presence of magistrates. It was therefore invalid. Furthermore, because it was written only by a notary, "much mischief may be concealed."[44] The court had never before made such pronouncements.

Janse wrote nothing about these unaccountable and disturbing changes. Yet if he was not alert to the curtailment of his practice, the other town notary, Ludovicus Cobus, was. He was wilier than Janse and eager to cooperate with officials. Yet even for him, things were unpredictable. For example, he could not get compensation now for taking a deposition—and, in any case, the court referred to taking statements as "swearing a person," as though the validity of statements rested on the word, or oath, of the deponent and not the license and signature of the notary. Nevertheless, he had found an expanded role for himself as an "attorney." He had conformed to some new definition of notary; so he sometimes identified himself as notary and, at other times, as "attorney admitted to practice before this court."[45] He also took over cases that had once been prosecuted only by the *schout*, the law enforcement officer and president of a Dutch court.

Janse, during these years, seldom made an appearance in the courtroom. If he had, he would have recognized that it was still the place of his own language but also a room filled with new words and phrases. They were words like "defective" evidence, "subpoenaed" witnesses, and consent given "per superabundance." Did the magistrates, we must wonder, know the meaning of such words? Were they insulted when a plaintiff who knew English took it upon himself to teach them another new phrase: "Yesterday," he instructed, my suit "remained *in mora*, or otherwise, in English, nonsuited." Did it disturb them—

44. Robert Sanders to Secretary Matthias Nicolls, May 30, 1677, in Peter R. Christoph and Florence A. Christoph, eds., *The Andros Papers: Files of the Provincial Secretary of New York during the Administration of Governor Sir Edmund Andros, 1674–1680*, trans. Charles T. Gehring (Syracuse, N.Y., 1990), 64, 65 (hereafter *Andros Papers*); Ext. Sess., Apr. 17, 1677, Ord. Sess., July 3, 1677, in *CRA, 1675–1680*, 223, 224 (and see 240), 255 (quotations).

45. Ord. Sess., Aug. 14, 1677, in *CRA, 1675–1680*, 258, and see 19, 21.

did they think the townspeople would find it contradictory—to read the duke of York's laws to one plaintiff and, four months later, entertain the case of another supporting his position by citing the popular Dutch commentator on civil and criminal law, Joost de Damhouder?[46]

The courtroom was now busy with new ways of presenting disputes. It was a meeting place for adversaries, not parties expecting to haggle but finally arbitrate. Evidence was sometimes marshaled in a military tone. One man, an English soldier, asked the court to arrange the parties standing before it as if they were two battalions facing off in combat: "The plaintiff requests that his witnesses may be heard," he said, and soon, "Now follows the testimony for the defense." Most litigants carried on in the old way, expecting the court to make its decisions without referring to precedents, just judging the circumstances of each case. Yet even the most eminent burghers were being drawn up short and called ignorant. In 1673, Philip Pietersz Schuyler was told by his opponent's attorney that he could expect his case to fail because he was proceeding "according to the old custom" and was "ignorant of any other form."[47]

No one spoke about the cause of these changes. Certainly not Janse, and not the magistrates who carefully muffled complaints. Yet one man uttered what they dared not say. Two peoples lived here now, Dutch and English. Everyone knew there was a divide. An "unjust" court decision brought against the man was proof enough for him. He had been mistreated, he alleged, for "being an englishman." He would carry his case to the governor in New York.[48] No one offered public comment.

For everyone, it was a time of mangled words and attempted translations. Many were trying to reproduce the new English language sounds and signs that either met some requirement or served as a safety net. Even important men and women were mixing Dutch and English. One wealthy merchant made a try at it, describing land he meant to sell as "*Seventigh Acres of five en Dartigh Morgen,*" seventy acres or thirty-five morgen. The magistrates tried "scandalous" and came up with "schandilas." They tried "justice of the peace" and wrote "Justes of de Pees" and "Justice of peace."[49] They were not excep-

46. Ext. Sess., Apr. 7, Aug. 23, 1676, Ord. Sess., Mar. 6, 1677, Ext. Sess., Mar. 9, 10, 1677, all in *CRA, 1675–1680,* 89 n. 1, 146, 147, 204 (and see 321), 206.

47. Ord. Sess., May 7, 1678, Ext. Sess., Apr. 3, 1683, in A.J.F. van Laer, ed., *Minutes of the Court of Albany, Rensselaerswyck, and Schenectady, III, 1680–1685* (Albany, N.Y., 1932), 316, 317, 338 (hereafter cited as *CRA, 1680–1685*).

48. Complaint of William Loveridge, Apr. 23, 1678, in Christoph and Christoph, eds., *Andros Papers,* 317, and see 329.

49. Sale of land from Stephen van Cortlandt to Dirck Teunis van Vechten, Oct. 20, 1681, Van Vechten Papers, LZ15213, folder 25, Special Collections, New York State Library, Albany;

tional. Everyone was found groping along the walls of the new language. Livingston, who knew both Dutch and English, in fact meant to make money out of it. He alone could put on the market the English words that the provincial authorities had to have and that a man like Janse could never give them. Particularly, Livingston expected a salary increase for keeping the town's account books: after all, he said, he has "more trouble in making translations, etc., than any secretary has ever had heretofore." For Janse, too, language was central. He was expected to be at home in the native language of his clients. The learned writers had repeatedly said so. But what was the native language? Not that long ago, tapsters were paying for their licenses and, of course, calling it the *"spinhuiyssedeel,"* the fee that supported the poorhouse.[50] *Spinhuiyssedeel* was part of a ready-made language passed down from generation to generation. Now there were Dutch and English.

Janse, then, was not alone in feeling clumsily along the dark wall of language. He tried to spell a few English words, names like Frazier and Connell and Willson, but he distorted each of them. Twice he tried to write the name of a sloop, *The Royal Oak,* and misfired both times. He altered the initial solemnities of wills. Rather than writing "Appeared before me"—words that signaled the privacy of the document—he changed to phrases that marked it as public. "In the name of God, Amen," he began. "Know all men by the contents of this present public instrument . . . ," and he went on.[51] Why he felt the need to emphasize the public nature of a will and of himself as a maker of public documents, he did not record. If he was worrying about the privacy that had always surrounded wills, he had the best Dutch authorities on his side. What was disturbing him?

Language, and the importance of the legal language of the English, came dramatically to the townspeople's attention in the early 1680s. By those for whose fortunes it could make a difference, there was already a search for the language of the English lawyers in London. Maria van Rensselaer, trying to administer the patroonship against the designs of Livingston, learned with alarm that he meant to discover from them how to carry his claim to her lands

---

Lawrence H. Leder, *Robert Livingston, 1654–1728, and the Politics of Colonial New York* (Chapel Hill, N.C., 1961), 19; Deed from Willem Ketelhuym, Nov. 1, 1684, Deed from Sybrant van Schaick, Nov. 17, 1684, Deed from Cornelis van Dyck and Johannes Provoost, Oct. 14, 1684, in A.J.F. van Laer, ed., *Early Records of the City and County of Albany and Colony of Rensselaerswyck,* II, *Deeds 3 and 4, 1678–1704,* trans. Jonathan Pearson, New York State Library, History Bulletin 9 (Albany, N.Y., 1916), 246, 247, 253 (hereafter cited as *ER2*).

50. Ord. Sess., Apr. 27, 1677, *CRA, 1675–1680,* 226 (quotation); Ord. Sess., Nov. 12, 1668, *CRA, 1668–1673,* 36.

51. See, for example, Will of Gerrit Harttenberch [*sic*] and his wife Jaepje Schepmoes, Dec. 24, 1678, in *ER3,* 466, and, for orthographic errors, 400, 403, 345, 467, 468, 573, 577.

through the English courts. A friend countered by promising to consult lawyers there as well.[52] Soon Livingston placed an order to London for five law
books. Before that time, however, the burghers witnessed a remarkable court
drama. Legal words and notions were enunciated that they could never have
composed, even imagined. English law had come to Livingston's doorstep and
mocked him.

Livingston was deriving some of his income from collecting excise taxes in
the old Dutch way. He had, however, tripped up. In August 1681, a wealthy New
York merchant, John deLaval, came before the Albany magistrates to answer
charges brought by Livingston for failing to pay duty on imported spirits. In
the course of his defense, the six magistrates and twelve jurymen heard a legal
position never before put in the courtroom. DeLaval caught the secretary out
for collecting taxes that *were* the financial base of any Dutch city or town. He
asserted, however, that they had no place in English law. "I request to know," he
went on, "whether we are not considered to be free born subjects of the king? If
not, during which king's reign and by which act passed during such king's
reign we were made otherwise than free?" Pursuing that, he asked: "When did
the king, lords and commons empower . . . a governor of New York to levy
taxes on his Majesty's subjects, since such right belongs to all three of them
jointly, and not to one of them alone?"[53]

DeLaval persisted. If the excise is legal, show me "on what page or in which
book" it may be found? If it cannot be discovered, shouldn't one who demands
such an unlawful tax be considered a disturber of his majesty's peace and
consequently be prosecuted for arousing the anger of the people against the
king, "making him out to be most severe who by all nations is regarded as the
most benevolent king in the whole world?"[54]

Janse wrote nothing about these words, about laws made during the reign of
one or another king, about legal empowerment by "king, lords and commons." Yet if he had to worry about being examined again as notary, how
much law would he have really known? At home, stealing from a church, mill,
bridge, or sluice was a special kind of crime. Were there such categories of
misdemeanors under English law? And if so, how could he, not knowing them,
counsel townspeople about them? He was sworn not to write an act that
violated the laws of the land. Yet, even if he could consult them, what books
were there pointing out such laws? It was of no use to learn the laws of England

52. See Maria van Rensselaer to Richard van Rensselaer, Jan.? 1683, and Pieter de Lanoy to
Maria van Rensselaer, Endorsed 1683, in A.J.F. van Laer, *Correspondence of Maria van
Rensselaer, 1669–1689* (Albany, N.Y., 1935), 86, 118.

53. Ext. Sess., Aug. 29, 1681, *CRA, 1680–1685*, 153–155.

54. Ibid.

when, even as English-speaking New Yorkers knew, the laws here were those of the duke of York. Or more confusing, actions were lawful if they accorded with the methods and practices of England *or* the laws now established—that was how the provincial Assembly put it.[55] Moreover, if he had discovered a guide to English legal practices, he would have found a capacious space made for constables and justices of the peace. But not notaries.

The burghers knew that the law was there. But something was changing, breaking apart. One man, a baker, put it down to the transition from producing written evidence in court to—what the English seemed to want— swearing oaths. He could only identify the shift as something happening "nowadays." Taking an oath "nowadays makes little difference to the people." For twenty or thirty guilders, "they readily take an oath," and "I lost my money." Back in 1665, a man on Manhattan Island, when asked to take an oath in court, said he needed an explanation of "what an oath means."[56] That was not the way things were now.

Late in 1684, Janse earned some income as tax assessor for his ward in the city. Six months earlier, another set of assessors had tried their hand at following the governor's instructions about laying the taxes. They had, however, made a mistake. They had taxed movable property like Indian goods. Somehow, that was unlawful. Janse had made no blunders during the last year, but neither had he attracted a substantial clientele. In fact, he had met with clients on only thirteen occasions. Trusting acts written in Dutch was no longer wise. The Assembly, for example, had now decreed that all mortgages were to be

55. Pieter Spierenburg alerts us to the localism of Dutch laws regarding theft in *The Spectacle of Suffering: Executions and the Evolution of Repression: From a Preindustrial Metropolis to the European Experience* (Cambridge, Mass., 1984), 135. The uneven development of English law and legal practice in 17th-century New York is traced by Julius Goebel, Jr., in *Law Enforcement in Colonial New York: A Study in Criminal Procedure (1664–1776)* (Montclair, N.J., 1970). He argues that the English legal treatises that finally reached early New York were out-of-date. That is confirmed by Conyers Read, ed., *William Lambarde and Local Government: His "Ephemeris" and Twenty-Nine Charges to Juries and Commissions* (Ithaca, N.Y., 1962); and the work of a London jurist writing in 1668, George Meriton, *A Guide for Constables, Churchwardens, Overseers of the Poor, Surveyors of the High-Ways, Treasurers of the County-Stock, Masters of the House of Correction, Bayliffs of Mannors, Toll-Takers in Fairs, etc. . . .* (London, 1685). Like Lambarde, Meriton ascribes no role for the notary. For the failure of the *notariaat* to develop in England as it did on the Continent, see inter alia, M. T. Clanchy, *From Memory to Written Record: England, 1066–1307* (Oxford, 1993).

56. Ext. Sess., Nov. 8, 1682, *CRA, 1680–1685*, 300; Court Sess., Apr. 20, 1665, in Fernow, ed., *Records of New Amsterdam from 1653 to 1674*, V, *Minutes of the Court of Burgomasters and Schepens, Jan. 8, 1664, to May 1, 1666, Inclusive*, 226.

drawn up in English form. Those written before the ruling were invalid. By 1686, a mortgage Janse had executed in the early years of his practice was referred to as "old" and "Dutch."[57]

In the same year, Janse would have known that Livingston was also occupied as a scribe but doing a far greater volume of business than he. For each act that he had written over the year, the secretary had drawn up at least five. Yet, he would have known too that Livingston's paperwork—except for a few depositions—was not siphoning work away from him. Much of Livingston's business, as clerk of the town or county, was in writing up deeds, whereas Janse's work was in authenticating the informal agreements of sale prior to the final transfer of property.

Yet although the volume of work of the two men differed greatly, their papers were alike in one respect: almost all had to do with land. It was not so in van Schelluyne's day. If Janse had cared to compare his predecessor's papers with his own, he would have discovered that 103 of 321 documents van Schelluyne drew up, about 31 percent, had to do with the Low Countries or New Amsterdam (and less so Long Island and Wiltwijck [Kingston]). Without the townspeople's negotiations with parties outside the Mohawk Valley, he would have earned only 69 percent of his income. For Janse, only a little more than 2 percent of his earnings came from acts involving the Low Countries or residents outside the immediate area. On the other hand, 50 percent of the acts that he wrote involved local land negotiations; only one of six acts that van Schelluyne wrote did the same. Livingston's papers were much the same. From 1675 (when he arrived in Albany) to the time of Janse's death in 1686, about 80 percent were deeds to land.[58] For Livingston, there was profit in this. However, for a Dutch notary whose livelihood depended on the fluidity of goods and people beyond city gates and across seas and customs barriers, and who expected residents to conduct their commercial affairs beyond the jurisdiction of the local court, it was a disaster.

Late in January of 1685, Janse put his signature to a completed document. He had been meeting with four men, two engaged in the sale of land, the others acting as witnesses. The vendor was disposing of land north of the town, beyond one of the farms of the Schuyler family. He made his mark on the paper. Then Janse signed and identified himself as notary. He tried to write

57. Mortgage from Adriaen Appel, Jan. 26, 1686, in ER2, 296. "Preface," in ER3, 9, refers to the Assembly's laws regarding mortgages drawn before June 13, 1684.

58. I have used the Livingston papers edited by van Laer, in ER2, 15–270, and those few in ER4, 117–119, 127–129, with no pretense at complete accuracy, since we have to think that many would not have been included.

English. He signed himself as "Note Republic."[59] No one that we know of laughed at his error. He must have known that he was experimenting with English words. Perhaps he *had* felt himself becoming increasingly worthless all these years because he could not write English. Maybe he did recognize that, in the politics of colonialism, language was a powerful weapon that he had no way of handling. Whatever his reasons for experimenting on this day, the fact was that in the language where power now resided he couldn't even spell what he was.

Fourteen months later, he hanged himself. On July 29, the governor and Council agreed that a cousin from out-of-town might dispose of the property of "Adriaen Johnson van Elpendam," a suicide.[60]

III

More than two hundred years later, Arnold J. F. van Laer, New York state archivist and publisher of Janse's notarial register, tried to interpret Janse's suicide. As I have suggested, he thought he found it in the proclamation of the Albany City Charter that occurred on July 26, just days before Janse's estate was first processed. He explained it this way: "Not long before July 29, 1686, almost at the very time of the chartering of Albany as a city which to him may have meant further curtailment of his business as thenceforth all records were kept in English style, he committed suicide by hanging."[61]

Van Laer was both wrong and right. He was mistaken because Janse died— as van Laer later knew—four months before the charter was passed. Nor was there anything specific in the charter about the use of English, although it was certainly implied. His insight lay in seeing the charter not so much as a beginning to be later remembered and glorified—"Albany as a city"—but as a moment of erasure. The charter drew a line through Dutch-made institutions as determinants of public life, and it ran through Janse's life as well. His suicide was a political event. Taking van Laer's insight further, we can look to the

59. Agreement between Sybrant van Schaick and Tierck van Visscher, before Adriaen van Ilpendam, Jan. 20, 1684/5, Albany Papers, folder, 1680–1689, Collections, New-York Historical Society.

60. "Preface," in *ER3*, 17. See also New York (Colony) Council, *Calendar of Council Minutes, 1668–1783*, comp. Berthold Fernow (Harrison, N.Y., 1987), 49 (reprint of New York State Library, *Calendar of Council Minutes, 1668–1783*, Bulletin 58 [Albany, N.Y., 1902]).

61. "Preface," in *ER3*, 17. See also A.J.F. van Laer, "Albany Wills and Other Documents, 1668–1687," *The Dutch Settlers Society of Albany Year-Book*, X (Albany, N.Y., 1934–1935), 8–9. Schiltkamp, *Geschiedenis van het Notariaat*, 206, and I, in *Possessing Albany*, 197, followed van Laer in his error.

public memory of Janse's life and death and find that its erasure over the subsequent three hundred years was a series of political events as well.

For all the reasons that diminish any community's memory of the dead, Albany began to forget Janse in the years immediately after his death. Those closest to him had always been few and silent. His wife—her name written just once in the records—leads us to a story of a companionable old age, but little more. There were no children to bring his story, even a genealogy, forward through the years. No tales were told, and retold, of his suicide.

In the city's public records, his name also started to fade and be misspelled. He became Adriaen van Elpendam. His house and lot began to tell stories of lives other than his. The young cousin who had been granted his estate had no reason to retain property in Albany and had soon sold it to a local merchant. The next owner seems to have placed his own character on it, and, as nineteenth-century antiquarians liked to write, he "settled in Albany and for many years occupied the west corner of Maiden Lane and Broadway." At the same time, the memory of the Dutch notary moved into the past. The two men who had served off and on as notaries while Janse was alive were dead by the late 1690s. In New York City, it was becoming necessary to invent procedures to cover what notaries did, such as calling three witnesses in order to authenticate something like a power of attorney. One Dutch resident explained it to an Amsterdam notary in 1693. The precaution was needed because "there were no Dutch notaries there any longer."[62]

It was, however, the English conquest that worked most powerfully to erase the memory of Janse. In the course of it, the cultural systems with which New Netherlanders had lived familiarly before 1664 disappeared into distant, and distorted, memory. One of them was the legal system. All the performances that had previously actualized it became infrequent. The acts of presenting and recording testimony in local courtrooms, the articulations of a discourse sprinkled with the commentaries of de Damhouder or Rooseboom, the appearance before the bench of nonlawyers like notaries, the daily dramas of notary and client, the sight of a woman bent effortfully over an account book that might be required in court—these performances slowly gave way, until the show folded.

Actors like Adriaen Janse lost their audiences. Dutch viewers, those who

62. For an example of the misspelling of Janse's name, see Receipt by Bennony van Curler for payment of land, June 24, 1701, in *ER2*, 389. For the next owner of Janse's house and lot, see Agreement of John Corneel [*sic*] and Jonannes de Wandelaer, Dec. 3, 1668, in *ER1*, 452 n. 1. For the Dutch resident's reference to Dutch New York notaries, see Deposition of Willem Bancker, May 19, 1693, Notarial Archives 2342, Collections 51–69, Notary Jacob de Winter, GA.

had been "native" to the performances, now sat uneasily, either bewildered or looking to accommodate to the new ways. English people, the strangers, saw what was foreign and, as often, laughable. Over time, the unspoken rules that had governed how the Dutch performances had been assembled and how parts had certified one another for their efficacy went out of memory. Messages that lay behind the lines delivered by the company's judge advocate, stage effects that a *schout* could get in a given scene, meanings conveyed by the right law book used as a prop on a magistrate's table: these were forgotten as "Closed" went up on the billboard. The next generation in Albany saw the props change greatly. Just three men, two of them English, followed by their sons, began to divide the city's local law business. They made the mayor's court a stage of "bewildering English procedures." An officer of the garrison had introduced them.[63] In his spare time, he was a lawyer.

Performers like Adriaen Janse were out of work. Along with other townspeople who could only say that somehow "nowadays" things had changed, he had been present to see the stage sets slowly altered, then the old pieces carted away. Those considering the old performances much later, like the New York historian Thomas Janvier, thought that they knew what the merits of the old plays were anyway. Writing in 1903, he looked to the new performances of English law that had replaced those of the Dutch. Only in them did he find enactments of a political culture that nourished civic rectitude. It was the good government of men like Richard Nicolls and Richard Coote, Lord Bellamont, that, he said, helped New York achieve "that civic rectitude which was an unknown virtue in the Dutch times."[64]

Janvier's statement would seem an outlandish one were it not for the force of the power to forget. We now know—from anthropologists, literary critics, art historians, and those who have studied cross-cultural encounters—something of how forgetting works. Many strategies are available to serve the colonizers' need to block remembering. Representations of the vanquished natives as primitives, grotesques, living without the blessings of law, all are constructed alongside those that present the strangers as civilized and purposeful lawgivers. They call up, often inadvertently, the darker and simpler feelings of which the lawgivers' propositions and statutes on paper, the seemingly neutral paraphernalia of governing, are only shadows.

The seventeenth-century Dutch were ridiculed as ignorant before the century ended. The observations of an army chaplain or the report of an admin-

63. Alice P. Kenney, *The Gansevoorts of Albany: Dutch Patricians in the Upper Hudson Valley* (Syracuse, N.Y., 1969), 28.

64. Thomas A. Janvier, *The Dutch Founding of New York* (New York, 1903), 195.

istrator: there were many artful forms to carry the message. Governor Bellamont's remarks in 1699 must have seemed commonsensical. He wrote that
those who were honest among the Dutch were nonetheless "very ignorant."
They could "neither speak nor write proper English."[65] By 1899, a local Dutch
historian noted that it had become the fashion to laugh at the early Dutch
settlers. They were, she wrote, "an excellent subject for a jest."[66] The "lingering
echo of sneers"—her phrase as well—sounded through the decades of the next
two centuries: the Dutch preferring to let their history be told by "the more
expert tongues and the more eloquent pens of Englishmen"; the Dutch mid-
way on a scale of civilization between the early New York natives and the
Anglo-Americans; the Dutch blameworthy for failing to adopt the common
law of England.[67] Clumsily participating in the new legal system, Dutch justices
of the peace were a constant source of amusement for their "ignorance and
peculiarities."[68]

Much to their credit, members of New York's historical societies continually
(and often against their own prejudices) introduced a degree of ambiguity to
this repertoire of representations. Although they adopted the general view that
English law was not a replacement for but the introduction of legitimate government in early New York, they also made themselves into hunter-gatherers
of the state's earliest relics, entering the chase for early records as others looked
for evidence of ancient geological strata. They turned over early artifacts,
dusted off Dutch inscriptions, and waited for someone who could make sense
of them. Performances that played on the stage before "Closed" went up began
to be reexamined—and a rewriting of the history of the conquest made a
possibility. In 1918, van Laer translated and published Janse's notarial papers.
Warmed by the politics of progressivism, he felt that the study of registers like
Janse's would reveal "the effect of the community upon the life of the individual." The "home surroundings, daily occupations, customs and intimate busi-

65. Bellamont, quoted in Hugh Hastings, ed., *Ecclesiastical Records, State of New York*, II
(Albany, N.Y., 1902), 1299. For a chaplain's reference to the Dutch as ignorant, see John Miller,
New York Considered and Improved, 1695, ed. Victor Hugo Palsits (Cleveland, 1903), 40.

66. Gertrude Lefferts Vanderbilt, *The Social History of Flatbush, and Manners and Customs of the Dutch Settlers in Kings County* (New York, 1899), 16.

67. Walton W. Battershall, "Albany," in Lyman P. Powell, *Historic Towns of the Middle
States* (New York, 1899), 9, 10; James Fenimore Cooper, *The Chainbearer: or, The Littlepage
Manuscripts . . .* (Boston, n.d.) 10; Egbert Benson, *Memoir, Read before the Historical Society
of the State of New York, December 31, 1816* (New-York Historical Society, *Collections*, 2d Ser.,
II, pt. 1 [New York, 1848]), 98, and see 139.

68. Charles Edwards, *Pleasantries about Courts and Lawyers of the State of New York* (New
York, 1867), 112.

ness and family relations of all classes of society" would be revealed.[69] In many ways, Janse was not the individual van Laer was expecting to emerge from his papers. But he had assigned him some positive significance. His existence, variously configured during his lifetime out of his role as schoolmaster, counselor to the court, and notary, was useful enough to be reconfigured in at least one of the narrative forms that called upon the past to better understand and manage the present. He gave Janse a place, a useful place, in academic history.

The Dutch New Netherlanders as comic is still, however, a mythic chord upon which New York writers can play. Even in 1994 and in a learned journal, a historian (innocently) wrote of a meeting between a minister and a resident director-general of New Netherland in the 1630s as playing out "the last act of a comic opera." The editor, either on his own choice or that of the author, enlarged the point by printing an illustration taken from a history of New York written in 1910 and not unlike the satirical drawings of George Cruikshank used in an 1866 publication of Washington Irving's sketches. The caption, like the illustration, played the purposeful English against the grotesquely careless Dutch. Here was a "silly incident" when New Amsterdam's soldiers were defending the fort in so bizarre a way that it was much "to the confusion of an intruding English vessel." More than a score of defenders appear in the illustration, one inebriate quaffing a drink, another already collapsed on the ground, the obese director grasping a tankard of liquor and, as weaponry, a golf stick.[70]

The depiction of such ludicrous characters works by reducing the differences between Dutch and English to a stereotype of English probity and Dutch animality. The power to enforce such stereotyping lay in all the social and cultural systems that postdated Dutch New Netherland and that classified the strange and the familiar, the acceptable and the unacceptable. Dutch men were made strange as the victors, the English and then the Yankee-Americans, exercised their power to be rulers over knowledge and the story of the past.

Janse's life was inescapably caught up in the English conquest of New Netherland. However, the consequences for those who shared the experience with him were like those set in train by dozens of armed conquests elsewhere. Those who were conquered had to read their environment, their social and moral space, in a radically different way. They had to change. The first Dutch invaders

69. "Preface," *ER3*, 8. For a biography of a man who was indefatigable in collecting and publishing early Albany records, see David S. Edelstein, *Joel Munsell: Printer and Antiquarian* (New York, 1950).

70. Oliver A. Rink, "Private Interest and Godly Gain: the West India Company and the Dutch Reformed Church in New Netherland, 1624–1664," *New York History*, LXXV (1994), 256, 257.

had forced native Americans to reread their way of life against the text of an overseas Dutch way of life. Now, in the same places, Dutch colonists were made to read their cultural systems against those of the victorious English.

It became Janse's task to do this kind of reading. He had to find in the performances of each cultural system enough meaning to survive, if not to prosper or acquiesce with equanimity. Although others could do it, he could not. If Brueghel were to have put on canvas a historical allegory of the English conquest, he would have presented people—some standing as individuals, others gathered in small groups—offering a range of responses. It is fearful to think how the story of Janse's response, off to the edge of the painting, would have been made to appear.[71]

71. For the importance to Brueghel of figures painted "smallest and furthest from the viewer," see Jane Susannah Fishman, *Boerenverdriet: Violence between Peasants and Soldiers in Early Modern Netherlands Art* (Ann Arbor, Mich., 1979), 24.

PART II: TEXTS OF SELF

TEXTS OF SELF

There are many occasions that provide texts of self. They come mostly in those moments of cultural edginess when contradictory demands are made on the individual. That was never so true as for those confronted by the impossible choice between gentility and brutality in dueling. Dueling can be our analogue for all the tensions that created texts of self.

There used to be such a text of self come of dueling in Buccaneers' Cove in the Galapagos Islands. It read:

> Sacred to the memory
> of Lieut. John S. Cowan,
> of the US Frigate Essex,
> who died here anno 1813
> Aged 21 years.

> His loss is ever to be regretted
> by his country
> And mourned by his friends
> and brother officers.

Cowan's commander, Lieutenant David Porter, was only partially as accommodating of that text as Cowan's "brother officers." Porter was aware of the transgression in such a gentlemanly act. He called the duel, in which Cowan had died on the third exchange, "a practice which disgraces human nature." But he bowed to its hegemony. "I shall, however, throw a veil over the whole proceedings and merely state that without my knowledge the parties met on shore at daylight."[1]

The Galapagos Islands seem a most uncivilized place to perform that most exquisitely civilized theater of honor, a duel. "A shore fit for pandemonium," Captain Robert Fitzroy, commander of the *Beagle*, called it. A place of no charm at all, "where the chief sound of life is a hiss," Herman Melville thought. And Charles Darwin himself, for all his wonder at a place in which he saw creation at work, felt that the Galapagos had a cyclopean air, like some hell

---

1. David Porter, *Journal of a Cruise Made to the Pacific Ocean . . . in the United States Frigate Essex, in the Years 1812, 1813, and 1814,* 2d ed., 2 vols. (New York, 1822), I, 222.

made by the devils of satanic mills in the industrial valleys of Staffordshire.[2] The Galapagos had none of the green and misty romanticism of Bloody Island at St. Louis or the Duelling Oaks in New Orleans, or even of that private little coign on the cliffs above the Hudson where Aaron Burr killed Alexander Hamilton.

Punctilio is a word of the duel. In a duel, honor is honed down to its most punctilious moment in a word or a gesture. It is an occasion for self-definition like no other. It was theater like no other, too, in which groups played out their distinctiveness before others—aristocrats before bourgeoisie, bourgeoisie before working class, slaveowners before slaves, officer corps before troops and people. The duelists were forced to the edge of things in all sorts of ways—to the limits of their own self-love, to precise definitions of social protocol, to the boundary of legal and unacceptable behavior. To sustain them at this moment, there are a code of language and formality and an audience who accepts their absurdities as real. Such texts of self demand con-texts of extraordinary power.

Karl Marx and Alexis de Tocqueville had something to say about dueling in the United States. Marx, who had some experience of dueling's hegemony in his own life, saw dueling as a relic of a decayed class system and mocked its prevalence in the southern United States as the sort of ersatz chivalry that the dying elite of the slaveowners would pursue. Tocqueville thought, on the other hand, that American dueling had no class at all. "In America one only fights to kill." The Bowie knife and James Bowie's murderous exploits were signs to fastidious Europeans that the Americans had not understood how very civilized dueling was.[3] But neither Marx nor Tocqueville looked very deeply into the soul of gentility.

In the soul, gentility—for an officer in the early navy such as Cowan, but for gentlemen and gentlewomen of Virginia and Massachusetts also, as we shall see—had a sharp edge. The edginess created many texts of self.

There are some distinctions to be made that are pertinent to an anthropology of experience and texts of self. Wilhelm Dilthey, philosopher of history, made them first. John Dewey, polymath, took them up, and Victor Turner, anthropologist, developed them.[4] There is life as lived, reality in its infinite

2. Adrian Desmond and James Moore, *Darwin* (London, 1991), 169; Herman Melville, *The Encantadas, or Enchanted Isles,* in *Selected Writings* (1854; reprint, New York, 1952), 51; Charles Darwin, *The Voyage of the Beagle* (1836; reprint, New York, 1972), 323, 326, 344.

3. V. G. Kiernan, *The Duel in European History: Honour and the Reign of Aristocracy* (Oxford, 1989), 277–279, 309; George Wilson Person, *Tocqueville in America* (Garden City, N.Y., 1959), 404–405.

4. See Edward M. Bruner, ed., *Text, Play, and Story: The Construction and Reconstruction of Self and Society* (Washington, D.C., 1984); Victor W. Turner and Edward M. Bruner, eds.,

complexity, "one damn thing after another." There is experience, the way reality presents itself to consciousness. And there is expression, the way experience is articulated, performed, told.

When we talk of self, we are a little bedeviled by the double-sided element of the word *persona*, a word from Latin and Greek theater. There is *persona*, the mask, comic or tragic in the sifted-down realism of the stage. There is *persona*, the agency that gives life to the mask. Perhaps, the *persona* (the person, the experiencing self) across time, across cultures, across genders, across individuals is inaccessible. Or perhaps, more certainly, it is the *persona* (the mask, the shaped and externalized experiencer) that is accessible. Let us call the expressions of experience, the masks, the texts of self. The self is materialized in these expressions, in song, dance, sculptured stone, words on paper. Being texts, they are available to be read. They are presented to an audience. By that they are theater too, performances. The selves that we experience, *our* selves and the selves of others, are always textual in some way. They are subject then to all the complex processes that readings are. That's all right. History above all is a text-reading discipline.

The words "performance" and "experience," as Victor Turner has pointed out, share an Indo-European element: the hypothetical **per*, "to attempt, venture, risk."[5] Experience is not just stream of consciousness. Experience is something reflected upon, something pulled out of the flow of things. There is an element of gamble in that. Any interpretation is risk taking. Performing the experience is even more a venture. It means letting go of self and putting it in the hands of someone else, a reader, an audience. "Performance" has an older meaning, as well, of completion. That is a risk, too. Closure is always a risk. Closure is the platform for somebody else's critique. The performances of self in the texts of self are always uncomfortable. We are never now what we have just said we have been. Perfection—there is that **per* again—as any writer is likely to know, strikes us dumb.

Texts of self are everywhere—in monument, in art, in sermon, in the canon of literature, in sacred history, in ritual—everywhere where the relationship between self and otherness is performed. Saying that the texts of self are everywhere, however, can mean that they are nowhere to be seen. In movements of historical understanding, "discovery" is usually a re-seeing, a re-vision. Texts that have been plainly read by custom and assumption are read

The Anthropology of Experience (Urbana, Ill., 1986); Turner, *The Anthropology of Performance* (New York, 1987).

5. Victor W. Turner, "Dewey, Dilthey, and Drama: An Essay in the Anthropology of Experience," in Turner and Bruner, eds., *Anthropology of Experience*, 35.

for something else. The four essays that follow are re-visions of texts that have been seen for some time as showing something else.

Perhaps there are no texts as immaterial or as evanescent as dreams. Dreams are Mechal Sobel's texts of self. Not uncontextualized dreams in a Freudian sense—not dreams seen as signifiers of some universal psyche—but dreams very much contextualized in the time and place and the occasions that inspired them. The dreamings Sobel writes of are of people who felt themselves ordinary, not famous nor notorious. Culture and society are made of them rather than by them, at least in their own eyes. But they are dreamings of people who wanted to change themselves. The otherness by which they know themselves is in themselves. It is alien and hateful. To know that terrible fact is to make a penitent self. That is liberating from forces that do not want to see them change. But it is an enslavement too. That is why they seek interpretation of their dreams—from *Universal Dream-Dictionaries,* from the autohistories of those in change, from spiritual counselors and soothsayers, from cross-cultural, cross-class, cross-gender experiences. The menagerie of divine and devilish presence is large and fashionably and culturally changing. There is more than enough reading in these dream texts of self to last one lifetime and numerous spiritual rebirths.

Rhys Isaac reminds us that the texts of self are continually being transformed. So the "oldest" text of an African American self in Virginia is a French translation of Thomas Jefferson's granddaughter's memory of her mother's explanation of slave folklore set against *her* father's skepticism of its poetic worth. The self so seen is of necessity seen "through a glass darkly." But there are glimpses of it to be seen in the portrayal of the cunning weak prevailing over the predator. But it is in Landon Carter's portrayal of an aging self that Isaac's interests lie. Carter's "book of self," his diary, presents himself as innovating manager and maintainer of efficient production on his plantation. He is confronted by the otherness of his own old age in which his strengths are unappreciated, his power questioned, and his own body plays the trickster. Isaac looks at the diary and finds theater in it. Stories of the mundane and ordinary become presentations of self with all the theatricality that "presentation" implies. The theatricality of everyday life creates a reflexivity about role, gender, and age that makes the self audience to its own acting.

Hannah Barnard's "moveable"—marked exuberantly with many signs of immovability—is Laurel Thatcher Ulrich's text of self. Ulrich masterfully "reads" a piece of furniture for the persona encapsulated in it. Hers is a re-vision of a text that has been displayed in museums and by historians for all sorts of antiquarian and aesthetic purposes. Of course, such texts are never isolated. There are always con-texts as well—wills, birth certificates, inscriptions on gravestones. There are always other "moveables" marked with the same or developing signs. Hannah's cupboard is as palindromic as her name. It joins a line of women's selves from generations before to generations after Hannah. These women find strength in a shared name, in shared skills, and in a sense of the longevity of their relationships. Texts of self are relics of boundaries made around some part of an environment. They are reflections of ownership in the broadest sense of the word. Hannah Barnard's cupboard, empty as it might have been of "moveables," was very full of things that lasted.

"Commonplace books" have been traditionally considered intransigent texts. Kenneth A. Lockridge opens them up anew for us. To read them, he first takes us to Norbert Elias and his notions of the terrible contradictions suffered by the exquisitely civilized and to Peter Stallybrass and Allon White who argue that the point of no return in the civilizing process is a moment of transgression. William Byrd's "commonplacing" of "The Female Creed" is one text of self. Robert Bolling's poems and drawings in a raw, unrestrained notebook are the other. "Looking glass," as Lockridge reminds us, was an eighteenth-century euphemism for a chamber pot. Byrd and Bolling find reflections of their own gentility in a chamber pot, and it is not a pretty sight. Both see that the demands made of them to mimic an English gentility required successful marriage. Their rage and hatred of women whom they see as the cause of their failures and frustrations make awful texts of self. There is a darkness in their commonplace books that is ominously commonplace. As Lockridge himself shows, the civilizing process leads to a transgression that is near pathological.

There are more than enough texts of self to employ the historians. But there are silences of self that are not so easy to catch: silences of pain, and of happiness for that matter; silences of guilt, silences of the poor, of victims; silences of exclusion; silences of forgetting. And the language of self is so often bland, trite and without apparent depth, difficult to read for the forces hidden in it. There is a paradox that elements of the highest human importance in living are unlikely to have cultural or external elaboration. That is a sort of silence, too. These silences are not likely to be an emptiness. They are more likely to be, in Paul Valéry's words, "the active presence of absent things." Finding these absent things is a historical problem. Richard Rorty has suggested that they are more likely to be found in imagination than by inquiry.[6] Imagination is rather unnerving to most historians. But it need not be. Imagination is not necessarily fantasy. Imagination is restoring to the past all the

6. Richard Rorty, *Contingency, Irony, and Solidarity* (Cambridge, 1989), xvi.

possibilities of its future. The sort of imagination that Charles Dickens or Vladimir Nabokov had would help. But there are poets, too, and painters and musicians and literary critics and even philosophers who catch the closed-down-but-full-of-possibilities nature of self. They all can help describe our selves, the better to describe other selves.

Greg Dening

THE REVOLUTION
IN SELVES: BLACK AND
WHITE INNER ALIENS

Mechal Sobel

"What happened to you in the past has yet to be determined."
—Sam Keen and Anne V. Fox, Telling Your Story

I: THE SELF-CREATION PROJECT

The extraordinary outpouring of research and writing about the nature of the self in the last few decades leaves little room for doubt both that the self is a central concern of our own period and that self-perception and self-goals, or ideal selves, are deeply influenced by culture and history. Key research in this field deals with the historical changes in the self within Western culture and with the significant differences between the selves of people in Eastern cultures and those in the West (see Bibliographic Note below).

In the modern West, an autonomous self has long been regarded as both ideal and normative. Whereas postmodern thinkers have suggested that the autonomous self is a fiction that no longer serves society's best interests, many leading researchers in the field of individual development still seem to regard such a self as natural and view deviation from it as immature, unhealthy, or abnormal, often without taking note of how deeply cultural their conception is. Augusto Blasi and Jane Loevinger's working definition of the self is "the subject, the actor, the knower," and they maintain that

> its salient characteristics are (a) a sense of agency, that I am the author of my actions, manifest, among other ways, by control of my actions and by self-mastery; (b) distancing, the ability to reflect on oneself, something like being aware of being aware, something like 'inner space'; (c) individuality, differentiation, and separateness from other agents; (d) self-appropriation,

I want to thank Fredrika Teute and Greg Dening for extremely helpful critiques of this essay.

unity, and ownership of all my thought and actions, though not necessarily their mutual consistency.

This value-laden definition might more accurately be viewed as a description of what became the goal or ideal of male self-development in the modern West. That this goal is, not a natural one, but the result of a particular historical development is abundantly clear when it is contrasted with the "interdependent construal of the self" fostered in premodern Europe and in most Eastern cultures. In these cultures, it is accepted that behavior should be guided by relationships "to a specific other in a particular context" and not by concern for individuality.[1] In most Eastern societies, fitting in, adjustment, and the goals of family, clan, or social group are primary. The individual who aids in bringing such group ends about is succeeding in developing a good self, whereas the autonomous individual, who thinks primarily about his or her individual success, is regarded as immature or antisocial.

Alan Roland, a psychoanalyst who has practiced in Japan and India as well as America, views Indians and Japanese as having a "familial self," or a "we-self," at the core of their personalities. Roland describes this self as formed by "intensely emotional intimacy relationships" based on "symbiosis-reciprocity" within families whose members are further embedded "in relationship-centered cultures where there is a constant affective exchange through permeable outer ego boundaries."[2] He found that in these cultures individual spiritual development is encouraged but viewed as private and sharply separated from social development, which is tied to family, clan, and "we-ness."

Eastern goals of personal development, as posited by Roland, are virtually the opposite of those in modern Western society: physical and psychological separation from family is discouraged, "empathic awareness of others' feel-

1. Augusto Blasi and Jane Loevinger, "Development of the Self as Subject," in Jaine Strauss and George R. Goethals, eds., *The Self: Interdisciplinary Approaches* (New York, 1991), 150–167 (quotation on 150). For a postmodern view, see Elizabeth Fox-Genovese, *Feminism without Illusions: A Critique of Individualism* (Chapel Hill, N.C., 1991), 7–9, 123, 154, 225–241. See the Bibliographic Note below for various definitions and discussions of the development of this concept. On the (imposed) goal in psychoanalysis, see Roy Schafer, *Retelling a Life: Narration and Dialogue in Psychoanalysis* (New York, 1992), 94: "A whole person acts knowingly without profound reservations about the fact of acting, and so acts with presence and personal authority and without anxiously introducing serious disclaimers— such as the claim of being passively moved by natural forces, by the mind, or by a split-off self." On the "interdependent construal of the self," see Hazel R. Markus and Shinobu Kitayama, "Cultural Variation in the Self-Concept," in Strauss and Goethals, eds., *The Self,* 18–48 (quotation on 26).

2. Alan Roland, *In Search of Self in India and Japan: Toward a Cross-Cultural Psychology* (Princeton, N.J., 1988), 7, 8, 225.

ings" is encouraged and expected, the self is "oriented toward libidinal strivings and fulfillment" but is expected to reach sensual fulfillment only through adherence to clan and family dictates and "rigorous codes of [social] conduct."[3]

There do seem to be certain significant parallels between the nature of Western self-views prior to the Renaissance and those of these Eastern cultures extant today: in the medieval West, the self was viewed as embedded in concern with family, clan, and ascriptive role as well as with each individual's duty. Although there was the fostering of a collective, or we-self, it was not the we-self of contemporary Japan or India. Spiritual aspects of self, which in the East are far more private, were generally an important part of the persona in the West. In the early West, libidinal strivings were almost always tinged with sin, whereas certain individual strivings were recognized as having positive aspects. Children's ties with parents and kin were widely broken early, and the establishment of firm ego boundaries was encouraged for a minority. Although concerns for family, kin, and clan were considered primary, character was early recognized as having reality beyond the social structure that positioned it.

When, in the modern period, the West moved from a role-based society in which individuals were born into and by and large assumed to have to accept a position determined by their birth (that is, their ethnicity, class, family, sex, and birth order) to one in which personal attributes were supposed to be considered most important, the commonly accepted sense of what the self was and how it was to be protected underwent very significant change. It had been widely accepted that power was at the basis of social order and that those without power could not expect to have individuated selves that would be respected; the modern worldview came to hold that God-given, or natural, rights protect individuals and individuality. As Richard A. Shweder and Edmund J. Bourne remind us, however, "Our sense of personal inviolability is a violatable social gift, the product of what *others* are willing to respect and protect us from, the product of the way we are handled and reacted to, the product of the rights and privileges we are granted by others in numerous 'territories of the self.' "[4]

The "territories of the self" underwent a rapid and radical transition in the

---

3. Ibid., 7–8, 228–229. "Linked to each other in an interdependent system, members of organic cultures take an active interest in one another's affairs, and feel at ease in regulating and being regulated. Indeed, others are the means to one's functioning and vice versa"; see Richard A. Shweder and Edmund S. Bourne, "Does the Concept of the Person Vary Cross-Culturally?" in Shweder and Robert A. LeVine, eds., *Culture Theory: Essays on Mind, Self, and Emotion* (Cambridge, 1984), 194.

4. Shweder and Bourne, "Concept of the Person," in Shweder and LeVine, eds., *Culture Theory*, 194. Although Erving Goffman is cited as using the phrase "territories of the self" in

early modern period. It is generally believed that before the modern era almost all women had a limited territory of autonomy and that they were enmeshed in a communality (or had a we-self). There is, however, little awareness of the extent to which men shared in this limited situation, as it is generally thought that men were significantly more individuated. That was apparently not the case. In a careful study of developments in England, John R. Gillis concludes: "Throughout the seventeenth and eighteenth centuries, men experienced a sense of connectedness very similar to that of women. Their sense of self was no less porous; and they thought of themselves not as autonomous individuals but as part of an interdependent whole." David Warren Sabean has found that much the same was true in Germany. It seems likely that until the mid-eighteenth century most Western men and women had "as yet no notion of the person as a single, integrated center of awareness." By the last third of the eighteenth century, however, the Western world was engaged in a vast self-change project in which new territories were being mapped and colonized. This project extended and reified "a split along gender lines between the ideal of a separate, autonomous, objective male self and a relational, connected, and empathic female self." The autonomous male self came to be seen, not as an ideal, but as a fixed reality: males were expected to have a basic true self that would (or should) remain fixed or constant through life.[5]

The mapping of new territories of the self demanded a new cartography. The writing of self-narratives was quickly ritualized into a sacred method for this mapwork. Self-narratives were records of the great changes occurring in the self and were also agents of change in and of themselves. Creating narratives of their lives gave individuals coherence and purpose and gave structure to the self itself. Writing an autobiography became a ritual act that reframed the past.

When the writing of self-narratives became a ritual act, it was, in part, because these documents were seen as "making a home for certain images that

---

Relations in Public: Microstudies of the Public Order (New York, 1971), 242, he used the term "circles of the self," and Shweder and LeVine apparently transposed it.

5. John R. Gillis, "From Ritual to Romance: Toward an Alternative History of Love," in Carol Z. Stearns and Peter N. Stearns, eds., *Emotion and Social Change: Toward a New Psychohistory* (New York, 1988), 95–96; David Warren Sabean, *Power in the Blood: Popular Culture and Village Discourse in Early Modern Germany* (Cambridge, 1984), 35 (which refers to German men); Judith V. Jordan, "The Relational Self: A New Perspective for Understanding Women's Development," in Strauss and Goethals, eds., *The Self*, 146. On the self as a fixed reality in 18th-century literature, see Patricia Meyer Spacks, *Imagining a Self: Autobiography and Novel in Eighteenth-Century England* (Baltimore, 1989), 8–9; Stephen D. Cox, *"The Stranger within Thee": Concepts of the Self in Late-Eighteenth-Century Literature* (Pittsburgh, 1980), 7.

[had] . . . been transforming." These transforming images were often first seen in visions and dreams, dramatic envisionings that when described in writing were much like plays that could be replayed in reading. A large number of the autobiographical narratives from the early modern period contain such dream and vision reports.[6]

In the eighteenth and nineteenth centuries, thousands of individuals, most of them of the middling sort or poor, including many at the margins, were enjoined or volunteered to write narratives of their lives, most to be saved for posterity (see Bibliographic Note below). Some were published, often by the writers themselves, who sometimes marketed them as well. In publicly sharing their private lives, the writers were confirming both their subjectivity and their objectivity, laying claim to rights to both good values and material goods.[7] It is now fairly widely believed that this type of writing served the interests of middle-class holders of private property. What has not been recognized is how early and how significantly the poor and disadvantaged participated in writing their selves. These were new and even revolutionary acts: the writing and selling of selves by those without power or pretense to high culture. Well-diggers, wall-plasterers, mechanics, farmers, robbers, rapists and murderers sentenced to death, cross-dressers, madmen, wanderers, and spiritual seekers wrote narratives of their lives. By writing themselves onto the public stage, they too were making a public claim to newly recognized rights.

The extensive body of self-narratives from the early modern period provides graphic and detailed evidence of the changing conception of the self. Although alternative conceptions of the self were always in existence (even in small and isolated communities), there were dominant views that changed over time. In light of this, the writing of selves by the marginal, which *was* revolutionary, was at the same time a move to participate in the creation of the emerging view of the self and involved the acceptance of new limits on self.[8]

Regarding the narratives as maps to the new territories of the self, one can

6. Thomas Moore, *Care of the Soul: A Guide for Cultivating Depth and Sacredness in Everyday Life* (New York, 1992), 12. C. G. Jung termed the dream "a theater, in which the dreamer is scene, player, prompter, director, author, audience, and critic"; "General Aspects of Dream Psychology," in *Dreams,* trans. R.F.C. Hull (Princeton, N.J., 1974), 52. More than half of the 150 narratives analyzed for this study contained dream reports. Dreams recorded by Americans have not been widely analyzed by historians.

7. Jürgen Habermas, *The Structural Transformation of the Public Sphere: An Inquiry into a Category of Bourgeois Society,* trans. Thomas Burger (Cambridge, Mass., 1989), 54, 56, 49, 50; Charles Taylor, *Sources of the Self: The Making of the Modern Identity* (Cambridge, Mass., 1989), 201–207, 305–318, 319.

8. Sabean, *Power in the Blood,* 30–36, 48–49. See Norbert Elias, *The Society of Individuals* (Oxford, 1991), 169, 182–183.

catalog three diachronically developed categories. First in time (but continuing throughout the period) were the repetitive tales of events the narrator passively endured. In these autobiographies, the narrators, who had a collective sense of self, present themselves as passive witnesses of life. They did not see themselves as having fashioned their lives or as being responsible for their selves. This was an ancient view of self, and indeed these narratives are apparently much like those Georg Misch found in classic Egyptian, Greek, and Roman sources or those H. David Brumble believes were characteristic of the oral narratives of native Americans before Western contact. These were lives seen as the sum total "of deeds done, of hardships endured, of marvels witnessed, of crops harvested, of . . . [animals] killed, of ceremonies accomplished." Although some of these acts were clearly purposefully undertaken, the writers had no sense of paths not taken, nor any awareness of character development. They did not view their lives as having alterable patterns, nor did they recognize stages or turning points. They were also given to much repetition, seemingly to establish the existence of "things" and to record life as it seemed to be lived.[9] These narratives were, in part, records of material possessions. As such, they included powers gained in governing or through knowledge of magic or medicine, which were tantamount to possessions and indeed could often be inherited or purchased. Dreams too, often recorded, were seen as potentially valuable: they could disclose hidden treasures and reveal potential harm, aiding the dreamer in avoiding evil.[10]

These early narrative writers wrote very little about childhood and many times did not mention marriage or name a spouse. Children were often referred to only at their death. It was not considered proper to record personal

9. H. David Brumble III, *American Indian Autobiography* (Berkeley, Calif., 1988), 135; Georg Misch, *A History of Autobiography in Antiquity*, 2 vols. (Westport, Conn., 1973). For an example of an autobiography in which the narrator is a passive witness, see William Lee, *The True and Interesting Travels of William Lee . . .* (London, 1808). There was development of the self in antiquity as well, and an interiorized self might well have develped then. David Lowenthal notes that "well into the eighteenth century even reflective men took life to be 'a discontinuous succession of sensory enjoyments' interspersed with abstract reflections, in Starobinski's phrase, with 'chance events and momentary excesses' featuring successive unrelated episodes"; see *The Past Is a Foreign Country* (Cambridge, 1985), 198; Jean Starobinski, *The Invention of Liberty, 1700–1789*, trans. Bernard Swift (Geneva, 1964), 206–207.

10. See Alan Taylor, "Rediscovering the Context of Joseph Smith's Treasure Seeking," *Dialogue: A Journal of Mormon Thought*, XIX (1986), 18–28; Taylor, "The Early Republic's Supernatural Economy: Treasure Seeking in the American Northeast, 1780–1830," *American Quarterly*, XXXVIII (1986), 6–34; D. Michael Quinn, *Early Mormonism and the Magic World View* (Salt Lake City, Utah, 1987), 16, 114; Ann Fabian, *Card Sharps, Dream Books, and Bucket Shops: Gambling in Nineteenth-Century America* (Ithaca, N.Y., 1990).

happenings or much emotion. In fact, the great majority of American life narratives of the eighteenth and early nineteenth centuries were written by individuals who apparently sought to limit or eliminate their personal concern with self. A large number of narratives might be better titled "Accounts of Pain Endured in the Process of Trying to Lose Self."[11]

Although these passive witnesses retained a collective sense of self, by writing their selves they were inaugurating a re-vision of self. Their witnessing involved selection, an unacknowledged evaluation of the content of their lives. Paradoxically, their written presentations of self as virtually unselfconscious generated concern with responsibility and purpose. Writing of one's self, and of goods and powers possessed by the self, led to a growth in self-possession. Trying to lose this self, punishing the self for its self-concern, also helped bring about the sense of an inner self.

During this same period, a growing number of narrative writers began to present parts of their accounts as dramas in which they acted. To varying degrees, these dramatic narrators began to picture themselves as characters who changed over the course of time, whose lives did have turning points, suggesting they might have decided to go different ways. Dreams were often experienced at these turning points, indicating the direction the dreamer should go. These dreams challenged narrators, demanding commitments, and clarified what was to be abjured.

Narration of "self," seeing oneself as part of a dramatic story that begins at birth or before, with beginning, climax, and end in mind—which we have come to regard as the normal or natural way to see the self—was expanded significantly in these narratives and was as well at the core of the fictive autobiographies in so many of the novels of this period.[12] This idea of the self was transmitted by this literature as well as by mothers, fathers, and others who

11. See, for example, Seth Coleman, who, at age 21 in 1761, wrote in his diary that he "longed to go out of self entirely" and to be "impotent"; *Memoirs of Doctor Seth Coleman, A. M., of Amherst . . .* (New Haven, Conn., 1817), 102. For an excellent discussion of the concern with pain in this period, see Karen Halttunen, "Humanitarianism and the Pornography of Pain in Anglo-American Culture," *American Historical Review*, C (1995), 303–334, and the essay by Elaine Forman Crane, " 'I have Suffer'd Much Today': The Defining Force of Pain in Early America," in this volume.

12. Arnold Weinstein, *Fictions of the Self: 1550–1800* (Princeton, N.J., 1981), 3–18, discusses self in 12 fictive autobiographies from the early modern period; Spacks, *Imagining a Self*, parallels fictive and "true" English autobiographies of the 18th century. Marie-Paule Laden maintains that "most novels written in the first half of the eighteenth century in France and England were fictive autobiographies"; *Self-Imitation in the Eighteenth-Century Novel* (Princeton, N.J., 1987), 9.

now talked to young children about the stories of their lives.[13] It was culturally developed and transmitted further by many of the narratives under study here. Some of the dramatic narrators seemed ambivalent about these changes and possibilities, seeking them and yet fearing them, partially aware of their implications and closing themselves off to them as well.[14] Dramatic narrators, by definition, saw themselves as characters and generally viewed character as influencing life patterns, but many were nevertheless unsure of their control over their own life stories.

A third group, a small number, came to openly see themselves as self-fashioners who were, to a marked degree, responsible for the direction their lives were taking. In their autobiographies, the former "episodic style made up of chance events and momentary excesses, was replaced by *a style of willpower or purpose,* in which life was organized, given precise ends, 'finalized.'" In this group too, dreams were often used to further work on the self, but many began to fear that concern with dreams was a throwback to an earlier worldview. As a result, self-fashioners began to report fewer dreams. At the same time, emotions, earlier viewed as virtually possessing the individual, were increasingly "owned" as a product of the self; values were identified as legitimating action, and personal acts were seen as part of a story or drama.[15] Some of this small number, however, perhaps frightened by the hubris of believing themselves self-fashioners, seemed to retreat from this radical new view, apparently wanting to return to a belief that forces outside themselves were responsible for their life's path.

Stephen Greenblatt, in his seminal study of Renaissance self-fashioning, suggests that in order to achieve a new identity an individual had to discover or invent an "alien, strange or hostile" other which had to be "attacked and

13. See, for example, *American Mother; or, The Seymour Family* (Washington, D.C., 1823), identified by Fredrika J. Teute as written by Margaret Bayard Smith, and Margaret Bayard Smith, *The Diversions of Sidney* (Washington, D.C., 1805), both of which script proper selves and futures for the white and black children presented, who apparently are given the names of those in her own family. Smith and her works are discussed by Teute in "'A Wild, Desolate Place': Life on the Margins in Early Washington," in Howard Gillette, Jr., ed., *Southern City, National Ambition: The Growth of Early Washington, D.C., 1800–1860* (Washington, D.C., 1995), 47–68. I am indebted to Fredrika Teute for bringing this text to my attention.

14. Tom Verhave and Willem Van Hoorn, "The Temporalization of the Self," in Kenneth J. Gergen and Mary M. Gergen, eds., *Historical Social Psychology* (Hillsdale, N.J., 1984), 334.

15. Starobinski, *Invention of Liberty*, 207. On Benjamin Franklin as a "self-actualizer," see Phyllis Franklin, *Show Thyself a Man: A Comparison of Benjamin Franklin and Cotton Mather* (The Hague, 1969); Ormond Seavey, *Becoming Benjamin Franklin* (University Park, Md., 1988). On the history of autobiographies, see Karl Joachim Weintraub, *The Value of the Individual: Self and Circumstance in Autobiography* (Chicago, 1978), 228–260.

destroyed" and had to submit "to an absolute power or authority."[16] Application of this thesis to the early modern life narrations, and particularly to the dreams reported in them, provides a crucial key to understanding the development of modern individuality. The issues of self-other conflict and submission to authority were central both in the dreams and the lives described by dramatic narrators and self-fashioners.

The recognition of otherness was, of course, not new to the early modern period. The recognition of sexual and out-group otherness was no doubt one of the basic ways in which human beings always defined themselves. All individuals begin with a potential for a range of gender and cultural characteristics and learn to reject aspects of their own potential while creating their selves. These rejected aspects do "not consist of elements that are outside of and irrelevant to the self, but rather those that are consolidated into an *anti-Me*." Throughout history, the opposite sex and the foreign other have been of significance in creating an oppositional identity or negative role model.[17] When identities were widely shared within traditional cultures, however, males and females were other in fairly stable categories, as were other peoples who were communally alienated. Both men and women, sharing common enemy others, grew up and into shared and fairly stable senses of self, coming to maturity with the familial or we-selves referred to above. In the early modern period new pressure was felt by individuals to develop an I-self through heightened personal concern with difference. Males felt a heightened pressure to view themselves as consciously and aggressively not female; Western whites felt a new pressure to view themselves as far superior to racial others. Increasingly, each self projected the negative of its own ideal image on an enemy alien in order to better establish itself, and new institutions were developed in part to legitimate and support these new selves. However, inasmuch as the enemy other is created of rejected inner characteristics, it remains an important part of the self as well, an inner alien.

It is generally assumed that Europeans in early America naturally came to view Indians and then enslaved Africans as their most dangerous and threaten-

16. Stephen Greenblatt, *Renaissance Self-Fashioning: From More to Shakespeare* (Chicago, 1980), 9.

17. Marc Augé, *Non-Places: Introduction to an Anthropology of Supermodernity* (London, 1995), 19–20; Gary S. Gregg, *Self-Representation: Life Narrative Studies in Identity and Ideology* (New York, 1991), 47 (quotation). Other analysts, from the ancient period to the modern, have viewed opposites as preexistent: "The world of our experience is made up of pairs of opposites and . . . any aspect of reality derives its substance or concreteness from the existence of its opposite"; Paul Watzlawick, John H. Weakland, and Richard Fisch, *Change: Principles of Problem Formation and Problem Resolution* (New York, 1974), 18. See also Vamik D. Volkan, *The Need to Have Enemies and Allies* (Northvale, N.J., 1994).

ing enemies. Although both groups were objective threats to European settlers, the dangers posed by both native Americans and enslaved Africans were significantly inflated and the opponents demonized so that they could be used by white Americans for important self-work. These alien others were made to play the role of the "not-me" for individual white males seeking both to refashion themselves and to justify genocide and the renewed and vastly expanding institution of enslavement.

As more white males sought individuation through demarcation of a racial "not-me," they also sought to distance themselves from the collective or we-self they had shared with women, and they did so in part by characterizing that self as feminine.[18]

It would thus appear that emphasis on racial and sexual difference or, more correctly, on white male superiority was at the core of the process that led to the heightened sense of individual value in America. Although, over time, white male individuality did come to widely rest on intensified sexual and racial hostility, this process was a complex one and did not lead to unidimensional characters—a danger that singling out these aspects poses for this analysis. If, in order to create an alien other, an individual has to project or displace rejected personal attributes onto the other, self-fashioning individuals are likely to be involved in complex love-hate relationships with their enemy figures. Furthermore, this paradigm of self-development suggests that such individuals are likely to be openly inconsistent inasmuch as these core symbols of the self are "*structurally ambiguous.*" "They can and do encode formal contradiction, so that a reconfiguration of their relations can reverse a symbol's meaning by calling out the figure concealed in its ground."[19]

If, as posited, racial and gender otherness was central to early modern white male self-fashioning, racial and gender inequality is part of the essence of modernity. The implications of this thesis are of great contemporary concern. Demands for black and female rights have popularly been viewed as attacks on white male domains or territories of the self. If, indeed, the modern white male self is built on the assumption of the gender and racial inferiority of the other, racial and sexual equality *are* deeply threatening. Moreover, if such alienation is at the core of modern Western individuation, neither females nor black males were or are protected from it. As individual white and black women and black men moved from traditional to more individuated development, they too shared in the need for positioning themselves against clear enemy others. We all share in this history and participate in these developments.

18. The issue of the demarcation of the we-self as feminine is not discussed at any length in this essay but will be considered in an extended study of these narratives.

19. Gregg, *Self-Representation*, 47.

The numerous dreams of blacks by whites and whites by blacks reflect the deep concern with the racial other and, in many cases, suggest that individuals significantly changed their perception of race in their dreams. Changes in behavior in waking life often followed.

The posited need for an authoritarian power, in part outside the self, seems antithetical to the growth of a self-fashioning individual, but many theories of growth recognize this seemingly contradictory need. These theories maintain that, in order to change, an individual must reframe the past. A person with a fixed self-view and a fixed worldview is highly unlikely to reconstruct the past differently inasmuch as "a rule for the change of . . . rules . . . must be introduced from the outside." To change, an individual must accept new values and in light of these values can then reevaluate the past. Although such a new evaluation can come about as a result of a traumatic or "corrective emotional experience," without such an experience it appears that reframing occurs only through submission to an ideology, a movement, or a leader. Submission, in and of itself, especially if one accepts the need for an initiating ordeal, immediately reframes reality and reorients values. Under these conditions, one can target a new enemy other and project a life for a changed self.[20] Often individuals in this cohort made their first and crucial submissions in their dreams and afterward regarded these actions as committing them to new behaviors in their waking life.

In this historic period, the new churches were the formal authorities most often submitted to, although the new nation played a significant role as a reframing authority as well. These authorities legitimated projecting hated

20. Paul Watzlawick, *The Language of Change: Elements of Therapeutic Communication* (New York, 1978) 134 (quotation). "To reframe . . . means to change the conceptual and/or emotional setting or viewpoint in relation to which a situation is experienced and to place it in another frame which fits the 'facts' of the same concrete situation equally well or even better, and thereby changes its entire meaning"; Watzlawick, Weakland, and Fisch, *Change*, 95. Franz Alexander and Thomas Morton French hold that change can come about owing to a "corrective emotional experience"; *Psychoanalytic Therapy: Principles and Application* (New York, 1946), 66. Arthur Burton, reviewing 14 therapies, concludes that, "regardless of the healing system which is proffered, in order to be healed the patient must accept—yes, have a readiness to believe in—the values, circumstances, and efficacy of that particular system"; Burton, ed., *What Makes Behavior Change Possible?* (New York, 1976), 323. Modern psychoanalysis can be seen as based on the acceptance of its ideology and submission to its practitioner. It often involves participation in an ordeal and leads to a reframing of past reality that enables the individual to create a new future; see Watzlawick, *The Language of Change*, 131. Milton Erickson shared this view; see F. William Hanley, "Erickson's Contribution to Change in Psychotherapy," in Jeffrey Zeig, ed., *Ericksonian Approaches to Hypnosis and Psychotherapy* (New York, 1982), 36.

parts of the self on an other and helped the individual reframe the past and begin a new path in life. The new church institutions asked for total commitment or for individuals to give up their old lives and make new ones. Sins were recounted publicly, and, since all of one's earlier life was reviewed, life histories were necessary. Histories were often told to ministers or to the community. Since old lives were to be given up in whole, they needed to be encapsulated, and with the great expansion of literacy the oral testimonies gave way to written narratives. The recountings of past evil were followed by those of saintly lives in the new order. These narratives were often edited and completed after the death of the subject. This project was a vastly expanded version of the lives of the saints, new in its encompassing a massive cohort. An extraordinary example can be found in the vast number of autobiographies collected by the Moravians: thousands of German, American, and African converts wrote or dictated their lives, which were stored in archives for posterity. They, like most of the sects, saw these collections of lives as virtual pattern books for future generations to emulate.[21]

The Moravians, like the Puritans and the Quakers who over time came to promote the keeping of journals and the writing of autobiographies, called for control over the self, limits to be put upon the self, and self-abnegation. But the self was to be limited through concern with the self: through daily documentation of the acts of the self and periodic evaluation of the life of the self. Caught in a bind, these methods and concerns contributed to an opposite end: enlargement of self. No scrutinized behavior remains the same, and someone constantly observed, stimulated, and pressed in a particular direction often alters, grows, and goes in unpredicted (but perhaps covertly sought) ways. In the very course of the prescribed analyses, individuals emerged more individuated and certainly with more self-concern than the sects wanted or thought they were leading toward.

The very act of joining these new groups was a mixed one. It meant the submission to a new authority, but it involved the rejection of old authorities. It enabled sons and daughters as well as wives and husbands to distance themselves or break away entirely from mothers and fathers, husbands and wives. Many grew thereby in self-possession, at least to the extent of deciding who would be their authority figures and their (fictive) families.

Thousands were in these sects, and thousands more became Baptists and Methodists. These groups too demanded a personal decision to submit to authority, which, in the early period, often meant a harsh break with the family

21. For a discussion of the development of the idea of self as narrative, see Jerome S. Bruner, *Acts of Meaning* (Cambridge, Mass., 1990), 111–116.

of origin and a continuing self-analysis. Often the act of joining such a new group, and breaking with parents or spouse, was legitimated in a dream or vision reported in a self-critical autobiographical narrative. The new fictive families generally criticized the new member's self as well, as in Baptist business meetings and in Methodist classes. The business of life was the business of everybody in the group. Although charismatic sectarian leaders played a special role, by and large the self was shared with the new communities, and the dyadic relationship of priest and communicant was opened to more democratic forces that made for a new conformity to group norms and expressed a new common will. The changing self was thus enmeshed in a process that demanded change in a commonly dictated direction.

The new state too was a "jealous institution": sons and daughters of liberty owed it filial honor and the commitment of time.[22] Men spent much time in the new committees, and some of those in the congresses left grass widows and abandoned children, who suffered both emotionally and materially, as did the families of those who went to war. But those abandoned were also left to act on their own, and a great many grew in individuality, submitting to the new authority of the state and accepting the new enemy other, both in their dreams and in their waking lives.[23]

While dreams played a very significant role in helping individuals attain a new sense of their self, shared dreams were part of the life of both the new

22. Lewis A. Coser, "Greedy Organizations," Archives européennes de sociologie/European Journal of Sociology, VIII, no. 2 (1967), 196–215. Coser, discussing organizations that "require total commitment and exclusive loyalty," notes that celibacy and promiscuity fulfill "essentially similar . . . functions" in that they "assure that a person's total loyalty and affective involvement remain with the group and at the disposal of the leadership." On psychosocial development and the Revolution, see Jay Fliegelman, Prodigals and Pilgrims: The American Revolution against Patriarchal Authority, 1750–1800 (New York, 1982).

23. See W. D. McCrackan, ed., The Huntington Letters, in the Possession of Julia Chester Wells (New York, 1897). This revealing correspondence of Benjamin H. Huntington of Norwich, Connecticut (a lawyer who between 1775 and 1798 became a member of a Committee of Safety, the Continental Congress, the first U.S. Congress, and the Connecticut legislature, and was as well a mayor of Norwich and a judge of the Connecticut Superior Court) with his wife Anne and children, 1761–1799, provides ample evidence of his virtual abandonment of family in order to fulfill what he took to be his responsibilities to the new state. On several occasions, Huntington wrote: "I have been a Slave to the Public these 24 Years Pass'd" (81, 127). His wife began with requests that he make decisions for her but soon came to act on her own, noting in her letters that she was sure her husband would have acted as she had. Helen K. Brasher noted in her diary that during the Revolution her husband, Abraham Brasher, put the country before family; see "The Narrative of Mrs. Abraham Brasher, Giving Her Account of Her Experiences during the Revolutionary War . . . ," New-York Historical Society, 23–46. I am indebted to Laurie Wolberg for this reference.

churches and the new state.[24] They helped develop common symbols, common webs of meaning, common expectations for the future, and common patterns for self-development. Their function was recognized, and Revolutionary literature used the format of fictive dreams in the hope of creating a new future.

II: INNER ALIENS AND THE DREAM SELF

Christopher Bollas has suggested that "the fundamental contribution of the dream to human sensibility was its offering a place for . . . interplay of self and Other."[25] As increasing numbers of people created a personal alien other, they recorded their play with this other in their dream reports. Passive witnesses, however, were less likely to personalize their alien others and, because they did not posit an enemy within, did not recognize dreamed others as parts of their own self. They generally understood their dreams to predict good or bad fortune and to warn of enemies without in encoded forms. By means of explication, they hoped to avoid predicted dangers and to recognize predicted rewards. They did not seek to change themselves through analysis of their dreams or in the lives they recorded. As Paul Auster has written, however, "In the process of writing or thinking about yourself, you actually become someone else."[26] That was true, even for the passive narrators.

At any given time during their lives, narrators viewed themselves (or can be viewed) as at a particular point along a continuum from we-self–witness to I–self-fashioner, sometimes having moved, as it were, forward and sometimes backward. Some individuals developed alien others but could not commit themselves to an outside authority; some came to commitment and could not focus on an alien other. Some created aliens that consumed them, others entered into a moratorium, and some became totally immobilized. (Erik H. Erikson's view of vectoral development, tied to age-linked tasks, is a description of the expected changes in self that came about after the patterning of the life cycle became essentially uniform. This process was under way in the period under discussion, but, as with other changes, including death, the develop-

24. Dreams and visions were shared in most sects and new churches. See Bibliographic Note below.

25. Christopher Bollas, *The Shadow of the Object: Psychoanalysis of the Unthought Known* (New York, 1987), 68.

26. See Taylor, "Rediscovering the Context of Joseph Smith's Treasure Seeking," *Dialogue: A Journal of Mormon Thought*, XIX (1986), 18–28; Taylor, "The Early Republic's Supernatural Economy," *American Quarterly*, XXXVIII (1986), 6–34; Paul Auster, *The Red Notebook and Other Writings* (London, 1995), 107.

mental ones were then far more likely to occur at random times in the life cycle than they are today.[27])

When individuals in the process of fashioning themselves began to posit an enemy other, ironically the first enemy that many became aware of was their own self, and they did indeed set out to destroy it. Seventeenth-century Puritans had been adjured, " '*Hate* our *selves.*' " By the eighteenth century, this call had been internalized by many American Protestants. Congregational minister Samuel Hopkins revealed: "I . . . have generally reflected on myself, character and conduct, . . . with a *painful shame* and self condemnation. . . . I am truly ashamed of myself." Congregationalist Seth Coleman "longed to go out of self entirely" and to be "impotent." Ann Byrd and Elizabeth Collins, both Quakers, castigated themselves, the first for "the unlawful indulgence of *self* "; the second endeavored to be "much reduced, and centred in nothingness of self."[28]

Susanna Anthony (1726–1791) also experienced her self as an enemy alien, and, as a leader of a women's group, became an important role model of a painfully successful self-attacker.[29] She particularly hated her own "carnality and self confidence" and sought to destroy it, praying, "Lord, empty me of self." She was so tortured by what she suspected was inside her that she came to

27. See Erik H. Erikson, "Eight Ages of Man," in Erikson, *Childhood and Society,* 2d ed. (New York, 1963), 247–275; Erikson, *Young Man Luther: A Study in Psychoanalyis* (New York, 1958); Martin Kohli, "The World We Forgot: A Historical Review of the Life Course," in Victor W. Marshall, ed., *Later Life: The Social Psychology of Aging* (Beverly Hills, Calif., 1986), 271–303; and Joseph F. Kett, *Rites of Passage: Adolescence in America, 1790 to the Present* (New York, 1977).

28. See Sacvan Bercovitch, *The Puritan Origins of the American Self* (New Haven, Conn., 1975), 17; Thomas Shepard, *The Parable of the Ten Virgins . . .* (London, 1660), 6 ("Fear not enemies without, but your selves at home"); Samuel Hopkins, *Sketches of the Life of the Late, Rev. Samuel Hopkins, D. D. Pastor of the First Congregational Church in Newport, Written by Himself. . .* (Hartford, Conn., 1805), 87; Coleman, *Memoirs,* 102; Ann Byrd, *Narratives, Pious Meditations, and Religious Exercises, of Ann Byrd, Late of the City of New York, Deceased. . . ,* 2d ed. (Byberry, 1844), 97; [Elizabeth Mason Collins], *Memoirs of Elizabeth Collins . . .* (Philadelphia, 1833), 38.

29. Susanna Anthony and Sarah Osborn were founding members of a religious female society that introduced a large group of New Haven women to their values. See Edwards A. Park, "Memoir," in *The Works of Samuel Hopkins . . . with a Memoir of His Life and Character,* ed. Park, 3 vols. (Boston, 1852), I, 98–99; Susanna Anthony, *The Life and Character of Miss Susanna Anthony,* comp. Samuel Hopkins (Worcester, Mass., 1796), 7–8; Sarah Osborn, *Memoirs of the Life of Mrs. Sarah Osborn,* comp. Samuel Hopkins (Worcester, Mass., 1799), 53; Sarah Osborn and Susanna Anthony, *Familiar Letters, Written by Mrs. Sarah Osborn, and Miss Susanna Anthony . . .* (Newport, R.I., 1807), 11; Charles E. Hambrick-Stowe, "The Spiritual Pilgrimage of Sarah Osborn (1714–1796)," *Church History,* LXI (1992), 408–421; Mary Beth Norton, " 'My Resting Reaping Times': Sarah Osborn's Defense of Her 'Unfeminine' Activities, 1767," *Signs,* II (1976), 515–529.

"fear [she was] offering strange fire" to God. A climax to her crisis was brought about by a dream that promised her immortality: "And my mind was much more calm." This dream acceptance enabled her to finally leave her parents' faith (The Society of Friends) and join a Congregational church: "I sealed to be the Lord's; and here God sealed to be mine, my Father, my Redeemer, and my Sanctifier; my only, everlasting refuge and hope."[30] Anthony's dream life did not end her self attacks, but it did enable her to live a life of devotion and spiritual development and to play a very significant role in her community of believers.

Dramatic narrators, such as Anthony, beginning to own their emotions and their selves, generally recorded significant dreams as related to important marker events. Unlike the passive witnesses, they did not simply see their dreams as foretelling the future; they believed that they had to follow through on tasks suggested by dreams or to find ways to achieve goals posited in dreams in order to change themselves and their lives. Although, as noted above, many of the conscious self-fashioners used dreams in this way as well, they also began to have doubts about the source of dreams and tended to be more concerned about their use of them.

Narrators in all three categories interpreted dreams in terms of their "*mundus significans*," or signifying universe—the "rhetorical and symbolic vocabulary," or "storehouse of signifying capacities potentially available to each member" of a culture.[31] Each person, however, has access to a unique combination of the signifying capacities extant, in part determined by class, ethnicity, and gender and in part by historical accident and personal choice. When eighteenth-century Americans, white and black, sought to understand the meaning and import of their dreams, they could draw on rich traditions with ties to biblical and Greco-Roman exegesis as well as to those of the peoples who had converted to Western Christianity over the generations, including those of recent African and native American converts.

The early modern tradition of dream analysis still had ties to ancient Greco-Roman practices, particularly as mediated by Artemidorus of Daldis. In his five-volume work on dream explication, compiled in the second century A.D., Artemidorus held that dream analysis should always take into account the acceptable social behavior in a dreamer's society; he suggested that all dreamed events that violate acceptable behavior signify "trouble." He enjoined dream interpreters to "learn local customs and the peculiarities of every place." Artemidorus also maintained that class, sex, and family position should be taken

30. Anthony, *The Life*, 8, 33, 38.
31. Thomas M. Greene, *The Light in Troy: Imitation and Discovery in Renaissance Poetry* (New Haven, Conn., 1982), 20.

into account. He held that dreams might clearly foretell the future, but they might also express meanings through opposites (especially with regard to emotions). He considered more hidden meanings as well, explicating anagrams, homonyms, emblems, and symbols. (He considered the symbolic meaning of dreamed sexual acts at length, most often explaining them as betokening the future economic condition of the dreamer.) In addition to these complex methods of explication, Artemidorus's work encompassed a vast encyclopedia or dictionary of symbols based on the widely accepted understandings that he had come to know through his research. In making this compilation, Artemidorus provided a model for what became standardized dream-symbol dictionaries in the West.[32]

Artemidorus's five-volume study was passed down through generations, copied, abbreviated, and widely translated. Over time, much of Artemidorus's sensitivity to normative values and problems of interpretation was dropped. As Western culture delimited and exteriorized its view of the proper self, dream manuals became simple listings of the supposed symbolic meanings of dreamed objects or events, ascribed to Joseph or, more commonly, to Daniel (*The Somnia Danielis*).[33] The use of such manuals did not call for sensitivity to culture or to the dreamer. This static and deterministic view of the dream was tied to a static and deterministic view of the self.

Early Jewish sources had raised serious doubts about the validity of much dream interpretation, both in dreams recorded in the Bible and those in daily

---

32. Artemidorus, *The Interpretation of Dreams; Oneirocritica . . .* , trans. Robert J. White (Park Ridge, N.J., 1975), 58, 188, 189. This work was translated into English in 1606 and by 1800 was in its 33d edition. For an extensive, and very suggestive, discussion of sexuality in Artemidorus, see Michel Foucault, *The Care of the Self* (New York, 1988), vol. III of *The History of Sexuality*, 4–68.

33. Lisa M. Bitel, "*In Visu Noctis*: Dreams in European Hagiography and Histories, 450–900," *History of Religions*, XXXI (1991), 39–59; Lynn Thorndike, "Ancient and Medieval Dream-Books," in *History of Magic and Experimental Science*, 8 vols. (New York, 1959–1964), II, 290–302; Steven R. Fischer, *The Dream in the Middle High German Epic: Introduction to the Study of the Dream as a Literary Device . . .* (Bern, 1987), 17–36. The earliest volume with the *Somnia Danielis* was apparently a Greek work from the 4th century. Many variants were written between the 7th and 15th centuries, with English translations appearing in 1481 and 1500. Fischer suggests that the *Somnia Danielis* was "but a collection of self-perpetuating topics stemming from the ancient tradition"; Fischer, *The Dream*, 31. See Steven R. Fischer, *The Complete Medieval Dreambook: A Multilingual, Alphabetical Somnia Danielis Collation* (Bern, 1982), 8, 9; Fischer, "Dreambooks and the Interpretation of Medieval Literary Dreams," *Archiv für Kulturgeschichte*, LXV (1993), 1–20. See Steven F. Kruger, *Dreaming in the Middle Ages* (Cambridge, 1992); Jacques Le Goff, "Dreams in the Culture and Collective Psychology of the Medieval West," in Le Goff, *Time, Work, and Culture in the Middle Ages* (Chicago, 1980), 201–351.

life and had suggested that dream interpretation might alter the self. In contrast, there is substantial evidence that, before the mass conversions to Christianity, Europeans, "both ordinary people and intellectuals considered the vast majority of dreams to be true and reliable" and concerned with events that would happen *to* the dreamer.[34] The church saw this complete acceptance as dangerous and, in trying to exert control over this cultural production, held that dreams stem from "three sources: this world, heaven, or hell." True, or heaven-sent, dreams were regarded as powerful significations from God that were believed to shape reality. Those from the world or from hell were not only unlikely to be of predictive value; they might well be evil.[35]

Notwithstanding the church's attempts to control attitudes toward dreams, European converts widely retained their faith in dreams and also added an important genre to dreams not found in the Bible: otherworld journeys and meetings with the dead. This genre continued to dominate early European Christians' dream reports after conversion as well as those of succeeding generations. Myriad reports of such dreams have been recorded over the last two thousand years. The dream journey to the otherworld is a basic Western culture pattern dream of major importance.[36]

In the early modern period, the radical shifting of thought that brought about the Reformation affected ideas about dreams. Luther, participating in perhaps the most important shift under way, suggested that dreams could bring self-knowledge, but he maintained the fear that the devil might also

34. In post-biblical literature, the statement, "'All dreams follow the mouth,' together with the accompanying stories, comes perilously close to hinting that every interpretation alters reality"; Ken Frieden, *Freud's Dream of Interpretation* (Albany, N.Y., 1990), 93. See also Joel Covitz, *Visions of the Night: A Study of Jewish Dream Interpretation* (Boston, 1990), 2; Yoram Bilu, "Sigmund Freud and Rabbi Yehudah: On a Jewish Mystical Tradition of 'Psychoanalytic' Dream Interpretation," *Journal of Psychological Anthropology,* II (1979), 443–463; *Talmud Bavli, Berakhot: The Talmud with English Translation and Commentary,* ed. A. Zvi Ehrman (Jerusalem, 1976), IV; David Bakan, *Sigmund Freud and the Jewish Mystical Tradition* (Boston, 1958); Jacques Le Goff, *The Medieval Imagination,* trans. Arthur Goldhammer (Chicago, 1985), 197.

35. Bitel, "*In Visu Noctis,*" *History of Religions,* XXXI (1991), 50; Patricia Cox Miller, "'A Dubious Twilight': Reflections on Dreams in Patristic Literature," *Church History,* LV (1986), 164. Fears of democratization from such direct access to God's messengers and messages were well founded: sectarians did indeed claim legitimation through dreams and visions; see Le Goff, *The Medieval Imagination,* 207.

36. Bitel, "*In Visu Noctis,*" *History of Religions,* XXXI (1991), 42, 45; Le Goff "Dreams," in Le Goff, *Time, Work, and Culture in the Middle Ages,* 201–204; Le Goff, *The Medieval Imagination,* 225. A culture pattern dream is an archetypal dream, that is, one that has assumed central importance in a particular culture. For use of this concept, see Jackson Stewart Lincoln, *The Dream in Primitive Cultures* (London, 1935), 22.

work through them. Other Reformation leaders were not as open to new views of dreams and were increasingly unsure about the old ones. Calvin believed that God sometimes spoke through dreams but found it was "always in an allegorical or obscure way leaving the person in a quandary." Ironically, those in the left wing of the Reformation seemed to retain a more traditional attitude toward dreams. Although they were more likely to rely on dreams, they still worried about the devil's role as well as the power that those who misinterpreted dreams might wield. Radical Protestants did, however, open decision making about the validity of dreams to an expanded lay group rather than limit it to the professional clergy. Dreams were still to be carefully considered, but the people were freer to judge whether the word of God was in them.[37]

John Bunyan used the dream of the journey to the otherworld for a revolutionary purpose that he consciously recognized: change in self. He believed he had been a sinning youth and had suffered "fearful dreams and dreadful visions" as punishment for his immoral behavior. His spiritual development was marked by dreadful nightmares of the underworld, which led him to change his behavior, and he was then rewarded with glorious visions of the journey to heaven. He first wrote a personal narrative of these happenings in his life in *Grace Abounding to the Chief of Sinners* (1666) and then reworked them into an archetypal version of spiritual death and rebirth in *The Pilgrim's Progress* (1678). It was this volume that was extraordinarily successful, providing a pattern for proper Christian dream and vision experiences as well as for the narrative construction of an ideal self; it was widely read in America and reached the poor and the enslaved.[38]

With the proliferation of printed material in the early modern period, the people had increasing access to published dream manuals, both chapbooks and lengthier versions, as well as to printed images of symbolic objects that might appear in dreams. People of this period, educated and uneducated, apparently gave much thought to emblems and betokenings, accepting that visual and verbal meanings were intertwined.[39] *The Pilgrim's Progress* was issued in illustrated form, as was Bunyan's emblematic poetry and many other popular books, including works that dealt with interracial contacts, such as

37. Carl W. O'Nell, *Dreams, Culture, and the Individual* (San Francisco, 1976), 36. See the experience and advice of George Fox in relation to dreams, in Fox, *Journal*, ed. John L. Nickalls (Cambridge, 1952), 9.

38. John Bunyan, *The Complete Works of John Bunyan*, ed. Henry Stebbing, 4 vols. (London, 1859), I, 1–42, II, 9–135, IV, 445–458.

39. See Michael Bath, *Speaking Pictures: English Emblem Books and Renaissance Culture* (London, 1994); William B. Ashworth, Jr., "Natural History and the Emblematic World View," in David C. Lindberg and Robert S. Westman, eds., *Reappraisals of the Scientific Revolution* (Cambridge, 1990), 303–332.

Daniel Defoe's *Life and Strange Surprizing Adventures of Robinson Crusoe . . .* (1719), which had illustrations of his African manservant, Friday. Even the Bible was printed in illustrated, or hieroglyphic, form, picturing the Holy Ghost as a dove flying downward and life as "a child, or youth, with a flaming torch . . . blowing bubbles from . . . a common tobacco-pipe." In one volume, hope, peace, and righteousness were pictured as women, each with a different symbol: an anchor, an olive branch and a dove, and a sword and a balance. The devil was a mixed but seemingly male figure, with bats' wings, horns, a double barbed tail, and goats' legs and hooves. All of these images were taken from a pool of commonly shared visual symbols, part of the signifying universe. These images did change over time, but they seem to have had a long life. The dove, for example, was apparently once the symbol of the sexuality of the goddess Venus. Perhaps it was due to the femininity of the soul in biblical Hebrew that early Christians adopted the dove as the symbol of the Holy Spirit. The devil was moving from a perverse collection of attributes (clawed or cloven feet, hairy body with batlike wings and animal ears, sometimes part female with exposed breasts, and often with dark skin) to a figure more recognizable as a black male.[40]

In analyzing tenth-century dreams, Paul Edward Dutton realized that "when metaphors change we should watch carefully, for an entire world of

40. See W. A. Clouston, *Hieroglyphic Bibles: Their Origin and History . . .* (Glasgow, 1894), 66. The first picture bible was published by J. A. Comenius in Nuremberg in 1657, and the first English version by Charles Hoole appeared in 1658 in London. Clouston cites a New England edition of 1794. *The Hieroglyphic Bible; or, Select Passages in the Old and New Testaments for the Amusement of Youth,* 2d ed. (Boston, 1814), includes all of the above discussed images. See Elizabeth Carroll Reilly, *A Dictionary of Colonial American Printers' Ornaments and Illustrations* (Worcester, Mass., 1975), for an important compilation of colonial visual images, including a large number of Africans. On the dove as a symbol, see Barbara G. Walker, *The Woman's Dictionary of Symbols and Sacred Objects* (New York, 1988), 100. See also Matthew 3:16; Fischer, *Complete Medieval Dreambook,* 60; Walker, *Women's Dictionary,* 206, 367, 399, 400. The dove also symbolized sadness in the pre-Christian period. Frederick Douglass suggested that "moans of the dove" symbolize sorrow and "the grave at the door"; *Narrative of the Life of Frederick Douglass, an American Slave* (1845; reprint, Cambridge, Mass., 1973), 78. Freeborn Garrettson compared the church to a dove, and Rebecca Jackson saw God's city as a dove; Garrettson, *The Experience and Travels of Mr. Freeborn Garrettson . . .* (Philadelphia, 1791), 266; Jackson, *Gifts of Power; The Writings of Rebecca Jackson, Black Visionary, Shaker Eldress,* ed. Jean McMahon Humez (Amherst, Mass., 1981), 247. For changing images of the devil, see Barbara D. Palmer, "The Inhabitants of Hell: Devils," in Clifford Davidson and Thomas H. Seiler, eds., *The Iconography of Hell* (Kalamazoo, Mich., 1992), 20–41. In the early pictures of the devil as a black man, he was not shown as having Negroid features. See collected illustrations in Rosemary Ellen Guiley, *The Encyclopedia of Witches and Witchcraft* (New York, 1989), 97–98. A devil with "dark skin and

perception and ideas may have changed with them." It would appear that the significant changes in perception and ideas of the eighteenth century were reflected in the visual imagination as well. Further evidence of this can be found in the fact that Masonic imagery was filtering into popular usage. The Masonic compass, which stood for the "circumscribing of desires" and the "all-seeing eye," which represented the "Supreme Being's" ability to see inside the individual heart, were becoming common images.[41] Both suggest a new conception of inner-directedness and of the need for inner control.

Some Masonic symbols were color-coded: checkerboard blocks of black and white pavement, supposedly as in Solomon's Temple, stood for evil and good. This symbolism was, of course, not new. Black and white were very widely seen this way. It is not surprising that the pre-Revolutionary diary, or "Monitor," of young Mary Osgood Sumner had a "Black Leaf" for wrongdoings and a "White Leaf" for duties performed. Africans as well shared in this use of black and white to symbolize evil and good.[42]

Color-coding can be found in the early dream manuals published in America, but it was inconsistent.[43] With regard to faces, white or pale skin was seen as "a sign of trouble, poverty and death," whereas "a black face denotes long

---

negroid features" was painted by Charles Deas in 1838. Titled *The Devil and Tom Walker*, it was used as an illustration for a story of that title written by Washington Irving. A print appears in Guy C. McElroy, *Facing History: The Black Image in American Art, 1710–1940* (San Francisco, 1990), 26.

41. Paul Edward Dutton, *The Politics of Dreaming in the Carolingian Empire* (Lincoln, Nebr., 1994), 258 (quotation). Dutton discusses the 10th-century introduction of a new symbolic language "crowded" with wild animals. Some of these could be found in 18th- and 19th-century literature, where a roaring lion was occasionally the symbol of the devil. See Jackson, *Gifts of Power*, 246. For Masonic symbols used in American decorative arts, see Mimi Handler, "Masonic Symbols: Decorating Our History," *Early American Life*, XXIV (August 1993), 45–55 (quotations on 47).

42. Alice Morse Earle, *Child Life in Colonial Days* (New York, 1889), 166–167. On the symbolic meanings of black and white for Africans, see Mechal Sobel, *Trabelin' On: The Slave Journey to an Afro-Baptist Faith* (Westport, Conn., 1979), 115; John S. Mbiti, *African Religions and Philosophy* (London, 1969), 212.

43. The first known American publication of a dream manual was that of *The New Book of Knowledge* (Boston, 1767). This was a motley collection taken from English dream books, as was the far more extensive *Universal Interpreter of Dreams and Visions* (Baltimore, 1795). The first volume was an edited copy of an interesting English volume, Thomas Tryon's *Pythagoras, His Mystick Philosophy Reviv'd* (London, 1691). The second volume, separately titled *The Universal Dream-Dictionary, or Interpreter of Dreams and Visions*, was also based on English sources. It was reprinted separately at least five times between 1797 and 1821 by print shops in Philadelphia, Baltimore, Wilmington, and New York. See the excellent bibliography in Harry B. Weiss, "Oneirocritica Americana," *Bulletin of the New York Public Library*, XLVIII (1944), 519–541 (reprinted by the library as a pamphlet in 1944).

life." The color of flesh was considered separately, as if not connected to the same body as the face: "If any one dreams his flesh is grown spotted, or black, like a moor, it signifies he will deceive those he trades with by lying and craft. If a woman dreams thus, she will be taken in adultery, and put away or repudiated by her husband." Spirits could also be identified by the color of their garments. White clothing signified joy, whereas black clothing betokened the temptation to sin.[44] Bodies were thus in conflict with faces or heads: a black head was a positive sign of long life, whereas a black or black-robed body betokened evil or sexual license.

It is impossible to establish how widely dream dictionaries were read or how directly they influenced dream interpretation. (A rare glimpse of a case in which a dream book was treasured and dreams were consciously used to guide life can be found in letters describing their influence on Joseph Noyes, son of Mary Fish and John Noyes.[45]) Certainly many of the printed associations were part of the oral culture as well and had long since become common knowledge. When the enslaved African American Dolly worried Lucy Breckinridge by telling her that "to dream of fruit out of season is trouble without reason," we cannot be sure of the immediate source of the idea, but it certainly seems to have been an echo of Artemidorus coming down through some sixteen hundred years. (Artemidorus had written: "For all things, with few exceptions, that are out of season are bad.") Breckinridge recorded that she was troubled by Dolly's comment but apparently came to accept that it applied to her self.[46]

Parallel to the problems raised about dream dictionaries, the contribution of traditions other than the English to the American signifying universe is difficult to evaluate. The significance of dreams was strongly emphasized in the traditional (pre-European-contact) cultures of both Africans and native Americans. The seventeenth-century Récollect missionary, Louis Hennepin, believed that the intensity of native American dream belief severely hampered Christian missionizing:

44. *Universal Dream-Dictionary,* 132, 138, 189.

45. John Noyes to Mary Fish, Feb. 18, 1810, Silliman Family Papers, Yale University Library, reprinted in Joy Day Buel and Richard Buel, Jr., *The Way of Duty: A Woman and Her Family in Revolutionary America* (New York, 1984), 264.

46. Breckinridge had dreamed of peaches on the night of Jan. 18, 1863, prompting Dolly's comment. Breckenridge's diary provides what might have been her association with peaches and what might have led Dolly to caution her. On Sept. 28, 1862, Lucy visited the grave of her beloved brother, and she then went walking in the adjacent garden, where there was a peach tree. That night she dreamed that her brother asked her to join him in the grave; see Lucy Breckinridge, *Lucy Breckinridge of Grove Hall; The Journal of a Virginia Girl, 1862–1864,* ed. Mary D. Robertson (Kent, Ohio, 1979), 52, 98; Artemidorus, *Dreams,* 25.

Their Dreams are to them instead of Prophecy, Inspiration, Laws, Com-
mandments, and Rules, in all their Enterprizes, in War, Peace, Commerce,
and Hunting: They regard them as Oracles. The Opinion they have of their
Dreams draws them into a kind of necessity to be ruled by them; for they
think 'tis an Universal Spirit, that inspires them by Dreams, and adviseth
them what to do.

By the eighteenth century, missionaries were no longer fighting native Americans' dreams. In fact, they were making use of their reliance on dreams as a
bridge to bring them to Christianity.[47] In doing that, they were unwittingly
opening themselves up to the influence of Indian beliefs.

Native Americans and Africans widely believed that the spirits that inhabit a
person can leave the body during sleep and that a dream might be the narrative
of the soul's travels or of a visit to the dreamer's soul made by "a dead person,
such as an ancestor, or of some still living." As in the West, dreams were
believed to demand proper interpretation, and professional interpreters existed in most societies. African dream interpreters used specialized techniques,
such as the throwing of bones, but they also engaged in symbolic exegesis to
reach their understandings. Restorative acts, such as offerings and sacrifices to
the spirits, were generally suggested, and amulets and medicine were provided
for protection.[48]

African cultures had differing approaches to dreams, but both the evil that
might befall the dreamer and the human cause of that trouble were generally
emphasized. Among the Ashanti, dreams were believed to describe the actions
of the dreamer's soul, for which the dreamer was held responsible: "If you
dream that you have had sexual intercourse with another man's wife and any
one hears of it, and tells her husband, then you will be fined the usual adultery
fees, for your soul and hers have had sexual intercourse." Zulu elders said:
"Dreams are our eyes in the work" and held that "without dreams, true and
uninterrupted living is not possible." The Temne of the Guinea Coast region,
who believed in multiple worlds, regarded dreams as one of the "means of
mediation" between these worlds. Dreams were relied upon by the Igbo in
choosing candidates for religious office, as well as at other significant junc-
tures. The Yunsi of Zaire were one of the groups that practiced dream explication at funerals: members of a deceased's household were adjured to tell their

47. L. Hennepin, *A New Discovery of a Vast Country in America*... (London, 1698), II, 66.
See James Axtell, *The Invasion Within: The Contest of Cultures in Colonial North America*
(New York, 1985), 15–17; Barnett Richling, " 'Very Serious Reflections': Inuit Dreams about
Salvation and Loss in Eighteenth-Century Labrador," *Ethnohistory*, XXXVI (1989), 148–169.

48. Akinyele Omoyajowo, *Your Dreams: An Introductory Study* (Ibadan, Nigeria, 1965),
11, 15, 22.

dreams, which were then analyzed to determine who had caused the death. The dreams had to be "turned the right way up," "opened up," and "picked over" by an interpreter.[49]

Given this widespread and serious concern with dreams, which was shared by African Muslims, it is not surprising that dreams were significant in African and African American conversions to Christianity.[50] Many African Americans cited their dreams in their conversion narratives. African beliefs about dreams certainly had come into the Americas, perhaps merging with each other and also with those of Anglo-Christians and native Americans. Spirits were believed to actually travel, and into the twentieth century "some go so far as to say that a bucket of water should be left in the room [where one sleeps] so that one's spirit may drink, or else it may wander so far away in search of water that it can't get back." In the eighteenth and early nineteenth centuries, African Americans reported dreams of conversion, of calls to preach, of warnings of troubles and enemies, and of promised rewards.[51] These dreams too needed to be "turned the right way up," "opened up," and "picked over."

49. R. S. Rattray, *Religion and Art in Ashanti* (Oxford, 1927), 192–196 (quotation on 193); C. G. Seligman, "Appendix to Chapter 21," in Rattray, *Religion*, 197–204. In M. C. Jędrej and Rosalind Shaw, eds., *Dreaming, Religion, and Society in Africa* (Leiden, 1992), 11 contemporary analysts have problematized attitudes to dreams and dreaming in Africa in a very suggestive manner. Citations above are from Pamela Reynolds, "Dreams and the Constitution of Self among the Zezru," 33, Rosalind Shaw, "Dreaming as Accomplishment: Power, the Individual, and Temne Divination," 40, and Mubuy Mubay Mpier, "Dreams among the Yansi," 108.

50. See Humphrey J. Fisher, "Dreams and Conversion in Black Africa," in Nehemia Levtzion, ed., *Conversion to Islam* (New York, 1979), 217–235. An 1862 account tells of an Ijaye captive who had but "slight contact . . . with Christianity" and was devoted to his *orisha*: Osun, Ibeji, and Ifa (*orisha* are "deities under God"). In several of his dreams, he saw himself and his *orisha* "chained" near "a large fire" in which they were to be burned. He saw his *orisha* put into the fire, and saw himself set free. In the final dream in this series, the dreamer was commanded never to bow down to *orisha* again. The captive awoke in great torment and could not be comforted until he was converted to Christianity. He was certain that his dream had mandated this action. See Peter McKenzie, "Dreams and Visions from Nineteenth Century Yoruba Religion," in Jędrej and Shaw, eds., *Dreaming*, 129, who cites dream reports in Church Missionary Society Archives, Birmingham University Library. On *orisha*, see Robert Farris Thompson, *Face of the Gods: Art and Alters of Africa and the African Americas* (New York, 1993), 20.

51. A. P. Watson and Clifton H. Johnson, eds., *God Struck Me Dead: Religious Conversion Experiences and Autobiographies of Ex-Slaves* (Philadelphia, 1969); Newbell Niles Puckett, *Folk Beliefs of the Southern Negro* (1926; reprint, New York, 1968), 110 (quotation). Examples of dream reports by African Americans in the 18th and 19th centuries can be found in George White, *A Brief Account of the Life, Experience, Travels, and Gospel Labours of George White, an African* (New York, 1810), and throughout Jackson, *Gifts of Power*. For examples of

African and native American dream interpreters came from societies with a model of self similar in many ways to the we-self posited above. Their recognition of the dreamer's responsibility for dream actions, however, and the tradition of legitimating roles bestowed in dreams easily served the needs of individuals in transition to more individuated selves.[52]

In the antebellum Sea Island black communities, where many African traditions (as well as language patterns and vocabulary) were preserved, there were spiritual guides, who helped individual "seekers" work with their dreams.[53] A key feature of the method used by these analysts was to seek a central image in each dream that they would then use as a key to unlock the dream's meaning. Recognition of the image that would suit the particular individual's problems was supposed to come to the guide in a dream as well. No doubt there were well-established traditions of dream interpretation and a specific repertoire of key elements, but there was an individualized aspect as well, based on the personal assessment of the seeker by the guide. The guide sent the seeker back to pray, fast, and dream "until the seeker reports a vision which, because of the whiteness of the object envisaged, the activity of the one seen, the meaningful message spoken, or some other clue, seems to the spiritual teacher to compare favorably with or fit into his own dream or vision concerning this particular seeker." This key image marked what was regarded as the climax dream of the seeking process, signifying that the seeker had "come through" or been accepted by the spirit and was vouchsafed salvation. Although detailed evidence of this type of work has only been recorded in the Sea Islands, it is possible that

the extensive use of dream reports in contemporary African churches, see Richard T. Curley, "Dreams of Power: Social Process in a West African Religious Movement," *Africa: Journal of the International African Institute*, LIII, no. 3 (1983), 20–37; and S. R. Charsley, "Dreams in an Independent African Church," *Africa: Journal of the International African Institute*, XLIII, no. 3 (1973), 244–257.

52. See Robert A. LeVine, "The Self in an African Culture," in David H. Spain, ed., *Psychoanalytic Anthropology after Freud: Essays Marking the Fiftieth Anniversary of Freud's Death* (New York, 1992), 37–47; Godfrey Lienhardt, "Self: Public, Private; Some African Representations," in Michael Carrithers, Steven Collins, and Steven Lukes, eds., *The Category of the Person: Anthropology, Philosophy, History* (Cambridge, 1985), 141–155.

53. In the mid-1930s, a revealing study was made of Sea Island beliefs and practices by Samuel Miller Lawton, who lived on Port Royal Island for more than a year. Lawton interviewed 55 adult believers, "28 of whom were ex-slaves." Of all the adults, 86% were "directed by the Spirit in a dream or vision" to choose their particular guide. Of 55 adults, 54 had a vision during the period they were "seekin'" salvation; see "The Religious Life of South Carolina Coastal and Sea Island Negroes" (Ph.D. diss., George Peabody College for Teachers, 1939), 131–150, 160. I am indebted to Grey Gundaker for bringing this work to my attention. See also Margaret Washington Creel, *"A Peculiar People": Slave Religion and Community-Culture among the Gullahs* (New York, 1988), 284–302.

such advisers once functioned over a wider area or that the religious leadership on the plantations, both prior to Christian conversions and after, played a similar role.[54] Dreams were reported in African American spiritual life in all locations.

The hundreds and no doubt thousands of black dream visions recounted in church love feasts and conversions, at Baptisms and funerals, revealed to whites that many blacks possessed extraordinary means of understanding dreams. Both dreams and dream interpretations were shared by whites and blacks, enriching and changing both traditions. This was not, however, an isolated aspect of interracial exchange. Inasmuch as black alien figures were *very* significant for whites, whereas perhaps the most significant inner aliens for blacks were white, the sharing of dream life was an addition to a complicated counteridentification that was taking place.[55] The examination that follows of white and black individuals' dream images of their black and white inner aliens reveals the extent to which the dreamscape provided a protected space for negotiations with the other and a reacceptance of part of the abjured self. This group of five individuals is taken from the 150 that are the cohort selected for the project. It includes three men and two women, one black and four whites, two Baptists, one Methodist, one Quaker, and one Shaker. It is not a representative group, however, but is chosen to illustrate the role of dreams in the changing lives of the three groupings, with one passive witness, three dramatic narrators, and one self-fashioner. This brief selection was made to suggest the ways in which dreams opened inner worlds to penetration from the other and prepared the self for change in the outer world.

James Ireland (1748–1806) likely heard many African women and men discuss dreams in Virginia. He also, no doubt, heard white preachers talk of biblical dreams and likely read of Joseph before he came to believe that he himself had "got to be a Joseph, a great dreamer." While thinking of himself as a biblical figure, he regarded his dreams much as an African would have and learned from them who were his enemies and how they were planning his downfall: "It

54. Lawton, "Religious Life," 138–139, 164, 166. In the contemporary African conversion dreams reported by Curley, "Dreams of Power," *Africa: Journal of the International African Institute*, LIII, no. 3 (1983), 28–29, bright light often signifies conversion, and preachers play a significant role in suggesting interpretations. For evidence of the practice of seeking in other locales, see Charles A. Raymond, "The Religious Life of the Negro Slave," *Harper's New Monthly Magazine*, XXVII (1863), 680–682.

55. See Gregg, *Self-Representation*, 47; Watzlawick, *The Language of Change*, 18; Jill Savege Scharff, *Projective and Introjective Identification and the Use of the Therapist's Self* (Northvale, N.J., 1992), 89–95, 205, 209; Thomas H. Ogden, "On Projective Identification," *International Journal of Psycho-Analysis*, LX (1979), 369.

pleased God graciously to condescend to give me information in the visions of the night, pointing out the persons and the way they were pursuing, by which I was prepared before hand."[56]

In his narrative, Ireland presented himself as a passive witness, and, as such, he expected his dreams to inform him of what would happen to him. Although his dreams were thus important to him, they did not lead him to try to alter his self. He saw guides in them and followed their directions literally. Going south, as he was directed, he had himself baptized, together with many African Americans telling of their dreams, at the place he believed his dream had foretold. Ireland's rich signifying universe helped him understand a red horse he had seen in his "remarkable dream," as that from Revelations 6:4. He thus associated it with the opening of the second seal and expected violence would follow. When racial violence did disrupt his early preaching to blacks and whites, he believed it was a realization of his dream. He had also dreamed of being imprisoned in a jail, and he was literally on the lookout for the physical substantiation of this aspect of his dream. He believed he saw the very building where he would be (and indeed later was) incarcerated. He associated the mountains he crossed in his dream with trials and troubles, much as an English or early American dream book would have told him to.[57] And relying on what seem like African beliefs in his signifying universe, he confronted his enemies with his shamanistic knowledge of their evil intentions gained in his dreams. Black people had been in his dreams and were in his life, but he did not own their presence in his soul. Although he submitted to the authority of a new church and changed his life, he did not grapple with the meaning of the racial other in his self.

Unlike Ireland, Freeborn Garrettson (1752–1827) wrote of his life as a dramatic narrative in which his character and changing actions played a crucial role. In June 1775, he came to a parting of the ways and had to make life-determining choices. At this point, twenty-three-year-old Garrettson, son of a slaveowning Anglican family in Maryland, experienced a series of dreams and visions; his developing understanding of their meaning and his reactions changed his life. Above all, his understanding of his dream life stopped him from being pushed into behavior he did not feel morally committed to and supported him in acting in socially unacceptable ways. On the day that he was to have gone to a review of Revolutionary troops with the intention of volunteering, he was awakened by a thunderous "alarming" and "awful voice" shouting out: "Awake sinner, for you are not prepared to die." He understood

56. James Ireland, *The Life of the Rev. James Ireland* . . . (Winchester, Va., 1819), 192.
57. Ireland, *The Life*, 123; Sobel, *Trabelin' On*, 84–85, 97, 102, 107, 188, 296; *Universal Dream-Dictionary*, 100, 165.

this bivalent message, which he might well have thought suggested his un-willingness to die in battle, as signaling his unpreparedness for eternity. That very day, in place of joining the Revolutionary army, Garrettson went to a Methodist meeting. The following week, he experienced an inner battle in which "two spirits" tore his soul apart. Garrettson violently argued with these two—a "good spirit" and the "devil"—as "with two persons." He was describ-ing what one of his slaves might have said was a battle between Freeborn and little Freeborn, or with the "little me" within. Garrettson tried to put this battle off, but he was violently shaken by a voice telling him he had no more time and must immediately " 'chuse or refuse.' " He cried out, "Lord, I submit."[58]

Through submission to this outside authority met with in his dream and vision experience, Garrettson began to attack parts of his inner self and to change his life. Preaching to the enslaved, he heard the voice of God telling him: "You must let the oppressed go free." He freed his own slaves almost immediately, and, in response to this act and to his continued preaching to the enslaved, he was beaten by a relative. Deciding that he should not "have any hand in shedding human blood," he took the dangerous route of opposing the war publicly and faced a violent mob with passive resistance. Notwithstanding these heroic acts precipitated by his dream commitment, he was again attacked in his dreams by the devil. He decided that he had to resubmit to God in order to free himself from the devil's threats. He interpreted the dream that followed as a demand that he renege on a marriage proposal he had made so that he would be free to devote his life to preaching the word. Another dream sup-ported him in the adoption of what were regarded as a feminine means of protection—passive resistance—to defend himself, helping him to develop a more androgynous self in a way that was not generally approved of. Garrettson emerged from this time of inner turmoil and outer conflict with slaveowners, Revolutionary mobs, and the temptation of a sexual and family life as a recog-nized leader in the new Methodist Church, a man free to dedicate all his time and all of his self to his oppressed people.[59] Through the incorporation of

58. Garrettson, *Experience and Travels*, 27, 28, 29, 30, 31. On the "little me" within, see Sobel, *Trabelin' On*, 108–109, 112, 229. Following Julian Jaynes, this might be viewed as an example of a debate occurring between the two halves of the brain; see Jaynes, *The Origin of Consciousness in the Breakdown of the Bicameral Mind* (Boston, 1976), 208, 269. Rodge M. Payne has compared Garrettson's journals with his published autobiography and finds that the autobiography contains more visions and self-concern; see Payne, "Metaphors of the Self and the Sacred: The Spiritual Autobiography of the Rev. Freeborn Garrettson," *Early American Literature*, XXVII (1992), 31–48.

59. Garrettson, *Experience and Travels*, 36, 42, 165–167. Garrettson did not marry until he was in his forties, and then only after Catherine Livingston convinced him that theirs was a

alienated parts of himself, he became more loving toward other males and to himself and more open to female figures of authority as well as to blacks.

With the words, "You must let the oppressed go free," the voice of God had spoken to Garrettson as though he were both Pharaoh and Moses. He responded by freeing both his own slaves *and himself*. Afterward, although he spent much of his free time with the enslaved and became aware of his adoption of shouting and other African patterns, he too did not indicate that he was conscious of inner black figures. Nevertheless, he had changed his self, achieving freer emotional expression and broader moral commitments through his use of his enslaved black (and female) alien others and through dreamed commitment.

Like Garrettson, Sarah Beckhouse Hamilton (1745–1806) wrote as a dramatic narrator and also used her dream work to help assert her values and to take responsibility for her actions. Going beyond what Garrettson did, she also used her dream work to openly avow repressed parts of herself and openly embrace spiritual interaction with blacks. Hamilton's dream life helped her to reject her wealthy Georgia plantation and slaveowning fiancée and to join the congregation of a poor white Baptist preacher whose outreach was primarily to the enslaved. A recurring dream, in which a white man had pulled her from a deep pit, had prepared her for this action. While attending a slave baptism with the intention of mocking the "dirty wench" who was to be baptized, Hamilton recognized the preacher as the man who had saved her in her dream. Moreover, she recognized a crucial parallelism with her dream: at the baptism, as in the dream, it was "a negro" who enabled her to begin her journey to redemption by pushing her into the waters that stood between her and heaven. She became a convert and a runaway from family, fiancée, and slaveowning.[60]

In her dream, Hamilton saw heaven as populated by "a great company of shining people, dressed in white robes, with white palms in their hands. They all sang with melodious harmony, such singing as I had never heard before." The phrase "shining people" (possibly a reference to the oiling of the skin practiced by some African Americans), the pun on "white palms" (betokening both Palm Sunday and Africans' palms), and the reference to "singing . . . never

---

God-ordained union. On Garrettson's role in the church, see William Henry Williams, *The Garden of American Methodism: The Delmarva Peninsula, 1769–1820* (Wilmington, Del., 1984), 41, 47, 112.

60. Sarah [Beckhouse] Hamilton, *A Narrative of the Life, of Mrs. Hamilton . . .* (Greenwich, Conn., 1806), 4, 7. Born in Frankfurt, Germany, Hamilton was brought to Charleston, South Carolina, by her Catholic father in 1752. She later married a Charleston merchant, who was killed in the Revolution. Her dream and baptism took place sometime after the Revolution and before 1800.

heard before" (a common comment on black singing) all suggest that the heavenly population she envisioned was probably African. Envious of the "melody, union and harmony" she had seen in her dream vision (and perhaps remembered from the enslaved Africans who had no doubt cared for her when she was a motherless child), Hamilton joined the mixed-race congregation, courageously rejecting both her natal family and her future social status. She gave up her social position and potential wealth to associate with the enslaved and the outcast and become thereby a poor runaway, sought by her father, who thought he could reprogram her.[61]

Hamilton's black other was within, but rather than attack this figure she sought to unite with it, going to live with her savior-preacher's black-and-white congregation in North Carolina. After some three years, however, she ran away from the South, ostensibly running from her father but in doing so abandoning this congregation as well.[62] However, she was not willing to allow her move to be seen as such a rejection; her publication of her autobiography after her trek north was a public affirmation of the black other and of the change in her self that she had brought about through her new commitment.

John Woolman (1720–1772) would not have thought of himself as a Joseph or a Daniel, but dreams were important in his life and in his written narrative. He used them to become a self-fashioner.[63] Although Woolman can perhaps be viewed as *the* archetypal figure of a moral man in the second half of the eighteenth century, he nevertheless mounted a major attack on himself that was centrally concerned with the morality of his relations to blacks. His alien other was tied to the enslaver within and yet also (in part through projection, in part through extraction) connected to the black without. It was the ambiguous ground that reversed color, much as he chose to substitute white clothing

61. Ibid., 3–4. Rev. 7:9 notes, "People of all nations" stood before God with "palms in their hands." In 1775, Samuel Davies termed black singing a "seraphic exercise" and "a kind of ecstatic Delight in Psalmody"; see *Letters from the Rev. Samuel Davies, etc., Shewing the State of Religion in Virginia, Particularly among the Negroes,* 2d ed. (London, 1757), 30. James Meacham, in Virginia in 1789, "awaked in raptures of Heaven by the sweet Echo of Singing in the Kitchen among the dear Black people (who my soul loves). I scarcely ever heard anything to equal it upon earth"; see "A Journal and Travels of James Meacham, *Trinity College Historical Papers,* IX (1912), 79.

62. Hamilton's three-year stay with this community might have been 1799–1802. See Hamilton, *A Narrative,* 14, 21.

63. John Woolman, *The Journal and Major Essays of John Woolman,* ed. Phillips P. Moulton (New York, 1971), 24, 46–47, 161–162, 184–186, 297–298, 304. Woolman included some ten dreams in his journal (seven of his own and three that were told to him), but a Friends editorial committee eliminated them, and many published versions do not include them. Four of the dreams, two of his own and two of his friends', were understood by him to be about slavery.

for the proper black so that he would not use dye produced by slaves. Although he accepted that whiteness stood for purity and knew that others took it as a badge of his antislavery stand, he recognized that it did not cover his own impurity but rather constantly reminded him of it.

Woolman attacked his inner self, the unnamed blackness within. One of his most moving dreams revealed the nature and depth of his conflict:

> On the night between the 28th and 29th, 5th month, 1770, I dreamed a man had been hunting and brought a living creature to Mount Holly of a mixed breed, part fox and part cat. It appeared active in various motions, especially with its claws and teeth. I beheld and lo! many people gathering in the house where it was talked one to another, and after some time I perceived by their talk that an old Negro man was just now dead, and that his death was on this wise; They wanted flesh to feed this creature, and they wanted to be quit of the expense of keeping a man who through great age was unable to labour; so raising a long ladder against the house, they hanged the old man.
>
> One woman spake lightly of it and signified she was sitting at the tea table when they hung him up, and though neither she nor any present said anything against their proceedings, yet she said at the sight of the old man a dying, she could not go on with tea drinking.
>
> I stood silent all this time and was filled with extreme sorrow at so horrible an action and now began to lament bitterly, like as some lament at the decease of a friend, at which lamentation some smiled, but none mourned with me.
>
> One man spake in justification of what was done and said the flesh of the old Negro was wanted, not only that this creature might have plenty, but some other creatures also wanted his flesh, which I apprehended from what he said were some hounds kept for hunting. I felt matter on my mind and would have spake to the man, but utterance was taken from me, and I could not speak to him. And being in great distress I continued wailing till I began to wake, and opening my eyes I perceived it was morning.[64]

This dream can be seen as a reflection of the troubled life space Woolman lived in, revealing aspects that he did not discuss in any other way in his narrative. The associations he gave and the symbols he explicated provide a good "feeling sense," as Friends said, of what it might have meant to him. In the margin of this manuscript, he wrote, "A Fox is cunning; a cat is often idle; hunting represents vain delights; tea drinking with which there is sugar points

64. Ibid., 161.

out the slavery of the Negroes, with which many are oppressed to the shortening of their days." Woolman's limited gloss, when applied to the dream, suggests far more. "A man had been hunting," which Woolman associated with "vain delights," and the catch, which he brought to the town where Woolman actually lived, was "a living creature." Slavecatchers generally caught living creatures. The creature caught in the dream was described as unnatural, half cat, half fox, suggesting that it betokened a mixed-race figure. Woolman's gloss tells us it was lazy but cunning, and the dream warned it was dangerous, with sharp "claws and teeth."

Mixed-race and black individuals were often regarded as both lazy and dangerous by whites. Their bodily characteristics were seen as indicating these traits. In the "Register of Free Negroes" kept in York County, Virginia, 1798–1831, which included brief physical descriptions, two-thirds were of mixed race, and many of these people were described as having "fierce black eyes." In John Saffin's published description, "The Negro Character," he wrote: "He that exasperates them, soon espies / Mischief and Murder in their very eyes." A terrifying dream reported in a Massachusetts life narrative told of a "sable countenance" with frightening "fiery eyes" that the dreamer could not put out of mind.[65] Woolman's gloss on his own dream suggests that he too was frightened. It is likely that it was his own self that frightened him; he apparently feared that he too might want to take "vain delights" such as the hunter had. In his dream report, Woolman twice repeated that the persecutors "wanted flesh" and noted that the "mixed breed" was "active in various motions," all of which indicate that he feared that these "vain delights" involved sex with the other.

Ladders appear in many recorded dreams, from Jacob's through Woolman's, and have stimulated much comment. (Sigmund Freud saw ladders as representing the sex act. James Fernandez has suggested: "The ends of the ladder and the ladder itself constitute a system of understanding—ladders are good to think with and stairs, too, I suppose. . . . The ladder has polarity, a satisfying binary quality. It has mediation. And best of all it has . . . measurement along an equally divided continuum.") Ladders appear in many published woodcuts from the colonial period: they were often shown as leaning

---

65. "Register of Free Negroes," York County, Virginia, Guardian Account Books, 1780–1823, i–xv, 417–428, 1823–1846, 1–11 (I would like to thank Lou Powers for bringing this source to my attention); John Saffin, *A Brief and Candid Answer to a Late Printed Sheet, Entituled, The Selling of Joseph . . .* (Boston, 1701), 5. See Lawrence W. Towner, "The Sewall-Saffin Dialogue on Slavery," *William and Mary Quarterly*, 3d Ser., XXI (1964), 40–52. Lewis Still's dream is reported in George Peck, *The Life and Times of Rev. George Peck . . .* (New York, 1874), 97–98. I am indebted to Jon Butler for this last reference.

against the gallows on which a criminal was to be hanged.[66] They clearly were associated with guilt and with death as well as with stairways to heaven.

In a dream report that Woolman was fairly certain to have been aware of, Quaker Robert Piles described his ascent up a ladder to heaven as having been made dangerous and in fact impossible, owing to the "black pot" he was carrying. He believed this pot betokened an enslaved black, and Woolman is most likely to have shared this interpretation. Woolman himself had expressed earlier concern with ladders: in the one dream he illustrated, he pictured what he termed red streams leading to heaven; he drew these much like ladders. He was likely to have associated their color with slavery as well. When a friend told him of a dream of "a great pond of blood" and of blood-colored clothes, he believed the red blood "represented the state" of "hardhearted" men responsible for the enslavement of Africans.[67]

It is also likely that Woolman associated a ladder with a particular African blocking his own route to heaven. In 1753, Woolman and a colleague had settled the estate of one Thomas Shinns and had put Gamaliel and Aquilla "to trades" until age thirty. Had they been white youths, they would have been apprenticed until age twenty-one. Woolman came to feel that, in denying them their freedom for an additional nine years, he had committed a sinful act. In 1769, he noted that one of these young men, then "upward of twenty-four years of age and now a servant . . . frequently attends the meeting I belong to" and sits "in the uppermost seat," a seat he might have had to climb a ladderlike stairway to reach. Woolman sat at these meetings "with my heart exercised toward that awful Being who respecteth not persons nor colours." He tried to expiate his guilt by buying this young man's freedom for half of the extra nine years he had to serve, as he had shared responsibility for the sale.[68]

66. James W. Fernandez, *Persuasions and Performances: The Play of Tropes in Culture* (Bloomington, Ind., 1986), 225; Reilly, *Dictionary of Colonial American Printers' Ornaments and Illustrations*, 277–280.

67. Robert Piles, "Paper about Negroes" (1698), reprinted in Roger Bruns, ed., *Am I Not a Man and a Brother: The Antislavery Crusade of Revolutionary America, 1688–1788* (New York, 1977), 9–10. For red streams, see Woolman, *Journal*, 46–47; Dream of Peter Harvey of "pond of blood," Oct. 9, 1771, in Woolman, *Journal*, ed. Moulton, 191.

68. Woolman probably wrote of this youth's family in *A Plea for the Poor* (published with the *Journal*, ed. Moulton, 271), where he stated: "Suppose an inoffensive youth, forty years ago, was violently taken from Guinea, sold here as a slave . . . and hath children who are now living." He then totaled up the money and interest that would be due his family, some 141 pounds. The young man in question might have been born in 1745; he would have been eight in 1753, when Shinn's estate was settled, and due to serve until thirty in 1775. Woolman signed a note to relieve him of four and a half years, so he might have finished his service in 1771. See Woolman, "Book of Executorship," 3, Historical Society of Pennsylvania, Philadelphia.

When the whites murdered the old black man in Woolman's dream report, it was, not because he was dangerous, but because he was weak and unproductive and because his body was wanted for food. This was parallel to, and yet also the reverse of, what Woolman had done to the young black man as an executor of a will: he had sold the black child to make money for the white family. He had indeed been an executor.

In his dream, Woolman "stood silent all the time." He was a silent witness to crimes against humanity. Silence was central to Quakers, and Woolman had often used silence as a tool, sitting quietly with slaveowning Quakers who had to do inner battle with his unspoken criticism.[69] But he might well have been deeply ambivalent about silence. He had put off publishing his first work on slavery for some years, until he felt he could gain the Quaker publishing committee's approval. However, he knew that other Quakers, Ralph Sandiford and Benjamin Lay, had not waited for approval, nor had they been careful in what they wrote. They had harshly criticized Quaker slaveholding and had been willing to risk (and did incur) punishment. His dream suggests that he had a deep need to cry out, to act, yet he often had to be silent and patient. His dream indicates that he was in psychic pain over his own silence. The cannibalism of the whites in his dream caused him to wake screaming or wailing, "like as some lament at the decease of a friend." Part of his own self, possibly a part that Africans had enriched, was being killed. He was the Friend who was dying, but he was also the executioner. This dream brought Woolman to enter a plea to be "witnessed against." In "the words of that righteous judge in Israel [Samuel]: 'Behold here I am; witness against me before the Lord and before his anointed.'" The dream had enabled Woolman to accuse himself, although it also displaced the guilt onto others.[70]

Self-fashioning Rebecca Jackson (1795–1871) also experienced inner turmoil over her own "besetting sin" and over skin color.[71] As she was a black woman

69. On the use of silence as a form of pressure with regard to manumission, and for another dream involving African Americans, see Philip J. Schwarz, "Clark T. Moorman, Quaker Emancipator," *Quaker History*, LXIX (1980), 27–35. On the ideological justification for silence, see Richard Bauman, *Let Your Words Be Few: Symbolism of Speaking and Silence among Seventeenth-Century Quakers* (Cambridge, 1983), 20–31.

70. Ralph Sandiford, *A Brief Examination of the Practice of the Times . . .* (1729), Benjamin Lay, *All Slave-keepers That Keep the Innocent in Bondage, Apostates . . .* (1738), reprinted in Bruns, *Am I Not a Man*, 31–38, 52–54. Both men had been forced to leave the Quaker fellowship after publishing these works. Woolman's crucially important essays against slaveholding were published in 1754 and 1762, after receiving committee approval. The first was written in 1746; see Woolman, *The Journal of John Woolman: And a Plea for the Poor* (New York, 1961), 28, 31; Woolman, *Journal*, ed. Moulton, 161, 272.

71. Jackson, *Gifts of Power*, 98.

who was overtly concerned with white spirit figures and her spiritual absorption of pure whiteness, the influence of the values of white people must be raised. In considering this issue, it should be emphasized how African this color-coded view of purity was. It should also be noted that, although Jackson was born to a free black family in Philadelphia, she lived in a world of blacks and whites and spent many years first as a disciple of white Shakers and then as a spiritual leader of both blacks and whites. Her outer and inner worlds were always inhabited by figures of both colors.

Jackson's inner life was expanded by her mixed-race (and mixed-gender) visionary experiences. Her earliest dream memory (from 1805) was of a white witch killing her siblings. Rebecca, flying faster than the white witch, reached heaven safely. There she met with her dead African grandmother, who was busy tending white children. God (whom she did not look at, and so could not report on his color) gave her a "great" life task and sent her back to the earth.[72] She later returned to memories of this dream and saw it as her first anointment, but she did not begin to follow a special path until she was a married woman, caring for her husband as well as her widowed brother (a prominent black Methodist minister) and his children. Her call (1830–1831) included a call to practice chastity, and from this point on her dreams and her life involved significant power struggles with men as well as women. Her first spirit guide was a female, whom she followed, approaching closer and closer. In 1834, this female spirit guide merged with her soul. In 1836, on Easter Sunday at midnight, after three weeks of fasting and prayer: "A white ball . . . entered into my heart. And as soon as it entered it became a man, and my heart became an arch, and a chair in it. He had a mantle on him. He raised himself up three times, wrapping his mantle around him every time. Every time he wrapped his mantle, it caused black specks to rise up out of my heart and pass away into nothing." With this union, Jackson felt fully redeemed. A Sea Island dream analyst would, no doubt, have shared her recognition that this white object in her dream signified her "coming through." The chair in her bosom suggests a parallel with the thrones so important in African societies, recreated in the African American visual universe, from gardens to folk sculpture, whereas the elimination of black specks of evil is

72. Ibid., 236. Major J. Jones suggests that the color of God was not a question in Africa before the coming of white Christians but that since that time "the tendency to color God black recurs in a broad base of Christian Black religious thought." He cites a Congolese woman, Kimpa Vita/Beatrice, who in San Salvadore in 1700 saw Christ and the apostles as black; see Jones, *The Color of God: The Concept of God in Afro-American Thought* (Macon, Ga., 1987), 38, 39.

reminiscent of Western visualizations, suggesting the richness of her "*mundus significans.*"[73]

Only after she believed her black sins were gone did Jackson feel it was time to dedicate her work to her "people in bondage." Whiteness within remained her mark of purity, but now she became more aware of it as marking her enemy as well. In an earlier vision, she had been graphically violated by a white man who "took a lance and laid my nose open and then he cut my head on the right side, from the back to the front above my nose, and pulled the skin down over the side." He then did the same to her left side. She was crucified, but the cross was not external. It was cut into her body, much as the marks of punishment that were on so many enslaved African American bodies. "The skin and blood covered me like a veil from my head to my lap. All my body was covered with the blood. Then he took a long knife and cut my chest open in the form of the cross and took all my bowels out and laid them on the floor by my right side."[74] Both Christ and Jackson's suffering people were memorialized in this image.

Although Jackson had been cut open and emptied out, she saw this violation by a white male as strengthening her. She came to believe that she herself had to slaughter parts of her own inner self in order to continue on the path she had chosen. Jackson had visions of killing her sense of feeling, hearing, seeing, smelling, tasting, and "understanding." In an epiphany of death and resurrection, she saw whiteness come out of her mouth, "like the purging of a dead body." She emerged with her taste, mouth, and chest "clean as a little child's."[75]

In an important study of the process of change, Watzlawick, Weakland, and Fisch maintain: "There can be no doubt that a large part of the process of socialization in any society consists in teaching the young that which they must *not* see, *not* hear, *not* think, feel, or say. Without very definite rules about what should remain outside one's awareness, an orderly society would be as unthinkable as one that fails to teach its members what they must be aware of and communicate about." Clearly Jackson's socialization as a young person had brought her to see, hear, and think of too many too deeply disturbing aspects

73. Jackson, *Gifts of Power*, 92, 133, 148. On the significance of chairs, see Grey Gundaker, "Tradition and Innovation in African-American Yards," *African Arts*, XXVI (April 1993), 58–96. See also James Hampton, "The Throne of the Third Heaven of the Nations Millenium General Assembly," 1950–1964, National Museum of American Art, Smithsonian, Washington, D.C. For the elimination of black specks of evil, see Samuel King's "Portrait of Ezra Stiles," Yale University Art Gallery, plate in John Dillenberger, *The Visual Arts and Christianity in America: The Colonial Period through the Nineteenth Century* (Chico, Calif., 1984), 73.

74. Jackson, *Gifts of Power*, 94–95.

75. Ibid., 191.

of white behavior. Jackson had many trials over accepting (white) absolute power and probably could not fully submit until she retrained her senses and greatly enlarged the arena of "what should remain outside [her] . . . awareness."[76] It was only after she had purged herself in her dream vision that she could act as if she did not have an alien white other or an inner white part-self.

Dream reports and dream analysis were extremely important at turning points in the lives of a large proportion of dramatic narrators and self-fashioners. Narrators believed that dreams warned them of dangers they had not appreciated, provided answers to pressing problems, awakened or called them to a richer spiritual life than they had expected, and, of utmost significance, supported deviant behavior that they would not have undertaken without the legitimation of what they regarded as spiritual direction. Work with their dreams often enabled the dramatic narrators and the self-fashioners to recognize their enemy others and to make new submissions and commitments and thus to work on and change their selves. Although the racial other had become more significant, dreams helped many to recognize the possibility of reclaiming parts of themselves that had been cut off and demonized.

Nevertheless, in the post-Revolutionary period, ambivalence about dreams was increasingly expressed. Those who regarded themselves as modern among the elite and the growing middle class increasingly saw themselves as rational and felt that reliance on dreams was part of an old-fashioned, irrational worldview. By the 1830s, many whites, viewing themselves as superior to or above this practice, took note of black reliance on dreams; putting credence in dreams began to become something the other did.[77] Over time, narrators were less likely to cite dreams as the legitimation for particular actions in life.[78] In

76. Watzlawick, Weakland, and Fisch, *Change*, 42.

77. Ralph Waldo Emerson, in his lectures on human life, given in Boston in 1839–1840, spoke of dreams as part of what he termed "Demonology," regarding them as revealing aspects of the self but viewing belief in their predictive value as superstition; see Emerson, "Demonology," in *Lectures and Biographical Sketches* (Boston, 1888), 7–32. For white criticism of black reliance on dreams, see Robert Ryland, "Reminiscences of the First African Church, Richmond, Virginia, by the Pastor," *American Baptist Memorial*, XIV (September–December 1855), 211, 262–263. Renatus Shmidt, Moravian pastor to blacks in North Carolina, writing in 1833 on the spiritual state of Lucas, noted: "It is to be regretted that he bases his conversion so much on dreams, visions and other fantasies"; cited in Jon F. Sensbach, "A Separate Canaan: The Making of an Afro-Moravian World in North Carolina, 1763–1856" (Ph.D. diss., Duke University, 1991), 497.

78. "My notion about conversion was very incorrect; I thought it was nothing more than a dream or some strange sight"; see James Jenkins, *Experience, Labours, and Sufferings of Rev. James Jenkins of the South Carolina Conference* (n.p., 1842), 10. For doubts about the

losing this support, the poor and the weak lost an important bulwark in their attempts to act or behave in ways that were not in keeping with the demands of those in power. The loss was a serious one.

In the process of fashioning their selves, increasing numbers of individuals were rejecting part of themselves and responding to these rejected aspects as other and alien. As a result, the need for addressing dreams actually became more acute among all segments of the population, not only the marginal. In relating to dreams, individuals had often found ways of understanding the dilemmas they faced and had sometimes found extraordinary legitimation for solutions that violated traditional norms. Most important of all, however, by relating their dreams, often in ludic ways, a wide spectrum of the population had become reconnected with disassociated parts of their selves. As dreams were increasingly ignored, these aspects became more alien and more dangerous and selves began to develop in more polarized and menacing directions. The "power of the world of dreams" was by and large lost sight of, ostensibly owing to the growth of rationality, while the power of the irrational hatred of the other grew apace.[79]

BIBLIOGRAPHIC NOTE ON DREAMS AND THE SELF

For an introduction to the analysis of the self, see Clifford Geertz, " 'From the Native's Point of View': On the Nature of Anthropological Understanding," Michelle Z. Rosaldo, "Toward an Anthropology of Self and Feeling," and Richard A. Shweder and Edmund J. Bourne, "Does the Concept of the Person Vary Cross-Culturally?" all in Richard A. Shweder and Robert A. LeVine, eds., *Culture Theory: Essays on Mind, Self, and Emotion* (Cambridge, 1984), 123–136, 137–157, 158–199; Jaine Strauss and George R. Goethals, eds., *The Self: Interdisciplinary Approaches* (New York, 1991); Grace Gredys Harris, "Concepts of Individual, Self, and Person in Description and Analysis," *American Anthropologist*, XCI (1989), 599–612; Ralph H. Turner, "The Real Self: From Institution to Impulse," *American Journal of Sociology*, LXXXI (1976), 989–1007; Charles Taylor, *Sources of the Self: The Making of the Modern Identity* (Cambridge, Mass., 1989), 211–392. J.W.T. Redfearn discusses the broad range of current definitions

---

significance of dreams, see Thomas Smith, *Experience and Ministerial Labors of Rev. Thomas Smith . . .* (New York, 1848), 18, 22. Joseph Smith was originally believed to have been given his esoteric knowledge in a dream, but this was later referred to as a vision; see Quinn, *Early Mormonism*, 114.

79. Wendy Doniger O'Flaherty, *Dreams, Illusions, and Other Realities* (Chicago, 1984), 304.

of self (which he terms "The Present Muddle") in *My Self, My Many Selves* (London, 1985). I use what Redfern disparagingly calls "the lay word which implies personal identity and carries the feeling of 'myself'" (14). Jack D. Douglas, after much difficulty voicing his working definition, came to a formulation that I would also agree with: "The inner self is a vastly complex, open-ended, slowly evolving set of intuitive senses that our mind has about our entire being-in-the-world"; see "The Emergence, Security, and Growth of the Sense of Self," in Joseph A. Kotarba and Andrea Fontona, eds., *The Existential Self in Society* (Chicago, 1984), 95.

Comparative studies of the self include Anthony J. Marsella, George DeVos, and Francis L. K. Hsu, eds., *Culture and Self: Asian and Western Perspectives* (London, 1985); Alan Roland, *In Search of Self in India and Japan: Toward a Cross-Cultural Psychology* (Princeton, N.J., 1988); Richard A. Shweder and Joan G. Miller, "The Social Construction of the Person: How Is It Possible?" in Kenneth J. Gergen and Keith E. Davis, eds., *The Social Construction of the Person* (New York, 1985), 41–69. Studies of changes of self in Western history include Richard D. Logan, "Reflections on Changes in Self-Apprehension and Construction of the 'Other' in Western History," *Psychohistory Review*, XIX (1991), 295–326, Thom Verhave and Willem van Hoorn, "The Temporalization of the Self," in Kenneth J. Gergen and Mary M. Gergen, *Historical Social Psychology* (Hillsdale, N.J., 1984), 325–337; Richard D. Brown, "Modernization and the Modern Personality in Early America, 1600–1865: A Sketch of a Synthesis," *Journal of Interdisciplinary History*, II (1971–1972), 201–228; Louis P. Masur, "'Age of the First Person Singular': The Vocabulary of the Self in New England, 1780–1850," *Journal of American Studies*, XXV (1991), 189–211; John O. Lyons, *The Invention of the Self: The Hinge of Consciousness in the Eighteenth Century* (Carbondale, Ill., 1978); Robert Elbaz, *The Changing Nature of the Self: A Critical Study of the Autobiographic Discourse* (London, 1988); Patricia Meyer Spacks, *Imagining a Self: Autobiography and Novel in Eighteenth-Century England* (Cambridge, Mass., 1976); Felicity A. Nussbaum, *The Autobiographical Subject: Gender and Ideology in Eighteenth-Century England* (Baltimore, 1989). Locke's ideas of self have been seen as marking a turning point in the Western conception. "Locke had severed substance from selfhood and had paved the way for the ultimate denial of the abiding self"; see Christopher Fox, "Locke and the Scriblerians: The Discussion of Identity in Early Eighteenth Century England," *Eighteenth Century Studies*, XVI (1982), 11. Nevertheless, belief in the "true self" and the "real self" have played a role in the West through the modern period. Although many analysts would accept Daniel C. Dennett's definition that "a self . . . is . . . an abstraction defined by the myriads of attributions and interpretations . . . that have composed the biography of the living body whose Center of Narrative Gravity it is," others, this author among them, use as a working concept Heinz Kohut's thesis of the self as agent, developing out of a given or "true" basis; see Dennett, *Consciousness Explained* (Boston, 1991), 412; Kohut, *Self Psychology and the Humanities: Reflections on a New Psychoanalytic Approach* (New York, 1985), 10–11, 33. Ronald R. Lee and J. Colby Martin review the development of Kohut's idea of self and hold that, "in its final form," Kohut came to view "the self as a supraordinate agency, [and] an independent center of initiative," which is present in the infant "in a rudimentary form"; see *Psychotherapy after Kohut: A Textbook of Self Psychology* (Hillsdale, N.J., 1991), 178, 182.

For an analysis of American dream reports by historians, see the survey by Merle Curti, "The American Exploration of Dreams and Dreamers," *Journal of the History of Ideas*, XXVII (1966), 391–416; William H. McGowan, "The Dream of Ezra Stiles: Bishop Berkeley's Haunting of New England," *Studies in Eighteenth-Century Culture*, XI (1981), 181–198; Susan Sleeper-Smith, "The Dream as a Tool for Historical Research: Reexamining Life in Eighteenth-Century Virginia through the Dreams of a Gentleman: William Byrd, II, 1674–1744," *Dreaming*, III (1993), 49–92; Carl A. L. Binger, "The Dreams of Benjamin Rush," *American Journal of Psychiatry*, CXXV (1969), 1653–1659; L. H. Butterfield, "The Dream of Benjamin Rush: The Reconciliation of John Adams and Thomas Jefferson," *Yale Review*, XL (1950–1951), 297–319.

For published American autobiographies written in this period, see Louis Kaplan, comp., *Bibliography of American Autobiographies* (Madison, Wis., 1962). Arthur E. Imhof, "Life-Course Patterns of Women and Their Husbands: Sixteenth to Twentieth Century," in Aage B. Srenson, Franz E. Weinert, and Lonnie R. Sherrod, eds., *Human Development and the Life Course: Multidisciplinary Perspectives* (Hillsdale, N.J., 1986), 247–270, notes that 200,000 early German funeral orations, several pages each, are extant. These are biographies, but some were based on self-reports, such as the late-18th-century collection of autobiographies edited by Karl Philipp Mortiz, in *Magazin zur Erfahrungsseelenkunde*, noted by Martin Kohli, in "The World We Forgot: A Historical Review of the Life Course," in Victor W. Marshall, ed., *Later Life: The Social Psychology of Aging* (Beverly Hills, Calif., 1986), 285. Early Quaker autobiographies and British working-class autobiographies have been collected and republished on microfiche. See, for example, Society of Friends, *Early Quaker Writings from the Library of the Society of Friends, London, 1660–1750* (London, 1977–1979); and *The People's History: Working Class Autobiographies* (Woodbridge, England, 1986), which is based on John Burnett, David Vincent, and David Mayall, eds., *The Autobiography of the Working Class: An Annotated Critical Bibliography* (New York, 1984). The Society of Friends Archive in Haverford, Pennsylvania, has extensive autobiographical holdings from the early modern period, as do Moravian archives in Herrenhut, Germany, and Bethlehem, Pennsylvania.

Dream reports can be found in the collection of writings by the followers of the Universal Friend, recorded in "Rachel Malin's Dream and Date Book," Otter-Wilkinson Papers, 1768–1872, Cornell University Library, Department of Manuscripts and University Archives, Ithaca, N.Y. Baptist and Methodists often reported soul travels from their dreams in their sermons and testimonies. Almost every Baptist and Methodist narrative from the period 1740–1840 includes dream reports, which were shared with congregations. See, for example, Baptist John Leland, *Some Events in the Life of John Leland, Written by Himself* (Pittsfield, Mass., 1838), 10, 14, 15; Methodist James Jenkins, *Experience, Labours, and Sufferings of Rev. James Jenkins of the South Carolina Conference* (n.p., 1842), 9, 11, 34, 39, 47, 97, 159. Early Quaker narratives, prior to committee editing, were full of dreams. See, for example, John Richardson, *An Account of the Life of That Ancient Servant of Jesus Christ: John Richardson . . .* (Philadelphia, 1783), 33, 48, 53, 62.

There is ample evidence that dreams were also recounted in family circles and at more public places, were entered as evidence in court trials, and were published in newspapers. Dreams played an important role in letters, were preserved in diaries as well as the narratives, and were created for fictive autobiographies and early novels. Elizabeth Drinker recorded that "George Churchman was reading to night to us a Dream of a woman friend, he did not tell us her name, it was of scourgeings that the people were to experience"; see Elaine Forman Crane, ed., *The Diary of Elizabeth Drinker*, 3 vols. (Boston, 1991), July 23, 1799, II, 1192. I want to thank Elaine Forman Crane for this reference. For a selection of dreams in the various types of sources, legal documents, newspapers, diaries, and literature, see the following: Jesse Lemisch, "Listening to the 'Inarticulate': William Widger's Dream and the Loyalties of American Revolutionary Seamen in British Prisons," *Journal of Social History*, III (1969–1970), 1–29; James Walcot, *The New Pilgrim's Progress; or, The Pious Indian Convert* (London, 1748), esp. 74; John Vandeluer [pseud.], *A History of the Voyages and Adventures of John Van Delure* (Montpelier, Vt., 1812), 34, presents what is claimed to be the lengthy dream of his native American mother-in-law. A dream report of a man who turned into a "Beast with a pair of Horns" was printed in *New-York Gazette*, Apr. 3, 1738. William Jenks (1778–1866) recorded his dreams of 1798 in a notebook he titled "Somnia," William Jenks Papers, Massachusetts Historical Society. Zuriel Waterman recorded a six-page dream in the "Memorandum Book for the Sloop Retaliation, May 1780," Zuriel Waterman Papers, History of Medicine Division, National Library of Medicine, Bethesda, Maryland. I am indebted to Manfred Wasserman for bringing this work to my attention. See Edgar Allan Poe, "A Dream" (1831), in Raymond Foye, ed., *The Unknown Poe: An Anthology of Fugitive Writings by Edgar Allan Poe* (San Francisco, 1980), 55–57, which reports a dream in which the dreamer participated in the crucifixion of Christ, "driving the sharpest nails through the palms." In *The Prodigal Daughter . . .* (Boston, 1769), Rev. Williams of Newport wrote of the parents of an immoral daughter being warned in a dream that their child was planning to poison them. Revolutionary newspapers printed many fictive dreams, clearly hoping to establish the bona fides of the Revolution as a God-sent event, and at least one Revolutionary soldier later claimed to have been given a vision of the war in 1763. See David Perry, *Recollections of an Old Soldier . . .* (Windsor, Vt., 1822), 40–41. See Thomas Paine, *Examination of the Passages in the New Testament . . . To Which Is Prefixed an Essay on Dreams . . .* (New York, 1807). For concern with dreams in Revolutionary journals, see "An Extraordinary Dream," *Pennsylvania Magazine; or, American Monthly Museum*, I, January 1775, 16; "The History of Dream Interpretation," *Pennsylvania Magazine; or, American Monthly Museum*, II, March 1776, 119–122.

After many years of struggling with how I should approach the dreams in this study, I have come to accept a "hermeneutic model" in which " 'interpretation' involves an interaction between the world of the text and the world of the interpreter." See Carol Schreier Rupprecht and Kelly Bulkley, "Reading Yourself to Sleep: Dreams in/and/as Texts," in Rupprecht, ed., *The Dream and the Text: Essays on Literature and Language* (Albany, N.Y., 1993), 1–12 (quotation on 3), and the book as a whole, for an excellent introduction to the issues in contemporary dream text interpretation, particularly with regard to historical and cultural concerns. On the dream and culture, two of the most important collections of essays are that of G. E. von Grunebaum and Roger Caillois, eds., *The Dream and Human Societies* (Berkeley, Calif., 1966), and Barbara Tedlock, ed., *Dreaming: Anthropological and Psychological Interpretations* (Cambridge, 1987). Virtually all schools of interpretation are paying serious attention to the manifest dream. For a summary of current views, see Judith Marks Mishne, *The Evolution and Application of Clinical Theory: Perspectives from Four Psychologies* (New York, 1993), 4–5, 7–10, 27, 379–380; Ross Levin, "Psychoanalytic Theories on the Function of Dreaming: A Review of the Empirical Dream Research," in Joseph Masling, ed., *Empirical Studies of Psychoanalytical Theories*, 3 vols. (New York, 1990), III, 1–53. Levin emphasizes that many Freudians now hold "that the dream revealed the individual's attempt to adapt and work through emotional problems, past or present." Distress, anxiety, and depression in daily life are found to be directly reflected in dreams, as are styles of coping. "Manifest dream content clinically and statistically discriminated between individuals with varying levels of coping effectiveness in response to a major life change." Levin concludes that dream work may "lead to highly creative and novel solutions to old conflicts." "While many of Freud's formulations continue to be useful, and indeed invaluable, the evidence overwhelmingly indicates that dreams are active, organized, and sometimes even rational attempts to process meaningful information from past and present and that the manifest content of these dreams are meaningful and valid sources of data for systematic study" (4, 21, 38–39). Heinz Kohut, George E. Atwood, and Robert D. Stolorow, among others, have seen dreams as a significant arena for the strengthening of self. See Kohut, *The Restoration of the Self* (New York, 1977), 109; Atwood and Stolorow, *Structures of Subjectivity* (Hillsdale, N.J., 1984). Alan Moffitt, Milton Kramer, and Robert Hoffmann have edited an exceptionally fine book of essays, *The Functions of Dreaming* (Albany, N.Y., 1993). Virtually all the authors in this volume share Harry Fiss's view: "Dreams do not conceal. On the contrary, they *reveal,* and they reveal extraordinarily well." See Fiss, "The 'Royal Road' to the Unconscious Revisited: A Signal Detection Model of Dream Function" (397).

STORIES AND CONSTRUCTIONS OF IDENTITY: FOLK TELLINGS AND DIARY INSCRIPTIONS IN REVOLUTIONARY VIRGINIA

Rhys Isaac

In the end, we become *the autobiographical narratives by which we "tell about" our lives.*
—Jerome Bruner

Personal identities are above all sustained by their stories. Narrative is one of the most powerful forms of knowledge. Jerome Bruner, prominent cognitive psychologist, proposes that it is through acquiring narratives and learning to enter into narratives that the infant first gains not just understanding of social realities but also the necessary forms needed for constructing those social realities.[1]

It has become a truism—understood first among contenders for the women's cause but generally accepted wherever issues of equity and access are taken seriously—that full personhood requires having a validating story of one's own, just as collective identity requires that one's gender or ethnic group have a duly acknowledged place in the master narratives that are taken for the society's history. With regard to individuals in a highly individuated world— where concern seems to have moved inward from an externally presented persona to a self experienced within—it may be nearer the mark to suggest that for full selfhood one needs a story appropriate to that desired self.

Four story clusters are presented in this essay for illustrative review—some African American songs and tales, some British American ballads, and two

The author gives thanks for the critique of one or more drafts of this essay by the following persons: Alton L. Becker, Inga Clendinnen, Katie Holmes, Colleen Isaac, and Lotte Mulligan, a great authority and source of insight into early English diaries. Many persons have helped in many ways. I am grateful to them all.

1. Jerome Bruner, "Life as Narrative," *Social Research*, LIV (1987), 11–32 (quotation on 15). For further elaboration of cognitive psychological fundamentals in this area, see Jerome Bruner, "The Narrative Construction of Reality," *Critical Inquiry*, XVIII (1991), 1–21.

very different book-readers' diary self-presentations. None are in traditions peculiar to the Revolutionary Virginia from which they come, and I shall seek to interpret and compare them so as to open the American phase of the wider Atlantic Revolution rather than to define distinctive local characteristics. Most attention will be given to the diary narratives of the two literate persons; although of different generations and of opposite sex, both were from Virginia gentry families that supplied active leadership to the Revolution. I hope in this way to advance understanding of the growing sense of the individuated, feeling-oriented self that was fundamental to reconceptualizing individual and society—the transformation of subject into citizen—that was at the heart of the Atlantic Revolution.

NARRATIVES AND IDENTITIES

The "story" in its many, many varieties is a developed form of narrative that pervasively orders our worlds. Stories generate and sustain most of our knowledge of human affairs through their terse presentation, review, and evaluation of particular actions, great and small. In telling, interpreting, and commenting on our own and others' actions, we gain our most valued knowledge of ourselves and of those others. In establishing a sense of person and a sense of self, stories do essential cultural work. ("Story," it should be noted, is an everyday category that scholars have almost obscured; we know one when we hear or see one—and such common-sense recognition is the only essential understanding requisite for the discussion that follows.)[2]

Stories that are already known have told the community that shares them what *has* happened, and so indeed by extension they reveal what *does* happen or *can* happen in the world. Knowing stories is indispensable to following sequences of action even as they unfold. Stories frame a mundane world of

2. The best formal account of the story form that I know is in William Labov, *Sociolinguistic Patterns* (Philadelphia, 1972), 354–396. Labov, however, replaces the categorization "story" (which would have been familiar to his informants) by the social-scientific designation "natural narrative." Mary Louise Pratt, *Toward a Speech Act Theory of Literary Discourse* (Bloomington, Ind., 1977), 38–78, gives a valuable overview of Labov's anatomy of storytelling and shows how all the essential elements are—and must be—transposed into written forms. Bruner, in "Narrative Construction of Reality," *Critical Inquiry,* XVIII (1991), 6–20, outlines a more extensive set of requirements for what he simply designates "narrative"; the word "story" slips into his account only by revealing accident, it seems (9, 11, 13, 15, 17, 19). I would insist—for all the very high esteem in which I hold Bruner's contribution—that there is an important distinction to be maintained between "narrative" (a hold-all category) and "story" (a more constrained one) and that only "stories" fulfill all Bruner's 10 criteria.

supposed actual happenings, even as they present much larger, more fascinating domains of what should or might happen. In doing so, stories constitute for their audiences a realm of worlds within worlds and of worlds beyond the everyday world. They show humans what kinds of being each person might be; they show what kinds of actions, leading to what kinds of outcomes, may be entered into by all the different kinds of beings in the known and imagined world.

Storytelling is therefore a special form of action that suspends for its duration other forms of action. In stories, action is replayed so that meanings may be imposed on it and drawn from it. Storytelling is, therefore, one of the most powerful forms of that large and pervasive set of social activities directed toward the making, sustaining, and intensifying of meanings—activities that the anthropologist Victor Turner and the historian and anthropologist Greg Dening have designated "entertainment." In the entertainment of storytelling, we are, as the etymology of the word implies, held in an in-between time, as we are taken out of the realm of action and into a powerful one where the possible meanings of actions are contemplated. It is in such realms of entertainment that societies, and groupings within society, assemble many of the resources available for individuals to construct their own "subjectivities"—for them to identify what personae they may present to the world, what self they may experience and sustain inwardly.[3]

Every story, every entertainment, requires its "theater"—its moment, its situation, and its medium—for performance. We discover and reveal our self and find revealed the personae, and perhaps sense the selves of others, in the entertainments of their theaters of interaction, narration, communication.

The revelatory and constitutive entertainment provided by stories makes them important contributors to and draws on the "mythology" of any society at any given time. (By "mythology," I do not mean, positivistically, a stock of stories known to be untrue; anthropologically, I adopt "mythology" as a term for the collective knowledge that is *the* indispensable ground of "truth"—reality—in any cultural system.) Self and persona can be sustained in any society only from that society's "mythology"—from the stock of stories that both enter into and arise from shared knowledge of what has been, what is, and what might be. Sex is assuredly at the head of the permanent agenda of mythologies. Since newborn humans are anxiously scrutinized at birth for their

3. See Victor Turner, "Process, System, and Symbol: A New Anthropological Synthesis," *Daedalus*, CVI (1977), 73; and Greg Dening, *History's Anthropology: The Death of William Gooch* (Lanham, Md., 1988), 3–4, 14, or Dening, *The Death of William Gooch: A History's Anthropology* (Honolulu, 1995), 15, 25, 31, 87, 104. See also Greg Dening, *Performances* (Chicago, 1996), 47–48, 49, 52, 55–56, 167, 199.

sex and then enter on a lifelong pervasive, insistent education of the gender roles appropriate to their declared male or female category, mythologies, and the stories in which they exist have to be deeply and intensely concerned with the narration, contestation, and negotiation of gender roles. Within the framework of always-contested masculine hegemony, (un)feminine transgressions provide ever recurrent stories for the dominant mythology. Important changes in gendered persona and in self will be traceable historically in a changing mythology and in the changing stories that carry and indicate such changes.[4]

White Women Communicate African Performance

In 1816, there met in Washington Miss Ellen Randolph, Thomas Jefferson's grandaughter, and M. Eugène Vail, a visiting Frenchman, who—like so many of his kind—thought he might write a book recounting to his countrymen a sojourner's experiences of the New World and of its emergent republican culture. Perhaps he questioned Miss Ellen about the poetry of the African Americans. If so, the young woman seems to have passed the questions on to her mother, Mrs. Martha Jefferson Randolph; or else Vail followed up the acquaintance himself, visiting the Jefferson-Randolph menage at Monticello. Mrs. Randolph thus found herself communicating African Virginian song and story to an interested Frenchman.[5] She showed an appreciation of it that she

4. The conception of myth that I advance here owes much, it will be seen, to Northrop Frye, *Fables of Identity: Studies in Poetic Mythology* (New York, 1963)—except that I see "myth" more historically, as a living medium that is continuously added to as well as drawn upon rather than as some primal cultural capital. I am much indebted to Roger Abrahams for searching discussions of this topic—and for a timely caution concerning the "lightness" of many genres of "floating" stories when compared with "the chartering stories of a culture" (personal communication). In addition, I have gained from Hildred Geertz and Jerry Sider a strong sense of the partial character of all tellings of myth—only a fragment is given at any time. The partiality of these fragments resides also in the interested claims always being advanced by the tellers, both in their selection and in their manner of telling (Shelby Cullom Davis Seminar, Princeton University, 1981). I have been further influenced by Marshall Sahlins, *Historical Metaphors and Mythical Realities: Structure in the Early History of the Sandwich Islands Kingdom* (Ann Arbor, Mich., 1981). Literary-critical discussions are ably summed up in K. K. Ruthven, *Myth* (London, 1976).

5. Ellen W. Randolph to Mrs T. M. Randolph, Dec. 30, [1816], MSS 9090, box 1, Alderman Library, Charlottesville, Va. The results of this transmission of information were published later in Eugène A. Vail, *De la littérature et des hommes de lettres des Etats-Unis d'Amérique* (Paris, 1841), 322–333. (I am deeply indebted to Mechal Sobel for sending me a

could never have shared with her own circle—especially not with her father, whose disparagement of African American poetic and narrative art is notorious. Perhaps her familiarity with these songs and stories was in any case understood as part of women's knowledge, since it derived from the intimacies of the lady of the house as supervisor of slave work in kitchen and nursery. Thomas Jefferson had surely also encountered such song and story in his infancy, but he had—in his embrace of a gentleman's polite European culture (as well as in his strong rejection of a biracial Virginia)—determinedly repressed that knowledge. His daughter, Martha, by contrast, valued her knowledge and shared that valuation with her own daughter, Ellen. Only the advent of a foreigner who was interested in exotic forms was likely to get past the prudent reserve by which ladies were taught to avoid putting forward their women's knowledge in conversation with gentlemen.

In what Martha Jefferson Randolph presented to Vail, she was explaining—and identifying with and defending—the powerful musical and narrative imagination of the African American singers and storytellers that she recalled from her own and her children's upbringing in Virginia.[6] Martha, who had been partly raised in Paris while her father was United States envoy to France, doubtless had some distanced perspective and even perhaps delight in the rediscovery of exciting performances whose sounds had surrounded her during infancy. If so, she was, in the entertainment of her presentation of this folklore to the Frenchman, surely discovering a woman's household-based Virginian American identity.[7]

In presenting M. Eugène Vail with an account of old Titus, a street performer with a "banjar," who was a familiar figure in the Virginia capital city of Richmond, Martha opened up for the enquiring Vail the realm of songs. Here were

———

copy of these pages of this rare book.) An English translation of the songs and stories given to Vail was published in Elizabeth Langhorne, "Black Music and Tales from Jefferson's Monticello," *Folklore and Folklife in Virginia*, I (1979), 60–67.

6. Vail named his informant only indirectly—"one of the noble daughters of Virginia, offshoot (*rejeton*) of a name which figures at the head of the most illustrious of our presidents." The known connection of the Frenchman, however, with the Jefferson Randolphs led Elizabeth Langhorne to assume that Vail's informant was Martha Jefferson Randolph; see Langhorne, "Black Music," *Folklore and Folklife in Virginia*, I (1979), 60.

7. There certainly seems to be an older woman's appreciative but distanced eye and ear—rather than a fascinated child's memory—at work collecting the observational details of Mammy Ursula's performance style. As the wife of a legislator and then governor of Virginia, Thomas Mann Randolph (1819–1822), she would have resided in Richmond with opportunities to take note of such street performers as Titus. (I am extremely grateful to

musically sustained stories that may well be—despite historians' continuing neglect—one of the most powerfully pervasive forms of entertainment in all culture. Vail later published translations of what had been shared with him, and thus in 1841 there appeared in Paris in French one of the earliest collections of African Virginian folklore to be printed.[8]

Vail had learned not only about Titus and his songs but also about Mammy Ursula, an old nurse at Monticello, and about her notable narrative style. One story was especially memorable—the tale of Old Día, a woman of great power, who had three wonderful dogs, whom she was able to summon magically to her rescue whenever she was in danger. In this story, Old Día called on these dogs one day when the devil—perhaps an African wood spirit, Vail thought—had chased her up a tree. The devil had set about chopping down the tree; "ducka, ducka, ducka" went the sound of the axes that he wielded, one in each hand. The manner of the telling of this tale was shown to be as vital as the story itself: there was not only the rhythmic imitation of the sound of the axe to heighten suspense, but also—and evidently crucial to the whole dramatic effect—there was the way the singing voice of the old woman, "slow and plaintiff," and of the devil, "quick and jerky," were alternately represented by Mammy Ursula in her narrations. Here then, conveyed to us by the chance encounter of a folklore-conscious Virginia lady and a French litterateur, is a fragment of an undoubtedly vast stock of stories that was part of a mythology of beings with powerful personae and forms of action.[9]

In a different but equally expressive genre, there was the old nurse's tale of how a fox tried both to gain protection in a hare's burrow and to devour the hare who had given him shelter—only to be himself tricked and destroyed by the resourceful hare. Through Vail's publication, we thus know that white women and children at Thomas Jefferson's Monticello had already heard a version of a story belonging to the most famous of all cycles of trickster tales. This story would change little before it came to be written down again in the

---

Lucia Stanton of the Monticello Foundation for helping me with this matter, including the assurance that the absence of any record of Vail's visiting Monticello is not a reason to assume that he did not do so [personal communication].) On Thomas Jefferson's rejection of the African heritage open to him from his childhood (and throughout his life), see Rhys Isaac, "The First Monticello," in Peter S. Onuf, ed., *Jeffersonian Legacies* (Charlottesville, Va., 1993), 79–81, 99–101. On Jefferson's expectations concerning a responsive rather than an initiating role for ladies in conversation, see Jan Lewis, " 'The Blessings of Domestic Society': Thomas Jefferson's Family and the Transformation of American Politics," in Onuf, ed., *Jeffersonian Legacies*, 134.

8. Vail, *De la littérature*, 322–333.

9. Ibid., 327–330.

later nineteenth century, except that the more African hare, at some later time, became the decidedly African American Brer Rabbit.[10]

Although these stories come to us through so many filters, the African spirit world and animal trickster tales can be here perceived flourishing in Revolutionary Virginia. We can only guess at the entertainment slaves found in such stories, but they were evidently parts of a powerful collective mythology—a mythology that told not of inward self so much as of strong personae directed outward to action in the world.

British American Balladry

Alongside African American mythology and the narratives in which it had its being, there existed another active oral tradition that, although different, was no less vigorous in its representations of strong, outward-directed action and personae. The Anglo-Virginian oral tradition is also mainly known from later folklorists' collections, but there exists at least one clearly documented instance—like the Randolph-Vail transcriptions—of early performances occurring in an identifiable setting.

In his autobiography published in 1804, Devereux Jarratt gives us a glimpse of Anglo-Virginian tales in the theater of their telling. He was recalling his remarkable powers of memory as a child, but that led him to mention some of the stories that had early shaped his consciousness. As a farm boy in the 1730s and 1740s, he had come to know, and had incorporated strongly into his personal mythology, the story of Samson and Delilah from the Bible—a strand of folklore that would make a large subject on its own. The young Jarratt had also internalized a cycle of the ballads that the English settlers had brought with them, stories these folk were so attached to that they preserved them in active oral repertoires until well into the twentieth century.[11]

"The Ballad of Chevy Chase," the only one of these songs that Jarratt mentioned by name, was a longtime favorite in Old England. This song carries the story of warrior boldness, of a challenge that was met with defiance, and of an ensuing great slaughter of Englishmen and Scots, neither of whom would yield—although they would make speeches celebrating their dying enemies'

10. Ibid., 330–333. On the hare as African trickster, see Lawrence W. Levine, *Black Culture and Black Consciousness: Afro-American Folk Thoughts from Slavery to Freedom* (New York, 1977), 103; and also—from this author's own childhood—Frank Worthington, [trans. and comp.], *Kalulu the Hare* (London, 1930).

11. Devereux Jarratt, *The Life of the Reverend Devereux Jarratt . . .* (Baltimore, 1806; facsimile reprint, New York, 1969), 19. For the persistence of the ballads, see Arthur Kyle Davis, Jr., ed., *Traditional Ballads of Virginia: Collected under the Auspices of the Virginia Folk-Lore Society* (1929; reprint, Charlottesville, Va., 1969).

valor. It is a tale of men. But women are always present in such tales. In this one, women's roles appear indirectly but powerfully: in the lament at the relentless killing that "the chylde may rue that ys un-born" and in the narration of how, "on the morrowe . . . many wedous with wepyng tears" came to fetch their husband's bodies away.[12]

Most of the other ballads that crossed the Atlantic—to be relished and kept alive among white farmfolk in parts of Virginia—were stories of courtship, of the jealousy of siblings, of the fierce and fatal guarding of wealth and women by their fathers and brothers. Or else they were stories of unrequited love leading both true and false lovers to graves from which then sprang entwining roses and briars. The most insistent, ever recurrent story in these ballads told that romantic love was a fatal, dooming passion. These ballads thus underscore how, in property-based patriarchal systems (such as the English brought to and adapted in Virginia), women and the love that may bond them to outsiders are a troubling source of dangers and potential betrayals. Their affections can bring enemies within the gates. Even when daughters are given in marriage, that gift in itself alienates them from their fathers' or brothers' households as human resources; their dowries are subtracted from the material wealth of the patrilineage.[13]

Transforming Theaters: Changing Identities

I have thus far reviewed fragments of two different mythologies among two largely unlettered peoples. We have these stories and we do not have them. As I find them and as I present them, they are no longer the stories of the people from whose oral repertoire they have been taken. Mammy Ursula's stories as presented here are a historian's taking up of a litterateur's rendition of a white mistress's record of stories told by an African American woman to amaze and stretch the eyes of the white gentlefolk children in her care. Such tales when printed (first by M. Eugène Vail and now by me) are at a far remove from the same stories as they had originally been learned by Mammy Ursula in performance. Then they had been at once drawn from and woven back into the shared mythologies that were sustained among Mammy Ursula's own people at the quarter. Likewise, Devereux Jarratt's favoring "The Ballad of Chevy Chase"—because, as he wrote, Mr. Addison had celebrated it!—also marked

12. James Kinsley, ed., *The Oxford Book of Ballads* (Oxford, 1989), 497, 506.

13. Davis, ed., *Traditional Ballads*. Societies retain in their repertoire what is meaningfully relevant. Roger Abrahams has pointed out to me that the old ballads collected in early-20th-century Virginia mostly came from mountain communities where clan feuding was endemic, where holding together a fighting band of men was vital, and where complicating love relationships *were* apt to be fatal (personal communication).

his own decisive transference of it out of the realm in which he learned it and into a quite other print-sustained mythology. In the printed form in which the historian finds them, these tales tell differently, in one case of an incipient elite interest in folk culture and in the other case of a characteristic autobiographical nostalgia for a neighborhood-community world on the part of an upwardly mobile American, who had become, in maturity, a more cosmopolitan man of letters. Noticing the transitions through which the stories have gone draws attention again to an important truth that is too easily forgotten: every story, indeed every entertainment, gets its meaning in *each* theater of *each* performance and from the interactions of that particular theater, as much as (or more than) from its formal resemblances to previous performances or its supposed structural identity with the story it notionally reproduces.[14]

These instances of folk narrative, available to the historian because serendipitously they were caught up in written records, are included here to stand as reminders of the oral recitals in spontaneous theaters of face-to-face interaction that then sustained the vast bulk of the stories in circulation in early America. Both samples are out-of-context fragments, but they do nevertheless represent two distinct mythologies out of which two peoples who inhabited different imaginative universes were in their eighteenth-century times entertained.

The distinctness of the family systems here represented almost certainly kept the African American and Anglo-American mythologies poles apart: slave society was on the defensive and was systematically denied the resources of property as a means to reinforce relationships; the masters' society was aggressive for the accumulation of property to sustain and extend patriarchal dominion and its family strategies. Furthermore, the masters' mythology was relentless in its stigmatizing repression of the stories of the Africans, which might indeed have had appeal for the weaker, the women and children, within the strong hegemony of the adult white male patriarchs. In the African American stories, one predominant theme was the struggle and the means to prevail of the cunning weak—the woman armed with special knowledge, the hare with quick wit—against the predatory strong; in the British American ballads, a pre-

14. The same story—with regard to contents or plot—can be told straightly and ironically to make opposite points. Historians must avoid being mesmerized by textual formalism and attend always to the *actual* theater of any performance—and so seek out what might *actually* have been communicated there. For a masterly set of treatments of theaters in specified social settings, see Greg Dening, *Mr Bligh's Bad Language: Passion, Power, and Theatre on the Bounty* (New York, 1992). Conference discussion initiated by Laura Rigal, and then the wise counsel of Roger Abrahams, helped me to better appreciate the parodic translations that were probably happening in the Monticello nursery theater when Mammy Ursula told stories to the Randolph children. (I here assume that Martha Jefferson Randolph was recording stories that she heard Mammy Ursula telling the children in her care, including Ellen.)

dominant theme already noted was the fatality of love, of the very attraction between the sexes, then, that must be the means to renew life. In both cases, whether shown by talking animals or by the entwining rose and briar from the lovers' graves, there was an ancient assumed continuity between human life and the natural world. This was an assumption already heavily undermined by the rational functionalism pervading European print culture and the habitual violence toward forests and rivers practiced on the Anglo-American frontier.[15]

These sung-and-told worlds, both of the colonial balladists and of the tellers of African American magical and trickster tales, were all worlds of strong personae and not, it seems, worlds of the developed self; they were like the world of the Homeric epics that had provided models for literature and education in the West for countless generations. The imaginative universes of those oral narratives were not peopled by characters inwardly sustained by elaborated self-knowledge; these tales were not psychologized stories of the self. The storyteller too, although assuredly assuming a powerful persona, was scarcely an introspective self but was rather the voice through whom a well-known imaginary world was conjured up in a vividly shared present so as to entertain all participants with the possibilities of reflecting on deeper meanings. In such oral performances, it was not just the underlying mythology (always a shared system) but the story itself that was a collective possession. Authorship could not even be an issue here, because the story was already owned by the group before, during, and after each teller-led interactive performance. In such enacted stories of such heroic-action worlds, contemplative and introspective modes played little if any part.[16] These oral narrative traditions were present in

15. Robert Darnton, "Peasants Tell Tales: The Meaning of Mother Goose," in *The Great Cat Massacre and Other Episodes in French Cultural History* (New York, 1984), 9–72, is a good place for historians to start revisiting the phase in the European preprint cultural tradition when the animals still spoke—although Darnton does not review the continuities of man and nature assumed in the animal tales. Keith Thomas, *Man and the Natural World: Changing Attitudes in England, 1500–1800* (Harmondsworth, England, 1984), deals with the hardening of rational-functionalist positions rather than the preceding animist beliefs. For a famous English example at the interface of oral and literary culture, see Geoffrey Chaucer, *The Parlement of Foules* (composed c. 1380). The ranking of bird and beast there—noble and base—is a reminder of another ancient and enduring form of assumed correspondence with the human, indeed cosmic, order. On the violence against nature of the English frontier in America, see William Cronon, *Changes in the Land: Indians, Colonists, and the Ecology of New England* (New York, 1983), esp. 159–170; and Frederick Turner, *Beyond Geography: The Western Spirit against the Wildnerness* (New Brunswick, N.J., 1992), 255–259. (I am grateful to Karri Giles for presenting me with the republished version of this strong book.)

16. On oral performance there is now a vast literature; my formulation here is still guided by one of the paradigm-building interpretations; see Walter J. Ong, *The Presence of*

Virginia, and in early America generally, in ethnically diverse forms; they are an indispensable context for the beginnings of a historical appreciation of the kinds of stories and performances—the personae, the actions, and the forms of self—that writing, reading, and personal recordkeeping were sustaining.

IDENTITY IN WRITING

An increasingly individual sense of self belongs in the distinctive mythologies that have been created and sustained in *written* forms of entertainment. A sense of unique, inwardly complex selves has long been growing in Western mythology as fostered by alphabetic script. That means, then, that this particular form of Western mythology has been associated closely with elite white males, who so long had a near monopoly of the written medium and thus dominated the traditions from which writing-sustained Western constructions of the self at first emerged.[17]

Particularly revealing of distinctive selves were stories about the self as written into diaries, into autobiographies, and into the first-person novels that had such prominence in the eighteenth century. (Indeed, with the powerful advent of the novel, each published narration conjured a vast, continually extending array of ostensibly new stories about humans who characteristically had an elaborated sense of a unique self that was more or less sustained by an introspective story of that self.)[18]

---

the Word: Some Prolegomena for Cultural and Religious History (New Haven, Conn., 1967). For an excellent brief discussion of a heroic-mode sense of the active human agent (or person) that leaves no room for a complex inward self, see Charles Taylor, *Sources of the Self: The Making of Modern Identity* (Cambridge, Mass., 1989), 118–120.

17. Susan Stanford Friedman, "Women's Autobiographical Selves: Theory and Practice," in Shari Benstock, ed., *The Private Self: Theory and Practice of Women's Autobiographical Writings* (London, 1988). The subject is also constructively reviewed in Charlotte Linde, *Life Stories: The Creation of Coherence* (New York, 1993), 98–111. I have further been helped conceptually by essays in George Levine, ed., *Constructions of the Self* (New Brunswick, N.J., 1992).

18. The long history of a sense of the self as a complex inwardness is effectively traced and its peculiarity to modern Western and westernizing traditions from the time of Plato to the present is persuasively suggested in Taylor, *Sources of the Self*. Taylor does not use the term "persona" to designate the *outward* manifestations of humans in action—the manifestations that are managed by the agent and responded to by interactants—but I have introduced it as necessary to my discussion. My account of the emergent novel and the self is principally formed from Patricia Meyer Spacks, *Imagining a Self: Autobiography and Novel in Eighteenth-Century England* (Cambridge, Mass., 1976); Jay Fliegelman, *Prodigals and Pil-*

In the balance of this essay, two diaries—coming also from Revolutionary-period Virginia—will serve as illustrative examples. First is the long-kept diary of one of the richest and most powerful of late-colonial Virginia gentlemen; the second is drawn from the small range of women's diaries from Virginia in this period. It is a two-month letter journal kept by a young lady and is chosen because in its youthful lightness it reveals the diarist as a self constructing herself out of the new narratives. She was an avid reader of novels who was finding a new subjectivity in the burgeoning novel-sustained mythologies. I shall explore the instructive contrast apparent in this pair of personal writings and in the stories they tell, the better to open a discussion of what such records may reveal of myths of the self in written stories of the self.

Since diaries are inscribed, kept, and archived, they are one of the prime means by which the emergent self-conscious introspective self and its stories can be the object of historical study. Samuel Pepys—one of the first great English-language accumulators of such a narrative of the self—was so identified with his painstaking project that, when he was impelled to abandon it for the preservation of failing eyesight, he felt that the breaking off was "almost as much as to see myself go into the grave." And so, Robert Fothergill, a perceptive student of the diary genre, finding such an intense identification between diarist and diary to be quite usual in the case of long-sustained diary-writing projects, designated these lovingly accumulated records as being, each for its keeper, truly "the book of the self."[19]

With this concept of "the book of the self," I would associate another concept that strictly applies to oral forms current among twentieth-century middle-class Americans. The sociolinguist, Charlotte Linde, has made a milestone study of what she calls the "life story" among her American contemporaries. What she found was in fact composite sets of stories that are for their bearers an essential part of their equipment for living. Being part of their bearers' oral repertoire, these stories cumulate as "life story" and are, she explains, a "temporally discontinuous" "unit" whose component narratives are differently told upon different occasions and are subject to revisions as the lives of their bearers unfold.[20]

A key feature of these "life stories," as Linde characterizes them, is that they "have as their primary evaluation a point about the speaker, not a general point about the way the world is." This is a feature usually shared by the stories

---

grims: *The American Revolution against Patriarchal Authority, 1750–1800* (Cambridge, 1982); and Felicity A. Nussbaum, *The Autobiographical Subject: Gender and Ideology in Eighteenth-Century England* (Baltimore, 1989).

19. Robert A. Fothergill, *Private Chronicles: A Study of English Diaries* (London, 1974), 43.
20. Linde, *Life Stories*, 21.

in diaries. Although diary stories of the self differ from Linde's life stories in that they do not usually tell and retell in revised form the same perceived "turning points" of a life, they do tend to tell—through day-by-day little episodes showing changed perspective with changing phases of the life—a continuous set of evaluations of the self. Furthermore, a diary is also an identifiable theater in which the life stories as performed by the diarist are preserved for the historian, unlike the theaters in which the folk oral repertoires were performed. The interactive dynamics of the diary theater, like those of any written document, are elusive to be sure but may, by painstaking attention to genre and to voice, be at least partially discovered and presented in our histories.[21]

Phases of a Patriarchal Diary

The self that is known through the stories that gather to make a life story is not a constant. Far from it. There is a shifting repertoire of stories—stories are added (or revised) as we go on our way through the world, and stories (or versions of stories) are discarded. The perspective of the story-bearer is continually changing, and markedly so with the major role transitions in the phases of a whole life. Such transitions are clearly manifest in the changing book of the self inscribed over a period of more than twenty years by one of early America's most remarkable diarists, Colonel Landon Carter of Sabine Hall, 1710–1778.[22]

The stories in the earliest part of Colonel Carter's book of the self accord with the character of its keeper at the time of writing. He was then a Virginia grandee scarcely past his prime, entering slightly late but confidently into what he took to be his inheritance as a dominant man of affairs in his province. The colonel's first extant day-by-day plantation record was headed "Farming Observations etc. continued." It was in spirit an at-home continuation of the 1752–1755 procedures book and parliamentary diary. Indeed, the diarist had dedicated a handsome black-bound quarto notebook to his purpose when he had commenced his career as legislator in 1752. In 1756, he literally turned the book over to begin a plantation procedures book from what had been the back—that now became the front—of that same volume.[23]

In the theater of the initial surviving plantation record, stories had small place. That is not surprising, since there is always a negotiation of power in storytell-

21. Ibid., 25. On the theaters of discourses, see Dening, *Mr Bligh's Bad Language*.
22. Jack P. Greene, ed., *The Diary of Colonel Landon Carter of Sabine Hall, 1752–1778*, 2 vols. (Charlottesville, Va., 1965).
23. The MS quarto notebook from which the quoted heading is taken is among the Sabine Hall Papers, Alderman Library, University of Virginia.

ing, and there is necessarily a problematic negotiation of self in relation to the world at stake in the kind of stories that may enter into the life story. Overwhelmingly, the contents of the first years of the plantation diary were "Observations"—as the heading had declared. There were also accompanying analyses, with reflections upon them, and there were resolutions for action that should follow. The dominant genres were planning reviews, construction projects, and the like. This was the book of the self of a man who felt himself in command and who was confidently developing, as a new project for his life, the introduction of "English husbandry" in his tobacco growing; stories properly so called would be almost out of place in this book.[24]

The small number of action stories that were included in the colonel's first plantation journal were of a kind in keeping with the diarist's project; they were intended to record his tough, measure-and-calculate managerial self. On January 21, 1757, for instance, he discovered that his "threshers of oats made a shift to thresh no more per day than they did when the days were 20 minutes shorter"; unwilling to tolerate "such evident lazyness," he "ordered them Correction . . . three days running" and devised a scheme to monitor them individually "by setting them on different floors to discover the lazy fellow." So pleased was he to note how, after this, they returned him "40 bushels per day," that he entered a coda, in which he evaluated the whole story and celebrated the self that he was recording in it: "This I minute down to shew that things are often judged impossible when obstinacy alone is the Cause of it."[25]

There is one notable series of exceptions to this early paucity of stories. Medical and veterinary narratives featured largely in the first sustained year of plantation journal keeping. I count some thirty such performances for 1757 and find that nearly half of these are fairly low-key case reports written with the self suppressed and the observation of symptoms, dosages, and outcomes strongly emphasized. The other half of this assemblage, however, transcended the constraints of the case-report genre and tended toward the fully told story of particularized intentional actions. In these stories, the colonel was not just the managerial, improving gentleman planter who was well read in contemporary medicine, natural philosophy, and agriculture; he also found it important to narrate himself as the caring patriarch whose eye ran over his estate and all its quarters to survey the health of his "people." He was both the benevolent master who nursed those who fell ill and the widower who was a solicitous father to his own sickly children. In sum, the colonel evidently needed to

24. Greene, ed., *Diary of Landon Carter,* I, 163. For purposes of analysis and counting, I have needed a definition of "story," which I have adapted from Labov's concept of the "natural narrative"; see *Sociolinguistic Patterns,* 354–396.

25. Greene, ed., *Diary of Landon Carter,* I, 138.

narrate himself as one who gave "humane Care" to those under his protection. (It is in these stories that we can also see—as in his lamentations about the weather in the agricultural entries—how the whole diary, with all its stories, was framed within a biblical worldview. According to this view, God was sometimes explicitly, and always implicitly, the ultimate doer and disposer, whereas the diarist did what he could, "knowing that God is Mercyfull and that he requires no more of us but our own proper humane Care and that he will protect where it shall seem good to his infinite wisdom.")[26]

One narrative stands on its own in the pages of 1757's "Farming Observations"; it is a story of a father-son quarrel told in the very familiar "I said-and-then-do-you-know-what-he-said?" conversational form. This narrative was so out of keeping with the rest of the record in which it was included that the diarist explicitly transferred it from the nonfarming, nontechnocratic part of his life story with an explanation: "This I write down the moment it passed that I might not through want of memory omit so Singular an act of great filial disobedience in a Child that I have thought once my greatest happyness but as a just Father kept it concealed." He could not have known it in 1757, but variants on this kind of narrative intrusion, incorporating a great diversity of items toward his socially interactive life story, were in time to superimpose themselves and to take over his working "Observations," making his later journal much more comprehensively a book of the self, even as it negotiated the self more and more often in dangerous relation to others.[27]

Stories for an Age of Uncertainties

The active, planning, reasoning, engineering gentleman planter that had been the dominant self of the notebook in the 1750s when the colonel was in his forties still appears on nearly every page of the great series of extant 1770s diaries—but the character and composition of the performances is so changed that a notably altered self is now evidently being presented, developed, and reviewed in these later pages by a man now in his sixties.

In the journal for 1757 (excluding mere case reports from this tally), I counted some twenty-one stories inscribed more or less complete; of these, seventeen, or 85 percent, were medical cases presented as stories. In the diary

26. Ibid., I, 143. I have, in an earlier study, addressed the way—in the manner of the "moderate enlightenment"—Colonel Carter straddled the ancient mythology of the biblical worldview (with the curse of labor) and the modern mythology of "improvement." See Rhys Isaac, "Imagination and Material Culture: The Enlightenment on a Mid-18th-Century Virginia Plantation," in A. E. Yentsch and M. C. Beaudry, eds., *The Art and Mystery of Historical Archaeology: Essays in Honor of James Deetz* (Boca Raton, Fla., 1992), 401–423.

27. Greene, ed., *Diary of Landon Carter*, I, 185.

for 1770, there are, at the most conservative estimate, more than one hundred stories; of these, only about 10 percent are medical narratives, and the remaining 90 percent are taken up with a wide variety of stories. These cover a whole range: contretemps on the estate (about 40 percent), family quarrels (about 20 percent), and neighborhood conflicts (also about 20 percent). (There is another nearly 10 percent of truly dramatic narrations of the weather!) The performances of journal writing were evidently no longer constrained by the original workbook intentions. They had come to be powerfully subsumed in an altered project of day-by-day passionate accumulating, a much more comprehensive book of the self.

What had occasioned this transformation in the diary? What self or selves was the colonel negotiating in all these stories? The short answer is that the diarist had entered consciously into old age. In 1768, after sixteen years in the House of Burgesses, his most elevated role in public life had been terminated; he had been—as he put it—"turned out" by the voters of his county. He had already, more than ten years before, been widowed for the third and last time. (This had occurred about the period of the commencement of his household and plantation journalizing and was, perhaps, a motivation for his taking it up.) Now, increasingly through the 1760s, and even more so in the 1770s, he felt himself painfully confronted in his own house by his own family—by his married eldest son (Robert Wormeley Carter), by his detested daughter-in-law (Winifred Beale Carter), and by their brood of (as it seemed to him) ungoverned children. He transposed his book of the self into readily extendable form and began to fill it out with a stream of life stories.

There is a longer answer to how we may understand Colonel Carter's reconfiguration of his diary—an answer that can only be indicated here. The colonel was keeping his diary through the decades of a coming revolution. He was living in a time of increasing contestation of traditional forms of authority. Can it be an accident that the first diary volume to contain extended story negotiations of challenges to his own patriarchal authority was the same 1766 volume in the front of which he had penned a revealing note of troubled times? "This almanack," he wrote, "came enclosed under cover with nothing hinting from whom. I examined it to see if it had been stampt, but finding none I ventured to set my name on it"—which he did, signing with flourishes on March 8, 1766. Here was a little epitome of the contradictions that his diary sustained. He was an ardent leader in opposition to the sovereignty of king-in-Parliament as confronted in the Stamp Act, but he was a jealous upholder of his own sovereignty at Sabine Hall. Furthermore, he wrote the stories that now filled out his diaries with a sensibility that was resonant of the humane concern for personal feelings that was expressed in the novels of this time and that problematized patriarchal authority. But he carried to the situations he narrated the expectations of deference to position within a ranked order that had been more secure in his father's and his grandfather's time. In other words, his humane sensibilities led him to narrate contested situations in his little world and to construct these stories out of the emergent new mythology of person, feeling, and relationship. In the great world, this same mythology was preparing the way for the American Revolution, the first great wave of the Atlantic Revolution.[28]

Patriarchal Nemesis: Age, Gender, and Labor Resistances

Divided thus, the diarist constructed himself as a man of feelings in order to justify himself by self-explication; at the same time, he cast his narratives (and his understandings of situation) in a profoundly traditional folkloric mold. The life stories now flowed in two great streams. One continual outpouring drew deeply on familial folklore: it told endlessly of the readiness of the rising generation to discount and displace the declining one. (Had not Landon Carter entertained himself, indeed, with the story of King Lear, when he addressed that rejected father in the margin of his text of the play, passionately identifying the story of the tragic hero with his own? "Oh Lear, others have acted the same foolish part that you did, and have been as handsomely rewarded as thou wast by their offspring.") The other major stream of stories was a form of what I shall call "gentrylore"—a manor house counterpart to the trickster tales of the cottage and the quarter.[29]

Told as they were—expressing a sense of profoundly challenged authority and with it an enhanced need for personal understanding—both the colonel's two streams of diary stories served to sustain the indignant telling of a sadly unappreciated self; both undertook a continual vindication of the diarist to

28. On the advancing ethos of humanity and sensibility, see Garry Wills, *Inventing America: Jefferson's Declaration of Independence* (Garden City, N.Y., 1978). On the problematization of patriarchal authority in the British Atlantic world, manifest in both political philosophy and in novels, see Fliegelman, *Prodigals and Pilgrims*, esp. 9–28, 67–89. On the ways novelistic storytelling might overtly confirm traditional order—in gender relations especially—by an explicit "moral," while subverting it by the disturbances of the "tendency" of the narrative's plot, see Patricia Meyer Spacks, *Desire and Truth: Functions of Plot in Eighteenth-Century English Novels* (Chicago, 1990), esp. 1–11, 114–146. For an earlier discussion of Landon Carter's dividedness, understood as straddling between modes oriented toward personal feelings and those oriented toward social rank, see Rhys Isaac, "Communication and Control: Authority Metaphors and Power Contests on Colonel Landon Carter's Virginia Plantation, 1752–1778," in Sean Wilentz, ed., *Rites of Power: Symbolism, Ritual, and Politics since the Middle Ages* (Philadelphia, 1985), 297–300.

29. The apostrophe to King Lear is penned at the end of an extract from the play printed in the colonel's copy of the periodical anthology *The Adventurer*, ed. J. Hawkesworth et al., 3d ed., 4 vols. (London, 1756), no. 113, 67, in Alderman Library, University of Virginia.

himself, to his son and daughter-in-law, and to his grandchildren and posterity whenever they might read it. He certainly intended that they should. In February 1770, after a severe domestic storm (or "gust," as he characteristically metaphorized such episodes), he followed the turbulent story he had told with a declaration: "I have written this, let who will read it, only to show that I have long seen this little cloud ready to burst[,] and after I am gone let such people clap their hands upon their hearts and say whether it was not their own determined pride. . . . Yes! There is no Christian conscience that can deny this truth."[30] Thus reads one of his recurrent highly rhetorical addresses to an imagined audience for all these writing performances; thus is sharply revealed the affinity of all these stories to the life story. Set in the context of the decade in which they were written, these stories can be read as little epitomes both of the more emotionally demanding self and of the simultaneously more troubled traditional systems of rule in household and state in the age of revolutions. Colonel Carter's diary, as well as the radical intensity of Virginia's engagement in revolution, suggests that the extreme and distorted forms of patriarchy in the extended, composite plantation households might have created particularly acute tensions in a gentry that was now open to the newer sensibilities of polite culture.

Five months after that expostulatory address to his posterity, the old colonel inscribed an even more explicit version of the life story toward which all these narratives contributed. "I cannot help taking notice," he wrote, "that the long time I have lived, the care I have taken of my family, the paying off Children's fortunes, and putting out 3 sons with an Estate very well to pass in the world, still maintaining a large family at home, and all this without being in debt but a very trifle, I say, I cannot help taking notice that these circumstances well considered as they ought to be . . . [,] do not preserve to [me] with my Son the character even of a tollerable manager." Behind that account of the "perverse disposition" of his son, there lurked another continuing drama—the story of "Madam," his daughter-in-law. "This woman," he called her in one of the versions of a story that he kept repeating: "This woman every day discovers [that is, reveals] who is at the bottom [of] all the ill usage that I receive." He narrated her story as intertwined with his own according to a deep folkloric patriarchal wisdom about family. She was, he declared: "A mean spirited creature . . . that cannot see her All, alredy rising out of me: but unless I part with my all, she will not be satisfied. And I am certain then I should be turned a grazing, and by her means."[31]

30. Greene, ed., *Diary of Landon Carter*, I, 359.
31. Ibid., I, 310, 447, 485.

Willful Slaves

The long series of stories of the diarist as the master of slaves and the well-informed manager of a large plantation was almost as defensive as the familial series in this old-age, revolution-age continuation of the book of the self. Colonel Carter continually told stories to show the difficulties he encountered everywhere with his workforce and to vindicate himself (to his son mostly?) as a "manager." He attempted that by recounting his constant endeavors to sustain order and to see the work properly done. He was, it seems, both recording his setbacks and drawing on a Virginia version of an ancient English (and indeed European) fund of manor house wisdom. He was inscribing a gentry-lore counterpart of folklore; in this mythology, the peasant tricksters raise for their masters the perennial question: Are they most knaves or fools? His story-telling in such a mode is all the more striking, since there is a fatalism running through all these stories that continually subverts the life story he wants to tell of the self as improving manager. Whether the overseer or slave is fool or knave, the remedy—a whipping, a tongue-lashing—is the same, and there is no expectation that it can provide a lasting reform.

Behind the mockery or scorn that often evaluates the stories of recalcitrant workers, the wording reveals clearly a certain knowing, accepting self. Thus, when the old colonel summarily narrated how, "during my [twelfth night] entertainment the Gentlemens' servants not only took the hay from the Cow yard to litter their horses but used all the blades out of the stack," he concluded with the judgment: "My Scoundril Nat, the ringleader of this impudence, it seems was too fat to go to the hay house."[32]

Colonel Carter's acceptance of the world as he found it sometimes, but rarely, enabled him to ease up on his strenuous enactment and defensive presentation of self as the effective manager and stern judge of his plantation workers. In these instances, he could hear them and almost acknowledge their skills and experience. Thus, in July 1770 he noted: "I sometimes divert myself with talking to my old people," as they "worm and top" the growing tobacco crop. He was always on guard nevertheless: "As they had told me it was all in the main very well standing I could not help seeing through their treachery." But he let himself be—perhaps—persuaded of what he wanted to believe: "Sukey told me there were now buds spreading [on] the hill where it was said to be missing and she would answer by September I would see a good Crop of Tobacco for she knew the ground."[33]

It was Landon Carter's dual project in the new-format 1770s diary to show

32. Ibid., I, 348.
33. Ibid., I, 454.

on the one hand the ill-usage and lack of appreciation accorded him by his son and daughter-in-law and on the other hand his estimable conduct as the manager of a plantation. Nowhere is the perilous aspect of negotiating the self in stories of the self more clearly revealed than in the way the victim role—proper to his accusatory family project—was apt to spill over into the plantation narratives with their project of vindicating himself as manager of slaves. In these performances, that role repeatedly undermined the very claims he sought to establish. Here is a clear example, involving his personal attendant, Nassau, and his coachman, Nat, who was Nassau's son:

> I came home but without Nassau or Nat, a drunken father and Son. The [father] first mired my horse . . . in crossing a marsh that none but a blind drunkard could ever venture upon[,] and Mr. Nat [was] so engaged with boon companions as never to get my chariot by which means I was to plung[e] home 5 or 6 miles upon this mired horse without one person to assist me. I got home near sunset and about 8 o'clock came the Chariot with the drunken father and Son. This morning I ordered the son his deserts in part. The father I shall leave till another opportunity for though my old Servant I am too old a Master to be thus inhumanely treated.

Although, or perhaps because, Landon Carter despised the theater—"Stupidity and nonsence delivered from the mouths of Walking Statues"!—the term "farce" was a ready word in his vocabulary of scorn. Here he had, however, narrated (unintentionally, no doubt), a perfect exemplar of farce; it was complete with the valet and coachman riding home in the master's chariot after the master himself had "plung[ed] home" through the late winter gloom on the horse that one of them had mired. The diarist's own evaluation of the story, the attempted pathos of his being too old to be treated "inhumanely" by his servants, only heightened the sense of self revealed as victim.[34]

A Silence? The Stories of the Others?

A self so strongly revealed in stories of the self as Landon Carter's makes problems for the appreciation of those persons—indeed all the rest of the people—who are represented as other. Have we access to their stories, their selves, or the personae they assumed for themselves? Probably there is some kind of fit between lores, between gentrylore and folklore. We can perhaps imagine, or at least faintly sense, the versions that might have been told from the other side. At the quarter, Sukey no doubt knew how to make a mocking

---

34. Ibid., I, 103, 373. I surmise that Carter, though he wrote "the latter" where I have suggested "the father," meant to specify Nassau's delinquency at this point.

story of herself persuading the master to believe what he wanted to believe about the crop. A filmmaker would readily reconstruct Nat in the yard, telling, and miming in the firelight, his version of how he drove his own father home in the chariot after the party. We can sometimes sense more directly from the reported altercations how the daughter-in-law, Winifred, would have told her side of the rows over household management, child-rearing, and gratitude.

To be sure, the others, the antagonists, of the old colonel's life story had, like him, to inhabit the world as they found it; they had to try to bring their own constructed selves into alignment with their constructions of the world. Such aligning would surely be one function of the life stories that *they* generated and cumulated. But the approximate fit of stories and assumed personae could not be altogether complete; there were cruel disjunctions. Often, the world as it was could not be accepted. The daughter-in-law's position, although subordinate, was among the highly privileged, yet the old patriarch not infrequently reduced her to tears, perhaps even to despair. More ominous, looking outside the circle of the privileged, we may certainly sense the despair in one of the overseers, who alternately sought drunken escapes, and then—a "pitiful puppy," the colonel called him—found himself "crying" not to be dismissed and turned out destitute into the world. Most ominous, there was the harsh, often arbitrary treatment of those who could not even be threatened with dismissal, although they might face an ultimate banishment of being sold away.[35]

Perhaps some of the whippings were part of life as it was found and perforce accepted, but we surely see more than the self the colonel meant to put on display in the following story. Did he see more? Would those he wrote to impress—especially his daughter-in-law—have seen a sound manager or a failed one? Would she have seen a racist misogynist entering into violence as a desperate last resort? These are *our* questions and our categories, but we may wonder nevertheless whether the daughter-in-law might have condemned (as cruelty) at least one recorded woman-hating excess on the part of the patriarch whom she encountered repeatedly trying to crush her also. We can only guess at alternative ways in which this cluster of stories might have been retold by the others of the colonel's world; we do know that the victims themselves in several instances registered their refusal of acceptance by running away:

March 22 1770
The 2 sarahs came up yesterday pretending to be violent ill with pains in their sides. They look very well, had no fever, and I ordered them down to their work upon pain of a whipping. They went, worked very well with no grunting about pain[,] but one of them, to wit Manuel's sarah, taking the

35. Ibid., I, 410.

advantage of [the overseer] Lawson's ride to the fork, swore she would not work any longer and run away and is still out. There is a curiosity in this Creature. She worked none last year pretending to be with Child and this she was full 11 months before she was brought to bed. She has now the same pretence and thinks to pursue the same course but as I have full warning of her deceit, if I live, I will break her of that trick. I had two before of this turn. Wilmot of the fork[,] whenever she was with Child[,] always pretended to be too heavy to work and it cost me 12 months before I broke her. Criss of Mangorike fell into the same scheme and really carried it to a great length[,] for at last she could not be dragged out. However[,] by carrying a horse with traces the Lady took to her feet run away and[,] when catched[,] by a severe whipping has been a good slave ever since[,] only a cursed thief in making her Children milk my Cows in the night.

When Manuel's Sarah—"this infamous jade"—was caught three weeks later, the colonel "had her corrected" [that is, whipped], and he told his diary that: "I intended to lock her up till I could sell her. She begs hard and is turned out to work." Three years later, the same pattern of actions recurred, only this time she was actually locked up. She was released illicitly (by her father?), and the master resolved to sell her away when she should be caught again.[36]

"Marchlands" Identity?

No doubt there was a Virginia slaveowners' folklore about how to prevent slave women from claiming more protection from heavy manual labor than self-interested necessity suggested to the masters they be given, but the frank intrusion of such lore here—its translation into literature by being inscribed in a literary gentleman's diary—points up deep contradictions in the very project of the diary. Undoubtedly drawing on the literature of his age, Landon Carter incorporated the sensibility of that age into the diary in order to construct and present his self as that of a "humane" gentleman, who was unkindly denied "humane" treatment by his ungrateful brute of a son and all his household. But when he calmly described the horse and traces brought to the slave cabin door to drag out the possibly pregnant woman, he had momentarily revealed a different self.

Colonel Carter probably justified the occasional revelation of a cruel self as an unfortunate product of the circumstances that constrained him to work his lands with slave laborers. That in turn reminds us of what has been called the "marchlands" character of the colonial world—a world sustaining forms and intensities of violence that the metropolitan culture had moved, and was still

36. Ibid., I, 371, 389, II, 777, 779.

moving, to segregate and distance from legitimate civil society—or at least from the domestic life of the literate upper and middle classes. It is a characteristic of such a "marchland" culture—which must be prominent in any discussion of identity in early America—that a gentleman like Colonel Landon Carter could, with little or no sense of strain, both tell of his violence to the pregnant women and study so hard to inscribe his own self as humane. He wanted to appear devoted to the bodily and spiritual welfare of his immediate family and, indeed, of all in his care; and yet he could calmly tell these stories of such brutal enforcement of his will.[37]

Bringing Gender to the Foreground

Georges Gusdorf has said of the impulse that sustains autobiography, that it comes from the individualistic self in which a "man knows himself . . . [the] gatherer of men, of lands, of power." Charles Taylor, focusing on René Descartes and John Locke as prime examples, provides the chronological precision that is lacking in Gusdorf's unreflectively masculinist description of a certain kind of Western autobiographical self-construction. Taylor finds that it was the seventeenth century that saw the advent of a phase in the Western tradition when a growing interest in individual identity found expression in an increasing autobiographical preoccupation and a more developed sense of an inward self. The new, commanding self was being called upon to be self-detached as well as self-regarding in order to maximize two kinds of control—control of self and control of environment.[38]

Certainly, projects of control of self and other gave a distinctive white male character and purpose to Colonel Carter's diary, both in its confident improving-and-methodizing phase and in its later defensive coming-to-terms-with-subverted-authority phase. This was assuredly a white *man*'s diary—or, in the language of its day, a white *gentleman*'s. A most instructive contrast to the slave master's diary can be made by turning to the writings of a young lady,

37. On the "marchlands" aspect of the colonies, using Landon Carter as a case in point, see Bernard Bailyn, *The Peopling of British North America: An Introduction* (New York, 1986), 120.

38. Georges Gusdorf, "Conditions and Limits of Autobiography," in James Olney, ed., *Autobiography: Essays Theoretical and Critical* (Princeton, N.J., 1980), 31. See also Taylor, *Sources of the Self*, 143–176. There might indeed have been contrasting modes of diaristic autobiography, as epitomized by James Boswell—although he could be seen as "gathering men" by his literary and other self-dramatizing exploits. Perhaps, however, Boswell's diary is better related to yet another great Western tradition. At least from Montaigne onward there was emerging a way of seeking self and identity in a celebration of individual particularity and idiosyncrasy (177–184). I thank my colleague Lotte Mulligan for posing the countercase of Boswell.

Lucinda Lee, in her remarkable journal of a spell of house-to-house visiting in northern Virginia in 1787. (Lucinda had—it appears—made an agreement with her best friend, Polly Brent, that each would keep a journal of their time apart, to be exchanged when they had opportunity.)[39]

A Young Woman in Search of Her Story

Lucinda Lee's letter diary is one of a small number of women's diaries from eighteenth-century Virginia. Its inclusion in a review of life stories is certainly warranted because it reveals so much of the ways that its writer drew on the momentously new mythology of the romantic novel that was revolutionizing self and society in the North Atlantic world by the 1780s. Lucinda's writing expressed vividly what has been identified as a feminine contrast to the masculine self just epitomized—forms of subjectivity in which the "woman's sense of self exists within a deep awareness of others." In this regard, Lucinda's journal, like the novels on which it drew, stands very much in the Western tradition of another form of search for identity that, since Montaigne, has been more concerned with the expressive *particularity* and idiosyncrasy of the self than with its powers of *control* over itself and its environment.[40]

Lucinda Lee did not tell many stories in developed form; instead, she almost made an epistolary novel of her life at the time of writing. She presented herself with an immediacy that was revealed in cherished activities whose value is in the relationships they sustain, including the relationship of letter-journal writer to the recipient Polly:

> Lucy Gordon and myself are just returned from walking out. I was delighted: we walked to a river. . . . The banks of it are beautiful, covered with moss and wild flowers; all that a romantic mind could form. I thought of my Polly . . . and how delighted she would have been had she been a Spectater of the scene . . . , but her dear Company was denied. Lucy Gordon

39. Emily V. Mason, ed., *Journal of a Young Lady of Virginia, 1782* [1787] (Baltimore, 1871). The date assigned to this journal has been revised from 1782 (E. V. Mason's reading of the MS) to 1787 on the basis of the calendar of dates and days of the week and through datable events; see *National Union Catalog: Pre-1956 Imprints* (London, 1976), CLXXXIII, 235. Mrs. Mason published the journal—Polly Brent's copy, surviving in her family's papers—as a fund-raiser for Confederate veterans. The whereabouts of the original manuscript is now unknown, but Mrs. Mason declared that the printed text was a faithful transcription without editorial correction.

40. The quotation is Susan Stanford Friedman's summing up of the paradigm developed in Mary Mason's introduction to Mary G. Mason and Carol Hurd, eds., *Journeys: Autobiographical Writings by Women* (Boston, 1979), xiv. See Friedman, "Women's Autobiographical Selves," in Benstock, *The Private Self*, 47. On the tradition of which Montaigne is seen as the archetype, see Taylor, *Sources of the Self*, 177–184.

is a truly good Girl, but nothing of the romance in her. So much the better, say I; she is much happier without. I wish to Heaven I had as little.

Here is another example of intensely self-presenting diary writing:

> Interrupted again. They are come to tell me a Mr. Grimes and his Lady are come to wait on us. I must throw aside my pen. . . . I will write more when we retire to dress. . . . Mrs. Grimes is very handsome, though appears to be a little proud. Sister is almost drest; I shall have but little time to smart myself.[41]

There is a great deal of play in the high-spirited interaction of the young women, and the self-inscription in the letter diary is itself an extension of that play. And yet the play of the writing is "deep play," involving no less than simultaneous self-discovery and self-construction.

Role Models?

Observation and reporting were keen because Lucinda had to make what she could of the world into which she was coming out; she must find her place in it. Seeking her place meant attention to hierarchy—looking up, not down. This diarist was therefore very selective, and her references to slaves were rare and incidental—a very active silence in this record indeed. Lucinda both identified with other ladies and evaluated them detachedly, learning at once ideals and realities from their dress, deportment, and characters. Occasionally, she felt she truly glimpsed the ideal, as when she wrote: "I saw a beauty at church, a Miss Thaskkel. She has hazel eyes, fine complexion, and Beautiful Auburn hair, which hung in ringlets upon her neck." More usually it was a perception of a composite, as with "one of the Miss Ballendine's—truly Amiable, I believe, but not handsome." To which was added the reflection: "But how preferable is good sense and affability to Beauty: more pleasing a thousand times!" (In this, no doubt, Lucinda was at the same time regarding herself obliquely in the looking glass of her diary and negotiating the blend of good qualities she hoped to observe there.) Lucinda also related to and strongly valued older women, such as "old Mrs Gordon," into whose bedroom the girls retreated for safety from a frolic with the young men, finding that "she sat laughing fit to kill herself at us. She is a charming old lady."[42] The appreciation of an elder

---

41. Mason, ed., *Journal*, 8–9, 12–13. Lucinda was not singular in this sort of effusiveness. On the great shift in forms of expression in personal letters and diaries, see the important work of Jan Lewis, *The Pursuit of Happiness: Family and Values in Jefferson's Virginia* (New York, 1983).

42. Mason, ed., *Journal*, 7, 20, 35, 42–43.

generation—such as she would not have sought or secured from her own mother—was no doubt reassuring in these daring games.

The Opposite Sex

Of course Lucinda observed and keenly evaluated one class of males in particular—the "*Beaux,*" whose otherness she tried to fathom. "The Gentlemen," she once reported, were "all in high spirits"; they were "thinking," she supposed, "of the pleasure of to-morrow." With this she could identify, since it was a horse race meeting they anticipated—although she was firmly resolved not to go herself. She distinguished the "handsome," the "uncouth," the "polite," and the "clever" (a term of general approbation, matching, perhaps, the word "neat" in a twentieth-century usage). A more favored young man she declared to be "one of the cleverest young Beaux I have seen for some time." She eyed the unmarried men warily, mockingly, especially when they were seeking to be suitors to her friends. "Nancy had an admirer lately," she noted; but then, with satisfaction: "He got his discard yesterday." Marriage was a doom at the end of courtship; it threatened the separation that was "the bane of Female Friendship" by creating a category apart, as when, "Lucy and myself had a pleasant walk back," while "the married folks went on before."[43]

Men were excitement and danger both—mostly the latter, unless they could be drawn into the games the young women played. Perhaps she found the experience disagreeable and alarming when two "horred Mortals, Mr. Pinkard and Mr. Washington [both married to cousins of Lucinda], . . . seized me and kissed me a dozen times in spite of all the resistance I could make." But similar action later was turned around by the young women collectively when Mr. Washington had found them "mighty busy cutting thistles to try our sweethearts" and had, as she reported, "plagued us—chased us all over the Garden, and was quite impertinent." The men had, nevertheless, been taken into a subsequent "frolic." Mr. Washington was then "dressed in Hannah's [his wife's] short gown and peticoat" and burst into their bedroom, where the girls were noisily having a midnight feast. It was evidently not so upsetting to Lucinda this time, when, once again, as she recorded, he "seazed me and kissed me twenty times, in spite of all the resistance I could make; and then Cousin Molly." It was certainly a continuation of an agreeable frolic when the young women went "down in the Seller" to get oysters, and Mr. Washington followed them "to scear us just to death." Only four days later, diary writing was again interrupted: "It is Cousin Molly. She is come to propose dressing Mr. Pinkard

43. Ibid., 15, 22, 29, 48.

in Woman's cloaths. I assent, so away goes the pen." (Once more the very writing here is part of the exuberant play.)[44]

The self as represented in these episodes was both excited by and contending against experiences of men. The perhaps troubling kisses of Messrs. Pinkard and Washington surely gave her a sense of what kisses from the right beau might be. She and her friends and cousins could, in the safety of the domestic setting, break the barriers of decorum. What could it have meant to dress these men in women's costume? Perhaps a surrogate undressing *for* men and *of* men or a making a man familiar with women's clothes and how they were shaped for women's bodies. The adolescent's pent-up sexual state could be released in this horseplay in counterpoint to the other more serious self she wanted to reveal to Polly.

Lucinda was a loyal and respectable young lady, who valued real friendship more than frolic. The comfort of conformity, alternating with the fascination of cross-dressing, both provide the little stories of games in this Virginia country house and advance the letter diary's whole metanarrative of self-discovery and self-definition as a sexed social being. The innocent-seeming stories are indeed profoundly mythic in their exploration of gender through transgression. (Gender in the conventional forms of women's and men's clothing was indeed rendered deliciously, dangerously sexual by the intimate body reference of the "petticoat.") In the narrative of this play, the men were at once tamed (rendered girls among the girls) and demonized by the story of their boldness in using the situation to assert their manhood in "seizing" the young women. The playful inscription of all this at once courted danger and, by rendering both the action and the writing as play, contrived innocence.[45]

Negotiating Alternatives

There were other precious (and safer) escapes from the conformities of the social round; these included cherished reveries no doubt also charged with sexuality but given shape by the reading of romantic literature. One evening, Lucinda recorded: "Nancy and myself have been to visit our little garden." She went on to remember another garden she and Polly formerly had made as a "pledge" of their very special friendship: "How often do I think with rapture on the happy hours we spent sitting on the [garden] fence, singing and looking at

44. Ibid., 29, 41–42, 45.

45. The speculative interpretations in this and the next paragraph were mostly proposed to me by Colleen Isaac, with some further suggestions by Fredrika Teute. The construction of innocence through play—in action and in writing—was the suggestion of my colleague Dr. Katie Holmes, who has written very insightfully on diaries (see Holmes, *Spaces in Her Day: Australian Women's Diaries of the 1920s and 1930s* [Sydney, 1995]).

the river with the Moon shining on it. Oh, how beautiful it look't!" Indeed, Lucinda and her companions seem to have sought in night walks a desired escape into such reveries. One evening they "took a walk to the river," and the diarist recorded that "Nancy observed [how] walking by moonlight, she thought, reminded us of our absent Friends." And again, some days later, when "Milly and myself took a walk . . . by Moonlight," Milly had felt impelled to declare that she knew Lucinda's special friend, Polly, and thought her "beautiful."[46]

Beyond reverie and lingering upon the close friendships that marriage would imperil or dissolve, Lucinda used her journal for exploring alternatives to the conformities of her woman's lot—the often irksome feminine requirements that she come downstairs upon summons to pour tea and that she coif and dress to be an ornament at dinner. Upon one occasion, she was moved to comment on a visiting lady's sadness: "Mrs. Graem, poor creature, appears much distressed at the death of her Children"; Lucinda added the reflection: "When we come to consider, I think it much better for them [than to endure the trials of life?]: but how seldom can a Mother reason in that manner!" Although her implied censure was of the grieving parent, there might just also have been in the protesting comment something of a young woman's subconscious revolt against a lifetime's bondage to child-rearing.[47]

Lucinda experimented at intervals with possibilities of self-fashioning. She recorded having "almost determined not to go to the races this Fall" and faced down the fact that "every one appears to be astonished." They all "laugh, and tell me, while I am mopeing at home, other girls will be enjoying themselves at races and balls." She was evidently affirming her autonomy in the matter of such amusements: "I never will, I am determined, go to one unless I have an inclination." She added that, of course, she did not mean to "pay no regard to the opinion of the World," but still she maintained that such opinion was to take second place to "a good conscience." Similar searching for acceptable forms of self-determination seem also to have been at work when she and her cousin Nancy had, even as she wrote, "shut ourselves in a room up stairs, and intend not to go down till summoned to dinner." She went on to note revealingly that "the Topic of our Conversation is, regretting the manner in which we have spent our past life." On another occasion, she chid herself for being "too fond of Novel-reading" and advised the reading of "something improving," since she hoped that "Books of instruction will be a thousand times more pleasing (after a little while) than all the novels in the World." (The irony is that novels had indeed instructed her and given her this kind of wisdom both for the self-reproach and for these representations of her world

46. Mason, ed., *Journal*, 29–30, 43, 50.
47. Ibid., 19.

in writing.) In another mood, Lucinda explicitly praised two novels, *Evelina* and *Lady Julia Mandeville,* both of which narrate heroines of the same class and ambitions as herself.[48]

Novels were indeed a disturbing consumer product now coming into the better-off households of the North Atlantic world—a new drug almost. Ladies with the addiction were, to that extent, withdrawn from the domestic chores and social compliances demanded of them; they reproached themselves and no doubt felt also the disapproval of the men. Furthermore, the entertainment of these books that gave women a story promoted a self-absorption that was at odds with the selfless dedication to familial service that was the prescribed norm for women.[49]

Sentimental Education

More important than games and reveries and experiments in autonomy as resources for subjectivity and self-construction were the readings aloud that punctuated this busy round of young persons' social activity. The intensely patriarchal Sunday ritual when the household were all "collected in the Chamber, reading the Lessons of the day" indicates, no doubt, a pervasive constraining mythology in Lucinda's world; but the Bible did not supply the mythology on which she drew for recording her life and for reflecting upon it. The diary narratives and the sensibilities they rehearsed were continually informed by the reading aloud of novels and plays rather than of Scripture. Sometimes the young women read to each other. Once, after being so "much affected" by *Lady Julia Mandeville,* Lucinda confided: "I think I never cried more in my life reading a Novel." So much so that, when the two were called downstairs, she found she was suddenly "affraid both Sister's and my eyes will betray us." A

48. Ibid., 11, 26, 48. Fanny Burney's epistolary novel, *Evelina,* is told through the lively letters of a young lady whose social standing was problematic but who displayed exquisite sensibility. During visits to wealthy connections, she meets desirable (titled, sensitive, genteel) and undesirable (crass, brutal, plebeian) persons; her adventures range from high drama to low farce before she finally achieves wisdom and marriage to her ideal lord. Published in London by Thomas Lowndes in 1778, the work was acclaimed, with Dr. Johnson, Sir Joshua Reynolds, and Edmund Burke among its admirers. *The History of Lady Julia Mandeville* (1763), by Mrs. Frances Brooke, tells, also through letters, a complex tale of the courtship of young persons. Both these novels include strong depictions of an idealized benevolent gentry.

49. On the disturbances and self-reproach that continued to be called forth by ladies' novel reading, see Elizabeth Fox-Genovese, *Within the Plantation Household: Black and White Women of the Old South* (Chapel Hill, N.C., 1988), 260–263. For the intensity of such concerns, in the very world in which Lucinda Lee was coming out, see Spacks *Desire and Truth,* 44–52.

young married gentleman also might sit "all the evening" reading a satiric literary narrative to the young ladies and the whole company. Fanny Burney's *Evelina* was commended by Lucinda as a model of pretty sentiment in a novel, and, whereas Lucinda's journal is much freer and more of a tête-à-tête conversation in style than the stilted periods of that epistolary romance, it seems certain that she could not conceivably have found herself empowered to produce such a written life story—such an intense book of the self—without her sustained engagement with novelistic representations of young ladies' passionate sensibilities.[50]

Lucinda could write of courtship and the young married state, not as participant, but as observer, at once apprehensive and filled with anticipation. Nevertheless, her perceptions and her narratives were charged with the mythology of romantic novels and the decisive refiguration of true love that they had helped bring about—*from* being the fatal passion narrated incessantly in the old English ballads *to* being the indispensable basis for happy marriage.[51]

IDENTITIES AND REVOLUTION

Women's New Stories

When we pursue stories, we begin to open up the imaginative universes—indeed, the cosmos—of past peoples. In fragments of recorded oral performances, we, indeed, encounter the powerful personalities of storytellers like the old nurse of Monticello and the true-to-myth worlds of the extrovert beings with which she deeply entertained her hearers. When we pursue diaries, we may enter a distinctive cultural tradition in which the myth of the self-contemplating self began to loom large and to sustain the keeping of books of the self, and so of a record of the cumulation of self-evaluating narratives toward a life story. Colonel Landon Carter's diary reminds us forcibly how much that myth of the self—especially that self as expanded and elaborated in

50. Mason, ed., *Journal*, 12, 25, 26, 27. Interestingly, Fanny Burney herself saw parallels between women's lives and novels. When Maria Allen, her scatty, indiscreet stepsister, eloped, Fanny recorded in her 1772 journal: "Miss Allen—for the last time I shall so call her—came home on Monday last. Her *novel* is not yet over, nevertheless, she was married last Saturday" (Sarah Kilpatrick, *Fanny Burney*, [London, 1980], 33). Novel and play reading in Virginia, including references to Lucinda Lee, are discussed in Jane Carson, *Colonial Virginians at Play* (Williamsburg, Va., 1965), 40–48.

51. On the representation in novels of issues about love-derived marriage, parental choice, and partners' choice, see Fliegelman, *Prodigals and Pilgrims*, esp. 27–29, 83–93. See also Lawrence Stone, *The Family, Sex, and Marriage in England, 1500–1800* (New York, 1977), for discussion of "affective individualism."

forms of written projects for improvement—has been a myth empowering the extension of control by white males. Women and the colonized are currently engaged in challenging and replacing that myth in order to construct their own stories into powerful texts. Lucinda Lee's little journal provides a small point of access to a late-eighteenth-century time in which romances, rather than pious self-humblings, had become generally available as stories out of which to create a young lady's book of the self. This epistolary diary is an active writing down of Lucinda's life story—resistances as well as compliances—at the moment of her approach to the crucial courtship phase.[52]

The sentimental novel had for decades before 1787 been reconfiguring a crucial role for courtship as the prelude to a version of marriage that was more and more idealized as arising from romantic love. In that same mythology, marriage was, however, the denouement that ended the woman's story. Lucinda's journal might have owed some of its bright intensity to an urgent sense that the phase she was then entering would be brief and that this kind of book of her self would soon succumb to "matrimony" as "the bane of Female Friendship"—friendship such as this letter diary was expressly intended to serve. But, looking north from Virginia to Maine at the same time and after, we may take up Martha Ballard's diary as a most powerful demonstration of the forms of a book of the self and the cumulative writing of a life-story collection that could be used by a *married* woman to bear witness to the powers as well as the trials of her station and to record her mature roles in society. Assuredly, we may see how Martha Ballard's diary stands there to do that, since Laurel Thatcher Ulrich has taken it up to entertain deeply our times with the histories to be made into *A Midwife's Tale*.[53]

The Revolutionary Power of the Self

The magical tale, the trickster story, the heroic warrior epic, and a multitude of other forms of narrative sustained in the oral tradition go back into the

52. Many of the complexities of only partially secularized women's autobiographies and books of the self are explored in Nussbaum, *The Autobiographical Subject*.

53. For a perceptive novelistic, literature-conscious account of another 18th-century colonial elite—that of New England—and an entanglement in the paradox of fantasizing a paradise of married love even while intensifying concerns for family connections and property settlements, see Laurel Thatcher Ulrich, *Good Wives: Image and Reality in the Lives of Women in Northern New England, 1650–1750* (New York, 1982), 119. On marriage as "the end" of the woman's story, see Carolyn G. Heilbrun, *Writing a Woman's Life* (New York, 1988), 79–95, and her "Marriage Perceived: English Literature, 1873–1944," in the collection of her essays titled *Hamlet's Mother and Other Women* (New York, 1990), 131–157. For the married woman's book of the self, see Laurel Thatcher Ulrich, *A Midwife's Tale: The Life of Martha Ballard, Based on Her Diary, 1785–1812* (New York, 1990).

mists of time and certainly have persisted strong through the Revolutionary era to the present day. But for centuries in the West, there has been an intensification of narratives—stories of the self cumulating as life stories—that have entertained by revealing and constructing, constructing and revealing increasingly individuated selves. These stories have drawn from writing and print and have increasingly found expression in such written forms as the diary. The newer stories have drawn on changing mythologies that have over time given ever more prominence to an introverted self; each such story has, when told, in its turn contributed to those mythologies.

Within the intensifying inward-self-regarding mythologies, there were many varied stories available as resources for the formation and transformation of the subjectivity—the self-telling, self-representation—of continuing generations in America and Europe. It might be stories of a self given to scientific improvement or to humane sensibility—two of the mythologies out of which Landon Carter has been shown to have shaped many of his stories of his self; it might be stories of a self preparing herself for "a pursuit of happiness" that was in part inspired by the novels that were making a new sort of epic concerning this "pursuit" by ordinary persons. Prominent among the subversive protagonists of such quests were young women, hence the mythologies that Lucinda could draw on vividly to construct her story of herself for the friend who was also on the threshold of womanhood.[54] There were many other thematic stocks of stories from which individuals could construct stories of their own selves. These included the traditional religious conversion narratives that seemed in the era of the Great Awakenings, like the novel, also to dramatize every person as potentially the bearer of a significant individuated story of the self.

All these dramatized personal stories—these little but newly significant theaters of self—did not just contribute to the great spectacle that we call the American Revolution, but, in a profound sense, they *were* the Revolution. The same is true of the global transformations of which the American Revolution was an early dramatic episode. Without these little theaters—these cumulating stories spotlighting a self in a "pursuit of happiness"—the great new refigurings and enactments of the story of the origins and nature of authority, of the individual and of society, that we call the Atlantic Revolution could neither have occurred nor have entertained with such deep meanings.

54. For a strong, persuasive account of the novel—especially for women—as a subversive, individuating medium for the continuing of the American Revolution, see Cathy N. Davidson, *Revolution and the Word: The Rise of the Novel in America* (New York, 1986).

HANNAH BARNARD'S
CUPBOARD: FEMALE PROPERTY
AND IDENTITY IN EIGHTEENTH-
CENTURY NEW ENGLAND

Laurel Thatcher Ulrich

Ah, when she moved, she moved more ways than one:
The shapes a bright container can contain!
—Theodore Roethke, "I Knew a Woman" (1961)

Hannah Barnard's cupboard was the most engaging, if not the most elegant, object in an exhibit of Hadley chests mounted at Israel Sack in New York, at the Wadsworth Atheneum in Hartford, and at Memorial Hall Museum in Deerfield, Massachusetts, in the spring of 1993 (Figure 1). In describing the installation at Israel Sack, curator Suzanne Flynt told a reporter for *The Hartford Courant:* "No doubt about it. It was the dominant object of the show. I set up the other chests like so many little pews leading up to the cupboard, which sat there like a kind of throne or altar at the end of the line." "Altar" seems like the right word to describe this exuberant cupboard with its electric blue columns flanking a symbolic garden. But who or what did it celebrate? Could it have been Hannah Barnard herself? The Hartford reporter thought so. Expressing amazement that a woman could emblazon her own name on an article of furniture in "this rigidly patriarchal period," he pronounced it "a remarkable cupboard with a proto-feminist message." A Hartford collector, on the other hand, reverted to a more traditional interpretation of family life in time past. Surely the cupboard must have been

This essay owes a special debt to William Hosley of the Wadsworth Atheneum, who invited me to keynote a furniture conference even though I knew nothing about furniture. He and Karen Blanchfield introduced me to the topic and, in the initial stages of my research, provided photocopies of key sources as well as advice and direction. Later Suzanne Flynt of Memorial Hall and David Proper and Philip Zea of Colonial Deerfield gave generously of their time and knowledge, correcting many errors in earlier drafts of this essay.

FIGURE 1. Hannah Barnard Cupboard. *Henry Ford Museum and Colonial Greenfield. Photo courtesy of Pocumtuck Valley Memorial Association, Memorial Hall Museum, Deerfield, Mass.*

an extravagant gift from Barnard's future husband. It was "a Valentine in furniture."[1]

The authors of the exhibit catalog were more circumspect. Although acknowledging that the woman's name "made a strong statement" about her role

1. Owen McNally, " 'Furniture from New England Towns': Window to the Past," *Hartford Courant*, Feb. 6, 1993.

"as keeper of the household and a major portion of its assets: valued textiles and silver," they concentrated on stylistic analysis ("The Barnard cupboard was a stage for new Baroque concepts conveyed through traditional Hampshire County ornament") and on details that could be empirically affirmed (under polarized light microscopy the paint on the columns turned out to be a mixture of white lead and Prussian Blue, an artificial pigment first synthesized in Berlin in 1704). Their choice was understandable. In an effort to avoid the romantic excesses of early-twentieth-century collectors, decorative arts scholars are often cautious about exploring the social implications of their materials.[2] Unfortunately, social historians have been even more indifferent to the decorative arts. Most turn to objects, if at all, in the last stages of their projects, looking for illustrations to enliven arguments developed from written sources.[3]

My own interpretation of the Barnard cupboard, therefore, has both a methodological and a content objective. I want to make a particular argument about female identity in early America, and I want to demonstrate the value of object-centered research in social history. These two objectives came together quite by accident. Asked in the same season to write an essay on female identity and to keynote a symposium held in conjunction with the Hadley chest exhibit, I decided to see what would happen if I brought the two projects together. Although I had begun working with museum textile collections in an effort to expand available sources in women's history, I had never considered furniture. I thought of wood and things made of wood as belonging to the male domain. Hannah Barnard's cupboard took me by surprise.

Here was a seemingly expressive, highly personal object marked with a woman's name, but what did it mean? Were the words on the cupboard idiosyncratic or representative of some larger pattern in early American culture? Combined with vines and flowers, were they symbols of fertility, assertions of self, markers of one woman's command of her household goods, or emblems

2. Philip Zea and Suzanne L. Flynt, *Hadley Chests* (Deerfield, Mass., 1992), 20, 28. An exception to the cautious approach of decorative arts scholars is Richard Lawrence Greene, "Fertility Symbols on the Hadley Chests," *Antiques*, CXII (1977), 250–257. One of the first scholars to urge a cultural approach to the study of early American furniture (and later to decorative arts scholarship in general) was Robert Blair St. George (*The Wrought Covenant: Source Material for the Study of Craftsmen and Community in Southeastern New England 1620–1700* [Brockton, Mass., 1979], 13–17). For a vigorous statement of the problems of what he calls "scientific antiquarianism" in the decorative arts, see Michael J. Ettema, "History, Nostalgia, and American Furniture," *Winterthur Portfolio*, XVII (1982), 135–144.

3. Even Richard L. Bushman, whose work has done so much to bridge the gap between the two disciplines, explains that he did not attempt to learn "the methods of curatorial scholarship with its emphasis on vast quantities of highly specific and exact knowledge"; see *The Refinement of America: Persons, Houses, Cities* (New York, 1992), xiii.

of everywoman's subordination to domestic duty? Or were they merely design conventions or expressions of style? At the most basic level, I wanted to know what the cupboard could tell me about property. In a world where most forms of wealth were controlled by male heads of household, were certain objects in fact owned by women? The cupboard led me backward and forward between objects and documents, suggesting new ways of looking at gender and material life in early America. Hannah's cupboard is neither a protofeminist statement nor a valentine in furniture. It is an index to the shifting sources of female identity in early America. Surviving through three centuries, it exposes the contradictions in our inherited notions of family and the potent mix of violence and refinement in our history.

Hadley, Massachusetts, is a town rich in both history and antiquarian lore. Founded in 1658 by disaffected Puritans from Wethersfield, Windsor, and Hartford, Connecticut, it became one of the founding towns of Hampshire County, Massachusetts, in 1662. Battered during King Philip's War, the town still had only 50 families in 1682, but by the end of what the town history labels the "Fourth Indian War, 1722–1726," there were 117 households. Hadley entered the annals of furniture history in the next century, when in 1883 a Hartford banker began to speak of an antique chest he had found on a summer excursion as his "Hadley chest." By then, similar chests had already found their way into the exhibition space of the Pocumtuck Valley Memorial Association in Deerfield, one of the nation's landmark regional museums. Founded to commemorate the deaths of Deerfield settlers in the French and Indian attack of 1704, the PVMA soon became the guardian of antiques of every description— from a massive door bearing the marks of Indian hatchets to delicate silk embroideries.[4]

The conjunction of war and refinement is not an invention of the nineteenth century. Those who thrived in the "rough, rude, violent, and unpredictable world" of frontier Massachusetts were determined to conquer their French and Indian antagonists and to perpetuate an English culture expressed not only in sermons but in things. Men like Deerfield's famous minister John Williams returned from captivity in Canada to commission carved chests and silver tankards as well as to write of God's providence.[5] Hannah Barnard's

4. Sylvester Judd, *History of Hadley . . .* (Springfield, Mass., 1905), 10–14, 85, 283, 284; Zea and Flynt, *Hadley Chests,* 5–6; Suzanne L. Flynt, Susan McGowan, and Amelia F. Miller, *Gathered and Preserved* (Deerfield, Mass., 1991), 5–15.

5. Richard I. Melvoin, *New England Outpost: War and Society in Colonial Deerfield* (New York, 1989), 287; Douglas Edward Leach, *The Northern Colonial Frontier, 1607–1763* (New York, 1966), 208. Also see Kevin M. Sweeney, "From Wilderness to Arcadian Vale: Material

cupboard reflects this combination of frontier exigency and English aspiration. Decorated with conventional emblems of fecundity and equally stylized symbols of British sovereignty, it celebrates the wealth and ambition of Hannah's family. The cupboard relates to two important and well-documented furniture traditions—the Connecticut Valley joined-oak cupboard and its close cousin, the equally famous and exhaustively researched "Hadley" chest.

In seventeenth-century New England, a cupboard was an ostentatious and expensive form owned primarily by ministers, merchants, and government officials. When the Reverend Mr. Solomon Stoddard of Northampton, Massachusetts, died in 1729, he left silver, "needle wrought cushions," and fine linens as well as a "cupboard in the Parler." Mary Rowlandson, the author of the famous captivity narrative, inherited a cupboard when her first husband, the Reverend Mr. Joseph Rowlandson, died in Wethersfield, Connecticut, in 1678. The Rowlandson cupboard is typical of the so-called sunflower furniture made in Wethersfield (Figure 2). The maker of the Wethersfield cupboards used black paint to imitate the ebony turnings on English cupboards, which were often ornamented with exotic woods or mother-of-pearl. Such cupboards were designed both to store and to display wealth. Turned columns supported an overhanging top shelf that was draped with a rich textile called a "cupboard cloth." Often the cupboard, though valuable, was worth much less than the textiles stacked in its dark and almost inaccessible lower section. The textiles in the Rowlandson inventory, for example, were valued at almost fifty pounds. The cupboard, appraised at two pounds, was roughly equivalent to twenty-eight towels and napkins, worth less than ten pillowbeers (pillow cases).[6]

Life in the Connecticut River Valley, 1635–1760," in Gerald W. R. Ward and William Hosley, eds., *The Great River: Art and Society of the Connecticut Valley, 1635–1820* (Hartford, Conn., 1985), 17–21.

6. Gerald W. R. Ward, "Some Thoughts on Connecticut Cupboards and Other Case Furniture," *Old-Time New England,* LXXII (1987), 66–69 (Ward attributes the phrase to Charles Montgomery); Hampshire County Probate Records, V (1719–1738), 15, Hampshire County Courthouse, Northampton, Massachusetts. The so-called Rowlandson cupboard now stands in the public library in Lancaster, Massachusetts, the town the Rowlandsons fled after their house and possessions were destroyed in the war that took Mary into captivity. Since Rowlandson apparently had a prenuptial contract reserving her inheritance at the time of her second marriage, the "great cupboard" listed in the estate of her second husband, Samuel Talcott, was probably a different piece of furniture (Estate Records, Hartford District Probate Court, nos. 4658, 5380, Connecticut State Library). On Mary Rowlandson's second marriage, see David L. Greene, "New Light On Mary Rowlandson," *Early American Literature,* XX (1985), 24–38. On the cupboard, see Ward, "Some Thoughts," *Old-Time New England,* LXXII (1987), 67–69; Walter A. Dyer, "The Tulip-and-Sunflower Press Cupboard," *Antiques,* XXVII (1935), 140–143. On the textiles, see Rowlandson Inventory, Estate Records,

FIGURE 2. Mary Rowlandson Cupboard. *Lancaster Public Library, Lancaster, Mass.*

If few families in this period had cupboards, fine linen, or silver, most had at least one chest. An ordinary chest was merely a large box with a hinged lid. The cheapest ones were made of plain boards, nailed together, but the sturdiest and most valuable were constructed like a cupboard (or a house), with panels fitted into a heavy frame with mortise-and-tenon joints. Some of these "joined" chests had one or two drawers beneath. In probate inventories, they are often

Hartford District Probate Court, no. 4658. On the inaccessibility of storage space in early cupboards, see Ward, "Some Thoughts," *Old-Time New England,* LXXII (1987), 70.

described as "chests *with* drawers." Joiners also made "chests *of* drawers," a furniture innovation that abandoned the hinged top of the conventional chest, allowing easier access to stored linens or clothing by devoting all of the space to drawers. Hannah Barnard's cupboard is a compromise between a traditional cupboard, like the one inherited by Mary Rowlandson, and a chest of drawers. The upper half has doors, like a cupboard; the lower half drawers, like a chest. In fact, a chest of drawers with dark blue (almost black) paint at Historic Deerfield is almost identical to the lower half of Hannah's cupboard and was perhaps made by the same joiner.[7] (In the eighteenth century, the "joiners" who made the Rowlandson and Barnard cupboards and hundreds of chests, chests of drawers, and chests with drawers in rural towns like Hadley were succeeded by "cabinetmakers" who made lighter, more modern pieces using dovetailed boards and fine veneer. These were sometimes called "cases" rather than "chests" of drawers.)

Furniture scholars have identified at least sixteen variants of the so-called Hadley chest, made in Hadley and nearby Hampshire County towns from the 1680s to about 1730.[8] Some have drawers, some do not. Since most are marked with initials or a name, genealogists have been able to link many to young women born in nearby towns. In contrast, plain nailed chests made during the same period often have men's initials. Although early collectors wrote of the Hadley chest as a "folk" form, furniture scholars today emphasize its dynamic origins in a cluster of seventeenth-century shop traditions, ranging from Wethersfield, Connecticut, to the north-country joiners employed by John Pynchon at Springfield, Massachusetts. The name derives from an early piece, found in Hadley, carved with a distinctive, two-petaled tulip. The exu-

7. Patricia E. Kane, "New Haven Colony Furniture: The Seventeenth-Century Style," *Antiques*, CIII (1973), 950–962; William N. Hosley, Jr., "The Wallace Nutting Collection at the Wadsworth Atheneum, Hartford, Connecticut," *Antiques*, CXXVI (1984), 860–874; Ward, "Some Thoughts," *Old-Time New England*, LXXII (1987), 74–77; Dean A. Fales, Jr., *American Painted Furniture, 1660–1880* (New York, 1972), 16, 17; Zea and Flynt, *Hadley Chests*, 22, fig. 14. On the distinction between chests *with* drawers and chests *of* drawers, see Brock Jobe and Myrna Kaye, *New England Furniture: The Colonial Era* (Boston, 1984), 130–131.

8. Although some Hadley chests, like the Barnard cupboard, did indeed originate in Hadley, Massachusetts, related examples are found throughout the Connecticut River Valley. See Zea and Flynt, *Hadley Chests*, 5, 16; Clair Franklin Luther, *The Hadley Chest* (Hartford, Conn., 1935), xix–xxvi; Patricia E. Kane, "The Seventeenth-Century Furniture of the Connecticut Valley: The Hadley Chest Reappraised," in Ian M. G. Quimby, ed., *Arts of the Anglo-American Community in the Seventeenth Century*, Winterthur Conference Report, 1974 (Charlottesville, Va., 1975), 79–122; Philip Zea, "The Fruits of Oligarchy: Patronage and the Hadley Chest Tradition in Western Massachusetts," *Old-Time New England*, LXXII (1987), 1–65.

berant and varied decoration led early collectors to label them "dower" or "marriage chests."[9]

Although what furniture scholars consider true Hadley chests include tulips in some form, the variety of styles is really quite remarkable. Two initialed chests made about the same time as Hannah's cupboard suggest the range. The "MS" chest, with its undulating vines and explicit sexual imagery in the central panel, places the owner's initials in tight lozenges to the right and left. The "SH" chest, in contrast, splashes tulips over the entire ground, the shallow carving highlighted in red paint over a stippled background. The initials on the SH chest command the central panel, standing out all the more boldly because, with the exception of a small area just above, they occupy the only plain field on the chest (Figures 3 and 4).

Almost all Hadley chests are marked in some way. Like the linens they were designed to protect, most have two initials, though a handful have three.[10] Only 8 of the more than 120 marked chests have complete names. With one exception, all of those with full names seem to have been made for women from the towns of Northampton and Hadley. Esther Lyman, Sarah Strong, Esther Cook, and Mary Burt all came from Northampton, and Elisabeth Warner and Thankful Taylor from Hadley, though they married men from Enfield and Suffield (now in Connecticut). Mary Pease, who was born in Enfield, was related to Warner by marriage (Figure 5).[11] The 4 Northampton chests employ a distinctive fleur-de-lis pattern as well as a variant of the Hadley tulip, though there are differences in the way the names are handled. Esther Lyman's uses the curling tendrils typical of the SH and many other Hadley chests; on the other chests,

9. William N. Hosley, Jr., and Philip Zea, "Decorated Board Chests of the Connecticut River Valley," *Antiques*, CXIX (1981), 1146–1151.

10. Kane, "Seventeenth-Century Furniture," in Quimby, ed., *Arts of the Anglo-American Community*, identifies 126 chests, 102 with two initials, 6 with three, 11 with none, and 7 with full names. Philip Zea believes the NDM/1700 chest might have been made for Nathaniel and Margaret (Pynchon) Downing; see Zea, "Oligarchy," *Old-Time New England*, LXXII (1987), 9, fig. 12.

11. Further research may refine the connections between Mary Pease and Elisabeth Warner, who married a Pease. The information in Figure 6 is based on my own research in the International Genealogical Index, on genealogies in Judd, *Hadley*, and George Sheldon, *A History of Deerfield, Massachusetts*, 2 vols. (1895–1896; reprint, Deerfield, Mass., 1983), II; Luther, *The Hadley Chest*, 98, 121, 144; C. F. Luther, "The Hadley Chest," *Antiques*, XIV (1928), 338–340; Preston R. Bassett, "Collectors' Notes: An Unrecorded Hadley Chest," *Antiques*, LXXV (1959), 460–461; *Catalogue of the Bertram K. Little and Nina Fletcher Little Collection* (New York, 1994), 71; "Researches among Funeral Sermons," *New England Historical and Genealogical Register*, VIII (1854), 180–183; and telephone conversations with Lynne Bassett, curator, Historic Northampton, and Olive Blair Graffam, curator of collections, Daughters of the American Revolution Museum, Washington, D.C.

FIGURE 3. "MS" Chest with Drawers. *Hatfield, Mass., area, c. 1715. Wadsworth Atheneum, Hartford. Wallace Nutting Collection. Gift of J. Pierpont Morgan, by exchange and the Evelyn Bonar Storrs Trust Fund*

the names are carved in unadorned letters. The placement of the names also varies. On 5 chests, including 3 from Northampton, the name marches boldly across the upper rail (Figure 6). Mary Pease's appears on the lower rail, just above the drawers; Esther Cook's, which seems to have been altered or replaced in the twentieth century, sits somewhat awkwardly in the central panel.[12]

All of that suggests consumer choice. At any given point, several joiners were capable of creating carved chests, varying the final product, including the placement of names and initials. Ironically, as Philip Zea has observed, "re-

12. See illustration in Edith Gaines, "Collectors' Notes," *Antiques,* LXXXII (1962), 172. Philip Zea doubts the authenticity of the name panel in the Cook chest.

FIGURE 4. "SH" Chest with Drawers. *Hadley or Hatfield, Mass., c. 1710. Pocumtuck Valley Memorial Association, Memorial Hall Museum, Deerfield, Mass. Gift of George Sheldon, before 1886*

gional acceptance of these hybridized expressions of American joinery was accelerated by the devastation of King Philip's War, particularly in Hampshire County where wholesale rebuilding and refurnishing was required."[13] The Hannah Barnard cupboard, probably made just after the end of Queen Anne's War (1713), explodes with new adaptations of old ideas. It builds on the Hadley chest tradition, but it is not carved. Although many Hadley chests were painted before assembly, not so with the Barnard cupboard. In fact, it belongs to a small cluster of Hampshire furniture related by surface decoration alone. The

13. Simpler versions of the same design elements appear on a nailed chest owned by a Northampton woman; see Zea, "Furniture," in Ward and Hosley, eds., *The Great River*, 187.

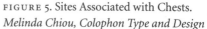

FIGURE 5. Sites Associated with Chests.
Melinda Chiou, Colophon Type and Design

"SW" chest at Memorial Hall in Deerfield is a chest *with* drawers (Figure 7). A chest *of* drawers at Winterthur was made in a different manner by a different joiner, yet both seem to have been decorated by the person who painted Hannah's cupboard. This unknown painter could have been the joiner who made Hannah's cupboard, one of the men who made the other chests, or a different person entirely. The character of the painting suggests someone used to working with wood, however. The designs were laid out with a straightedge and compass, the outlines incised into the wood, then filled in with pigment.[14]

The Barnard cupboard draws from most of the Hadley variations, interpreting each motif in paint rather than carving. It has undulating vines like the MS chest, curling letters like the Esther Lyman chest, inverted hearts like those on the SH chest, leaf and diamond constructions like those on the "EE" and "LB" chests, and a row of half-circles like those on the bottom rail of an uninscribed example. But it doesn't stop there. The painted drawer "moldings" are shaped like the actual moldings on early cupboards or chests. Glorying in paint, the

14. Fales, *American Painted Furniture,* 20–23; Zea and Flynt, *Hadley Chests,* 19–23. For early images and the provenance of the three pieces, see "The Editor's Attic: The Frontispiece," *Antiques,* X (1926), 188–190; "Connecticut Valley Polychromed Press Cupboard," *Antiques,* XXV (1934), 129; "The Editor's Attic: Which Hannah Barnard?" *Antiques,* XXVI (1934), 168; "The Editor's Attic: The Vindication of Hannah," *Antiques,* XXIX (1936), 139–140. The SW chest has been heavily repainted, but enough of the original work remains to demonstrate the technique. Although the Winterthur chest was stripped of a later coat of paint, the original paint, when exposed, was in excellent condition. The design, pigments, and methods of application are strikingly similar to the Hannah Barnard cupboard. I would like to thank Suzanne Flynt for looking at the Barnard cupboard and the SW chest with me and Brock Jobe for showing me related physical evidence in the Winterthur chest.

FIGURE 6. Sarah Strong Chest with Drawer. *Northampton, Mass., early eighteenth century.*
Historic Northampton

creator of Hannah's cupboard bent tradition in yet another way. The turned
posts of cupboards were meant to be black. The flamboyant blue on Hannah's
cupboard shows off a vibrant new tint unavailable before. An awareness of
European imports is also evident in the segmented roses that march across the
drawers. Although they might have been laid out with a straightedge and
compass, they look very much like the roses on a tin-glazed plate owned by
Esther Williams of Deerfield, who married in the same year as Hannah Barnard (Figure 8). In English delftware, flat "roses" were sometimes combined
with checkered "thistles." The upright blossom in the central panel of Hannah's cupboard is in fact a thistle. The plump fruits on either side of the central panel are pomegranates, another widely used motif in English decorative
arts.[15]

15. Fales, *American Painted Furniture,* 19, fig. 16; Kane, "Seventeenth Century Furniture,"
in Quimby, ed., *Arts of the Anglo-American Community,* 94, 101, 102, figs. 9, 10, 17, 19; Zea,
"Furniture," in Ward and Hosley, eds., *The Great River,* 202, 206, figs. 81, 84.

The rose-and-thistle motif connects Hannah's cupboard to a large group of unrelated
chests, chests with drawers, chests of drawers, and standing high chests made in Guilford

The designer brought all of these elements together in a unified and powerful composition. Hannah's name is integral to the design, yet its placement sets it apart from the Hadley and Northampton chests, perhaps because the cupboard form demanded a different treatment. A chest, with its lidded top, left several unbroken surfaces for decoration. A cupboard required a vertical opening. Unless the designer wanted to string the name across a drawer, he (or she) had to fit it into one of the panels on the top, easy to do with an initial, hard to accomplish with a full name. The solution was brilliant. The name "Hannah" is a palindrome, a word that reads the same backward or forward. The composition takes advantage of this repetition allowing the three letters H, A, and N to form two strong columns. "Barnard," despite its tantalizing internal rhyme, was more difficult, since seven letters required four rows rather than three. Again the painter allowed A and N to dominate, keeping the curved letters, B, R, and D somewhat narrower, filling in the extra space with a square.[16] (The handling of the curved letters seems to be typical of Hadley chests, however, as the narrowness of the S on the SH chest shows.)

---

and Saybrook, Connecticut, between 1700 and 1725. The Connecticut chests are painted in a flowing and lyrical style, yet they too employ some version of the stylized rose and thistle that was so much a part of English decorative arts from the early seventeenth century onward. The Guilford-Saybrook chests are closely related to printers' ornaments that combined the rose and thistle with the fleur-de-lis, symbolically linking the crowns of England, France, and Scotland. I do not know whether there was any political significance to the appearance of these ornaments in 18th-century New England. Using a different painting style, a Connecticut chest of drawers from the same period alternates roses and thistles on the four drawers. Among the Hadley chests, the carved Northampton chests seem to be the only ones with fleur-de-lis. See Fales, *American Painted Furniture*, 24–29, 36–38, 39, 42–43; Charles F. Montgomery, "Country Furniture: A Symposium," *Antiques*, XCIII (1968), 357–358, figs. 3, 3a; John T. Kirk, "The Tradition of English Painted Furniture; Part 1: The Experience in Colonial New England," *Antiques*, CXVII (1980), 1082–1083, figs. 8, 8a, b; and Elizabeth Carroll Reilly, *A Dictionary of Colonial American Printers' Ornaments and Illustrations* (Worcester, Mass., 1975), 187. See, for an example of the pomegranate motif, the slip-decorated plate made by John Burslem in Staffordshire in exactly this period, in Leslie B. Grigsby, *English Slip-Decorated Earthenware at Williamsburg* (Williamsburg, Va., 1993), 10, 41, figs. 2, 46.

16. The visual rhymes formed by the repeated A's might have been accidental. When the cupboard was restored in 1994, the conservator discovered faint marks of an E below the first A, suggesting that the painter had been uncertain about the spelling of Hannah's name (Conversation with Susan Buck, Society for the Preservation of New England Antiquities Conservation Center; Zea and Flynt, *Hadley Chests*, 28 n. 56). Variant spellings of names were common in this period. A piece of silver owned by one of Hannah's relatives was marked "Bernard"; see Silver Beaker, "The Gift of Samuel Bernard to the Church in Deerfield 1723," c. 1723, L-20-85, Historic Deerfield.

FIGURE 7. "SW" Chest with Drawers. *Hadley, Mass., area, c. 1718. Pocumtuck Valley Memorial Association, Memorial Hall Museum, Deerfield, Mass. Gift of George Sheldon, 1892*

Inside the columns formed by Hannah's name are two bold towers formed of seemingly unrelated things—paired leaves, pomegranates, hearts, and diamonds. Nothing on the cupboard seems more "folklike," yet the composition is probably an abstracted version of the borders often used in late-Renaissance tapestries and engravings. A cushion cover owned by Edward Taylor, the pastor of nearby Westfield, Massachusetts, shows a central vase of flowers bordered by pillared constructions of fruit, flowers, leaves, urns, and masks, the massing strikingly similar to the borders on the Barnard cupboard (Figure 9). The busy turnings on seventeenth-century cupboards are, of course, a three-dimensional version of the same thing.

Thus, Hannah's cupboard is both idiosyncratic and representative of larger

FIGURE 8. Plate. *Tin-glazed earthenware, England, early eighteenth century. Pocumtuck Valley Memorial Association, Memorial Hall Museum, Deerfield, Mass. Gift of Mrs. Bessie Gamons, 1954*

patterns in the decorative arts. Looking backward to the sober seventeenth-century households that sent the first settlers up the river toward Hadley, it embraced the expanding world of eighteenth-century commerce. Made by an unknown local joiner who knew how to construct both chests of drawers and cupboards, it was likely decorated by a second person who added a flamboyant new pigment to a repertoire of designs familiar from local carved furniture and English ceramics to create a highly personal rendition of a traditional "woman's chest." The cupboard itself can tell us that much.

One of the staples of social history—probate records—can tell us a bit more. In Hampshire County, Massachusetts, as elsewhere in the English-speaking world, cupboards and chests, like the textiles, ceramics, and silver they were designed to store, belonged to that category of property known as "movables."

FIGURE 9. Tapestry Cushion Cover. *England, c. 1610–1615. Pocumtuck Valley Memorial Association, Memorial Hall Museum, Deerfield, Mass. Gift of the Reverend John Taylor to Deerfield Academy Museum, before 1806. Brought by the Reverend Edward Taylor from England in 1662*

According to English law, movables, or "personalty," formed the core inheritance of women. Unless other circumstances required a different arrangement, sons received buildings and land, daughters a combination of household goods, animals, and occasionally servants or slaves. There was a principle of equality in seventeenth-century New England, but it assumed differential treatment of males and females. When John Billings of Hatfield died unmarried, the court divided his worldly possessions among his siblings "in Equall and proportion, the said Brothers to have all the Lands Equallie divided to them and the said Sarah to have her share in the Moveable goods." The court used similar language when it ordered that Joseph Barnard's sons were "to injoy all the lands in Equall proportions . . . and the daughters to be payd out of the moveable Estate so farr as they will Extend." When another man willed his lands to his sons and brother but neglected to provide for his daughters, the court added "that the daughters of the said deceased shall have their portions Out of the Movables."[17]

Anthropologist Annette Weiner suggests that the Western concepts of "real property" and "movables" are one manifestation of "the world's most ancient and profound economic classification"—the distinction between alienable and inalienable possessions. "What makes a possession inalienable," Weiner explains, "is its exclusive and cumulative identity with a particular series of owners through time." In English property law, that series of owners was the patriline. Movables might pass freely, but real property was protected from indiscriminate inheritance. Typically, widows inherited the use of land rather than the land itself. At death or remarriage, real estate reverted to male heirs. For the possessors, Weiner argues, inalienable possessions resolved the paradox of "keeping-while-giving."

> Some things, like most commodities, are easy to give. But there are other possessions that are imbued with the intrinsic and ineffable identities of their owners which are not easy to give away. Ideally, these inalienable possessions are kept by their owners from one generation to the next within the closed context of family, descent group, or dynasty.[18]

The association of males with land and females with movables was not, therefore, a neutral division of resources. The possession of "real" property secured male identity. A man who passed his name and land to a son transcended his own mortality as he validated his own authority. He kept while giving.

In the classic "thirds" offered to a widow, land reverted to the male line at the woman's death. In the Connecticut River Valley, as Toby Ditz has shown, daughters received land only when personalty was lacking; the value of that land was always significantly less than that inherited by their brothers. By custom and law, fathers "could simply exclude all daughters and members of daughters' families from heritable rights in land and confine their share of property to personalty."[19] In such a system, women themselves became "movables," changing their names and presumably their identities as they moved

17. John Billing Distribution, Sept., 8, 1698, Joseph Barnard Distribution, n.d., Charles Fierre Will and Distribution, July 29, 1699, Hampshire County Probate Records, Book 1690–1700.

18. Annette B. Weiner, *Inalienable Possessions: The Paradox of Keeping-while-Giving* (Berkeley, Calif., 1992), 6 (quotation), 32, 33, 37, 42–43, 154.

19. Toby L. Ditz, *Property and Kinship: Inheritance in Early Connecticut, 1750–1820* (Princeton, N.J., 1986), 65. In the case of daughters, Ditz argues, bequests of land were substitutes for personal property. She notes, however, that wills undervalue bequests to daughters, since most probably received all or part of their portions of movable goods at marriage (69–70).

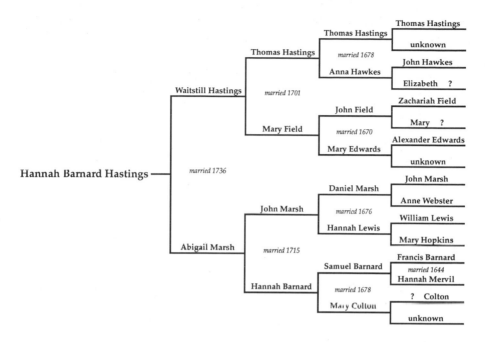

FIGURE 10. Hannah Barnard Hastings Pedigree. *Melinda Chiou, Colophon Type and Design*

from one male-headed household to another. But what if some portion of these goods retained the daughter's maiden name even as she lost it? That is the puzzle presented by Hannah Barnard's cupboard.

Hannah Barnard married John Marsh in 1715. She died in 1717, leaving an infant daughter Abigail. That daughter married Waitstill Hastings in 1736, and in 1742 Abigail and Waitstill had a daughter. They named her, not just Hannah, but Hannah *Barnard* Hastings (Figure 10). The use of middle names is extraordinarily rare in Hadley (or anywhere else in New England) in this period. Hannah Barnard Hastings may be the only child in eighteenth-century New England named for a cupboard. Not surprisingly, she inherited it.[20] The cupboard preserved her grandmother's name, but the name also transformed the cupboard. Marked in this way, it became less portable, less exchangeable. It had become an inalienable possession.

Hannah's cupboard points toward invisible and little understood notions of inheritance lying just beneath the surface of early probate records. Hannah

20. Court Cupboard, 36.178.1, Henry Ford Museum and Greenfield Village Files; "Connecticut Valley Polychromed Press Cupboard," *Antiques*, XXV (1934), 129; "The Editor's Attic: Which Hannah Barnard?" *Antiques*, XXVI (1934), 168; "The Editor's Attic: The Vindication of Hannah," *Antiques*, (1936), 139–140. I can find only three girls in colonial Hadley given a surname for a middle name, none before Hannah Barnard Hastings; see Lucius M. Boltwood, "Family Genealogies," in Judd, *Hadley*, 8, 64, 91–92.

Barnard had been John Marsh's second wife. He had married the first time in 1704, the summer following his return from captivity in Canada. After Hannah's death, he married a third time. He was only in his forties when he died in 1725, but he was already a wealthy man, in part, one suspects, because of the goods brought to marriage by three wives, all daughters of substantial families.[21] He owned parcels of "meadow," "woodland," "upland," and "outland" in addition to his homestead with its buildings and orchard. He owned horses as well as two yoke of "fat oxen" and tools for farming and lumbering. He also owned an "Indian [perhaps West Indian] Boy Sippey about 14 Years Old," and at the time of his death he had five minor children, including Hannah's daughter Abigail.

His will and inventory make clear what the cupboard only suggests, that within the clutter of household goods defined as "movables," certain objects were marked, literally or figuratively, with female lineages. The inventory lists household goods in three separate places, in the general list following land and cattle and under the subtitles: "3d Wives Goods" and "2d Wives Goods." Marsh's only son, then two years old, was promised all of his father's real estate, but Abigail was to receive £120 "to be paid in what was her own Mothers," plus "her Mothers Wearing Cloaths . . . to be given her free." The younger girls were to receive portions worth £100. The inventory suggests that these goods, too, were to come from property their mother brought to marriage.[22]

The three lists are strikingly parallel in both organization and value. Each includes brass, iron, and pewter, earthenware and glass, "wooden ware," including furniture, and a range of valuable textiles divided into "Woolen," "Linnen," and "Bedding." The household goods on the general list amount to seventy-two pounds, Hannah Barnard's goods total eighty-five pounds, the third wife's goods eighty-seven pounds. The goods on the first list, some of which might have originated with Marsh's first wife, include "A Carved Work Chest" valued at thirty shillings. One can easily imagine a Hadley chest here, perhaps one marked with initials or a name. The furniture listed with the "2d Wives Goods," our Hannah Barnard, includes "a floward Chest" valued at

21. Sheldon, *Deerfield,* II, 298. Of the 117 names in the Hadley valuation list of 1720, Marsh's father-in-law, Samuel Porter, ranked first, his father, Daniel Marsh, was fourth, and his father-in-law, Samuel Barnard, was seventh. On the valuation list of 1731, "Heirs of John Marsh, and Widow Sarah Marsh" rank fifteenth out of 87 (Judd, *Hadley,* 278, 283). Marsh's third wife, Sarah Williams, was the daughter of Isaac Williams of Newton and a first cousin of Deerfield's minister, John Williams; see Sheldon, *Deerfield,* II, 376–377.

22. John Marsh Will, June 5, 1725, Hampshire County Probate Records, IV, 134, Microfilm, Latter-day Saints Family History Library, film number 0879184. As it turned out, little John never did come of age. He died July 3, 1726, age three; see Boltwood, "Family Genealogies," in Judd, *Hadley,* 92.

thirty-two shillings and another "ditto" at ten. There is no mention of a "cupboard," though there must have been one at some point because the list of linens includes "2 Cupboard Cloths." The furniture listed with the "3d Wives Goods" includes a more modern (and expensive) item: "A case of drawers," valued at four pounds. The third wife, like Hannah, had a store of sheets, towels, tablecloths, and napkins, but she had no cupboard cloth.[23]

Perhaps the more expensive "floward chest" on Hannah's list was the "cupboard" that survives today, though it is strange that the inventory takers, who carefully distinguished between the "carved" and "floward" chests and who knew the difference between a "chest" and a "*case* of drawers," would call a cupboard a chest. Perhaps the cupboard was too visible a reminder of the dead wife to remain in the household after Marsh married again. Hannah's section of the inventory includes nine pounds, "money due for sundries in Ensign Moses Cooks hands." Moses Cook was Hannah Barnard's brother-in-law. Could Mary Cook have taken the cupboard (and perhaps little Abigail) at the time of her sister's death? We cannot know. There is no question, however, about the intent of Marsh's will. The goods Hannah Barnard brought to marriage formed the core of her own daughter's inheritance.

Marsh's inventory has been known to furniture researchers since the 1930s, yet none has noted the importance of the separate listing of each wife's goods. When Hannah's cupboard surfaced in the antiques market in 1936, the Reverend Clair Franklin Luther, the first systematic cataloger of Hadley chests, was certain Marsh's inventory contained the clue to the identity of the similar SW chest. Marsh's third wife was named Sarah Williams. Surely the first flowered chest in the inventory was Hannah's cupboard and the second belonged to Sarah. It was an attractive notion, yet it ignored the structure of the document. Unless one assumes that Hannah Barnard conveniently anticipated the initials of her successor, the least likely place to find a chest marked "SW" was with her goods![24] Surprisingly, the 1992 catalog of the Hadley exhibit repeated the error. The problem was not so much faulty scholarship as an inability to break free of patriarchal paradigms.

In scholarly as well as common usage we speak of the "Marsh family," the "Barnard family," or the "Hastings family." Biologically, of course, there is no such thing. One can speak of a particular family through time only by ignoring the fundamental basis of reproduction, that every child requires both a mother

23. John Marsh Inventory, Hampshire County Probate Records, IV, 138–140. I thank Suzanne Flynt for the suggestion that the cupboard might have left the household. The identity of Moses Cook reinforces the possibility.

24. "The Editor's Attic: Which Hannah Barnard?" *Antiques*, XXVI (1934), 168; Zea and Flynt, *Hadley Chests*, 22.

and father. Barring sibling incest, in each generation half of the genes must come from outside the original group. But law, culture, and convenience conspire to make us forget that. The pedigree of Hannah Barnard Hastings illustrates the fragility—and complexity—of female lineage (Figure 10). Notice how easy it is to trace the "Hastings" line, reading along the top of the chart from Hannah to her father Waitstill Hastings, then to Waitstill's father, grandfather, and great-grandfather, all named Thomas Hastings, the repetition of names illustrating Weiner's concept of "keeping while giving." Everywhere on the chart, going from child to father to grandfather is simple—from Abigail Marsh to John Marsh to Daniel Marsh to John Marsh, for example, or from Hannah Barnard to her father and grandfather. But to trace daughter-mother lineages is more difficult. The names of all eight of Hannah's great-great-grandfathers survive; only three of her great-great-grandmothers have complete names. Two are simply "unknown."

Even though biologically the notion of descent from mother to daughter makes every bit as much sense as from father to son, it is extraordinarily hard to define such a "line" within Western genealogical conventions. To enfold a female lineage in the patrilineal line of descent, a girl would have to carry a chain of surnames that grew heavier with each generation. Abigail and Waitstill Hastings acknowledged just one link in that chain when they named their daughter for her maternal grandmother. Yet the name persisted for two more generations. Hannah Barnard Hastings had a daughter named Hannah Barnard Kellogg (born 1769) and a granddaughter named Hannah Barnard Hastings Kellogg (born 1817).[25] The cupboard perpetuated one woman's identity for more than a century after her death.

In the Marsh family, demographic accidents—the early deaths of two wives, the husband's own premature demise—exposed female lineages. More commonly, the formulaic dispersal of movables, as in "one-third of my household goods," concealed the female labor that created and maintained those goods and the social customs if not the female voices that directed their disposal. Because daughters customarily received their portions at marriage rather than at the death of their father, wills and inventories actually mask much of what moved from one generation to another. Land can be traced in deeds, but movables, by definition, flowed outside the constraints of law. That is why object-centered research is so useful. Probate records can tell us what sorts of objects people possessed at any one time and what kinds of things fathers (and

25. [Lydia Nelson Hastings, ed.], *The Hastings Memorial: A Genealogical Account of the Descendents of Thomas Hastings of Watertown, Mass., from 1634 to 1864* (Boston, 1866), 7, 8, 11; Thomas Hopkins, *The Kelloggs in the Old World and the New*, I (San Francisco, 1903), 172, 369. The last of the Hannah Barnards died childless in San Jose, California, in 1889.

occasionally mothers) willed to their children at the end of life, but well-documented histories of surviving objects can tell us how certain movables were actually transmitted—or lost—over time.

Almost inadvertently, decorative arts historians produce a great deal of social history simply by pursuing their most basic enterprise—establishing provenance. Challenging the attribution of a Hadley chest first documented in 1935, Marius Peladeau demonstrated lineal descent from mother to daughter. Making a slight detour to include a posthumous stepdaughter, the line stretched from 1700 to the early twentieth century. Museum curators can no doubt point to many other examples of this sort, on unmarked as well as marked objects.[26] One need not assume awareness of a "female line." All that is required is a belief in each generation that certain objects ought to pass from mother to daughter. Establishing provenance is seldom that easy, however, nor is direct transmission from mother to daughter the only alternative to patrilineal descent.

The mystery of the SW chest suggests the complexity of the enterprise. The first accession records for Memorial Hall listed the chest as an "Ancient oak cabinet—not carved but painted—bought of Jonathan A. Saxton about 1870 Long in the Saxton [——] / Geo. Sheldon." The blank is in the original, perhaps reflecting Sheldon's uncertainty. By 1908, he had in fact changed his story, writing that the "Oak chest, marked SW . . . came down in the White family." A printed catalog published at the same time attributes it to Susanna White of the Mayflower.[27] The 1991 exhibit catalog understandably debunked the Mayflower connection, noting the propensity of nineteenth-century antiquarians to assign English origins to every piece of old furniture, yet they too offered a somewhat fanciful explanation of the origins of the chest. Since George Sheldon purchased it from Jonathan Saxton about 1870 and since the only payment to Saxton recorded in Sheldon's daybook relates to the estate of Charles Williams, "The 'SW' Chest was probably a Williams family heirloom." Their reasoning was straightforward. Since Charles Williams was a "collateral descendant" of John Marsh's third wife, Sarah Williams, the Barnard cupboard and the SW chest were probably "successively brought into the Marsh house-

26. Marius B. Peladeau, "A Hadley Chest Reconsidered," *Antiques*, CXVII (1980), 1084–1086. But such lineages are difficult to trace. Some scholars seem to assume descent from male, some through female lines. See, for example, entries concerning different objects inherited by the same woman, discussed by Philip Zea, "Furniture," and Jane Nylander, "Textiles, Clothing, and Needlework," in Ward and Hosley, eds., *The Great River*, 223, fig. 103, 374–375, 380, figs. 245, 249.

27. Suzanne Flynt to Laurel Ulrich, Mar. 10, 1995, citing Pocumtuck Valley Memorial Association Accession Book, I, 181, and *1908 Catalogue of Relics in Memorial Hall*, 94, MH 702, PVMA Library, Deerfield; Zea and Flynt, *Hadley Chests*, 22, 29 n. 67.

hold in 1715 and 1718."[28] Notice once again how patrilineal constructions ("Williams family heirloom," "Marsh household") simplified the story. The catalog does not explain why an object ostensibly belonging to the third wife was listed with the second wife's goods, nor does it attempt to show how a piece of furniture belonging to a woman married successively to a Marsh and a Grey ended up, six generations later, in the "Williams family."

Working with the same set of documents but with a different set of assumptions about family history produces alternative routes to Jonathan Saxton. One of these even connects to a Sarah Williams who died in Deerfield in 1720. This Sarah was a second cousin of John Marsh's Sarah and a first cousin of the Esther Williams who owned the tin-glazed plate with the rose that looks so much like the ones on the Barnard cupboard and the SW chest. Born in Roxbury, this Sarah Williams married Samuel Barnard, Hannah's cousin, in 1718. Like Hannah, she died giving birth to an only child. Sarah's infant, however, did not survive. Samuel Barnard left Deerfield after his wife's death and though he married again had no children. When he died in 1762, he left land and property to the sons of his brother Ebenezer Barnard. Although there is no way of proving this, at any time between 1720 and 1762 he could also have given movables to his brother's daughters. One of those daughters became the grandmother of Jonathan Saxton, whose sister Tirza was the wife of the Charles Williams mentioned in George Sheldon's daybook.[29] Thus, the SW chest, if it belonged to Sarah Williams Barnard, could easily have been both a Saxton and a Williams "family heirloom."

It could also have come down "in the White family" either as an heirloom or as a piece of junk left behind in one of the many family migrations. Jonathan Saxton's mother-in-law, Mercy White, was the daughter of Salmon White, a *male* with the initials "SW." Although Salmon was too young to have been the original owner of the chest, his aunt Susannah Wells, who became Susannah White at marriage, might have been the "Susannah White" who inspired the Mayflower legend. She moved to Hardwick, Massachusetts, and later to Vermont. But this trail, too, leads back to Hannah Barnard's cousin Samuel and his wife Sarah Williams. Samuel's sister Sarah Wells was Susannah White's adoptive mother. One can imagine the initials directing the chest from Sarah Williams to Sarah Wells to Susannah White and then by some forgotten

28. Zea and Flynt, *Hadley Chests*, 20–23.

29. Stephen W. Williams, *The Genealogy and History of the Family of Williams* . . . (Greenfield, Mass., 1847), 21, 33, 34; *Vital Records of Deerfield, Massachusetts*, I (Boston, 1920), 2, 264; *Vital Records of Roxbury Mass.*, I (Salem, Mass., 1925), 383; *Vital Records of Roxbury Mass*, II (Salem, Mass., 1926), 437; Sheldon, *Deerfield*, II, 66, 67, 279–280. Sheldon incorrectly states on page 377 that Sarah, daughter of Samuel Williams, Jr., married John Polly.

path, perhaps through Salmon White, to Jonathan Saxton. By then the chest might have been less a treasure than a burden. The first Hadley chests were often discovered on back porches, in barns, or in slaughterhouses. One even traveled to the Midwest as a shipping crate.[30]

Barring the discovery of a forgotten will, inventory, account book, or letter with an explicit reference to the SW chest, there is no way of knowing how it reached Jonathan Saxton, nor can we know for certain whether the S stands for Sarah, Susannah, or Salmon, or the W for White, Wells, Williams, Wright, Wait, or any other of the ubiquitous W's in Hadley or Deerfield. The first families of Deerfield and Hadley are so intertwined that it is almost impossible to trace one line of descent without encountering another. The very difficulty of establishing provenance reinforces the central insight of this essay, however. Families are social constructions, made and remade over time. Family identities, like personal identities, are built from selective fragments of the past—names, stories, and material objects.

Fortunately, enough well-documented objects survive to help us see how gender intersects with property in the continuing struggle to define the meaning of family. Historian Barbara Ward became interested in the subject of female inheritance when she was researching provenance for the silver entries in *The Great River*, a catalog produced for a major exhibit of Connecticut Valley objects. Probate records revealed, for example, that the silver caudle cups John Davenport bequeathed to his minor daughters in 1731 were to be engraved "D/IE" to represent the girls' parents. But a surviving cup, belonging to an older daughter and not mentioned in the will, is engraved "AD." Since the daughter's name was Abigail, the initials were appropriate, but the form of the cup marked it as much older. Ward believes it was made for the paternal grandmother, a woman whose name also happened to be Abigail Davenport. The "AD" cup might well have been a prototype for later gifts from the father and mother to their younger daughters. The same process was at work in the case of Prudence Stoddard, who owned two pieces of Stoddard silver, a teapot with the family coat of arms given her at marriage in 1750 and a standing salt made half a century earlier and inscribed with the initials of her paternal grandparents the Reverend Solomon Stoddard and his wife Esther Mather. Prudence, in turn, passed these objects on to her daughters.[31] Ward's catalog

30. Sheldon, "Genealogies," *Deerfield*, II, 66, 67, 281, 358, 393. Sarah and Thomas Wells both left property to nieces and nephews; see Thomas Wells Estate, Hampshire County Probate Records, VII, 272–273; Sarah Wells Estate, Hampshire County Probate Files, box 9, 25; Zea and Flynt, *Hadley Chests*, 3–4.

31. Barbara McLean Ward, "Women's Property and Family Continuity in Eighteenth-

FIGURE 11. Silver Tankard. *C. 1700–1710. Jeremiah Dummer, Boston, 1645–1718. Historic Deerfield, Inc., Acc. #59–88. Photograph by Helga Studio*

entries demonstrate the power of combining object analysis with genealogical research.

Women did not always pass on their gifts to female descendants, however, as a silver tankard from the collections of Historic Deerfield shows. Fortunately, the tankard, dating from 1700–1710, bears its genealogy on its handle (Figure 11). The first set of initials belonged to Mary Williams Cook of Newton, Mas-

---

Century Connecticut," in Peter Benes and Jane Montague Benes, eds., *Early American Probate Inventories*, Dublin Seminar for New England Folklife (Dublin, 1987), 74–85; catalog entries in Ward and Hosley, eds., *The Great River*, 279, 281–282, 288–289.

sachusetts, who bequeathed it to her nephew, Dr. Thomas Williams of Deerfield. It then descended to several generations of Williamses, each heir adding his or her initials in turn. In this case, a lineage obscured in marriage returned to the paternal line in a gift from a woman to her brother's son. The inscription on another Deerfield piece, also associated with the Williams family, shows a different line of descent. The inscription reads: "This Cann Is Presented to Mrs: Anna Williams/By her Uncle and Aunt Hindsdale/1754." Aunt Hinsdale, born Abigail Williams, was Anna Williams's paternal aunt. Although Anna might already have married Jacob Cushing, the "Mrs" before her name denotes social rather than marital status. The cann, which symbolized a familial relationship between two women whose maiden names were "Williams," bore the Hinsdale coat of arms and descended in the Cushing family. Meanwhile, "Aunt Hinsdale" was widowed twice, becoming first Madame Hall and then Madame Silliman. When she died in 1783, she left more silver with the Hinsdale arms to the church at Deerfield and to her niece Sarah Williams. She also manumitted her slaves, honoring gendered notions of property by giving her male servant, Jockton, one hundred acres of New Hampshire land and her female servant, Chloe, "a Bible, a cow, a feather bed, a brass kettle, a pot, 2 tramels, chests, hand irons, chairs and pewter things." In addition, she gave clothing, jewelry, and other valuables to seven female relatives including nieces Abigail Norton and Abigail Woodword and stepgranddaughters Frances Silliman and Abigail Williams Hall.[32] Such bequests assert an expansive, almost fluid, notion of family that undercuts simple notions of patrilineal *or* matrilineal descent. It also suggests how a woman, particularly a much-married woman, might accumulate multiple lineages. Identity for such a person derived less from membership in a group than in the ability to move between and among groups.

In a legal system that required the subordination of women, one might imagine a female identity that was inherently fragile and derivative, shaped through attachment to others rather than assertion of self. Yet, ironically, the force of patriarchy might have encouraged certain women to develop a more complex and in some ways autonomous sense of self than their brothers or sons. Never able to step into a ready-made identity, they learned to mediate between a family of origin and one or more families of marriage. Surely, for men as well as women, "family" meant brothers and sisters, aunts, uncles, and cousins as well as husbands, wives, parents and children, but for women lived relationships almost always cut across patrilineal markers. In Annette Weiner's

32. Registration Records, Historic Deerfield. In 1777, Madame Silliman occupied pew number one, next to the pulpit, in Deerfield Church. See Sheldon, *Deerfield,* I, 479, II, 744, 904, "Genealogies," II, 204–205, 378, 380, 382.

words, "To draw on other social identities, to enhance one's history, and to secure the appropriate transmission of inalienable possessions for the next generation involve voluminous exchanges, elaborate strategies, and productive efforts." The bequests of Mary Cook and Abigail Hinsdale point to one of the central themes in Weiner's work—exchanges between brothers and sisters and their offspring, "the kinship counterpart of keeping-while-giving."[33]

Such exchanges did not require marked objects, of course, only a continuing effort to cultivate and maintain associations across generations. Still, the marking of objects, like the naming of children, tightened connections. Since brothers and sisters commonly named children for each other, relationships between a woman and her namesakes might take on heightened significance. At her death in 1720, Joanna Dyer of Exeter, New Hampshire, divided her pewter among her sisters' daughters, Joanna Perryman, Joanna Leavitt, and Joanna Thing, though her ring marked "JG" went to a brother's daughter who like herself had been born Joanna Gilman.[34] A sister might honor a sibling with a given name, but only exchanges between a sister and her brother's daughter fully returned the gift to the giver.

With that insight, we return once again to Hannah Barnard, moving back a generation to consider the life of her paternal aunt and namesake, Hannah Barnard Westcarr Beaman, a childless and twice-married woman who left a fragmentary but colorful history. Born in Hartford, Connecticut, about 1646, she was already the wife of John Westcarr (or Wescar) when she was charged at the county court in Springfield, Massachusetts, in March 1673 for wearing silk "contrary to law." She was presented again in 1675 and in January 1677 was admonished "for wearing silk in a flaunting garb, to the great offence of several sober persons in Hadley." Hannah was not alone in her rebellion. In 1673, her brother Joseph Barnard and his wife Sarah were presented as well as Sarah's two unmarried sisters, daughters of Elder John Strong of Northhampton. In 1675, "38 wives and maids and 30 young men" were charged, "some for wearing silk and that in a flaunting manner, and others for long hair and other extravagancies." At a 1677 court, Abigail, the wife of Mark Warner, and Hannah Lyman, the sixteen-year-old daughter of Richard Lyman of Northampton, were among the defendants. Hannah Lyman was fined ten shillings for "wearing silk in a flaunting manner in an offensive way and garb, not only before, but when she stood presented, not only in ordinary but in extraordinary times."[35]

If the names Warner, Strong, and Lyman sound familiar, they are. Like

33. Weiner, *Inalienable Possessions*, 67.
34. Albert S. Batchellor, ed., *Probate Records of the Province of New Hampshire*, II (Concord, N.H., 1907), 128–130.
35. Judd, *Hadley*, 91–92.

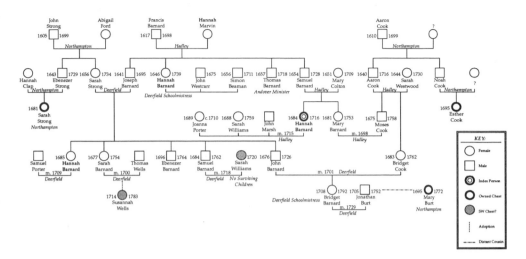

FIGURE 12. Hannah Barnard Relatives. *Melinda Chiou, Colophon Type and Design*

Hannah Barnard Westcarr, several of these silk-wearing offenders of late-seventeenth-century Hampshire County were paternal aunts of young women who many years later put their full names, in an assertive if not a flaunting manner, on chests and cupboards (Figure 12). The fathers of the silk wearers were not the river gods of the upper Connecticut, the Stoddards, Williamses, Dwights, Ashleys, Porters, Partridges, and Pynchons who dominated religion and politics in Hampshire County for generations, but a group of ambitious families a step down on the social scale. Their children's insistence on the right to wear clothing reserved only for elites suggests as much. Hannah's father, Francis Barnard, was one of the "perpetual pioneers" of early New England. Born in England, he was first in Hartford, then Hadley, then by the 1670s in Deerfield. In a frontier environment, his children moved from rebellion to respectability. The oldest son, Thomas, graduated from Harvard College in 1679 and was ordained pastor of the First Church of Andover, Massachusetts, in 1682. The middle son, Joseph, was convicted in 1681 of selling liquor to Indians but by 1687 was clerk of the Deerfield town meeting, serving until he died from wounds received in an ambush of "Enymy Indians" in August 1695. Joseph's widow soon married Captain Jonathan Wells, a man who had also overcome his youthful transgressions to become a military and political leader.[36]

Hannah Westcarr Beaman's own trajectory was similar. A year after her

36. Zea, "Oligarchy," *Old-Time New England*, 23–24; Melvoin, *New England Outpost*, 85, 138, 145, 150, 163, 167, 171, 184, 199; Sheldon, "Genealogies," *Deerfield*, II, 65. When Francis Barnard died in 1698, he left his son "Mr Thomas Barnard Minister of the Gospel in

presentation in court for outraging "several sober persons" with her flaunting apparel, Hannah Westcarr had acquired at least one serious book. By 1694, she had become Deerfield's schoolmistress, though we know of her work only because she hustled the town's children to the fort during an attack. The book, Richard Baxter's *Reformed Pastor,* bears her name, the inscription somewhat obscured by the effort of a later hand to copy it (Figure 13):

Hanah Wescar

Ejus Liber

1678

[Hannah Wescar, Her Book.][37]

The use of Latin in the inscription led Deerfield's nineteenth-century historian, George Sheldon, to conclude that the gentle school dame could never have written it herself.[38] Yet there is no reason why an educated woman of her generation could not have used a common Latin phrase like "Eius Liber." Minus the flourishes, the inscription is quite compatible with her later signature. Regardless of who wrote it, the flourishes in the handwriting are characteristic of the time and strikingly similar to the curling tendrils on many Hadley chests (Figure 14). A flowing inscription in a book—or on a chest—set a person apart. Even the letters on Hannah Barnard's cupboard, which appear at a distance to be straight Roman letters, have tiny curls at the tips.

Hannah Westcarr was a widow in 1678. Because she had no children and her husband no competing male heirs, she had inherited everything. At the estate settlement, witnesses, including her own sister Sarah, testified that "Mr John Wascarr sayd upon his Death Bed that he would Leave all his Estate to his Wife and that it was not his minde to take away One Penny of it from her." An inventory taken by Hannah's father, Francis Barnard, documents Westcarr's work as a frontier trader, listing "mooseskin" as well as fifty-nine pounds-worth of "English goods," the latter still at Hartford. Other goods in the

---

Andover the full and just sum of fiftie pounds money . . . which I give him to be improved towards the bringing up one of his Sons to Learneing"; see Francis Barnard, Will, Hampshire County Probate Records, III, 46.

37. I am grateful to Deerfield librarian, George Proper, for finding and photocopying this inscription. George Sheldon, "The Hannah Beaman Book and the Regicides," *History and Proceedings of the Pocumtuck Valley Memorial Association, 1912–1920* (Deerfield, Mass., 1921), 25–33, argues that Wescar got the book from English Civil War general Edward Whalley, who got it from Baxter himself.

38. Ibid., 30. Sheldon was unable to connect the signature with that of any other educated contemporary but thought it looked a bit like three autographs of General William Goffe, the second of his "Regicides." It came to Sheldon's museum from a descendant of Samuel Williams, an associate and teacher of the third Thomas Barnard.

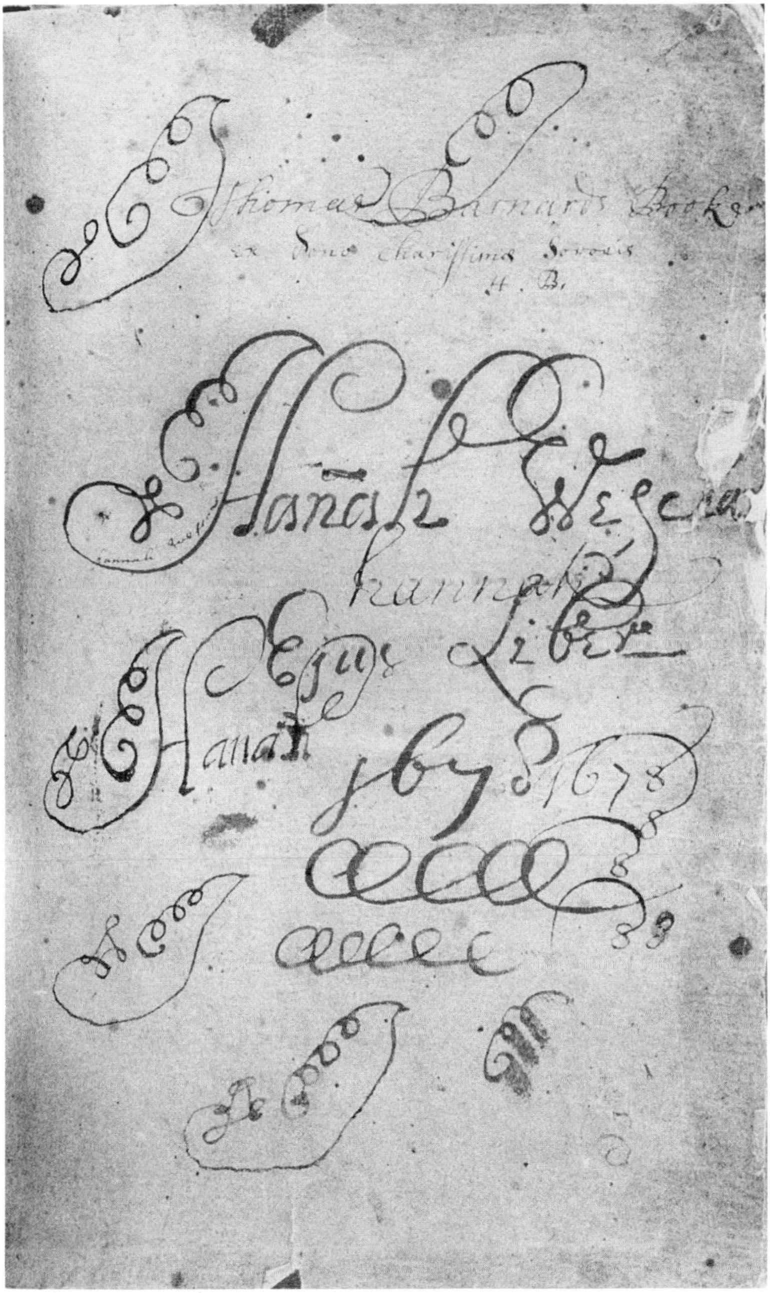

FIGURE 13. Handwritten Inscription, Hanah Wescar Ejus Liber. *In Richard Baxter,* Gildas Salvianus: The Reformed Pastor . . . *(London, 1656). Pocumtuck Valley Memorial Association, Deerfield, Mass. Photo by Amanda Merullo*

FIGURE 14. "RA" Chest with Drawers (detail). *Hadley or Hatfield, Mass., c. 1700. Pocumtuck Valley Memorial Association, Memorial Hall Museum, Deerfield, Mass. Gift of Chester Graves Crafts, 1887*

inventory, a chest of drawers, cupboard, carpets, and cushions might have been part of Hannah's portion.[39] The Baxter book might have been among the unnamed volumes valued in the inventory at more than seven pounds. Whether Hannah inherited it from her first husband or acquired it later, she eventually gave it to her brother, Thomas Barnard, pastor of the church at Andover, Massachusetts. On the title page of the book is *Thomas's* name and a tiny inscription in Latin, "Ex dono charissima Sorosis, H.B." (a gift from my dear sister, H.B.). The "H.B." stands for "Hannah Beaman." Hannah had married for the second time in 1680. She and her second husband, Simon Beaman, were among the Deerfield captives taken to Canada in 1704. There is no other record of her life in Deerfield until 1718, when widowed again she is listed among household heads. When she died in 1739, she left ten shillings to each of her brothers' children and the rest of her estate to the town of Deerfield for the support of schools.[40]

39. Hampshire County Court Records, Book I, 177, and on Westcarr's dealings with Indians, I, 89, 99, 121, 133.

40. Hampshire County Probate Records, V, 66, VI, 22, 58, 59, 77; Sheldon, *Deerfield*, I,

Perhaps Hannah Beaman bequeathed her brothers' daughters and grand-daughters more than shillings. It is not farfetched to think that she was her niece's first teacher. The invisible work of some schoolmistress surely lies behind the bold assertion of literacy on Hannah's cupboard and on other Hampshire County chests. Perhaps some of the owners of these chests were themselves schoolmistresses. Hannah Barnard was almost thirty when she wed John Marsh. Could she, like her aunt, have been a teacher? There is no way to know, since proprietors of "dame schools" were paid by parents, leaving no record in town accounts. In 1728, however, Deerfield did pay a female teacher. Significantly, she was Bridget Barnard, Hannah Beaman's grandniece.[41] A comparison between Hannah Barnard's cupboard and an illustration from a Renaissance writing manual broadens the point (Figure 15). On the cupboard as in the engraving, a row of half-circles underlays the central panel. In the engraving, a woman, a writing master, and a neatly printed text stand at the center of a windowlike opening, flowering stalks at the side. On the cupboard, the symbolic woman, through the letters of her name, frames the flower. Although the cupboard and the engraving have no direct connection, both partake of design conventions common in the early modern era. Hannah's cupboard may be less a valentine in furniture than a protosampler, a deft combination of letters and flowers marking femininity, gentility, and literacy.

Early American historians have had a great deal to say about "consumer revolutions," but the social implications of the expansion of material goods have remained elusive. Material culture studies, like much scholarship in the decorative arts, have concentrated on defining differences among regions and on tracing the spread of "amenities" from one status group to another. Even so powerful a work as Richard Bushman's *Refinement of America* is fundamentally a "diffusion" study. Somewhere between the broad contours of "refinement" and the microscopic examination of paint pigments, there must be room for a social history of objects that focuses on the small politics of everyday life. As Amanda Vickery has written, "Social emulation and conspicuous consumption are useful concepts . . . but as portmanteau descriptions of eighteenth-century consumer beheaviour and material culture they are dangerously misleading." Material goods not only served as markers of status but as "crucial props in unobserved, intimate rituals." A woman might use them

---

244, 272, 303, 308, 624, II, 840; Richard E. Birks, "Hannah Beaman, Deerfield's First School Mistress: Her Times and Her Experiences," in *History and Proceedings*, 496–513.

41. Judd, *Hadley*, 56–58, 418; Sheldon, *Deerfield*, II, 840. The town also enjoined farmers "to procure School Dames to teach their children."

FIGURE 15. Giovanni Bapttista Verini, *Alla Illustra . . .* , title page. *John M. Wing Foundation, Newberry Library, Chicago, Ill.*

not only to assert status and define relationships but "to create a world of meanings and ultimately to transmit her history."[42]

Although few families in rural Massachusetts owned press cupboards, silver, fine textiles, or embroideries, many owned chests, sheets, blankets, and cheap imported ceramics. As Gloria Main has demonstrated, the stock of movables in the Connecticut Valley, as elsewhere in New England, was growing in the second quarter of the eighteenth century. Thus, the opportunity for people to attach names, genealogies, and stories to material objects, to create inalienable possessions, was expanding. At the same time, more and more women were learning to write their own names not only on documents but on personal possessions—bed rugs, sheets, towels, weaving drafts, books, letters, and diaries.[43]

The meanings of those names were highly variable, never fixed. Some women claimed ownership: "Martha Ballard, Her Diary." "Polly Lewis, Her Verses." "Mary Comstock, Her Rugg." Others made claims on posterity:

> When I am dead and in my grave,
> And all my bones are rotten.
> When this you see remember me,
> That I won't be forgotten.

Similar verses appear in the meditations of the seventeenth-century poet, Anne Bradstreet, in the autobiography of an eighteenth-century Connecticut farm woman, Hannah Heaton, on schoolgirl embroidery from the seventeenth through the eighteenth century, on nineteenth-century patchwork quilts, and even in graffiti on Virginia furniture.[44]

42. Amanda Vickery, "Women and the World of Goods: A Lancashire Consumer and Her Possessions, 1751–81," in John Brewer and Roy Porter, eds., *Consumption and the World of Goods* (London, 1993), 294.

43. See Gloria L. Main, "The Distribution of Consumer Goods in Colonial New England: A Subregional Approach," in Benes and Benes, eds., *Early American Probate Inventories,* 153–168. In an effort to measure the distribution of consumer goods in early America, Main has created an "Index of Amenities" that includes some of the things we have been discussing here, particularly linens, earthenware, and silver. "In the Valley," she writes, "the only subregion for which we have a useful sample in the period 1725–1729, the index rose to an extraordinarily high level for householders in the lower and middling class." Although the distribution of amenities varied over time and by region, nearly everyone was accumulating a broader range of consumer goods over the course of the century. See also Gloria L. Main, "An Inquiry into When and Why Women Learned to Write in Colonial New England," *Journal of Social History,* XXIV (1990–1991), 579–589; William J. Gilmore, *Reading Becomes a Necessity of Life: Material and Cultural Life in Rural New England, 1780–1835* (Knoxville, Tenn., 1989).

44. Betty Ring, *American Needlework Treasures . . .* (New York, 1987), for example, fig. 5, Margret Palfrey Sampler, 32, fig. 51, Cordelia Bennet Sampler, 4, and computations based on

Cary Carson has argued that the growth of marked objects in England and America in the seventeenth century was part of a social revolution that predated and helped to stimulate the so-called commercial revolution of the eighteenth century. He contrasts the inscribed drinking vessels of rural England, the "pot laureates" of a forgotten world, with the labeled chests, textiles, silver, and ceramics that became increasingly common in the eighteenth century. In an earlier world, a pot might speak for itself, advising all who saw it to take their "mery fill." In the more individualized world of an emerging middle class, "inscriptions on ordinary utilitarian objects bespeak not comradeship, but ownership." As we have seen, however, ownership took different forms for men and women. Marked objects appear everywhere in early America, but the forms they take vary widely. Among German-speaking settlers, for example, cupboards frequently bear the names of married couples rather than individuals. Does that suggest differences in the meaning of property or simply contrasting methods of outfitting young women for marriage? There are also significant differences in the same region over time. In Hampshire County (as elsewhere), heavy joined chests bearing women's initials or names gave way in the early eighteenth century to sleek cabinetry with no marks at all. Did refinement mean greater anonymity for women as well as greater freedom to purchase and display movable goods? Finally, the relationship between the construction and the ownership of objects bears more study. What did it mean when women became producers as well as purchasers of household goods? Did other women share the exuberant materialism of the Vermont woman who in the early nineteenth century wove into the center of her decorative all-white coverlet: "The Property of Susan Bailey"?[45]

Hannah Barnard's cupboard forces us to consider the so-called marriage chest, not as a romantic relic of a bygone day, but as one element in a complex gender system. About the time the first Hadley chests were being carved, the Hamp-

Ethel Stanwood Bolton and Eva Johnston Coe, *American Samplers* (Boston, 1921). Heaton wrote, "i leaue you her a little book for you to look upon / that you may see your mothers face when she is dead and gone" (Barbara E. Lacey, "The World of Hannah Heaton: The Autobiography of an Eighteenth-Century Connecticut Farm Woman," *William and Mary Quarterly*, 3d Ser., XLV [1988], 280–304 [quotation on 282]). Jonathan Prown pointed out to me a white pine and poplar desk, Norfolk, Virginia, ca. 1790–1820, Colonial Williamsburg, G1988-427, with a succession of female names inside the lid and the penciled phrase, "If you see remember me."

45. Cary Carson, "The Consumer Revolution in Colonial British America; Why Demand?" in Cary Carson, Ronald Hoffman, and Peter J. Albert., eds., *Of Consuming Interests: The Style of Life in the Eighteenth Century* (Charlottesville, Va., 1994), 533–541, 555; Tufted Counterpane, 1985–0639.01, National Museum of American History, Washington, D.C.

shire County minister Edward Taylor wrote a poem entitled "Upon Wedlock and Death of Children." Taylor's poem, like Hannah's cupboard, uses flower imagery to celebrate marriage and the establishment of a new household. The poem puns on the word "knot," which in seventeenth-century usage could connote a decorative flower bed, a bud on a plant, a calligraphic flourish, sexual intercourse, marriage, a believer's relationship with God:

> A Curious Knot God made in Paradise,
>   And drew it out inamled neatly Fresh.
> It was the True-Love Knot, more sweet than spice,
>   And set with all the flowres of Graces dress.
>
> . . . .
>
> When in this Knot I planted was, my Stock
>   Soon knotted, and a manly flower out brake.
> And after it my branch again did knot:
>   Brought out another Flowre; its sweet breath'd mate.

In the poem, Taylor's sweet flowers are both children and the words used to remember them. When his children die, he writes, "I piecemeale pass to Glory bright in them."[46] His description of reproduction is lush, yet curiously asexual, almost parthenogenetic. There is no female presence, unless it is the earth itself. Taylor's poem may unconsciously reflect the ancient notion of the womb as a passive receptacle for male seed.

A cupboard, too, is a container. Yet framed with a woman's name, Hannah Barnard's cupboard lays claim both to the garden and the branching flower. Whether or not she willed it, her name asserts her identity as an educated person, an heir to the material wealth of an ambitious family, and the future mistress of a household. The hearts, vines, pinwheels, thistles, and roses that embellish it are both traditional and imitative, relics of English tradition and emblems of a new possessive individualism as it developed among aspiring gentry in the Connecticut River Valley. Hannah's cupboard tells us that, in a world where most forms of wealth were controlled by male heads of household, certain objects were in some sense owned by women. Ownership of precious household goods offered the power not only to shape a material environment but to build lineages and alliances over time. Yet Hannah's cupboard is also a sign of the fragility of life and the transience of female identity in a world circumscribed by the cycles of marriage, childbearing, and death. When Hannah Marsh gave birth to a daughter, then died, her cupboard became both a monument and a knotted puzzle for future generations.

46. Edward Taylor, "Upon Wedlock and Death of Children," in Thomas H. Johnson, ed., *The Poetical Works of Edward Taylor* (New York, 1939), 117, 118.

COLONIAL SELF-FASHIONING: PARADOXES AND PATHOLOGIES IN THE CONSTRUCTION OF GENTEEL IDENTITY IN EIGHTEENTH-CENTURY AMERICA

Kenneth A. Lockridge

But whatever the level at which one operates, and however intricately, the guiding principle is the same: societies, like lives, contain their own interpretations. One has only to learn how to gain access to them.—Clifford Geertz, The Interpretation of Cultures

A good portion of our intellectual effort now consists in casting suspicion on any statement by trying to uncover the disposition of its different levels. That disposition is infinite, and the abyss that we try to open up in every word, this madness of language, we call scientifically: "enunciation." It's this enunciatory abyss that has to be opened up first, and for tactical reasons: in order to break down the self-infatuation in our statements and to destroy the arrogance of our sciences.—Roland Barthes, Roland Barthes par lui-même

What did it mean to Jefferson, slave owner and philosophe, *that he grew up in this far western borderland world of Britain, looking out from Queen Anne rooms of spare elegance onto a wild, uncultivated land? We can only grope to understand.—Bernard Bailyn,* The Peopling of British North America

I believe as all good Catholicks ought to do, in Spirits, Demons and Hobgoblins, that like the Prisoners in New-Gate, they are let out of their Hole anights, and suffer'd to play their Pranks at large in the World. That they appear for the most part to Women and children, their Faith and Imagination being exceeding Strong. I believe that these Spectres with their Horns and cloven feet, and with the Hurly-burly they make in the Dead of night, unluckily scare both the maid and her mistress into a Diabetis. Hence it comes to pass that so many Females in all countrys can scarce hold their precious water, haveing been terrify'd in the Nursery with Bul-beggars and Apparitions. This is the case of the unfortunate Dripabunda, who when She

I would like to thank the National Endowment for the Humanities for the Summer Stipend and support for 1994 and Ronald Hoffman, Director of the Institute of Early American History and Culture. I would like to thank as well my remarkable colleagues at the University of Montana Julia Watson, Chris Anderson, Michel Valentin, Stewart Justman, and

fancy'd She saw the Ghost of her deceast Husband, dy'd away for fear the good man was come to life again. From that fatal moment she lost her Retentive faculty, beyond the Relief of Turpentine Pills and Bristol-water, nor can even Dr. Friend, or Apollo himself intirely stop the Leak, but stil whenever she laughs beyond a Simper or a Broad Smile, the liveing Salalmoniac flows from her. I believe most commonly Spirits delight to haunt old rambleing Houses in the Country, because all sorts of Devils have a passion for Solitude and irregularity. nor do they ever fail to walk in ancient Abbys and Nunnerys, because of the Impurity that was formerly committed therein. In short I believe that all Ghosts hurry back to their dark abode a little before day, because they cant stand the Purity of morning air, Besides every body knows they detest the crowing of a Cock worse than the prayers of a Doctor of Divinity, because it brought St. Peter to the bitter Tears of Repentance.

With these words, in or around the year 1725, William Byrd II began his parody of credulous womanhood known as "The Female Creed." The essay continues in the fictional voice of the archetypal woman through nineteen more such passages, reeking with the author's contempt for female credulity and corporeality, yet using a woman's purported voice as a platform for jabs at the male British establishment and ending with the words, "O Woman, Great is thy Faith."[1] The initial passage cited above and the essay it opens raise the central question of my essay: How can I explain to you what I feel is going on here?

As you know, we are long past the days when we could regard such essays only as the amusing literary efforts of moderately sensual colonial gentlemen.[2]

Linda Frey; also Susan Juster, Julie Ellison and the members of their seminar at the University of Michigan; Carroll Smith-Rosenberg for her painstaking critique and assistance; Alfred F. Young, Laura Edwards, Linda Lee Sturtz, Mary Kelley, Charlotte Sussman, Katherine Eggert, Linda Gregerson, James Winn, Daphne O'Brien, Richard Bushman, Jill Lepore, Kevin Hardwick, and Terri Snyder; Linda R. Baumgartner and the other members of the Collections staff at Colonial Williamsburg; Michael Plunkett, Curator of Manuscripts at the Alderman Library, University of Virginia; Mary Robertson, Karen Kearns, and Peter Blodgett, at the Huntington Library, San Marino, California; and John Stagg and Jean Cross at the Papers of James Madison, Alderman Library, University of Virginia. Special thanks to Marianne Farr, former Head of Interlibrary Loan at the University of Montana, and her assistant Matthew Dreissen.

1. William Byrd, "The Female Creed," in Maude H. Woodfin, ed., *Another Secret Diary of William Byrd of Westover, 1739–1741*, trans. Marion Tinling (Richmond, Va., 1942), 445–475. Hereafter page references to "The Female Creed" will be given in parentheses in the text.

2. One scholar still of the old school is Richard Dunn, who in his review of Kenneth A. Lockridge, *The Diary, and Life, of William Byrd II of Virginia, 1674–1744* (Chapel Hill, N.C.,

They possibly were this, and these gentlemen certainly wanted to convince both themselves and us that such writings were merely exercises in an easy and automatic gentility, sallies in an inevitable and balanced war of the sexes. But our investment in their gentility, and through it in our own, is considerably less than it was thirty years ago. So we are able to see that what is going on in "The Female Creed" and in sallies of its ilk in public and private is also the complex process known as the construction of gentility. Or rather, what we see is the construction, reconstruction, and maintenance of gentility under the sometimes inhospitable conditions of the colonial enterprise.

I think I can easily take you this far with me in explaining why "The Female Creed" is more than it seems to be. But what I need to explain further, and to ask your help in explaining, is my conviction that in William Byrd's case and perhaps in others genteel self-construction in Britain's North American colonies was an unusually harried, intense, brittle, visible, vulnerable, and dysfunctional process. In a sense that is difficult to explain, and I know I shall retreat from this word, it was almost pathological.

The path I am going to take in trying to explain this troubled reflection begins with an initial excursion into the theory of genteel self-construction as developed from the work of Norbert Elias. Thereafter it consists largely of applying Elias to a deeper look at gender and misogyny in William Byrd's "Female Creed"—a text I have already treated briefly in *On the Sources of Patriarchal Rage*—and then to the poetics of misogyny in Thomas Jefferson's relative, the poet and Revolutionary Robert Bolling. The misogyny seen in these two cases will be the primary opening, or door, to this study of colonial self-creation. I would like then to ask to what degree we can generalize from such cases to the behavior of other would-be colonial gentlemen and to end with some reflections on this kind of history in general.

What is at stake here is not the psychodynamics of a few individuals; it is the operation of an entire culture, the genteel culture of eighteenth-century Virginia and perhaps of the colonies at large. Like *Patriarchal Rage,* though hopefully with more subtlety, this is a study in the ways in which the stresses of genteel self-creation in the colonial context seized vulnerable individuals, in this case William Byrd and Robert Bolling, turning them into raging misogynists on private occasions and publicly into the great mythmakers of their New World gentry class. These men were at once unusual and typical: unusually vulnerable, they nonetheless reflected strains felt in varying degrees by many of their peers. Unusually intense in their expressed misogyny and in their incessant mythmaking, they were nonetheless recognized by many, then and now,

---

1987), in the *William and Mary Quarterly,* 3d Ser., XLV (1988), 779–782, labels Byrd simply "a self-confident and self-indulgent Anglo-American gentleman" (782).

as leaders, precisely because the strains they so intensely epitomized were the strains of their gender, class, and time.

II

It is a commonplace of postmodern or at least of post-structuralist thought that if a self exists at all it is discursively formed. The self is an ambivalent, multivalent, constantly reenacted social construction. George Herbert Mead developed the core of this idea several generations ago, though we feel more comfortable associating this sense of the dialogic self with Mikhail Bakhtin.[3] Just now, however, in giving the theoretical background that will permit me to provide a context for Byrd's "Female Creed" and to reflect on the processes of self-construction entailed in it, it is not this generalized truism of the dialogic self that I wish to invoke.

Rather, the theoretician of self-construction I reach back to is Norbert Elias. This European scholar was active from the 1930s to the 1970s, but some of his work became available in English as late as 1982 or 1983; so, although once much neglected, he is now at least cited by such scholars as Stephen Greenblatt and Richard L. Bushman. Elias is the great chronicler of what he calls "the civilizing process." He is a student of a historically conditioned moment in Western culture, that moment in the fifteenth through eighteenth centuries when "civility" and "civilization" rose to the head of the cultural agenda for the powerful and reflective classes of Europe. He is also, quintessentially, the student of that historically conditioned self that arose out of the civilizing process. That self becomes the self entailed in what we now call genteel self-construction. His work is filled with the most stunning examples of actual human behavior illustrating his points. I take Elias seriously because he helps me explain the intensities of what I find in "The Female Creed," in William Byrd's life in general, in Robert Bolling—to whom we shall come later—and in Thomas Jefferson. Elias helps me explain that the long project of the construction of gentility and of the genteel self could be a destructive enterprise, especially in particular settings.

3. See George Herbert Mead, *On Social Psychology: Selected Papers,* ed. Anselm Strauss (Chicago, 1964). Mead's concept of the socially constructed self was extended by Peter L. Berger and Thomas Luckmann in *The Social Construction of Reality: A Treatise in the Sociology of Knowledge* (Garden City, N.Y., 1966). And see Mikhail Bakhtin, *The Dialogic Imagination: Four Essays,* ed. Michael Holquist, trans. Caryl Emerson and Michael Holquist (Austin, Tex., 1981). Subsequent to these sources, of course, postmodernist thought has rendered it customary to regard the self as multivalent, porous, conflicted, and shifting— implications that follow from the idea of a socially constructed self.

Elias's view of the civilizing process is presented in three books: *The History of Manners; Power and Civility;* and *The Court Society.*[4] Elias notes that, while there has been a gradual increase in emphasis on what might loosely be called manners from the early Middle Ages to the present day, there was also a special focusing of this process in the sixteenth through eighteenth centuries. What was new in this period was the rise of the centralized monarchial state. With its monopoly of force, it was able to render a decentralized warrior aristocracy either outmoded or subservient to its purposes. The state's near-monopoly of revenue drew would-be elites, whether from the older aristocracy or from other social groups, into its capital, its court, and ultimately into its service. In France, this magnetic process went to extremes of centralization in the royal court itself. It reached toward this extreme in seventeenth-century England, then retreated somewhat from it, and was in general characteristically European. In the crucible of the swelling courts, administrations, and capital cities of the new European monarchies, says Elias, a new model of elite behavior and indeed of the ideal human personality emerged, characterized by a deepening emphasis on "civility."

These things occurred as part of what Elias calls a "social formation," a phenomenon rather like Michel Foucault's "episteme." The modern state and the civilizing process arose together in an untraceable tangle of cause and effect, creating a paradigm shift without simple linear causation. But some lines of development can be traced. Circumstances alone pushed matters in the direction of "civility." In the competition between would-be courtiers for attention and for official positions, violence no longer carried credibility. The nobility's armed followers were suppressed, as these implied regional revolts that could be the death of the new state. Military matters were left to officials of the state. Eventually even dueling was discouraged. In the place of such harsh displays, an ever more refined courtly behavior acquired value in the struggle to be noticed. This courtly manner initially came to define "civility." Soon steady, predictable behavior and literate learning, both of which had obvious advantages for the state, also got wrapped into the new concept of "civility."

Beyond circumstance, however, lay craft and intention. In Elias's view, it was above all a small coterie of humanists, courtly and otherwise, who took on the task of developing and explaining to would-be elites the full ramifications of the civilized behavior that would lead to advancement in the new monarchical state. Their goal was to create a new aristocracy and so to increase their own power. Foremost among these was Erasmus of Rotterdam, whose books on

4. Norbert Elias, *The History of Manners,* trans. Edmund Jephcott (New York, 1982); Elias, *Power and Civility,* trans. Jephcott (New York, 1982); Elias, *The Court Society,* trans. Jephcott (New York, 1983).

manners, behavior, and education became the school texts for many succeeding generations of European gentlemen, among them William Byrd II. Byrd in
fact kept an Erasmian commonplace book, a genre originally intended as a
school exercise book for practicing civilized learning, throughout his life.

In one sense, the humanists' "civility," the deepest features of which I am
about to sketch, was intended as a pattern for young men of the elite classes. It
provided them with a personality and a perceptual and literal language of
learning and of politeness that would make them acceptable in the court cities
of their nations and throughout "civilized" Europe. In a further sense, as Elias
notes, civil behavior and the civil personality became in turn a model for
human behavior and personality at large. In subsequent years, one of the
projects of the modern state would be to reduce its peasant populations to
civilized as well as to pious and obedient behavior. This did not work very well
before the nineteenth century, largely because these populations were also
treasured as reservoirs of uncivilized persons who defined by contrast the
civility of the elite. The state both did and did not want all its people civilized.

At its heart, as a model personality, what was "civility"? As Elias looks at the
advice literature and at human behavior from the twelfth century on, what is
new about the intense civilizing the humanists are recommending is an ever
increasing *aversion* to the bodily self and to strong emotions, coupled with a
powerful *internalization* of restraint on the body and on feelings. External
controls—"Don't wipe your nose on your sleeve, don't spit on the floor, others
will ridicule you or the prince may fine you"—became internal controls "One
does not spit." Internal controls relate not so much to what one does as to who
one is. One is not one's own snot or spit, one's own arousal or anger. This
pervasive alienation of the self from the bodily, the sexual, and the emotional is
perhaps the central event in Elias's history. From it stem the neurotic behaviors
one might expect to follow. Elias is here grounding both Sigmund Freud's
Civilization and Its Discontents and the modern neurotic personality in the
history of the sixteenth through nineteenth centuries.[5]

Many other personality traits follow from this self-alienated, self-as-control
personality that underlay the civility cultivated in the Renaissance. Competition was one ground on which this personality was built, and service to the
state was the other; so intense sociability was a given. The ability subtly to be
aware of the feelings of others was necessary in order not to give offense and in
order to sense enemies and find allies. Intellectualization was prized as well.
Brilliance rose above the bodily, deflected or disguised one's own feelings, and
demonstrated ability to serve the state. Curiously, for a long time intellectual-

5. Sigmund Freud, *Civilization and Its Discontents*, trans. Joan Riviere (London, 1930).

ization took the form of the sometimes seemingly mindless collection of isolated topoi, or commonplaces, of classical and modern authors, an enterprise that if anything betrayed true intellectualization and undermined the personal integration the humanists supposedly strove for. Control and steadiness were, however, always paramount to the truly integrated self, and such collections certainly expressed control.

At the time, this civilized personality was always seen as the artful product of a lifelong effort at self-construction. As a result of such ceaseless self-constructions, two orders of humanity were created, the higher nominally justified by its services to the common welfare and the lower present largely as a foil for the higher. As Bernard Mandeville put it:

> To introduce, moreover, an Emulation amongst Men, they [the humanists] divided the Species into two Classes, vastly differing from one another: The one consisted of abject, low-minded People, that always hunting after immediate Enjoyment, were wholly incapable of self-denial, and without regard to the good of others, had no higher aim than their private Advantage; such as being enslaved by Voluptuousness, yielded without Reisistance to every gross desire, and made no use of their Rational Faculties, but to heighten their Sensual Pleasure. These vile grov'ling Wretches, they said, were the Dross of their Kind, and having only the Shape of Men, differ'd from Brutes in nothing but their outward Figure. But the other Class was made up of lofty high-spirited Creatures, that free from sordid Selfishness, esteem'd the Improvements of the Mind to be their fairest Possessions; . . . and making a continual War with themselves to promote the Peace of others, aim'd at no less than the Publick Welfare and the Conquest of their own Passion.[6]

Long before the eighteenth century dawned, in the reordering of human life entailed in the advent of the modern state, to be civilized or genteel was to be saved—to rise into the sunshine of elite sociability, influence, and state "service"—and to be uncivilized or common was to be damned—consigned to contempt and to earning a living as best one could by common means. Money alone would not determine gentility. As everyone knew, as often as not it was the ability to craft a semblance of gentility that validated money and that led to the further ability, through access to influence and to legal and state power, to

6. Bernard Mandeville, *The Fable of the Bees, or Private Vices, Publick Benefits,* 2 vols., ed. F. B. Kaye (1723; reprint, Oxford, 1924) I, 43–44, as cited in Richard Halpern, *The Poetics of Primitive Accumulation: English Renaissance Culture and the Genealogy of Capital* (Ithaca, N.Y., 1991), 95–96. On the artifice of self-construction, see further references in note 8, below.

defend and increase that wealth. The social access that gentility permitted opened the door to a treasure trove of legislation, contracts, grants, bribes, and offices that constituted the most direct avenues to achieve or to enhance wealth. From the sixteenth to the eighteenth century, gentility and the state, not land, were the primary currencies of rapid success. These facts taken together guaranteed that what was at stake was not mere behavior but a thoroughly crafted personality. It became impossible to separate this personality's usefulness from its status as a desirable end in itself. John Locke himself aimed quite frankly at a genteel, crafted, and controlled personality, not at mere behavior. To pick one example of many, Dudley Ryder, an ordinary English judge and diarist, made it his whole project to follow Locke's advice in constructing a truly genteel personality. Locke would scarcely have written had there not been other Dudley Ryders listening.[7] Although some *colonial* efforts in this direction began with the externals of civil behavior, to one degree or another most also proceeded to some version of an internalized self-civilization.

Elias's examination of this social figuration called "civilization" and of the personality it epitomized (or epistomized) was raised to a further level of intensity in his third book, *The Court Society.* Here, in studying the superheated atmosphere at the court of Louis XIV, Elias achieves what could truly be called a study in sociopathology. In some respects, its conclusions are generalized beyond Versailles, indeed beyond the boundaries of any European court or capital. At Versailles, in the ultimate crucible of centralization and of courtly competition for the resources of the monarchical state, the wilder fauna of the civilized personality, at its most savage, flourished. In the palace of the Sun King, the assiduous self-construction intended by Erasmus and practiced throughout Europe truly became hysterical. "Hysteria" is not my word; Elias uses it and other, equally strong terms. By hysteria Elias seems to mean first of all the divorce of the civilized self from the bodily. Because the body is ultimately inescapable, loss of "civilized" control is inevitable, hence hysteria. But he seems also to mean by hysteria an obsessive pursuit of the signs of civility within a controlled personality that is, if only by reason of that pursuit, always and inevitably nearly out of control.

Describing the self-crafting of persons in the French court, he observes that in such a context luxuries became necessities. "In a society [as competitive as the court] in which every outward manifestation of a person has special significance, expenditure on prestige and display is for the upper classes a necessity

7. Dudley Ryder and his uses of Locke are treated extensively in Robert A. Fothergill, *Private Chronicles: A Study of English Diaries* (London, 1974).

which they cannot avoid. [These expenditures] are an indispensable instrument in maintaining their social position, especially when—as is actually the case in this court society—all members of the society are involved in a ceaseless struggle for status and prestige." He continues: "A duke must build his house in such a way as to tell the world: I am a duke and not a count. The same applies to every aspect of his public appearance. . . . Thus the most real way of asserting one's rank is by documenting it through an appropriate social appearance." The result is a compulsive, consuming, display-oriented, other-directed personality, perpetually jockeying for position.

> If one grows up in a society in which the possession of a title is rated higher than that of earned wealth, and in which membership of the royal court or even the privilege of access to the king's person . . . ranks exceptionally high on the scale of social values, it is difficult to escape the compulsion to base one's personal goals on these social values and norms and to join in the competition for such opportunities, as far as the social position of one's family and one's own abilities allow. The goals one deems worthy of pursuing laboriously over long periods are never determined solely by the increase in satisfaction and value that each step taken towards them gives a person in his own eyes; they are also affected by confirmation of one's value or an increase in respect in the eyes of others. . . . Many—if by no means all—of the opportunities to the possession of which people of court society dedicated all the efforts of their lives, have since lost their lustre and meaning. How could people become excited over trivialities, one may ask, or devote their whole lives to attaining such futile goals? . . . One does not need to share the values of court people to understand that they formed part of the compulsions of their social existence.[8]

8. The preceding quotations are both from Elias, *The Court Society*, 63–64, 75–76; and thanks are due Mary Kelley for key phrasings and perspectives on these paragraphs. The court became a world of almost unbelievable semiotic complexity; see Linda Gregerson, "Narcissus Interrupted: Specularity and the Subject of the Tudor State," *Criticism*, XXV (1993), 1–40. This article appears as a chapter in Gregerson's *The Reformation of the Subject: Spenser, Milton, and the English Protestant Epic* (Cambridge, 1995). The artificiality of self-fashioning became such a problem that the advice literature had, finally, to insist on at least a semblance of naturalness; see Anna Bryson, "The Rhetoric of Status: Gestures, Demeanor, and the Image of the Gentleman in Sixteenth- and Seventeenth-Century England," in Lucy Gent and Nigel Llewellyn, *Renaissance Bodies: The Human Figure in English Culture: 1540–1660* (London, 1990). See also Jay Fliegelman, *Declaring Independence: Jefferson, Natural Language, and the Culture of Performance* (Stanford, Calif., 1993), for an example of how this need to restore naturalness spread, apace with the problematic tendencies of courtly artifice, to a wider genteel population by the mid-18th century.

Elias tells the story of a nobleman who gave his son some money. He later asked his son what he had done with the money. "I still have it," said the boy. His father promptly threw it out the window. "Like this!" the father was saying. Not consumption but display, *necessary* display, was his point. In such a world, where items of consumption are really items of display, and in which one's standing is also measured by the most exact placings in the etiquette of public ceremonies, both consumption and ritual position acquire a fetishistic character.

> For the king to take off his nightshirt and put on his dayshirt was doubtless a necessary procedure; but in the social context it was at once invested with a different meaning. The king turned it into a privilege distinguishing those present from others. The Lord Chamberlain had the right to assist; it was precisely ordained that he should cede this right to a prince and to no one else; and it was exactly the same with the right to be present at the *entrées*. . . . Each act in the ceremony had an exactly graded prestige-value that was imparted to those present, and this prestige-value became to an extent self-evident. It became, like the size of the courtyard or the ornamentation of a noble's house, a *prestige-fetish*. It served as an indicator of the position of an individual within the balance of power between the courtiers, a balance controlled by the king and very precarious. The direct use-value of all these [items and] actions was more or less incidental. What gave them their gravity was solely the importance they conferred on those present within court society, the power, rank and dignity they expressed.

> Etiquette and ceremony [like consumption] increasingly became, as the above examples showed, a ghostly *perpetuum mobile* that continued to operate regardless of any direct use-value, being impelled, as by an inexhaustible motor, by the competition for status and power of the people enmeshed in it—a competition both between themselves and with the mass of those excluded—and by their need for a clearly graded scale of prestige. In the last analysis, this compelling struggle for ever-threatened power and prestige was the dominant factor that condemned all those involved to enact these burdensome ceremonies.[9]

It is this compulsive, fetishistic element in the court personality that I label hysterical.

In *The Court Society*, Elias also foreshadows later work by other scholars in linking the intensified self-construction identified here to the Enlightenment and to a species of romanticism. His thought here is Tocquevillian, reasoning

9. Elias, *The Court Society*, trans. Jephcott, 67, 85–87.

from observations of behavior to its genesis and logic, for Elias is the Tocqueville of the predemocratic elite personality. In his view, the controlled, calculating, rational, intellectualized side of the court personality found a natural expression in the Enlightenment. Naturally that same personality found the Enlightenment not inconsistent with judicious forms of opulence and display. This personality's romanticism, on the other hand, was the result of a need to escape the relentless competition of control-and-display. Creeping out long before its time in our textbooks, this early romanticism took the form of a hunger for escape to the bucolic, to grottos in the woods and rural retreats. Enlightenment and romanticism, which eventually in a bourgeois age were to become somewhat detached from each other, in fact went hand in hand in the eighteenth century as expressions of a central ambivalence of the courtly, civilized mind. Both, of course, soon became forms of display as well. Here Elias's discussion is so evocative of American gentries in general and of Thomas Jefferson in particular as to be startling.[10]

But leaping from Versailles to the master of Monticello is not so startling, for the court personality, which is simply an intensified extension of the civilized personality, was by no means confined to the courts of Europe. That is why, if Elias's *Court Society* is his final reflection on the civilizing process, it is a disturbing one: he is emphatic that the court society extended far beyond Versailles, or Whitehall, or Vienna. Elias observes specifically that the court society was a social figuration, a culture, that spread outward from any particular set of rooms, gardens, or city walls. Court was to country, he implies, as, in our own day, city is to country, the source not only of many of the administrative and financial resources around which human life was increasingly focused but also of the very orientation, standards, fashions, manners, rituals, and values that permeated the provincial gentry and bourgeois.[11] In my own view, country gentry, even if permanently sequestered and in opposition to court values, could not help but reflect the values and behaviors of court society. So central were its mentalities that opposition elites merely rang a few changes on its personality and fetishes. Thus, a Virginia gentleman, enjoying the bucolic pleasures of "going native" in the woods and juxtaposing this excursion to the claustrophobia of the English court became by this very act the aspiring imitator of one of the court's own values. To use English terminology, court and country were curiously the same.

Yet Elias seems to suggest further that provincial gentries, professionals, and

10. Ibid., 110–113, 214–217, 224, 250–264. For Jefferson's romantic streak, see Rhys Isaac, "The First Monticello," in Peter S. Onuf, ed., *Jeffersonian Legacies* (Charlottesville, Va., 1993), 77–108, esp. 84. Likewise, Elias beautifully explains Monticello on 41–65, esp. 51.

11. Elias, *The Court Society,* trans. Jephcott, 36; see also 64, 65, 76, 250–265.

certain bourgeois might have actually *intensified* the processes of genteel and courtly self-alienation, self-construction, and compulsive display in their eagerness to rise by attaining fluency in the forms prevailing in the center.[12] They mimicked more intensely in their eagerness, one might say, not to be provincial. This suggestion is vital for our consideration of colonial society. It is only a small extension of Elias to suggest of distant provincial demi-bourgeois that, in turning in corrosive soil and from too great a distance toward the great sun at the center of all society, they could become twisted. In the end, Elias himself virtually makes that extension.

Elias's final passages in *The Court Society* open with a moving appeal to consider the constraints and distortions entailed in high "civilization" in general.

> It is understandable that up to now research has often concerned itself only with the constraint to which less powerful groups are exposed. But in this way we gain only a one-sided picture. . . . The constraints to which lower strata are exposed cannot be understood without also investigating those affecting the upper strata. . . . Princes and aristocratic groups are apt to appear as people leading a free and unconstrained life. [Yet] . . . it emerges very clearly to what constraints upper classes, and not least their most powerful member, the absolute monarch, are subjected. They are subjected to them in good part in the form of constant self-discipline, precisely because the preservation of their high position, their distinction, their superiority over others, has become an end in itself dominating their whole existence.[13]

But for me his three-volume work culminates with a matched pair of brief passages from *Power and Civility* that reveal most pointedly the competitive stresses inherent in civilized self-construction. The second of these, which focuses on the peculiar nature of the attempt to *rise* socially in such a system, could serve as an appropriate introduction to this essay on the problems of colonial self-construction.

> Finally, this permanently smouldering social fear [of rising inferiors] also constitutes one of the most powerful driving forces of the social control that every member of this courtly upper class exerts over himself and other people in his circle. It is expressed in the intense vigilance with which members of courtly aristocratic society observe and polish everything that distinguishes them from people of lower rank: not only the external signs of status, but also their speech, their gestures, their social amusements and man-

12. Ibid., 64, 65, 76, 250–265. Elias's thought is very complex here.
13. Ibid., 266.

ners. The constant pressure from below and the fear it induces above are, in a word, one of the strongest driving forces—though not the only one—of that specifically civilized refinement which distinguishes the people of this upper class from others and finally becomes second nature to them. . . .

By contrast, the feelings and gestures of inferiority in people rising socially as individuals take on their particular coloration from the fact that these people identify to a certain extent with the upper class. . . . People in this situation acknowledge in one part of their consciousness the upper-class norms and manners as binding on themselves, *without being able to adopt them with the same ease and matter-of-factness. It is this peculiar contradiction between the upper class within themselves, represented by their own super-ego, and their incapability of fulfilling its demands, it is this constant inner tension that gives their affective life and their conduct its particular character.*[14]

Norbert Elias's view of aristocratic self-construction explains why, when one scholar says that William Byrd was just a moderately sensual gentleman, or another, working on Byrd's library, identifies it primarily as the instrument of a provincial man of learning, I have some reservations. In such statements, there is no room for bodily self-alienation, for emotional repression, for compulsive display and positioning, or for any of the possible distortions in civility caused by provincial and bourgeois mimesis.[15] Even if these were only occasionally displayed, they are nonetheless basic features of the civilizing process and of genteel self-construction. To ignore Norbert Elias's concerns is to ignore the historical world of which William Byrd was a part. To ignore Elias is also to ignore how closely some of Byrd's texts and most notably "The Female Creed" reflect the very strains of the self-construction Elias depicts.

Before taking up "The Female Creed," I should mention some further scholarship in the tradition of Elias that extends his analysis of Renaissance self-fashioning and will be employed here. Several of these scholars focus on the particular distortions of that process which seem to arise when it is practiced on the periphery, in one case including intense misogyny. In a book titled *The Politics and Poetics of Transgression,* which I shall apply shortly, Peter Stallybrass and Allon White explore the ensuing and problematic history of that self-aversion and self-control central to Elias's version of the civilized personality, specifically by examining the projection of the rejected physical

14. Elias, *Power and Civility,* trans. Jephcott, 304, 313 (emphasis added).
15. For the former, see Dunn's review of Lockridge, *Diary, and Life,* in *WMQ,* 3d Ser., XLV (1988), 779–782; the latter is Kevin J. Hayes, *The Library of William Byrd of Westover* (Madison, Wis., 1997).

self into the other. These authors greatly intensify Elias's analysis of the central psychological syndromes of self-fashioning. In his *Renaissance Self-Fashioning,* Stephen Greenblatt deals with the elite self-construction of figures who are peripheral because they are middle class, rather than provincial or colonial. He observes that in such cases "self-fashioning is achieved in relation to something perceived as alien, strange, or hostile," a threatening other, whether heretic, savage, witch, adulteress, traitor, antichrist, that must be discovered or invented in order to be destroyed. Greenblatt adds the corollary, central to his book, that "self-fashioning is always, though not exclusively, through language." This is a corollary that Elias neglected and that permits Greenblatt to extend Elias's considerations of the compulsions, fetishes, and dilemmas of self-fashioning and of its ambivalent relationship to power—particularly on the figurative or literal periphery—into the realm of personal literary productions. Homi Bhabha has illuminated further the compulsive, narcissistic pathologies of genteel self-construction in modern colonial and postcolonial contexts.[16] Stallybrass and White, Greenblatt, and Bhabha extend Elias conceptually, and also chronologically, to encompass the eighteenth-century texts, men, and places I shall consider here. Perhaps at this point I should add Ivory and Merchant to my list, or rather E. M. Forster, because for me the movie *Howard's End* epitomizes the aversion for the other and the savage boundary maintenance that can characterize genteel self-construction in all settings. Through these works, the full dimensions of Elias's process of genteel self-construction will become available.

III

What Elias tells us, then, is that the civilized self was characterized by self-aversion, by self-control yet by hysterical fetishistic consumption and positionings, by attacks on the other and on the "low" which were really attacks on something uncontrolled in the self, and by fiercely policed boundaries. He tells us further that aspiring peripheral members of the civilized class were in a constant state of tension between the values they aspired to and their own incapability of achieving those values.

To look at "The Female Creed" in this context is perhaps to begin to understand what is going on in it. This essay has always seemed to me to epitomize

16. Peter Stallybrass and Allon White, *The Politics and Poetics of Transgression* (Ithaca, N.Y., 1986); Stephen Greenblatt, *Renaissance Self-Fashioning: From More to Shakespeare* (Chicago, 1980), 9 (quotations); Homi Bhabha, "Of Mimicry and Men: The Ambivalence of Colonial Discourse," *October,* XXVIII (Spring 1984), 125–133.

the inexplicable intensity, weight, and nervous contradiction in many of Byrd's writings. I knew I had failed fully to explain my sense of the man through his manuscripts in my essay on Byrd's peculiar diary, and even before it appeared I had already turned to Elias and Greenblatt for help. Several years ago, I had explained something of the intensities of colonial self-construction in an essay on the misogynistic outbursts in Byrd's and in Thomas Jefferson's common-place books *(Patriarchal Rage)*.[17] Rejection by women in possession of the resources needed to construct gentility in a context of intensive and threatened colonial self-construction seemed to me to explain outbursts of misogyny like that found in Byrd's commonplace book. Like the commonplace, the simulta-neous "Female Creed" was written after a series of rejections both by imperial authorities and by possessing women. Yet even though *Patriarchal Rage* in-cluded a brief chapter on "The Female Creed," I still felt that this remarkable text had much more to reveal along these lines. Anna Foa, an Italian scholar familiar with Elias, had already suggested that this text was unusual even by European standards. Then a colleague at the University of Montana gave me Stallybrass and White. Their book did everything to describe what was going on in "The Female Creed" save to name it. In the perspective offered by Elias, then, and with the assistance of Stallybrass and White and of other new critical works, let us look again at this text and at some of the cultural acts I now see going on in it.

I want to look first at the *technique* Byrd uses to create this essay, a technique I will label "commonplacing," and at the way he focuses this technique on women, setting these technical elements of his essay in the context of the civilizing process. Then I will explore at some length the central misogynistic *intent* of "The Female Creed," which consigns not only superstition but also a grotesque corporeality to women and in so doing sets Byrd's misogyny in the context of the civilizing process or of genteel self-construction, examining at the same time some peculiar further things he does with gender, things that are part of the civilizing process but that partly undermine his misogynistic intent. Implicit throughout is the argument that "The Female Creed" is not only one of the more typical, if refined and grotesque, products of the civilizing process but that its techniques and misogynistic intents and paradoxes were almost uniquely intense and that this genteel intensity might have been caused by the particular pressures of self-construction brought to bear on ambitious British colonials. I will suggest the latter possibility—an extension of the central theme of *Patriarchal Rage*—as I go through "The Female Creed" but will develop

17. Kenneth A. Lockridge, *On the Sources of Patriarchal Rage: The Commonplace Books of William Byrd and Thomas Jefferson and the Gendering of Power in the Eighteenth Century* (New York, 1992).

the full case that this tortured text is a distinctively colonial product only at the end, when its dimensions are fully available. In studying colonial self-construction in William Byrd and, eventually, in other gentlemen, we will also be considering the social construction of emotions among genteel early American males.[18]

One of the fascinating things about "The Female Creed" is that the central literary *technique* used is that of the commonplace book. True, the "Creed" as genre is nominally a parody of a purported female credo, or rather it is a nominally female credo that turns out to be a parody of a Christian credo. Byrd had a Christian credo of his own inside the cover of one of his diaries, so he knew the genre well. Parody and satire were the standard fare of the early eighteenth century.[19] But underneath this initial rubric, the body of the essay has been assembled by gathering a list, or rather twenty sublists, of human superstitions. These are all attributed to "woman" and are framed together as "her" parodic creed. This gathering and framing of topoi is precisely what is involved in making a commonplace book, something Byrd did all his life.

In her book *Framing Authority,* Mary Thomas Crane points out how strange it is that commonplacing, the mere accumulation of brief quotes, observations, and facts out of their original and more organic contexts, should have become the characteristic device of humanistic self-construction.[20] How, she asks, could Erasmus and his circle, all of whom wished to create whole, harmonious human beings, have urged so fragmented and fragmenting, so primitive and merely accumulative a form of identity construction on their pupils? The commonplace book, the humanists' characteristic genre, required only tactically manipulative recastings and superficial framings of the items assembled and could not lead to the person of reflection they purported to create.

18. On the social construction of emotions among genteel males, see Philip Greven's pioneering work, *The Protestant Temperament: Patterns of Child-Rearing, Religious Experience, and the Self in Early America* (New York, 1977).

19. Byrd might have had as example a French model of the parody-satire aimed at women, namely the *caquet d'accouchée,* in which male writers portrayed the lustful, credulous gossip of women attending another woman's lying-in and subtly turned this gossip into social and political satire. See Domna C. Stanton, "Recuperating Women and the Man behind the Screen," in James Grantham Turner, ed., *Sexuality and Gender in Early Modern Europe: Institutions, Texts, Images* (Cambridge, 1993), 247–266. But Byrd's immediate use of the credo as model cuts closer to the heart of the matter where he is concerned, namely that female credulity and crude corporeality, before they are appropriated for social and political satire, are directly juxtaposed to male control and enlightenment.

20. Mary Thomas Crane, *Framing Authority: Sayings, Self, and Society in Sixteenth-Century England* (Baltimore, 1993). Byrd's commonplace book is treated in Lockridge, *Patriarchal Rage;* see also note 30, below.

Crane has no answer, noting only that the commonplace technique *is* a betrayal of humanistic ends and in her view a historical dead end as well. In an earlier work, Richard Halpern suggested that commonplaces were a form of primitive accumulation and as such a precursor of capitalism. Although this may be so, Norbert Elias seems to put the commonplace phenomenon in particular and its use in works like "The Female Creed" in a wider and more persuasive context not necessarily inconsistent with Halpern's. In Elias's terms, the commonplacing technique is a not very successful attempt to humanize the compulsive acquisition of goods, positions, and ornaments characteristic of the court society and of the gentility at its core. It is not a very successful effort because the accumulation is so primitive, a sort of hysterical collection of displayed moral postures functioning as much through volume as through digestion. Thus, while commonplace books occasionally achieved incidental therapeutic functions never envisioned by the humanists, at their heart, at the heart of "The Female Creed," lay the ceaseless collection of civilized merits essential to gentility. This compulsive process, it seems to me, accounts for some of the tension I sense in Byrd's essay. He is showing us yet again how *much* he can assemble. Both the one surviving commonplace book that Byrd kept at this same moment in his life and "The Female Creed" leave little doubt that the compulsive quality of his efforts to be civilized and of his incessant commonplacing in particular was driven by a lifelong effort to overcome the disadvantages of colonial peripherality. As Homi Bhabha notes, such efforts are doomed by their very intensity to failure, and by their very failure, to intensity.[21]

In "The Female Creed," the commonplacing technique is, furthermore, given a rare and intense focusing. The rules of the commonplace genre call for variety and detachment. Civility required controlling excesses of anything, so one must not go on too long about anything, and certainly not about emotionally laden issues. Byrd was already breaking these rules briefly in his commonplace book, in a seven-page-long psychosexual tirade of appropriated quotations hostile to women. Now, simultaneously, in "The Female Creed," these rules of variety and detachment are thrown completely to the winds. The "Creed's" impressive, if somewhat frantic, gathering of excerpts is nominally entirely about superstition, and its framing almost relentlessly places these on women. Beneath his screen of wit, Byrd violates the conventions of the very technique he uses by going on obsessively about a single, emotionally laden issue.

21. Halpern, *Poetics of Primitive Accumulation;* Bhabha, "Of Mimicry and Men," *October,* XXVIII (Spring 1984), 125–133.

Why would a civilized man again violate the rules essential to the very civilizing genre, commonplacing, whose techniques he is employing to give content to "The Female Creed"? On one level, the answer is that he is writing, not a commonplace book, but a parody and so has leave to take the commonplacing technique and focus it obsessively. On a parallel but deeper level, the answer goes a bit beyond this, and Greenblatt has already offered one version of it. In peripheral figures, the civilized self was often fashioned with unusual intensity in juxtaposition to an alien other. Among these others were women. Women, as witches, as adulterers, or merely, as in this case, as inherently superstitious beings, served the intensified needs of men struggling hardest to fashion themselves into gentility amid deadly competition. In "The Female Creed," courtly competition and peripheral self-construction have raised gender to the status of a negative fetish, something that had to be distanced in order to achieve civility.[22] Civility could also entail uncivil savageries toward fetishized versions of other races and classes as well as toward a fetishized version of the other gender. On such intense occasions, civility could break its own rules of detachment while commonplacing. In William Byrd's case, as I have suggested elsewhere, the specific gender fear and savagery that led him to violate the rules of the commonplacing technique employed in the "Creed" were driven not only by vaguely peripheral necessities but also by the specifically *colonial* needs and frustrations entailed in his effort at self-construction.[23]

"Savagery" may seem too strong a term based on the evidence offered so far, but it will appear better justified if we leave literary techniques behind and focus directly on the central misogynistic *intent* of "The Female Creed." For as assembled excerpts on woman's superstition give way to contemporary gossip about prominent women—in a voice still nominally woman's but increasingly Byrd's own—what we discover is that, in drag, he is dumping on women not only superstition but also corporeality, lust, greed, and lack of control. Let us explore for a moment the intensification of the essay's misogynistic message, which I have taken up briefly in *Patriarchal Rage.*

On the most superficial level, "The Female Creed" celebrates Byrd's entry into the full intellectualized rationality of the Enlightenment, an entrance he accomplishes by transferring to women, in "woman's" purported voice and credo, all the realms of superstition, credulity, and magic he himself once avowed but now jettisons in the latter stages of his own civilizing process. For

22. On gender as a fetish, see Ann Rosalind Jones and Peter Stallybrass, "Fetishizing Gender: Constructing the Hermaphrodite in Renaissance Europe," in Julia Epstein and Kristina Straub, eds., *Body Guards: The Cultural Politics of Gender Ambiguity* (London, 1991), 80–111. The idea of fetishism as a cultural construct derives from Elias.

23. Lockridge, *Patriarchal Rage.*

example, in the strophe offered at the beginning of this essay, women, children, and Catholics are presented as the sole possessors of spirits, demons, hobgoblins (and later, of devils and ghosts), which "like the Prisoners in New-Gate, they are let out of their Hole anights, and suffer'd to play their Pranks at large in the World." What a prefiguration of William Butler Yeats's "mere anarchy is loosed upon the world"! Asserting that these spirits "appear for the most part to women and children," Byrd-as-woman narrows the field to the female and the infantile and lets the papists somewhat off the hook. In and of itself, this seems a relatively polite distancing of adult males in general and Byrd in particular from their "female," childish, dark past in order to establish a credulous and largely female antitype for their own enlightened civilization. But if the essay is relatively polite to women on this level, this may only be because making females literally into demons and devils would only plunge Byrd himself back into the very unenlightened credulity he consigns to them. As the essay progresses, however, superstition gives way to "womanly" gossip about women, and it becomes clear that Byrd has found a way to demonize women that is consistent with the Enlightenment. Beyond mere credulity and lack of mental control he now relentlessly associates women with the body at its most corporeal. In the most grotesque terms, he renders women as beings plagued with urine, lust, greed, and impending excrement and with the inability to control these urges.

Thus, as the first strophe extends from superstition into gossip:

I believe that these Spectres with their Horns and cloven feet, and with the Hurly-burly they make in the Dead of night, unluckily scare both the maid and her mistress into a Diabetis. Hence it comes to pass that so many Females in all countrys can scarce hold their precious water, haveing been terrify'd in the Nursery with Bul-beggars and Apparitions. This is the case of the unfortunate Dripabunda, who when She fancy'd She saw the Ghost of her deceast Husband, dy'd away for fear the good man was come to life again. From that fatal moment she lost her Retentive faculty, beyond the Relief of Turpentine Pills and Bristol-water, nor can even Dr. Friend, or Apollo himself intirely stop the Leak, but stil whenever she laughs beyond a Simper or a Broad Smile, the liveing Sal-almoniac flows from her.

Or, to pick later examples from other strophes:

I believe these Bel-dames can make a Love-powder so very strong, that the proudest Female in Great Britain, even madame Lofty herself, wou'd be humble enough to marry her Foot-man, if she swallow'd but half a scruple of it before she made water in a morning (451).

I believe when we are utterly undisturb'd with passion, sudden Impressions are made on our minds by some invisible power. . . . I remember Philo had an Impression not long ago, that Gloriana wou'd infallibly wed a man with a great nose in his face, and have into the bargain all the advantages, which according to the doctrine of Proportion, are promis'd by that comely Feature (457–458).

My good Lady Junket carrys her destestation [sic] of this unlucky number [13] much farther and tho' she loves her gut more than other Females do a coach and six, or Fine Cloaths, yet she once refus'd to tast a Pye, because it had 13 ortolans in it, and this too when Lent was just ended, and there was not a morsel of any think else for Supper. How unfortunate was the Curiosity which made [her] inquire how many of those rare Birds were immur'd in the Crust? But . . . the moment her question was answer'd, She lay'd down her Knife and Fork, retir'd from the Table, and pretended she cou'd not eat, tho' her poor Guts croakt all the while at their disappointment (472–473).

Tis a certain piece of History that Mademoiselle Frizzle was 26 [when, several] years ago[,] [she was] put into so mortal a Fright with one of these Deathwatches [a beetle, ticking out the years of her life from its hole in the wall], that her very Heart-breakers, that lay upon her Toilet, turn'd as grey as a Gander, yet blessed be God she is stil alive, and strong enough to open her Self a passage to the King with her Elbows, every Drawing-room night let the Throng be never so great . . . [knowing that] she may stil receive her pension, and carry that hideous Smile upon her face full 30 years longer, because the fatal Insect tickt 56 times (458).

Recommend me to discreet Fartamira, who never pretends to wipe her Backside on Such a day as this, for fear of bedaubing her taper Fingers. I was acquainted with a wise Woman once, who always kept her bed on Childermass day, believing her Self safe in that Snugg Situation, but that precaution fail'd her once very cruelly. For poor Mrs. Straddle, (the Gentlewoman's name) pearching with all her weight upon the Pot, the brittle Utensil flew to pieces, filling the Bed with water of high-perfume, and at the Same time makeing a Wound, which none but a female Surgeon cou'd have the honour to dress (462).

There were also seven Wondows [sic] of the world, and Seaven champions to destroy monstors, and relieve distressed Damsels. For these Reasons whenever Madam Wool-sack thinks it proper to purge for the benefit of her complexion, she conjures her Apothecary to prepare a Dose that will give her exactly Seaven Stools (469).

What is going on here is a powerful engendering of that civilizing dichotomy portrayed by Norbert Elias. In this text, the uncivilized and credulous and also the physically coarse and uncontrolled lesser orders into whom this newly civilized man is projecting his fear of his own credulity, corporeality, and lack of control while he distances himself from them in constituting his own identity are chiefly *women*. Byrd's fears of a lack of bodily control and of the inability to master his own lust and greed are relieved by projecting these incontinencies onto women. In "The Female Creed," therefore, the dawn of the Enlightenment means that the civilizing process has become deeply gendered, casting uncontrolled woman into that dark night where the demons in whom she still believes reside.

By the early eighteenth century, the civilizing project was well under way in England. As Stallybrass and White point out, some of William Byrd's literary contemporaries, such as John Dryden and Alexander Pope, and some of his specific models, such as the *Spectator/Tatler* series and Sir Robert Southwell, were engaged policing the popular, the low, the filthily corrupt, and the grotesque in order to clarify the boundaries of high culture. Elsewhere in Europe, the state itself undertook the same task. While gender was always to some degree implicit in this drawing of the line, Byrd's "Female Creed" is the purest example we have of how, in certain hands, the great dichotomy of the civilizing process could become a seemingly unbridgeable gender divide. Men were mind and women the disgusting body. Men were saved and women damned. Women, that is, and children and Catholics. In the proceedings of Byrd's essay, with its focus on woman, children exist only to infantilize women, and Catholic men implicitly become infantilized and feminized, like the men of who knew what superstitious, corporeal races. In the case of women alone, however, Byrd's vignettes raise the possibility that in truth women were gaining too much skill at civility and sensibility, monopolizing this new cultural trend and forcing men to counterattack by seizing possession of the civilizing reason of the Enlightenment. "Civilization" may have become the battleground, above all, of gender.[24]

24. Stallybrass and White, "The Grotesque Body and the Smithfield Muse: Authorship in the Eighteenth Century," in *Politics and Poetics of Transgression*, 80–124; Lawrence E. Klein, "Gender, Conversation, and the Public Sphere in Early Eighteenth-Century England," in Judith Still and Michael Norton, eds., *Textuality and Sexuality: Reading Theories and Practices* (New York, 1993), 100–115. The specific gendering of the bodily, and consequent contempt for "leaky women," is treated in Gail Kern Paster, "Leaky Vessels: The Incontinent Women of City Comedy," in *The Body Embarrassed: Drama and the Disciplines of Shame in Early Modern England* (Ithaca, N.Y., 1993), 23–63. Paster puts Elias's civilizing process, and so Stallybrass and White, in the larger context of European state building and social control.

Had Stallybrass and White had this text and Susan Gubar's work on Pope and Jonathan Swift, they would surely have emphasized this renewed gendering of civilization much more. Taken together, Byrd's commonplace book and this text further suggest that it is above all colonial contexts that evoke civilizing misogyny in unusually intense forms.[25] This colonial theme will soon emerge more fully, but certainly it should be clear by now that "The Female Creed" is not simply an amusing essay by a moderately sensual gentleman. It is a powerfully revealing early modern European text. It is also, or could be, an important text in colonial history.

We can go still farther. Byrd's little essay next reproduces in a special form an ambivalence at the very heart of the civilizing process. This ambivalence in its general form is the subject of Stallybrass and White's title, *The Politics and Poetics of Transgression*. Their entire point is that, having displaced the corporeal, in its sexual as well as gustatory and eliminative functions, onto the low and having distanced along with lack of control profound physical pleasure—and note here that in their book the displacement is more onto the lower classes than onto the other gender—the civilized mind finds that it regards the low with irrepressible feelings of loss and desire. It has consigned something necessary in itself to the other. Desire cannot in fact be fulfilled nor therefore identify itself completed save through transgression in thought or in deed. Wholeness is not possible without crossing over the very boundary just created into the sensual realms imaginatively projected there. The civilized man must transgress, through fear or desire, into the realm of the low, the other, where his sense of the forbidden resides alongside his sense of magic, his emotions, and his desiring body. Transgression becomes a constituent of identity in civilized Western culture. As Stallybrass and White put it, "What is socially peripheral becomes symbolically central" to identity.[26]

But the transgression often takes the form of a phobic fascination with "low" corporeality, excrement, sexuality, a fascination that is recursive, obsessive, terrifying, hysterical, and necessary. The energy of this process derives from the very emotions that have been suppressed as well as from the terrors of transgression itself. Freud deals with some of the neuroses and hysterias that result from these feared and desired transgressions. Surely there could be no

---

For a similar commentary on the way civilization fits the needs of the state, see David Warren Sabean, *Power in the Blood: Popular Culture and Village Discourse in Early Modern Germany* (Cambridge, 1984).

25. Susan Gubar, "The Female Monster in Augustan Satire," *Signs*, III (1977), 380–394; Lockridge, *Patriarchal Rage*, discusses the Byrd commonplace book as a colonial product.

26. Stallybrass and White, *Politics and Poetics of Transgression*, 20. Their theory here is essentially Lacanian.

bètter description of Byrd's own evident focusing on the bodily, sexual, excremental self he has projected onto women in the "Female Creed." He is plainly both horrified and fascinated by the corporeality he has displaced onto women. Here, then, is a further source of the special energy this text radiates and of the fascination it holds for the reader. It is a text of loss, of transgression, of desire.

It follows from Stallybrass and White that there is also a need to reappropriate that which has been lost, to repossess the sensual through a form of transgression that can best be described as a reoccupation of the lost sensuality. Repossession of this sort can be literal. The sexual possession of servant girls became one common means for the ultracivilized to regain that which had been lost in the nether regions of class and gender to which it had been consigned. Stallybrass and White document some remarkable cases and depict the sick fascinations of transgression that accompanied them. Here, their work is uncannily descriptive of Byrd's life, and of "The Female Creed." To begin with, we cannot escape noting the sexual focus on servant women that comes to mark Byrd's own life in the years just before and long after he writes "The Female Creed."[27] In possessing these women, was he repossessing the sensual self he had so distanced in his essay and in his life? Does transgression explain the guilt he felt on each occasion? Was guilt also delight?

Transgressions into the low in the desire to repossess the distanced sensual self could be vicarious as well. That, it seems to me, is what we see in the final movement of Byrd's thoughts within "The Female Creed." Ever more intensely, as each strophe wears on, "woman's" voice becomes William Byrd's voice. That is, when "woman" is being credulous, she is plainly woman, but as soon as "she" begins to link "her" superstitions to gossip about corporeal females, "she" becomes ever more the voice of the misogynistic William Byrd. By the end of each strophe, the voice of "woman" has begun to attack the priests, physicians, and officials of the British establishment, and at that point "she" becomes very plainly the outraged man who has been rejected in his ambitions to be royal governor of Virginia and to marry English money, in both cases because he was a colonial.

> I believe in astrologers, coffee-casters, and Fortune-tellers of every denomination, whether they profess to read the Ladys destiny in their faces, in their palms, or like those of China in their fair posteriors. . . . [etc., etc.] . . . I believe from my heart that the Pretender to the crowne of Great Britain has no other hopes of ever putting it on his head, but what the Mistresses of this

27. See, most notably, ibid., 151, 155. For references to Byrd's sexual focus on servant women and the sources, see Lockridge, *Diary, and Life*, 101, 148.

art inspire him with. I believe if a Bull or a Goat appear in a mans cup, he must needs be a Whore-master, tho' he be a Lord Chancellor or an Arch-Bishop, and if a Bear or a Munky be seen in a Ladys she'll need a vast deal of Grace to keep her honest. If an ass or an owl chance to be there, the happy caster will have a fair Hit to be an alderman, but if the Beast's ears appear longer, or the Bird's countenance graver than ordinary, there are hopes he may come to be a Judge or at lowest a Sergeant at Law. If a ravening wolfe be in the cup, the man may rise in the navy and grow to be a Captain of a man of War, or if he be a Land officer, and good for nothing else, he may live to be a Governour in His Majesty's Plantations.

Time and again, then, in most of the twenty miniature essays that make up the "Creed," Byrd, having set out to distance women in order to establish his own enlightened civility, ends up ever more thoroughly assuming woman's voice. He takes on that voice initially in order to distance women and the bodily even more by becoming the voice of woman commenting on the failings of specific women, but in the end, as in the example above, he reverses his whole intent, truly becomes woman, and as woman conducts a devastating attack on the male establishment of Britain. He seems to be saying, "Even I, as credulous woman, coarse and out of control, can see how much more corrupt and beyond control the establishment is." But in his colonial rage, he has thereby repossessed the very femininity he started by rejecting. He has both seized the Enlightenment from women and then for his own purposes repossessed the bodily self he had consigned to them! Surely there was sensual as well as political delight in this vicarious repossession. Delight, yes, and a compassionate reintegration of the human self. For in the very end of the "Creed," Byrd-as-woman admits that he/she is Byrd after all, by uttering as his/her/his final condemnation of women the fact that they have faith in men. He here appears again as a man, only technically in woman's voice, warning "woman," who he has just been, against men! For just a second, here at the end, speaking as man/woman/man, he has made himself whole again.

Julie Ellison has shown us that this sort of vicarious repossession of women, of other races, and of the low is characteristic of oppositionist thought in the early eighteenth century.[28] It usually arose from a sense that politically marginalized men, whether colonials, radical whigs, or even opposition Tory intellec-

28. Julie Ellison, "Cato's Tears" (paper delivered at the University of California, Berkeley, in 1991 as "The Passionate Empire: North Africa and the Cato Tradition," and part of a larger project on "Vicarious Emotions and Colonialism in Anglo-American cultures," conducted under a fellowship from the Institute for the Humanities at the University of Michigan).

tuals, were like these victimized others, and, specifically, they were like women because they shared a feminine sensitivity to the wrongs done them. The problem in such cases was dealing with a femininity that was inappropriate to manly politicians. But the projection of oppositionist sensitivities onto woman, or onto Africans, where these emotions could most dramatically be portrayed—again, because *even* degraded women, Africans, etc., could see the abuse and because victimized women and colonized Africans could best portray the degradation oppositionists felt—at least had the advantage of reuniting the civilized male authorial self with its detached sensual as well as sensitive components and so of restoring a certain wholeness. In such masquerades lay the possibility of accepting submission and loss.

As far as women and Africans were concerned, however, the process meant only a triple colonization by marginalized men, first a colonization by the otherness projected onto them and then a colonization by the need to use that otherness to propel a critique of established power while repossessing it in order to be whole. Byrd's "Female Creed" skirts around the edges of this game. Rhys Isaac's account of Thomas Jefferson's contradictory stories about gender and race also incorporates some features of this ambivalent multiple colonization of the other.[29]

But the situation is even more volatile than the word "ambivalence" suggests. Gender in Byrd's commonplace book and in "The Female Creed" taken together is at once a fetishized concept—based on arbitrary signs that have no stable basis in reality and are the subject of obsessive attention—and yet a wildly unstable one. In his commonplace book, the "female" is at first identified with sexual and reproductive anatomy, but when that frightens and eludes Byrd as a reliable locus for femininity he turn to lust, which is also inherently unstable when identified only with women. In the "Creed," he frames femininity as superstition only to lapse into grotesque corporeality as a better sign and then promptly destabilizes these definitions by actually taking on the voice of woman himself. The less he could stabilize "woman," one might speculate, the more "she" alarmed him, particularly as to reunify himself with "her" was at once to regain a part of himself he had alienated through aversion and to concede the implicit feminization of himself as a marginal, colonial male.

Inescapable in all our considerations of "The Female Creed," from its hysterical gathering and obsessive framing, through its intense distancing of the bodily self bound up with a ferocious misogyny, to this repossession yet apprehension of the unstable feminine, is the haunting possibility that it is Byrd's

29. Isaac, "The First Monticello," in Onuf, ed., *Jeffersonian Legacies*, 77–108.

colonial situation that makes this document so extraordinary. It is time to face this issue fully.

Much more is happening in "The Female Creed"; my desk is covered with notes on further resonances, but to follow further lines of development is to run the risk of becoming too much like William Byrd, too intensely gathering and framing because the object is to establish my own form of gentility. I hope I have brought you with me along at least some of the straight and narrow if still complex path I have taken through this text. I hope you will at least agree that "The Female Creed" is a complex text of distancing, civilizing, intellectualizing, of fetishizing gender, loss, fascination, reappropriation, and instability. Most of all, I hope you will agree that it is potentially a powerful *variation*, in its unusually compulsive gathering, its unusually intense focus on gender, and in the unusually rough form and accusative purpose of its transgression and reunification of the gender-divided self, on the literature of self-construction as it comes down to us from Elias, Greenblatt, and Stallybrass and White. The exact source and nature of this variation is of great concern for our task.

We have here a man from the colonies desperate for gentility, deeply in debt, searching for resources, recently rejected as a suitor by at least one well-off woman (and possibly recently rejected for a colonial governorship as well) on the grounds that he was a colonial. He has just married a woman essentially without dowry. His commonplace book shows a growing focus on women's voracious sexuality as one source of his sense of failure and of fear.[30] Simultaneously, this same man frames a frantically gathered text entirely, compulsively, repetitively—and the twenty miniature essays within "The Female Creed" do quickly become repetitive once one gets past the slightly different superstitions at the start of each—around civilizing himself by rejecting the credulous and the bodily in himself and by projecting these in grotesque form onto woman. In explosive proximity to this very act, he then repossesses in all seriousness the voice of woman in order to drive a critique of the British establishment. His assault includes (see preceding quotation) an attack on the very British gentleman, the "Land officer," Alexander Spotswood, whom he had failed to displace as royal governor of his own colony. In this context, our text does more than echo the compulsiveness, aversion, fetishism, implied hysterics, and transgressive complexities invoked by Elias, Greenblatt, and Stallybrass and White. It plainly suggests that there was also a peculiarly *colonial* dilemma that produced a *unique* combination of a compulsive gathering,

---

30. Since some of the references to Byrd's commonplace book in the foregoing passages go beyond the discussion of it in *Patriarchal Rage*, I should mention that the manuscript itself is in the Virginia Historical Society in Richmond.

an obsessive focus on gender, and a breathtaking sequence of profound self-alienation followed by sudden, vicarious repossession of the feminine voice in order to conduct an attack on the imperial establishment.

The mechanism behind the special furies in Byrd's text is, of course, a simple one. A variation on the special convolutions and narcissistic rages of colonial self-fashioning as explained by Homi Bhabha, it is derived from studying the powerful outbursts of misogyny in William Byrd and Thomas Jefferson's commonplace books in *Patriarchal Rage*, and it provides the setting for "The Female Creed" in all its subtleties.[31] As Virginia planters' aspirations to gentility rise, they find themselves trapped on an accelerating treadmill. The standards of genteel display—in goods and in intellectualization—are constantly rising. Further, no matter how hard they try, elite Virginians' efforts to achieve this rising standard of gentility are doomed to failure, because the very intensity and visibility of their efforts—their desperate orders of fashionable goods, their accumulating libraries—mark them as imitations. Further, in a world increasingly inclined to sympathy and benevolence, their possession of slaves also marks them as less-than-genuine gentlemen. They are imitations both in British eyes and, especially after 1760, in the eyes of an increasingly evangelical populace for whom the whole civilizing process is a disorderly and immoral appropriation of power. Perhaps for these very reasons, our self-fashioners strive on and, in an economy where tobacco prices have long since leveled off and merchants and the crown have learned to siphon off the real profits, there are only two ready sources of the cash needed to achieve genteel display: public office and wealthy women. Since truly profitable posts in the colonies are few, they turn to women, and risk humiliating rejections. Failing to become truly genteel, the rejected men remain colonial and feminized.[32]

31. See Lockridge, *Patriarchal Rage*, 75–102; Bhabha, "Of Mimicry and Men," *October*, XXVIII (Spring 1984), 125–133.

32. On the various ways in which gender came to be caught up in the metaphors of colonial status, including "feminization," see Susan Juster, "Body and Soul: The Modernist Impulse in American Puritanism," *Reviews in American History*, XXI (1993), 19–25, esp. 24. Julie Ellison's argument, in "Cato's Tears," could, in this context, easily be extended from the oppositionist politicians who flirt with "effeminacy" as well as with colonial status (by using images such as those used in Joseph Addison's *Cato: A Tragedy* . . . [1713]) directly to actual colonials, who, however, could not flirt with such images because they could not evade them. Hence, Juster's argument that "a more feminine version of religious humanism took root in the New World in tacit recognition of the inherently 'feminine' nature of its proponents' colonial status." Unable to evade "effeminacy," then, some colonials simply embraced it. But, as Juster's book on evangelicals and gender, *Disorderly Women: Sexual Politics and Evangelicalism in Revolutionary New England* (Ithaca, N.Y., 1994), points out, even in evangelical circles an equal number of men reacted to feminization by struggling all the harder

Byrd is a case in point. Like most colonials, he had trouble generating the resources his aspirations demanded. Denied access to lucrative colonial governorships, he turned to women. But women with fortunes also rejected him, one because her father had said that an estate in Virginia was "little better than an Estate on the moon."[33] Taken together, these circumstances explain the intensities and variations on the process of genteel self-construction, most notably the compulsive gatherings, the intense, distancing misogyny, the gender instability, and the fury at the establishment evident in "The Female Creed."

Colonial need and recursive failures ever to *be* recognized as genteel aside for the moment—and these furies would of course lead to revolution—what interests me most is that the intersection that generates misogyny is the one of desperately needy men with women commanding necessary resources. Usually these are the women being courted. Sometimes, as I have suggested with Thomas Jefferson, they are mothers commanding inheritances, though in Jefferson's case he was also facing his entry into the uncertainties of courtship. Rejection in such confrontations provokes a misogynistic fury we can understand only if we go all the way back to Norbert Elias and if we comprehend the special pressures on self-creation in the colonies. "The Female Creed" thus reveals that in colonial settings genteel self-fashioning was a particularly intense, poignant, gender-laden business for the self fashioners. At a minimum, this text stands for a culture, genteel self-fashioning, for a place, Britain's American colonies, and for a personality, William Byrd's, which we have scarcely begun to reconstruct.

IV

Perhaps it is Byrd who is peculiar, Byrd and, in a similar way, his successor as Virginia mythmaker, Thomas Jefferson. Perhaps I am taking extreme cases. In *Patriarchal Rage*, I suggested that colonial self-fashioning generated unusually intense pressure and unusually intense misogyny in unusually driven men, such as these incessant self-constructors and mythmakers. If they epito-

---

to assert their masculinity. It is this reaction we are seeing in Byrd as, shortly, in Robert Bolling and in Thomas Jefferson. Bolling equates himself, as rejected colonial poet, with his female muse in one poem, actually becoming "she" and so feminized through his rejection by Britain. See "Reseration" at the opening of "A Collection of Diverting Anecdotes, Bon-Mots, and Other Trifling Pieces 1764," BR163, Huntington Library, San Marino, California; and Daphne Hamm O'Brien, "From Plantation to Parnassus, Poets and Poetry in Williamsburg, Virginia, 1750–1800" (Ph.D. diss., University of North Carolina, 1993), 146, discussed in the text, below.

33. Lockridge, *Diary, and Life*, 92, 182.

mize colonial self-construction, perhaps they epitomize its pathologies as well. I want always to leave the door open to the possibility that other Virginia and other colonial gentlemen were less drivenly self-constructed, less misogynistic, more easy, more gracefully artful, full of joy, flexibility, spontaneity, and natural grace, and, even in times of crisis, characterized by charity, forgiveness, and compassion. What a terrible vision I should otherwise be offering. Logic alone suggests that must have been so. Should a culture be epitomized by its most extreme cases?

Let me address this issue by telling a story about Robert Bolling, a Buckingham County planter who was born in 1738 and lived until 1775. Bolling's misfortune was that he was the third of five sons of a wealthy and prominent planter. His inheritance was therefore relatively modest and at first consisted of a small cottage, eight hundred acres near the Piedmont, and thirty slaves. He pursued a number of courtships that promised to augment these resources. He acquired other distinctions along the way, becoming pre-Revolutionary Virginia's greatest poet, published repeatedly in England, and a young patriot and political ally in the crisis leading to the Revolution of his relative by marriage Thomas Jefferson. In *Patriarchal Rage*, this young gentleman of the 1760s and early 1770s was my primary example of a less-driven and thus a less-misogynistic Virginian. I called him that because, in two literary commonplace books or literary exercise books at the Huntington Library, as read both by myself and, for a later book, by J. A. Leo Lemay, Bolling seemed supremely able to overcome what neither William Byrd nor Thomas Jefferson quite could, rejection by a possessing woman.[34]

In 1760, Anne Miller, daughter of Hugh Miller, a Scots merchant resident in Virginia, target of Bolling's second-ever attempt at courtship, and evidently a young woman whose considerable resources would have nicely supplemented the acres and slaves inherited by Bolling, seemed about to consent to marry him. Suddenly, her father took her back to Scotland. She seemed neither to have warned Bolling adequately of her father's disapproval nor to have resisted her father's act, so in a jilted suitor's mind she undoubtedly seemed culpable. Since the Millers were Scots, that same jilted lover could have read their departure as dissatisfaction with his colonial status. Yet my original reaction, based on Bolling's own "Circumstantial Account" of the failed courtship as well as on the two literary notebooks, which also date from the early 1760s, was that

34. The Bolling notebooks in the Huntington Library are "La Gazetta di Parnasso; or Poems, Imitations, Translations, etc.," BR73, and "A Collection," BR163. J. A. Leo Lemay's account of the courtship and rejection is *Robert Bolling Woos Anne Miller: Love and Courtship in Colonial Virginia, 1760* (Charlottesville, Va., 1990).

Bolling was not all *that* angry and that he quickly digested his anger.[35] In any event, this feeling was primarily directed at Anne Miller's father and at a male colleague of her father and was channelled, in the notebooks, into some fairly polished poetry. He seemed to have incorporated any anger at Anne Miller herself into a single, moderately misogynistic poem in one of the notebooks. Bolling eventually gained a few publications out of all that and appeared to have returned to other subjects. Leo Lemay's judgment is that the "Circumstantial Account" and the poems in the Huntington notebooks gave Bolling perspective on his rejection. What a relief! How glad I was to meet Robert Bolling.

My trail has since crossed Bolling's again, and he now seems a substantially different man. A year after *Patriarchal Rage* was published, I was looking for eighteenth-century commonplace books in the Special Collections rooms at the Alderman Library in Charlottesville, and the first name I chose to check was that of Robert Bolling. Under his name, there was a reference to the microfilm of a privately held notebook, which he titled the "Hilarodiana." This seemed to be a new manuscript, so I asked for it and put it on the machine.[36] What I found was quite surprising to me.

Many things are still not clear, and I hope hereby to obtain some help, but let me give as good an account as I presently can. The notebook dated from 1760, with most entries dating from 1760 to 1762. Although there are later interpolations, no items appear to have been entered later than 1767. The notebook begins with an urging to secrecy not found on either of the two volumes at the Huntington (Figure 1):

> *Nota bene*
> Bob Willis
> It is rather too familiar to take up a
> Gentleman's Manuscripts and peruse them
> without his Permission
> But to divulge any Matter to
> the Knowledge of which a Person

35. Bolling's "Circumstantial Account" of his courtship is published in Lemay, *Robert Bolling Woos Anne Miller*, 47–73, as are the poems from Bolling's three notebooks (the two in the Huntington Library, cited in note 34, above, and the "Hilarodiana" (listed as "Robert Bolling's Commonplace Book"), #8708-B, Private Collection, microfilm in the Manuscripts Division, Special Collections, Alderman Library, University of Virginia, Charlottesville, which Lemay judges to be contemporary with and relevant to the courtships.

36. Bolling, "Hilarodiana"; I would like to thank Michael Plunkett, Curator of Manuscripts and University Archivist, for permission to quote from the "Hilarodiana."

comes by so great a Piece of
Rudeness is highly dishonest and reproachful.

This unusual warning was added later, as it is dated October 25, 1766, subsequent to nearly all the entries in the notebook. Aimed perhaps at a specific person, Bob Willis, it is, in any event, clearly an effort to keep someone or everyone from reading or reporting on the contents of the "Hilarodiana."[37] The significance of this date will shortly become apparent.

The entries in this notebook are frequently amended by means of excisions and marginal additions, and the entire appearance is one of haste and frequent, equally hurried revision. Some pages have been torn out. All this stands in contrast to the neatly copied out notebooks at the Huntington. Leo Lemay, who had in fact seen this manuscript, though he uses it only a little, agrees that, despite later incursions, it appears to be the raw original in which, together with his "Circumstantial Account," Robert Bolling first recorded his reactions to his rejection by Anne Miller and her father. Shortly thereafter, sometime between 1761 and 1767, many of the poems from the "Hilarodiana" were copied in better form, and a few originals added, in the notebooks now in California. Some of these poems were published in Virginia and others in London in the middle 1760s.[38] So what occurs here is a process in which a gender confrontation is being absorbed into a continual literary self-construction, which explains why all these notebooks also contain translations and seemingly unrelated poems, including satires on Virginia politics. What we see is a sustained editing of the author's reactions to his confrontation with Anne Miller and her father and a transmitting of these into, while placing them within, a wider spectrum of polite literary discourse.

Yet what is striking is how very raw the raw form of Bolling's reaction to his rejection by the Millers really is in the "Hilarodiana." It is not simply that the whole notebook has a raw, worked-over, involuted appearance. More important, there are misogynistic poems that seem never to have made it into Bolling's subsequent copybooks. One of these seems innocuous enough, insofar as I can decipher it on film, though it uses a baroque image of female fickleness,

---

37. *Nota bene* is on what seems to be the third in a series of unnumbered pages, including the title page, preceding what seems to be, and is listed in Bolling's table of contents near the end of the volume as, page 1. Identifying exact pages is a problem even with the subsequent pages. Many contain numbers and are identified by number in the table of contents, but these do not always agree with the numbers on the pages where the poems listed in the contents are actually found. Some pages have simply been removed from the volume, leaving only stubs, and several unnumbered pages follow the table of contents at the end.

38. Lemay, *Robert Bolling Woos Anne Miller,* 80–81.

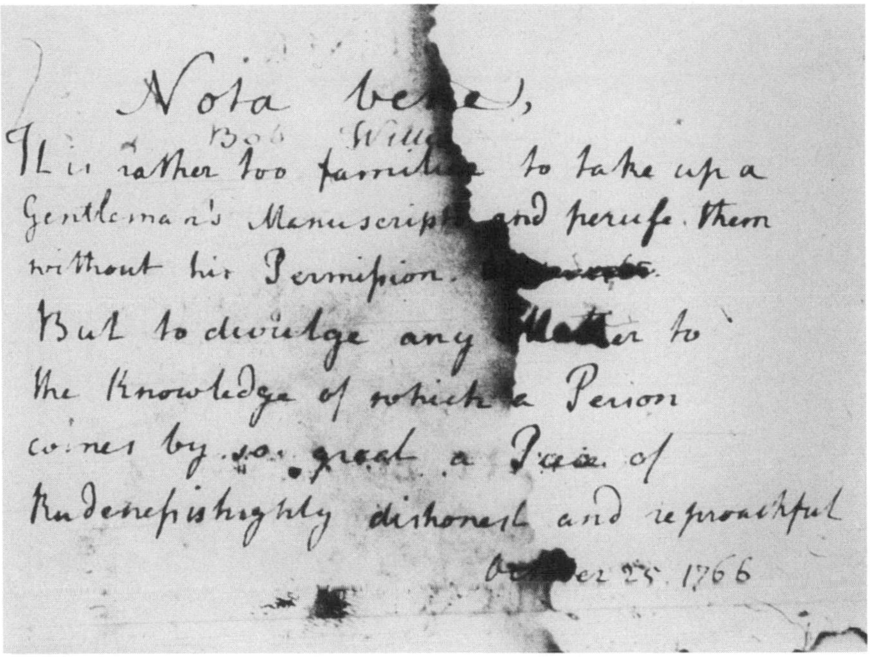

FIGURE 1. "Nota Bene." *The opening inscription added to Robert Bolling's notebook,* *"Hilarodiana," on October 2–5, 1766, shortly after the suicide of Colonel John Chiswell.* *Reproduced with permission of the Special Collections Department, Alderman Library,* *University of Virginia*

the resonances of which I do not fully grasp. (Note that Anne Miller was taken back to Scotland in October 1760.)

> Epigram written on a looking glass. Oct. 1760
>
> Like this dear Girls, you're [frail?] and Fair
> You gentle Belles but [Glass?] are.
> Breathe on the [glass]—the s[mearing?] Dew
> Shows how [seductors?] act on you.
> Two [*sic*] fierce a Heat [and] 'tis [understood?]
> Will break a Glass, o'ercome a Prude.
>   Robert Bolling

Bolling's real point, however, is expressed in a drawing just below the poem, to which the word "this" in line 1 of the poem seems to refer: "Like this dear Girls. . . ." The drawing shows a standing woman whose back is turned; she is bending over lifting her skirts to reveal her posterior and possibly her sexual anatomy while looking around invitingly at the reader (Figure 2). Beneath her is a blotched latin epigram I am still attempting to translate, but the drawing

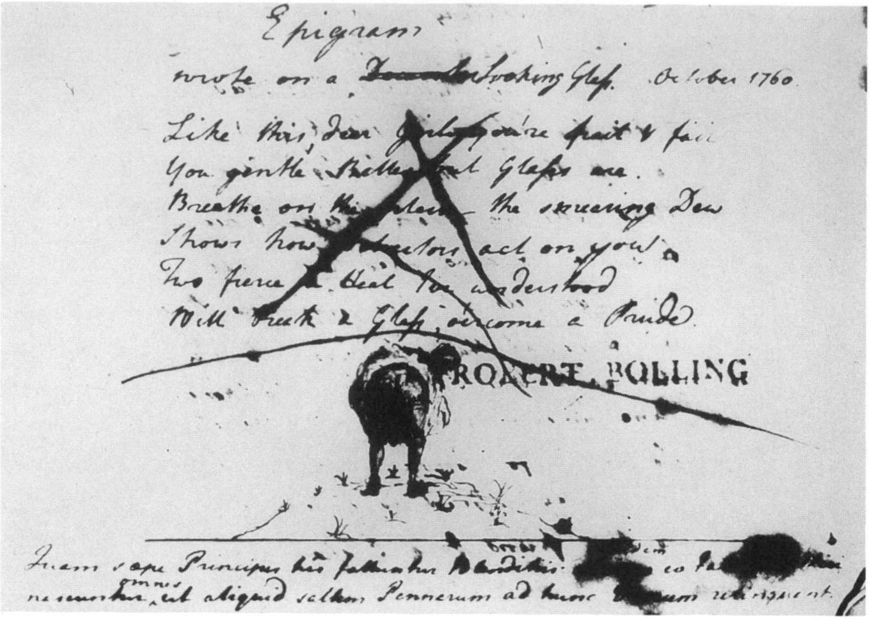

FIGURE 2. "Epigram Wrote on a Looking Glass." *Dated October 1760, immediately after the failure of Robert Bolling's courtship of Anne Miller. From Bolling's "Hilarodiana." Reproduced with permission of the Special Collections Department, Alderman Library, University of Virginia*

alone leaves no doubt of the momentary fury that Bolling has put into the seemingly polite poem.[39] "They are instantly sexually available," he seems to be saying, "to whoever breathes on them last and most warmly." Perhaps the poem said too much, for, even without the drawing, it seems not to have made it into the more refined Huntington notebooks. In fact, someone has gone back and violently crossed it out, carefully leaving the drawing beneath intact as if to say that the visual text, with its intense emotional message, had been the point all along.

There may be more dimensions to this poem and drawing. The raw slashes across the poem could be an attempt to portray a cracked looking glass,

39. The poem and drawing are in Bolling, "Hilarodiana," 3, as listed in his table of contents and in Figure 2. The Latin epigram beneath does not seem to appear in any of the concordances to the classics, and crucial parts are obscured by smeared ink, deletions, and faded ink. It appears to read: "Quam [or Quem?] saepe Principes his falluntur Blenditiis equidem eo Fato ——?—— Viri/nascuntur omnes ut aliquid saltem Pennerum ad hunc [Viscum?] Uti—rquent [or something like ul—i—quant]." Bolling seldom used Latin, and virtually never his own Latin, so the obscurities of this particular effort may reveal what a poor Latinist he was. The only way my colleague, John Madden, can presently make sense of

shattered, presumably by the image of the promiscuous woman it sees. The idea of a too-truthful looking glass recalls Hogarth's contemporary use of truthful mirrors in his devastating satire on courtship and marriage in a series of etchings he called *Marriage à la Mode*. Here, the foppish, aristocratic groom is first seen studying his stylish face in a mirror while his wife-to-be flirts with her lover, the charming young lawyer Silvertongue. The mirror is held at such an angle that it in fact reflects Silvertongue, her true lover. His frivolous bride, on the other hand, captured at a later moment in conversation with her lover, leaves no reflection at all in a mirror carefully placed on her dressing table. In the end, when the groom has surprised his wife in bed with Silvertongue, and the lawyer has run him through with a sword, the groom's face in its death agonies is framed by a mirror on the wall behind him.[40] In every instance, the mirror has told the truth, first of betrayal, then of emptiness and death. Yet Bolling's too-truthful mirror, shattered by the lasciviousness of women, may be more than a mirror. In the popular language of the seventeenth century, at

most of this passage is to read the final verb as "ulciscant," or rather as a stab at this proper form of the verb "ulciscor," to take revenge. This calls for reading what seems to be a *t* in that word as an *l*, but in the poem above, Bolling has in fact crossed an *l* to make the word "frait," when clearly he means "frail."

If "ulciscor" is the verb and "Viscum" is also correct (as some special techniques for penetrating the blots covering certain words indicate) then the passage suddenly becomes clear as an epigram on Bolling's drawing immediately above of a woman displaying her sexual anatomy, to wit: "*Although great men are often taken in by these attractions, yet such is Fate that all men are born so that* [a wordplay also implying "when all men are born"] *they take at least some revenge on [women's] soft/sexual/reproductive parts.*" This rendering leaves "Pennerum" unaccounted for, unless Bolling meant "Perneum" and was trying to evoke by this word the fat "hams," or thighs, of the woman in the drawing, adjacent to her soft/sexual/reproductive parts.

The kind of sentiment this rendering entails is consistent with the whole tone of William Byrd's earlier commonplace book (See Lockridge, *Patriarchal Rage*), in which the war of the sexes is profoundly anatomical, sexual, and reproductive and certainly entails revenge. Moreover, a few pages later ("Hilarodiana," 20, in Bolling's table of contents but marked 21 in his hand on the actual page), Bolling has drawn another mysterious quasi-female figure, this one in the birthing position, whose "hams" are displayed though the reproduction or sexual parts are again obscured by ink, and who is pointing to and so presumably birthing Bolling's male lineage (Figure 4). Obviously Bolling had the birthing of males by women's soft parts on his mind. Conversely, then, the Latin epigram as rendered here would reveal that his intent in this "birthing" drawing was not so much to honor women or to put them in their place as to depict men's revenge on them! Is the ink obscuring the genital area in both drawings, then, a fierce blotting out of the female organs on which Bolling wishes to take revenge?

40. Robert L. S. Cowley, *Marriage á la Mode: A Review of Hogarth's Narrative Art* (Manchester, 1983).

least, "looking glass" was a common euphemism for a chamber pot.[41] If Bolling intended this double meaning, then what is stored in the chamber pot, cracking it, is the promiscuous woman he pictured below.

What Bolling is doing with the poem and drawing combined is teaching us how to read his poetry of rejection. The drawing in particular reflects his frustrated sexuality and the sexuality of his misogyny at the moment both his desires and his plans were thwarted. Like Byrd in his commonplace book, Bolling is reading his rejection by a possessing woman primarily as a rejection of his inner (and outer) sexual self. His actual language in this, as in most other poems in the "Hilarodiana," is already somewhat polite. Without the drawing of a woman offering herself, and the slashes across the poem, we could never estimate his initial fury with Anne Miller in particular or with women in general.

There are other poems, some nearly enigmatic, save that beside them are still other sexually explicit drawings. The theme of poems with associated drawings seems to be an erect and aggressive, even an animalistic, male sexuality, exhausted or eluded by cryptic woman. There is also a poem, "Vespilla, that Voluble Tongue [Who] Dispenses Distraction Around." The titles of the poems from the nine later pages torn out of the "Hilarodiana" may suggest further the turmoil of Bolling's emotions in the early 1760s. These titles are preserved in the table of contents and include "Hilarodiana on the Death of Lovers," "Hilarodiana Obscaena and Another Vile [word blacked out]," "The Bourgeois Gentilhomme" (a poem copied into the Huntington manuscripts and full of bitterness at the rejections faced by bourgeois who reach for aristocratic status), and "Hilarodiana for the Display of Dignity." These titles alone give the title of the notebook, "Hilarodiana," its indelibly bitter and sarcastic tone.[42] Yet I am not sure that the fierce misogyny of the looking glass poem and its drawing was ever fully sustained by these missing poems. Bolling's anger at women seems to be ebbing a shade as the surviving pages of the notebook wear on, though the fierceness of what must have been its initial expression is quite remarkable, and how much of it ever ebbed in the long run is doubtful.

What does not ebb at all is Bolling's rage at Anne Miller's father. Out of it seems to grow a pattern of association that leads him to colonial rage at the

41. James Deetz, "The Link from Object to Person to Concept," cited in Phyllis K. Leffler and Joseph Brent, *Public History Readings* (Malabar, Fla., 1992), 491–492. The Deetz essay originally appeared in Zipporah W. Collins, *Museums, Adults, and the Humanities: A Guide for Educational Programming* (Washington, D.C., 1981).

42. See, for example, "Hilarodiana," 5, the missing page 13–19 stubs, 38 (listed as 39 in the table of contents, it contains "Admonition," with voluble Vespilla), 48, 65 (table of contents).

metropolis, or rather at its more pretentious provinces. Angry poems aimed at Hugh Miller, Anne's Scots merchant father who took her away, give way to a poetic tale of Bolling's grandfather, who was "forced" to return to Yorkshire, "where men were surprised to behold him so white. All thought that Virginians were blacker than night." "But when he began in English to speak," Bolling continues, their ignorant surprise knew no bounds.[43] Bolling gets his grandfather out of this embarrassing confrontation with a witty reply to the effect that Virginians speak better English than Yorkshiremen, but what he is clearly doing here, on the occasion of a personal crisis, is reviving a two-generation-old family tale of colonial rejection. Like Robert Beverly's similar tale, Bolling's story is part of Virginians' folklore of cultural rejection. Not only can they not get access to Scotsmen's daughters, Bolling is saying, but Yorkshiremen classify Virginians racially with their slaves. He will repeat this poeticized folk tale in a later notebook.

Plainly, then, behind its injunction to secrecy, the "Hilarodiana" is a literary notebook arising in significant part from a rejection by a woman with the resources Bolling could have used further to establish his gentility, a rebuff that was also a rejection of Bolling as a Virginian and so as a colonial. It documents his rejection by the two categories he might be thought to be superior to, women and Scots merchants, but whom he needed to enlarge his fortune and so his gentility. It also documents still other British provincials, Yorkshiremen, reclassifying his ilk as equivalent to the one group over whom Virginia gentlemen thought themselves to have achieved total mastery, their slaves. Constructing a genteel self out of such rejections entailed at least an initial fury, a misogynistic and colonial rage, which Bolling later decided, for reasons we shall see, he wanted kept secret. Less of the misogyny crept into his later notebooks and still less into his publications.

In combining rejection by an actual British family with sexual rejection and the denial of resources, Bolling's courtship of Anne Miller was an unusually focused version of the sort of provincial courtship and rejection Bolling himself had earlier faced and that most would-be Virginia gentlemen had to face. In the more usual case, the potentially rejecting female was a native of Virginia and so could merely reject them sexually—as they read it—and deny them her resources. In this more normal instance, the British were represented only by the eternal presence and contempt of the mother country, setting an ever rising standard of gentility that neither Virginia's economy nor the contempt of the metropolis would ever let them reach, forcing them all the more energetically

43. See "Hilarodiana," 6–7 (reprinted in Lemay, *Robert Bolling Woos Anne Miller*, 113–114), 20.

to seek propertied young women who might in turn also reject them. Bolling seemed unable to distinguish between the former case and the latter. The syndrome, as far as he and we are concerned, was the same.

Every man has a right to edit himself. As has every woman. Yet every historian has an obligation to ask what are the sometimes painful grounds on which a given form of gentility is constructed. That way lies compassion. In his "Hilarodiana," as he smoothed the surface of his gentility, Robert Bolling let the painful truths out.

I would like to be able to say that in Robert Bolling's case, as I originally thought and as Leo Lemay subsequently suggested, the agonizing process of editing and re-editing his notebooks and himself did finally give him perspective on his furies. But a closer reading of Lemay's book on Bolling, *Robert Bolling Woos Anne Miller,* convinced me that Bolling never escaped from these furies despite heroic and successful lifelong efforts to transform them into fine poetry. Lemay is an excellent scholar and, although he does not mention the drawings in the "Hilarodiana," emphasizing the finished poetry instead, he has done his homework well. Here is the result, some facts from Bolling's life before and after the notebooks. Lemay identifies him as an independent, even willful young aristocrat, unwilling to admit error, full of pride. He had been rejected earlier by a very wealthy Virginia woman, Susanna Chiswell, whose father, Colonel John Chiswell, was connected with the dominant and wealthy Robinson-Randolph faction then at the top of Virginia politics. Susanna then married fifty-five-year-old John Robinson, speaker of the House of Burgesses and a leader of this faction. In his second courtship, that of Anne Miller, Hugh Miller had in fact invited Bolling to follow Anne to Scotland, there to wait two years to see whether his love was true, but it appears that, while he was then twenty-two and of age, his mother objected to his departure—having no-one-knows-what power over him—and he did not go. By 1763, another young Virginian, one of many suitors to Anne Miller, had pursued her to Scotland and married her. That same year, Bolling married the well-off Mary Burton of Virginia and, while courting her, but before her acceptance, wrote a poem he called "Neanthe." "Neanthe" is a mock epic about the clownish courtship of the fat, lustful daughter of a nouveau riche gentleman of mundane origin, by two young friends who lust for her body but above all are desperate for her resources. In the end, the would-be suitor favored by Neanthe kills the other, is hanged, and Neanthe then hangs herself. Lemay describes this poem as inventing "one of the most disgusting sluts in American literature, the subject of a grotesque [sexual competition followed by a deadly] fight between her suitors," a poem drawing on anti-Petrarchan Italian models to create "one of the

FIGURE 3. Drawing of a man resembling Robert Bolling, replying tartly to what seems to be a rejection by a woman. *The clothing and woman's hair seem to date from 1764–1766, possibly indicating an unrecorded courtship and rejection for Bolling. From the "Hilarodiana."* Reproduced with permission of the Special Collections Department, Alderman Library, University of Virginia

most savage satires in American literature."[44] Mary Burton evidently brought Bolling a great fortune, and when she died in 1764 he lamented her death in rather narcissistic terms and then, possibly after still another courtship and rejection, married a woman without a fortune (Figure 3).

Beginning in May 1765, Bolling was instrumental in hounding to suicide John Chiswell, the father of the first woman who had rejected him. The "aristocratic" Chiswell had run another man through with a sword and been set free on bail. Bolling challenged his bailment as a case of privilege, forcing the authorities to order Chiswell back to prison. Chiswell then committed suicide, in October 1766, the very month Bolling added his injunction to secrecy designed

44. Lemay, *Robert Bolling Woos Anne Miller*, 20–21. "Neanthe" is printed in J. A. Leo Lemay, "Southern Colonial Grotesque: Robert Bolling's 'Neanthe,'" *Mississippi Quarterly*, XXXV (1982), 97–126.

to conceal the contents of the "Hilarodiana."[45] Bolling also became one of the few Virginians—but, since his poetry dominated the poetry pages of the Virginia *Gazette,* a most influential one—to ridicule the anglophilic cult of admiration that grew up around Virginia's first lordly governor, the earl of Botetourt. Bolling later became a fervent American patriot. When he died of a heart attack at the age of thirty-six, in 1775, it was said of him that he was "an amiable and accomplished gentleman, a firm patriot." His abilities, the eulogy went on, made him "an ornament to his country."[46] He was Virginia's foremost poet.

At this point words become superfluous. But let me underline the obvious. Some of this avidly self-constructing young Virginian's fury at women and at Scots in the "Hilarodiana" might have been anger displaced from its true target in a powerful mother, who had blocked the courtship's extension to Scotland. In this, Bolling might have resembled the Thomas Jefferson depicted in *Patriarchal Rage* more than he resembled William Byrd. Yet Bolling had two known courtships in addition to this one. Years after the first ended in rejection, he pursued the woman's father, John Chiswell, even to death. After the second, that of Anne Miller chronicled here and the only one involving a British woman, also ended in rejection, he wrote the "Hilarodiana" and its sequels. During the third, his courtship of his eventual first wife Mary Burton, when rejection was still possible, he created "Neanthe," a poem about a "disgusting slut" of a rich young lady surrounded by grotesque suitors. He seems to be saying at the end of this poem that the desperate desire for sex and for resources combined is reducing all Virginia men of his class to the low and to the grotesque in their pursuit of low and grotesque, but wealthy, women. Rejection, in turn, both in the "Hilarodiana" and in "Neanthe," calls forth fears of sexual inadequacy that I take to be also a metonymy for the cultural inadequacy that awaited failed colonial self-constructors and that looms behind every line of "Neanthe." After his marriage, in the very month he drove Susanna Chiswell's "aristocratic" father to suicide, Bolling set a seal of secrecy on his "Hilarodiana," with its intense misogyny, fears of inadequacy, and hatred of British superiors, as if to tell us that such creations were deadly and to hide them forever from view. His hostility to things British remained intact the rest of his short life.

Courtship was an agony for this intensely self-shaping young gentleman,

---

45. Lemay gives a fuller account of the Chiswell episode in "Robert Bolling and the Bailment of Colonel Chiswell," *Early American Literature,* VI (1971–1972), 99–142. As Ronald Hoffman has pointed out, Bolling did not actually *destroy* the notebook, which indicates that in some way he wanted to preserve the emotions it contained, even while holding them from another's/others' view.

46. Lemay, *Robert Bolling Woos Anne Miller,* 25.

and, after his first rejection, it took place in an aura of fury toward women, toward the other suitors clustering around them, toward rejection, and toward a Britain that not only literally rejected him in one courtship but that also set the very standard it kept unattainable, the standard of gentility whose vain pursuit had sent him to these wealthy women only to expose himself to another form of rejection, one that only confirmed his larger cultural rejection. His disgust in "Neanthe" with the whole business of courtship and his hatred of Britain and of the aristocratic John Chiswell were also a distaste for something in himself, of the recursively doomed ambition to possess that had repeatedly exposed him to rejections and that he could not control. Or, rather, he began to control these rejections only once his wife had died and left him in possession of her contribution to his estate. But even then, in 1766, in hounding Chiswell to suicide and later in attacking the Botetourtians, he was attacking ambitions still within himself. That these ambitions still lived within him is shown by the fact that in 1767 he scrapped his "lonely . . . little cottage" whose philosophical virtues he had once extolled, and built himself a new Chellowe, a fine "seat" in the Piedmont possibly modeled on the Palladian mansion drawn in the Huntington notebooks at about this time (Figures 4, 5, 6)![47] Chiswell died for Bolling's continuing sins of ambition as well as for his own and so that Bolling could be reborn as a patriot. I know of no other way to interpret poor Robert Bolling's life. He was bound by the terms of a recurring dilemma he did not create.

47. Shortly before building this house, in an undated entry in the "Hilarodiana" (49), which seems to come from 1764 or 1765, just before he attacks Chiswell, Bolling draws the little house he had inherited at Chellowe (see Figure 8; another drawing is on 20; see Figure 4) and writes the following partly decipherable verses on it:

> Little Cottage, lonely cell
> Poor retreat (in which I dwell)
> Tho so lonely poor and small
> Thou'rt to me my Bolling Hall
> House of mine house of mine
> however small thou art
> Thou seemest to me an Abby

The sequence seems to be that he then attacked the "aristocratic" Chiswell, built his new "seat," and then attacked the fawning Botetourtians! See Lemay, *Robert Bolling Woos Anne Miller,* 148. Observator [Pierre Etienne Du Ponceau], "An Account of Two Americans of Extraordinary Genius in Poetry and Music," *Columbian Magazine,* II (April 1788), 211-B, and Du Ponceau's letter to his daughter in 1837, reprinted in James L. Whitehead, ed., "The Autobiography of Peter Stephen Du Ponceau," *Pennsylvania Magazine of History and Biography,* LXIII (1939), 321–322, both mention the new Chellowe, Du Ponceau describing it as a "seat" like other impressive houses. The drawing of a house is in "La Gazetta," 156.

FIGURE 4. Robert Bolling's drawing of his inherited cottage, "Chellowe," and of a woman in birthing position pointing to his male lineage. *From the "Hilarodiana," circa 1761. Reproduced with permission of the Special Collections Department, Alderman Library, University of Virginia*

The conclusion I draw from this accomplished man's life history, then, is that Robert Bolling spent much of his youth as we first see him in 1760, caught between women who possessed, but did not easily yield, the sexual, reproductive, and financial resources he needed to reach the ever rising standard of display gentility required, and the simultaneous contempt and demands of British culture. I use these terms because my view is that Bolling still felt the contempt of the metropolis for mere colonials, who might actually be black, yet felt the mother country's escalating cultural demands and its demands to acquire the resources to become a real and not just a colonial gentleman. This last is the one part of his case I cannot prove, but I find it significant that Bolling, like Jefferson, turned from British to European models, in Bolling's case to Italian Renaissance poetry, in his assiduous crafting of his intellectual gentility. This was a low-cost strategy and avoided comparison with the British. His aspiration to sumptuous display needs further study, but his new "seat" at Chellowe and the elegant coaches and furnishings depicted in his drawings point to a lifelong desire for a more than bourgeois standard and status. I am convinced that British contempt and Britain's implicit cultural demands sent him to the only source of quick capital in a Virginia where tobacco and wheat yielded only slow returns, where office was hard to come

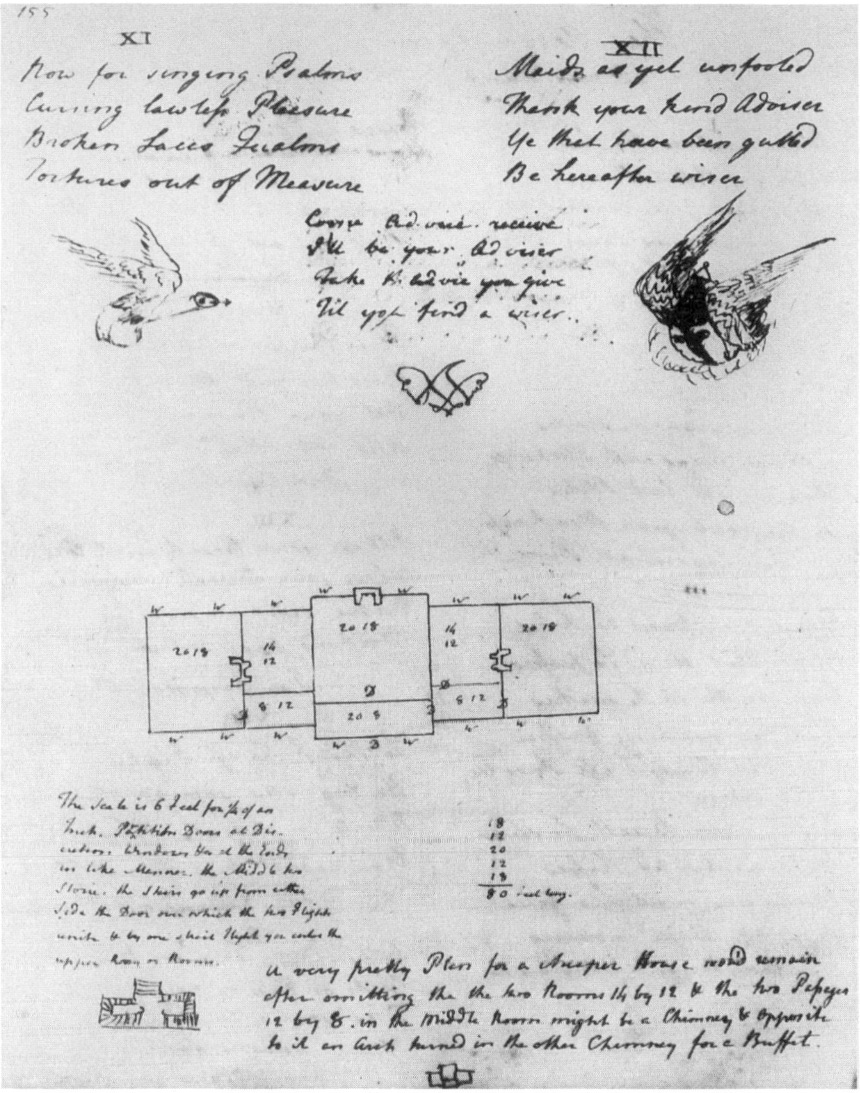

FIGURE 5. Beneath a winged and triumphant male sexual organ, Robert Bolling's plan for a large house. *C. 1765, with notes that "a cheaper house" might be built by omitting the rooms 14 by 12." From Bolling's notebook, "La Gazetta di Parnasso. . . ." Reproduced by permission of the Huntington Library, San Marino, California. Call number BR73*

by, and where the law—which he tried—was a bit déclassé.[48] Thus sent to possessing women, he found them surrounded by a swarm of other likely suitors and was twice rejected. Yet where else could he go to escape being

48. Evidently, Thomas Jefferson shared Bolling's distaste for the law as a source of status; see Willard Sterne Randall, *Thomas Jefferson: A Life* (New York, 1993), 83, 109.

FIGURE 6. Plan of a Palladian seat. *From Robert Bolling's "La Gazetta . . . ," circa 1765. Reproduced by permission of the Huntington Library, San Marino, California. Call number BR73*

mistaken for a slave—or a woman—and to pursue the colonial's doomed effort to become truly genteel? This whipsaw, I would guess, generated fury in him much of his life, fury at women and at the mother country. Fury also at himself. Caught between the merely bourgeois and the merely colonial on the one hand, and a gentrification that led inevitably toward the attractive, consuming, frightening, unattainable aristocratic culture of the eighteenth century on the other, Bolling is a study in the most agonizing of conflicts.

Robert Bolling has himself given us the confirmation of the heart of his crisis, namely that he was caught up in a recursive dilemma of unresolved class and status identity. Daphne O'Brien has done a preliminary analysis of "Reseration," a poem from "A Collection," the most polished of Bolling's notebooks, which to my mind leaves little doubt of the terms in which this dilemma existed in Bolling's own mind. Casting himself as the colonial poet, his one sure identity amid all his confusions, Bolling asks why he has been rejected, why his poetry has found neither market nor fame. He blames his prospective audiences. Assuming the identity of his rejected muse, his feminized self, "she," Bolling finds no fame in Williamsburg because "she treated no Law case." "She" is equally a failure in Philadelphia because "Trade and Tax distract" prospective audiences there. The inescapably bourgeois character of American audiences guarantees rejection for a learned and genteel American artist. Yet Britain, where "her" poetry ought to receive acclaim, is fascinated only by the trashy but fashionable poetic toys and gew-gaws of "other" foreign poets, Italian, French, and Dutch. Britain has no place for the "honest" and "manly" colonial gentleman-poet. Bolling's own poem beautifully captures his agonizing position, too artistic, learned, and genteel to be one with his bourgeois colonial neighbors, he is yet too "manly" and "honest" to be accepted in a metropolitan culture where high civilization has become aristocratic foppery. Feminized, "vagrant," and "hapless," Bolling-the-poet lacks audience and home and becomes the perfect metaphor for Bolling-the-man, unable to be merely bourgeois, yet equally unwelcome as genteel unless he abandons his colonial manhood for the worst excesses of the very aristocratic recognition he sought. But this is exactly what Bolling had already done, for most of his poems are deliberately cast as imitations of Italian models. Feminized by this imitation, he has been further feminized by rejection. What Bolling is saying in "Reseration" is that as poet he is guilty over his cultural capitulation, has been feminized both by this act and by its failure, and is still unrelievably trapped between the colonial bourgeois and the metropolitan aristocratic.[49] I believe that this describes his life.

Robert Bolling's ambitions for himself and for his poetry may demonstrate a particular instability in the conceptions of class and status *in Virginia* that made the repeating dilemmas of pursuit and rejection encountered by colonials seeking to establish their genteel status unusually frantic in the Tidewater regions. In the poem "The Bourgeois Gentilhomme," Bolling places himself in the position of a bitter bourgeois who has aspired to, indeed married into, the aristocratic life, and who has been ruined as a consequence. The poem is nearly a justification of his attacks on Colonel Chiswell, who had burned Bolling by blocking the younger man's marriage to his daughter. Similarly, in the early stages of the Revolution, Bolling, like Jefferson, spoke of Spartan, rural, almost bourgeois leaders, who would slay the dragon of aristocracy. Yet plainly from his courtships, his drawings, and his eventual standard of living, he aspired to something far beyond the bourgeois, possibly beyond the merely genteel. Surely the particular circumstance that blocked the Tidewater gentleman Robert Bolling from accepting anything like bourgeois status, and so kept him from abandoning the doomed merry-go-round of colonial self-fashioning by accepting a gentrified middle-class position in keeping with his democratized

49. O'Brien, "From Plantation to Parnassus," 148–151. The clue to the aristocratic nature of the metropolitan audience Bolling is invoking is in his use of the term *"virtuosi"* to describe that audience—an unmistakably aristocratic if often irredeemably trivialized culture of connoisseurship that had evolved in late-17th-century England. The reference is half-sarcastic, half-longing.

society, limited resources, and colonial taint, was that the planter's life simply could not be construed as bourgeois. The planters' isolation, their vast acreages, their unchallenged power over their families, slaves, and self-sufficient plantations partook inescapably of the aristocratic. Not simply of the genteel, but of the aristocratic.[50]

And so, perhaps, Bolling, like other Tidewater self-constructors and they uniquely among colonial would-be gentlemen, had a hard time taking the one exit from the dreadful carousel of colonial striving for genteel status readily available to other colonial gentlemen, namely to accept, even embrace, that theirs was a bourgeois gentility. By virtue of the way they deployed their resources, Bolling and perhaps others of his plantation culture simply could not get off the terrible mental shuttle that had the unacceptably bourgeois at one end and the unattainably aristocratic at the other. In this system, rejection by propertied women became a metonymy not so much for his poetic career as for his life.

As he shuttled between aspiration, rejection, feminization, and fury, Bolling revealed instabilities and conflicts not least in the areas of gender and sexuality that were far more problematic than I have so far revealed. To pick one example, there is in Bolling as in Byrd a fascination, as the overall crisis of self-construction comes to focus on gender, with the low and the grotesque. Neanthe herself is a crude, repulsive, lusty woman, reminiscent of Byrd's "Dripabunda" and "Fartimira." But in Bolling's case, the corresponding transgression, in which he implicitly places himself in this realm of uncontrolled corporeality, desire, and greed, is immediate and profound. Neanthe's suitors are nearly as crude and lustful as she, and their desires and greed are more uncontrolled than hers. His drawing of Neanthe, of her doomed suitors, and of the sickening

50. "The Bourgeois Gentilhomme" is in Bolling, "La Gazetta"; the drawings are primarily in his "Hilarodiana" and show furnishings, dress, and coaches. Bolling's rhetoric in the Revolution can be seen here and there in Lemay, *Robert Bolling Woos Anne Miller*, but is best seen in the Bolling work reprinted in Lemay, "Robert Bolling and the Bailment of Colonel Chiswell," *Early American Literature*, VI (1971–1972), 99–142. The best depiction of the plantation owner as a god-like patriarch clearly beyond the merely genteel is William Byrd's, in a letter from the 1720s, as quoted in Lockridge, *Diary, and Life*, 123–124: "Like one of the patriarchs, I have my flocks and my herds, my bond-men and bond-women . . . so that I live in a kind of independence on everyone, but Providence. . . . I must take care to keep all my people to their duty, to set all the springs in motion." Curiously, Byrd's version of the planter's life, like Bolling's, also contains large doses of practicality, economy, and virtue, again demonstrating the peculiar ambivalence of planters' status with respect to the convental bourgeois-genteel-aristocratic spectrum customary in British social categories. Hence Bolling's ambivalence, amid flirtations with it in "The Bourgeois Gentilhomme," about accepting merely bourgeois status *or* a bourgeois status lightly veneered with mere gentility.

So sung the Berd and he sung well.
The Muse has nothing more to tell.

FIGURE 7. Narrative drawing of the plot of Robert Bolling's poem "Neanthe." Accompanies *the copy of the poem in Bolling's notebook, "A Collection of Diverting Anecdotes. . . ." Drawing tentatively dated at 1763. Reproduced by permission of the Huntington Library, San Marino, California. Call number BR163*

events of the poem in one of the Huntington notebooks scrawls all the characters with an agonized crudity unmatched until the Weimar drawings by George
Grosz and, like them, places even the artist in hell (Figure 7). Bolling ends the
poem with an elegy whose overstated gentility seems to be saying, "Beneath this
gentility lurks primitive desire, which can make fools, or corpses, of us all."[51]
Virginia maids and their suitors are all potentially this gross, this grotesque,
acting out a sham of gentility over a ground of profound corporeal crudity and
uncontrolled desire for sex and for status. Nominally, Bolling is aiming this dart
at the more aristocratic Virginians, whose superior position he so resented. But
in view of the fact that he writes this poem on the occasion of his own still-
doubtful courtship, and considering the lust for the same high status shown in
his first two courtships, particularly that of Susanna Chiswell, he is clearly also
placing his own and probably his friends' aspirations in "Neanthe's" realm of
the low, and he transgresses this boundary, not primarily for literary purposes,
as with Byrd, but as an abiding self-condemnation.

Similarly, in the drawings in the "Hilarodiana," other boundaries, gender

51. This is close to Lemay's reading in "Southern Colonial Grotesque," *Mississippi Quarterly*, XXXV (1982), 97–126, but adds the probability that Bolling is including or could have
included himself.

and even sexual boundaries, are often blurred and so are transgressed disturb-
ingly in ways not as self-consciously literary as in Byrd. The bending figure beneath the "Looking Glass" poem is curiously androgynous, its sexual anatomy
obscured by a dark mass of cross-hatching, which almost seems to be putting
male drawers beneath the clearly female petticoats, and by deep shadowing in
which the front edge of the petticoats and skirt, hanging down between the legs
of the figure, could be read as pendulous male genitals. She could be a man in
petticoats, saying "Kiss my ass." (Or, if the looking glass is also a chamber pot,
saying, "Shit on you.") A similar figure occurs on another page, reclining in the
classic birthing position, pointing up to Bolling's male lineage in Virginia
(Figure 4). As a woman, the figure's message is obscure; it seems to be saying,
"I, woman, birthed the lineage," as if this supine woman were the mere mediator or facilitator of the distinguished male genealogy to which she points.[52] But
is the figure female? Here again, we see the tightly gathered hair, characteristic
of both of these ambiguous figures, the cross-hatching that, inadvertently or
otherwise, presents the possibility of male drawers, and a great, dark pile of
unreadable clothing obscuring the genital area. Ambiguity and androgyny run
all through Bolling's drawings of women and men in the "Hilarodiana." The
women all have tightly gathered hair, far shorter than the pageboy length wigs
the men wear. The women's faces are always tight and linear, the men's occasionally full and sensual by comparison. The one woman clearly shown nude
has, to put it mildly, a boyish figure (Figures 3, 8).[53]

Finally, these ambiguous boundaries lead in turn to the fleeting evidence of
male homosocial, and even homosexual desire in Bolling's works. There is a
careful drawing of a friend's detumescent penis, following his wedding night,
next to a poem in which the friend is warned that going too enthusiastically
into sex with the bride can literally be deadly. In "Neanthe," the two rival
suitors at first try to settle their differences by a masturbating contest, to
see who can shoot furthest. Presumably, the winner will shoot the bride.[54]

52. "Hilarodiana," 20. For a less benevolent view of what the figure tells us, see note 39.
For another example of the birthing position, see Joan B. Landes, "Representing the Body
Politic: The Paradox of Gender in the Graphic Politics of the French Revolution," in Sara E.
Melzer and Leslie W. Rabine, eds., *Rebel Daughters: Women and the French Revolution* (New
York, 1992), 20.

53. "Hilarodiana," 20, 42, 48.

54. "Hilarodiana," 5; and Lemay "Southern Colonial Grotesque," *Mississippi Quarterly*,
XXXV (1982), 97–126. See also Eve Kosofsky Sedgwick, *Between Men: English Literature and
Male Homosocial Desire* (New York, 1985). Kevin Berland at Pennsylvania State University,
Shenango Valley, has found extensive marginalia focused on homosexuality in a French
dictionary owned by Byrd.

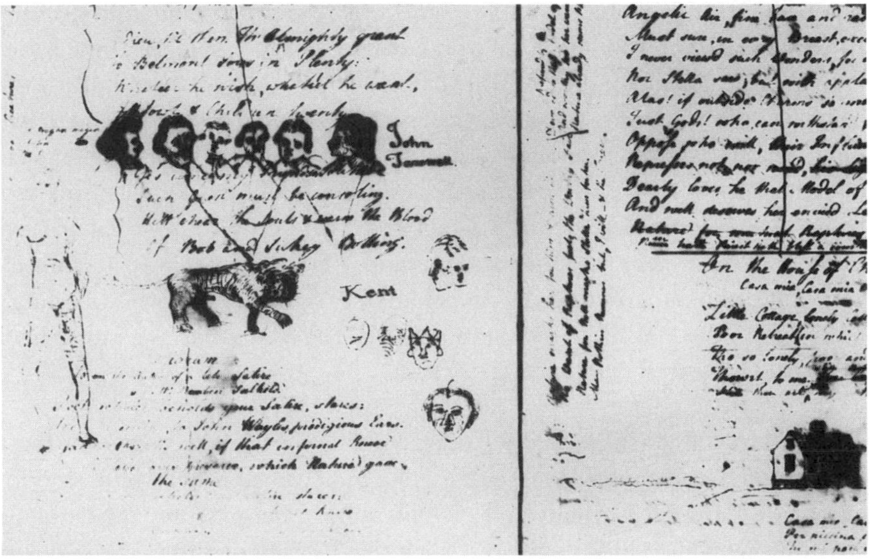

FIGURE 8. Robert Bolling's only sketch of a nude woman, along with "Der Hoogende Moogende," a sexually aroused lion, and Chellowe, "Little cottage, lonely cell. . . ." *From the "Hilarodiana." Reproduced with permission of the Special Collections Department, Alderman Library, University of Virginia*

Through these works run a subtle sense that men's rivalries in courtship interfere with their friendships.

So, transgression is the name of the game in Robert Bolling's psychosexual world. All boundaries are unstable, all things possible, his very identity uncertain. What does this tell us? In my mind, these multiple transgressions and boundary instabilities arise somehow from Bolling's self-hatred. As noted, his willingness to transgress class and gender boundaries in "Neanthe," by placing the suitors as firmly in the realm of the low as the woman, suggests, just as his subsequent attacks on the father of his first intended bride suggest, a powerful self-hatred: in "Neanthe," he implicitly placed his fellows and himself in the realm of lust for sex and property that neither he nor they could control and that made grotesque oafs of them; then, several years later, in the person of John Chiswell, he attacked and murdered the very lust after aristocracy that had earlier made a fool of him. Thus, in Bolling the transgression into their low is not so much a reunification of the masculine self with its sensual, bodily components as it is testimony of a deadly self-hatred. Was it this self-hatred that not only led to Chiswell's death but shattered Bolling's own heart at the age of thirty-six? The self-hatred and sense of failure expressed in his incursions into the low may also explain why Bolling, even more than Byrd, retains his fear of women, first occupants of the low and symbols of his failure, obscuring their genital areas with darkness or rendering them androgynous. And that fear of any but idealized women and the presence of these observed, androgynous females in the drawings may help us to understand in turn the overtones of the homosocial, if not the homosexual, in his writings and drawings. Among women, he found only enemies, whereas, if some men were enemies, others were close friends. Yet even on this level, the dilemma was recursive, for homosocial desire, if it had overtones of the homosexual, in turn implied an effeminacy that once again recalled his failures to construct himself as a gentleman, failures tinged with colonial, peripheral effeminacy. Bolling's mysterious notebook, even more than Byrd's "Female Creed," is a monument to a world we scarcely understand.

Troubled lives frequently yield great art. Bolling's art was to construct these emotions, himself, and his local culture in a public poetry that would smooth out its own troubled origins and give pleasure. The pressures on self-constructing gentlemen in Virginia were such that he did not always succeed. His triumph as an artist was that he often did.

I rank Robert Bolling with his predecessor William Byrd and with his contemporary, brother-in-law, and spiritual brother Thomas Jefferson as at once one of the supreme achievements of genteel self-construction in Virginia and as a symptom of the pressures of self-construction in that demanding environment.[55] I believe Byrd and Bolling were caught in the same recursive dilemmas of colonial self-construction, within which courtship and rejection were central and potentially traumatic occasions. In Thomas Jefferson's case, it was rather his mother's possession of resources during his minority that created a similar fury of obsessive but blocked self-construction. With Bolling, as in the other two instances, the misogynistic fury was quickly sublimated, but "Neanthe" and the fate of John Chiswell suggest that fury did not disappear from Bolling's life any more than from Byrd's or Jefferson's. Perhaps less so. In Bolling's case, the effort to put a smooth face on the fury with the mother country and implicitly with himself—a kind of colonial, mimetic fury—was even less successful, for he never quite matched the skill with which Byrd and Jefferson inverted their colonial furies with the mother country into their great legends of Virginia's superiority, simultaneously sublimating their self-loathing into self-glorification. Self-crafting in the colonial context could be a terrible task.

55. Again, for Jefferson, see primarily Lockridge, *Patriarchal Rage;* and see Isaac, "The First Monticello," Jan Lewis, " 'The Blessings of Domestic Society': Thomas Jefferson's Family and the Transformation of American Politics," and Lucia C. Stanton, "Those Who Labor for My Happiness: Thomas Jefferson and His Slaves," in Onuf, *Jeffersonian Legacies,* 77–108, 109–146, 147–180.

I do not claim that these three men are typical of their class. Generations of Virginia historians have done so, and indeed have raised them to epitomes of the plantation gentry. Perhaps it would be better to say that I also regard them as epitomes, but that an even better term would be "symptomatic." That is, I do not dispute that to some degree forces peculiar to each of these individuals made them the unusually driven self-constructors and mythmakers they so clearly are. Something in each man's childhood and youth made each the driven fabulist of the gentry experience that would make them all, to genteel historians, the epitomes of their class. What I do suggest is that these drives were also shaped by and expressed in ways revealing of the general pressures facing colonial self-constructors in Virginia. Thus, Byrd, Bolling, and Jefferson are symptomatic not only of their own individual histories but also of the problems of masculine self-construction in this class, place, and time. It remains to be seen to what degree other gentry, many less driven to fabulize, showed the same pressures and symptoms. But certainly if Byrd, Bolling, and Jefferson had their enemies, they also had their followers, then and now. To what wider needs did these men's fables speak?

Let me be clear then, that what I am attempting here is not a study of a peculiar man, or of his psychology, or of three peculiar men, Bolling, Byrd, and Jefferson, or of their psychologies. This is a study of the way three men, each, perhaps, with a peculiar psychology, each certainly unusually driven, intersect with the distortions genteel self-construction endures in a peripheral culture. This dramatic intersection produces two products, mythmaking and misogyny. I am after the way personal psychology and colonial culture combine to produce, in public writings, the myths of a Virginia gentry class—in Byrd and Jefferson—and to produce the mythic power of that culture's most self-conscious poet in Bolling's public writings. Their myths are the public product long regarded by historians as exemplary and as typical, and, indeed, as mythmakers these men, particularly Byrd and Jefferson, were variously witty, detached, imaginative, and creative, working nice variations on classic topics in order to liberate their class in a series of hard-won visions.[56] And I am after the way personal psychology and colonial culture produce, in private writings—the personal notebooks of all three men—a savage misogyny in which women become the metonymy of the metropolitan enemy responsible for their failure as colonial self-constructors and the symbol of the chaos and

56. See, particularly, two fine articles by Susan Manning, "The Pleasures of Indolence: James Thomson and William Byrd II," *Scottish Literary Journal*, XXI (1994), 39–54; and "Industry and Idleness in Colonial Virginia: A New Approach to William Byrd II," *Journal of American Studies*, XXVIII (1994), 169–190. For an earlier version of praises for Byrd's mythmaking, see Lockridge, *Diary, and Life*, 127–143.

effeminacy they feel this failure will entail in themselves. I am after, in an already gendered society—and racist and hierarchical—the wellsprings, in actual lives and events and in their intersection with the cultural politics of this milieu, from which gendering was renewed. And I believe that, in less-driven men, the same cultural dilemmas could produce milder versions of the same defensive mythologizing and of the same misogyny. How else can we explain the contemporary fame of such men as Byrd, Bolling, and Jefferson?

I would add that, if we want to know which other Virginia gentlemen were most likely to have shown the most intense desire to appropriate resources, control, and intellectuality from women and to have fetishized gender and been furious at women to the highest degree, we could do worse than to look at the list of impecunious but prominent gentlemen to whom in the 1750s and 1760s Speaker Robinson lent the public treasury. Alternately, we could look at those who, like Bolling, were either refused such loans or were too proud to ask for them. For, by Bolling and Jefferson's time, it is not the proud constructors at the top of the social order who need to construct themselves as intensely as William Byrd had a generation earlier. Rather, it is the downwardly mobile sons of the high gentry, such as Bolling, and upwardly mobile peripheral gentry, such as Jefferson, who are embarked on the hardest task of all, namely to break into the top ranks monopolized by the Robinson-Randolph-Chiswell-Byrd faction and *then* to create a gentility both accepted by Britain and yet not as aristocratic as the worst available local or British models. By "look," I mean look as closely as we have been able to look at Byrd, Bolling, and Jefferson.

v

Although perhaps few such men showed the full measure of misogyny and mythmaking seen in Byrd, Bolling, and Jefferson, it is fair to ask how many showed part of this reaction, namely misogyny. There is wider evidence that the steadily increasing requirements of genteel consumption and of genteel display and the recursive, narcissistic inability of male colonials to achieve true gentility no matter how much display was accomplished, taken together, perhaps, with growing skepticism of their social inferiors, bred an increasing misogyny in many eighteenth-century Virginia gentlemen and perhaps in their colleagues throughout the colonies. Misogyny arose widely because intensified display became an overcompensation for the cultural legitimacy that genteel colonials could never possess, because, before 1765 or so, economic and state growth failed to generate new resources from land or from office fast enough to meet the needs of display and because, in this context, inheriting women controlled or possessed the resources that alone seemed to offer these men any hope of secure gentility.

In a letter responding to this explanation of the dilemmas of colonial gentility, as initially developed in *Patriarchal Rage*, Ronald Hoffman offers his own Carrolls of Maryland as a striking example of this syndrome. The Carrolls reveal the degree to which women came to be associated with the problems of acquiring and maintaining genteel resources and the explicitness to which the associated misogyny could rise. The Carrolls saw the woman problem from an alternate perspective to that of obtaining resources through courtship. Charles Carroll of Annapolis (1702–1782) followed a strategy that regarded young women purely as reproductive resources. Prospective financial gain from a bride's inheritance and dowry, he seemed to feel, was counterbalanced by the larger threat that a man would die without a male heir, leaving his resources to leak out of the masculine line to the daughters and widow, who could then marry and carry these resources into another male line. Hence, the senior Charles Carroll, known to his son as "Papa," lived out of wedlock with a woman of lesser status until the son she produced was fully grown and educated. Although such a "wife" brought no financial assets to the family, she might produce sons and, because she was not by law a wife, was not a threat as a possible source of leakage of patriarchal resources through dowered inheritance claims. Similar cautious strategies can be found in European history, most notably in the republican city-states of Renaissance Italy, whose rising gentries, self-construction, culture, and misogyny are remarkably reminiscent of the American culture depicted here.[57]

The Carrolls' thoughts on women were quite explicit. As Hoffman observes, "[Papa] warned always about the dangers of widows carrying fortunes into 'strange families.'" Papa's son, Charles Carroll of Carrollton (1737–1832), "Charley," took these warnings to heart. In a letter to his father, he observed, "If I die young, which is not improbable as I am of a weak constitution, my widow may marry a second Husband and carry the greatest part of the estate

57. Ronald Hoffman to the author, June 12, 1992; and Ronald Hoffman, "Princes of Eile, Planters of Maryland: The Carroll Saga, 1500–1782." On women and inheritance in Italy, see Thomas Kuehn, "Some Ambiguities of Female Inheritance Ideology in the Renaissance," *Continuity and Change*, II (1987), 11–36; Maura Palazzi, "Female Solitude and Patrilineage: Unmarried Women and Widows during the Eighteenth and Nineteenth Centuries," *Journal of Family History*, XV (1990), 443–459. For related articles, see Eileen Spring, "Law and the Theory of the Affective Family," *Albion*, XVI (1984), 1–20. For other colonial settings, see Alida C. Metcalf, "Women and Means: Women and Family Property in Colonial Brazil," *Journal of Social History*, XXIV (1990), 277–298; and Patricia Seed, *To Love, Honor, and Obey in Colonial Mexico: Conflicts over Marriage Choice, 1574–1821* (Stanford, Calif., 1988).

into another family."[58] Women and resources are here again equated in a context where women are seen as necessary for male replication but—whether as a source of financial resources or as a source of leakage of these resources— are plainly difficult to control. The parallels with Byrd, potentially with Bolling, and with Jefferson as presented in *Patriarchal Rage* are obvious.

The Carrolls were Catholic as well as colonial, so the fragilities of their self-construction were doubled. It may be that they are a truly extreme example of the ways colonial self-fashioning produced misogyny. Yet Papa's willingness to live out the consequences of his warnings about women is striking. So is the explicitness of Charley's own language. Papa's association of women with money had further dimensions, for among his advice to his son was this:

> As to the Women of Town avoid them as you wou'd a Rattle Snake, by several Examples within my own knowledge they have proved as fatally nay almost as suddenly venemous, I have known some young men after as much time and Money spent on their Education as has been on yrs snatched from their Expecting Parents by the poison reced from Prostitutes, others I have known long to linger in a State of Rottenness and at last to die objects of horror.

Resources, aversion, sexuality, and dissolution mingle in a brew whose ingredients were foreseen but whose intensity and target were scarcely envisioned by Norbert Elias. Curiously, Thomas Jefferson later wrote a very similar letter.[59]

Hoffman also brings up a much more general phenomenon that extends far beyond the Carrolls, beyond Byrd, Bolling, and Jefferson, to illustrate what may be the threatened position of self-crafting patriarchs throughout much of late colonial America and to demonstrate further the ways in which their fragile position affected women. "It seems to me," he remarks, "that the pa-

58. Charles Carroll of Carrollton to Charles Carroll of Annapolis, Oct. 3, 1763, Carroll Papers, MS 206, n. 99, cited in Hoffman, "Princes of Eile," 320.

59. Charles Carroll of Annapolis to Charles Carroll of Carrollton, Oct. 6, 1759, Carroll-McTavish Papers, cited in Hoffman "Princes of Eile," 291; Thomas Jefferson to John Banister, Jr., Oct. 15, 1785, in Julian P. Boyd et al., eds., *The Papers of Thomas Jefferson*, VIII (Princeton, N.J., 1953), 635–637. Note that in this letter Jefferson himself is aware that his warning about a Europe characterized by "dissipation," most notably by "a spirit of female intrigue" and "a passion for whores destructive of [the] health," by adultery, and by the general "voluptuary dress and arts of the European women," involves excessive emotion on his part: "Did you expect so short a question to draw such a sermon on yourself? I dare say you did not. But the consequences of foreign education are alarming to me as an American. I sin therefore through zeal whenever I enter on the subject." Thus, to Jefferson as to Carroll, the only "chaste" women are American; that which is threatening in woman and which will dissolve a man's estate and being is placed primarily in Europe. Equally plainly, female seductiveness and desire could not be confined to Europe, for all Carroll's and Jefferson's efforts to place the threat "over there."

triarchal perspective you offer constitutes a useful way of looking at some of the probate research that has been the focus of the Chesapeake school for the last twenty-five years."

Certainly the eighteenth-century testamentary practices described and analyzed in several of the essays in *Women in the Age of the American Revolution* suggest a studied effort by men to extend patriarchal control. In general, the authors conclude that, as the eighteenth century wore on, sons did better at the expense of their mothers and sisters—instead of outright inheritances, widows got life estates which reverted at their deaths to their male rather than their female children. And even though inheritances shrank as a result of being divided among multiple sons, males—potential patriarchs, however paltry their domains—still got control of the property. It seems to me that these probate findings mesh with the patriarchal perspective to say something interesting about the late eighteenth-century family.[60]

The idea that many threatened self-constructors, desperate for the resources that they imagined would socially legitimate their male lines, would seek to control patriarchal resources by limiting the female inheritance of resources within the family is certainly consistent with the view of colonial self-fashioning presented here.

Greater restriction of female control of resources seems to have been the solution at both ends of the spectrum of gender risks faced by would-be gentlemen in colonial America, before marriage as well as after. Joan Hoff Wilson suggested back in 1979 that, in the late eighteenth century, courting men were successfully pressing women to surrender their dower rights, defined as their legal right during marriage to concur in decisions affecting the one-third of the husband's real estate they could reasonably expect to control as widows. By the early nineteenth century, the law itself was canceling these rights as outmoded relics of a past age.[61] The Carrolls in particular made their eventual wives—when they finally married them—surrender this right before marriage, and evidently many gentlemen managed to make this precaution prevail, some perhaps by adopting the Carroll strategy of marrying women lower on the social scale than themselves. Such women brought less to the marriage, but their dower rights during marriage as well as their inheritances,

60. Ronald Hoffman to the author, June 12, 1992. The probate research referred to appears or is cited in Ronald Hoffman and Peter J. Albert, eds., *Women in the Age of the American Revolution* (Charlottesville, Va., 1989).

61. Joan Hoff Wilson, "Hidden Riches: Legal Records and Women, 1750–1825," in Mary Kelley, ed., *Woman's Being, Woman's Place: Female Identity and Vocation in American History* (Boston, 1979), 7–25.

their administration rights after the husband's death, and perhaps their daughters' inheritances could more easily be limited. This strategy kept family resources securely under masculine control, in the male line, and out of the hands of the sorts of inheriting women who had made life hell for William Byrd, Robert Bolling, and Thomas Jefferson.

All the legal evidence together thus raises the possibility that an alternative system of marriage and resources was emerging, one quite different from that in which swarms of suitors buzzed around the few well-dowered daughters of rich men. That, after all, was a bitter experience for the suitors. Rejection was probable and, as the Carrolls discovered, rich fathers might insist on premarital agreements protecting the resources their daughters brought to marriage. Rich fathers certainly would not let their daughters surrender their legal dower rights to concurrent authority over one-third of the husband's real estate. Rich fathers would see to it that their daughters would inherit their husband's property whether they bore sons or not. But what about another strategy in which socially less-prominent and less-wealthy women, or women whose wealthy fathers did not want to commit great resources to female dowries, are sought out by men who can persuade such brides to forego premarital agreements and dower rights? The husbands thereby retain control both of whatever resources the bride brings to the marriage and of the legal dower right presumably destined by law for the widow. Such a strategy would imply as well efforts to restrict the leakage of patriarchal resources through inheritance to the widow, who might remarry. By also restricting dowries and inheritances to daughters, it would accomplish a similar end while perpetuating the system by providing low-dowered daughters for marriage to the next generation of men. This would be in all ways a strategy for maintaining masculine control of whatever resources did exist and for restricting rejections in courtship, though it meant trading the immediate assets that a well-dowered bride could bring for the long-run conservation of patriarchal resources as *masculine* property within the family. In his mundane second marriage, Robert Bolling, who had already inherited from his well-off first wife, may have been pursuing such a strategy to great advantage.[62]

62. Eileen Spring, *Law, Land, and Family: Aristocratic Inheritance in England* (Chapel Hill, N.C., 1993), suggests, in a revolutionary essay, that the famous "Strict Settlement" evolved among prominent families in England had already accomplished a similar strategy by permitting patriarchs to limit widows' rights and dowries while keeping most other property in the male line. As an alternate but parallel strategy, both in England and in the colonies, where men still pursued as brides women of family and of substance, the new cult of sensibility and of sentiment might have been the vehicle for getting women to agree to drop limits on the prospective husband's control of their estates and rights. There is an

Ronald Hoffman's remark on the existing legal evidence is provocative. If genteel self-construction in the colonies was widely subject to the kinds of whipsawing pressures for scarce resources and to the resultant misogynistic outbursts seen in the lives of William Byrd, Robert Bolling, and Thomas Jefferson, then the legal evidence should fall out exactly as it seems to, with evidence of increasing masculine efforts to arrange control of family resources, efforts ranging from courtship through marriage to probate and inheritance. Paul C. Nagel's book on the Lees, which depicts the young men of this family as infuriated with having to go to women for the resources with which to build gentility while watching resources already in the family leak out through mothers and sisters, leads us to the same expectations and evidence.[63] A study by Linda Lee Sturtz suggests that, in actual confrontations in the courts, women could have had a frustrating (for men) degree of success in maintaining their control of property in the face of male legal challenges under the law as it stood. The suppressed poetry of colonial misogyny found in the "Female Creed" and in Bolling's "To a Looking Glass" may have found its supreme expression in emerging marriage and inheritance practices by which some men sought to remasculinize property whenever possible within the framework of the law.[64]

The fact that patriarchal self-construction in the colonies and in Europe was threatened by the implications of the Enlightenment and by uncertainties over

---

engaging tale from Joy Day Buel and Richard Buel, Jr., *The Way of Duty: A Woman and Her Family in Revolutionary America* (New York, 1984), 82, which depicts Mary Fish as unwilling to insist on a premarital agreement by which she will retain control of the resources she herself will bring to the partnership. She seemed to feel that asking her suitor for such a legal protection would show mistrust of him as a prospective husband. If typical, this anecdote may explain why, save in South Carolina, we find few such premarital agreements in late colonial and early national America. It seems possible that the ideal of sentimental, companionate marriage might have served only to make it difficult for Mary Fish and for other women to insist on the legal protection of their initial property as well as of their legal dower rights as they entered marriage. See also Suzanne Lebsock, *The Free Women of Petersburg: Status and Culture in a Southern Town, 1784–1860* (New York, 1984).

63. Lockridge, *Patriarchal Rage*, 96; Paul C. Nagel, *The Lees of Virginia: Seven Generations of an American Family* (New York, 1990).

64. Linda Lee Sturtz, "Madame and Co.: Women, Property, and Power in Colonial Virginia" (Ph.D. diss., Washington University, St. Louis, 1994). But the difficulty of drawing conclusions from probate records about shifting practices within the areas left flexible by the law is notorious. See, for example, Amanda Vickery's comments in "The Neglected Century: Writing the History of Eighteenth-Century Women," *Gender and History,* III (1991), 211–219. Massive numbers may not be the way to approach the problem. Rather, as with the Lees and the Carrolls, we may need to reconstruct patterns of ambition, marriage negotiations, and inheritance family by family until the full range of strategies emerges. For an attempt nonetheless to unravel the relationship between aristocratic inheritance and gender conflict in England, see Spring, *Law, Land, and Family.*

patriarchal authority as well as locally by the specific insecurities of peripheral or colonial self-fashioners, may explain something more important than the steady appropriation of female wealth in local contexts, suggested here. It may explain the general masculine appropriation of new ideologies, such as the Enlightenment and the democratic revolution, by such clever self-crafters as William Byrd, Thomas Jefferson, and their European counterparts, but this latter is a Europe-wide phenomenon and so not one we need dwell on here.

VI

The implications of colonial self-construction developed in this almost psychological depth spin out surprisingly far. Think what a blessing the American Revolution was to men so plagued by the recursive dilemmas of colonial self-construction that they went into misogynistic rages that violated their claims to gentility. The Revolution replaced British contempt with American virtue. The rising hierarchy of British standards of genteel consumption and display was replaced by the low-cost image of a spartan gentry. A "manly" gentry.[65] No wonder the patriot gentry were euphoric! Jefferson's own love for muted luxury also indicates that, having exorcised their lust for possessions and gentility by symbolically killing the king, American gentlemen soon discovered that they had not come to terms with the fact that lust was still present in themselves. by intellectualizing and democratizing gentility, Jefferson showed post-Revolutionary gentlemen how to recast their luxuries, and their possessive self-constructions, in an acceptably republican style.[66] One doubts

65. These themes emerge in Bolling's manuscripts and published works in the years 1766–1770 (see references above) and are too familiar to bear repetition. But one wonders if the "killing the father" theme that appears alongside them (as in Jay Fliegelman, *Prodigals and Pilgrims: The American Revolution against Patriarchal Authority* [New York, 1982]), is not really the same thing: the king is not only the abusive father but the father who aspires to gentility, who has invited them to corrupt themselves with ambition while condemning them, through rejection, to colonial effeminacy and "slavery." Bolling's own agonies of desire and rejection suggest powerful motives for externalizing these conflicts in a father figure and executing him. The argument that the Revolution relieved the tensions of colonial inferiority was pioneered by Jack P. Greene; see his essays as collected in *Imperatives, Behaviors, and Identities: Essays in Early American Cultural History* (Charlottesville, Va., 1992).

66. Scholars are just beginning to see that this skill at "radical chic" is something Jefferson first encountered in a Paris of clearly impending revolution and that—for all his critical comments on European hierarchy and aristocracy—it quite bowled him over. Willard Sterne Randall suggests that Jefferson "brought back to the United States a sophisticatedly radical world view" and that he acquired this in very aristocratic company indeed;

whether, at first, this change greatly lessened patriot gentlemen's skepticism about women. Jefferson's life indicates that it did not.[67] But soon new sources of agricultural and industrial wealth opened up, so that inheriting women would at last escape some though not all of the immense pressures of genteel self-construction they had sustained. That construction itself became a sim-

---

see Randall, *Jefferson*, chaps. 15, 16, 17. I believe the central conception Jefferson acquired, in part from Lafayette, was the idea that a liberal, intellectualized aristocracy could lead and so survive the most powerful revolution. By 1784, when he arrived in Paris, Jefferson knew that the American Revolution had become far more democratic and popular than anyone had thought possible. He and Madison were already skilled at allying with such forces, notably with the evangelicals in Virginia, but Lafayette and others showed him how to combine liberal accommodation with aristocratic style in a new mode that included liberal, intellectualized, but still sumptuous libraries, dinner parties, and architecture. American gentlemen could survive as revolutionaries and still eat cake! The second Monticello, begun in 1794, was a crushingly expensive essay in conveying this radical-chic version of the aristocrat-as-liberal-intellectual in a medium that was not as flexible as rhetoric. It was all the more necessary because by then radical chic had failed Lafayette and his compatriots and the Terror had shown both them and Jefferson where that failure could lead. See Kenneth A. Lockridge, review of *Jefferson and Monticello: The Biography of a Builder*, by Jack McLaughlin, in *PMHB*, CXV (1991), 120–122. A superb book by Michael Dennis, *Court and Garden: From the French Hôtel to the City of Modern Architecture* (Cambridge, Mass., 1986), leaves no doubt that Jefferson's primary model for the new Monticello, the Hôtel du Salm, was an effort to replace the aristocratic Baroque hôtel marked by hierarchy and dependency with a still sumptuous pavilion posing as a one-story building and marked by personalism and egalitarianism. Dennis's opinion is that Jefferson adapted this still quite aristocratic "architecture of democracy" and brought it to America (136–158, 231 236). This architectural knowledge enables us to see the hidden agenda in Jefferson's entire intellectual project as well. Richard L. Bushman, *The Refinement of America: Persons, Houses, Cities* (New York, 1992), has a chapter on post-Revolutionary "Ambivalence" (181–203) that shows the strains on post-Revolutionary gentlemen as they tried to accommodate democracy yet maintain a quasi-aristocratic style of life. Jefferson brilliantly turned this post-Revolutionary ambivalence to synthesis by leading the way with his brand of radical chic. That is why he urged his styles and architecture so strenuously on others. For a parallel evolution in the area of rhetoric, see Jay Fliegelman, *Declaring Independence*. For an idea of just how aristocratic Jefferson's post-Revolutionary "aristocracy of merit" was, see Robert A. Gross "Educating a Citizenry: School and Society in the World of Thomas Jefferson" (paper presented to the Alumni College, College of William and Mary, Charlottesville, Va., June 26, 1993). Jefferson's pseudo-radicalism and inherent conservatism are nicely confirmed in James Oakes, "Was Madison More Radical than Jefferson?" *Journal of the Early Republic*, XV (1995), 649–655. See also note 10, above, and note 67 below; see also Gordon S. Wood, "The Trials and Tribulations of Thomas Jefferson," *Jeffersonian Legacies*, 395–417, esp. 410, 414.

67. In addition to the evidence of Jefferson's early and continuing misogyny offered in Lockridge, *Patriarchal Rage*, 47–73, there is his letter to Robert Skipwith, July 17, 1771, still recommending the same readings from which Jefferson had earlier (mis-)appropriated the

pler, native thing that soon faded into the bourgeois self-fashioning of the nineteenth century. It would be democracy and the specter of equal rights, rather than the impossible standards of a court society, that would threaten the bourgeois form of genteel self-construction. Although the future's more polite genderings would be in their way no less intense, this becomes a slightly different story, one I leave to Carroll Smith-Rosenberg, Linda K. Kerber, and E. Anthony Rotundo.[68]

Except in the South. For here slavery, and that region's eventual minority status in the new Republic, left some southern gentry with no options as they saw it but to continue to maintain a quasi-aristocratic gentility as the only proof of their superiority. And their superiority was the only justification for their peculiar institution. In isolation, with northern middle-class values eroding their constructions from within, they clung to a mythical version of a court society, one whose king was Walter Scott. It was no fiction where women and slaves were concerned, however. Stephanie McCurry has shown us that, although the North as an antitype nicely replaced the British court society as the machine driving this atavistic form of aristocratic self-construction, nonetheless, even more than in the eighteenth century, the fragile, misogynistic, exclusive gentleman's republicanism of the Italian city-state still reigned here as it had before the Revolution.[69] More than ever before everything rested upon a

---

fiercest of misogynistic quotes, and the letter to John Bannister, Jr., Oct. 15, 1785, treated in note 59, above. In a paper, "Jefferson and the Women of Paris," delivered at the 1993 meeting of the Western Society for French Studies, Elizabeth Marvick elaborates, with considerable evidence from the Parisian visit, the fear and mistrust of women, their sexuality and power, that had already marked and was to continue to mark Jefferson's life. This theme is touched on, as well, in the essays by Lewis, " 'The Blessings of Domestic Society,' " and Isaac, "The First Monticello," in Onuf, ed., *Jeffersonian Legacies,* 77–108, 109–146. Lewis in particular treats Jefferson's late decades. Evidence of Jefferson's continuing linguistic resort to the tropes of misogyny, compared with the absence of such usage in James Madison, can be found in Oakes, "Was Madison More Radical Than Jefferson?" *Journal of the Early Republic,* XV (1995), 649–655, specifically 652.

68. Carroll Smith-Rosenberg, "Domesticating Virtue: Coquettes and Revolutionaries in Young America," in Elaine Scarry, ed., *Literature and the Body: Essays on Populations and Persons* (Baltimore, 1989), 160–184; see also Smith-Rosenberg's unpublished "Federalist Capers: Reflections on the Nature of Political Representation and the Empowerment of the Political Subject," 1994, in which she treats the prior, inadvertent, further destabilizing of gender by urban-bourgeois political thinkers trying to ground their conservatism in pseudo-Revolutionary values; see Linda K. Kerber, "Separate Spheres, Female Worlds, Women's Place: The Rhetoric of Women's History," *Journal of American History,* LXXV (1988–1989), 9–39; and E. Anthony Rotundo, *American Manhood: Transformations in Masculinity from the Revolution to the Modern Era* (New York, 1993).

69. Stephanie McCurry, "The Two Faces of Republicanism: Gender and Proslavery

narrowly controlling, half-bourgeois, insecure form of hyper-masculine aristocratic gentility that rights for other men, for women, or for slaves threatened constantly to weaken. Controlling gender and race became for some southerners even more an obsession than in the eighteenth century. They were the last heirs of the civilizing process.

The world of genteel self-construction in early modern England and in her American colonies explains many things we have not understood. Misogyny is only one of these. This world speaks as eloquently of the very nature of the self under conditions of competition for gentility. What it tells us is not always attractive. George Washington's little copybook with precepts for the exact forms of bodily stance to adopt toward every class of superior and inferior, for example. We have seen him from the perspective of Samuel Smiles, as a kind of example of earnest American self-help. Certainly his earnestness was pathetic, but not pathetic in the mode of the nineteenth century, nor was his a nineteenth-century earnestness. Washington was entering a fierce and ruthless competition involving a total reconstruction of the self and the most intense pressures for the generation of resources in the face of metropolitan contempt. In this race, his constructions were as wooden as his teeth became, but the Revolution rescued him by needing such a figure, conveniently turning wood to marble. Still, Washington always saw where wealth lay. He married it and preserved it, and wealth would in any event have made up for a certain amount of clumsiness even had there been no Revolution. Jefferson, on the other hand, was the master. The exhibition at Monticello in 1993 shows that his standard of display was almost courtly, as Garry Wills noted in a review of the restored furnishings there. His compulsive need for display, the conflict between his heart and head, always won by the head, and between the Enlightenment and romanticized retreats, even his fury and misogyny were all transposed into a flood of the most beautiful language. He could manipulate the new conventions of democracy so as only to increase his own noblesse, as it became the nobility that obliges. He stuttered only once, in reconstructing Monticello on the French model of an aristocracy living in houses that were pavilions of the liberal intellect yet were subtly rich and imposing withal. Putting such noblesse oblige into the vocabulary of bricks and mortar required the most expensive revisions, yet, compulsively, Jefferson continued trying. He died successfully constructed in all media, but bankrupt.[70] I also ask myself, how much of the

---

Politics in Antebellum South Carolina," *Journal of American History*, LXXVIII (1991–1992), 1245–1264.

70. Charles Moore, ed., *George Washington's Rules of Civility and Decent Behaviour in*

murderous savagery used to distance the lesser classes in England can we read back into those times? Do we see Jefferson shifting it from the newly sacrosanct American yeoman onto his slaves?[71]

I don't mean it to end this way, but, insofar as pathology is an issue with which we started, we could return to it now. Jefferson is as good a subject as any, though my primary discussion of him is in *Patriarchal Rage* and not here. What strikes me about Rhys Isaac's lovely essay on him in *Jeffersonian Legacies*, and about Gordon Wood's review of the same book in the *New York Review of Books*, is that we are still in the "paradox" stage.[72] Both scholars still seem to be saying "how paradoxical Jefferson was to speak of liberty and to use Indians as examples of American superiority while in fact manipulating and controlling his family, subtly degrading women, degrading Indians severely, and disciplining his slaves with harsh punishments." Although I do not necessarily want to tumble all the way into pathology as a substitute, I would have hoped that by now we were well beyond astonishment at such supposed paradoxes. Jefferson is nothing if not a landmark in the career of genteel self-construction in America. His manipulative hunger to digest all material into his self-construction, his cleverness at substituting intellectual display for the display of luxuries he could not afford and in democratizing aristocratic gentility—these are part and parcel of more traditional strategies in his self-construction, including fury at women who deny him resources, a desire to keep women clean and

---

Company and Conversation (Boston, 1926), as discussed in Bushman, *The Refinement of America*, 39, 46; see Garry Wills's review, "The Aesthete," *New York Review of Books*, Aug. 12, 1993, 6–9. See references in note 66, above, to substantiate the rest of this passage.

71. See Stanton, "Those Who Labor for My Happiness," in Onuf, ed., *Jeffersonian Legacies*, 147–180. Whether displaced from the yeomanry or not, there is little doubt that the fury of driven and vulnerable self-constructors *did* descend upon slaves as well as upon women. A look at Landon Carter's diary will suffice; see Jack P. Greene, ed., *The Diary of Colonel Landon Carter of Sabine Hall, 1752–1778*, 2 vols. (Charlottesville, Va., 1965).

See also Gordon S. Wood, *The Radicalism of the American Revolution* (New York, 1992). Wood leads us to see how profoundly old-régime the mentality and to some degree the actuality of pre-Revolutionary America was. Wood's book stands as proof of Elias's applicability to pre-Revolutionary America and explains as nothing else can the behaviors we see in Byrd, in Bolling, and in Jefferson.

In an unpublished essay, "Soul Murder and Slavery: Toward a Fully-Loaded Cost Accounting," Nell Irvin Painter offers an account of the pressures of 19th-century planter self-construction like that offered here for the 18th century. She suggests that these pressures, combined with the willfulness and physical aggression indulged in against slaves, ultimately produced abuse of slaveowners' wives and children in a single syndrome of pressure and violence.

72. Rhys Isaac, "The First Monticello," in Onuf, ed., *Jeffersonian Legacies*, 77–108; Gordon S. Wood, "Jefferson at Home," *New York Review of Books*, May 13, 1993, 6–9.

under control, and the necessity of fetishizing and dichotomizing women and other races into a lesser realm where incontinency, the bodily, and the sexual reign and terrify. His ability to control women, slaves, and Indians is the figuration of his ability to control himself as well as the literal substance of commanding those resources on which the self-constructions of his own class are based. Having done so, he can then colonize them again as he does with Indians as examples of American superiority. From this point of view, Jefferson appears as just a variant—albeit a brilliant one—on the themes of colonial self-construction already established by William Byrd and Robert Bolling. I see no paradoxes here. I do see something that might be called pathology.

Pathology is a problematic word to use. On one level I mean it only to stand for the sense that all intense cultural (self) constructions carry their own twists and turns. On another level, I mean pathology in the sense that Byrd's, Bolling's, and Jefferson's efforts at genteel self-construction could be dysfunctional in their own terms. By his own admission, Byrd's vulnerabilities and hysterias repeatedly frustrated his own purposes. Bolling's attacks on Chiswell and Botetourt surely made him feared, even despised, and Chiswell's death evidently led him to go back and put a seal of secrecy on his own churning emotions as found in the "Hilarodiana." Jefferson stuttered himself into bankruptcy by trying to get his own democratic version of aristocratic self-construction built as architecture. Others made off with the entire public treasury of Virginia. William Byrd III committed suicide. Robert Carter threw over the whole effort and fled to the Baptists. Charles Carroll of Carrollton had to behave with almost perfect obedience to secure his inheritance and suffered agonies from which he never recovered in being exiled to Europe to acquire genteel skills and patina. Landon Carter fulminated endlessly at his family and his slaves alike.[73] How much evidence do we need before we conclude that colonial self-construction defeated its own ends frequently and sometimes spectacularly? Finally, I mean pathology in the modern and ahistorical sense that, from our point of view, the extreme fetishes of genteel self-creation and display, the savage distancing from the sensual self, and the intense misogyny and racism that could be part and parcel of self-construction, and evidently especially so in the colonies, are today becoming humanly and politically unacceptable.

It is not so extreme to play with the notion of a colonial pathology, or even of hysteria. Bernard Bailyn's career has been devoted largely to the ways in which peripheral status created educational frenzies and political paranoias

73. See Lockridge, *Diary, and Life*, 154–159, and notes for William Byrd II and William Byrd III, Robert Carter, Landon Carter, and for the appropriation of the treasury; see also note 71, above, for Landon Carter; see text and notes, above, for Charles Carroll of Carrollton.

on the far margins of the British cultural system. I see this essay's suggestions in that tradition. That is, I see similar processes distorting genteel self-construction, rather than merely education or politics, in the American colonies. I am willing to face a possibility Gordon Wood has argued, that the metropolitan model of any of these distorted processes might have had its own peculiarities, if not pathologies, so that it can be a fine-run thing to tell the pathologies of the original from those unique to the copy.[74] In *Patriarchal Rage*, I discuss several crises of patriarchy that might have been broadly European rather than specifically American, not least of which is that socially peripheral self-constructors were in crisis within the metropolitan countries themselves, for such was the nature of the competition under way. Further, Gail Kern Paster and others have linked Elias's civilized personality to the effort of the emerging European state to control its subjects and specifically its female population, so for this reason, as well, a "civilizing" misogyny was not necessarily only a colonial product. Lawrence Stone has posited a crisis of gender relations within English genteel families around the turn of the eighteenth century.[75] Any of these might be what we see operating in Byrd, Bolling, and Jefferson. Yet that is why I value Byrd and Bolling so much. For neither leaves any doubt that a specifically colonial rage is also at work in his more distorted moments. The fact that Byrd's diary is unique for its perceptual rigidity and compulsiveness among all known English diaries of the period, that Bolling's "Neanthe" is exceptional even by British standards, and that he was implicated in Chiswell's suicide certainly raises the possibility that such distortions of the genteel image were unusually intense or were found associated with furious colonials with an exceptional frequency. While this troubled colonial self-construction was perhaps one of many marginal variations that to some degree resembled the wider European process, it seems troubled indeed.

74. Bernard Bailyn, *Origins of American Politics* (New York, 1968); Bailyn, *Education in the Forming of American Society: Needs and Opportunities for Study* (Chapel Hill, N.C., 1960); Bailyn, "New England and a Wider World: Notes on Some Central Themes of Modern Historiography," in *Seventeenth-Century New England* (Publications of the Colonial Society of Massachusetts, *Collections*, LXIII [Boston, 1984]), 323–328; Gordon S. Wood, "Conspiracy and the Paranoid Style: Causality and Deceit in the Eighteenth Century," *WMQ*, 3d Ser., XXXIX (1982), 401–441.

75. Lockridge, *Patriarchal Rage*, 88–90, 103–108; Paster, *The Body Embarrassed*, i–63, and I thank Katherine Eggert and Charlotte Sussman of the Department of English at the University of Colorado, Boulder, for demonstrating to me how much of the phenomenon considered here could be European rather than specifically colonial; Lawrence Stone, *Uncertain Unions: Marriage in England, 1660–1753* (Oxford, 1992); Keith Thomas, "The View from the Keyhole," *New York Review of Books*, Nov. 4, 1993, 22–24; and Stone, *Broken Lives: Separation and Divorce in England, 1660–1857* (Oxford, 1993), 28–29. Stone may draw support from Spring, *Law, Land, and Family*.

Yet, if I do embrace the word "pathology" to describe our colonials' behavior, it is only very tentatively, and I do not want to take this word to its logical conclusion in postmodernist discourse. You will notice that references to Jacques Derrida, Jacques Lacan, Roland Barthes, Jean Baudrillard, Julia Kristeva et al. are by and large missing from the footnotes. My desk is covered in them, and in some cases they are revealing and appropriate. But I have chosen not to take this theoretical line, descending instead from Elias through the theoretically powerful Stallybrass and White to things we are all more familiar with, for three reasons. One, I am a poor theoretician. Two, ornamental footnotes vulgarizing these theoreticians have become the new form of self-construction, one I wish to avoid lest I be obliged to deconstruct it as well. Three, I am concerned that it is above all some of the American descendants of the postmodernist theoretical line who are creating what—in an uncharacteristic burst of honesty around 1989 or 1990—many of them acknowledged was an "over-determined" interpretive space. There is a feminist version of this same space. In such spaces, all is known in advance, every critical pyrotechnic leads us back with a chilling inevitability to the conclusion that Western culture has constructed the world by segregating the other on the basis of race, class, and gender.

There is a powerful truth in this body of theory, and you can see clearly that I participate in it. On the Virginia scene, a divided subjectivity increasingly characteristic of high civilization in the West is deploying class, race, and gender simultaneously, both constituting and dividing itself by mobilizing categories of the other that are in fact as much categories of the self. All of that is taking place in a peripheral, and specifically colonial, context steeped in contradictions and slippages that make the process of civilizing more unstable and more difficult. Our practitioners of gentrification are at once metropolitan and colonial. As colonials, they are feminized victims of metropolitan contempt even while they become also hypermasculinized patriarchs or revolutionaries in their efforts to evade that contempt. They deploy race and gender with unusual intensity in order to distance categories in which, in the metropolitan mind, as colonials they may be included, and only succeed in dividing their own subjectivities the more intensely as a result. They then struggle to cross in various and self-serving ways the very boundaries they must so energetically maintain. Colonized and colonizers, effeminate and masculine, they are divided within, and their reunification with that which might be called race and gender in themselves takes peculiar, unstable, sometimes self-serving forms. Nor is class itself a stable concept, for, at least by Robert Bolling's time, the specter of the bourgeois, itself unstable, tempts and haunts these would-be gentlemen continually. The Revolution relieves some of these contradictions and slippages only to create still others. It is a world I find as bewildering as I believe they often did. But I object to the self-constructing and obscuring displays of theoretical "knowledge" often found along the way to such realizations. Above all, I object to the sense of inevitability with which this body of theory is sometimes applied, and to its formulaic application without regard to the politics, complexity, and surprises of each local instance.[76]

What I would like to ask is that we keep the problematic of historical writing alive. By "problematic" I mean a sense that, in the contrapuntal weavings of race, class, and gender through an evolving early modern colonial culture, much is to be learned that we do not know, that sources of understanding are available, together with the unexpected, sources of surprise, of awe, of pity and compassion.[77] Many of us, I think, feel this way, and there is a wonderful article by Nancy Partner in *Speculum*, which makes the very same plea.[78] In this perspective, it is not where Byrd, Bolling, and Jefferson are going that concerns me. In the largest sense, I know where they are going in terms of race, class, and gender. Historically speaking, what concerns me is how they got there. In their surprising twists and turns within the tropes of self-fashioning, I sense, as I can in no other way, what it was, and is, to be human. For this reason alone, in fact, I am glad to surrender the use of the word pathology.

My ultimate plea is a simple one. I wonder that we have so easily accepted that carefully wrought, smooth surface that our colonial gentlemen have presented to us. I wonder that we have not seen, by its very smoothness, that it was an artifact and asked how it was wrought. I wonder what investment our predecessors made in their subjects' easy and affable gentility that was really an investment in their own. I wonder that a man who wrote the most peculiarly codified diary in the English and possibly in the European tradition, and who wrote one of the most vicious essays on women, could be regarded simply as a moderately sensual gentleman. Perhaps it is not time for pathologies, but—and it is a point to which this volume attests—it is certainly time to grow out of this business of paradox, a halfway house by which we still cling to something of our subjects' unalloyed, unexamined gentility. I am not asking that their joys—

76. I thank Carroll Smith-Rosenberg for making these contradictions and slippages in gender and class positions clear to me and for related references.

In broadest perspective, to give an example of my point here, Virginia is a special case of the colonial psychology described in Ashis Nandy, *Intimate Enemy: Loss and Recovery of Self under Colonialism* (Delhi, 1983). But in Virginia, "race" is far more complex, as *European* colonists are arbitrarily "black" in English eyes and displace the resultant fury and self-hatred onto women, Africans, and Indians. Each case is different.

77. For example, see Kathleen M. Brown, *Good Wives, Nasty Wenches, and Anxious Patriarchs: Gender, Race, and Power in Colonial Virginia* (Chapel Hill, N.C., 1996).

78. Nancy F. Partner, "No Sex, No Gender," *Speculum*, LXVIII (1993), 419–443.

the good marriages, the romps in the sun, the loved children, their local pride—
be surrendered, nor that their humanity be abandoned. Nor do I wish to
obscure the fact that there were many voices at work in this society. But I want
my histories and my lives whole. My plea is for American scholars to rise above
parochialism, and above erecting their own gentility in any form, into the
brilliant world of historical and literary scholarship in early modern Europe,
where alone our nation's early gentlemen find their true, multiple, and multivalent contexts, and by use of which alone we can explain their uniqueness.

Histories so informed, steering between current mythologies, unite us with
our European past and, in a postcolonial world, link us with nations everywhere. If we do not understand the sun toward which these colonials turned,
the compulsions and twistings that could be evolving in the colonial setting,
and the peculiar ways gender entered into this system, we can never have a
proper compassion for them, for their wives or their slaves, for ourselves, or
for anyone else.

PART III: REFLECTIONS
ON DEFINING SELF

REFLECTIONS ON DEFINING SELF

Early America reached out to the Central Pacific for a brief moment in 1814. Lieutenant David Porter learned that the inhabitants of "Madisonville" on the islands he called Washington (but more ordinarily are called the Marquesas Islands) "have requested to be admitted into the great American family whose pure republican polity approaches so near their own." Porter took it upon himself to admit them and to assure them that "our chief will be their chief." "Our Chief," President James Madison, was not so enthusiastic and was reported as saying that he had enough Indians of his own already. So the excursion into empire was short-lived.

The characteristics of empire building were not so short-lived, however. Commenting on a search-and-destroy campaign against the Taipi (better known to a later American public as the "Typee" among whom Melville sojourned), Porter had this to say: "Wars are not always just, and are rarely free from excesses. However I may regret the harshness with which motives of self-preservation, that operate everywhere, compelled me to treat these high-spirited and incorrigible people, my conscience acquits me of any injustice; and no excesses were committed, but what the Typees had it in their power to stop by ceasing hostilities. . . . Had no opposition been made, none would have been killed."[1]

The sea, in a sense, was the true marchlands of early America, east in the Atlantic and west in the Pacific. The sea was a marchlands because its ambivalences gave no guarantee that either civilization or savagery would prevail. Few of the ordinary rituals of extension of state power and authority that had engaged Europe in the civilizing process from the fifteenth to the eighteenth century worked out of sight of land. The protocols of making the sea "as if" it were the land were still being elaborated in early America. Letters of marque and reprisal were a key element in these charades. Letters of marque defined as lawful what otherwise was unlawful piracy. Of course, the letters were not just pieces of paper that, in hand, might save a privateer from being hanged as a pirate or legitimate looting, robbery, and murder. They were backed by all the legal paraphernalia of contracts, investment, adjudication of prize money, admiralty courts, and modern shipbuilding technology in the enterprise sys-

1. David Porter, *Journal of a Cruise Made to the Pacific Ocean . . . in the United States Frigate Essex, in the Years 1812, 1813, and 1814*, 2d ed., 2 vols. (New York, 1822), II, 79, 99–100.

tem. Privateering was a sort of legalized derring-do that lent a theatrical air to adventure capitalism in the Pacific and Atlantic.

There are two sides to an understanding of marchlands. The one is the behavioral reality of the marchlands with which Bailyn is primarily and revisionistically concerned. The behavioral reality was ugly and silent. The other, more hindsighted and rationalizing, is theatrical and exuberant. Michael Nerlich called attention to it in his *Ideology of Adventure*.[2] Nerlich explained a seeming paradox: the mythologizing needs of free enterprise, which were experienced in the glorification of the chevalier and hidalgo and the romanticizing of the gambles of merchant adventurers, called on narratives that both sustained civic virtue and made a virtue out of the brutality and mayhem of free spirits. "Adventure" is a marvelous word and worth Nerlich's two volumes of explanation of its meanings and consequences. Perhaps "derring-do" might be a better word to characterize the self being defined in the marchlands of the sea. "Derring-do" is a word as old as Chaucer. There is enough mocking playfulness in it to suggest that the heroic rhetoric of adventure might hold some ironies.

From the perspective that I take on early America—from the sea around it— the violence inherent in trade and territoriality among other and indigene peoples is sustained by a spirit of derring-do. Derring-do is the cultural thespianism that makes the ugliness of the marchlands look something different. That would be my contribution to reflections on defining self.

A modern translation of 1 Cor. 13:12, "For now we see through a glass darkly," reads: "For now we are seeing a dim reflection in a mirror."[3] Narcissus is our cultural and mythological warning on what too much reflection will do. But we should remember that Narcissus was running away from Echo at the time. There is not much to choose between plagiarist repetition and vain self-display. On the whole, however, historians would seem to prefer to be reflective rather than theoretical. Historians seem more comfortable with a narrative that is full of images, contextualizing events and characters within the narrative itself, shaping analytical concepts rather than operationalizing them in an anticipatory model.

These four essays on defining self, then, are reflections on reflections. They are reflective histories on the reflective moments in which self is defined. John Dewey made a distinction between "experience" and "an experience."[4] Reflection made the difference. "An experience" turns us back on ourselves, makes us

2. Michael Nerlich, *Ideology of Adventure: Studies in Modern Consciousness, 1100–1750* (Minneapolis, Minn., 1987).

3. *The Jerusalem Bible* (New York, 1966).

4. John Dewey, *Art as Experience* (1934; reprint, New York, 1980), 35.

sensitive to the authorship of what we do, creates theater and catharthis, enlightenment. The flow of living, personal and social, is given pulse by these reflective moments. They might be moments of ritual, or crisis, or memory, of empowerment or disempowerment, or of art. They might be calendric and regular. They might come out of happenchance or disaster. They can be "traditional," in Dilthey's sense of the word: the reflection in them makes us scan the past to see similarity with the present.[5] They are rarely replicative: they are rarely Echo. And insofar as structure is conceived as an imposed template on living, they are rarely structural. There is always a way in which "an experience" is new, invented by the reflection in it and on it.

Of all the historians in this volume, Philip Greven has the right to be reflective. The very writing of *The Protestant Temperament* (1977) and *Spare the Child* (1991) has been "an experience" for him. His essay itself is a historical document. He looks at himself in the mirror of his work and sees the ways in which the past and present reflect and refract one another. He cannot escape his discovery that the self is defined in an early America (and a later one, too) by violent rebirths. "I have begun to govourn Sally," Esther Edwards Burr reported of her ten-month-old daughter. "She has been whip'd once on *Old Adams* account and she knows the difference between a smile and a frown as well as I do." Child abuse, be it emotional, verbal, physical, or sexual, Greven argues, creates a permanent mixture of negative adult feelings that survives through generations. The advantages of a historian's reflection on defining self as against a psychiatrist's or social psychologist's is that a historian can review whole lives, not just transient partialities of the present.

Elaine Forman Crane alerts us to an issue that most historians find impossible to handle, the history of feelings. It should be no surprise that historians find it difficult to find measurements of difference in something as immeasurable as pain. It is the normality of pain that Crane discovers as a defining force of self. The ambiguities that unrelievable pain created—"God's method of behaviour modification," Crane suggests—left a sense of ambivalence, shame, and guilt. Or it could justify being one's real self, free of the bonds of systems that said she or he should be otherwise. Men and women were expected to suffer differently. Pain was "an experience" that discovered gender. The litany of suffering from which one had no relief in the eighteenth century is long. Crane muses at one point on how the language to describe such extensive and diverse pain is so ordinary and sparse. Words fail, it seems, when there is only self and God to blame.

Richard White takes us to the "middle ground" between Algonquian and

5. Wilhelm Dilthey, *Selected Writings*, ed. H. P. Rickman (Cambridge, 1976), 203.

Jesuit, between "Indian" and "French." Such middle ground is a true limen. It is an in-between social space that prompts reflection on self and other. In that limen all sorts of polarities are unsafe: self/person, feelings/reason, life/death, guilt/innocence. In such an in-between space, the definition, the defining, and the thing defined are each "multiple realities." White asks: What is self in such a space? To answer the question, he strikes a distinction between self (the auto-conscious agent) and person (the socially constructed being). Across cultures, self and person mix differently. Cross-cultural encounters inevitably sparked conversations and conflict about who people were and who they would become. So it became possible for a Jesuit priest and an Indian warrior to remake themselves. Identity being so malleable, it is possible "to be dead but not entirely so" and to appreciate how that could be true.

W. Jeffrey Bolster reflects on the dynamics of self-definition in conditions where self would seem—and had assumed to have been—degraded. He discovers a diasporic spirit among slave sailors. A resonant cultural heritage out of Africa, occupational mastery over their sailing skills, experience of otherness in their travels—especially of black freedom—made for an independent identity despite the strong forces of slavery and racial oppression. These are the ways tradition invented a cultural self. Ironically, although white seamen in a white world were being marginalized and deprived, black seamen in an enslaved society were given privileged status as possessing a new self shaped by old and new experiences alike.

The experiences inviting reflection in "Reflections on Defining Self" are qualitative rather than eventful. In an early America in which hegemonic and explicit religious belief was in an intervening God who graced and shaped individual lives in a period of trials and then rewarded or punished eternally, there was some urgency in bonding oneself rightfully. An experience of a willful self in one's own person or in others for whom one was responsible sparked all sorts of reflections on how to master and direct that self. Philip Greven's reflections on these reflections seem pertinent to today as well as yesterday. The problem of evil is as old as the belief in a God who is good. How early America coped with the evil of unrelievable pain is Elaine Crane's reflection. It is not so much the mystifying otherness of the supernatural that prompts Richard White's and Jeffrey Bolster's reflections. It is the otherness experienced across and within cultural boundaries. They discover that the experience of otherness itself creates a sense of malleability in self. They catch a freedom in self-definition that any over-socialized model of the human self might miss.

There are other looking glasses. White rabbits disappear through some: probably a theorist in disguise. There are halls full of funny mirrors, too: postmodernist halls, perhaps. Reflections can be very bright, and are blinding for that. Reflections can be dim, "through a glass darkly." In an age of hype, spectacle, and frenetic certainties, to feel satisfied with such dim perceptions might seem a little unambitious. Those who have not seen themselves in a mirror dimly, however, have not seen themselves at all.

Greg Dening

THE SELF SHAPED AND MISSHAPED:
THE PROTESTANT TEMPERAMENT
RECONSIDERED

Philip Greven

When I began, more than twenty years ago, to do the research that ultimately became *The Protestant Temperament: Patterns of Child-Rearing, Religious Experience, and the Self in Early America* (1977), I discovered that the life
experiences of early Anglo-Americans revealed a set of common themes that
pivoted on the issue of the self. Accordingly, my book was organized around
three modes of being: one suppressed the self, another controlled the self, and
the third asserted the self—ways of being that I associated with evangelicals,
moderates, and the genteel. Although I created the categories, the divergent
senses of selfhood were embedded in the sources for anyone to observe and to
fathom.

The three distinctive forms of selfhood explored in *The Protestant Temperament* were present continuously in the Anglo-American world for more than
two centuries, with varying concentrations, to be sure, but always vocal and
always visible.[1] No aspect of people's being failed to bear the imprint of these
different designs of selfhood. Neither time nor space mattered, for these distinctive forms of self recurred in the transatlantic community throughout this
entire period and beyond. Why was this so?

My central discovery was that the theological and religious doctrines and
beliefs that set people apart—and that historians have studied at length—
corresponded to aspects of their life experiences that most historians ignore:
the earliest and most formative experiences of childhood. Virtually all twice-
born Protestant Christians talked and wrote repetitively about the human
will's being broken and unfree. Their theologies elaborated their preoccupa-
tions with issues such as predestination, divine sovereignty, and free grace.
Moderates and the genteel, on the other hand, were confident that human wills

---

1. For another nonchronological analysis of early American patterns of behavior and
belief, see David Hackett Fischer, *Albion's Seed: Four British Folkways in America* (New York,
1989). Fischer examines child-rearing and other topics regionally.

were free to make choices and thus focused upon the process of transformation and the gradual growth of grace. The issues concerning the will that obsessed many Protestants—whether it was free or not, whether it was possible to be saved by acting on one's own behalf, or whether one must await the gift of free grace—were doctrinal issues that divided people profoundly for more than two centuries on both sides of the Atlantic. Significantly, these were also issues grounded in the innermost realms of experience and feeling rooted in the very core of people's sense of self formed in childhood and youth.

CHILDHOOD, CHARACTER, AND PIETY:
PURITANS, EVANGELICALS, AND OTHERS

The discovery that childhood experiences made theology explicable psychologically as well as intellectually troubles many historians. For example, at the outset of his book *God's Caress: The Psychology of Puritan Religious Experience* (1986), Charles Lloyd Cohen notes that, although *The Protestant Temperament* promises "to establish the connections between the way in which parents raise their young and the devotional stances their children adopted," it fails to take into account that "the sources of individual experience are also those that provide information about child-rearing; the people who enunciate their religiosity are the same ones who tell how they raised their own brood."[2] Although it is true that a lack of documents written by children about their experiences means that everything known about childhood reflects the beliefs, values, and experiences of adults, Cohen neglects to note that adults report both upon their own memories of childhood and their observations as parents. We do not know what Sally Burr, age ten months, felt or thought when being corporally punished by her mother Esther Edwards Burr, but we do know what Esther said on February 28, 1755, after she decided to whip her infant child: "I had almost forgot to tell you [Sarah Prince] that I have begun to govourn Sally. She has been Whip'd once on *Old Adams* account, and she knows the differance betwen a smile and a frown as well as I do."[3] We also know, however, that Sally Burr was but one of countless numbers of children on both sides of the Atlantic who were whipped, spanked, and beaten. If we deny these realities, we falsify the past in a profoundly consequential way.

2. Charles Lloyd Cohen, *God's Caress: The Psychology of Puritan Religious Experience* (New York, 1986), 18.
3. Carol F. Karlsen and Laurie Crumpacker, eds., *The Journal of Esther Edwards Burr, 1754–1757* (New Haven, Conn., 1984), 95. Also quoted in Philip Greven, *The Protestant Temperament: Patterns of Child-Rearing, Religious Experience, and the Self in Early America* (New York, 1977), 35–36.

The realization that theology mirrors the lived experiences of people with uncanny accuracy led me to use discipline for children as the pivot for constructing a typology of self in the three modes that I explored. Evangelicals consistently sought to break their children's wills, moderates preferred to bend their wills, and many genteel parents were content to let their children's wills be expressed freely.[4]

Accumulating evidence has confirmed my belief in the varieties of modes of discipline—from extremely severe to extremely indulgent or negligent. Lawrence Stone's massive study *The Family, Sex, and Marriage in England, 1500–1800* (1977) provides historians with an immense array of examples of child-rearing attitudes and practices over the course of three centuries. Although emphasizing change rather than continuity, his work confirms the recurrence of severe and authoritarian modes as well as gentler and permissive modes and indicates the persistence of both harsh and benign forms of upbringing among the middling ranks of English society.

Specifically, Stone argues that English methods of rearing and disciplining children altered over the course of the eighteenth and early nineteenth centuries, with middle-class parents becoming more affectionate and much gentler in the raising of their children. "There can be no doubt that between 1660 and 1800 there took place major changes in child-rearing practice among the squirarchy and upper bourgeoisie. Swaddling gave way to loose clothing, mercenary wet-nursing to maternal breast-feeding, breaking the will by force to permissiveness, formal distance to empathy, as the mother became the dominant figure in the children's lives."[5] Stone actually perceives the presence of six distinctive patterns of child-rearing during this period but focuses upon the

4. See also David Leverenz, *The Language of Puritan Feeling: An Exploration in Literature, Psychology, and Social History* (New Brunswick, N.J., 1980), 71–72; and John Putnam Demos, *Entertaining Satan: Witchcraft and the Culture of Early New England* (New York, 1982), 396. Readers of my book *Spare the Child: The Religious Roots of Punishment and the Psychological Impact of Physical Abuse* (New York, 1991) will discover that the practice of breaking children's wills has remained a constant part of evangelical and fundamentalist Protestant doctrine and parenting from the early 17th century to the end of the 20th century. Children's wills are still being broken today. Continuity, not change, is the key here.

5. Lawrence Stone, *The Family, Sex, and Marriage in England, 1500–1800* (New York, 1977), 447–448. However, the evidence from British "public" schools in the 19th and early 20th centuries provides abundant evidence of the persistence of corporal punishments as the ordinary and often brutal method of discipline for boys; see Ian Gibson, *The English Vice: Beating, Sex, and Shame in Victorian England and After* (London, 1978); and Jonathan Gathorne-Hardy, *The Public School Phenomenon, 1597–1977* (London, 1977). Also see Gathorne-Hardy's marvelous and underappreciated study of British discipline and child-rearing, *The Unnatural History of the Nanny* (New York, 1973). Physical punishments and other nasty methods of disciplining upper-class boys are amply evident in these books.

most permissive mode. His evidence is generally consistent with the evidence that I delineated for both moderates and the genteel, although he does not draw such a sharp distinction between these types of upbringing and discipline.

What is remarkable is that two scholars arrived concurrently yet independently at the conclusion that between three and six distinctive patterns of child-rearing and discipline were to be found in England and the American colonies throughout the seventeenth and eighteenth centuries. Moreover, *The Protestant Temperament* and Lawrence Stone's *Family, Sex, and Marriage* offer readers today something quite different from what they seemed to offer historians when they first appeared. Both books now can be read as case studies in alternative methods of rearing and disciplining children. Both books explore the diverse ways in which a person's sense of self is shaped and misshaped as a result of various degrees of pain, fear, anxiety, and suffering or, alternatively, love, nurture, respect, and guidance experienced in childhood. Both books implicitly explore a disciplinary continuum that ranges from severe violence to no violence, from much pain to little or no pain, from total control to virtually no control.

Having spent the past decade analyzing the practice of corporal punishment and its psychological and social consequences and subsequently writing *Spare the Child: The Religious Roots of Punishment and the Psychological Impact of Physical Abuse* (1991), I realize now that the rod and other forms of physical punishments that Stone explores in the context of England also were commonplace throughout most of the colonies, with profound consequences for the shaping and misshaping of both individual psyches and selves and collective behaviors and beliefs. Having examined in some depth the impact of corporal punishment upon the psyche, life, and writings of the Reverend Michael Wigglesworth, I have no doubt whatsoever about the centrality of the rod both as metaphor and as an instrument of painful punishments in early New England.[6]

Although breaking children's wills was obligatory for evangelicals, the ways in which this goal could be accomplished were rarely discussed in any detail. When I wrote the section on evangelicals, I made a serious mistake when I observed that "the use of the rod in discipline . . . has been exaggerated in our portraits of the early American past," because I fostered the impression that physical punishments in colonial America were less common than nonphysical forms of discipline.[7] An abundance of evidence in my own book actually

6. See my essay " 'Some Root of Bitterness': Corporal Punishment, Child Abuse, and the Apocalyptic Impulse in Michael Wigglesworth," in James A. Henretta, Michael Kammen, and Stanley N. Katz, eds., *The Transformation of Early American History: Society, Authority, and Ideology* (New York, 1991), 93–122.

7. Greven, *The Protestant Temperament*, 50.

belied my contention about evangelicals, if only I had been more sensitive to it, listened to the voices more carefully, and been more open to the implications of their language about the rod.

Much the same can be said for my portrait of the temperaments of the genteel, which also was flawed because I did not emphasize sufficiently that the genteel who had been subjected to physical punishments as children were very different adults from those who were not—more aggressive, more sensitive to threats to their autonomy, more domineering, more self-assertive.[8] In general, genteel southerners bore the scars of physical violence more visibly than did the genteel in New England and the middle colonies. The detailed accounts of whippings of Robert Carter's son by his New Jersey Presbyterian tutor Philip Fithian or Landon Carter's threat to whip his grandson reveal the presence of violence against children even in the households of the richest, most genteel Virginians in the latter part of the eighteenth century.[9] No such threats are recorded in the family papers of Thomas Hutchinson's kindred in New England or England, nor in the papers of many others, such as Belcher Byles and others who eventually fled their native land to escape the violence that threatened their lives and fortunes. Genteel people throughout the colonies were alike in many ways, but so different in others—the result, I believe, of different attitudes toward discipline and different experiences in childhood that remain to be explored.[10]

For the period in which New England took shape, Lawrence Stone's brilliant delineation of the severity of English child-rearing practices provides the obvi-

8. See, for example, Kenneth A. Lockridge, *The Diary, and Life, of William Byrd II of Virginia, 1674–1744* (Chapel Hill, N.C., 1987), and *On the Sources of Patriarchal Rage: The Commonplace Books of William Byrd and Thomas Jefferson and the Gendering of Power in the Eighteenth Century* (New York, 1992). Also see my review of *On the Sources of Patriarchal Rage* in the *Journal of American History*, LXXXI (1994–1995), 245. Unfortunately, Lockridge does not explore the issue of discipline or punishment in childhood, concentrating primarily on the youth and adulthood of these men. Richard L. Bushman also ignores childhood and child-rearing among the genteel, whom he examines in *The Refinement of America: Persons, Houses, Cities* (New York, 1992).

9. That some of the genteel in the Chesapeake region became evangelicals during the late 18th and early 19th centuries probably is linked to the traumas of their childhood experiences. See Jan Lewis, *The Pursuit of Happiness: Family and Values in Jefferson's Virginia* (New York, 1983), 40–68; Louis Morton, *Robert Carter of Nomini Hall: A Virginia Tobacco Planter of the Eighteenth Century* (Charlottesville, Va., 1941); Donald G. Mathews, *Religion in the Old South* (Chicago, 1977).

10. See Greven, *The Protestant Temperament*, 276–281. Bushman's analysis of the genteel in *The Refinement of America* portrays them as a remarkably homogenous group. See also Rhys Isaac's brilliant reconstruction of adult genteel culture and selfhood in *The Transformation of Virginia, 1740–1790* (Chapel Hill, N.C., 1982).

ous background for any understanding of the colonial experience in the first and subsequent generations. According to Stone, "During the period from 1540 to 1660 there is a great deal of evidence, *especially from Puritans,* of a fierce determination to break the will of the child, and to enforce his utter subjection to the authority of his elders and superiors, and most especially of his parents." Both at home and in schools, "more children were being beaten in the sixteenth and early seventeenth century, over a longer age span, than ever before."[11]

Stone also observes, with respect to the early nineteenth century:

It seems not unlikely that in many lower-middle-class homes, there was carried over from the seventeenth century the concept of the innate depravity of children and therefore the need and the incentive for an unremitting and stern effort to break the child's will and so repress his impulses to sin. There seems to have been an uninterrupted connection between the caring but authoritarian discipline of the Puritan bourgeois parent of the seventeenth century and the caring but authoritarian discipline of the Evangelical bourgeois parent of the late eighteenth and early nineteenth centuries.[12]

Stone is surely correct in his assessment of the severity of parenting in this period.

Stone's portrait of sixteenth- and seventeenth-century English people, both Puritan and non-Puritan alike, focuses upon the impact of violence and brutality both in childhood and adulthood. "The violence of everyday life seems to have been accompanied by much mutual suspicion and a low general level of emotional interaction and commitment. Alienation and distrust of one's fellow man are the predominant features of the Elizabethan and early Stuart view of human character and conduct." Because of the severity of their upbringing, Stone finds a pattern of " 'psychic numbing,' which created many adults whose primary responses to others were at best a calculating indifference and at worst a mixture of suspicion and hostility, tyranny and submission, alienation and rage." Puritans, of course, provide much of his evidence, and anyone who thus intends to analyze their psyches and sense of self must contend with Stone's unflattering portrait of their characters in this period.[13]

Readers of early American texts also confront an abundance of evidence

11. Stone, *The Family, Sex, and Marriage,* 162–164 (emphasis added). Additional evidence can be found in Linda A. Pollock's studies of Anglo-American child-rearing; see *Forgotten Children: Parent-Child Relations from 1500 to 1900* (Cambridge, 1983), 143–203, and *A Lasting Relationship: Parents and Children over Three Centuries* (Hanover, Mass., 1987), 165–200.

12. Stone, *The Family, Sex, and Marriage,* 466–467.

13. Ibid., 95, 101–102. Unfortunately, Cohen ignored Stone's book altogether in *God's Caress.*

that twice-born Protestants in the seventeenth and eighteenth centuries were victims of violence and abuse in childhood. Their sense of self was systematically suppressed in childhood, with lifetime consequences of feelings of anxiety, fear, anger, depression, obsessiveness, and paranoia that were directed against the body and the self and against other people. The self was dangerous and had to be repressed and denied, sometimes to the edge or even over the edge of suicide, but always to the point where a person's sense of willfulness, of self-fulfillment, of self-expression, was stifled and extirpated as fully as possible. The quest for submission to divine power and authority was endless and consuming for vast numbers of twice-born Christians. Listening to the voices of evangelicals in the pages of *The Protestant Temperament* may make many readers uncomfortable, but their words necessitate a confrontation with the self-hatred, anguish, guilt, and suffering that so many twice-born Christians still felt, long after being reborn. Their joy and ecstatic assurance were fleeting, whereas anxiety and fear remained embedded in their psyches for life.[14]

My portrait of evangelicals has been confirmed by other scholars as well in a series of studies both of individual Puritans and collective analyses of Puritans and evangelicals in England and the British colonies in the seventeenth, eighteenth, and early nineteenth centuries. David Leverenz's *Language of Puritan Feeling: An Exploration in Literature, Psychology, and Social History* (1980) explores many aspects of Puritan psychology, stressing the theme of obsessiveness. As he observes, "Puritans sought, with varying degrees of success, to remold themselves into what we would now call an 'obsessive-compulsive' personality, and their religion into obsessive ordering." He also notes that "Puritan sermons appear to be paradigms of the obsessive style." His depiction of this style is notable: " 'Precisianists,' we recall, was the other name for Puritans. Obsessives tend to suppress anger against parents or displace it, often against the self. . . . Feelings are split into exaggerated love for an authority figure and repressed hate, repressed because of the enormous fear of aggressive feelings toward those whose love is all-important. There is also great dread of rejection and abandonment." He adds: "The real threat is unacknowledged ambivalence. Because the hate side of ambivalence is so fearful, the hate becomes terrifyingly magnified into omnipotent, apocalyptic destructiveness that must be caged at all costs. Obsessional states are linked with depression and paranoia. . . . Obsessives tend to be intolerant, unable to accept bad qualities or imperfections, authoritarian even as they seek authority." He roots

14. According to Cohen, "The portrait of the evangelical style [in *The Protestant Temperament*], wonderfully evocative of personalities writhing in the throes of constricted self-abnegation, omits the joy that sometimes broke through their ordeal and misses the sense of power that humiliation brought"; see *God's Caress*, 18.

at least some of these psychological states in the particular forms of child-rearing and discipline characteristic of Puritans. Although Leverenz evades the issues of physical abuse and violence as roots of the obsessiveness that he observes, at least the feelings are transparently clear to anyone who reads his book.[15]

A similar interpretation of Puritans is to be found in *The Iron of Melancholy: Structures of Spiritual Conversion in America from the Puritan Conscience to Victorian Neurosis* (1983) by John Owen King III, which also emphasizes obsessiveness as well as the forms of depression labeled "melancholy" during this early period. King does not agree with me about the centrality of child-rearing in any account of psychological states, preferring to argue that language and texts reveal meaning more than childhood experiences might. "What one does find in Puritan culture, and particularly within Puritanism as it developed in America, is a certain literary genre and style of self-examination—the idea that to be of the saints is to be mentally beset." He notes that "one might argue that the Puritans' theology created such suffering and that what one is observing is a strong relationship between culture and personality—that an obsessional personality, in other words, was the creation of Puritan child-raising techniques," citing case histories from *The Protestant Temperament* as primary examples. "But," he adds, "theories of culture and personality, as well as culture and abnormality, remain fluid and vague; they are, in any event, open to attack from several points of view." He, like Cohen, believes that "certainly, in the confessions Greven employs, more is required than a circular argument that patterns of child rearing caused the expressions, and the expressions in turn created the patterns of child rearing."[16]

Nevertheless, the evidence of Puritan psychopathology embedded in King's study is entirely consistent with the evidence in my book concerning states of obsessiveness and melancholic depression. He observes: "The charge of melancholy against the Puritans survived Robert Burton [who wrote the classic *Anatomy of Melancholy* in 1621]. The psychologism survived because Puritan

---

15. Leverenz, *The Language of Puritan Feeling*, 3, 72, 111, 117, 138. For comparable arguments and evidence, see "Soldiers for Christ: Anger, Aggression, and Enemies," in Greven, *The Protestant Temperament,* esp. 109–113, 141, 143–144. For an analysis of "Obsessiveness and Rigidity," see Greven, *Spare the Child,* 135–141. For another perspective that takes issue with mine, see "The Great Care of Godly Parents: Early Childhood in Puritan New England," in Gerald F. Moran and Maris A. Vinovskis, *Religion, Family, and the Life Course: Explorations in the Social History of Early America* (Ann Arbor, Mich., 1992), 112–117.

16. John Owen King III, *The Iron of Melancholy: Structures of Spiritual Conversion in America from the Puritan Conscience to Victorian Neurosis* (Middletown, Conn., 1983), 331, 337–338.

authors provided the evidence for their own psychopathology, celebrating in their writings this sickness of soul." According to King:

> The psychomachia was not a Protestant invention. Its roots lay deep in the lives of the saints, most profoundly in the *Confessions* of Augustine. It remained for the Protestant to develop the self's examination in a peculiar way, however. . . . If one reads the words of trauma without a sense of the words required to express the excellency of [John] Bunyan's broken heart, then the Puritans stand revealed as the selves they celebrated: broken, nervously strained, even suicidal. Historians may then argue that seventeenth-century Americans suffered from the composition of the self that the sectarians themselves conceived of: crises of identity, high rates of suicide, an abnormal number of nervous breakdowns.

King adds, "To argue that one can look behind words into the emotional piety of New England, assumes that one can read through the texts into the heart of the writer." At the same time, he also recognizes: "It is not a question of choosing between words and experience, or between a language of conversion and conversion itself. Prescription is not opposed to experience; prescription is language with which to order and craft experience."[17]

What unfolds in King's narrative is a description of Puritans that focuses upon recurrent and widely experienced states of depression and obsessiveness. He asserts that John "Winthrop's own life is quite open to an interpretation of obsessional psychopathology." Much the same was true for Michael Wigglesworth. For Cotton Mather and Jonathan Edwards, as for others, melancholy was the central motif explored by King, who could describe the feelings and experiences even when he lacked an explanation for these persistent psychological sufferings among these twice-born Protestants—sufferings that King himself pursued through the nineteenth century among Victorians. In his conclusion, King acknowledges that "the evidence for such trauma is there, but the question again is why it is there, why the text appears as it does, why indeed the self is expressed, and *so* expressed." But his book, alas, offers no answers to these questions.[18]

For answers, however, we can turn to Julius H. Rubin's analysis, *Religious Melancholy and Protestant Experience in America* (1994), which provides a powerful and persuasive linkage of severe child-rearing practices (including

---

17. Ibid., 36, 41–42, 49. For additional evidence about suicidal tendencies and depression, see *The Protestant Temperament*, 82–83. Also see Stanley W. Jackson, *Melancholia and Depression: From Hippocratic Times to Modern Times* (New Haven, Conn., 1986); and Julius H. Rubin, *Religious Melancholy and Protestant Experience in America* (New York, 1994), 150–155.

18. King, *The Iron of Melancholy*, 59, 331.

corporal punishments) with persistent patterns of depressive and obsessional behaviors on the part of twice-born Protestants for more than three centuries. One of the most original arguments of his book is that "evangelical anorexia nervosa emerged as a prevalent distinctive expression of religious melancholy among evangelical Pietist sects in England and New England from the seventeenth through the mid-nineteenth centuries." He notes:

> The behavioral manifestations of this syndrome include food refusal, generalized anxiety, sleep disorder, and obsessive-compulsive conduct or repetitive neurotic ceremonials designed to alleviate feelings of personal sinfulness. The inner subjective meanings associated with these symptoms, the expressions of hopelessness and the certainty of eternal damnation reflect important theological contradictions of evangelical Pietism as enacted in the lives of believers who attempted and failed to forge a religiously grounded personality. The evangelical anoretic waged a lifelong battle against the self in search of self-denial.[19]

Rubin demonstrates the relevance of the evidence and arguments from my scholarship for a far broader analysis of the psychological manifestations of depression and other forms of mental suffering.

Puritan and evangelical Protestant theologies, in Calvinist forms especially, rationalized the abuse people experienced early in life and legitimated their felt need for total obedience and selflessness. John Stachniewski grasps the stinging nettle of Calvinist theology by asking—in *The Persecutory Imagination: English Puritanism and the Literature of Religious Despair* (1991)—"what it felt like to be an early protestant." He also asks these crucial questions: "Why was this discourse, especially in its repellent aspects, so successful in putting roots down in the community? What gave it purchase on the psyche?" He finds answers through the autobiographical writings and sermons of Puritans, although acknowledging: "It is difficult to grasp the experiential actuality of Puritanism. Much (too much) comment has simply refused to face Calvinist extremism, to inhabit imaginatively its assumptions about the world."[20]

Stachniewski, too, probes the harsh and brutal childhood experiences of so many of those whom we identify as Puritans. He observes: "The sense of divine

19. Rubin, *Religious Melancholy and Protestant Experience in America*, 83. For similar examples, see King's analysis of Susanna Anthony, *The Iron of Melancholy*, 42, 340–341 n. 1, and my analysis of Anthony in *The Protestant Temperament*, 24, 72, 76, 81–82, 86, 104. Also see Greven, "Melancholy and Depression," *Spare the Child*, 130–135.

20. John Stachniewski, *The Persecutory Imagination: English Puritanism and the Literature of Religious Despair* (Oxford, 1991), 5–6, 52. Although he did not read or make use of

rejection was often related to feelings about fathers, father-surrogates, or the social hierarchy. Frequent, often discriminatory or arbitrary, beatings; banishment from the father's presence and the threat of being disowned; guilt-feelings arising from lack of filial affection or hatred as a reaction to punishment; the desire to escape from paternal anger; the knowledge that paternal power circumvented any infantile plot: in all these experiences God and actual fathers seem to have been imaginatively conflated." Out of such experiences came the psychic wounds that persistently shaped the Puritan's character, leading often to the despair, anxiety, and paranoia that Stachniewski explores in depth. As he observes, "preachers wrapped people who were drawn into puritanism's cultural ambit in theological barbed wire."[21]

In mid-eighteenth-century New England, Jonathan Edwards, more precise and explicit than anyone else, spoke directly to the experiential and emotional impact of harsh physical discipline and breaking wills. His theology, which historians have explored in elaborate and admiring detail, is rooted in a fantasy of power, domination, control, and submission that made sense to many people in his audiences because of their personal life experiences.[22] Edwards's God is the absolute and arbitrary abuser of nearly every human whose life has ended—except for those few individuals who are able and willing to become his obedient slaves through eternity.

Punishment is the core experience that Edwards foresees awaiting sinners in hell, and his sermons left nothing to one's imagination concerning the degree of torment and pain that would be experienced. How can such theologies of wrath, retribution, punishment, and torture be explained unless we root them in experiences of suffering and pain and repression of feelings in childhood? Theology always reflects the innermost layers of human psyches and selves.

The Protestant Temperament, his portrait of Calvinists and Puritans is entirely consistent with my portrait of evangelicals. Clearly his study confirms my own reading of these autobiographical texts in ways that I could not anticipate. There is little joy to be found in Stachniewski's Calvinists.

21. Stachniewski, *The Persecutory Imagination,* 89, 95. His portrait of Puritans confirms my own assumption about the analogies between actual fathers and God the Father.

22. See, for example, Norman Fiering, *Jonathan Edwards's Moral Thought and Its British Context* (Chapel Hill, N.C., 1981), chap. 5, "Hell and the Humanitarians." Even Fiering acknowledges (254 n. 143) the connection between Edwards and the Marquis de Sade, thus recognizing the sadomasochistic quality of Edwards's sermons on hell. For an analysis of sadomasochism in connection to corporal punishments and sexuality, see Greven, *Spare the Child,* 174–186. See also Robert J. Stoller, *Pain and Passion: A Psychoanalyst Explores the World of S and M* (New York, 1991); Jessica Benjamin, *The Bonds of Love: Psychoanalysis, Feminism, and the Problem of Domination* (New York, 1988); Lynn S. Chancer, *Sadomasochism in Everyday Life: The Dynamics of Power and Powerlessness* (New Brunswick, N.J., 1992).

Many of Jonathan Edwards's contemporaries, like many of his predecessors and successors, were intensely aware of the repellent cruelty and tyranny of the Calvinist divinity as well as the need for parents to be tender and compassionate with their children. As Jonathan Mayhew said: "Were God a malevolent Being; were he an unreasonable Tyrant; were he an hard Master; were he an implacable and revengeful Being; instead of a merciful and faithful Creator; a compassionate Parent; a gentle Master; a righteous Judge; we might well think of him with horror and dread; and even wish a period put to his existence. . . . But God forbid that we should conceive of him in this manner."[23] Charles Chauncy, Edwards's chief opponent during the Great Awakening, came to believe that hell would never be the final destination for any soul, since every soul ultimately would be saved by a forgiving God, but he kept his universalist views quiet during most of his lifetime, knowing how eccentric they were, then as now. He was one of my moderates, whose sense of self was different from most evangelicals. Chauncy's God was incapable of sending anyone to suffer in hell forever.[24] Most other moderates, although they believed in the reality of hell and eternal punishments, felt confident that God was more benign and predictable and less vindictive than Edwards and other evangelicals thought. According to moderates, fathers did not punish their children excessively or severely, preferring to bend and shape rather than to break and crush their emergent wills and selves. Most, not surprisingly, felt an enduring sense of confidence that their own souls would be saved ultimately by God, their heavenly father, who, having given them free will, would appreciate their efforts to be dutiful and obedient and relatively free of sin throughout their lifetime.

As a result, the moderates' personalities, like their piety, were markedly different from those Puritans and evangelicals whose wills had been crushed and suppressed in childhood. Moderates—those middling sorts who provide historians with a sort of norm between the extremes of severity and permis-

23. Jonathan Mayhew, *Seven Sermons* (New York, 1969), quoted in Greven, *The Protestant Temperament*, 238. Lyle Koehler observes, with respect to Rhode Island dissidents in the 17th century: "The Gortonists were like the Quakers in accepting the civil 'magistracy' of parents over their children, while arguing against discipline enforced by fear. 'We profess right unto all men, and do no violence at all, as your prescripts threaten to do to us,' they wrote to the Massachusetts Puritans, '*for we have learned how to discipline our children or servants without offering violence unto them.*' The Gortonists were the first 17th-century New England group to assert outright that sparing the rod did *not* spoil the child"; see *A Search for Power: The "Weaker Sex" in Seventeenth-Century New England* (Urbana, Ill., 1980), 304.

24. See Charles H. Lippy, *Seasonable Revolutionary: The Mind of Charles Chauncy* (Chicago, 1981), 111–112, 118–121, 128–129; and Edward M. Griffin, *Old Brick: Charles Chauncy of Boston, 1705–1787* (Minneapolis, Minn., 1980), 109–127, 170–176.

siveness—were shaped by modes of rearing that allowed them to confront life and the world without most of the acute anxieties and extreme self-denial and self-suppression that haunted the repressed personalities of so many other people. The genteel, of course, were set apart from both of these sorts of people, consciously acting and thinking and feeling in ways that were anathema to many and distressing to most people of evangelical and moderate temperaments.

Anyone who reads *The Protestant Temperament,* however, must surely come away with a realization that those who suffered the most—those who bore the most visible and enduring scars of trauma and repression from childhood into adulthood—were those whom I called evangelical. It thus is accurate to say that their sense of selfhood was misshaped by the sufferings of their early life experiences. No matter how historians might wish to account for such anxiety and enduring anguish and suffering—by either including or excluding childhood experience—that such feelings were experienced by vast numbers of people over a long period of time on both sides of the Atlantic Ocean is simply undeniable. This remains a fact of immense importance for scholars who seek an understanding of the self and selfhood.

FROM PAST TO PRESENT: THE IMPLICATIONS OF ABUSE

Given the diverse forms of child-rearing and selfhood in Anglo-America during the seventeenth and eighteenth centuries, we need to ask this question: Is our quest for an understanding of the self in early America relevant to our understanding of ourselves and other people today? Having written both *The Protestant Temperament* and *Spare the Child*—which together span the entire period from the early seventeenth century to the present—I am more certain than ever that the past is never fully past. For all the vast changes and transformations that historians and others have charted that make colonial and Revolutionary America seem so distant and foreign, for all of the extraordinary technological and scientific revolutions that make our world so utterly alien in relation to the one we seek to fathom, I am convinced nevertheless that some aspects of human experience are still fundamentally the same.

Many historians, unfortunately, have proven to be intensely resistant to the thought that knowledge of the past might contribute something valuable to the quest for an understanding of the ways in which human beings in our own contemporary nation and world are formed, take shape, and emerge with a sense of self in adulthood that either sustains or inhibits their experiences of life. General indifference to the question of relevance is profoundly disturbing, for it implies that our knowledge of the seventeenth and eighteenth centuries in Anglo-America has little or nothing to contribute to our sense of our selves and our world at the end of the twentieth century.

What historians actually have to offer to anyone who is seeking an understanding of selfhood in our contemporary world is a vast array of information, evidence, and insights into the entire life histories of many generations of human beings. Unlike contemporary students of the self, historians have the unique advantage of studying people whose lives have been completed, being able to track them in many cases from birth to death. We therefore know, as few others can, what the outcomes of various types of upbringing actually were. We have long-term studies of individual human beings—we call them biographies—and groups of human beings—we call them prosopographies—that can be read as case studies similar to those being done today by psychologically-minded clinicians, therapists, and others. The problem with most contemporary psychological studies is that they usually deal with individuals whose lives are still continuing. Longitudinal studies thus are extremely rare in the field of psychology, especially in the emerging fields devoted to the analysis of the origins and outcomes of child abuse—emotional, physical, and sexual—and domestic violence. Violence and the abuse of children have been part of our world for as long as historians have tracked human behavior.

The shaping of character and a sense of self among twice-born Protestants, at least, has remained astonishingly constant for more than four centuries. There is an unbroken chain, generation after generation, from the early seventeenth century to the end of the twentieth, of corporal punishments, broken wills, and other forms of harsh and severe methods of disciplining and rearing children. Most contemporary fundamentalist and Pentecostal Protestants, together with many charismatics and other twice-born evangelicals, still believe in corporal punishment as the "Christian" method of disciplining children. The goal for present-day authoritarian fundamentalists is still the breaking and conquest of children's wills.[25] Such methods of child-rearing—rooted as

25. For evidence concerning these continuities into the present, see Greven, *Spare the Child*, esp. 60–81. For contrary views, see the assumptions by John Demos and David Leverenz. Demos, in the conclusion to *Entertaining Satan*, 396, roots some of the changing attitudes toward witches and witchcraft in changing child-rearing practices, noting that "the old emphasis on 'breaking the will,' the old preoccupation with early manifestations of 'original sin,' had faded considerably by the mid-nineteenth century." Leverenz noted, with respect to his own interpretation of Puritans: "I emphasize Puritan love . . . because others have concluded that Puritan child rearing consisted primarily in breaking the will. Michael Walzer and Lawrence Stone . . . find anxiety, rigid self-control, and harsh patriarchal upbringing almost everywhere they look. Philip Greven, with somewhat more justice I

they are in pain and fear and coercion—have formed an enduring source of profound human anxiety, aggressiveness, and suffering for successive generations of people on both sides of the Atlantic Ocean.

The psychological damage arising from physical punishments and will breaking in terms of the misshaping of the self was and is profound and enduring. Foremost among the repetitive feelings and thoughts characteristic of so many evangelicals, Puritans, and other twice-born Protestants from the seventeenth century to the present are (as we have seen) anger, anxiety, fear, self-loathing, depression (or melancholy), obsessiveness, and paranoia. Although there is an abundance of evidence embedded in *The Protestant Temperament* concerning such psychological states, numerous other studies now make overwhelmingly clear that many Protestants have been victims of such painful emotional states long after they have been filled with the ecstasy, joy, and happiness that they often felt during their rebirth and conversion. Nevertheless, the connections of these emotional, behavioral, and intellectual configurations with the life experiences that brought them into being still elude most historians and need to be explored.

Few historians, as yet, have been able or willing to see what someday may be self-evident: these repetitive modes of human suffering are grounded in the abuse of children and the traumas of growing up in families in which wills are broken, selfhood is denied, and fear pervades, families in which authoritarianism dominates and patriarchs force everyone—wives and children and servants alike—to submit to their power and control.[26] When we move beyond the temporal confines of the early American era into the nineteenth and twentieth centuries, it becomes increasingly clear that the psychological impact of child abuse is actually the same today as it was centuries ago. The psychological manifestations of child abuse that clinicians and others are exploring today— depression, anxiety, obsessiveness, dissociation, paranoia, sadomasochism, anger, and rage—were present already in the selves of many (but not all) of the people who inhabited British North America.[27] Their pasts—and ours—are connected in ways we have scarcely begun to recognize.

---

think, finds zealous evangelical families in New England breaking the will of children as young as ten to fifteen months, especially in the eighteenth century, *although he wrongly claims the pattern is constant over a 200-year period*, while contrasting it with another constant pattern of moderation" (emphasis added); see *The Language of Puritan Feeling*, 72.

26. To confirm my argument that some things do not change significantly, see the arguments in favor of patriarchy and obedience of wives and children by contemporary fundamentalist Protestants, such as Larry Christenson, whose book has sold more than one million copies; see *The Christian Family* (Minneapolis, Minn., 1970), esp. 32–54.

27. See, for example, John Demos's essay "Child Abuse in Context: An Historian's Perspective," in Demos, *Past, Present, and Personal: The Family and the Life Course in*

We need to grasp the fact that child abuse—whether in the form of emotional and verbal abuse, physical abuse, or sexual abuse—creates the permanent matrix for negative adult feelings, thoughts, and behaviors. Physical assaults against children in the form of corporal punishments result in a wide variety of outcomes over the course of a person's lifetime and shape different people in different ways. There is no single outcome for all people. What emerges from early abuse and violence is a spectrum of psychological harms. Abuse provides the most basic underpinning for the malformation and mis-shaping of character, of identity, of a sense of self, whether in the past or the present. The abuse of children—in all of its multiple forms—is the most enduring fact that historians need to reckon with if we are ever to grasp the complex ways in which human beings have reacted to and resolved their traumatic childhood experiences.

Alice Miller's brilliant analysis of the psychological impact of corporal punishments among German-speaking peoples in *For Your Own Good: Hidden Cruelty in Child-Rearing and the Roots of Violence* (1983) ought to be read in tandem with *The Protestant Temperament*. Much of her evidence about German modes of discipline from the eighteenth century to the mid-twentieth century—which she labels "poisonous pedagogy"—is virtually indistinguishable from the evidence on will breaking in my books. Among the various German sources that Miller cites is J. Sulzer's *Essay on the Education and Instruction of Children* (1748), which states: "It is quite natural for the child's soul to want to have a will of its own, and things that are not done correctly in the first two years will be difficult to rectify thereafter. One of the advantages of these early years is that then force and compulsion can be used. Over the years, children forget everything that happened to them in early childhood. If their wills can be broken at this time, they will never remember afterwards that they had a will, and for this very reason the severity that is required will not have any serious consequences." Miller, of course, knows that such a statement is false. What she demonstrates is an unbroken chain of violence and abuse, disguised as loving discipline, among German-speaking peoples. For many people, these life experiences culminated in the fascist and Nazi totalitarian governments of the pre–World War II era and fed the sadistic impulses that took their ultimate form in the deliberate, intentional, and systematic anni-

---

American History (New York, 1986), 68–91. Unfortunately, Demos specifically excluded corporal punishments from his definition of abuse: "Harsh discipline (which falls short of causing injury) and a seeming lack of empathy for childhood also fall outside our definitional boundaries" (75). For the psychological manifestations of child abuse, see Greven, *Spare the Child*.

hilation of six million Jews and millions of other people, including homosexuals and Gypsies, in the Holocaust.[28]

Alice Miller makes clear the long-term outcomes, both for the self and for others, of the methods of child-rearing that involve assault, pain, and suffering, forms of punishment that she knows to be abusive. The children whose wills are broken hide their true selves (which are obviously unacceptable to their parents, teachers, and other adults), and thus their anger and desire for revenge for the pains they suffer at the hands of their beloved parents are denied, buried, but not dissipated. Asking, "What becomes of all those people who are the successful products of a strict upbringing?" Miller answers as follows:

> It is inconceivable that they were able to express and develop their true feelings as children, for anger and helpless rage, which they were forbidden to display, would have been among these feelings—particularly if these children were beaten, humiliated, lied to, and deceived. What becomes of this forbidden and therefore unexpressed anger? Unfortunately, it does not disappear, but is transformed with time into a more or less conscious hatred directed against either the self or substitute persons, a hatred that will seek to discharge itself in various ways permissible and suitable for an adult.

Readers of *The Protestant Temperament* may note that

> the full measure of the aggressiveness and anger of evangelicals has never been taken by historians, even though the actions of evangelicals provide an unending record of their warfare with the unregenerate world in which they lived. Much of the time, their aggressiveness was confined to words rather than to deeds. . . . The very violence of their language and the ferocity of their denunciations—both of individuals and of doctrines—revealed the powerful impulses of hostility that erupted from deep within these repressed individuals. Yet such anger emerged only under stress and only occasionally in the course of a lifetime. Revivals were a major outlet for such feelings.

Although the contexts for these observations are utterly different, both Alice Miller and I agree that the earliest traumas arising from harsh authoritarian modes of rearing and discipline continue to shape people's sense of self and to

---

28. Alice Miller, *For Your Own Good: Hidden Cruelty in Child-Rearing and the Roots of Violence,* trans. Hildegarde Hannum and Hunter Hannum (New York, 1983), 13, 61. For a powerful and persuasive analysis of the linkages between corporal punishment and other forms of physical and mental abuse of children, the Nazis, and the Holocaust, see 64–91, 142–197.

warp their ability to live their lives fully, joyfully, and lovingly. Aggressiveness, hatred, rage, the desire to control and to dominate—feelings rooted in child-hood—still mold the thoughts, selves, and behaviors of these grown-up vic-tims of violence.[29]

Similar arguments and evidence can be found in Judith Lewis Herman's *Trauma and Recovery* (1992), which does not focus upon childhood discipline or physical punishments but does explore a wide range of traumatic experi-ences—emotional, physical, sexual—both in childhood and adulthood. What is most remarkable about her analysis is her insistence that the outcomes are the same, no matter what form the original trauma took. She, too, finds a spectrum of psychological responses to traumas, noting: "The capacity for induced trance or dissociative states . . . is developed to a fine art in children who have been severely punished or abused. Studies have documented the connection between the severity of childhood abuse and the degree of famil-iarity with dissociative states." Herman also notes that "the profound sense of inner badness becomes the core around which the abused child's identity is formed, and it persists into adult life." As Herman observes: "The emotional state of the chronically abused child ranges from a baseline of unease, through intermediate states of anxiety and dysphoria, to extremes of panic, fury, and despair. Not surprisingly, a great many survivors develop chronic anxiety and depression which persist into adult life." She also comments: "Though some child or adolescent victims may call attention to themselves through aggressive or delinquent behavior, most are able successfully to conceal the extent of their psychological difficulties. Most abused children reach adulthood with their secrets intact." Perhaps this is one reason why historians have such problems connecting childhood experiences with the adult selves of the people whom they study: the subjects themselves are usually unaware of the roots of their own psychological sufferings and thus cannot reveal them to us directly.[30]

The long-term psychological and behavioral outcomes arising from the experience of being physically punished in childhood and youth are explored and documented by Murray A. Straus in his *Beating the Devil Out of Them: Corporal Punishment in American Families* (1994). As a sociologist and a spe-cialist in the analysis of family violence, Straus demonstrates persuasively, from empirical evidence drawn from interviews with a large sample of people done in the mid-1980s, that one of the most common psychological outcomes in adulthood is depression. This finding confirms my arguments concerning the relationship of early experiences with authoritarian upbringing in which being hit and hurt and broken by parents produces subsequent proclivities

29. Ibid., 61; Greven, *The Protestant Temperament*, 121.
30. Judith Lewis Herman, *Trauma and Recovery* (New York, 1992), 102, 105, 108, 110.

toward self-denying, self-hating, and self-destroying feelings and behaviors, in addition to various forms of aggressive and violent behaviors.[31]

Although historians of early America have barely begun to reckon with the long-term impact of child abuse (because so few have taken the subject of child-rearing seriously), the exploration of the implications of early trauma and assaults against children's bodies and selves being undertaken by scholars today has much to teach us about the complex ways in which early life experiences are connected to the formation, the experience, and the expression of the self.[32] We now know enough about the psychological manifestations of early abuse among adults today to be confident that their emotional and behavioral problems did not come about by accident.

The long-dead evangelicals who populate *The Protestant Temperament* are no different from vast numbers of the clients and patients of modern-day psychologists and clinicians who specialize in the treatment of emotional distress and disturbances. Their anxiety, their intense self-scrutiny, their hostility toward their bodies, their alienation from their innermost selves, their sense of guilt, of shame, and of despair, and, overwhelmingly, their profound and enduring sense of depression reflect states of being that today would surely be recognized as the long-term outcomes of life experiences rooted in abuse and trauma.

When I immersed myself in the texts of the seventeenth and eighteenth centuries, I discerned repetitive outcries of both dismay and ecstasy in the voices of Puritans, evangelicals, and other twice-born people, but I did not fathom fully the implications of the evidence. In retrospect, however, my subsequent concentration on nineteenth- and twentieth-century accounts of analogous forms of suffering has led me to realize that my earlier work also was focused upon victims of violence and abuse who expressed, through their religious experiences and beliefs, the identical symptoms and feelings that so many patients grapple with in psychotherapy today. What is common to such people both then and now are the childhood experiences of assault, hurt, and suffering arising from authoritarian forms of discipline designed to break children's wills and sense of self. Although religious experiences provide a

---

31. Murray A. Straus with Denise A. Donnelly, *Beating the Devil Out of Them: Corporal Punishment in American Families* (New York, 1994), 67–80.

32. For an important exception to this observation, however, see Demos's exploration, "Child Abuse in Context," in Demos, *Past, Present, and Personal*, 68–91. Unfortunately, neither Helena M. Wall's *Fierce Communion: Family and Community in Early America* (Cambridge, 1990), 54–55, 59, 73, 76–80, 116–118, nor Karin Calvert's *Children in the House: The Material Culture of Early Childhood, 1600–1900* (Boston, 1992), seeks to do this. The issues of physical, sexual, verbal, and emotional abuse in early America remain enigmatic and largely unexplored.

means for many to grapple with and often to transcend many of the traumas of early life, many people find other, nonreligious ways of dealing with their past pain and suffering in the contexts of their secular experiences.[33]

The time has come for historians of early America to discover the psychological insights produced throughout the twentieth century and to use these many perspectives to probe and interpret the people who once inhabited the Anglo-American worlds of the seventeenth and eighteenth centuries. We need to read and use the studies by Alice Miller, Judith Herman, Murray Straus, and countless others because they have insights that are invaluable in our own quest for understanding people whose lives have been completed centuries ago. We need to use the evidence and the theories of contemporary explorers of child abuse to make sense of the evidence that we confront when we write about Puritans and evangelicals and other such people long ago. To stick, as most do, to the surface of texts and sermons and lives is to miss the core of human experience that gives permanent shape to virtually every aspect of our being: how we feel, how we think, how we behave. It is simply not enough to argue that "the primary task is to make sense of conversion in Puritan terms."[34] We also must make sense of Puritans, conversions, and religious experience in general in our own terms as well as theirs. That is why the vast literature on the deformations of the self written in this psychologically minded century need to be incorporated into our historical interpretations and analyses.[35]

Making use of contemporary studies of the psyche and the self also will help us understand that evidence can be read in more than one way: we can start at the outset, with evidence about children and childhood, or we can start later, with evidence about adults. Despite historians' cavils about the circularity of arguing about the childhood roots of adult religious experience and selves, the fact is that one can deduce childhood experiences without any evidence whatsoever being available by knowing about the theoretical origins of adult psy-

33. See, for example, the sections on "Sadomasochism," "Aggression and Delinquency," and "Authoritarianism," in my *Spare the Child*, 174–186, 193–198, 198–204. Also see Straus's *Beating the Devil Out of Them;* and Judith Herman's *Trauma and Recovery*.

34. Cohen, *God's Caress*, 20.

35. One notable example of a historian who has done so is Demos, whose *Entertaining Satan* is one of the most sophisticated and compelling psychological studies of New England Puritans yet done. See, however, my review essay of his book in *History and Theory*, XXIII, (1984), 236–251. One crucial point that he misses, in my opinion (249–251), is the impact of child abuse upon the psyches and fantasies of those whom he associates with witchcraft.

Many psychologists, of course, have been insensitive or indifferent to the issues of abuse in childhood, which only now is becoming a major issue in the field. See, for example, my discussion of Sigmund Freud in *Spare the Child*, 130–132, 155–157.

chological disorders. Only now, however, at the end of the twentieth century, are even psychologists and clinicians themselves beginning to grasp what has become obvious in recent years: child abuse, in all its multiple forms, is the progenitor of most of the emotional and behavioral disturbances manifested by adults. Alice Miller and Judith Herman are surely right in their convictions that childhood traumas have enduring and analyzable outcomes. Although the specific form that the early abuse took might not be knowable—whether physical, sexual, or verbal—the fact that abuse did occur (based upon adult evidence) is now beyond dispute.

One final thought. The evidence on selfhood in the seventeenth and eighteenth centuries in Anglo-America demonstrates something else that we need to reckon with—that human nature is more fixed than many historians are inclined to believe. Whenever a historian dismisses the use of psychoanalytic or other modern psychological theories in the interpretation or analysis of early American religious experience, belief, or behavior, the often unarticulated presumption is that people in the seventeenth and eighteenth centuries somehow were different from us. Rarely, however, are such differences explored explicitly. The common assumption is that, although the psychological theories might be applicable to us and to our contemporaries, they are not useful in terms of understanding people in the past who, being long dead, are unable to speak for themselves in response to our questions.[36] Implicit in this assumption is the belief that their psyches and ours are differently constituted, differently shaped, differently felt, differently experienced, and differently expressed.

In relation to the studies being done today on the psychological and behavioral outcomes of child abuse (whether as physical punishments, verbal and emotional abuse, or sexual abuse), my evidence concerning evangelicals demonstrates that the abuse of children creates a sense of self that is profoundly damaged and distorted, a sense of self misshapen in particular ways that transcend time and space. If we know that children have been subjected to modes of discipline that focus upon the infliction of physical pain and are designed to crush the emergent wills and sense of autonomy in children, we then know that these children will grow up to experience a wide range of emotional and behavioral problems. The same experiences of suffering and trauma in childhood result in predictable forms of suffering and trauma in adulthood, creating patterns of psychic damage and alienation that are manifested in multiple ways emotionally, intellectually, and behaviorally.

Simply by comparing the outcomes of the child-rearing experiences associ-

36. See, for instance, Cohen, *God's Caress,* 14–22.

ated with evangelicals with those of moderates and the genteel in *The Protestant Temperament*, it is now possible to assess the long-term results of various types of upbringing. It would be hard for most historians not to conclude that the moderates—who were preoccupied with self-control, balance, and reasonableness—were less traumatized and less inclined to assaults upon the self than were most evangelicals. Certainly, the genteel—as Rhys Isaac and Richard Bushman as well as myself have made clear—gave every appearance of having a degree of self-worth and self-confidence that set them apart from most of their contemporaries across a broad span of time. Although the psychological and emotional configurations of selfhood are immensely complex and varied, their distinctive roots in childhood are now clear, as never before.

Precisely for this reason, the study of past experiences of child-rearing in early America has much to offer in terms of our understanding of the shaping of selfhood and in terms of the complex manifestations of alternative modes of rearing and disciplining children so evident today. The same spectrum, from severe to moderate to permissive to negligent, that was visible in the seventeenth, eighteenth, and nineteenth centuries is to be found in the late twentieth century in the literature on child-rearing and discipline. If the patterns of experience, thought, behavior, and belief that I have reconstructed convince readers that the ways in which we rear children have long-term consequences—in terms of shaping the diverse ways people feel, experience, and express the self, both positively and negatively—I know that I have not written in vain.

"I HAVE SUFFER'D MUCH TODAY": THE DEFINING FORCE OF PAIN IN EARLY AMERICA

Elaine Forman Crane

PAIN: DISCOURSE AND REALITY

If human beings, separated by millennia and miles, share any experience, it is the sensation of pain. The discovery of anesthesia, aspirin, and antibiotics has enabled people to control pain, but these relatively recent developments only underscore the length of time that pain controlled people. In the not so distant past, pain was persistent and pervasive enough to make it a normal (rather than aberrant) condition of life, and one that acted as a dynamic of human society. Moreover, even though theological considerations dictated personal conduct consistent with a painful existence, the reality of pain ultimately frustrated behavior that attempted to approach standards prescribed by the clergy.

Poised on the threshold of modern science and technology, late-eighteenth-century Americans were no more advanced than any other human community in the struggle to conquer physical pain. Intellectual currents, such as sensibility and rationalism, had heightened sensitivity to the anguish pain produced, but, in fact, such discourse had done little to mitigate the ravaging effects of pain on both mind and body. Receptivity to such rhetoric might have reduced the pain one person inflicted upon another, but a wealth of evidence from that era suggests that pain from disease or injury continued to mold early republican lives.

The author wishes to thank Edith B. Gelles (Stanford University), George Rappaport (Wagner College), and Joan Gundersen (California State University, San Marcos) for their thoughtful comments and suggestions. Thanks are also due to Susan Klepp (Rider College) for drawing the author's attention to the Elizabeth Coates Paschall Recipe Book at the College of Physicians of Philadelphia, and to Stephen Greenberg (National Library of Medicine) for alerting the author to Roselyne Rey's *History of Pain,* trans. Louise Elliott Wallace, J. A. Cadden, and S. W. Cadden (Paris, 1993). The Fordham University Library staff went to unusual lengths to obtain material on interlibrary loan for this project, and gratitude is extended to them as well.

Pain was embracing and relentless. Family, friends, and neighbors testified to being "surrounded with infirmities." One diarist compared the world to a lazar house where "the ills and dolors of the human race" outweighed the pleasures of life.[1] Pain was aggressive and unyielding. Writers described unremitting suffering that lasted for months on end without reprieve. Pain was a trespasser, the alien other. It invaded without warning, striking here and there with a capricious abandon that incited emotions and left foreboding and dread to fester just below the surface of consciousness.

End-of-the-century literature indicates that pain influenced human self-identity, interpersonal relationships, and the community as a whole. As a common social denominator, pain encouraged spirituality—and spirits. It qualified economic productivity and reinforced gender-related attitudes. It conditioned child development and adult behavior. Pain altered looks and outlooks. It shaped one's impression of the world and one's performance in it. Pain hampered the ability to cope with what life meted out. Indeed, Benjamin Franklin was not far from the truth when he argued that pain (or what he called "uneasiness") was integral to "the Order and Design of the Universe."[2]

Although each individual experiences pain subjectively, the subject lends itself to objective study through a bifurcated approach: an analysis of the continuing (and often contradictory) discourse on pain and an examination of ways in which people actually responded to the experience of pain. As a general rule, pain forced people to dismiss the importunities of prescriptive literature (at least so far as suffering with forbearance was concerned), but even when public response approached the behavioral model that response might have only reflected contemporary social values, rather than actual feelings or emotions.[3] Praying for patience was not equivalent to enjoying an internal sense of equanimity, and in the war between composure and emotion pain lent aid and sustenance to the latter.

In short, although social scientists know what people said about pain and

1. Eliza Cope Harrison, ed., *Philadelphia Merchant: The Diary of Thomas P. Cope, 1800–1851* (South Bend, Ind., 1978), Aug. 16, 1800, 7; William Maclay, *The Journal of William Maclay: United States Senator from Pennsylvania, 1789–1791*, ed. Charles A. Beard (New York, 1965), July 12, 1789, 103.

2. Benjamin Franklin, *A Dissertation on Liberty and Necessity, Pleasure and Pain* (1725; reprint, New York, 1930), 16. For an expansive discussion of pain and the creation of identity, see Roy Porter and Dorothy Porter, *In Sickness and in Health: The British Experience, 1650–1850* (New York, 1988), esp. chap. 12.

3. Peter N. Stearns with Carol Z. Stearns, "Emotionology: Clarifying the History of Emotions and Emotional Standards," *American Historical Review*, XC (1985), 813–836; and Carol Z. Stearns and Peter N. Stearns, "Introducing the History of Emotion," *Psychohistory Review: Studies of Motivation in History and Culture*, XVIII (1990), 263–291.

how they reacted to it, from a distance of two hundred years the reasons behind such language and actions are less clear. We cannot even be certain of the
source of a painful experience: periodontal disease or colic may lend themselves to historical diagnosis, but a pounding headache could be stimulated by
any number of psychological or physiological agents. Furthermore, because
pain is so private and personal, the literature cannot resolve the longstanding
controversy over whether humans have become more sensitive to it in the
modern world. Do people feel pain more sharply than they once did? Pundits
disagree, although there appears to be little that distinguishes Augustine's
toothache in A.D. 387 from Nancy Shippen's more than a millennium later.[4]

No matter. For the purposes of this discussion, the causes and relativity of
pain are somewhat immaterial. Pain existed. The response to it, the way in
which it modified human behavior, the disjunction between advice and action,
the mental ambiguities it created, and the impact it had on identity are the
subjects of this exploratory essay.

Attitudes toward suffering have changed over time. Assumptions about the origins of pain, as well as the appropriate responses to it, have undergone a transformation since the Middle Ages, when God was held solely responsible for its
presence and self-flagellation was valued as a holy experience by those who
sought to identify with Christ. Because modern medicine is able to both prevent and alleviate a substantial amount of pain, religious explanations about its
genesis are less credible than they once were, and there is an undisputed
readiness to distance oneself from its company. Seventeenth-century theoreticians, such as René Descartes, might have linked body and soul through the
experience of pain, but for the vast majority of Americans today constant pain
is an abnormal condition, and one that is controlled rather than controlling.[5]

This modern perspective brings the eighteenth century into stark relief,
since early American ministers preached that pain stemmed from original sin
and that it was God's method of behavior modification. God meted out pain
for two reasons: as a test to his faithful in order to offer them the opportunity
to exhibit spiritual excellence or as a direct reproach for sin. The latter explanation implied that the self *deserved* pain, and it might have been of more than

4. See Daniel de Moulin, "A Historical-Phenomenological Study of Bodily Pain in Western Man," *Bulletin of the History of Medicine*, XLVIII (1974), 540–570, for an introduction to
this controversy (the reference to Augustine is on 564); Ethel Armes, ed., *Nancy Shippen:
Her Journal Book* (New York, 1968), Jan. 13, 1784, 174.

5. See Roselyne Rey, *History of Pain*, trans. Louise Elliott Wallace, J. A. Cadden, and S. W.
Cadden (Paris, 1993), for changes in attitudes toward pain in the classical age and the age of
Enlightenment, chaps. 4, 5.

passing interest that the Latin root of the word "pain" is "poena," or punishment. For many churchgoers, therefore, pain, religion, and self-identity were inseparably intertwined.

Yet even if the clerical establishment agreed on the source of and reason for human suffering, they parted company when it came time to explain God's intentions. For some, pain was regarded as essential to divine order. They believed that God dispensed such misfortune to divert people from sin and the condemnation of eternal punishment. By reforming themselves, humans had some control over the duration of that pain. Others were less optimistic about the human potential to avoid sinful behavior. They regarded human calamities as a sign of the approaching millennium, the test of suffering as a sign of grace, and remained unconvinced of the human ability to mitigate bodily pain through repentance. Although both camps preached discipline, the latter group more strongly emphasized resignation in the face of suffering. All ministers reminded their flocks that, just as Christ "cheerfully submitted to the pains and reproach of the cross," good Christians should bear their own pain with patience and an agreeable disposition; only extremists were persuaded that faith alone could triumph "over pain, disease, and mortality."[6]

Life would have been a lot simpler for early American Christians if their ministers had agreed on providential purpose. Alternative reasons for human suffering posed a quandary: how was anyone to know for which reason she or he was being subjected to pain? Was it for a sin committed unconsciously? Or was God merely challenging his best and brightest? To turn from sin would presumably usher in a release from pain; but what if God was proctoring a test? When would it end? A dilemma, to be sure, and one that conceivably had a significant effect on the American psyche.

Late-eighteenth-century ministers tirelessly expounded on variations of these themes both in the pulpit and in their private diaries. According to a sermon delivered by the Reverend David Barnes, God made pain more memorable than pleasure: "If we were as forgetful of pains, as we are of pleasures, we should be much oftener in trouble, than we commonly are. The recollection of past errors is the way to avoid them. . . . The school of affliction is the school of

6. Boyd Hilton, *The Age of Atonement: The Influence of Evangelicalism on Social and Economic Thought, 1795–1865* (Oxford, 1988), 8–11, 17; Nathan Williams, *No Cause nor Need of Pain in Heaven, Illustrated in a Sermon Preached at the Funeral of Eliakim Hall, Esq. of Wallingford* . . . (New Haven, Conn., [1794]), 20; David Barnes, *Thoughts on the Love of Life and Fear of Death: Delivered in a Sermon* (Boston, 1795), 9, 11; William Lockwood, *A Sermon Delivered at the Funeral of Mrs. Jerusha Woodbridge* . . . (Middletown, Conn., 1799), 14; Henry Channing, *A Sermon, Delivered at Hartford, at the Funeral of Mrs. Anna Strong* . . . (Hartford, Conn., 1789), 10.

wisdom." As the minister Henry Channing summed it up, God dispensed pain for the "improvement of the christian temper," a theory that elevated pain to a positive good. By denying people the ability to enjoy life, pain encouraged undistracted concentration on God.[7]

Channing and his colleagues appear to represent what psychologists refer to as the "old American group," a collective (albeit somewhat amorphous) body that set communal standards by denying approval for either public admission of pain or overt grievances against it. Accordingly, a show of frustration, an open display of anger, an admission of fear were evidence of resistance to a condition set in motion by God. Not only were these emotional responses dangerously akin to "murmuring against our Maker," but such resistance to God's will could subject "impenitent sinners" to the further pain of everlasting torment.[8]

Despite their role as creators and interpreters of permissible behavior, however, clerics were no more or less impervious to pain than anyone else. Whether or not such personal distress subconsciously molded a minister's outlook toward life and religion and whether that attitude was articulated between the lines of each sermon is unclear, although the Reverend Silas Constant's exceptional diary entry hints that his preaching might have occasionally lacked cheer: "Not well, pain in head and neck. O what a barren heart! . . . O useless instrument cold of feeling and zeal none, the Lord help."[9] If an unintentional lack of enthusiasm invaded a homily, what effect would this have had on a congregation that, theoretically at least, took its attitudinal key from its minister? And if a minister suffered from consistent poor health and pain, could this not indicate God's lack of endorsement—if bodily pain and divine punishment were actually interrelated?

Popular literature reinforced ministerial prescriptions and reached an even wider audience. *The Economy of Human Life* was an international best-seller within a generation of its publication in 1750, and its author, Robert Dodsley, reminded his readers that "the sickness of the body affecteth even the soul." Dodsley urged them to make the former "subservient" to the latter, since suffering was "a necessity" from which there was no escape. Given these unalter-

7. Barnes, *Thoughts on the Love of Life*, 11; Channing, *A Sermon Delivered at Hartford*, 11.

8. Kenneth D. Craig, "Social Modeling Influences: Pain in Context," in Richard A. Sternbach, ed., *The Psychology of Pain* (New York, 1986), 73; H. B. Gibson, *Pain and Its Conquest* (London, 1982), 21–22; Richard A. Sternbach, *Pain: A Psychophysiological Analysis* (New York, 1968), 74; James Fordyce, *A Discourse on Pain; Preached at Bath* (London, 1791), 12, 56.

9. Emily Warren Roebling, *The Journal of the Reverend Silas Constant, Pastor of the Presbyterian Church at Yorktown . . .* , ed. Josiah Granville Leach (Philadelphia, 1903), Mar. 10, 1784, 22.

able conditions, Dodsley charged his audience to "submit with modesty" and to "suffer with an equal mind"—advice more easily advanced than applied.[10]

Yet neither ministerial exhortations nor popular manuals went unchallenged in the age of Enlightenment. Pain was becoming secularized to the extent that the medical profession had begun to concentrate on nerve and muscle function and scientific experimentation. Their interest in sensory physiology was inextricably bonded to the culture of sensibility, although doctors took greater interest in pain as a symptom of some deeper problem: a warning to change one's habits or activities and thus avoid greater physical affliction. To them, there was nothing intrinsically beneficial about pain; it was merely a diagnostic tool.[11] On one level, both ministers and physicians could agree on the usefulness of pain as a signal to alter behavior, but their incompatible positions on the source of pain might have produced tensions between the two professions as well as confusion in the minds of those who sought advice. Was it bad diet or sinful behavior that caused a colicky episode? Or was it a combination of both, since God's overall scheme might have included temptation in the form of ill-advised edible delicacies?

The eighteenth century saw philosophes as well as physicians attempt to subvert religious doctrine. Denouncing submission and resignation as unrealistic, secular humanists such as Benjamin Franklin argued that avoidance of pain was intrinsic to human motivation. Franklin maintained that "we are first mov'd by *Pain*, and the whole succeeding Course of our Lives is but one continu'd Series of Action with a View to be freed from it." Some years later, the popular Scottish philosopher Francis Hutcheson projected Franklin's argument to another level by suggesting that the prospect "of avoiding bodily Pain" could engage desperate people "into actions really evil," an assessment seconded by the Reverend Nathan Williams, who noted that "indecency of behavior" frequently followed "extreme bodily pain."[12] Pain invoked the dark side of human nature by forcing people to act contrary to their better character. And although such behavior was obviously at odds with Christian doctrine, Franklin, Hutcheson, and Williams were unable (or unwilling) to translate their theories into practice, the likely reason being that there was little

10. Robert Dodsley, *The Economy of Human Life* . . . (1750; reprint, Hawick, 1814), pt. 2, bk. 5, 136–137.

11. For an extended discussion of the secularization of pain in the 18th century, see Rey, *History of Pain*, trans. Wallace, Cadden, and Cadden, esp. chap. 5.

12. Franklin, *A Dissertation*, 15; Francis Hutcheson, "An Essay on the Nature and Conduct of the Passions and Affections" (1728), in Bernhard Fabian, ed., *Collected Works,* 7 vols. (1745–1755; facsimile edition, Hildesheim, 1969–1971), II, 133–134; Williams, *No Cause nor Need of Pain*, 19.

anyone could do—morally or immorally—to escape the uninvited attention of pain, thus giving the advocates of resignation and submission the last word after all. But in this context, resignation was not a positive, uplifting force; it was a negative response to what could not be altered.

At the end of the century, resignation and submission were still the most potent palliatives offered, but some writers conceded that pain refused to be "talked down by bold speeches, fine reflexions, or moral maxims." Only "hope of relief sooner or later" helped people to bear the greatest "external" calamity known to man, admitted the English clergyman James Fordyce. Forty years earlier, Robert Dodsley had rejected the possibility of escape; Fordyce, caught in the crosscurrents of optimism and sensibility, allowed hope. Furthermore, Fordyce acknowledged the inherently evil nature of pain, despite its service to the twin causes of piety and virtue.[13] Yet even as he championed hope, he knew that pain without surcease undercut optimism.

Fordyce's allusions to speeches, reflections, and maxims might have been veiled references to the literature of sensibility that flowered so prolifically in the late eighteenth century and of which he was an ardent exponent. Its guidelines called for greater sensitivity to and sympathy for human suffering, while its adherents denounced pain as unacceptable and eradicable. Implicitly, sensibility validated at least some measure of self-pity, although the dividing line between permissible and nonpermissible complaints was rather murky.

As a result of this movement, moreover, humanitarian reformers urged the abandonment of publicly inflicted pain as a means of social control.[14] Benjamin Rush, whose intellectual interests resulted in a series of essays on various topics, argued that public punishment actually encouraged recidivism: "A man who has lost his character at a whipping-post, has nothing valuable left to lose in society. Pain has begotten insensibility to the whip; and infamy to shame." Instead, wrote Rush, such punishment bred a spirit of revenge. In addition, a spectacle of this nature, far from acting as a deterrent "by exciting terror in the minds of spectators," really produced the opposite effect. Eighteenth-century sensibility, which Rush added to the catalog of natural laws, elicited sympathy and a disposition to relieve all kinds of distress.[15]

13. Fordyce, *A Discourse on Pain*, 24–25, 28.

14. I am indebted to Michael Meranze, whose paper "A Criminal Is Being Beaten: The History of Punishment and the Politics of Body," delivered at the *Possible Pasts* conference, sponsored by the Institute of Early American History and Culture and the Philadelphia Center for Early American Studies, June 3–5, 1994, stimulated my thinking in this area.

15. Benjamin Rush, "An Enquiry into the Effects of Public Punishments upon Criminals, and upon Society . . ." (1787), in Rush, *Essays, Literary, Moral, and Philosophical* (Philadelphia, 1798), 136, 138, 139, 141.

All this is to say that end-of-the-century literature convincingly demonstrates a heightened awareness of suffering and a mentalité that repudiated the infliction of pain on others. Nevertheless, evidence is wanting that these intellectual trends actually lessened the pain arising from disease or accidents. Pain was still a fact of life, defying its unacceptability by its continued presence. The culture of sensibility could not act as a mediator between the self and pain because pain was so self-absorbing. As Dr. Alexander Anderson confided to his diary in 1796, "I have suffer'd much today—It cannot therefore be expected that I have much to say on any other subject than my complaints."[16]

Thus, even if one could distance oneself from the pain and violence to which others were subjected, even if such suffering filled the viewer with revulsion, it was impossible in the premodern era to divorce oneself from pain. Temporarily, at least, discourse and reality were forced to endure a discordant relationship. One might even say that although the culture of sensibility stimulated penal reform and intensified the search for effective painkillers—a search that culminated in the discovery and use of anesthesia and more efficient (and thus pain-reducing) medical instruments—the concept has perhaps been given too much credit for altering the nature of American society.

Sympathy, a staple of sensibility, had limits, according to Adam Smith, who argued that people were basically unsympathetic to the bodily suffering of others unless the fear and anxiety of death accompanied such distress. "The gout or the tooth-ach, though exquisitely painful," he asserted, "excite very little sympathy." Furthermore, external pain emanating from a surgical operation, wound, or fracture tended to excite more sympathy than pain that proceeded from an internal source: "I can scarce form an idea of the agonies of my neighbour when he is tortured with the gout, or the stone; but I have the clearest conception of what he must suffer from an incision, a wound, or a fracture."[17]

Smith did not address this issue further, although it might have been that people were inured to the internal distress of others because they were dulled by its very pervasiveness. Nevertheless, the implications of Smith's position put him at odds with Benjamin Rush, who portrayed sympathy as a natural response. Smith implied that sympathy required cultivation.

Compassion might also be expressed in such a way as to exclude the person most in need of it. When Thomas Cope received a letter from a friend whose

16. Diary of Dr. Alexander Anderson, May 20, 1796, New-York Historical Society, New York City.

17. Adam Smith, *The Theory of Moral Sentiments,* ed. D. D. Raphael and A. L. Macfie (1759; reprint, Oxford, 1976), 30.

wife suffered from a painful illness, he recorded in his diary: "My soul deeply and fervently sympathizes with her husband in the distress which her condition imposes on him. I feel for him. I feel for myself."[18] It is of some interest that his sympathy did not extend to the patient herself—a point which on the one hand confirms Adam Smith's observation and on the other suggests that pain might have elicited a particular network of responses.

An essential ingredient of sensibility, the language of refinement, might also have acted to mask rather than expose pain. Gentility precluded explicit references to genitalia, and, by concealing the sexual nature of a painful episode, the expurgated version tended to conceal the pain as well. Elizabeth Drinker, an eighteenth-century Quaker Philadelphian, surreptitiously recorded that her thirty-year-old son William "brulez son —— cett matin, he took a walk out this morning so that it cant be very bad." That she disguised the entry in French, and left blank the particular point of William's anatomy at which the burn occurred, suggests a reluctance to elaborate on what must have been an extremely painful incident. That it was more than minor is corroborated by a subsequent entry: "WD. in pain for two days past, and a little lame, occasion'd by a burn."[19]

Furthermore, even if the infliction of pain on others did in fact become culturally unacceptable, it does not necessarily follow that the *desire* to inflict pain was commensurately reduced. If Americans (for whatever socially constructed reasons) still retained aggressive or hostile tendencies, then perhaps the art depicting such violence served as a substitute—a fantasy—an acting out of what had become socially reproachable among refined people, rather than a rejection of it.[20] Perhaps it was even an attempt to distance the self from pain by projecting it onto others through drawings and prints. Or maybe the portrayal of men beating women was a sign of resistance to the feminization of American culture. But whatever role sensibility might have played in the development of this genre, husbands still beat wives, masters whipped slaves, soldiers slew Indians, parents abused children, and boys tortured animals. Those who, at a distance, eschewed such violence were rarely in a position to effect change, and the beneficiaries of humanitarian reform were members of a highly selective group. In this scenario, class, race, and gender intersected with pain.

Power intersected with all of the above as well. Acting on the presumption

18. Harrison, ed., *Philadelphia Merchant,* May 13, 1802, 108.

19. Elaine Forman Crane, ed., *The Diary of Elizabeth Drinker,* 3 vols. (Boston, 1991), Dec. 13, 16, 1797, II, 986.

20. Karen Halttunen, "Humanitarianism and the Pornography of Pain in Anglo-American Culture," *American Historical Review,* C (1995), 303–334, esp. 304.

that pain aroused fear, slaveholders continued to apply corporal punishment to reinforce power relationships and to deter slaves from unacceptable behavior, long after such punitive measures were abandoned among whites. If God was the source of pain for Christians and slaveowners were the source of pain for slaves, the unmistakable implications might have strengthened a sense of human majesty at the same time that the subliminal link sought to intensify deferential attitudes.

Yet in one sense, all this was compatible with the advance of civilization. If refinement meant that "better" people enjoyed a deeper appreciation of and response to pain, such an interpretation implied that "primitive" people tolerated pain with greater equanimity because their faculties were less developed. This construction justified equating Indians with savagery, given their reputed stoicism in the face of pain, and it justified brutality toward slaves. Thus, the dark side of sensibility exaggerated class and racial distinctiveness and allowed for the perpetuation of violence toward others. In the latter part of the nineteenth century, social Darwinism, with its emphasis on survival of the fittest, reinforced this concept.

The intellectual currents of the later eighteenth century offered such mixed messages about pain that many Americans exhibited mental conflict, confusion, and anguish in their diaries as they tried to sort out their private ambivalence about God's motives. The Reverend Seth Williston accepted his illness as a reproach for a "wicked heart," but Ephraim Bateman questioned the logic of God's apportionment plan:

> Is it for my sins I am chastised so? . . . But am I more sinful than many of my companions who I see daily basking in the open sunshine of uninterrupted health? Here I must confess that I think it is not the case. The inference then to be drawn is plainly this that as Vice is not always fully punished nor virtue fully rewarded in this life a Future State is morally certain where every one will receive the due rewards of his deeds.

Presumably, Bateman's afterlife promised better health than his present one, but he could not be certain. Perhaps Bateman *was* "sinful" and his pain signaled God's displeasure over that ethical deficiency. Although Bateman appears to have rejected this alternative, his qualified optimism might have repressed a subconscious self-image that identified more with moral failure than Bateman was ready to admit.[21]

21. Rev. John Quincy Adams, ed., "The Diaries of the Rev. Seth Williston, D. D.," *Journal of the Presbyterian Historical Society*, IX (1918), 381; "Journal of Ephraim Bateman of Fair-

And what if pain overwhelmed composure—as it often did—despite every effort to yield with patience? Presumably that would incite a sense of shame—even guilt—and compound the personal sense of failure: pain would have been not only a rebuke by God for moral dereliction but the force that prevented endurance of that reproach with resignation. Elizabeth Drinker found a way around this dilemma. Her mental accommodation to pain did not result from her own exertions "altogether," she reasoned, but rather from "dependance . . . on a supereor power." Should she fail, God could be held accountable for her inability to submit with grace.[22] Carried to its logical conclusion, Drinker's assessment relieved her from responsibility for sin altogether. An omnipotent God whose "supereor power" regulated human response to pain might just as well be held accountable for stimulating the sin that precipitated such a sequence of events. But although this particular interpretive twist would have been rejected by Drinker, she, like many of her contemporaries, was strikingly creative in amending doctrine to meet her needs.

Furthermore, just as individual and cultural pain thresholds varied widely, and just as internal belief systems underwent adjustments in order to accommodate religious theory, the simple existence of unrelieved pain precipitated behavorial patterns that only sometimes corresponded with prescriptive literature. The clerical army might have advanced standards of conduct, but the emotional forces unleashed by pain frequently overwhelmed attempts to conform to the ideal. Only when pain was "not very acute" could one become "measurably reconciled" to it, asserted Elizabeth Drinker, thus illustrating the tension between God's will and the demands of her own body.[23]

There is no way of knowing, of course, how many people actually subscribed to the paradigm, no way of quantifying those for whom religious values resonated so powerfully that they even attempted to conform to the prescriptive model. Nevertheless, for nonbelievers as well as believers, pain-sponsored behavior was remarkably similar—at least for those who recorded their responses. Ministers preached submission; those in pain resisted. Religion taught resignation; sufferers sought escape. Doctrine sanctioned patience; patients exhibited anger. And because even the most devout were often unable to comply with culturally defined responses, they also succumbed to conflicting emotions: ambivalence, guilt, and shame.

---

field Township, Cumberland County," *Vineland Historical Magazine*, XIV (1929), Oct. 26, 1800, 106. See also Claudine Herzlich and Janine Pierret, *Illness and Self in Society*, trans. Elborg Forster (Baltimore, 1987).

22. Crane, ed., *Diary of Elizabeth Drinker*, Feb. 28, 1801, II, 1389–1390.

23. Ibid., Dec. 11, 1794, I, 626.

The expectation, experience, and empirical observation of physical discomfort was so widespread in early America that it was memorialized in song, embroideries, drawings, and verse.[24] And because cultural approval for public weeping and gnashing of teeth was lacking in the eighteenth century, Americans recorded their personal sufferings in the privacy of their diaries. Admissions of despair, ill-temper, and resentment mingled on the pages with hope for resignation and patience. Writing about pain seems to have been more than a catharsis, however. It appears to have been a compromise between a public challenge to God over the grand design of the universe and a private conversation with friends and family—an exchange surely fraught with complaints. Confiding in a personal diary might have substituted for the public discourse about pain that could not take place. Open condemnation of pain was subversive of Christian doctrine, but one could plausibly argue that a diary—even one that circulated among friends—remained private.

Taken as a whole, diary literature confirms an incessant preoccupation with health and an effort to contain disease through constant vigilance. Moreover, if autobiographical writing is a (re)creation of the self, then writing about pain integrates that condition into any (re)construction of self. And by absorbing pain into its pages, the diary not only manufactures a self that identifies with a painful existence but is a record and reminder of the future potential of pain: "what we may hereafter possibly suffer."[25]

Yet only a few people who wrote about pain in their journals philosophized about it; most simply noted its existence, tried to alleviate it, and endured it when all else failed—which suggests that Franklin had a keener sense of reality than his more godly contemporaries. Accommodation to pain might have brought its own rewards—privileges, respect, sympathy, tenderness, or moral authority—but most sufferers would have gladly waived the honors.

24. See the poem "Upon Some Distemper of Body," by Anne Bradstreet, in Charles E. Hambrick-Stowe, ed., *Early New England Meditative Poetry: Anne Bradstreet and Edward Taylor* (Mahwah, N.J., 1988), 66. The following lines were embroidered on a sampler by Hannah C. Wolcott (1785–1843) in Boston, c. 1800: "Music the fiercest grief can charm / And fates severest rage disarm / Music can soften pain to ease / And make despair and madness please." See also Sherry Babbitt, ed., *The Picture of Health: Images of Medicine and Pharmacy from the William H. Helfand Collection* (Philadelphia, [1991]); and John Edmunds, comp., *A Williamsburg Songbook: Songs, Convivial, Sporting, Amorous, etc., from Eighteenth-Century Collections Known to Have Been in the Libraries of Colonial Virginians* (Williamsburg, Va., 1964), 4.

25. For development of this thesis, see Patricia Meyer Spacks, *Imagining a Self: Autobiography and Novel in Eighteenth-Century England* (Cambridge, Mass., 1976), esp. chap. 1; Smith, *The Theory of Moral Sentiments*, 30.

The language of pain was almost formulaic. Given the richness of the English language, the relative paucity of adjectives and adverbs used to describe the nature of pain and suffering is surprising. People were in "agony," they experienced "tormenting pain," or were exposed to "constant," "extreme," or "violent" pain, but diarists wasted precious little time searching for creative synonyms and dramatic phrases.[26]

Still, diary literature abounds with instances of physical distress and is extremely suggestive of the ways in which the individual was molded by and responded to such conditions of life. One of the most revealing illustrations of a painful society is the journal of Elizabeth Drinker, written in the half-century between 1758 and 1807. Drinker filled her three dozen manuscript volumes with information on every subject imaginable. Nothing was too routine, no daily event too trivial for inclusion in her journal. She consistently documented her own physical pain but refused to inflict psychological pain on others in the form of criticism or backbiting.

Drinker's self-imposed censorship notwithstanding, it is evident from the amount of space devoted to such issues as health and medicine that she considered her world replete with pain of all kinds. To take her at her word, she and almost everyone she knew suffered from some physical discomfort a substantial part of the time. Yet despite the considerable space devoted to this topic, Drinker left even more unsaid: "Were I to make a memorandum when ever I felt my self indisposed, I should daily say I was unwell." Shared expectations and experience as well as a common understanding about the ubiquity of pain and illness made further detail unnecessary. Only when she was "very poorly" did she bother to record it—either for her own recollection or for another reader's edification.[27]

Yet, the circulation of diaries in eighteenth-century America meant that a small, literate elite could commiserate with each other through a journal. It is impossible to determine whether the reader sustained any comfort from numbers, insight from others, or a sense of bonding from the similarity of circumstances, but the accumulation of evidence from diary literature implies that, although people tried to control pain, they were generally unsuccessful in their attempts to secure relief. If that is true, there is reason to believe that their world was considerably different from ours—at least to the extent that aspirin has made a difference.

Drinker's remarks were not unique, nor was she exaggerating. Contempo-

---

26. British diarists were as uncreative as their American cousins, although the Porters maintain that later in the century the English described their pain more expansively and intimately. See Porter and Porter, *In Sickness and in Health,* 103–104.

27. Crane, ed., *Diary of Elizabeth Drinker,* Dec. 31, 1799, II, 1252–1253, Dec. 2, 1795, I, 757.

raries up and down the eastern seaboard echoed her comments, and collectively these journals document both the existence of and the response to chronic and acute pain. Read as a human mosaic, they demonstrate that, at each stage of life, pain added a dimension to the development of self. The experience of suffering molded childhood expectations and adult attitudes. Pain negotiated intrafamilial and extrafamilial relationships to the extent that it became a defining force in early America. According to James Fordyce, whose works were extensively quoted and widely reprinted in America, pain darkened "some of the fairest characters" and interrupted "the flow of the finest affections." Pain generated "impatience, fretfulness, and nameless misgivings," as it spread "a general gloom" over life. Even worse, complaints about pain tended to "disturb the peace" and "destroy the comfort" of those who surrounded the sick or injured.[28] Thus, pain was a formative experience. It shaped individual perceptions, stimulated confrontation between emotion and intellect, and molded personal as well as communal behavior.

In the early American household, pain and personal development began their intimate relationship during childhood. Benjamin Franklin maintained that an infant's consciousness was only stimulated by its first sensation of pain. "Thus is the Machine set on work; this is Life." John Gregory, whose writings went through many editions as a testament to their popularity among his English and American readers, argued that very young children only cried from "pain or sickness." If left unattended, "their violent struggles to get relief . . . disorder their constitutions; and when a child's first sensations partake so much of pain and distress, and when the turbulent passions are so early awaked . . . there is some reason to suspect they may have an influence on the future temper."[29] A contemporary of Gregory, Dr. Elihu Hubbard Smith, confirmed that a painful childhood episode was not easily forgotten. He recalled that as a very young child he had two blisters applied to his legs, which caused "painful sensations" and that he was wakened "by the pain they occasioned." The incident had been "powerfully fixed" in his memory for decades, and it is fair to say that Smith had incorporated it into the persona he created through his journal.[30]

In a familial context, pain was also infectious. A child who grew up in what is called a "painful family" was (and is) likely to develop similar symptoms in later life. Chronic headache patients have been found to have had headache

28. Fordyce, *A Discourse on Pain*, 10, 12.

29. Franklin, *A Dissertation*, 15; John Gregory, *A Comparative View of the State and Faculties of Man with Those of the Animal World* (London, 1798), 51.

30. "Notes from Recollections of My Life from My Birth till the Age of Eleven," in James E. Cronin, ed., *The Diary of Elihu Hubbard Smith, 1771–1798* (Philadelphia, 1973), 17–18.

models in their families. People reporting persistent pain usually had a parent with persistent pain. Psychologists have also found that intrafamily arguments can stimulate physical pain.[31] If so, these factors must have had a disproportionate impact on family dynamics in an early American society marked by large families and a lack of privacy.

It was not only the residual effects of illness and injury that affected child development but the memory of corporal punishment as well. Philip Greven argues persuasively that the physical punishment to which early American children were sometimes subjected bred long-term resentments that in turn influenced personality development and adult behavior, particularly as far as parent-child relationships were concerned. And as a corollary to his argument against the use of corporal punishment in the legal system, Benjamin Rush advocated an end to such methods in the schools. Boys who were thumped on the head or boxed on the ears, wrote Rush, lost all sense of shame and thus "all moral sensibility." Pain begot a spirit of violence, a resistance to instruction, and long-lasting hatred of the schoolmaster.[32]

Thus, children learned early that physical pain from a variety of sources would be part of their lives. Although the "small lump cut out" of little Robert Pott's breast or breastbone was not an operation "of great consequence" according to Elizabeth Drinker, the doctors made "a great matter of a little business and enough to frighten the Child."[33] This episode suggests that the pain of such surgical intervention was initially of little concern to Drinker (and presumably to young Potts) and that children might have been threatened by the prospect of bodily pain only at a threshold that was higher than that of twentieth-century standards.

Adult attitudes and behavior were also molded by pain. Admonished to meet suffering with patience, resignation, and an even disposition, few diarists ever recorded the achievement of these goals. On the contrary, Elizabeth Drinker admitted that her sore throat, fever, and need to take pills put her "out of sorts" and offered her opinion that Betty Carmor, the whitewasher, was "very bad tempered, oweing . . . to infirmity of body." In a funeral sermon preached in 1794, the Reverend Nathan Williams noted that pain often resulted

31. Craig, "Social Modeling," in Sternbach, ed., *The Psychology of Pain,* 78; Gibson, *Pain and Its Conquest,* 153.

32. Philip Greven, *The Protestant Temperament: Patterns of Child-Rearing, Religious Experience, and the Self in Early America* (New York, 1977), esp. pt. II; and Greven, *Spare the Child: The Religious Roots of Punishment and the Psychological Impact of Physical Abuse* (New York, 1991), 134–135; Benjamin Rush, "Thoughts upon the Amusements and Punishments Which Are Proper for Schools . . . ," in Rush, *Essays,* 64–66 (quotation on 65).

33. Crane, ed., *Diary of Elizabeth Drinker,* May 23, 26, 1799, II, 1171, 1172.

in "a peevish spirit." In such circumstances, Williams asserted, people found "fault with all about them, even their best friends."[34] Try as they might to conform to Christian doctrine, human emotion, not intellect, controlled behavior.

This is not to argue that late-eighteenth-century America was marked by nearly three million irritable people, but it is likely that pain affected one's outlook on life in ways that are less common today because of our ability to control or at least reduce its worst effects. Elizabeth Drinker speculated that "good health does or ought to occasion Chearfullness," although the qualified nature of her remark suggests either that reality did not conform to theory or that her circle of acquaintances did not include enough people with good health to test her thesis.[35]

Although some people did, in fact, exhibit the patience and resignation that was expected of good Christians who suffered from painful disorders, and although others "appear'd . . . composed" in the face of "mesry and pain," these were exceptions, at least as far as diary literature offers evidence of attitude and behavior. In spite of Fordyce's insistence that hope was the "one cordial drop" that made pain bearable, most writers registered low expectations of improvement, and even Elizabeth Drinker admitted that her chronic pain challenged any hope of relief.[36]

Irritability and pessimism were two responses to physical pain, depression another. Indeed, it is possible that pain-sponsored depression might have led to despair deep enough to elicit consideration of suicide. There is some reason to believe that the British had a propensity for suicide (or self-murder) in the face of intractable pain, but the evidence is too sparse to justify any conclusions about this side of the Atlantic. Although the act was usually condemned, one of America's European mentors, Jean Jacques Rousseau, condoned suicide in circumstances where acute, incurable bodily pain distracted the mind to the extent that a person lacked both will and reason.[37]

Although Christian belief decried the act of suicide, was a *wish* for death within the prescribed boundaries? Lucy Cranch reported to Abigail Adams that when their Aunt Tufts died, "she bore her sickness with the resagnation of

34. Ibid., June 19, 1798, May 11, 1806, II, 1046, III, 1927; Williams, *No Cause nor Need of Pain*, 19.

35. Crane, ed., *Diary of Elizabeth Drinker*, July 24, 1794, I, 576.

36. Jonathan Evans, comp., *A Journal of the Life, Travels, and Religious Labours, of William Savery* . . . (Philadelphia, 1873), Oct. 13, 1797, 369; Fordyce, *A Discourse on Pain*, 28; Crane, ed., *Diary of Elizabeth Drinker*, June 30, 1802, May 17, 1806, II, 1539, III, 1930.

37. Porter and Porter, *In Sickness and in Health*, 241; Jean Jacques Rousseau, *Eloisa: or, A Series of Original Letters Collected and Published by J. J. Rousseau*, 4 vols. (London, 1776), II, 273.

a Christion yet longing to be released from that frail tenement which had always been a sourse of pain to her." On the one hand, Aunt Tufts's behavior was said to be exemplary; on the other, she was impatient with God's time-table, which was antithetical to ministerial advice. According to Reverend Williams, those who made an effort to suffer "in the exercise of grace" did not "wish for death to get rid of present pain."[38]

Suicide might not have been an option for people suffering from intense pain not only because of religious scruples but because both chronic and acute pain were frequently linked with impending death—thus obviating the need for an active role to achieve the same result. The association of pain and death (and the assumption that one accompanied the other) was a legacy of medieval theology, and one that Protestantism continued to perpetuate despite its Catholic roots.

The spatial intimacy of early American households guaranteed that pain would affect intrafamily dynamics as well as individual outlook and conduct. Since pain can spawn aggression toward others as well as toward oneself, it probably exacerbated the tensions already present in ordinary marital relationships, leading in extraordinary situations to the physical abuse of a spouse or child. Conversely, as Daniel Blake Smith suggests, physical distress could promote stronger kinship bonds, since family members became dependent on each other for their everyday needs. Even the strongest bonds could become strained, however, as the helpless patient surrendered all pretensions to modesty, cognizant that he or she was "giving trouble to others" and "causing grief" to the "kindest friends." And although nursing the sick with compassion imbued the caregiver with moral righteousness, even the most tender attendant must have suffered an occasional twinge of exasperation at his or her role. Which sequence was played out depended on many variables, but it is unlikely they were mutually exclusive.[39]

Surely it must have been frustrating for parents, spouses, and children to see their loved ones suffer. How hard it could become is illustrated by William Oliver of Salem, Massachusetts, who admitted that he was "happy" to see his nephew die after watching him suffer during an aggravated case of measles. Convinced that in the "Worlds beyond the Grave . . . pain or trouble can never

38. Lucy Cranch to Abigail Adams, Dec. 8, 1785, in L. H. Butterfied et al., eds., *Adams Family Correspondence* (Cambridge, Mass. 1963–), VI, 484–485; Williams, *No Cause nor Need of Pain*, 16.

39. Daniel Blake Smith, *Inside the Great House: Planter Family Life in Eighteenth-Century Chesapeake Society* (Ithaca, N.Y., 1980), 259; Fordyce, *A Discourse on Pain*, 38; Miriam Bailin, *The Sickroom in Victorian Fiction: The Art of Being Ill* (Cambridge, 1994), 11.

come," Oliver's ambivalence over the loss of a loved one was resolved in favor of release from pain.[40]

In another family scenario, pain might have been associated with one parent, whereas remission of pain was connected to another. The Drinker diary suggests that a father's strength was needed for a painful operation such as a tooth extraction: Jacob Downing (Drinker's son-in-law) pulled two large eye teeth from his daughter's mouth. At the same time, it was the mother, as primary caregiver, who usually attempted to relieve pain.[41] On one level, the different roles allowed parents to compete for power over their children; on another, these associations, repeated over time, might have exaggerated familial relationships (fear of father, affection toward mother). If such tendencies did in fact exist, they might have been altered over time by the professionalization of medicine and the development of effective pain remedies.

Alexander Anderson lived in New York with his parents. In his dual role as son and physician, he cared for his mother, who frequently complained of stomach pains and toothaches. In April 1795, Bellevue Hospital offered Anderson a position that required his residence at the institution, and Anderson recorded that his mother's feelings were "not a little agitated on this change in our family." The evidence does not link Mrs. Anderson's pains to her desire for attention from her son, yet this possibility should not be discounted. Psychologists agree that pain may be used as a means of empowerment by people who seek attention and compliance from those who surround them.[42]

If physical discomfort disciplined the worldview of household members, it also subjected household routine, social relationships, and community dynamics to its vagaries. Occasionally, people took advantage of pain when it invaded their lives; more often it was an intrusion that both inhibited and defined continuing and customary activities.

Ordinarily, the modest homes and large families of early America relegated solitude and privacy to the category of infrequent luxuries. Admission of pain, however, allowed people to engage in self-centered activities that were otherwise impermissible. Elizabeth Drinker loved to read but expressed guilt about indulging herself instead of attending to household chores. Her disabilities circumvented such ambivalence by sanctioning reading and justifying the

40. "Journal of William Wait Oliver of Salem, 1802–1803," *Essex Institute Historical Collections,* LXXXI (1945), July 8, 1802, 129.

41. Crane, ed., *Diary of Elizabeth Drinker,* Aug. 31, 1801, Mar. 16, 1804, Aug. 29, 1807, II, 1440–1441, III, 1732, 2070.

42. Diary of Dr. Alexander Anderson, Apr. 24, 1795; Thomas S. Szasz, *Pain and Pleasure: A Study of Bodily Feelings,* 2d ed. (New York, 1975), xxi.

abandonment of domestic duties to her sister. By the end of 1793, a little more than a year before her sixtieth birthday, she admitted that she found the "retirement" occasioned by her "present indispossion" "rather pleasing." Similarly, Elizabeth Cranch (a New England contemporary of Drinker) noted that her "indisposition" confined her to her chamber. In a revealing afterthought, however, she admitted that "the body alone suffers confinement—the mind has Liberty to range wheresoever it wills."[43] In this context, pain was empowering; it permitted Drinker and Cranch to elude socially prescribed routines.

In a society without telephones where reciprocal visits were the chief means of socializing, unexpected callers might have been an occasional intrusion. Grace Galloway might well have been "so bad in the colic" that she "could hardly converse," or she might have been feigning to rid herself of a tedious guest. In any case, when she excused herself on the grounds that she was indisposed, the visitor left. Similarly, pain could be used as an excuse to refuse an invitation: "Martha Rough . . . was to have dined with us she sent word . . . that she had the head-ach to bad to come out."[44]

Julia Cowles could not very well admit that she disliked school or that she lacked enthusiasm for Sunday meeting. Yet was her "hard headache" bad enough to warrant absence from school one afternoon in 1799? Did it exist at all? Did other aches and pains justify poor performance in school? And was it merely coincidence that her only headaches throughout the following year erupted on occasional Sundays? "Had a very hard pain in my head . . . did not attend meeting." "Did not attend meeting on account of headache." On the latter Sunday, a fortuitous recovery by evening permitted company. In 1802, Cowles also rejected the advances of a suitor on the grounds of ill health, although her untimely death in 1803 at the age of eighteen suggests that she might, in fact, have been ill at the time.[45]

Live-in servants who were constantly on call had good reason to look for respite whenever they could. As a seasoned mistress, therefore, Elizabeth Drinker suspected that her daughter's servant only feigned sickness: "Nancys black girl Patience Gibbs is very ill or appears so, with a pain in her stomach."[46]

43. Crane, ed., *Diary of Elizabeth Drinker*, Dec. 1, 1793, I, 532; Lizzie Norton Mason and James Duncan Phillips, eds., "The Journal of Elizabeth Cranch," *Essex Institute Historical Collections*, LXXX (1944), Dec. 30, 1785, Jan. 1, 1786, 22, 23.

44. Diary of Grace Growdon Galloway, in Elizabeth Evans, ed., *Weathering the Storm: Women of the American Revolution* (New York, 1975), Mar. 11, 1779, 210; Crane, ed., *Diary of Elizabeth Drinker*, Dec. 13, 1796, II, 866.

45. Laura Hadley Moseley, ed., *The Diaries of Julia Cowles* (New Haven, Conn., 1931), 1799, 30, 31, 44.

46. Crane, ed., *Diary of Elizabeth Drinker*, May 24, 1799, II, 1171.

But who could tell? Physical discomfort was so pervasive, it was impossible to dispute Elizabeth Cranch's indisposition, Grace Galloway's colic, Julia Cowles's headache, Mrs. Anderson's toothache, and Patience Gibb's stomachache. Pain was a handy tool—if one chose to use it—to avoid unpleasant activities and manipulate other people.

Children as well as adults used pain for their own ends, and it is likely that youngsters in large families vied with each other for the attention of their parents by expressing pain—whether it existed or not. Would this sibling rivalry have been reinforced by expressions of sympathy on the part of family members or caregivers? The possibility of such behavior was confirmed by Dr. Elihu Hubbard Smith, who noted that parents were not as solicitous of healthy children as they were of progeny disposed to ill health.[47]

Although it might have been difficult to separate the dissemblers from those who were truly suffering, some people were more adept than others at discerning fraudulent complaints. It was a relatively easy matter for Colonel Landon Carter, because, in his opinion, *all* expressions of pain from his slaves were suspect. In response, Carter countered pain with the threat of more pain, thus escalating the confrontation and accentuating the power relationship between master and slave: "The 2 sarahs came up yesterday pretending to be violent ill with pains in their sides. They look very well, had no fever, and I ordered them down to their work upon pain of a whipping."[48] Carter "ordered" his slaves punished for a variety of infractions, but the whip was only one method of maintaining control over his subordinates. In eighteenth-century terms, Carter possessed extensive medical knowledge. He demonstrated his expertise by ministering to his slaves so excessively as to give the phrase "medical arsenal" a concrete meaning. His remedies were weapons, and his use of harsh purges, emetics, and bloodletting appear to have been means of enforcing obedience. When one slave either "sham[med] her fits" or "pretend[ed]" a pain, Carter insisted that he was being manipulated by her complaints. As a result, and even if "it would possibly be barbarity," Carter planned to "cut an issue or a Sector to drain her head of whims."[49]

Carter's physical abuse of others left him in undisputed command of people and probably enhanced his own sense of superiority—an important dimension of his self-identity. Conversely, each time Carter forced an alleged remedy

47. Cronin, ed., *Diary of Elihu Hubbard Smith*, Sept. 1796, 36.

48. Jack P. Greene, ed., *Diary of Col. Landon Carter of Sabine Hall, 1752–1773* (New York, 1981), Mar. 22, 1770, I, 371–372 (see also June 4, 1773, II, 754).

49. Ibid., July 27, "Old Style," 1771, II, 604–605, "The last of old july," 1771, II, 610. An issue was an incision made for the purpose of causing a discharge.

on an unwilling slave, that person not only suffered the torment of the treatment but a loss of control over himself or herself.

Although some slaves did, no doubt, feign illness in order to escape the burden of work, many more probably suffered from the intractable pain of sickle cell disease. Marked by chronic pain and acute episodes, sickle cell disease is confined to the African American population as well as to people who are descended from inhabitants of malaria-infested regions.[50] Thus, the gene that protected a portion of slaves from contracting malaria interfered with their ability to perform physical labor, and they were punished as a result.

Unrelenting or intermittent pain could interfere with anyone's capacity to function on a daily basis. The evidence suggests that sleep loss was a common by-product of pain and that together they impeded one's ability to engage in normal activities by creating an unsteady hand, delayed reaction time, and the impairment of mental faculties. Although most men and women either ignored their discomfort or made an uneasy truce with it, sometimes pain made it impossible for them to function at all. In some cases, that had political implications, whereas, in other situations it imperiled economic productivity. Although Senator William Maclay made a valiant attempt to fulfill his obligations, illness prevented him from attending Congress for a week in 1789. The Senate postponed an important vote in hopes of a swift recovery, "but alas," recorded Maclay, "I can not attend if the whole Union were at stake." "I lie here fixed with so acute a pain through my loins that I can not move more than if I were impaled."[51]

Alexander Anderson's toothache got the better of him and required such strong medication that he was "unfit for any business 'till 10 o'clock." Edward Williams's wife "had a humour all over her hands Like very Bad Ring worms which lasted Several years and was So Sore that She was Allmost unfitt for any Business." And in December 1789, merchant John May, who noted, but rarely complained, of his ailments, "gott up with a head ake which was so seveer at three oClock" that he "was oblig'd to Quitt business." His frustration at being incapacitated was evident in the comment: "I should Nearly compleeted my buisness in this place if my head had not bin to full of Pain."[52]

50. *New York Times,* June 7, 1994; Peter H. Wood, *Black Majority: Negroes in Colonial South Carolina from 1670 through the Stono Rebellion* (New York, 1974), 88–89.

51. Maclay, *Journal of William Maclay,* Aug. 31–Sept. 2, 1789, 141–142, 147.

52. Diary of Dr. Alexander Anderson, July 30, 1797; Recipe Book of Elizabeth Coates Paschall (1702–1768), College of Physicians of Philadelphia, 5; Dwight L. Smith, ed., *The Western Journals of John May* (Cincinnati, Ohio, 1961), Dec. 1, 1789, 163.

Another merchant, Aaron Lopez, noted in his spinners book that "Sally Lewis has been absent 11 days being sick." Loss of work meant loss of income, and, although John May's economic vitality was not threatened by his short term inability to manage his affairs, Sally Lewis might not have been as fortunate. Employees could not count on an employer to compensate them for a sick day (or longer) and piece workers could not expect to be paid for work they did not produce. When a newly arrived worker complained of "an acute pain in his back . . . that he got . . . by lifting his hogsheads of tobacco where he came from," Landon Carter, with his usual magnanimity, unhesitatingly declared "that if he should be a Cripple I will not be obliged to pay his wages." Debilitating pain might have been the dividing line between economic viability and poverty, in which case the elderly would have been particularly vulnerable in a society without pensions or social security. Under these conditions, those who traded labor for room and board might have had a slight advantage, even on the Carter plantation, as long as they were provided (however reluctantly) with food and shelter: "My weaver truely with a scratch on his leg pretends he can't work; but he can eat."[53]

Pain affected both body and mind. Empirical observations aside, the physical experience of eighteenth-century Americans corroborated John Locke's philosophical position that pain was so basic as to be a test of human existence: "For if I know I feel pain, it is evident I have as certain perception of my own existence, as of the existence of the pain I feel."[54] Early Americans would have been just as happy, no doubt, to substitute different evidence for the same purpose, but they, as well as Locke, understood that, by validating their lives, pain was intrinsic to being.

Although certain attitudes toward pain varied from person to person, others were remarkably similar. An expectation of a painful existence permeated the collective consciousness, and expressions of discouragement and despair far outnumbered positive, uplifting sentiments. Acute pain and fear of death reinforced each other and thus exaggerated the severe anxiety produced by "the pains and agonies of a dying hour."[55]

53. Aaron Lopez, "Spinners Book," Feb. 28, 1769, Lopez Papers, Newport Historical Society, Newport, R.I.; Greene, ed., *Diary of Col. Landon Carter*, Dec. 4, 1757, Feb. 28, 1777, I, 192, II, 1087–1088 (quotation).

54. John Locke, *An Essay Concerning Human Understanding*, ed. Alexander Campbell Fraser, 2 vols. (1690; reprint, Oxford, 1894), bk. IV, II, 305.

55. Robert Breck, *A Sermon Preached at the Funeral of the Rev. Stephen Williams* (Springfield, Mass., 1792), 18, quoted in John Demos, *The Unredeemed Captive: A Family Story from Early America* (New York, 1994), 239.

Household structure, family dynamics, and social habits were subject to the influence of pain in ways that are uncommon today because of demographic changes, the professionalization of medicine, and technological advances. Pain exaggerated power relationships; it harbingered economic instability. More important, people used pain not only to manipulate others but, paradoxically, to manipulate their own lives. In an oddly convoluted sense, pain encouraged individualistic tendencies even as it suppressed them. Moderate suffering permitted a person to be him or her "self"; to indulge in behavior that would otherwise have been rejected.

PAIN AND GENDER

There is little doubt that the social construction of pain includes gender-related issues. Eighteenth-century women were expected to suffer more than men, a result of their delicate constitutions and the ills to which nature subjected them. And by claiming that female ill health was an inherent condition, women were thus afforded unparalleled opportunities to display other gendered characteristics. Cultural expectations required both men and women to suffer silently but for different reasons. A man in control of his passions eschewed cries of "bodily pain, how intolerable soever," because they were "unmanly." Indeed, "the man, who under the severest tortures allows no weakness to escape him . . . commands our highest admiration."[56]

Women, however, suffered with equanimity because they were naturally passive creatures, and their weaker nature allowed compromise of what was demanded of men. "Mild and gentle" complaints were acceptable if they were forced by pain and restrained as much as possible. A stronger expression of pain exhibited turbulence and rebellion—or a refusal to submit to God's will. Women who deviated from this prescribed role threatened to weaken the "affection and tender pity" to which they were generally entitled.[57] Furthermore, pain and illness were excellent justifications for confining women to their particular sphere: the privacy of the home—a notion that reinforces the idea that societies use pain to perpetuate social values.

If society had expectations about women and their response to pain, women themselves had expectations in terms of the pain they could anticipate

56. Antoine Leonard Thomas, *Essay on the Character, Manners, and Genius of Women in Different Ages* (Philadelphia, 1774), II, 45; John Gregory, *A Father's Legacy to His Daughters* (1765; reprint, London, 1784), 50–51; Smith, *Theory of Moral Sentiments*, 28–29, 30–31.

57. Hester Chapone, *Letters on the Improvement of the Mind, Addressed to a Young Lady*, 4th ed. (London, 1774), 101–103.

during their lifetime. Menstrual pain could be incapacitating. The physical discomfort of multiple pregnancies and childbirth was also a source of distress in the eighteenth century, and William Byrd was not the only husband who reported that his wife was "out of humor" because she was "indisposed with breeding and very cross." Francis Parkman's wife responded to a similar situation in much the same way. Dr. Jonathan Jackson reported to his colleague Edward Holyoke that "Mrs. Jackson . . . has for these several years past enjoyed but indifferent Health, owing to a weak and most irritable state of nerves and perhaps to frequent Childbearing." Pregnancy frequently caused as much severe discomfort as it did ill humor. "I have known several instances of women towards the later end of their Pregnancy, from Pain restlessness and anxiety, have been obliged to keep them almost all together in bed, and anodin almost every night till their delivery," wrote one Massachusetts physician to another.[58]

Slave women could not expect anodynes, much less bed rest, during pregnancy. Landon Carter indulged his visibly pregnant slaves by relieving them of weights on their heads and shoulders, but that was the limit of his beneficence. He refused to reduce their workload on the assumption that they were either faking pregnancy or they pretended "to be too heavy." In either case, the alleged pretense resulted in Carter's efforts to "break" them "of that trick." Carter permitted nursing mothers to breast-feed their infants three times a day. Those who abused the privilege were whipped.[59]

A crowded household and thin walls meant that children (especially female children) developed an awareness of the suffering that accompanied childbirth. Surely what they saw and heard made a lasting impression. Unmarried women were privy to labor and delivery, thus learning firsthand what lay in store if they married and sometimes even if they did not. Childbirth was so harrowing an experience that both Elizabeth Drinker and her daughter Nancy avoided assisting at the actual moment of birth if possible.[60]

Women grieved over a stillborn child not only because of the human loss but because they would subsequently undergo the agonies of childbirth sooner

58. Louis B. Wright and Marian Tinling, eds., *The Secret Diaries of William Byrd of Westover, 1709–1712* (Richmond, Va., 1941), 548; Marylynn Salmon, "Motherhood in Seventeenth and Eighteenth-Century Anglo America" (paper delivered at the Eighth Berkshire Conference on the History of Women, June 9, 1990); Jonathan Jackson to Edward Aug. Holyoke, n.d., [Silv. Gardner] to Edward Holyoke, Nov. 16, 1757, box 4, folders 7, 8, Holyoke Papers (Medical Correspondence, 1749–1769), Essex Institute, Salem, Mass.

59. Greene, ed., *Diary of Col. Landon Carter,* Mar. 22, Sept. 21, 1770, Mar. 28, 1771, I, 371–372, 496, 554.

60. Crane, ed., *Diary of Elizabeth Drinker,* Sept. 12, 1795, Oct. 23–24, 1799, I, 728, II, 1226–1228.

than if they had been able to breast-feed. On October 1, 1783, Susannah Hart-shorne delivered a daughter who died within two days, and on August 23, 1784, she gave birth to another girl. This sequence meant that she became pregnant within two months of the stillbirth. Elizabeth Drinker feared the same result when her daughter Molly's child was stillborn. Molly, Drinker worried, could experience "the same excruciateing trouble a year the sooner for this loss."[61]

Just as the pain of childbearing was part of the female life cycle, so were the ravages of breast cancer. Elizabeth Drinker's friend, Elizabeth Richardson, died of the dread disease in October 1804. "Poor woman! I trust she is out of misery and pain, which she has sustain'd for a long time past." Women's expectations were limited when breast cancer was diagnosed: either the torture of an un-anesthetized mastectomy or certain death. Breast cancer assaulted compara-tively few women, but the ever present threat might have heightened anxiety and a concentration on self, as it did in Elizabeth Drinker's case. The diary entries made while she experienced recurring breast pain in the fall and winter of 1784–1785 corroborate the apprehension she felt. Drinker was forty-nine that year and could hardly have forgotten her friend Dolly Saltar, who had succumbed, after much suffering, to breast cancer three years earlier at age forty-three. Nearly two decades later, Drinker had reason to be reminded of the anxiety her fear had occasioned: "I have filt frequent pain in my left breast laterly—whatever bodily pain I may suffer on that account, I trust and hope I shall never suffer so much in my mind, as I have formerly done." It was exactly as Adam Smith had theorized with regard to the prospect of pain: "The imagi-nation continues to fret and rankle within, from the thought of it."[62]

Diaries written by male physicians also offer insights into pain and gender, and the comments of these doctors not only reflect widespread attitudes toward women but reveal how those attitudes were translated into treatment for pain.

William Darlington (1782–1863) practiced medicine in West Chester, Penn-sylvania. His detailed diary for 1801–1802 indicates that American doctors treated women for hysteria long before the late nineteenth century, when this so-called disease reached epidemic proportions. On December 30, 1801, Dar-lington recorded that his patient, "Miss Gr—bb," had "a swelling in her throat." The discomfort apparently increased, because four days later on Janu-

61. Ibid., Oct. 1, 1783, Aug. 23, 1784, June 15, 1797, I, 415, 427, II, 930 (quotation).

62. Ibid., Apr. 27, 1781, Oct. 2, 6, 1784, Feb. 3, 1785, Feb. 28, 1801, Oct. 7, 1804, I, 386, 429, 433, II, 1389–1390, III, 1771. See the chapter on the death of Abigail Adams Smith as a result of breast cancer, in Edith B. Gelles, *Portia: The World of Abigail Adams* (Bloomington, Ind., 1992); Smith, *Theory of Moral Sentiments,* 29.

ary 3, Darlington noted that "Miss Gr——bb got frightened and thinks herself mighty bad—something *nervous* by the bye!"[63]

Darlington treated this patient with "anodynes, cathartics stimulating gums e.g. camphora." On January 5, the doctor recorded that "Gr——bb" had fainted two or three times during the preceding night and that he had administered an "antihysteria mixture." Darlington's patient improved enough over the next twenty-four hours so that he could report with confidence that "her disorder seems purely *nervous.*" His diagnosis: "Dr. thinks *qu'elle est en Amour!*" (for which he prescribed an anodyne). Some ten days later, "Miss Gr——bb—who was convalescent for some days past, was again attacked with a kind of *hysteric* affection of her throat," and once again the doctor prescribed an anodyne to compose her.[64]

At the same time that Dr. Darlington was treating Miss Gr——bb, another female patient, Deborah Spackman, was "affected with some kind of nervous derangement," which manifested itself by a "pain over her eye" and a "small frequent pulse." Spackman resisted the doctor's prescription, however, "having an idea that our giving it was in consequence of our thinking her disorder *hysterical!*" As it turned out, Spackman was "in possession of a gravelly Cyst."[65]

Between March and June 1802, William Darlington treated three other women with similar symptoms—two for hysteric colic and another who complained of "*pains in her bones* rising in her throat like *globus hystericus.*" Dr. Darlington decided that the latter's symptoms probably proceeded "from suppression of the Menses," for which he administered "a purge of Jalop, Nitre and calomel."[66]

With regard to Darlington's practice of medicine, several observations may be made. First, according to his diary, Darlington never treated a male with hysterical symptoms. His attitude suggests that pain articulated by men was organic, whereas discomfort reported by women was inconsequential, spurious, or linked to their sexual identity. Second, if female pain was trivialized, it was not only demeaning, but the actual source of the disability was left untreated—a point that did not escape Spackman's notice. Furthermore, women whose pain was merely nervous were presumably free to perform their usual duties without respite. Third, although Darlington deprecated blacks as a

63. Diary of Dr. William Darlington, Dec. 30, 1801, Jan. 3, 1802, NYHS. See also the papers of Dr. Edward Holyoke of Salem, Massachusetts (Essex Institute) for frequent references to female hysteria and nervous disorders.

64. Diary of Dr. William Darlington, Dec. 30, 1801, Jan. 5, 6, 15, 1802. Darlington thought his patient was in love.

65. Ibid., Jan. 2, 4, 6, Feb. 15, 1802.

66. Ibid., Mar. 11, 17, June 2, 1802.

group, his attitude toward African American women (or Negro wenches, as he called them) displayed a particular insensitivity.

Finally, investing so-called hysterical symptoms with a stamp of legitimacy gave nonphysician caregivers the opportunity to make the same diagnosis on the basis of what they perceived to be similar complaints. As early as 1757, Landon Carter reported: "Betty Oliver mended much yesterday . . . but in the night the Hysteric symptoms returned. . . . She says she was near Choaked by the usual lumps rising." And years later, Carter reviewed the case of a "healthy wench" who nonetheless was "full of Hysteric frights" and who complained of "something running up her arms and leggs which is a true Hysterick Symptom."[67]

Dr. Alexander Anderson also kept a diary, first as a medical student and thereafter as a practicing physician in New York City. He, too, treated women with allegedly hysterical disorders, one of whom was his mother. In December 1794, Anderson described his mother as suffering from "the Tooth-ach accompanied with hysteric symptoms." During the summer of 1796, he diagnosed her "violent" head pain as "symptoms of an hysterical nature," and on December 10 of that year Anderson's mother began to exhibit "those nervous complaints which have so often been a scourge to her." The next day, Anderson was pleased to report that his mother no longer suffered from a "pain in her eye and the ear-ach," which he now ascribed to a "false sensation." The remedy had been a large dose of opium—standard procedure in such cases.[68]

Anderson blamed his mother's distress on "the effects of her late exertions and agitation of mind," a theory supported by Erasmus Darwin's *Zoonomia,* which had been published in 1794. Darwin argued that pain was the consequence of excessive stimulation, and in the next century doctors such as S. Weir Mitchell would build on this hypothesis and argue for complete bed rest and total absence of intellectual stimulation for women who suffered from hysterical symptoms.[69]

That is not to argue that psychologically induced pain was nonexistent or that women and men were equally susceptible to it. Indeed, since women experience pain and sickness more often than men, it would not be surprising to find that much of it stems from what one author refers to as "life's lesions." Such "lesions," which produce anguish or pain, are initiated by stressful conditions, as when a woman either resists or finds it difficult to accommodate her socially determined gender role. Men, however, are shielded from such distress

67. Greene, ed., *Diary of Col. Landon Carter,* Feb. 24, 1757, July 10, 1771, I, 146, II, 609–610.

68. Diary of Dr. Alexander Anderson, Dec. 1, 1794, Apr. 16, July 7, Dec. 10, 11, 1796.

69. Ibid., Dec. 5, 10, 1796; David B. Morris, *The Culture of Pain* (Los Angeles, 1991), 115; Erasmus Darwin, *Zoonomia; or, The Laws of Organic Life* (New York, 1796), I, 21, 23, 24, 51.

by the ideology of gender roles, which defines them as superior and acts to cushion "life's lesions."[70]

It might not have been coincidental, therefore, that women took advantage of illness and pain to vindicate seclusion. On a late November day in 1793, Elizabeth Drinker cited fatigue and weakness in order to retire to her chamber to bathe a painfully sprained ankle. She noted in her diary that she felt released "from under a restraint, can set and think . . . and conceit I can do as I please."[71] In context, the immediate restraint to which Drinker referred applied to visitors, but it may also contain a gendered meaning. Because she was a woman, Drinker's world was full of restraints.

It is also possible that pain and birth control had an intimate relationship, given the dampening effect of physical pain on sexual desire and frequency of intercourse. Both women and men would have found that pain interfered with sexual activity, but it should be noted that Elizabeth Drinker's daughters, not her sons, suffered severe bouts of the "sick headache." Modern medicine attributes this disparity to hormones, and current studies show that adult women are far more susceptible than men to what are described as "life-disrupting headaches."[72]

Headaches are not only gender specific, but the sexual overtones of a headache in contemporary society (where relief is only an aspirin away) may be the legitimate legacy of a world where a headache could pound away for days at a time—making it either a calculated or unintended means of contraception. And in this context, headaches offered women a means of empowerment over their bodies in a society that rejected such independent tendencies.[73]

Since headaches are frequently hormone-related, menopause occasionally relieved the severity of these onslaughts. "My Sister and self were formerly much troubled with the sick head ach, but as we advanced in years, it left us," wrote Elizabeth Drinker in 1799, when she and her sister were in their sixties. Yet not all headaches were hormone-related, and, if a doctor peremptorily dismissed each one as a form of nervous hysteria, he stood the chance of misdiagnosing a more serious disease. Faith Trumbull Huntington, whose

70. Kaja Finkler, *Women in Pain: Gender and Morbidity in Mexico* (Philadelphia, 1994), 3, 15–16, 43, 46–47.

71. Crane, ed., *Diary of Elizabeth Drinker*, Nov. 28, 1793, I, 531.

72. *New York Times*, Jan. 8, 1992. Furthermore, the latest reports suggest that because of differences in brain circuitry, men and women do not experience pain in the same way and that the response to pain medication also differs according to sex. A class of opiate drugs that did little to mitigate male pain has been shown to relieve pain in women quite effectively; see ibid., Oct. 30, 1996.

73. Recipe Book of Elizabeth Coates Paschall, 17; Mercy Otis Warren to Abigail Adams, May 27, [1776], in Butterfield et al., eds., *Adams Family Correspondence*, I, 422.

"gloom and melancholy" degenerated into a depression that ended only with her suicide in 1775, complained of headaches.[74]

Pain was not gender-neutral. The social construction of pain and the gendered values associated with it reinforced and perpetuated patriarchal attitudes. At the same time, race, superimposed on gender, created ambiguities: if pregnancy was debilitating for white women, why not for black women? Certainly it was in the interest of every slaveholder to ensure the well being of a slave mother and the new addition to the slave family. Perhaps that is where the implications of sensibility caught up with Landon Carter: it was unnecessary to take any special precaution because African American women could be expected to suffer less than more sensitive white women.

The ambiguities that arose from the gendering of pain approached the level of paradox as women and men daily played out their respective roles. Female patients might be submissive, but their alternative performance as primary caregivers automatically conferred power over others—even men—each time they prescribed a successful remedy. Pain that incapacitated men permitted role reversal, as in a theater. Instead of male protection of the female, instead of male domination of the female, the female became cloaked with strength and authority, while the male remained passive and weak.[75] Moreover, to relieve pain and effect a cure must have enhanced female self-esteem in a society that denied women public recognition of their worth.

Yet despite the opportunities for casting aside deference, it is only as audience that we—two hundred years later—can appreciate the nuances and potential of such behavior. Similarly, it is obvious to us (although perhaps not to them) that, as the authorized arbiter of bona fide painful episodes, male physicians exercised considerable power through the gendered manipulation of pain.

PAIN AT THE END OF THE EIGHTEENTH CENTURY

As the nineteenth century approached, pain had been denounced as an inherent evil. Short of its diagnostic benefits, it had little redeeming value in and of itself, whether it emanated from God, germs, accidents, or human

74. Crane, ed., *Diary of Elizabeth Drinker*, Dec. 31, 1799, II, 1252; Ann Brandwein, "An Eighteenth-Century Depression: The Sad Conclusion of Faith Trumbull Huntington," *Connecticut History*, XXVI (1985), 28.

75. See Bailin, *Sickroom in Victorian Fiction*, 25, for further thoughts about pain and female assertiveness.

indifference. Yet even as the intellectual emphasis shifted from passive endurance to active resistance, pain remained omnipresent and demanding in the "great hospital of the world."[76] The cultural rejection of pain might have eased the shame and guilt that accompanied an inability to conform to religious precepts, but Americans continued to suffer from what they could not conquer. At best, the self maintained an uneasy alliance with pain; at worst, pain became so self-absorbing that it overwhelmed the self and dominated both attitude and behavior. Either way, pain remained integral to being.

Yet, many questions about the personal and social implications of pain remain unresolved. Did men and women unconsciously or deliberately avoid activities that might result in an accidental injury and lingering pain to themselves? Did people displace their own pain onto animals—which would explain Elizabeth Drinker's remark that the "marks of cruelty that have been exercised on . . . horses, Hogs, Dogs etc . . . in what is called a civelized land, is intolerable"?[77] Although the rhetoric of sensibility called upon people to repudiate such torture, it was still unclear whether animals had souls and therefore whether their susceptibility to pain required the same sensitivity bestowed on human life.

There is little doubt that pain reinforced the concept of human fragility and vulnerability. Just as the control of pain demonstrated power, the inability to dominate pain reflected helplessness, even humiliation. Although pain, by its nature, was an individual experience, incapacitating pain mocked the concepts of individualism, self-reliance, and self-determination at a time when these very attributes had taken on increased importance.

In this context, American independence was inconsistent with personal independence in that the absence, presence, or threat of pain controlled the extent to which a person could maintain such independence. And in a political context, pain and the virtuous self-sacrificing republican citizen were incompatible, because pain encouraged a preoccupation with self rather than the general good. Moreover, if it is true that eighteenth-century women and men were attempting to control their lives by eliminating violence, subduing emotions, and regulating bodily functions, their inability to arrest pain might have increased frustration levels since individualism held the self—not a whimsical God—responsible for personal incompetence. Conversely, the eventual suppression of disease and conquest of pain should have encouraged the growth of individualism and self-development, since people were not as reliant on one another for their essential needs. With the reduction of debilitating pain, the

76. Fordyce, *A Discourse on Pain*, 23.
77. Crane, ed., *Diary of Elizabeth Drinker*, Dec. 9, 1805, III, 1884.

fear of being immobilized with "no one to doe the least kind offis" was minimized as well.[78]

It is interesting, however, that, despite their various aches and pains, early Americans were a remarkably productive lot. One can only wonder whether the same dread of disabling pain that fostered personal anxiety and future insecurity was, paradoxically, a driving force that stimulated people to make the most of periods of physical well-being. Considered another way, the triumph of pain over productivity could be regarded as tantamount to failure in a society that equated success with results or achievement. Too often repeated, this scenario might have produced a self-image that included failure as part of one's profile, even as it blamed pain for each personal default. By forcing people to the sidelines, pain marginalized them, particularly if self-identity was associated with one's trade or profession.[79]

Even worse, to be paralyzed by pain was to be rendered powerless. And to be powerless was to be impotent, unmanned, castrated, or emasculated. In short, it was to be feminized—a label from which most men sought to distance themselves. In eighteenth-century terms, men who magnified petty disorders effeminated the soul.[80] Thus, gender construction and newly developed attitudes toward pain created another paradox: on the one hand, sensitivity encouraged expressions of anguish; on the other, it was unbecoming for men to vent such emotion.

Finally, further reflection about pain control raises questions about the relationship between piety and pain. Theoretically, one might argue that, if pain carried any weight on the moral scales, attempts to suppress it were nothing less than attempts to thwart God's will. From there it takes only a short leap of faith to conclude that the morally strong would eschew painkillers and that the demand for such suppressants came from only those of weak spirit. And surely some extremist, somewhere, took that last ideological step and equated pain relievers with the devil's handiwork, even as others championed laudanum as a gift from God.[81]

Ephraim Bateman theorized that God wrought havoc with his health to

78. See Jacquelyn Miller, "The Body Politic: Disease and Political Culture in the Age of the American Revolution" (paper presented at the Philadelphia Center for Early American Studies, Dec. 4, 1992), 24; "Diary of Rebecca Dickinson," in Daniel White Wells and Reuben Field Wells, *History of Hatfield, Massachusetts* . . . (Springfield, Mass., 1910), Nov. 15, 1787, 206–207.

79. Herzlich and Pierret, *Illness and Self in Society,* 178. The authors argue that this is a new phenomenon, dating from a more recent past where people are identified with a specific work or place in society. I believe the theory is applicable to the 18th century as well.

80. Fordyce, *A Discourse on Pain,* 10.

81. Rey, *History of Pain,* trans. Wallace, Cadden, and Cadden, 96.

remind Bateman of his "absolute dependence" on him. Yet the severity of such a reminder tempts one to ask whether Bateman harbored ambivalent feelings about God—just as he might have concealed ambivalent feelings about an earthly father who administered or withheld corporal punishment.[82] If resentment toward God did indeed exist at some subconscious level, then one might consider whether the power of effective painkillers has had unintended spiritual significance; God could be appraised as a more benign parent—and one to whom devotion could be shown with fewer conflicting emotions. Indeed, one might even ask whether the widespread faith in miracle drugs has undermined what was once a reliance on God's omnipotence—unless one argues that antibiotics are an example of God's beneficence, just as laudanum was once held to have been.

Few today still cling to the notion that God reproaches humans through pain, and thus the links between suffering, moral depravity, and the self have been all but sundered. If pain indicated a state of grace for some evangelicals, if God sent pain "as a seasonable warning from Heaven," if the self *deserved* pain and was inseparable from it in the eighteenth century, such beliefs barely linger in the twentieth.[83] So, too, the association between pain and death has been weakened by modern drugs that have the capacity to cure the underlying causes of acute pain.

The medical profession has routed the clergy as the arbiter of the social construction of pain, and science has brought theory and behavior into close harmony. Pain is not only philosophically unacceptable; the means to dismiss it are generally available. And just as pain has been disengaged from sin, so too has pain been distanced from the self. Contemporary public values encourage expressions of anger over a painful condition, with the expectation that a person will attempt to surmount or overcome it. If a few eighteenth-century diehards cherished pain and took pride in enduring it, such attitudes do not elicit respect today. Resignation and passivity do not inspire admiration; attempts to conquer pain, to disassociate oneself from disabilities, do. An inherent and inseparable part of eighteenth-century society, sickness and pain stigmatize the sufferer today.[84]

And yet, social values and personal behavior are still not completely congruent. As eager as people are to suppress pain, Americans retain an emotional

82. "Journal of Ephraim Bateman," Aug. 31, 1800, *Vineland Historical Magazine*, XIII (1928), 87; see also Fordyce, *A Discourse on Pain*, 51. Fordyce refers to God's punishment through pain as "the chastening of a father."

83. Fordyce, *A Discourse on Pain*, 62.

84. Bailin, *Sickroom in Victorian Fiction*, 13; Herzlich and Pierret, *Illness and Self in Society*, 53–54.

bond with their intellectual ancestors who believed that only the morally deficient succumbed to pain—and painkillers. Overtly confident in the ability to overcome pain (and in the righteousness of so doing), Americans still show private ambivalence, resisting appropriate levels of painkillers in the fear that excessive doses will create a drug dependency. Tenaciously held beliefs are not easily dismissed.[85]

Nothing—at least nothing perceptible—in eighteenth-century writing indicates that anyone really came to terms with pain. Authors themselves never appeared to achieve resignation; at least they never took written satisfaction in such. Perhaps they felt that any expression of self-praise smacked of unwarrantable pride. In any case, it was always someone else whose submissive behavior in the face of suffering merited approbation: an elderly aunt, a friend, a parent. Over the centuries, public values and expectations have only tangentially conformed to private, emotional behavior, because "the more the body is made to suffer, the more it objects, the less it accepts its suffering." With this in mind, it is easier to understand how, at the death of one of her grandchildren, Elizabeth Drinker was able to console herself with the thought that he was "out of all pain."[86] Since she believed that God both dispensed and eliminated suffering, this common expression contained more than metaphorical or figurative meaning to her and the other early Americans who used it.

BIBLIOGRAPHIC NOTE

Although many diaries in addition to the ones listed here were consulted, the entries in some were too terse to be of use. This study benefited most from the following journals: Diary of Dr. Alexander Anderson (1793–1799), New-York Historical Society, New York City; William G. McLoughlin, ed., *The Diary of Isaac Backus,* 3 vols. (Providence, R.I., 1979); "Journal of Ephraim Bateman of Fairfield Township, Cumberland County," *Vineland Historical Magazine,* XIII (1928), 55–64, 80–89, XIV (1929), 106–114, 127–135, 154–162, 174–182, XV (1930), 210–217, 235–246; [William Bentley], *The Diary of William Bentley, D.D., Pastor of the East Church, Salem, Massachusetts* (1905; reprint, Gloucester, Mass., 1962); Jack P. Greene, ed., *The Diary of Colonel Landon Carter of Sabine Hall, 1752–1778,* 2 vols. (Charlottesville, Va., 1965); Emily Warren Roebling, *The Journal of the Reverend Silas Constant, Pastor of the Presbyterian Church at Yorktown . . . ,* ed. Josiah Granville Leach (Philadelphia, 1903);

85. *New York Times,* Mar. 3, Apr. 3, Oct. 21, 1994.

86. Herzlich and Pierret, *Illness and Self in Society,* 88; Crane, ed., *Diary of Elizabeth Drinker,* Nov. 3, 1801, II, 1462.

Field Horne, ed., *The Diary of Mary Cooper: Life on a Long Island Farm, 1768–1773* (New York, 1981); Eliza Cope Harrison, ed., *Philadelphia Merchant: The Diary of Thomas P. Cope, 1800–1851* (South Bend, Ind., 1978); Laura Hadley Moseley, ed., *The Diaries of Julia Cowles* (New Haven, Conn., 1931); Lizzie Norton Mason and James Duncan Phillips, eds., "The Journal of Elizabeth Cranch," *Essex Institute Historical Collections,* LXXX (1944), 1–36; Diary of Dr. William Darlington (1801–1821), NYHS; "Diary of Rebecca Dickinson," in Daniel White Wells and Reuben Field Wells, *History of Hatfield, Massachusetts . . .* (Springfield, Mass., 1910), 206–207; "Extracts from Diary of William Faris of Annapolis, Maryland," *Maryland Historical Magazine,* XXVIII (1933), 197–244; Diary of Grace Growdon Galloway, in Elizabeth Evans, ed., *Weathering the Storm: Women of the American Revolution* (New York, 1975); "The Diary of Robert Gilmor," *Maryland Historical Magazine,* XVII (1922), 231–268, 319–347; William K. Bottorff and Roy C. Flannagan, eds., "The Diary of Frances Baylor Hill of 'Hillsborough,' King and Queen County, Virginia (1797)," *Early American Literature Newsletter,* II (1967), 3–53; Martin I. J. Griffin and Joseph Willcox, eds., "Extracts from the Diary of Rev. Patrick Kenny," *American Catholic Historical Society of Philadelphia,* VII (1896), 94–137; Virginia Steele Wood and Ralph Van Wood, eds., "The Reuben King Journal, 1800–1806," *Georgia Historical Quarterly,* L (1966), 177–206, 296–335, 421–458, LI (1967), 78–120; William Maclay, *The Journal of William Maclay: United States Senator from Pennsylvania, 1789–1791,* ed. Charles A. Beard (New York, 1965); Dwight L. Smith, ed., *The Western Journals of John May* (Cincinnati, Ohio, 1961); Emily V. Mason, ed., *Journal of a Young Lady of Virginia, 1782* (Baltimore, 1871); "Journal of William Wait Oliver of Salem, 1802–1803," *Essex Institute Historical Collections,* LXXXI (1945), 124–137, 227–256, 348–353; William Plumer, Jr., *Life of William Plumer,* ed. Andrew P. Peabody (Boston, 1857); Diary of Dr. Jotham Post, Jr. (1792–1793), NYHS; George W. Corner, ed., *The Autobiography of Benjamin Rush . . .* (Princeton, N.J., 1948); Jonathan Evans, comp., *A Journal of the Life, Travels, and Religious Labours, of William Savery . . .* (Philadelphia, 1873); Ethel Armes, ed., *Nancy Shippen: Her Journal Book* (New York, 1968); James E. Cronin, ed., *The Diary of Elihu Hubbard Smith, 1771–1798* (Philadelphia, 1973); David J. Jeremy, ed., *Henry Wansey and His American Journal, 1794* (Philadelphia, 1970); Rev. John Quincy Adams, ed., "The Diaries of the Rev. Seth Williston, D. D.," *Journal of the Presbyterian Historical Society,* VII (1913–1914), 175–208, 234–254, VIII (1915–1916), 40–48, 123–144, 184–192, 226–235, 316–330, IX (1917–1918), 25–40, 368–383, X (1919–1920), 24–35, 130–141.

"ALTHOUGH I AM DEAD, I AM NOT ENTIRELY DEAD. I HAVE LEFT A SECOND OF MYSELF": CONSTRUCTING SELF AND PERSONS ON THE MIDDLE GROUND OF EARLY AMERICA

Richard White

With all the attention given to the discovery of the other, it was only a matter of time before historians returned to the discovery of self. Since otherness presumes and demands a self, discovering or creating others implies discovering or creating oneself. Using encounters with the other as an avenue for examining colonial self-fashioning has a nice logic to it.[1]

During the seventeenth century and much of the eighteenth, many colonial Europeans and Indians presumed an ability to shape and change one's identity. Malleable identities put Indians and Europeans in complex relation with each other. On each side there was a presumption not just that self-fashioning was possible but that in the other—no matter how abhorrent—was also a self capable of change and self-fashioning. This mutual conviction created the opportunity for a dialogue about self and identity. This dialogue was the result of a dynamic encounter in a colonial America where cultures—and selves—did not simply clash like so many competing authenticities but instead intersected. Cultures and selves were porous and contested. As Inga Clendinnen has writ-

---

I would like to thank John Toews and Laurie Sears for help with this essay.

1. James Clifford, "Introduction," in James Clifford and George E. Marcus, eds., *Writing Culture: The Poetics and Politics of Ethnography* (Berkeley, Calif., 1986), 23. For "ethnographic self-fashioning" in general, see Clifford, "On Ethnographic Self-Fashioning: Conrad and Malinowski," in Clifford, *The Predicament of Culture: Twentieth-Century Ethnography, Literature, and Art* (Cambridge, Mass., 1988), 92–113. The issue of self-fashioning and the creation of identity precedes the explosion of interest in the other. Stephen Greenblatt, *Renaissance Self-Fashioning: From More to Shakespeare* (Chicago, 1980), 1–9; Michael Zuckerman, "Fabrication of Identity in Early America," *William and Mary Quarterly*, 3d Ser., XXXIV (1977), 184–214; Mitchell Robert Breitwieser, *Cotton Mather and Benjamin Franklin: The Price of Representative Personality* (Cambridge, 1984); and Sacvan Bercovitch, *The Puritan Origins of the American Self* (New Haven, Conn., 1975), are just four examples. Both Zuckerman and Greenblatt stress the role of the other in self-fashioning.

404

ten, "Colonial situations breed confusion." They "spawn multiple realities."[2] Conversion and adoption, for example, both assumed, though not necessarily in the same way, an ability in the other to change identity, to move from one reality to another.

Various soliloquies and dialogues about identity and self create a continual murmur in the records of both formal and everyday relations between colonial Europeans and Algonquian and Iroquoian peoples. The struggle to change oneself merged with the struggle to change the other. These were complicated conversations because they concerned not only who people were but who people might become. There were limits. From the beginning, these discussions of identity were gendered, but they were not usually racialized. Male and female were master categories that rarely were transcended. Race would not clearly limit the possibilities of self-fashioning among Indians and whites in the same way until later.

Such conversations about identity tended to arrange themselves around two axes. The poles of the first axis were self and person, with self, for now, understood as a self-conscious subject and person understood as a socially constructed identity. The poles of the second axis were feeling and reason. Europeans and Indian peoples could talk to and not past each other because in Eastern North America groups in contact shared overlapping categories of self and person, feeling and reason. The actual content of these categories differed from group to group and changed over time, but they were, like kinship, similar enough to permit a dialogue on self and identity (which was as much creative misunderstanding as mutual understanding). In the complications of this dialogue arose the possibility of colonial identities in which self and feeling, person and reason became open to reflection and revision.[3]

2. Inga Clendinnen, *Ambivalent Conquests: Maya and Spaniard in Yucatan, 1517–1570* (Cambridge, 1987), 127. Indians as well as colonial Europeans could see their lives as, in Mitchell Breitwieser's words, "conscious projects," although they were far less likely to seek to exemplify in individual lives what they regarded as universally human; see Breitwieser, *Mather and Franklin,* 3. Two books on the Iroquois underline the emphasis that people put on shaping identity. Indeed, the founding myth of the League of the Iroquois is about Deganawidah's effort at self-fashioning, his mastery of himself, and his ability to transform others. Hiawatha stands as an example of self-transformation. The Iroquois League of Peace, with its vision of indefinite extension, assumed that such transformations could continue. See Matthew Dennis, *Cultivating a Landscape of Peace: Iroquois-European Encounters in Seventeenth-Century America* (Ithaca, N.Y., 1993), 85–115; Daniel K. Richter, *The Ordeal of the Longhouse: The Peoples of the Iroquois League in the Era of European Colonization* (Chapel Hill, N.C., 1992), 30–35.

3. Natalie Zemon Davis has stressed both the changing contextual elements of self-definition and the way in which "virtually all the occasions for talking about or writing

To give this dialogue some substance, let me start with two emblematic moments in individual lives. In 1674, Father Claude Dablon ordered Father Jean Pierron to go among the Iroquois, despite his "very great natural repugnance" for them. Father Dablon recorded that Father Pierron was grateful for "sending him among the Iroquois, because in that I had acted against his own feelings." Father Pierron vowed to lose his own will and to "comply unquestioningly with the orders of his superiors."[4]

In 1655, during a council with the French and Hurons to propose peace, an Iroquois offered the last of a series of ritual presents. The speaker had once been a Huron captain, and then "a captive of the Iroquois, and now a Captain among them." He had a new name, new kinspeople, a new country, a new social place. He spoke of the Iroquois proposals as "our proposals." Yet he told the French and Hurons: "My brothers, I have not changed my soul, despite my change of country. . . . My heart is all Huron, as well as my tongue."[5]

These two brief glimpses of individual lives each contain illuminating flashes of self. Father Pierron was struggling not so much with the Iroquois as with himself. It was the difference the Iroquois embodied that excited a feeling of alienation and repugnance in him. These feelings were intensely personal. They were his own and not necessarily shared by other Jesuits. In order to change the Iroquois, he, in a real sense, needed first to change himself, a self that he fully discovered only by contemplation of the Iroquois.

The Iroquois captain, on the other hand, had seemingly already changed everything. He had become the other. The markers of his Huron identity had vanished. He had become a new person. Yet, he announced, he had only changed his country; he maintained the same heart. His speech and actions would match his heart. His heart corresponded to his old "self."

Both of these speeches are declarations of self that, as any proclamation of identity must be, are full of elaborate social and cultural cross-references. Father Pierron's identity takes shape with reference to the Iroquois, to his Jesuit superiors, to God. They prompt and organize his feelings. The Iroquois captain similarly speaks from an Iroquois body with a Huron heart. He needs to be accepted as honest and coherent by Frenchmen.

---

about the self involved a relationship"; see Davis, "Boundaries and the Sense of Self in Sixteenth Century France," in Thomas C. Heller et al., eds., *Reconstructing Individualism: Autonomy, Individuality, and the Self in Western Thought* (Stanford, Calif., 1986), 53–63 (quotation on 53).

4. Reuben Gold Thwaites, ed., *The Jesuit Relations and Allied Documents: Travels and Explorations of the Jesuit Missionaries in New France*, 73 vols. (Cleveland, Ohio, 1896–1901), LIX, 79.

5. Ibid., XLII, 57.

In different ways, Father Pierron and the Iroquois captain were searching for a coherent human self, and the proof of coherence seems to be a proper matching of affect and action. Father Pierron's feelings and will struggled against necessary action, so he sought to surrender his will. The captain declared a congruence between his heart and action, but the declaration was necessary because he spoke to an audience skeptical of the truth of such a congruence since he was no longer the person he had been.

The marking of incongruent selves was common among both seventeenth-century Indians and Europeans. In their own lives, they resisted feelings incompatible with culturally prescribed actions. And they marked otherness in part by this incongruity of affect and action. Europeans repeatedly observed, for instance, that Indian affect was inappropriate to Indian action. When the Jesuits in 1637 watched Hurons gruesomely torture an Iroquois at the stake,

> anger and rage did not appear upon the faces of those who were tormenting him, but rather gentleness and humanity, their words expressing only raillery or tokens of friendship and good will. There was no strife as to who should burn him—each one took his turn; thus they gave themselves leisure to meditate some new device to make him feel the fire more keenly.[6]

Indians noticed a parallel incongruence. Europeans were foolish and passionate over trivial things. In 1634, after watching a Frenchman in a fit of anger, a Montagnais shaman told Father Paul Le Jeune that the man had "no sense, he gets angry; as for me, nothing can disturb me; let hunger oppress me, let my nearest relation pass to the other life, let the Hiroquois, our enemies, massacre our people, I never get angry."[7]

These soliloquies on appropriate feelings—one's own and others'—are revealing, but only if we historicize feelings. Even now, we routinely expect differences in thought, belief, social organization, but we expect a set of feelings that, although culturally organized in particular ways, are universal in the manner that humans with two arms and legs are universal. We still tend to think of feelings as a sort of magma of human life—a hot-bloodedness, as we say, seething below a rational crust.[8] But emotions like Father Pierron's do not

6. The French often regarded the Algonquians as emotionally duplicitous. See ibid., XIII, 67, LII, 203–205; Gabriel Sagard, *The Long Journey to the Country of the Hurons* (Toronto, 1939), 86; A. Irving Hallowell, *Culture and Experience* (Philadelphia, 1955), 134.

7. Sagard, *The Long Journey*, 58; Thwaites, ed., *Jesuit Relations*, VI, 231; Hallowell, *Culture and Experience*, 134.

8. Peter N. Stearns with Carol Z. Stearns, "Emotionology: Clarifying the History of Emotions and Emotional Standards," *American Historical Review*, XC (1985), 813–836. The Stearnses, for example, although arguing for changes in emotional expression and organiza-

just burst forth like some paradoxical substance, at once universal and purely personal, before cooling and hardening into particular cultural forms such as stoicism, resignation, revenge, or mercy. We know emotions, like we know thought, *only* in a cultural form. "Affects," as Michelle Rosaldo wrote, "are no less cultural and no more private than beliefs."[9]

With the matching of affect to action as a common criterion for the creation of a coherent self, the colonial dialogue of self often revolved around feelings. And, again, there was a culturally exploitable convergence. Feelings were, in different ways for many of those concerned, both a mark of identity and something to be subdued. Like his seventeenth-century Puritan and Iroquois contemporaries, Father Pierron reacted to feelings and to the self they asserted by straining to conquer them.[10] To vanquish self by his own will, however, only ensured the triumph of the self in another form. The self was what was to be governed, not what governed.[11] His solution, the resort to the will of his superiors, was French and Catholic.[12] But self, of course, reappeared, for he had to willfully subject himself to the will of another.

The irony of self-denial and self-abnegation—so commonly praised by Protestants and Catholics in the seventeenth century—was that they depend on a constant monitoring of self and feelings. And an identity based on the monitoring of self and constant efforts toward its subjection makes self as central to the cultural identity of a human subject as does an identity based on

---

tion over time and from culture to culture, still sometimes write as if emotions themselves were basic and always present, although unevenly expressed (for example, 820–821, 824). At other times, they write as if emotions themselves change and as if emotions have a "cognitive element" and are not merely "glandular or hormonal reactions" (829, 834). This last statement would seem to indicate that emotions are not just culturally expressed but are social and cultural in their very makeup.

9. Michelle Rosaldo, "Toward an Anthropology of Self and Feeling," in Richard A. Shweder and Robert A. LeVine, eds., *Culture Theory: Essays on Mind, Self, and Emotion* (New York, 1984), 141–143. See also John Toews, "Cultural History, the Construction of Subjectivity, and Freudian Theory: A Critique of Carol and Peter Stearns' Proposal for a New History of the Emotions," *Psychohistory Review*, XVIII (1990), 303–318.

10. Bercovitch, *Puritan Origins of the American Self*, 15–25; Breitwieser, *Mather and Franklin*, 7, 24.

11. This formulation, made by Breitwieser for Cotton Mather, would apply as readily to Father Pierron; see Breitwieser, *Mather and Franklin*, 8.

12. Protestant submission was more direct. It was an annihilation of self by God; see Breitwieser, *Mather and Franklin*, 28–31. But, as Breitwieser also points out, the authority of the father imitates that of God (35–43). Fathers play the role of Jesuit superiors or, rather, vice versa.

self-fulfillment or self-indulgence.[13] The European colonial self proved protean. The Jesuit and Puritan attacks on the self only revealed how manifold were its forms and extensive its domains. Self-abnegation existed easily enough alongside vigorous attempts to promote and defend the reputation of the very same selves that ideally deserved suppression.[14] *The Jesuit Relations*—which publicized Father Pierron's self-denial—were, after all, a vehicle for the Jesuits' promotion of their own adventures, heroism, and success in order to raise funds for the missions.[15]

Father Pierron suffered real anguish at the incompatibility of his feelings and his action, and that is what makes the assurance of the Iroquois captain, who should be far more conflicted, so startling. It is, indeed, incidents like this that made Indian adoptions so mysterious to colonial whites. Europeans either marveled that Indian captives could take on a new identity and forget their former selves or they doubted that an individual could, in fact, do so. Yet here was a man claiming a Huron heart, soul, and blood in an Iroquois body. And though the Iroquois and Hurons were at war, he was supposedly not at war with himself.

This claim to coherence *is* suspect as long as it remains on the level of self. But to try to understand porous and contested selves involves entering a terminological tangle in which the person/self distinction is unavoidably embedded. I have, for better or worse, selected as a guide through this tangle an old essay by Marcel Mauss, and I have used anthropological terminology rather than current postcolonial categories of subject and subject positions.[16]

The basic issue that forces me into this terminological morass is that self as a

13. I would like to thank John Toews, whose reading of an early draft of this essay suggested this formulation to me. Also see Zuckerman, "Fabrication of Identity," *WMQ*, 3d Ser., XXXIV (1977), 196–200; Breitwieser, *Mather and Franklin*, 27.

14. A. Lynn Martin, *The Jesuit Mind: The Mentality of an Elite in Early Modern France* (Ithaca, N.Y., 1988), 30, 74, 79. Martin points out the parallels between Puritans and Jesuits (140). They shared the seeming Puritan paradox of self-abnegation and an emphasis on self-help and activity in the world (139). For praise of Father Leonard Garreau for his "total self-abandonment to God's will," see Thwaites, ed., *Jesuit Relations*, XLII, 241–243.

15. Similarly, colonial New Englanders, although a people devoted to self-abnegation, so valued their public reputation that, as John Demos has pointed out, they made suits for slander one of the most popular forms of legal action; see Demos, "Shame and Guilt in Early New England," in Carol Z. Stearns and Peter N. Stearns, eds., *Emotion and Social Change: Toward a New Psychohistory* (New York, 1988), 71–75.

16. Marcel Mauss, "A Category of the Human Mind: The Notion of Person; the Notion of Self" (1938), and J. S. La Fontaine, "Person and Individual: Some Anthropological Reflections," in Michael Carrithers, Steven Collins, and Steven Lukes, eds., *The Category of the Person: Anthropology, Philosophy, History* (Cambridge, 1985), 4–11, 124; Grace Gredys Harris, "Concepts of Individual, Self, and Person in Description and Analysis," *American Anthropologist*, XCI (1989), 599–612.

concept cannot stand alone. In terms of our current academic categories, it is connected with the categories of individual and person. These three terms are distinct but linked; they resemble a holy trinity of subjectivity. There is a move in anthropology to be more rigorous in drawing distinctions between human beings as biological entities (bodies, individuals), as self-conscious subjects (selves), and as socially constructed identities (persons, subject positions).[17]

The distinctions between individual, self, and person are important, but the significant issue for me is the relationship between concepts of self and concepts of person in the encounter of Indian peoples and Europeans. Person and self can never be free of each other. Persons are those individuals recognized by a society as possessing agency and juridical and moral standing. Person and self can conceivably be identical, but this was not the case with either colonial Europeans or Indians. European Christians came the closest. They regarded a moral person as a single entity, a "rational substance, indivisible and individual," that united soul and body.[18] Such persons were responsible for their own actions.

But in this Western formulation, selves and persons were not totally congruent. Not all human selves are fully persons (children before the age of reason, slaves, and, in many instances, women). Nor are all persons human. Religious institutions, universities, and corporations could and can be legal persons. The "category of 'self' " built around "self-knowledge and the psychological consciousness" thus remained distinct from that of a person.[19]

In the seventeenth and early eighteenth centuries, Algonquian and Iroquoian societies drew similar distinctions. Not all human selves were persons, and not all persons—for example, manitous who were other-than-human persons—were human selves. Indeed, Indian peoples probably tended to keep lines between these concepts clearer than did Europeans. It was this distinction between persons and selves among Indians that struck Marcel Mauss, who began his classic essay on notions of person and self with a discussion of North America. Mauss's own discussion is complicated and marred by a now outdated evolutionism, but his connection of Indian persons with a *personnage*—

17. Harris, "Concepts of Individual, Self, and Person," *American Anthropologist*, XCI (1989), 599–612 (quotation on 601). Like self, individual and person are our own categories, but we cannot escape using them in analyzing the past. Certainly they are necessary for talking coherently among ourselves.

18. Mauss, "Category of the Human Mind," in Carrithers, Collins, and Lukes, eds., *Category of the Person*, 20. Michelle Rosaldo was correct in arguing that, in other cultures, at other times, self and person "need not be conceptually opposed"; see Rosaldo, "Toward an Anthropology of Self and Feeling," in Shweder and LeVine, eds., *Culture Theory*, 147.

19. Mauss, "Category of the Human Mind," and see La Fontaine, "Person and Individual," in Carrithers, Collins, and Lukes, eds., *Category of the Person*, 4–22 (quotation on 20), 124.

a mask or role that an Indian subject might literally assume—remains useful. This role was named, and the temporary occupant of the position took the name as his or her own.[20] That is what the Iroquois with the soul of a Huron had done.

Both Indians and whites posited distinctive relations between persons and selves and created distinctive domains for each.[21] Contact demanded complicated cross-cultural understandings, or misunderstandings, of such relations.

Certainly on the level of formal political relations, the French and the Indians, and to a lesser degree the Dutch and English, agreed to act as if particular transitory selves were subordinate to enduring persons. Europeans pragmatically agreed to an Indian formulation of politics as a kinship relationship between a limited number of named persons. The name Onontio, by which Iroquois and Algonquians addressed the governor of Canada, or the name Corlaer, by which they addressed the Dutch and English, were not titles; they were not Iroquois equivalents of the word "governor."[22] Onontio was the name of a particular human self—Governor Montmagny—who had become the archetype for a character, a *personnage,* who was father to both the French and the Algonquians. It was a role with personal characteristics into which individual governors stepped. All the governors after Montmagny were Onon-

20. Mauss, "Category of the Human Mind," in Carrithers, Collins, and Lukes, eds., *Category of the Person,* 4–12. Mauss discussed the Pueblos and the Kwakiutl of the Northwest coast. He relied on anthropological sources created after the Pueblos had been in close contact with Europeans for more than three centuries and the Kwakiutl for more than a century. Mauss recognized the history these peoples shared with Europeans, but he argued that this history of contact had not affected their "aboriginal state."

Mauss's historical approach was evolutionary, and so Indians remained the ever popular primal peoples. Mauss used them to establish a baseline from which he could derive progress toward modern Western ideas about the self. For evolutionary aspects of Mauss's thought, see N. J. Allen, "The Category of the Person: A Reading of Mauss's Last Essay," in Carrithers, Collins, and Lukes, eds., *Category of the Person,* 26–27. For a discussion of names, identities, offices, and social roles among the 19th-century Iroquois, see William N. Fenton, "Structure, Continuity, and Change in the Process of Iroquois Treaty Making," in Francis Jennings et al., eds., *The History and Culture of Iroquois Diplomacy: An Interdisciplinary Guide to the Treaties of the Six Nations and Their League* (Syracuse, N.Y., 1985), 12. The creation of the *personnage* is a practice that has confused numerous historians (including myself) into thinking a single-named person was a single human self with a sometimes extraordinary lifespan.

21. In terms of colonial America, Michael Zuckerman noted this distinction between social role and inner identity some time ago; see Zuckerman, "Fabrication of Identity," *WMQ,* 3d Ser., XXXIV (1977), 184.

22. Daniel K. Richter refers to these as council titles, but since they carried so many duties as a personality and a way of acting, they are much closer to Mauss's *personnages;* see Richter, *Ordeal of the Longhouse,* 93, 141.

tio. There was one Onontio. Individual actors lived and died, the character lived on.[23]

Onontio existed in kinship relation to equivalent Indian persons. In 1740, the Ottawa Nagach8o "spoke" in council through an unnamed Ottawa speaker who addressed his French father.

> My father has always had pity on me during my life, and although I am dead, I am not entirely dead. I have left a second of myself at Michilmackinac before departing; he holds my place. This is my brother, Cabina. I hope that my father will have the same care of my younger brother that he had for me. I think that my brother will listen to the word of my father as I have always done.[24]

To be Onontio, to be Nagach8o, was to assume a very real and powerful identity; but particular human selves persisted. Cabina became Nagach8o, but he could still fashion himself. He did not, in fact, listen to his father. In 1750, "Nouk8ato," a Michilmackinac Ottawa, became a British chief.[25]

Colonial Europeans were able to accommodate this distinction between persons and selves, but Europeans, both Catholic and Protestant, had a particular understanding of the consequences of the distinction. Individuals as selves—as self-aware, individualized unions of souls and bodies—were all equal in the sense that they all possessed equivalent immortal souls. Individuals as persons, however, were radically unequal. They were ranked. Among Europeans, to stress selves was to stress equality; to stress persons was to stress inequality.

Europeans expected that a world organized on the basis of ranked persons would be a world of order, including emotional order. The French certainly accepted the universality and explosive consequences of emotion. But appropriate displays of emotions such as anger or pride varied according to rank. French pardon tales, designed to secure forgiveness from the king for crimes, were mimetic: they tried to re-create in listeners the anger or fear that prompted a killing. Anger could be understood by all, but rank legitimated

23. "Onontio" was an Iroquois word meaning "big mountain." It was the Mohawk rendering of the name of Charles Jacques de Huault de Montmagny, an early French governor. See W. J. Eccles, *The Canadian Frontier, 1534–1760* (New York, 1969), 201 n. 15; Mauss, "Category of the Human Mind," in Carrithers, Collins, and Lukes, eds., *Category of the Person*, 4–11.

24. Paroles des Outa8acs de Missilmakinac de la Bande de la fourche . . . , 6 juillet 1740, C11A, LXXIV, fol. 16, Arichives Nationales.

25. La Jonquière to Minister, Sept. 17, 1751, La Jonquière to Minister, Sept. 20, 1750, in State Historical Society of Wisconsin, *Collections,* 20 vols. (Madison, 1855–1931), XVIII, 67–68, 80–81; Parolles de Pemant8euns [Pennahouel], 5 juillet 1751, C11A, XCVII, NA.

displays of anger for some people and not for others. A gentleman rightfully reacted more forcefully to being called a knave by an inferior than a peasant might react to an identical insult. Feelings occurred among people of all social ranks, but their display was hierarchical.[26]

What alarmed the French in Canada was that the general equality of the Algonquians and Iroquois seemingly yielded emotional disorder.[27] Lacking a proper social arrangement of persons, they could not have a proper arrangement of feeling. According to Father Pierre de Charlevoix, the maxim of the northern Indians was that "one man owes nothing to another." Such independence yielded a characteristic set of feelings: "They are easily offended, jealous and suspicious, especially of us Frenchmen; treacherous when it is for their interest; great dissemblers, and exceeding vindictive."[28]

What was missing among Indians was a set of feelings—deference, respect, obligation, trust, subordination—appropriate to ranked persons. Hierarchy supposedly produced and properly routed these feelings. Indian societies were, so to speak, improperly wired. They were, in a reversal of the usual identification of Indians with nature, unnatural. In a metaphorical world of French fathers and Indian children, Father Charlevoix claimed that actual Indian children were unnatural, showing "no return of natural love for their parents."[29]

With the distinction between self and person in mind, the intricacies of the colonial conversation of feelings and selves become clearer. When Europeans and Indians sought to understand self, they both inevitably brought into play the distinct but allied conception of person. Similarly, when they talked about feelings and emotion, they brought into play the allied concept of reason. The meanings they attached to these concepts differed just as the appropriate domains of each differed. But both sides could use similar sets of paired concepts in their discussions of self.

26. Natalie Zemon Davis, *Fiction in the Archives: Pardon Tales and Their Tellers in Sixteenth-Century France* (Stanford, Calif., 1987), 37, 39, 43, 53, 67.

27. The English and French both perceived an Indian world lacking in subordination and therefore in order, civilization, and, at the most extreme, humanity. Father Membre's palpable relief at reaching the Muskogean Natchez—"all different from our Canada Indians"—came from the authority of their chiefs. "They have their valets and officers who follow them and serve them everywhere. They distribute their favors and presents at will. In a word we generally found men there"; see Chretien Le Clercq, *The First Establishment of the Faith in New France*, 2 vols. (1881; reprint, New York, 1992).

28. Pierre de Charlevoix, *Journal of a Voyage to North-America*, 2 vols. (London, 1761), II, 88.

29. Ibid., II, 88–89. Similar behavior could be defined as natural but inhuman; see Sagard, *The Long Journey*, 131. For an illuminating discussion of nature and what is natural in human nature in the 17th and 18th centuries, see Breitwieser, *Mather and Franklin*, 7–8, 101–116, 171–201.

A fundamental aspect of what I have elsewhere called the middle ground between Indians and Europeans was an agreement that the basis of formal relations would be a ranked hierarchy of persons. Europeans believed such ranked positions involved a set of appropriate feelings—honor, subordination, resignation—and saw as part of the colonial task the creation of such feelings among Indian peoples. For the French, the punishment of murderers provided an occasion for cultivating these feelings. Governor Philippe de Rigaud de Vaudreuil demanded of the Ottawa emissary Miscouaky, who had come to resolve a killing, "a great trust in my kindness . . . a real repentance for the fault that has been committed, and complete resignation to my will." "When your people entertain those feelings I will arrange everything." He wanted Indian murderers begging pardon of the governor to mimic the abasement of murderers of all ranks who, blaming their crimes on passion, sought pardon before the French king. In a ranked society, as Father Pierron knew, the shaping of self depended on subjecting one's will to that of a superior. In the case of murder among the French, when one's own will had been overwhelmed by passions, to seek pardon was to recognize that one's very life depended on the will of the king. Securing such a pardon depended on the rational cultivation and expression of proper feelings.[30]

Murder for the French and other colonial Europeans was largely about the murderer; it was primarily a crime of human selves. When Europeans explained the logic of murder, responsibility, and punishment to Indians, they did so largely in terms of self. A unique human self had died and would not return; specific human selves bore responsibility. The guilty self should vanish into death just as the victim had vanished. In fact, things were a bit more complicated. For if the human self who died at the hands of a murderer did not have the status of a person, punishment was far less likely. Murdering a slave was not the same as murdering a white freeman.

For Algonquians and other Indians, murder was about the victim; it was largely a crime of human persons. They understood both the victim and the murderer as persons. Without the loss of a person, a murder had not occurred. Thus when in 1655 an Onondaga warrior brutally killed a young captive girl of the Cat nation (Eries) at the behest of her mistress, the act was not regarded as murder because the victim was an unadopted war captive and a slave and thus not a person. The victim did, however, possess a soul, which had to be ritually driven from the town.[31]

30. Reply of Philippe de Rigaud de Vaudreuil to Miscouaky, Nov. 4, 1706, Michigan Pioneer and Historical Society, *Historical Collections* (Lansing, Mich., 1877–), XXXIII, 295 (hereafter, MPHC). For the French tradition of subordination and seeking pardon, see Davis, *Fiction in the Archives*, 53.

31. Thwaites, ed., *Jesuit Relations*, XLII, 137–139.

Similarly, punishing the actual killer—the human self who had performed the act—would not necessarily be the object of revenge. When those seeking to retaliate sought a victim, they demanded not so much the actual murderer as a person equivalent to the one they had lost. They would gladly kill a kinsperson or clan member of the murderer whose status equaled that of the deceased. But a retaliatory killing was not essential. Because persons existed within a clan, lineage, or other kin group, any individual accepted as occupying the proper social place of the deceased replaced the victim as a person. Sometimes the person was replaced with a slave—an individual who had already literally lost social identity. Sometimes the person's worth, value, or importance could be compensated for with payments—the victim was "covered" and no longer a source of grief. Because persons were not of equal importance, payments varied. Only in extreme circumstances would another life be taken. It was then that a person from the same lineage, clan, or village of the murderer could potentially pay the price. The group as a whole thus had an incentive to settle the murder by covering or raising the victim.[32] Dead persons, unlike dead selves, were not unique. They could be replaced.

French and Algonquian concepts of murder did, however, partially overlap in their understanding of the murderer. The French saw certain kinds of murders—the kind open to pardon—as outbursts of passion. In terms of retribution, Algonquians treated the murderer solely as a person, but in explaining murder and in dealing with the actual murderer Algonquians saw the murderer as a distinct and passionate self. Among Algonquians, murders—the acts of human selves overcome by their feelings—were also not the acts of rational people. Murderers were, as the Kaskaskia chief Kiraoueria told the French, madmen.[33] They had, so to speak, lost themselves. But they were only temporarily deranged. They could be redeemed. By the same logic, however, murder had the likelihood, indeed the virtual certainty, of deranging relatives of the victim who, mad with grief at the loss of a beloved son, daughter, father, or mother, could kill in turn. The emphasis on replacing persons had not erased the self from the equation, but the feelings of the murderer were not (as in the French ritual of pardon) of primary concern. The key to settling the murder was the victim's kinspeople, deranged by grief, who had to have their true selves restored.

The restoration of the true self among Algonquians or Iroquoians, although

32. The ancient peoples known to the Europeans had followed a similar system. For comparison of Indian and ancient treatment of murders and killings, see Joseph François Lafitau, *Moeurs des sauvages ameriquains comparées aux moeurs des premiers temps*, 2 vols. (Paris, 1724), II, 185–187.

33. Chefs du villages . . . , 17 juin 1793, F3, XXIV, fol. 157, Moreau St. Mery, NA.

it concerned feelings, was phrased as a transcending of strong feelings or passions altogether, rather than an attempt to find appropriate ones. People under the sway of passion, like people under the sway of alcohol or people who were bewitched, had lost themselves. The public culture of Iroquois was dominated by ceremonies for removing the emotion that "stupefies and blinds those who yield to it" and restoring reason.[34] The famed Iroquois condolence ceremony served both to reconcile individuals to the loss of loved ones and as the touchstone for Iroquois diplomacy. It aimed to remove the grief and anger that deranged people. The cultural ideal of Iroquois chiefs was to put themselves beyond "angry passions." "The thickness of their skin shall be . . . seven spans of the hand." Reason, calmness, and peace were the ideal states of the Iroquois self, but these were personal ideals that could only be realized with the aid of ceremonies performed by others. Algonquians shared this conception of a rational self beyond the parameters of passion.[35]

When Europeans killed Indians or when Indians killed Europeans, the axes of self/person and feeling/reason both governed possible solutions. Conceptions of murder as a domain of personal responsibility (self) and of social position and social responsibility (person) were in partial conflict. Europeans emphasized the action of the killer and put the responsibility on and demanded the punishment of a particular human self; they did not insist on compensation for or replacement of a deceased person. The "blood of Frenchmen [was] not to be paid for by beaverskins."[36]

Indians put the emphasis on the victim, the loss of a particular human person, and demanded that the person be replaced or compensation offered for his or her loss. Compensation was to be equal to the act. As a last resort, Indians would accept a life for a life, but they were often shocked by European excess, even when Europeans tried to demonstrate an impartial justice. The Iroquois, for example, objected vehemently when the French executed five Frenchmen for the murder of a single Indian.

The Algonquians and the French, and to a lesser extent the English, by the eighteenth century resolved these differences through what amounted to mu-

34. "These people believe that sadness, anger and all violent passions expel the rational soul from the body, which, meanwhile, is animated only by the sensitive soul which we have in common with animals. That is why, on such occasions, they usually make a present to restore the rational soul to the seat of reason"; see Thwaites, ed., *Jesuit Relations*, XLII, 51.

35. Dennis, *Landscape*, 96–97; Thwaites, ed., *Jesuit Relations*, I, 277. For a description of the ceremony, see William N. Fenton, "Structure, Continuity, and Change in the Process of Iroquois Treaty Making," in Jennings et al., eds., *History and Culture of Iroquois Diplomacy*, 18–21.

36. Reply of Vaudreuil to Miscouaky, Nov. 4, 1706, MPHC, XXXIII, 295.

tually acceptable ritual acts.[37] The French demanded surrender of the killer so that the murderer and his people might demonstrate proper feelings of remorse, deference, and trust. Then they almost always pardoned the murderer. Indians, for their part, sought to replace or cover the dead and to soothe the feelings of the Europeans and to restore them to reason.

They learned to do these things in tandem. In 1748, the wife of Agouachimagand, an Ottawa who had killed some French voyageurs, asked Gros Serpent, an Ottawa married to and living among Iroquois, to obtain pardon for her husband from the French. The ensuing dialogue was about feelings and reason, selves and persons. Gros Serpent conducted a condolence ceremony to restore the French to reason. He sought to remove the bile from the French heart. He sought also to offer proof of the Indians' own proper feelings as the French required. Speaking for the Ottawas, Gros Serpent told the French that the Ottawas asked for mercy and repented of their faults. This discourse of feelings was accompanied by the rituals necessary to replace lost persons: gifts to cover the bones of the dead and a slave to replace them. The French emissary replied with a parallel discourse on feelings and reason. He urged the Ottawas to visit their father. He was sure Onontio would take pity on his Ottawa children who had lost their sense *(esprit)*, and his speech would restore them to their senses.[38] Each side acted, in part, within categories defined by the other.

Contact put feelings and emotions on exaggerated display, and, in doing so, it promoted an increased awareness of self. Both the variety of selves on display in the colonial world and the possibilities of transformation embodied in these selves opened up self and person to reflection and possible revision. A universalism, whether Christian or of the Iroquois League of Peace, depended on a recognition of a common humanity and the ability of selves to fashion and transform themselves. This was a universalism that would not persist. A European construction of race on one side and an Indian construction of a separate Indian way on the other truncated and limited the ways the fashioning of selves might occur.

The possibilities for colonial fashioning of persons and selves along cultural borders would not, however, cease in the last half of the eighteenth century. In

37. The treatment of murders varied over time and according to context, but at no time did either Indian or French customs hold full sway. Nor, in the Great Lakes region, did British law hold sway. See Richard White, *The Middle Ground: Indians, Empires, and Republics in the Great Lakes Region, 1650–1815* (New York, 1991), 75–93, 343–351. For treatment of murders within the Canadian mission settlements of Sault-St.-Louis and Lac-des-Deux-Montagnes, see, Jan Grabowski, "Crime and Punishment: Sault-St.-Louis, Lac-des-Deux-Montagnes, and French Justice, 1662–1735," *Native American Studies,* VII (1993), 15–20.

38. Parolles du gros serpend, 8ta8ois . . . 1751, CllA, XCVII, fols. 401–403, NA.

ways I cannot examine in a short essay, Christian conversion, captivities, and captivity narratives, what might be called the cultural cross-dressing of the Sons of Liberty (who dressed as Indians) or Indian delegations (whose members dressed as whites), all continued the complicated tradition of discovering selves in relation to others. Contact opened new possibilities for hybrid cultural identities that probably did not seem hybrid to those who occupied them. There was continuity across what seemingly were most impervious boundaries. As Nagach8o said, "Although I am dead, I am not entirely dead."

~

AN INNER DIASPORA:

BLACK SAILORS MAKING SELVES

W. Jeffrey Bolster

On Christmas in 1747, Briton Hammon, a slave to Major John Winslow of Marshfield, Massachusetts, set out, as he put it, with "an Intention to go a voyage to sea" and shipped himself "on board of a Sloop, Capt. John Howland, Master, bound to Jamaica." When the sloop was "cast away on Cape Florida," only the prodigal Hammon survived—propelled by shipwreck on a thirteen-year odyssey embracing Indian captivity in Florida, imprisonment and enslavement in Cuba, Royal Navy service and combat against the French, hospitalization in Greenwich, dockwork in London, and a near voyage to Africa as cook aboard a slaver. Hammon's *Narrative of the Uncommon Sufferings, and Surprising Deliverance of Briton Hammon, a Negro Man,* the first voyage account published by a black American, indicates the extent to which enslaved sailors and nominally free men of African descent rode economic and military currents to every corner of the eighteenth-century Atlantic world, appreciatively comparing the regions they bridged. It also reveals Hammon's multidimensional sense of self. Among a crew of black and white sailors, he was one of "the people" chiding the captain; in Spanish Cuba, both a black Englishman and a slave; in Indian camps, a civilized man; in New England, a man of color; and aboard the slaver on which he planned to sail, a free seaman on wages or a Briton—not a captive African. Hammon clearly understood his identity in fluid terms that were not solely defined by color.[1]

More politicized than Hammon, John Jea took to the seas after his manumission from slavery in New York during the 1790s. Born in 1773 at Old Callabar, a notorious slaving port on the Niger Delta, Jea survived the Middle Passage as a child. By about 1800, he was on the road and at sea as an itinerant

1. Briton Hammon, *A Narrative of the Uncommon Sufferings, and Surprising Deliverance of Briton Hammon, a Negro Man—Servant to General Winslow, of Marshfield in New England* (Boston, 1760), in Dorothy Porter, ed., *Early Negro Writing* (Boston, 1971), 522–528, esp. 522, 523, 528. I would like to thank Greg Dening, Ron Hoffman, and Fredrika Teute for perceptive criticism of this article and to thank Greg Dening for the title.

minister, a quick-witted and powerful orator who embodied, according to his biographer, "Methodist evangelism, revolutionary egalitarianism, and a nascent black nationalism." Swept up in the black diaspora and mirroring its dispersed nature with his own voyages to North and South America, Europe, and the East Indies, Jea presented himself during the era of the Haitian Revolution as "a poor African" or an "African Preacher." He explicitly cultivated a sense of collective blackness among black audiences.[2]

Maritime skills and spiritual associations of a different sort shaped the meanings of self for an elderly African boatman in South Carolina named Cudjoe. "Very artful," explained his master at Charleston, Cudjoe had "been used to the Coasting Business Southwardly" in schooners, canoes, and pettiaugers. Like African vessels he might have known in his youth, canoes and pettiaugers were hollowed from the trunks of prodigious trees; like all vessels they carried associations of contact with the spirit world. When five slaves fled with Cudjoe in 1771, his master had little doubt that the elderly sailor had "enticed the others away." The master intuited correctly that the runaways trusted the old patroon's skill. But blind to Africans' spiritual associations with water and boats, he never entirely fathomed the nature of that trust.[3]

These sailors' stories suggest some of the processes and components with which eighteenth-century blacks constructed both a sense of self and a complex, although not homogeneous, African American identity. Too many histories assume implicitly that blacks were restricted by an a priori racial identity or that being black was more of a state than a process. But nothing like Aimé Césaire's "Negritude" existed in western Africa before European slave ships arrived. Thereafter, white men played little role in Africa except at coastal castles and slave barracoons. Without a white other, blackness remained virtually meaningless as a category of identity in African societies. Power, privileges, and fate were tied to kin, status, and ethnicity. It was the involuntary dispersal of people from the continent of Africa, especially into the degraded

2. Graham Russell Hodges, ed., *Black Itinerants of the Gospel: The Narratives of John Jea and George White* (Madison, Wis., 1993), 1, 12, 19–29, 126, 128, 145.

3. *South Carolina Gazette* (Charlestown), Apr. 11, 1771, in Lathan A. Windley, *Runaway Slave Advertisements: A Documentary History from the 1730's to 1790* (Westport, Conn., 1983), III, 299. "Pettiauger," or "periauga," referred to a long narrow canoe hollowed from one tree or, more generally, a boat built of two hollowed tree trunks with a flat bottom inserted between them. That made it more of a narrow barge or galley. Those in Georgia in 1744 were described as "long, flat-bottom'd Boats, carrying from 25 to 30 Tons." "They have a kind of Forecastle and a Cabbin; but the rest open, and no Deck. They have two Masts, which they can strike and Sails like Schooners"; Francis Moore, *A Voyage to Georgia Begun in the Year 1735 . . .* (London, 1744), 49.

conditions of New World slavery, that produced a new social psychology premised on race and new black cultural identities.[4]

Black Americans' social identities grew from expressions of particular African pasts and from a variety of social interactions.[5] Many of those identities centered on divisions among people of color. Such divisions contradict the "consistent assumption" identified by Henry Louis Gates, Jr., "that there exists an unassailable, integral, black self, as compelling and as whole in Africa as in the New World, within slavery as without slavery." Diasporic blacks' identities, then, should not be conceived as bounded or finite but as determined through a series of relationships and transactions.[6] Pivotal individuals like sailors, who were at once racial go-betweens straddling black and white worlds *and* channels of communications among dispersed blacks, illuminate the processes through which black people came to construct social identities.

Enslaved and free black seamen like Hammon, Jea, and Cudjoe established a prominent presence in every seaport and roadstead lapped by eighteenth-century Atlantic tides. Ships were important channels of escape for slaves and significant employers for the first generations of free blacks. At different times, then, ships were vehicles to unrequited hardship but also venues for black individuals' spirituality, reputations, skill, assertions of manliness, collective identity, and even—after the American Revolution—American patriotism.[7]

The nature of seafaring within and its impact on African American society changed with time. In 1740, deep-sea maritime labor in the Anglo-American world was largely white. Virtually all seafaring blacks were slaves, and the majority of black maritime workers were coastal boatmen in plantation so-

4. The term "Negritude" was first used in 1939 by Aimé Césaire, *Cahier d'un retour au pays natal*. See Clayton Eshleman and Annette Smith, eds. and trans., *The Collected Poetry of Aimé Césaire* (Berkeley, Calif., 1983), 2, 5, 67; Per Wästberg, "Themes in African Literature Today," in Sidney W. Mintz, ed., *Slavery, Colonialism, and Racism* (New York, 1974), 145–147. For the concept of African diaspora, see Elliott P. Skinner, "The Dialectic between Diasporas and Homelands," in Joseph E. Harris, ed., *Global Dimensions of the African Diaspora*, 2d ed. (Washington D.C., 1993), 11–40.

5. Most studies of the African diaspora focus on external forces imposed on blacks during their dispersal and reproduction rather than on the internal workings through which New World blacks came to envision themselves within that process. See, for example, Vincent Bakpetu Thompson, *The Making of the African Diaspora in the Americas, 1441–1900* (New York, 1987).

6. Henry Louis Gates, Jr., *Figures in Black: Words, Signs, and the "Racial" Self* (New York, 1987), 115–116. On identity as a process, see James Clifford, *The Predicament of Culture: Twentieth-Century Ethnography, Literature, and Art* (Cambridge, Mass., 1988), 344.

7. This essay suspends attention to the nature of seafaring work itself and to the class-based and racially based violence of the maritime workplace. See W. Jeffrey Bolster, *Black Jacks: African American Seamen in the Age of Sail* (Cambridge, Mass., 1997).

cieties. Between 1730 and 1779 in South Carolina, for instance, maritime work ranked as the third most common occupation among male slaves, after agriculture and woodworking. By 1803–1804, black men, mostly free, filled about 17 percent of seamens' jobs in many American ports, including New York, Philadelphia, and New Orleans, when roughly eighty thousand men manned the American merchant fleet. As their numbers grew, black mariners moved from billets as slaves, servants, and musicians to become skilled able seamen and to define as virtually their own the job of ship's cook. Most seamen of color thus made themselves in what was simultaneously a cramped interracial workplace and an expansive international arena.[8]

Skirting the Atlantic rim, sailors witnessed the treatment and accomplishments of far-flung blacks, who in turn watched the arrival and departure of sailing black strangers. Mariners became conduits for an emerging sense of transnational blackness and visible signposts of various black identities. They forged personal identities from ancestral traditions such as Africans' spiritual associations with water, from maritime work itself (including interactions with white officers and shipmates), from their pan-Atlantic mobility, and from communications with blacks elsewhere—notably Haiti. Detached from place unlike most predial slaves, they cultivated an extraterritorial African identity of symbolic importance, appropriating the entire African continent as their own, although they rarely intended to move back to Africa. That contradiction (among others) was central to black sailors' invention of a cultural self, a process that illuminates the formation of black American identities during the late eighteenth and early nineteenth centuries.

AFRICAN SPIRITUALITY, WATER, AND BOATS IN THE
CREATION OF BLACK SELVES

African sailors' lives were shaped not only by the social relations of production (in this case, by seafaring traditions, slave codes, and a multiracial, mobile labor force) but by their African understandings of and associations with maritime work. For many Africans, watery surfaces appeared as a conduit for communication with ancestors' spirits, and vessels themselves were idioms of mediation between this world and the next. African sailors' sense of self devel-

8. Philip D. Morgan, "Colonial South Carolina Runaways: Their Significance for Slave Culture," *Slavery and Abolition*, VI (December 1985), 57–78, esp. 64–65; New York and Philadelphia Crew Lists, Records of the U.S. Customs Service, RG 36, National Archives; New Orleans data from Martha S. Putney, *Black Sailors: Afro-American Merchant Seamen and Whalemen Prior to the Civil War* (Westport, Conn., 1987), 120–121.

oped in part through their appreciation of the particular powers of their workplace.

Recovering African perspectives on maritime experiences and the effect of those on the formation of black social identities requires a kaleidoscope of African maritime history, New World maritime slavery, free black seafaring, and African spiritual associations with water. Eighteenth-century Africans did not establish hard-and-fast boundaries between categories of experience such as work, art, the natural world, and the spiritual realm. All were intertwined. Although eighteenth-century whites still invoked the supernatural, their categories and conceptualizations remained distinct from those of Africans. Whites, for example, did not understand departed ancestors as a prominent presence in their own lives. Africans, on the other hand, as Igor Kopytoff points out, did not believe that ancestors' spirits affected their lives: they *knew* it. To understand African boatmen enslaved in America from African perspectives, one must pursue water and vessels simultaneously as historical memories, work environments, and sites or sources of spiritual power. That African mental world, constantly evolving as it was, provided sailors like Cudjoe an anchor for the self.[9]

Africans did not have an extensive oceangoing commerce in the manner of Europeans, and they did not build or navigate technologically complex ships like those in which Europeans dominated the world. Many slaves who ultimately came to America had never seen the sea until their coffle marched to the shore, and, with the exception of *grumetes*, or Africans from Upper Guinea who worked for Europeans on the coast, few had voyaged in deep-sea vessels. Yet long before fifteenth-century Portuguese seamen arrived in western Africa, sub-Saharan peoples had developed extensive commercial networks dependent not only on porters, caravans, and riverine traffic but on regionally based coastal canoe mariners as well. Much of West Africa was linked by commerce on the Niger, Senegal, and Gambia Rivers. The Niger itself was the main route

9. My understanding of historic African cosmology draws on Sterling Stuckey, *Slave Culture: Nationalist Theory and the Foundations of Black America* (New York, 1987), 3–97; Robert Farris Thompson, *Flash of the Spirit: African and Afro-American Art and Philosophy* (New York, 1983); Robert Farris Thompson, "Kongo Influences on African-American Artistic Culture," in Joseph E. Holloway, ed., *Africanisms in American Culture* (Bloomington, Ind., 1990), 148–184; Wyatt MacGaffey, "The West in Congolese Experience," in Philip D. Curtin, ed., *Africa and the West: Intellectual Responses to European Culture* (Madison, Wis., 1972), 51–56; Wyatt MacGaffey, "Kongo and the King of the Americans," *Journal of Modern African Studies,* VI (1968), 171–181; Wyatt MacGaffey, "Cultural Roots of Kongo Prophetism," *History of Religions,* XVII (1977), 186–187; Michael Mullin, *Africa in America: Slave Acculturation and Resistance in the American South and the British Caribbean, 1736–1831* (Urbana, Ill., 1992); Kopytoff, in Mullin, *Africa and America,* 73.

joining "the Hausa kingdoms, the Yoruba states, and the Nupe, Igala, and Benin kingdoms to a hydrographic system that was ultimately connected to the Atlantic." Farther south, canoemen from the Zaire and Kwanza Rivers connected inland and coastal people. American boat slaves thus looked back to African maritime traditions.[10]

A white seaman named John Willock noted with admiration in 1781 the small-boat handling abilities of slaves in Saint Kitts. As on most of the Leeward and Windward Islands, good harbors were rare; and a continual surf—like that on much of the West African coast—made beach landings difficult and dangerous. Willock believed "the negroes" were "by no means afraid of dying by water" and that this enabled them to perform "what would be very difficult to any other person." "They are very dextrous in the management of their canoes," he decided, both landing them and getting under way. "Each canoe is manned by two negroes, who, in an instant leap on board of her, and proceed to whatever ship they are destined."[11]

Canoes like the ones Willock saw and other small boats called periaugas, or pettiaugers (also constructed from hollowed logs in a variation of native American and African style), became the heart of the plantation transportation system from Chesapeake Bay to the Caribbean. Many were substantial. A pettiauger for sale near Charleston in 1764 was "eight feet wide and forty feet long, with a small cabin." The proprietor of Delegal plantation on Skidaway Island kept a six-oared canoe "painted white outside and red inside, with a black bottom, about 27 feet in length." Vessels like these were vital to slaves' visiting as well as to their work in the Carolina lowcountry and, to a lesser degree, in the Chesapeake. Such hybrid craft, with modified dugout hulls and European-style rigs, were similar in many ways to African small craft, including the sailing trade canoes built by grumetes in Senegambia. Slaves like Billy, "a very black short well made Fellow," born about 1738, who was "very handy at

10. Jean-Pierre Chauveau, "Une histoire maritime africaine—est-elle possible? Historiographie et histoire de la navigation et de la pêche africaine à la côte occidentale depuis le quinzième siecle," Cahiers d'études africaines, XXVI (1986), 173–235; Walter Rodney, A History of the Upper Guinea Coast, 1545–1800 (Oxford, 1970), 1–121; John Thornton, Africa and Africans in the Making of the Atlantic World, 1400–1680 (Cambridge, 1992), 1–71 (quotation on 19). Some scholars argue that African mariners sailed westward long before Columbus and influenced civilizations in Mexico and Central America. This intriguing hypothesis does not withstand scrutiny because of the lack of evidence. But see Ivan van Sertima, They Came before Columbus (New York, 1976); Leo Wiener, Africa and the Discovery of America, 3 vols. (Philadelphia, 1920–1922), esp. II, ix, x, 116–17, III, 365.

11. John Willock, The Voyages and Adventures of John Willock, Mariner; Interspersed with Remarks on Different Countries in Europe, Africa, and America; With the Customs and Manners of the Inhabitants; And a Number of Original Anecdotes (Philadelphia, 1798), 27–28.

building boats," undoubtedly felt a sense of proprietorship and possibly a spiritual connection to these vessels. Eighteenth-century Africans felt the power of water in profound and immediate ways as they envisioned themselves.[12]

Water's reflecting surfaces served variously in myth and ritual across western Africa as the boundary through which spiritual communications occurred. And intercourse with spirits, both benign and evil, affected all Africans' daily life.[13] For the Bambara in Senegambia, many of whom were transported to colonial America, an androgynous water spirit called Faro maintained an individual's soul or vital life force after death. Refreshed and purified under water, the soul would reappear in the next-born member of the family. Ibo peoples from near the Bight of Benin had similar associations with the transmigration of souls in water: a slave in Georgia testified that Ibos there intent on suicide would "mahch right down in duh ribbuh tuh mach back tuh Africa." For historic Congo peoples, a watery barrier called the Kalunga line divided the living from the spirit world. In Congolese minds, Kalunga conveyed powerful associations with the elderly and with those departed who had been exceptionally wise and strong. As Wyatt MacGaffey, a prominent anthropologist of the Congo, has written concerning twentieth-century Congolese: "The Atlantic Ocean is only one of a number of waters that may serve to represent the ideal barrier, which is called Kalunga. Boats of various kinds are vehicles for transporting souls or for returning to this shore such exceptional individuals as prophets, who are able to come and go." Twentieth-century thought, even in relatively undeveloped societies, does not necessarily mirror that of eighteenth-century people. But in this case, it is suggestive of a deeply historic cosmology concerning spirits (or the living dead) who were accessible across a watery interface, and without whom no conception of self could exist.[14]

Water was clearly a potent metaphor for life beyond this world, even if, as examples from Bambara, Ibo, and Congolese people reveal, it was understood

12. Rusty Fleetwood, *Tidecraft: An Introductory Look at the Boats of Lower South Carolina, Georgia, and Northern Florida: 1650–1950* (Savannah, Ga., 1982), 30–31, 62. For Billy, see *Maryland Gazette,* Apr. 4, 1765, in Windley, *Runaway Slave Advertisements,* II, 58.

13. Stuckey, *Slave Culture,* 12–15; Thompson, *Flash of the Spirit,* 72–83, 108–142; John S. Mbiti, *African Religions and Philosophy* (New York, 1969), 54–55, 78–91.

14. Gwendolyn Midlo Hall, *Africans in Colonial Louisiana: The Development of Afro-Creole Culture in the Eighteenth Century* (Baton Rouge, La., 1992), 41–55, esp. 49–50; William D. Piersen, "White Cannibals, Black Martyrs: Fear, Depression, and Religious Faith as Causes of Suicide among New Slaves," *Journal of Negro History,* LXII (1977), 153; MacGaffey, "West in Congolese Experience," in Philip D. Curtin, ed., *Africa and the West,* 51–56, esp. 55; MacGaffey, "Kongo and the King of the Americans," *Journal of Modern African Studies,* VI (1968), 171–181; MacGaffey, "Cultural Roots of Kongo Prophetism," *History of Religions,* XVII (1977), 186–187.

variously by different Africans. Beliefs of those sorts survived the Middle Passage, as the case of a slave called Minc suggests. During the late nineteenth century, a white American southerner named Harry Stillwell Edwards recalled that in boyhood he had watched the African-born Minc catch a terrapin "and with a bit of wire ground to an exceedingly fine point cut on its shell a number of curious signs or hieroglyphics" before releasing it, a process Minc repeated innumerable times. During the 1980s, Robert Farris Thompson, an American art historian, found "specialized ritual experts called *nganga nkodi* and *nganga nsibi*" in the northern Kongo conveying "intense messages to the dead" on the bodies of living fish or turtles. "They cut their signs *(bidimbu)* into the shell of a tortoise so that the reptile, diving back into the water, will carry them across the *Kalunga* line into the world beyond." Captive in America more than a century earlier, Minc had communicated similarly with his ancestors across the watery barrier. As Melville J. Herskovits noted years ago: "In all those parts of the New World where African religious beliefs have persisted, . . . the cult of water spirits, holds an important place." Although different Africans' spiritual associations with water were by no means homogeneous or universalizing, Africans shared underlying assumptions about water that were foreign to whites and that served to draw diverse eighteenth-century Africans and their descendants together as a corporate black people.[15]

Slave funerals provide another window to the multilayered appreciation of the sea shared by uprooted Africans. Dr. George Pinckard observed a late-eighteenth-century burial in Barbados attended by more than sixty slaves, of whom most were women clad in white—the African mourning color. Grave-diggers told the Englishman that Jenny, the deceased, was an African washer-woman. Slaves at the grave site, according to Pinckard, professed "full faith in Jenny's transmigration to meet her friends, at her place of nativity; and their persuasion that death was only a removal from their present state to their former home—a mere change from a state of slavery to a state of freedom"— seemed to alleviate their affliction. As the women each threw a handful of earth onto the grave, they cried out: "God bless you, Jenny, good-by! remember me to all friends t'other side of the sea, Jenny! Tell 'em me come soon! Good-by, Jenny, good-by!" Mourners also expected, as Pinckard relates, "to hear from poor Jenny . . . before morning" regarding their messages she bore to the ancestors.[16]

15. Thompson, "Kongo Influences on African-American Artistic Culture," in Holloway, ed., *Africanisms in American Culture*, 148–184, esp. 152; Melville J. Herskovits, *The Myth of the Negro Past* (New York, 1941), 232.

16. George Pinckard, *Notes on the West Indies*, 3 vols. (London, 1806), I, 271–274.

These Africans knew Jenny would simultaneously cross the sea to Africa and the Kalunga line to her ancestors. She would accomplish in death what some "new Negroes" tragically tried to do in life, misunderstanding the immensity of the Atlantic. A "Negro Fellow named Tom . . . imported from Africa about 2½ years ago" to Rock Creek, Maryland, "made an Attempt to get to Sea in an open Boat" in 1761. Home beckoned from across the sea, understood as both a physical and metaphysical connection to Africa.[17]

Congolese people still understand the "meaning of life as a process shared with the dead below the river or the sea—the real sources of earthly power and prestige," notes Robert Farris Thompson. Beliefs—and perhaps more important, belief systems—of this sort endured among eighteenth-century Africans transplanted to South Carolina. The volume of sacred pottery ritually thrown by slaves into South Carolina's rivers, and recently retrieved by archaeologists, indicates that Kalunga and other spiritual associations with water long remained a psychic compass for Africans set to work in a white-dominated world.[18]

African men in maritime occupations thus understood their experience in an intuitive and symbolic way. Even if their allegorical appreciation of the sea did not mitigate the harsh material conditions of their work, it did inspire a self-defining realm of experience safe from masters and an understanding of the workplace separate from that of white mariners.

Certain North American slaves put their own gloss on sea travel, coming to associate the successful navigator with spiritual power. Despite often disparaging mariners as people-out-of-bounds, many cultures have maintained awe and respect for voyagers who dare to drop below the visible horizon, who pursue their "business in great waters," and who nevertheless return through courage, skill, and divine assistance. Trobriand Islanders, celebrated by Bronislaw Malinowski as "The Argonauts of the Western Pacific," and Swahili dhow sailors in the East African port of Lamu come to mind, as do mariners immortalized in nineteenth-century romantic literature. Africans, especially those maturing under Bakongo and Angolan influences, associated vessels with "the ancient vision of return." Boats (and later, for slaves' descendants, automobiles, airplanes, and bicycles) did not exist simply in the three-dimensional world of daily life but were expressions of transcendence, means of traveling

17. *Maryland Gazette*, Oct. 22, 1761, in Windley, *Runaway Slave Advertisements*, II, 42.

18. Thompson, quoted in Stuckey, *Slave Culture*, 12; MacGaffey, "Kongo and the King of the Americans," *Journal of Modern African Studies*, VI (1968), 173, 177; Leland G. Ferguson, *Uncommon Ground: Archeology and Early African America, 1650–1800* (Washington, D.C., 1992), 109–120; Thompson, *Flash of the Spirit*, 135.

through time and space into the fourth-dimensional world of ancestral spirits. That explains the use of model boats and cars as grave adornments, but it also speaks to the potency of those who had mastered such vehicles in the here and now. "For a Kongo person in the 1930's or 1940's to say 'I am a driver,' " writes Robert Farris Thompson, "conveyed to the elders a very powerful message of strangeness and potentiality."[19]

That may further explain the respect in which slave sailors were held by other slaves—especially slave captains who had mastered the secrets of navigation. Brothers who departed and returned might have been seen to possess compelling powers. During the 1760s, the recently manumitted slave Olaudah Equiano was en route from Georgia to Montserrat as a seaman on wages when his captain died. Equiano had learned the essentials of dead reckoning while a slave and had made that passage several times. Thus armed, he navigated the sloop from midocean to Antigua, his goal, and was soon riding safely at anchor off Montserrat. "I now . . . was called 'Captain,' " he wrote, which "was quite flattering to my vanity to be thus styled by as high a title as any sable freeman in this place possessed. . . . The success I had met with increased the affection of my friends in no small measure." Like Equiano, an enslaved Virginian pilot earned respect from his accomplishments. African-born but raised from boyhood slavery as a river pilot, he *acted* as a free man during the era of the American Revolution, according to a white man who knew him, because of his skill and the estimation in which he was held. Although local whites called him "Uncle Mark," the pilot repeatedly introduced himself as "Capt. Starlins." Equiano's and Starlin's sense of self might have emerged not only from their occupational skill and perquisites but from the resonance of that skill with spirit mediation and public esteem.[20]

Some African-born seamen constructed a sense of self rooted in African spiritual associations with water and vessels. While such a cultural orientation was not compelling to all Africans, much less to all blacks, many shared a sense of water's spiritual power and of navigators' potency. Some sailors with African heritages thus created identities meaningful only to other blacks similarly oriented, even as they shared with white shipmates certain aspects of sailors' occupational identity based on working conditions, skill, and worldliness.

19. Bronislaw Malinowski, *Argonauts of the Western Pacific: An Account of Native Enterprise and Adventure in the Archipelagoes of Melanesian New Guinea* (London, 1922); Thompson, "Kongo Influences," in Holloway, *Africanisms in American Culture,* 167–180, esp. 178.

20. Olaudah Equiano, *The Life of Olaudah Equiano,* in Henry Louis Gates, Jr., ed., *Classic Slave Narratives* (New York, 1987), 106–107; "The Schooner Patriot," *Virginia Historical Register and Literary Advertiser,* ed. William Maxwell (Richmond, Va., 1848), I, 127–131, esp. 129.

Eighteenth-century black self-consciousness was more complicated than the Janus-faced opposition of black and white, even if a conceptual chasm existed between certain aspects of black and white sailors' spirituality and social identity. Depending upon specific circumstances, blacks defined themselves against other blacks *and* with other blacks, against whites *and* with whites. Black seamen constructed an occupational identity that transcended race even as that identity allowed expression of the racial awareness that seafaring enhanced. Skill, style, mobility, sexual prowess, contact with whites, and reputations as indefatigable runaways contributed to individual mariners' sense of self.

Many slaves were skilled in the arts of the sailor. According to their masters, 46 percent of slave mariners in South Carolina between 1732 and 1782 were "sailors," as opposed to boatmen or fishermen—men who either crossed oceans or sailed extensively coastwise. Able to "hand, reef, and steer," these sailors expressed themselves in no small degree through their workplace accomplishments. An African who "cost thirty pounds Sterling out of the ship" in Antigua was later sold by Walter Nugent. Describing him to Abraham Redwood in Rhode Island, where the man had been sent, Nugent wrote in 1731, "The Negroe man is a Peice [sic] of a Saylor." A Tidewater patriot responded to a plea for boats from the Maryland Council of Safety in 1781 by telling them that he would send "his schooner Cheerfully" but with "a Negro Skipper, as no whit [sic] man would go." Experienced sailors like that skipper, and Dick, a slave described in 1788 as "a very good seaman and rigger," instinctively understood shiphandling and had internalized the cause-and-effect relationships of wind speed, sail trim, and rudder angle. Slave sailors understood tyranny and abuse as well. Nevertheless, their skill allowed them to manipulate one of the most complicated pieces of machinery then known. Skill and worldliness also inspired an occupational identity distinct from that of slaves working in the fields.[21]

Nothing distinguished that occupational identity more than tattoos. Tat-

21. Morgan, "Colonial South Carolina Runaways," *Slavery and Abolition*, VI (Dec. 1985), 64 (N = 191 enslaved mariners); Walter Nugent to Abraham Redwood, Apr. 11, 1731, *Commerce of Rhode Island, 1726–1800*, 2 vols. (Massachusetts Historical Society, *Collections*, 7th Ser., IX [Boston, 1914–1915]), 15; Sidney Kaplan, *The Black Presence in the Era of the American Revolution, 1770–1800*, rev. ed. (Amherst, Mass., 1989), 44–45; *Virginia Independent Chronicle*, Jan. 2, 1788, in Windley, *Runaway Slave Advertisements*, I, 392–393.

tooed black sailors generally displayed the same designs as their white ship-mates, including initials, anchors, mermaids, dolphins, and crucifixes. Most white seamen, and an even larger proportion of black sailors were not tattooed. But in an era when tattoos were virtually never seen save on the weather-beaten skin of a seafaring man, they generally spoke to an identity as deepwater seamen that transcended race. Not always. Michael Jones, born in Louisiana in 1774, eschewed conventional designs: he had a figure representing "Justice" pricked into his skin. Jones's tattoo is a rare text for the study of an eighteenth-century black man's representation of self. His particularly sardonic wit permanently transformed the blackness with which he was stigmatized by whites into an emblem of "Justice." Although Jones might have been advocating "justice" within the black community, it appears that he chose to make a racially specific statement within the context of his occupational identity.[22]

As with tattoos, so with clothes: black and white sailors shared a distinctive style that nevertheless allowed room for racial expression. A "bright Mulatto Man Slave named Sam" sailed in 1771 aboard the sloop *Tryall* in Virginia, clad in "Cloathing . . . such as is worn by Seamen."[23] Jasper, a Virginian slave "accustomed to work on board vessels" sported "much the air of a sailor." These men presented themselves to the world with the clothing, gait, accessories, and style unique to their occupation. Contemporary oil portraits and etchings, however, establish clearly that some blacks set themselves apart from white sailors with hoop earrings and other sartorial flourishes. Commander of an all-black crew aboard the whaling schooner *Industry* in 1822, Captain Absalom Boston sported both the white shirt and tie that indicated command and prominent gold hoops in each ear.[24]

Along with a shared style, black and white sailors found common ground in the boxing ring and as fencing and wrestling opponents, although it is by no means clear that all of the underlying rules and meanings black sailors attributed to manly sports were identical with those of whites, even in this most common of arenas. Black sailors, for instance, competed in rough play and fought for real by butting heads. White sailors generally did not. Only in the rough-

22. Ira Dye, "The Tattoos of Early American Seafarers, 1796–1818," *American Philosophical Society, Proceedings*, CXXXIII (1989), 520–554. Descriptions of the tattoos of 54 African American seamen were kindly made available to me by Dye.

23. *Maryland Gazette*, Mar. 7, 1771, May 18, 1775, in Windley, *Runaway Slave Advertisements*, II, 85–86, 110.

24. *Virginia Gazette*, Nov. 26, 1767, July 18, 1771, *North Carolina Gazette*, Mar. 27, 1778, in Windley, *Runaway Slave Advertisements*, I, 56, 314, 449; Portrait of Absalom Boston at the Nantucket Historical Society, Nantucket, Mass.

and-tumble scrapping of the southern backcountry, where no holds were barred, do white men seem to have borrowed butting from black combatants.[25]

The African origins of head-butting are clear. Samba Jean, "a Mu-Kongo expert in the martial arts of Africa," explained to art historian Robert Farris Thompson in 1990 that several head-butt styles of combat are currently practiced in Kongo. Afro-Brazilians, Venezulans, and West Indians still rely on stylized kicks and head-butts, as did nineteenth-century South Carolinian and Georgian Sea Island blacks with their "knocking and kicking" combat. The butting characteristic of black sailors in the late eighteenth century survived the Middle Passage to take root in African America societies from New England to Brazil. Whether fighting pugnaciously or demonstrating martial skill, seamen propagated the art as they traveled from one region to another.[26]

If much of sailors' behavior and style suspended attention to racial distinctions, butting represented tendencies and historical traditions confined almost entirely to people of the African diaspora. It transcended cultural and linguistic divisions among blacks. Tarrying ashore at Guadeloupe in 1787, a group of black and white English-speaking sailors watched a Sunday gathering of slaves entertaining themselves. The males, according to one white sailor, regarded butting as a "favorite amusement . . . for which purpose their wooly hair is suffered to grow on the top of their heads, whilst that from behind is cut away, and frizzled in amongst that left on top, which forms a kind of cushion, or firm tuft of hair." Circled by onlookers, the "opposing combatants danc[ed]" to "African music" before darting "forward, head against head." Intent on reputation, a free seaman of color from Philadelphia named Tom Grace challenged the local champion, a patois-speaking Guadeloupean slave. Grace swore he would "capsize one of these fellows in a crack." He did, his white shipmates watching from the sidelines. But when Grace won, the locals drove him away, and he retreated with the white sailors. Connecting with the Guadeloupean slaves on one level through a characteristically black form of combat, Grace nevertheless remained divided from them by language, region, status, and occupation. As a free seafaring man of color, he maneuvered between the two groups, defining himself through transactions of different sorts with foreign blacks and white shipmates.[27]

Unlike sailors, most slaves lived in tight, land-based social networks. Even

25. Elliot J. Gorn, " 'Gouge and Bite, Pull Hair and Scratch': The Social Significance of Fighting in the Southern Backcountry," *American Historical Review,* XC (1985), 20.

26. Robert Farris Thompson, foreword to *Ring of Liberation: Deceptive Discourse in Brazilian Capoeira,* by J. Lowell Lewis (Chicago, 1992), xii–xiv.

27. William Butterworth, *Three Years Adventures of a Minor in England, Africa, the West Indies, South-Carolina and Georgia* (Leeds, [1831]), 301–307.

given the prevalence of runaways circulating widely within places like colonial South Carolina, most New World slaves were restricted to socializing with other blacks that lived nearby. Pass laws, terror, and limited transportation saw to that. Seamen, by comparison, existed within a far-flung maritime network that provided different possibilities—and different insecurities. Seafaring slaves had ties that were more extensive and more loose than those of slaves attached to one plantation, and they developed distinctive forms of collective and individual identities accordingly.

Maritime slaves had an employable skill and scattered contacts that together provided a kind of self-confidence. Historian Gerald Mullin has calculated that about one-quarter of the skilled runaway slaves in eighteenth-century Virginia were boatmen and sailors. Sufficiently poised to strike out into the world of masterless men but savvy enough to recognize that they would invariably need help in the future from others, runaway mariners acted with a degree of assurance that such help would be forthcoming. Some maritime runaways managed to elude their masters for years while remaining in a general geographic area between short voyages. John Emmanuel, for instance, passed as free for at least three years around Norfolk before being committed to jail in 1774. But most seafarers knew that by joining a ship's company they rapidly could find themselves alone in a strange place. Clearly a significant number of black seafaring men did not define themselves primarily through social networks established on "the plantation" or in "the quarter." Instead, they put their trust in themselves and in the fraternity of seafaring men. "Community" might have been defined more by shared values and social condition, within and across racial lines, than by geographic locale.[28]

Land-based and sea-based black men had opportunities to develop distinctive kinds of sexual identities. The notorious sexuality of sea chanteys from a later era, along with the blues sung by other working men, suggest that sexual prowess played no small part in black sailors' identity formation. Sailors in pursuit of love let the mystique of the water work its magic. They also capitalized on opportunities to win favors through pilferage or pay. During the American Revolution, Massachusetts blacks who went privateering brought "home their black Ladies such things, as enable them to look down, with Contempt, upon many of the whites." Enslaved sailors enjoyed the company of women like "a negro wench named BETTY . . . not unacquainted with coasting schooners"; and an "impertinent" Negro woman fleeing by water from Williamsburg, Virginia, to Hampton or Norfolk in 1773. "She is fond of Liquor,

28. Gerald W. Mullin, *Flight and Rebellion: Slave Resistance in Eighteenth-Century Virginia* (New York, 1972), 37–38, 94–95, 98, 111, 119–120.

and apt to sing indecent and Sailors Songs when so." Ned, whose mistress in Norfolk allowed him to hire himself out during the early 1760s, capitalized on "going by Water" (which he was "fond of") to have "a Wife at Mr. Parker's on the Eastern Shore." She would have remained inaccessible to him but for his boat work. All mariners enjoyed mobility that introduced them to many women, permitting multiple sexual contacts. That might have encouraged rakishness; it also might have allowed certain male slaves better chances to practice African-derived polygamy than would ever be the case for land-bound slaves. When Cambridge "run away from the schooner Sharpe" in 1768, his master believed he had "a wife at almost every landing on the Rappahannock, Mattapony, and Pamunkey rivers."[29]

Seamen's rolling gait, tarred trousers, and tattoos set them apart from landsmen, as did sailorly skill. All of those elements contributed to a specific occupational identity that transcended race. Within that shared style, however, black and white sailors often went their separate ways. Blacks were more likely to sport earrings and to fight by butting heads. They might have understood having "a wife in every port" differently from white sailors, and they were certainly more likely to be estranged from their land based social networks of origin because of sale or flight. Black sailors' particular social identity emerged out of workplace conditions in which they were at once racial go-betweens straddling black and white worlds *and* traveling men who spent more time moving between dispersed black communities than residing in any single one.

SEAFARERS' MOBILITY AND THE FORMATION OF AFRICAN IDENTITY

Situated on vessels connecting all corners of the Atlantic world, black seafaring men were newsmongers central to the formation of black America and to the elaboration of a multidimensional black identity. They broadcast accounts from blacks' perspectives regarding the Haitian Revolution, the movements to abolish the slave trade and emancipate slaves, and the debate over colonization that centered on the question of whether people of color would remain in the United States. Outside the pale of these transformative debates and events, the mundane ebb and flow of black sailors' daily lives brought into focus differences among diasporic blacks. A slave named Jim fled down the James River in 1802 to City Point, or Norfolk, and then went "to Philadelphia

29. H. Lee to Mary Robie, July 26, 1779, Robie Sewall Papers, Massachusetts Historical Society; *Virginia Gazette*, Jan. 16, 1761, Apr. 21, 1768, Jan. 20, 1774, *Charlestown Gazette*, Jan. 11, 1780, all in Windley, *Runaway Slave Advertisements*, I, 33, 59, 142–143, III, 706.

and New York on board of a vessel," "which," his master said, "I am inclined to think . . . he makes a practice of." Seamen like Jim compared the lives of black brothers and sisters in plantations and seaports; and, drawing on storytelling traditions prominent among sub-Saharan Africans and Atlantic seafarers, they talked.[30]

Seafaring elevated individual blacks' self-confidence and prominence. Worldly seamen achieved distinction as leaders within eighteenth- and early-nineteenth-century Afro-America. The list was long and included Prince Hall, James Forten, Denmark Vesey, Paul Cuffe, and Olaudah Equiano. Whereas white mariners were among the most marginalized men in white society, black seamen found access to privileges, worldliness, and wealth denied to most slaves. Nothing conveys that more strikingly than the fact that sailors wrote the first six black autobiographies published in English before 1800. Not only did their pens bridge oral black culture with what had been an exclusively white world of letters, but theirs was the opening salvo in what would become a barrage of antislavery literature by black authors dedicated to diasporic liberation. Seafaring men were in the vanguard of defining and creating a new black ethnicity out of the many African peoples dispersed and reproduced by Atlantic slavery. Reduced to subordination in New World societies, they began to envision their lost nation as the continent of Africa.[31]

Pioneering black men of letters chose not to identify themselves primarily as seamen, but as Christians and Africans—roles that served their antislavery cause and the creation of a diasporic consciousness. Relatively privileged compared to brethren toiling in the fields, they nevertheless understood seafaring as yet another form of compulsory and unpaid labor. Their wide-ranging maritime work informed their writing, however, as it honed their perspectives on variations in race and slavery throughout the Atlantic. Whereas nineteenth-century African American leaders often stepped out of the pulpit, those in the eighteenth century came out of the forecastle. Boston King, John Marrant, and John Jea were at home in both.

Early black seafaring autobiographers did not root their personal narratives

---

30. *Virginia Argus*, Apr. 9, 1796, June 23, 1802.

31. The six autobiographies are Hammon, *Narrative of the Uncommon Sufferings*; James Albert Ukawsaw Gronniosaw, *A Narrative of the Most Remarkable Particulars in the Life of James Albert Ukawsaw Gronniosaw, an African Prince . . .* (Bath, c. 1770; reprint, London, 1840); Olaudah Equiano, *Life of Olaudah Equiano* (London, 1789); John Marrant, *Narrative of the Lord's Wonderful Dealings with John Marrant, a Black . . .* (London, 1785); [Venture Smith], *A Narrative of the Life and Adventures of Venture, a Native of Africa . . .* (New London, 1798); Boston King, "Memoirs of the Life of Boston King, a Black Preacher," *Methodist Magazine* (1798), 105–110, 157–161, 209–213, 261–265.

in American or European locales. In fact, they were detached from place in a way that the authors of many later slave narratives were not, and in ways that few whites wished to be. Olaudah Equiano (in 1789) and James Albert Ukawsaw Gronniosaw (circa 1770) paid substantial attention to their African cultural and geographic origins, thus defining themselves in opposition to the societies in which they currently lived. But with little chance of repatriation to a now strange Africa, these black intellectuals envisioned themselves as members of an international black community.[32]

Whether professedly British or American or neither, seafarers like Equiano and Jea recognized the ability of blacks in the Atlantic world to redefine the term "African" in a characteristically creole way. Jea's consistent description of himself as an African illuminates the creation of "Africa" itself in the identities of late-eighteenth-century black people and refers to much more than his birthplace on the continent. Jea could have been born an Ibo, an Efik, an Ibibio, or into one of the other ethnic groups common in Old Callabar. His family probably had not long considered themselves Africans. Nondiscerning Europeans imposed "African" as a continental and totalizing label on blacks native to a host of ethnicities and polities. Ibo, Mandingo, and Ashanti people themselves, along with a multitude of others, then refashioned the term into a diasporic black identity in the ports and plantations of the New World. But in each individual's life, that did not happen immediately. Few eighteenth-century blacks born in Africa transformed themselves directly from their birthethnicity to an African identity. An intermediate, liminal, and detached stage of acculturation to Euro-American practices, and reassessment of the role of blackness in the New World, almost invariably intervened. Equiano's autobiography makes that clear. He declines to label himself an "African" in early chapters, referring instead to Benin or Eboe. After three years of slavery, he had become substantially acculturated to English ways, in a few particulars "almost an Englishman," he wrote, largely because of so much time aboard ship in the company of Englishmen. As his political consciousness developed, however, he referred to himself as "the African," or "the oppressed Ethiopian."[33]

African identity in the black Atlantic belonged, not to residents of sub-

32. On African origins, see Equiano, *Life*, 11–32; Gronniosaw, *Narrative*, 3–7.

33. Hodges, ed., *Black Itinerants*, 89, 93–94, 155, 164. Equiano, *Life*, in Gates, ed., *Classic Slave Narratives*, 1, 12, 17, 51, 182. Scholars disagree on how blacks' identity formation might have evolved, especially with reference to ethnicity. Stuckey argues that white oppression mitigated the importance of African ethnicity at once. Mullin argues that the perpetuation of specific African ethnic identities in America among enslaved immigrants deserves more study as an important component of slaves' identities; see Stuckey, *Slave Culture*, 3; Mullin, *Africa in America*, 268–277.

Saharan Africa, but to those swept up in the diaspora and struggling against great odds to define themselves. Their sense of being African honored ancestral cultural inheritance but acknowledged as well how people living in Africa were enduringly rooted in places and the past in ways that no liminal African American could be. The African identity cultivated by worldly diasporic blacks emphasized racial and political realities and was by no means synchronous with that of indigenous peoples of the continent. Nothing reveals that more clearly than the resounding refusal of most free African Americans to embrace their own deportation to Africa as part of the colonization movement. As James Forten wrote from Philadelphia to Captain Paul Cuffe in 1817: "We had a large meeting of males at the Rev. R. Allen's church the other evening. Three thousand at least attended, and there was not one soul that was in favor of going to Africa." Many African Americans' new African identity, like that of Equiano, was heavily laced with Christianity, civilization, and market values. Although less-educated black sailors were not as westernized as Equiano, they defined themselves no longer primarily through referents from the continent of Africa (even if they referred to themselves as "African") but through hybrid black American referents.[34]

Through their daily confrontations with the racial other, seamen straddling black and white worlds became more self-consciously African than were many slaves immersed in the black majorities of South Carolina or Jamaica. Much of black culture, unlike diasporic identity, was not racial. Cultural norms do not depend on an other the way that race (a specific social relationship) does. Ancestral spiritual communications, the dancing form of worship known as ring-shouts, and slave funerary practices, for instance, were heartfelt expressions of a people's cosmology, largely irrelevant to the existence of white folk. Blacks reflexively practiced African-derived cultural behaviors and attributed symbolic meanings to them for themselves and other blacks, but without a racial other in mind. This is not to minimize the fact that culture, as E. P. Thompson taught us long ago, can be an important means of conflict.[35] It is to suggest that many of slaves' cultural practices were inward-looking. The specifically African identity espoused by many African American sailors, on the

34. James Forten to Paul Cuffe, Jan. 25, 1817, in Wilson Jeremiah Moses, ed., *Classical Black Nationalism: From the American Revolution to Marcus Garvey* (New York, 1996), 50–52, esp. 51.

35. E. P. Thompson, *The Making of the English Working Class* (London, 1963); Thompson, "The Moral Economy of the English Crowd in the Eighteenth Century," *Past and Present*, no. 50 (February 1971), 76–136; Thompson, "Patrician Society, Plebian Culture," *Journal of Social History*, VII (1973–1974), 382–405; Thompson, "Eighteenth-Century English Society: Class Struggle without Class?" *Social History*, III (1978), 133–165.

other hand, emerged not so much out of blacks' cultural separation from whites as out of cultural and political self-awareness following contact with them.

The brilliant Ibo Equiano became politicized in an international arena in which race was emerging as a primary social referent. Such was not the case during his African boyhood, when class, ethnicity, and lineage superseded racial identity. Even African merchants, soldiers, and slave traders on the coast, with much more exposure to whites than most Africans, did not always make decisions as though race was the primary social distinction. A Fanti boy named John Quamino, for instance, was entrusted to a white man by his father in 1754, with the understanding he would be sent to Europe for education. Instead, he was enslaved. Quamino later played a central role in Rhode Island blacks' Christianization and died in battle aboard a Revolutionary war privateer. New World blacks learned quickly from stories like that to distrust whites and painfully that they would have little of the self-assurance of African kings. But with memories of the slave trade freshly in mind and with African ethnic diversity confronting them in America, they by no means assumed all blacks were one people. That required many transformations, not the least of which was the preaching of leaders like Quamino, Equiano, and Jea who sought to catalyze New World African identity.[36]

Grappling with their sense of self and with how that was connected to place, people of color split over the question of blacks' future in America. Captain Paul Cuffe, arguably the most influential black American before Frederick Douglass, ultimately advocated repatriation and colonization of African Americans in Sierra Leone. Only there, he believed after his extensive voyaging to Europe, Africa, and through the Americas, could blacks "rise to be a people." Raised in the midst of his mother's Wampanoag people in Massachusetts and much closer physically to them than to his father's Ashanti kin, Cuffe eventually favored his diasporic identity as an African. "My nature is Musta," he had written circa 1773. But by 1809, he stated unequivocally (despite his Indian mother and Indian wife): "I am of the African race." Indians, mustees, and Africans were amalgamated in coastal New England, and boundaries between them were difficult to establish. Compared to many plantation slaves in the South or West Indies, however, Cuffe was culturally "musta." Politics, he recognized, publicly defined him more than culture. As a prominent man of color, he refashioned himself into an African, subsuming his musta identity

36. Thornton, *Africa and Africans*, 72–128; Ralph E. Lukar, " 'Under Our Own Vine and Fig Tree': From African Unionism to Black Denominationalism in Newport, Rhode Island, 1760–1876," *Slavery and Abolition*, XII (Sept. 1991), 23–48, esp. 24–28.

to a larger cause. Most free blacks in his generation, however, whether they called themselves "black," "African," or "people of color," rejected colonization, defining themselves not only against whites but against inhabitants of Africa.[37]

Letters written by African American seamen impressed into the British navy at the turn of the nineteenth century expressed geographic and cultural attachment to America and asserted a radical African American patriotism demanding black inclusion (not assimilation) in the United States. These sources reaffirm not only inconsistencies within African American identity formation but the doubled identities of American and black selfhood. Consider, for example, the behavior of impressed blacks who refused to enter their signatures in British muster rolls. Doing so was to enlist officially in the Royal Navy and to become eligible for a bounty, wages, and prize money. Refusing to enter consigned a man to the same work, same food, and same service as those who joined—but without the pay. Financial incentives and bullying pressures thus acted like carrot and stick, confounding all but the most stalwart. Yet many black Americans refused. "I . . . was treated very Ill because I would not Enter," lamented William Godfrey in 1799. "Neither have I," he wrote, "knowing myself to be an american as well as for what reason, I do not wish to serve them." Jacob Israel Potter refused to capitulate in 1811 after more than nine years of unwilling service "because I was an American and likewise I was a Citizen and beside I had a wife and family." Through the rage, pain, and endurance of their impressment, sailors like Godfrey and Potter expressed an identity as black Americans at the turn of the nineteenth century. Their expressions were deeper than just a pragmatic and immediate response to their situation as impressed men and more than a Faustian bargain with the devil-nation that had stolen millions of black souls. Those ideas asserted their attachment to place, a place inhabited and shaped by numerous other people of color, and their right to belong.[38]

Eighteenth-century black society defined itself more through common folks' talking than through the extraordinary accomplishments of a handful of prominent leaders like Paul Cuffe. Black storytellers moved easily along the waterfront, where they sought shipping and added their voices to the yarns of men before the mast. Although the degree to which such people talked re-

37. Lamont D. Thomas, *Paul Cuffe: Black Entrepreneur and Pan-Africanist* (Urbana, Ill., 1986), 7, 71. See also John David Smith, review of *Paul Cuffe*, by Lamont Thomas, *American Historical Review*, XCV (1990), 906.

38. William Godfrey folder, box 4, John Backus folder, box 1, Jacob Israel Potter folder, box 6, all in Miscellaneous Correspondence Regarding Impressed Seamen, Records on Impressed Seamen, 1794–1815, RG 59, NA.

mains undefinable and, although it is clear that some slaves repressed painful memories and kept their own counsel, evidence suggests that itinerant mariners confided in other blacks. Equiano remembered visiting at New Providence, Bahamas, "about seventeen or eighteen days" on a voyage from Montserrat in the 1760s, "during which time I met with many friends who gave me many encouragements to stay there with them." In Savannah, Equiano "went to a friend's house to lodge."[39]

Sailors thus became for black people in the Atlantic world what newspapers and the royal mail service were for white elites: a mode of communication integrating local black communities into the larger community of color, even as they revealed regional and local differences. In November 1756, a Bermudian-born slave named Thyas, "an extraordinary good Caulker, and a tolerable good Ship Carpenter," fled from the master to whom he had been sold on Saint Eustatius. Eight months later, he was seen at Bermuda; fourteen months after that, his master "heard that he had got to South Carolina," where he was "harboured somewhere with a run away Wench." Thyas capitalized not only on his maritime skill to circulate between those places but on networks of information about how to proceed and what he might find. Other sailors appropriated ships as conduits for political dissent, as the careers of Equiano, John Jea, Denmark Vesey, and Robert Wedderburn clearly testify.[40]

Try as they might to stop the flow of blacks' ideas around the Atlantic world, whites could not. "We may expect therefore black crews, and supercargoes and missionaries . . . [from revolutionary Saint Domingue] into the southern states," wrote Thomas Jefferson after President John Adams reinstituted trade between the United States and Saint Domingue in 1799. "If this combustion can be introduced among us under any veil whatever, we have to fear it."[41]

Seamen like the ones who scared Thomas Jefferson by circulating revolutionary ideas were among the most worldly of all slaves. Many were well traveled and multilingual—talents useful for fostering links between otherwise discrete black communities. A "Negro man named LUKE" ran off from his master at Cainboy, South Carolina, in 1763. He "has been us'd to the seas,

39. Equiano, *Life*, in Gates, ed., *Classic Slave Narratives*, 116–117.

40. *South Carolina Gazette*, Nov. 10–17, 1758, in Windley, *Runaway Slave Advertisements*, III, 167; Iain McCalman, ed., *The Horrors of Slavery and Other Writings by Robert Wedderburn* (New York, 1991), 3. Black communication and consciousness around the Atlantic are examined in Julius Sherrard Scott, "The Common Wind: Currents of Afro-American Communication in the Era of the Haitian Revolution" (Ph.D. diss., Duke University, 1986); Paul Gilroy, *The Black Atlantic: Modernity and Double Consciousness* (Cambridge, Mass., 1993).

41. Thomas Jefferson to James Madison, Feb. 12, 1799, quoted in Scott, "The Common Wind," 299.

speaks English, French, Spanish, and Dutch, and probably may attempt to get off in some vessel." A "mustee man slave, born in Caracoa [that is, Curaçao, Dutch West Indies], about 50 years of age," ran off from the schooner *Hannah* in Charleston, South Carolina, in 1783. He had lived for a while in North Carolina but, more significant, had been "employed in the West Indies as a coasting sailor, [and] he speaks all the languages used there." His frustrated master felt that the man might have headed back to North Carolina or might "have gotten on board some vessel going to sea."[42] Multilingual men like these, with extensive knowledge of the Americas, had better-than-average chances to escape from their masters, and, perhaps more significant for black peoples' self-awareness, abilities to spin yarns that implicitly or explicitly dramatized commonalities (and differences) among widely dispersed and linguistically separated people of color. Throughout the Caribbean, then, legal and clandestine inter-island trade introduced slave sailors to interstices in the slave system and to the recognition that, whether they spoke English, French Creole, Danish, or Papiamento, they had a great deal in common throughout plantation and maritime America.[43]

That is not to suggest that boatloads of multilingual slaves broke down cultural barriers willy-nilly. Many slaves remained parochial and provincial, accustomed to an insular existence and unable—or unwilling—to look outward. Contemporary Caribbean societies, long cross-pollinated by multilingual sailors and migrant workers, remain oriented to the home island rather than to the region as a whole. The constant movement of eighteenth-century black sailors, however, became an integral part of the process through which blacks created both a sense of diasporic connectedness and of particularity within their new black ethnicity. Fundamental to diasporic identity was the recognition (like that of Paul Cuffe) that all New World blacks, whether in New England, North Carolina, Nevis, or New Spain, inhabited common ground. Divisions certainly existed, creating fear and suspicion. But time after time, in seaport after seaport, vessels arrived with strange black men who led local blacks to the revelation, during lengthy port stays, that those strangers inhabited a definably black cosmos of martial arts, spirituality, and resistance to slavery and that the African identity they imported had broad applicability.

42. *South Carolina Gazette*, June 25–July 2, 1763, *South Carolina Gazette and General Advertiser*, Aug. 12–16, 1783, in Windley, *Runaway Slave Advertisements*, III, 231, 719.

43. Scott, "The Common Wind," 59–113, esp. 75; N.A.T. Hall, "Maritime Maroons: *Grand Marronage* from the Danish West Indies," *William and Mary Quarterly*, 3d Ser., XLII (1985), 476–498, esp. 489; Jane Landers, "Gracia Real de Santa Teresa de Mose: A Free Black Town in Spanish Colonial Florida," *American Historical Review*, XCV (1990), 9–30.

The revolution that began on the scorched northern plain of Saint Domingue in the summer of 1791 and that ultimately liberated Haiti from the hemispheric slavocracy provided a focal point for black redefinition of self. Revolutionary Saint Domingue and republican Haiti became a source of refuge and
inspiration for blacks of many nationalities. Epitomizing the demise of slavery,
Haiti embodied a potent symbol for slaveowners and for free black spokesmen
like Richard Allen as well as for the group of foreign blacks most intimately
familiar with it—free and slave seamen who actually went there. Those men
pitted shipmasters and American officials against the Haitian government,
finding protection in Haiti simply because they were black.[44] Moreover, transient black seamen from Saint Martin, Martinique, London, Baltimore, Boston, and a host of other locales often became "citizens" of Haiti, but "citizens"
who returned to the sea and kept moving as roving ambassadors of the pan-
African sovereignty that they had found in Haitian ports. Significantly, these
men retained their particularistic national identities while doing so. For many
black sailors, then, a voyage to Haiti affirmed the value of blackness and helped
focus a black Atlantic sensibility, even as it reaffirmed national and linguistic
differences among men of color who went there.

No exact numbers exist, but well-founded estimates suggest that several
thousand black seamen voyaged to Saint Domingue/Haiti between 1791 and
1830.[45] African American sailors expressed palpable pride in what they found
there. When the brig *Traveller* arrived in Port au Prince about 1812 carrying
North Carolina shingles and herring, one of the sailors in her all-black crew
watched with fascination the bodyguard of President Jean Pierre Boyer. "They
appeared to understand military tactics to perfection," he wrote. "Boyer was

44. On free black spokesmen and Saint Domingue, see Gary B. Nash, *Race and Revolution* (Madison, Wis., 1990), 77, 78. The United States did not have diplomatic ties with Haiti,
so, instead of consular officials, "commercial agents" conducted business for the United
States government.

45. In 1797, 600 American ships traded there, bringing approximately 5,000 American
sailors, of whom probably no fewer than 15% were black. In 1830, 753 American seamen
arrived in Haiti, of whom again probably 15% were black; see Donald R. Hickey, "America's
Response to the Slave Revolt in Haiti, 1791–1806," *Journal of the Early Republic*, II (1982),
361–379, esp. 362–365; "Return of the American Trade at the Port of Cape Haytien," and
"Statistical View of the Commerce at Port-au-Prince," Consular Despatches, Cape Haitian,
microfilm M-9, roll 6, RG 59, NA. For numbers of African American seamen working on
American ships, see W. Jeffrey Bolster, " 'To Feel Like a Man': Black Seamen in the Northern
States, 1800–1860," *Journal of American History*, LXXVI (1989–1990), 1173–1199, esp. 1176.

most superbly dressed and equipped, and on horseback made an elegant appearance." Here was an incarnation of black achievement and power.[46]

Many seamen knew that Haitian governments actively encouraged black immigration and sought to transform New World blacks into Haitians. As early as 1804, the governor-general of Haiti had offered American ship captains financial incentives to carry African Americans there, hoping to enlarge the army and swell the war-ravished male population. While King Henri Christophe reigned in the north, his secretary-general Joseph Balthazar Inginac encouraged New York blacks to emigrate. So did other prominent Haitians. "Make known, sir, to the unfortunate descendants of Africans, in the United States," wrote one of President Boyer's aides to a Massachusetts correspondent in 1824, that "they will find in us brothers, ever ready to receive them." Haitian President Alexander Petion readily harbored African American seamen at the risk of angering the United States. "Petion is extremely obstinate," the commercial agent of the United States, William Taylor, wrote to James Monroe in 1814, "and claims every negro or mulatto (no matter of what nation), who enters this port and will go every length to seduce them from their bounden duty."[47]

Haitian officials did not have to "seduce" black sailors "from their bounden duty," because black sailors from around the Atlantic learned that they could desert in Haitian ports with impunity. Taylor lamented to Monroe again in 1814 "that among . . . seamen on board of our vessels . . . are sometimes found *natives of this island*." "Such men on their arrival here," continued the agent, "immediately desert their vessels and such is the situation of this country, that there is neither authority, nor inclination, to compel them to return." Taylor complained bitterly about non-Haitian nationals as well. A black sailor signed articles for a cruise in the American privateer *Fox* "at New Orleans where he had resided many years." In Port au Prince, the sailor took on a new identity: he "called himself a Haytian, but," wrote Taylor, "as far as I have been enabled to ascertain the fact, [he] is a native of Martinique, and was never until now in Haiti." For Taylor, this swearing and counterswearing was pure duplicity, a breach of the code of honor that supposedly regulated men's actions. For the unnamed French West Indian—resident of Martinique, New Orleans, and

46. Paul Cuffe, [Jr.], *Narrative of the Life and Adventures of Paul Cuffe, a Pequot Indian . . .* (Vernon, Conn., 1839), 5. This autobiography was by the namesake son of the famous captain.

47. Floyd J. Miller, *The Search for a Black Nationality: Black Emigration and Colonization, 1787–1863* (Urbana, Ill., 1975), 74–76; William Taylor to James Monroe, Aug. 30, 1814, Consular Despatches, Cape Haitian, microfilm M-9, roll 5, RG 59, NA.

Haiti—a declaration of Haitian citizenship at once freed him from his captain's power and affirmed a diasporic identity in which race transcended place.[48]

The Haitian constitution honored that diasporic identity by expressly forbidding slavery, and many Haitians took seriously the liberation of enslaved sailors. Captain Nathaniel Raymond sailed the American schooner *Baracoa* from Baltimore to Cape Haitian in December 1820, with a hired slave seaman named George Rayner. After Rayner absconded, the captain futilely tried to get him back. Although he received many empty promises from the commanding general of the port that Rayner would be returned, when the *Baracoa* departed for New Orleans George Rayner remained in Haiti.[49]

Color-conscious Haitian courts were especially receptive to black sailors' accusations of slavery and man-stealing. Robert Baker, cook of the American schooner *Hancock*, filed a suit in 1822 against Captain Ezra Ryan in a Haitian court, charging that Ryan had threatened to sell Baker as a slave in North Carolina. Commercial agent Andrew Armstrong interceded on behalf of the captain with the grand judge of Haiti. "The difficulties he would have met trying to execute such a plan," wrote Armstrong, "shows its almost impossibility and he knew that the laws punish such crimes with death." But seaman Baker and Judge Fresnel knew just the opposite. Hundreds of free seamen lost their liberty to man-stealers in precisely that fashion. Unfortunately, existing records do not indicate whether Baker appropriated a Haitian identity or even whether he prevailed in his suit.[50]

By the end of 1821, American officials grudgingly recognized that slave sailors could legally demand their freedom in Haiti, but they remained ruffled by the Haitian government's partial treatment of *free* black seamen. The American agent in Port au Prince conceded to President Boyer: "If a *slave* is brought to this country in a foreign vessel, he may take the benefit of the laws of Haiti, and leave the vessel with impunity, but the case is very different with a free man. . . . when a coloured free man ships on board of our vessels as a citizen of the U.S. he must be answerable to our laws."[51] Boyer ignored him, determined to maintain Haiti as an oasis for people of color. African American seamen arriv-

48. William Taylor to James Monroe, Port au Prince, Jan. 9, 1814, Consular Despatches, Cape Haitian, microfilm M-9, roll 5, RG 59, NA.

49. "Protest of the Master of the Baracoa for the Forcible Desertion of a Slave Belonging to the Vessel . . . at Cape Henry," Feb. 12, 1821, Misc. Letters on Seamen from Collectors of Customs, 1817–1824 (E 145), RG 59, NA.

50. Andrew Armstrong to John Quincy Adams, Sept. 24, 1822, Andrew Armstrong to the Honorable Fresnel, Grand Judge of Haiti, [n.d.], Consular Despatches, Cape Haitian, microfilm M-9, roll 5, RG 59, NA.

51. Armstrong to John B. Boyer, Sept. 26, 1821, Consular Despatches, Cape Haitian, Series 5, microfilm M-9, roll 5, RG 59, NA.

ing there, "either with or without cause of complaint" against their shipmaster, according to Armstrong, "have only to say they have been maltreated, wish to become, or are citizens of Haiti, and they immediately obtain their desire."[52]

Black sailors recognized the mountainous island nation as a place where race conferred more privileges than nationality. All nationalisms are symbolic fictions through which disparate individuals are united into a supposedly cohesive whole. But in the hemispheric politics of the early nineteenth century, race transcended nationality. Slavery and black oppression, after all, were international and transcultural systems against which the Republic of Haiti was valiantly struggling. Haitian nationalism erupted as a response to the history of slavery, and Haitian politicians resolutely defined Haitian citizenship in terms of African descent, especially for the benefit of foreigners.[53] After the cook of an American schooner from Philadelphia was "chastized" by his captain on a voyage to Aux Cayes in 1821, he deserted and "made his complaint before the justice of the peace, Mr. Solomon Fils, who immediately [c]ited the captain to appear before him." The American commercial agent at Aux Cayes attempted to intercede, explaining that, since the matter had occurred "between the master and Seaman of an American" ship, it should properly be resolved by the American agent. Fils interpreted the case as racial politics instead of Admiralty law. He commanded the captain to pay a fine and court costs, liberated the cook from his contract, and—in a blow to American nationalism—forced the captain to hand over the black seaman's official American protection certificate. In effect, Fils awarded the African American sailor dual citizenship by offering him asylum in Haiti and simultaneously letting him keep his American passport.[54]

That was exactly what most African American sailors wanted: the chance to manipulate the political situation in Haiti against their captains and employers but with the option to return to the United States when they chose. Most black seamen, even if they jumped ship in Haiti, did not want to become permanent

52. Armstrong to John Quincy Adams, Oct. 8, 1821, Consular Despatches, Cape Haitian, microfilm M-9, roll 5, RG 59, NA.

53. My thoughts on nationalism have been influenced by Benedict Anderson, *Imagined Communities: Reflections on the Origin and Spread of Nationalism* (London, 1983); and by Michel-Rolph Trouillot, *Haiti, State against Nation: The Origins and Legacy of Duvalierism* (New York, 1990).

54. Aaron Nouez to Andrew Armstrong, Sept. 20, 1821, Nouez to John B. Boyer, Sept. 20, 1821, Consular Despatches, Cape Haitian, microfilm M-9, roll 5, Series 5, RG 59, NA. Beginning in 1796, the United States government issued seamen's protection certificates to black and white American sailors as protection against British impressment. The certificates were also a form of job card, an identification for entitlements such as hospitalization or repatriation and, for black men, a tenuous form of free papers.

expatriates. Commercial agent Armstrong complained of black seamen in Port-au-Prince who petitioned him for passage back to the states. These sailors, like the several thousand African Americans who voluntarily emigrated to Haiti in the mid-1820s but then returned, found themselves in a foreign society that for all of its race pride still spoke Haitian Creole, practiced a creolized Catholicism, and countenanced an exploitative plantation agriculture.[55] If race transcended nationality in hemispheric politics, such was often not the case in individual psyches. Proud to be black in a place where blackness conferred privileges, American sailors of color nevertheless retained an American identity that confirmed their attachment to black American culture and American places. Clearly, these men had a complex and multilayered understanding of self grounded in their own versions of being black, American, and (perhaps temporarily) Haitian.

American agents had a more rigid understanding of nationalism and citizenship than did Haitian officials. They fumed that when African American seamen accepted the privileges and protections of Haitian citizenship, the sailors' American protection certificates should be surrendered. They did not want black men who circumvented their authority with instantaneous Haitian citizenship later to claim American entitlements, including hospital money, repatriation, or employment on American ships.[56]

Black sailors and Haitian officials understood Haitian citizenship in more mutable terms. Solomon Fils recognized that a transient black man's citizenship in Haiti did not preclude that same sailor's continued citizenship in the United States, because Haitian citizenship—as extended to seamen of color— was as much an affirmation of diasporic identity as it was an extension of specific national privileges and responsibilities. Desiring foreign men of color to settle there, Haitian officials did not hold them to it. The "Brig Saco, sold here," wrote the American commercial agent at Cape Haitian, "is now Haytien." "Her crew (all black) reshipped here as Haytiens, and returned to New York in the same vessel."[57] Refashioning themselves as "Haytians," those English-speaking black Americans returned to the United States under the red-and-black Hai-

55. Armstrong to Daniel Brent, July 30, 1825, Consular Despatches, Cape Haitian, microfilm M-9, roll 5, RG 59, NA; Miller, *Search for a Black Nationality,* 80–81. The new Haitian state was by no means a paradise for labor. King Henri Christophe instituted a form of militarized plantation agriculture reminiscent of the outlawed slavery. Throughout Haitian history, peasant labor has always supported the bureaucracy and the bourgeoisie. See Trouillot, *Haiti: State against Nation,* 35–58.

56. Nouez to John B. Boyer, Sept. 20, 1821, Consular Despatches, Cape Haitian, microfilm M-9, roll 5, RG 59, NA.

57. Consular Returns of American Vessels, Jan. 28, 1837, Consular Despatches, Cape Haitian, microfilm M-9, roll 7, RG 59, NA.

tian flag, with tales of resplendent black troops, obliging officials, and of a nation where all black people were citizens.

Black seamen welcomed the opportunity to become citizens of Haiti. Haitian sovereignty united sailors' pragmatic concerns about independence from their captains with the ideology of racial unity and black pride. Tales of triumphs told by ex-slaves like George Raynor, who had achieved the selfhood of freedom in Haiti, not only reinforced the diasporic consciousness of blacks around the Atlantic world but affirmed as well a multiplicity of black identities. When black American sailors looked at brothers in Haiti, they saw only a partial reflection of themselves.

SEPARATION AND INTEGRATION IN THE CONSTRUCTION OF BLACK SELVES AND RACE

Selves are made, not born. The Atlantic economy that propelled thousands of men of color into maritime work during the late eighteenth and early nineteenth centuries initiated a series of specific social transactions that simultaneously shaped sailors' individual identity formation and contributed to the creation of a complicated and multifaceted African American identity. As cases examined here reveal, however, race and self among sailors were not necessarily congruent. No "black self" existed, even though sailors were in the vanguard of redefining "African" in diasporic terms. In fact, the use of "black" as an adjective to modify "values," "behavior," or "self" belies the complexity of early American blacks' selfhood.

Contrapuntal pressures created separation within and integration among blacks in America. For instance, specific ethnic African spiritual associations with water and vessels, differing as they did, served to distinguish Africans in America from each other, perpetuating multiple African identities among "new Negro" slaves. Yet those cultural associations also had certain commonalities that separated Africans from white people and that contributed to the creation of a shared African (as opposed to white) cultural identity. Contrapuntal pressures also led blacks in certain circumstances to define themselves with other blacks and against other blacks, with certain whites and against all whites. Aboard ship, black sailors defined themselves against other blacks who did not share their worldliness, skill, and alienation from land-based social networks. Meanwhile, they shared an occupational identity with white shipmates based on mutuality and the conditions of their work. Yet the asymmetrical assignment of social power by race never disappeared. So black sailors created an occupational identity that asserted race in certain ways, even as it transcended race in others. Travel also separated and integrated New World blacks. Black sailors' extraordinary mobility introduced geographically separate black communities to knowledge of a far-flung black world, bringing into focus other blacks' exploitation and their accomplishments. Even as this established the basis for a diasporic identity, however, voyages to places like Haiti affirmed significant differences within blackness. If Haiti itself embodied the diaspora with its transnational racial identity, sailors of color in Haiti identified themselves against each other through their distinctive national and linguistic orientations. For them, as for others, the self was created in a dynamic and responsive fashion within certain parameters, including, but not limited to, race and occupation.

The final word on black sailors' self-representation, and thus on their relationship to blacks and to sailors, belongs to Joseph Johnson, a memorable superannuated merchant mariner frequenting London's Tower Hill during the early nineteenth century. Entitled to no naval pension and having no claim to parish relief on account of his foreign birth, the old seaman had no choice but to entertain and beg for his subsistence. A white Londoner suggested that "novelty . . . induced Black Joe to build a model of the ship Nelson; to which, when placed on his cap, he can, by a bow of thanks . . . give the appearance of sea-motion." The aged Johnson tramped the streets with his unique ship model, gracefully dancing his way to a beggar's livelihood. But neither novelty nor necessity alone, I suggest, inspired Johnson's elaborate headgear. Look instead to his memories of slave John Canoe or to African mummers. John Canoe, a prominent mummer at festivals in the Bahamas, Jamaica, and North Carolina, wore what whites considered outlandish masks and headdresses, regalia that, however, represented ancestral figures and spiritual power.[58]

In a classic case of cultural crossover, Johnson appropriated a European artifact, one that had become meaningful to him through his own years of sea service, and reinvested it with African meanings to create a characteristically black cultural hybrid. Most white contemporaries looked at Joe Johnson through the distorting glass of race and saw an old black sailor cleverly manipulating a full-rigged ship on his head. London blacks, on the other hand, saw an aged mummer bobbing through the streets, connecting them with his

58. On Johnson, see Paul Edwards and James Walvin, *Black Personalities in the Era of the Slave Trade* (Baton Rouge, La., 1983), 165–166. On John Canoe, see Matthew Gregory Lewis, *Journal of a West Indian Proprietor . . .* (London, 1834), 51; Stuckey, *Slave Culture*, 68–73, 104–106; Judith Bettelheim, "Jamaican Jonkonnu and Related Caribbean Festivals," in Margaret E. Crahan and Franklin W. Knight, eds., *Africa and the Caribbean: The Legacies of a Link* (Baltimore, 1979), 80–100.

coded ship to West Indian and Carolinian slaves and to people on the Gold Coast and Niger Delta. Forced to represent himself with fawning propriety to white almsgivers, Johnson undoubtedly took psychological refuge in their inability to comprehend him fully, even as he shook his creolized African past in their faces.

INDEX

identity, 173–174; and dreams, 176–181; and Christian conversion, 177–178, 187–188; and Christian missionaries, 184–185; and definition of pain, 372–372, 400–402. See also *individual denominations*

Renaissance: and American culture, 279–280, 286–287, 314, 325

Rensselaerswijck (Dutch vessel), 124

Republicans, 116–118

Rhode Island, 98–99, 437

Richardson, Elizabeth, 394

Richardson, John, 203

Richmond, Va., 210

Rights of the British Colonies Asserted and Proved, The (Otis), 83

Ritual, 2, 110–112, 166, 417

Robinson, John, 310

Rodes, Dorothy, 40, 45–46, 49

Rodes, Roger, 41, 46–47, 57, 59–60

Roland, Alan, 164

Rolo, Desiah Van Amburgh, 117 n. 41

Romanticism, 284

Rooseboom, Gerard, 136

Rorty, Richard, 161

Rough, Martha, 388

Rousseau, Jean Jacques, 385

Rowlandson, Joseph, 242

Rowlandson, Mary, 242, 243 (illus.), 244

Rubin, Julius H., 356–357

Rush, Benjamin, 376–377, 384

Rutland District, Mass. (Hutchinson, later Barre), 83–86, 93–94

Ryan, Ezra, 443

Sabean, David Warren, 166

Sabine Hall, 218

Saffin, John, 194

Sailors, 421–422, 429–433, 438, 443–445

Saint Domingue, 439, 441

Saint Kitts, 424

Saltar, Dolly, 394

Sandiford, Ralph, 196

Sattelihu, Andrew (or Andreas). See Montour, Andrew

Saxton, Jonathan, 259–261

Scarouyady (Oneida Indian), 27, 37–38

Schuyler, Philip Pietersz, 143

Sea Islands (S.C.), 187

Secular humanism, 375

Self: presentations of, 5–6, 9–10, 173, 200–205, 229–230 (*See also* Autobiography; Diaries); historical interpretation of, 10; autonomous, 163–164, 166; conceptions of, in East v. West, 163–165, 201; in Europe, 164–166, 278–281; and the inner alien, 171, 176–177, 191–194, 198–199, 279, 286–287, 337, 408–409; reflections of, 344–345; and perfectionism, 356

Seneca Indians, 20

Seven Years' War, 83

Sewall, Jonathan, 89

Sexual intercourse, 59, 397

Sexuality, 231–233, 295–296, 299, 305–307; and women, 59–61, 63, 207; and men, 60–63. *See also* Homosexuality; Identity

Shamokin (Indian town), 13–16, 21–23

Shawnee Indians, 20, 30

SH chest (Hadley chest), 245, 247 (illus.), 248

Sheldon, George, 259–260, 266

Shickellamy (Oneida Indian), 37–38

Shingas (Ohio Delaware leader), 35

Shinns, Thomas, 195

Shippen, Nancy, 372

Shweder, Richard, 165

Sickle-cell anemia, 390

Sijbinck, Madame (Mrs. Jan), 138–139

Sijbinck, Jan, 137–138

Silliman, Frances, 263

Silver, 261–262

Sin, 165, 372

Slavery: and role boundaries, 11, 80–95; and public opinion, 70–95; in country v. city, 84; symbolism of, 195; and discipline and punishment, 226–227, 379; rationalizations for, 300; and pain and illness, 389–390; and Middle Passage, 419, 426; and colonization, 436–438

Slaves: ownership of, by Indians, 21; in Northeast, 82–83, 92–95; as alien enemies, 171–172; and autobiographies, 174; and visual symbols, 182–184, 195, 197; and dreams, 185–188; and oral traditions, 209–212; and trickster tales, 211–212, 214–215; in Landon Carter's diary, 224–227, 389; and pregnancy and birth, 393; and maritime work, 421–422, 427–433, 441; and funerals, 426, 436

Smith, Adam, 376

Smith, Daniel Blake, 386

Smith, Elihu Hubbard, 383, 389

Smith, Gaines, 102

Social Darwinism, 379

Social hierarchy: and patriarchy, 98, 103, 213, 221–223; and behavior, 413–414

Solar eclipse (1806), 96–97

South, 332–333, 352

South Carolina, 427, 429, 439–440

Southwell, Sir Robert, 294

Spackman, Deborah, 395

Springfield, Mass., 244

Stachniewski, John, 357

Stacy, Mr., 44, 57, 60

Stacy, Nathaniel, 106–107, 113

Stallybrass, Peter, 161, 286, 288, 294–296

Stamp Act, 73, 82, 221

Starlings, Captain ("Uncle Mark"), 428

Stoddard, Prudence, 261

Stoddard, Solomon, 242, 261

Stolorow, Robert D., 205

Stone, Lawrence, 350

Stone, William Leete, 120

Stories and storytelling, 207–208, 214–215, 438, 440

Strong, John, 264

Strong, Sarah, 245

Structural Transformation of the Public Sphere, The (Habermas), 68–69

Stuyvesant, Petrus, 130, 132, 139

Suffolk, Mass., 63

Suicide, 122–153, 354, 356, 385–386, 398

Sukey (Carter slave), 224

Sulzer, J., 363

Sumner, Mary Osgood, 183

Susquehanna Indians, 20, 24, 35

Susquehanna River, 13–17, 102

Susquehanna Valley, 13–39

SW chest (Hadley chest), 248, 251 (illus.), 259–261

Symbolism: of dreams, 181–183, 193–197; Masonic, 183; of color, 183–184, 195, 197; of ladders, 194–195; of mirrors, 307–308; of boats, 421, 425, 427

Tattoos, 429–430

Taunton, Mass., 74–77, 79

Taylor, Charles, 68–69, 228

Taylor, Edward, 251, 273

Taylor, Thankful, 245

Taylor, William, 442

Temne (African people), 185

Textiles, 242, 256

Thaskkel, Miss, 230

Thing, Joanna, 264

Thompson, E. P., 436

Thompson, Robert Farris, 426–427, 431

Thuys, Jacques, 136

Thyas (Bermudian slave), 439

Tiepkesz, Jan (Dutch ship captain), 124

Titus (street performer), 210–211

Tocqueville, Alexis de, 158, 283–284

Tompkins, Daniel D., 117

Traveller (U.S. brigantine), 441

Tucker, St. George, 71–72

Turner, Victor, 2, 158–159, 208

Tuscarora Indians, 20

Tutelo Indians, 20

Tyos, Jane, 43–44

Tyos, John, 43–45, 48, 51, 57, 60, 65

Uffitt, Hannah, 55

Uffitt, John, 55

Upper Guinea, 423

Vail, M. Eugéne, 209–210

Valcooch, Dirck Adriaensz, 126

Valéry, Paul, 161

Van Amburgh, Betsey, 100–104, 106–107, 114–115

Van Eyck, Jan, 135

Van Gennep, Arnold, 2

NOTES ON THE CONTRIBUTORS

W. Jeffrey Bolster is Assistant Professor of History at the University of New Hampshire. He is the author of *Black Jacks: African American Seamen in the Age of Sail.*

T. H. Breen is William Smith Mason Professor of American History at Northwestern University. He is the author of *Imagining the Past: East Hampton Histories, Tobacco Culture: The Mentality of the Great Tidewater Planters on the Eve of Revolution,* and many essays on the consumer marketplace of the eighteenth century and the coming of the American Revolution.

Elaine Forman Crane is Professor of History at Fordham University. She is the editor of *The Diary of Elizabeth Drinker* and the author of *A Dependent People: Newport, Rhode Island, in the Revolutionary Era.*

Greg Dening is Emeritus Professor of History at the University of Melbourne. He is the author of *The Death of William Gooch: A History's Anthropology, Mr Bligh's Bad Language: Passion, Power, and Theatre on the Bounty,* and *Islands and Beaches: Discourse on a Silent Land, Marquesas, 1774–1880.*

Philip Greven is Professor of History at Rutgers University. He is the author of *Spare the Child: The Religious Roots of Punishment and the Psychological Impact of Physical Abuse* and *The Protestant Temperament: Patterns of Child-Rearing, Religious Experience, and the Self in Early America.*

Ronald Hoffman is Director of the Omohundro Institute of Early American History and Culture and Editor of the Carroll Family Papers. He is the author of *A Spirit of Dissension: Economics, Politics, and the Revolution in Maryland* and the coeditor of *The Transforming Hand of Revolution: Reconsidering the American Revolution as a Social Movvement,* the latest volume in the Perspectives on the American Revolution series published for the United States Capitol Historical Society.

Rhys Isaac is Professor of History at La Trobe University in Melbourne. He is the author of *The Transformation of Virginia, 1740–1790* and is a member of the Melbourne Group of Ethnographic Historians.

Kenneth A. Lockridge is Professor Emeritus of History at the University of Michigan and Professor of History at the University of Montana. He is the author of *On the Sources of Patriarchal Rage: The Commonplace Books of William Byrd and Thomas Jefferson and the Gendering of Power in the Eighteenth Century* and *A New England Town: The First Hundred Years.*

James H. Merrell is the Lucy Maynard Salmon Professor of History at Vassar College. He is the author of *The Indians' New World: Catawbas and Their Neighbors from European Contact through the Era of Removal* and is coeditor of *Beyond the Covenant Chain: The Iroquois and Their Neighbors in Indian North America, 1600–1800.*

Donna Merwick was Associate Professor of History and is now an Associate of the Department of History at the University of Melbourne. She is the author of *Possessing Albany, 1630–1710: The Dutch and English Experiences* and *Boston's Priests, 1845–1910: A Study in Social and Intellectual Change.*

Mary Beth Norton is Mary Donlon Alger Professor of American History at Cornell University. Her publications include *Founding Mothers and Fathers: Gendered Power and the Forming of American Society* and *Liberty's Daughters: The Revolutionary Experience of American Women, 1750–1800.*

Mechal Sobel is Professor of History and Director of the American Studies Program at the University of Haifa. She is the author of *The World They Made Together: Black and White Values in Eighteenth-Century Virginia* and *Trabelin' On: The Slave Journey to an Afro-Baptist Faith.*

Alan Taylor is Professor of History at the University of California, Davis. He is the author of *William Cooper's Town: Power and Persuasion on the Frontier of the Early American Republic* and *Liberty Men and Great Proprietors: The Revolutionary Settlement on the Maine Frontier, 1760–1820.*

Fredrika J. Teute is Editor of Publications at the Omohundro Institute of Early American History and Culture. She has been an editor of *The Papers of John Marshall* and *The Papers of James Madison.*

Laurel Thatcher Ulrich is Phillips Professor of Early American History at Harvard University. She is the author of *A Midwife's Tale: The Life of Martha Ballard, Based on Her Diary, 1785–1812* and *Good Wives: Image and Reality in the Lives of Women in Northern New England, 1650–1750.*

Richard White is Professor of History at the University of Washington. He is the author of *The Middle Ground: Indians, Empires, and Republics in the Great Lakes Region, 1650–1815.*